# Introduction to

# MACROECONOMICS

## EDWIN G. DOLAN
Ph.D. Yale University

## DAVID E. LINDSEY
Ph.D. University of Chicago

*Best Value*
*Textbooks*

EDITOR: Kristin Van Gaasbeck

TEXT DESIGN AND COMPOSITION: Archetype Book Composition

COVER DESIGN: Walker Printing

ISBN: 1-932856-03-X

Copyright © 2004 by Best Value Textbooks, LLC

# TABLE OF CONTENTS

# PREFACE

HE MOST RELIABLE constant of life in a market economy is constant change. Sitting down to work on this new edition of this textbook has brought many changes to my attention.

Some of them are trivial. One chapter mentioned some authors who were on the best-seller list at the time of the last edition—good books they wrote, but just as the market economy is in constant change, so is the publishing industry. Out they go, to be replaced by J.K. Rowling and Dan Brown.

Other changes are much more fundamental, such as the trend toward globalization of both the macro- and micro-economy. Professional economists will know that this trend is not really new. If one looks at the data, trends in imports and exports, integration of labor and financial markets, and global brand penetration started long ago. Yet, although statistically well established, these trends have clearly hit a new threshold of public awareness in the first decade of the 21st century. For that reason alone, a modern textbook must reflect the global nature of the economy.

One of the signs of its increased global outlook is the disappearance of a separate chapter on foreign exchange markets and international monetary policy. Because these topics are more important than ever, it is no longer appropriate to isolate them in the last chapter of the macroeconomics course, too easily skipped in the rush toward final exams. Instead, topics like the effects of exchange rates on aggregate demand and the relationship between price stability and exchange rate policy are now integrated directly into the various macro chapters that deal with related issues for the domestic economy. The result is a book that is both more up-to-date and more streamlined. Numerous globally-oriented cases and topics appear in the micro chapters as well.

One final change is in the textbook market itself. Earlier editions of this book reflected the college publishing world of the past: Fat, heavy volumes with fat, heavy price tags that, over time, came to be one of the most resented financial burdens of a college education. And students didn't even get their money's worth from those texts of an earlier era. The technology of the day meant long lead times and the sheer costs of production meant substantial intervals between revisions, so that textbooks were often several years out of date before they hit the classroom. Things were even worse for students who, because of financial pressure, depended on lower-cost used copies of earlier editions. Happily, that model of publishing is now in retreat.

It is a great pleasure to me to see this new edition come out through Best Value Textbooks at a price that offers a fair value to students. The advantages of working with a publisher who uses the latest technology to bring the book to market just a few months after final revisions are made makes the pleasure all the greater. I hope you, as a user of the book, will complete the cycle by providing me, as author, with your feedback so that your suggested changes can be quickly incorporated in future editions.

## Acknowledgments

My first thanks must go to my long-time co-author, David E. Lindsey, with whom I worked on earlier editions of this text over a period of many years. During his years as Deputy Director of the Division of Monetary Affairs of the Board of Governors of the Federal Reserve System, David was able to find the ideal balance between the theory and practice of economics. Although he did not contribute directly to preparation of this new edition, his strong influence can still be seen in both the macroeconomic and microeconomic chapters.

Second, I would like to thank Kristin van Gaasbeck, Ph.D for her innovative work in updating data sources, news items, and many other elements for the new edition. Her work has made a big difference in keeping the content of the book fresh and up to date, and in bringing it to market faster than could ever have been done without her able contribution.

Finally, I thank the entire publishing and editorial staff of Best Value Textbooks for introducing me to this great new concept in college publishing. I hope you, the user, benefit as much as I have.

EDWIN G. DOLAN
Lopez Island, Washington

## Features of This Edition

- *State of the art pedagogy*. An abundance of case studies introduce and illustrate the subject matter of every chapter.
- *Integrated international economics*. As the world economy itself comes closer together, international economics must be more closely integrated into the principles course. Accordingly, topics in international economic theory and policy, ranging from balance of payments accounts to the foreign exchange operations of the Fed, are introduced in the chapters in which they occur naturally, rather than presented separately in a single chapter.

# Supplements

## Test Bank

The accompanying Test Bank contains over 2,000 questions in a variety of formats including multiple choice, true/false, and essay questions..

## Instructor's Manual

The expanded Instructor's Manual contains material which can be easily included in lectures. The manual also includes all of its traditional elements, including instructional objectives, lecture notes, and suggestions.

## Study Guide

The Study Guide has hands-on applications and self-testing programs. It is available in two versions, *Macroeconomics*, and *Microeconomics*. Students can gain an advantage by reinforcing their reading and lecture notes with the following study guide features:

- *Where You're Going.* The objectives and terms for each chapter are recapped to tie concepts together.
- *Walking Tour.* The "Walking Tour" section provides a narrative summary of the chapter and incorporates questions on key points. Answers are given in the margin.
- *Hands On.* Geographical and numerical exercises clarify concepts and better prepare students for tests and quizzes.
- *Economics in the News.* A news item illustrates how concepts covered in the chapter can appear in the real world. Questions and answers reinforce the concepts.
- *Questions for Review.* These questions and answers follow the key chapter concepts, preparing students for the self-test.
- *Self-Test.* Extra test preparation increases a student's understanding and ability to succeed.
- *Careers in Economics.* Formerly an appendix in the text, this material provides students with an understanding of where the study of economics could lead them.

## Best Value Textbooks Online Student Tutorial

Created to support and enhance the student's comprehension of the economic principles discussed in the textbook. The online tutorial includes chapters objectives and study questions. To access the tutorial please visit our Students section on our Web site www.bestvaluetextbooks.com. Username: Economics  Password: DolanLindsey

*Best Value Textbooks Economic PowerPoint Transparencies*

This PowerPoint slide set combines graphics and text to further illustrate the economic principles discussed in the text.

*Best Value Textbooks Transparencies*

Graphs, charts, and illustrations from the text creates additional in-class support for the instructor and students.

## About the Authors

EDWIN G. DOLAN was born in Oklahoma and grew up in a small town in Oregon. He attended Earlham College and Indiana University, where he majored in Russian Studies and received the Certificate of Indiana University's famed Russian and East-European Institute. After earning a doctorate in economics from Yale University, he taught at Dartmouth College, the University of Chicago, George Mason University and Gettysburg College. In 1990, he began teaching in Moscow, Russia, where he and his wife founded the American Institute of Business and Economics, an independent, not-for-profit MBA program. Since retiring as President of that institution in 2001, he has lectured on global macroeconomics and managerial economics in Riga, Latvia; Budapest, Hungary; and Zagreb, Croatia. When not lecturing abroad, he makes his home in Washington's San Juan Islands.

DAVID E. LINDSEY comes from the university town of West Lafayette, Indiana. He received his B.A. from Earlham College, where he and Dolan were roommates. He then earned a Ph.D. from the University of Chicago under the direction of Milton Friedman. Lindsey taught economics for several years at the Ohio State University and Macalester College. From 1974 to 2003, he was on the staff of the Board of Governors of the Federal Reserve System, where he served for many years as Deputy Director of the Division of Monetary Affairs and Associate Economist for the Federal Open Market Committee.

# PART I

# Overview of Economics

# The Economic Way of Thinking

1. The subject matter of economics
2. The considerations underlying four fundamental economic choices:
   – What an economy will produce
   – How goods and services will be produced
   – Who will produce which goods and services
   – For whom goods will be produced
   – How to coordinate economic choices
3. How economists use theory, graphs, and evidence in their work

## CASE STUDY: LAND MANAGEMENT AND WILDFIRE

In autumn of 2003, wildfires spread through Southern California, closing schools, businesses, and freeways in San Diego and Los Angeles. The growing population in this region has created pressure to erect homes closer to forests and canyons, exposing more people to the threat of fire. Such wildfires not only damage buildings, but also destroy trees and wildlife. As metropolitan areas have spread closer to forests (8 million people live in wildland areas), the demand for fire protection has grown.

However, in working to prevent fire, these communities actually increase the chances of wildfire. California's climate and topography create ideal natural conditions for wildfire. To combat destructive wildfires, the California

Department of Forestry and Fire Protection (CDF) uses prescribed burning. Isolated forest fires occur naturally and serve many purposes. They cleanse the forest floor, removing brush and debris. This exposes the soil to essential sunlight, fostering the growth of healthier trees, grasses, and plants that provide wildlife habitat. The CDF hopes to recreate this process by igniting controlled fires in state parks. Prescribed burning not only serves an important purpose to support natural growth in forests, but reduces the chances of a devastating wildfire. By consuming brush, diseased trees, and other debris, forest fires consume fuel. Without fire, this debris builds up over time, making wildfires more of a threat.

In addition to prescribed burning, the CDF wants to establish larger Wildfire Protection Zones to buffer communities from forests and canyons. These zones would institute an area between wildland and development. This will prove more difficult as the pressures of a growing population create the need for more housing.

Source: California Fire Plan, California Board of Forestry, May 2000.

➥

**Scarcity**

A situation in which there is not enough of a resource to meet all of everyone's wants.

**Economics**

The social science that seeks to understand the choices people make in using scarce resources to meet their wants.

THE DIFFICULTY OF land management is an example of **scarcity**—a situation in which there is not enough of something to meet everyone's wants. Scarcity and the way people deal with it are the central topics of **economics**, which can be defined as the social science that seeks to understand the choices people make in using scarce resources to meet their wants.

**Economics**, as the definition makes clear, is a study not of things or money or wealth but of *people*. Economics is about people because scarcity itself is a human phenomenon. Although Southern California encompasses a certain amount of land, land became scarce when it became the object of human wants. The same is true of all other scarce resources—mozzarella cheese is scarce because people want pizzas, Manhattan real estate is scarce because people want to live and do business on that crowded island, and time is scarce because people have many things they want to do each day.

A second reason that economics is about people is that the choices it studies are made in a social context. That is why economics is considered a social science rather than a branch of operations management, engineering, or mathematics. Take, for example, the social context of decisions regarding the use of land and prescribed burning. People want to prevent fire because they want to protect their homes. The decision to use resources to build homes closer to forests reflects a judgment about which human wants should be given priority over others that the same resources could be used to satisfy. The California Department of Forestry and Fire Protection's desire to create Wildfire Protection Zones reflects the debate about how to allocate the world's scarce resources.

Economic choices are being made every day. You make economic choices when you buy clothes or groceries, when you work at a job—even when you choose to fill one of the scarce slots in your class schedule with a course in economics rather than with one in environmental toxicology. Economic choices are made everywhere: in the factory that made the computer this book was typed on, in the government offices that oversee affirmative-action policies, in nonprofit organizations such as churches and student clubs, and in just about any other situation you can think of.

All the examples just given come from the branch of economics known as **microeconomics**. The prefix *micro*, meaning "small," indicates that this branch of economics deals with the choices of small economic units such as households, firms, and government agencies. Although microeconomics studies individual behavior, its scope can be worldwide. For example, households, firms, and government agencies conduct worldwide trade in such goods as cars, chemicals, and crude oil. That trade and the policies regulating it fall within the scope of microeconomics.

Economics also has another branch, known as **macroeconomics**. The prefix *macro*, meaning "large," indicates that this branch deals with larger-scale economic phenomena. Typical problems in macroeconomics include how to maintain conditions in which people who want jobs can find them, how to protect the economy against the distortions caused by the widespread price increases called inflation, and how to provide for a continued increase in living standards over time. Government policies concerning taxes, expenditures, budget deficits, and the financial system are central concerns of macroeconomics. However, inasmuch as macroeconomic phenomena, such as inflation, represent the summation of millions of individual choices regarding the prices of particular goods and services, macroeconomics rests on a microeconomic foundation. Both microeconomics and macroeconomics study the problem of scarcity. While microeconomics focuses on individual choices, macroeconomics examines how society as a whole behaves.

Whether one is dealing with microeconomics or macroeconomics, with domestic or international economic relationships, all economic analysis comes down to a special way of thinking about how people choose to use scarce resources.

**Microeconomics**

The branch of economics that studies the choices of individuals, including households, business firms, and government agencies.

**Macroeconomics**

The branch of economics that studies large-scale economic phenomena, particularly inflation, unemployment, and economic growth.

## WHAT? HOW? WHO? FOR WHOM?

In every economy certain basic choices must be made. Among these, the most important are *what* goods will be produced, *how* they will be produced, *who* will do which jobs, and *for whom* the results of economic activity will be made available. Each of these choices is made necessary because of scarcity, and each can be used to introduce key elements of the economic way of thinking.

## Deciding What to Produce: Opportunity Cost

**Factors of production**

The basic inputs of labor, capital, and natural resources used in producing all goods and services.

The first basic choice is that of what goods to produce. In any real economy the number of goods and services that could be produced is immense. The essential features of the choice of what to produce, however, can be illustrated using an economy in which as few as two alternative goods exist—for example, cars and education. For many students, going without a car (or driving an older, used car instead of a new one) is a sacrifice that must be made in order to get a college education. The same trade-off that is faced by an individual student is also faced by the economy as a whole: Not enough cars and education can be produced to satisfy everyone's wants. Someone must choose how much of each good to produce.

**Labor**

The contributions to production made by people working with their minds and muscles.

The impossibility of producing as much of everything as people want reflects a scarcity of the productive resources that are used to make all goods. Many scarce productive resources must be combined to make even the simplest of goods. For example, making a table requires lumber, nails, glue, a hammer, a saw, the work of a carpenter, that of a painter, and so on. For convenience, productive resources are often grouped into three basic categories, called **factors of production**: labor, capital, and natural resources. **Labor** includes all of the productive contributions made by people working with their minds and muscles. **Capital** includes all the productive inputs created by people, including tools, machinery, buildings, and intangible items, such as computer programs. **Natural resources** include anything that can be used as a productive input in its natural state—for example, farmland, building sites, forests, and mineral deposits.

**Capital**

All means of production that are created by people, including tools, industrial equipment, and structures.

**Natural resources**

Anything that can be used as a productive input in its natural state, such as farmland, building sites, forests, and mineral deposits.

Productive resources that are used to satisfy one want cannot be used to satisfy another at the same time. Steel, concrete, and building sites used for automobile factories cannot also be used for classrooms. People who are employed as teachers cannot spend the same time working on an automobile assembly line. Even the time students spend in class and studying for tests represents use of a factor of production that could otherwise be used as labor in an auto plant. Because production uses inputs that could be used elsewhere, the production of any good entails forgoing the opportunity to produce something else instead. In economic terms, everything has an **opportunity cost**. The opportunity cost of a good or service is its cost in terms of the forgone opportunity to pursue the best possible alternative activity with the same time or resources.

**Opportunity cost**

The cost of a good or service measured in terms of the forgone opportunity to pursue the best possible alternative activity with the same time or resources.

Let's go back to the example of an economy that has only two goods, cars and education. In such an economy, the opportunity cost of producing a college graduate can be stated in terms of the number of cars that could have been produced by using the same labor, capital, and natural resources. For example, the opportunity cost of educating a college graduate might be four Ford Mustangs. Such a ratio (graduates per car or cars per graduate) is a useful way to express opportunity cost when only two goods are involved. More typically, though, we deal with situations in which there are many goods. Having more of one means giving up a little bit of many others.

In an economy with many goods, opportunity costs can be expressed in terms of a common unit of measurement, money. For example, rather than saying that a college education is worth four Mustangs or that a Mustang is worth one-fourth of a college education, we could say that the opportunity cost of a car is $20,000 and that of a college education is $80,000.

Useful as it is to have a common unit of measurement, great care must be taken when opportunity costs are expressed in terms of money, because not all out-of-pocket money expenditures represent the sacrifice of opportunities to do something else. At the same time, not all sacrificed opportunities take the form of money spent. *Applying Economic Ideas 1.1,* which analyzes both the out-of-pocket expenditures and the opportunity costs of a college education, shows why.

The importance of opportunity cost will be stressed again and again in this book. The habit of looking for opportunity costs is one of the distinguishing features of the economic way of thinking.

## Deciding How to Produce: Efficiency and Entrepreneurship

A second basic economic choice is that of how to produce. There is more than one way to produce almost any good or service. Cars, for example, can be made in highly automated factories using a lot of capital equipment and relatively little labor, or they can be built one by one in small shops, using a lot of labor and only a few general-purpose machines. Ford Mustangs are built the first way, Mercedes and BMWs the second way. The same kind of thing could be said about education. Economics can be taught in a small classroom with one teacher and a blackboard serving 20 students, or it can be taught in a large lecture hall in which the teacher uses projectors, computers, and TV monitors to serve hundreds of students.

**Economic efficiency**

A state of affairs in which it is impossible to make any change that satisfies one person's wants more fully without causing some other person's wants to be satisfied less fully.

**Efficiency in production**

A situation in which it is not possible, given available knowledge and productive resources, to produce more of one good without forgoing the opportunity to produce some of another good.

**EFFICIENCY**  Efficiency is a key consideration in deciding how to produce. In everyday speech, *efficiency* means producing with a minimum of expense, effort, and waste. Economists use a more precise definition. **Economic efficiency**, they say, refers to a state of affairs in which it is impossible to make any change that satisfies one person's wants more fully without causing some other person's wants to be satisfied less fully.[1]

Although the definition of economic efficiency may be unfamiliar, it is actually closely related to the everyday notion of efficiency. If there is some way to make you better off without making me worse off, it is wasteful (*inefficient*) to pass up the opportunity. If I have a red pen that I am not using, and you need one just for a minute, it would be wasteful for you to buy a red pen of your own. It is more efficient for me to lend you my pen; it makes you better off and me no worse off. If there is a way to make us both better off, it would be all the more wasteful not to take advantage of the opportunity. You lend me your bicycle for the afternoon and I will lend you my volleyball. If I do not ride a bicycle very often and you do not play volleyball very often, it would be inefficient for us both to own one of each item.

The concept of economic efficiency has a variety of applications: one such application centers on the question of *how* to produce. **Efficiency in production** refers to a

### APPLYING ECONOMIC IDEAS 1.1

## THE OPPORTUNITY COST OF A COLLEGE EDUCATION

How much does it cost you to go to college? If you are a resident student at a typical four-year private college in the United States, you can answer this question by making up a budget like the one shown in Figure A. This can be called a budget of out-of-pocket costs, because it includes all the items—and only those items—that you or your parents must actually pay for in a year.

Your own out-of-pocket costs may be much higher or lower than these averages. Chances are, though, that these are the items that come to mind when you think about the costs of college. As you begin to think like an economist, you may find it useful to recast your college budget in terms of opportunity costs. Which of the items in Figure A represent opportunities that you have forgone in order to go to college? Are any forgone opportunities missing? To answer these questions, compare Figure A with Figure B, which shows a budget of opportunity costs.

Some items are both opportunity costs and out-of-pocket costs. The first three items in Figure A show up again in Figure B. To spend $14,000 on tuition and fees and $1,200 on books and supplies, you must give up the opportunity to buy other goods and services—to buy a car or rent a ski condo, for instance. To spend $1,100 getting to and from school, you must pass up the opportunity to travel somewhere else or to spend the money on something other than travel. Not all out-of-pocket costs are also opportunity costs, however. Consider the last two items in the out-of-pocket budget. By

spending $7,000 a year on room, board, and personal expenses during the year, you are not really giving up the opportunity to do something else. Whether or not you were going to college, you would have to eat, live somewhere, and buy clothes. Because these are expenses that you would have in any case, they do not count as opportunity costs of going to college.

Finally, there are some items that are opportunity costs without being out-of-pocket costs. Think about what you would be doing if you were not going to college. If you were not going to college, you probably would have taken a job and started earning money soon after leaving high school. As a high-school graduate, your earnings would be about $16,000 during the nine months of the school year. (You can work during the summer even if you are attending college.) Because this potential income is something that you must forgo for the sake of college, it is an opportunity cost even though it does not involve an outlay of money.

Which budget you use depends on the kind of decision you are making. If you have already decided to go to college and are doing your financial planning, the out-of-pocket budget will tell you how much you will have to raise from savings, a job, parents' contributions, and scholarships to make ends meet. But if you are making the more basic choice between going to college and pursuing a career that does not require a college degree, the opportunity cost of college is what counts.

| Figure A | Budget of Out-of-Pocket Costs | Figure B | Budget of Opportunity Costs |
|---|---|---|---|
| Tuition and fees | $14,000 | Tuition and fees | $14,000 |
| Books and supplies | 1,200 | Books and supplies | 1,200 |
| Transportation to and from home | 1,100 | Transportation to and from home | 1,000 |
| Room and board | 7,000 | Forgone income | 16,000 |
| Personal expenses | 1,400 | | |
| **Total out-of-pocket costs** | **$24,700** | **Total opportunity costs** | **$32,200** |

situation in which it is not possible, given available productive resources and existing knowledge, to produce more of one good without forgoing the opportunity to produce some of another good. The concept of efficiency in production, like the broader concept of economic efficiency, includes the everyday notion of avoiding waste. For example, a grower of apples finds that beyond some certain quantity, using more fertilizer per tree does not increase the yield of apples. To use more than that amount would be wasteful. Better to transfer the extra fertilizer to the production of, say, peaches. That way more peaches can be grown without any reduction in the apple crop.

The economist's definition also includes more subtle possibilities for improving the efficiency of production in cases where the waste of resources is less obvious. For example, it is possible to grow apples in Georgia. It is also possible, by selecting the right tree varieties and using winter protection, to grow peaches in Vermont. Some hobbyists do grow both fruits in both states. However, it would be inefficient to do so on a commercial scale even if growers in both states followed the most careful cultivation practices and avoided any obvious "waste." To see why, suppose that initially apple and peach trees were planted in equal numbers in the two states. Then compare this with a situation in which 500 fewer struggling peach trees had been planted in Vermont, and 500 thriving apple trees had been planted instead. At the same time, suppose 500 fewer heat-stressed apple trees had been planted in Georgia, and their place had been taken by peaches. Clearly, the second alternative would increase the output of both fruits without increasing the total land, labor, and capital used in fruit production. This shows that the original distribution of trees was inefficient.

**HOW TO INCREASE PRODUCTION POTENTIAL**   Once efficiency has been achieved, more of one good can be produced only by forgoing the opportunity to produce something else, assuming that productive resources and knowledge are held constant. But over time, production potential can be expanded by accumulating more resources and finding new ways of putting them to work.

In the past, discovery of new supplies of natural resources has been an important way of increasing production potential. Population growth has always been, and still is, another source. However, as the most easily tapped supplies of natural resources are depleted and as population growth slows in the most developed countries, capital will increasingly be the factor of production that contributes most to the expansion of production potential.

**Investment**

The act of increasing the economy's stock of capital—that is, its supply of means of production made by people.

The act of increasing the economy's stock of capital—that is, its supply of productive inputs made by people—is known as **investment**. Investment involves a trade-off of present consumption for future consumption. To build more factories, roads, and computers, we have to divert resources from the production of bread, movies, haircuts, and other things that satisfy immediate wants. In return, we put ourselves in a better position to satisfy our future wants.

**Entrepreneurship**

The process of looking for new possibilities—making use of new ways of doing things, being alert to new opportunities, and overcoming old limits.

Increased availability of productive resources is not the only source of economic growth, however. Even more important are improvements in human knowledge—the invention of new technology, new forms of organization, new ways of satisfying wants. The process of looking for new possibilities—making use of new ways of doing things, being alert to new opportunities, and overcoming old limits—is called **entrepreneurship**. It is a dynamic process that breaks down the constraints imposed by existing knowledge and limited supplies of factors of production.

Entrepreneurship does not have to mean inventing something or starting a new business, although it sometimes does. It may mean finding a new market for an existing product—for example, convincing people in New England that tacos, long popular in the Southwest, make a quick and tasty lunch. It may mean taking advantage of price differences between one market and another—for example, buying hay at a low price in Pennsylvania, where growing conditions have been good in the past year, and reselling it in Virginia, where the weather has been too dry.

Households can be entrepreneurs, too. They do not simply repeat the same patterns of work and leisure every day. They seek variety—new jobs, new foods, new places to visit. Each time you try something new, you are taking a step into the unknown. In this sense you are an entrepreneur.

Entrepreneurship is sometimes called the fourth factor of production. However, entrepreneurship differs from the three classical factors of production in important ways. Unlike labor, capital, and natural resources, entrepreneurship is intangible and difficult to measure. Although entrepreneurs earn incomes reflecting the value that the market places on their accomplishments, we cannot speak of a price per unit of entrepreneurship; there are no such units. Also, unlike human resources (which grow old), machines (which wear out), and natural resources (which can be used up), the inventions and discoveries of entrepreneurs are not depleted as they are used. Once a new product or concept, such as the transistor, the toothpaste pump, or the limited-partnership form of business, has been invented, the required knowledge does not have to be created again (although, of course, it may be supplanted by even better ideas). All in all, it is more helpful to think of entrepreneurship as a process of learning better ways of using the three basic factors of production than as a separate factor of production in itself.

## Deciding Who Will Do Which Work: The Division of Labor

The questions of what will be produced and how to produce it would exist even for a person living in isolation. Even the fictional castaway Robinson Crusoe had to decide whether to fish or hunt birds, and if he decided to fish, he had to decide whether to do so with a net or with a hook and line. In contrast, the economic questions of who will do which work and for whom output will be produced exist only for people living in a human society—another reason economics is considered one of the social sciences.

The question of who will do which work is a matter of organizing the social division of labor. Will everyone do everything independently—be a farmer in the morning, a tailor in the afternoon, and a poet in the evening? Or will people cooperate—work together, trade goods and services, and specialize in one particular job? Economists answer these questions by pointing out that it is more efficient to cooperate. Doing so allows a given number of people to produce more than they could if each of them worked alone. Three things make cooperation worthwhile: teamwork, learning by doing, and comparative advantage.

First consider *teamwork*. In a classic paper on this subject, Armen Alchian and Harold Demsetz use the example of workers unloading bulky crates from a truck.[2] The crates are so large that one worker alone can barely drag them along or cannot move them at all without unpacking them. Two people working independently would take hours to unload the truck. If they work as a team, however, they can easily pick up the crates and stack them on the loading dock. This example shows that even when everyone is doing the same work and little skill is involved, teamwork pays.

A second reason for cooperation applies when there are different jobs to be done and different skills to be learned. In a furniture plant, for example, some workers operate production equipment, others use office equipment, and still others buy materials. Even if all the workers start out with equal abilities, each gets better at a particular job by doing it repeatedly. *Learning by doing* thus turns workers of average productivity into specialists, thereby creating an even more productive team.

A third reason for cooperation comes into play after the process of learning by doing has developed different skills and also applies when workers start out with different talents and abilities. It is the principle of division of labor according to *comparative advantage*. **Comparative advantage** is the ability to do a job or produce a good at a relatively lower opportunity cost than someone else.

An example will illustrate the principle of comparative advantage. Suppose two clerical workers, Bill and Jim, are assigned the job of getting out a batch of letters. Jim is a whiz. He can type a letter in 5 minutes and stuff it into an envelope in 1 minute. Working alone, he can finish ten letters in an hour. Bill is clumsy. It takes him 10 minutes to type a letter and 5 minutes to stuff it into the envelope. Alone, he can do only four letters an hour. In summary form:

> Jim: Type 1 letter 5 min.
> Stuff 1 envelope 1 min.
>
> Bill: Type 1 letter 10 min.
> Stuff 1 envelope 5 min.

Without cooperation, the two workers' limit is 14 letters per hour between them. Could they do better by cooperating? It depends on who does which job. One idea might be for Jim to do all the typing while Bill does all the stuffing, because that way they can just keep up with each other. But at 5 minutes per letter, that kind of cooperation cuts their combined output to twelve letters per hour. It is worse than not cooperating at all.

Instead, they should divide the work according to the principle of comparative advantage. Even though Bill is the slower typist, he has a *comparative advantage* in typing because the opportunity cost of typing is lower for him: The 10 minutes he takes to type a letter is equal to the time he needs to stuff two envelopes. For Jim, the 5 minutes he takes to type a letter could be used to stuff five envelopes. Thus, for Bill the opportunity cost of typing one letter is to forgo stuffing *two* envelopes, whereas for Jim the opportunity cost of typing one letter is to forgo stuffing *five* envelopes.

**Comparative advantage**

The ability to produce a good or service at a relatively lower opportunity cost than someone else.

Because Bill gives up fewer stuffed envelopes per letter than Jim, the principle of comparative advantage says that Bill should spend all his time typing. If he does, he can produce six letters per hour. Meanwhile Jim can spend 45 minutes of each hour typing nine letters, and the last 15 minutes of each hour stuffing all 15 envelopes. By specializing according to comparative advantage, the two workers can increase their total output to 15 letters per hour, their highest possible joint productivity.

In this example the principle of comparative advantage points the way toward an efficient division of labor between two people working side by side. But the principle also has broader implications. It can apply to a division of labor between individuals or business firms working far apart—even in different countries. In fact, the earliest application of the principle was to international trade (see *Who Said It? Who Did It? 1.1*). Today comparative advantage remains one of the primary motivations for mutually beneficial cooperation, whether on the scale of the workplace or on that of the world as a whole.

Whatever the scale, the principle of comparative advantage is easy to apply provided one remembers that it is rooted in the concept of opportunity cost. Suppose there are two tasks, A and B, and two parties (individuals, firms, agencies, or countries), X and Y, each capable of doing both tasks, but not equally well. First ask what is the opportunity cost for X of doing a unit of task A, measured in terms of how many units of task B could be done with the same time or resources (the opportunity

---

⟋ **WHO SAID IT? WHO DID IT? 1.1**

### DAVID RICARDO AND THE THEORY OF COMPARATIVE ADVANTAGE

David Ricardo was born in London in 1772, the son of an immigrant who was a member of the London stock exchange. Ricardo's education was rather haphazard, and he entered his father's business at the age of 14. In 1793, he married and went into business on his own. These were years of war and financial turmoil. The young Ricardo developed a reputation for remarkable astuteness and quickly made a large fortune.

In 1799, Ricardo read Adam Smith's *The Wealth of Nations* and developed an interest in political economy (as economics was then called). In 1809, his first writings on economics appeared. These were a series of newspaper articles on "The High Price of Bullion," which appeared during the following year as a pamphlet. Several other short works added to his reputation in this area. In 1814, he retired from business to devote all his time to political economy.

Ricardo's major work was *Principles of Political Economy and Taxation*, first published in 1817. This work contains, among other things, a pioneering statement of the principle of comparative advantage as applied to international trade. Using a lucid numerical example, Ricardo showed why it was to the advantage of both countries for England to export wool to Portugal and to import wine in return, even though both products could be produced with less labor in Portugal, as long as wool can be produced relatively less expensively in England.

But international trade is only a sideline of Ricardo's *Principles*. The book covers the whole field of economics as it then existed, beginning with value theory and progressing to a theory of economic growth and evolution. Ricardo held that the economy was growing toward a future "steady state." At that point economic growth would come to a halt and the wage rate would be reduced to the subsistence level. This gloomy view and the equally pessimistic views of Ricardo's contemporary, Thomas Malthus, gave political economy a reputation as "the dismal science."

Ricardo's book was extremely influential. For more than half a century thereafter, much of the writing on economic theory published in England consisted of expansions and commentaries on Ricardo's work. Economists as different as Karl Marx, the revolutionary socialist, and John Stuart Mill, a defender of liberal capitalism, took Ricardo's theories as their starting point. Even today there are "neo-Ricardian" and "new classicist" economists who look to Ricardo's works for inspiration.

cost). Then ask the same question for Y. The party with the lower opportunity cost for doing a unit of task A has the comparative advantage in doing that task. To check, ask what is the opportunity cost for each party of doing a unit of task B, measured in terms how many units of task A could be done with the same time or resources. The party with the lower opportunity cost for doing a unit of task B has the comparative advantage in doing that task.

## Deciding for Whom Goods Will Be Produced: Positive and Normative Economics

Together, the advantages of team production, learning by doing, and comparative advantage mean that people can produce more efficiently by cooperating than they could if each worked in isolation. But cooperation raises yet another issue: For whom will goods be produced? The question of the distribution of output among members of society has implications in terms of both efficiency and fairness.

**EFFICIENCY IN DISTRIBUTION** Consider first a situation in which production has already taken place and the supply of goods is fixed. Suppose, for example, that 30 students get on a bus to go to a football game. Bag lunches are handed out. Half the bags contain a ham sandwich and a root beer; the other half contain a tuna sandwich and a cola. What happens when the students open their bags? They do not just eat whatever they find—they start trading. Some swap sandwiches; others swap drinks. Maybe there is not enough of everything to give each person his or her first choice. Nevertheless, the trading makes at least some people better off than they were when they started. Moreover, no one ends up worse off. If some of the students do not want to trade, they can always eat what was given to them in the first place.

This example shows one sense in which the "for whom" question is partly about efficiency: Starting from any given quantity of goods, the allocation can be improved through trades that result in better satisfaction of some people's preferences. As long as it is possible to trade existing supplies of goods in a way that permits some people to satisfy their wants more fully without making others worse off, **efficiency in distribution** can be improved even while the total quantity of goods remains fixed.

Efficiency in distribution and efficiency in production are two aspects of the general concept of economic efficiency. When both aspects are taken into account, the relationship between distribution and efficiency is not restricted to situations in which the total amount of goods is fixed in advance. That is so because the rules for distribution affect the patterns of production. For example, the rules for distribution affect the supply of productive resources, because most people earn their incomes by providing labor to business firms, and the amount they supply is affected by the wages they are promised. Another reason is that rules for distribution affect incentives for entrepreneurship. Some people may work hard to discover new ways of doing things even if they expect no material reward, but that is not true of everyone.

**Efficiency in distribution**

A situation in which it is not possible, by redistributing existing supplies of goods, to satisfy one person's wants more fully without causing some other person's wants to be satisfied less fully.

**FAIRNESS IN DISTRIBUTION**   Efficiency is not the whole story when it comes to the question of for whom goods will be produced. One can also ask whether a given distribution is fair. Questions of fairness often dominate discussions of distribution.

One widely held view judges fairness in distribution in terms of equality. This concept of fairness is based on the idea that all people, by virtue of their shared humanity, deserve a portion of the goods and services turned out by the economy. There are many versions of this concept. Some people think that all income and wealth should be distributed equally. Others think that people have an equal right to a "safety net" level of income but that inequality in distributing any surplus beyond that level is not necessarily unfair. Still others think that certain goods, such as health care, food, and education, should be distributed equally but that it is fair for other goods to be distributed less equally.

An alternative view, which also has many adherents, judges fairness primarily in terms of the procedures through which a given distribution is carried out. In this view, fairness requires that certain rules and procedures be observed, such as respect for private property or nondiscrimination on grounds of race and gender. As long as those rules are followed, any resulting distribution of income is viewed as acceptable. In this view, equality of opportunity is emphasized more than equality of outcome.

**POSITIVE AND NORMATIVE ECONOMICS**   Many economists make a sharp distinction between the question of efficiency and that of fairness. Discussions of efficiency are seen as part of **positive economics**, the area of economics that is concerned with facts and the relationships among them. Discussions of fairness, in contrast, are seen as part of **normative economics**, the area of economics that is devoted to judgments about whether particular economic policies and conditions are good or bad.

Normative economics extends beyond the question of fairness in the distribution of output. Value judgments also arise about the fairness of the other three basic choices faced by every economy. In choosing what will be produced, is it fair to permit production of alcohol and tobacco but to outlaw production of marijuana and cocaine? In choosing how to produce, is it fair to allow people to work under dangerous or unhealthy conditions, or should work under such conditions be prohibited? In choosing who does which work, is it fair to limit access to specific jobs according to age, gender, race, or union membership? As you can see, normative issues extend to every corner of economics.

Positive economics, rather than offering value judgments about outcomes, focuses on understanding the processes by which the four basic economic questions are or could be answered. It analyzes the way economies operate, or would operate if certain institutions or policies were changed. It traces relationships between facts, often looking for measurable regularities in economic observations.

Most economists consider positive economics their primary area of expertise, but normative considerations influence the conduct of positive economics in several

**Positive economics**

The area of economics that is concerned with facts and the relationships among them.

**Normative economics**

The area of economics that is devoted to judgments about whether economic policies or conditions are good or bad.

ways. The most significant of those influences is the selection of topics to investigate. An economist who sees excessive unemployment as a glaring injustice may study that problem; one who sympathizes with victims of job discrimination may take up a different line of research. Also, normative views are likely to affect the ways in which data are collected, ideas about which facts can be considered true, and so on.

At one time it was thought that a purely positive economics could be developed, untouched by normative considerations of values and fairness. Within its framework, all disputes could be resolved by reference to objective facts. Today that notion is less widely held. Nevertheless, it remains important to be aware that most major economic controversies, especially those that have to do with government policy, have normative as well as positive components, and to be aware of the way each component shapes the way we think about those controversies.

# COORDINATING ECONOMIC CHOICES

To function effectively, an economy must have some way of coordinating the choices of millions of individuals regarding what to produce, how to produce it, who will do each job, and for whom the output will be produced. This section discusses how people, businesses, and the government interact in the coordination of economic choices.

## A Noneconomic Example

Everyone has had the experience of shopping at a supermarket where there are several long checkout lines. In such a situation, you and other shoppers want to get through the checkout process as fast as possible. How can the store avoid the frustrating situation in which some lines have a long wait for service while the cashiers in other lines stand idle for lack of customers?

One way would be for the store to direct certain customers to certain lines. The store could use a standard rule, such as customers with names starting with A–D go to line 1, E–H go to line 2, and so on. Or the store could hire an employee to sit in a special booth and direct shoppers to one line or another.

But supermarkets do not work that way. Instead, they leave shoppers to decide for themselves what line to join, based on information from their own observations. As you approach the checkout area, you first look to see which lines are the shortest. You then make allowance for the possibility that some shoppers may have carts that are heaped full, while others have only a few items. Using your own judgment, you head for the line you think will be fastest.

**Market**

Any arrangement people have for trading with one another.

## The Importance of Markets

In economics, the the coordination of decisions occurs through market activities. A **market** is any arrangement people have for trading with one another. Some markets have formal rules and carry out exchanges at a single location, such as the New York Stock Exchange. Other markets are more informal, such as the word-of-mouth networks through which teenage babysitters get in touch with people who need their services. Despite the wide variety of forms that markets take, they all have one thing in common: They provide the information and incentives people need to coordinate their decisions.

Just as shoppers need information about the length of checkout lines to coordinate their efforts, participants in markets need information about the scarcity and opportunity costs of various goods and factors of production. Markets rely primarily on prices to transmit this information. If a good or factor of production becomes more scarce, its price is bid up. The increase in the price tells people it is worth more and signals producers to make greater efforts to increase supplies. For example, when platinum first began to be used in catalytic converters to reduce pollution from automobile exhaust, this brought buyers into the market. With the discovery of its new use, platinum becomes more difficult to acquire because of the newly increased desire to use it. Competition for available supplies then bids up the price of platinum. This sends a message to buyers of its increased value. The producers learn that, where possible, they should increase the quantity of platinum mined.

Instead, suppose a new technology reduces the cost of producing platinum, for example, by allowing extraction of platinum from mine wastes that were previously discarded. Information about the reduced cost is transmitted by markets in the form of a lower price. People can then consider increasing the quantity of platinum they use.

In addition to knowing the best use for resources, people must also have incentives to act on that information. Markets provide incentives to sell goods and productive resources where they will bring the highest prices and to buy them where they can be obtained at the lowest prices. Profits motivate business managers to improve production methods and to design goods that match consumer needs. Workers who stay alert to opportunities and work where they are most productive receive the highest wages.

Adam Smith, often considered the father of economics, saw the achievement of coordination through markets as the foundation of prosperity and progress. In a famous passage in *The Wealth of Nations,* he called markets an "invisible hand" that nudges people into the economic roles they can play best (see *Who Said It? Who Did It? 1.2*). To this day, an appreciation of markets as a means of coordinating choices remains a central feature of the economic way of thinking.

## The Role of the Government

Important as markets are, they are not the only means of achieving economic coordination. Some decisions are guided by direct authority within organizations. The most important example is decisions made by government agencies. Government decisions are made not through the spontaneous choices of individuals, but via directives issued by a central authority.

Adam Smith is considered to have been the founder of economics as a distinct field of study, even though he wrote only one book on the subject: *The Wealth of Nations*, published in 1776. Smith was 53 years old at the time. His friend David Hume found the book such hard going that he doubted that many people would read it. But Hume was wrong—people have been reading it for more than 200 years.

The wealth of a nation, in Smith's view, was not a result of the accumulation of gold or silver in its treasury, as many contemporary theorists believed. Rather, it was the outcome of the activities of ordinary people working and trading in free markets. To Smith, the remarkable thing about the wealth produced by a market economy is that it is not a result of any organized plan, but rather the unintended outcome of the actions of many people, each of whom is pursuing the incentives the market offers with his or her own interests in mind. As he put it:

It is not from the benevolence of the butcher, the brewer, or the baker that we expect our dinner, but from their regard to their own interest. . . . Every individual is continually exerting himself to find out the most advantageous employment for whatever capital he can command. . . . By directing that industry in such a manner as its produce may be of the greatest value, he intends only his own gain, and he is in this, as in many other cases, led by an invisible hand to promote an end which was no part of his intention.*

Much of the discipline of economics as it has developed over the past two centuries consists of elaborations on ideas found in Smith's work. The idea of the "invisible hand" of market incentives that channels people's efforts in directions that are beneficial to their neighbors remains the most durable of Smith's contributions to economics.

*Adam Smith, *The Wealth of Nations* (1776), Book 1, Chapter 2.

Individuals and the government deal with one another through markets. Markets and the government thus play complementary roles in achieving economic coordination. Some economies rely more on markets, others on government planning. At one extreme, the centrally-planned economy of North Korea places heavy emphasis on government authority. Market economics, such as that of the United States, make greater use of markets. But no economy uses one means of coordination to the exclusion of the other. Government regulatory agencies in the United States establish laws to control pollution or protect worker safety; on the other hand, North Korea uses small-scale markets to distribute some goods. Likewise, in the United States, the government fosters coordination in markets by enforcing laws and providing national security. This protects an individual's right to property, encouraging market interaction.

In short, wherever one turns in economics, the question of coordination arises. Understanding economic coordination means understanding the complementary roles of markets and the government.

# ECONOMIC METHOD

The economic way of thinking is a very broad concept; economic method is a somewhat narrower idea having to do with the way economists go about their work. The chapter would be incomplete without a few comments about method.

## Theories and Models

At the beginning of the chapter we defined economics as the social science that seeks to understand the choices people make in using scarce resources to meet their wants. Later, in discussing positive economics, we noted that understanding something means discovering how its parts are related to one another. In economics, we want to know how each of the four basic types of choices are related to the context in which they are made, and how outcomes are related to those choices.

**Theory**

A representation of the way in which facts are related to one another.

**Model**

A synonym for theory; in economics, often applied to theories that are stated in graphical or mathematical form.

Any representation of the way in which facts are related can be called a **theory** or a **model**. The terms are synonyms, although economists tend to use the term *theory* to refer to more general statements about economic relationships and the term *model* to refer to more particular statements, especially those that take the form of graphs or mathematical equations.

Economics needs theories and models because facts do not speak for themselves. Take, for example, the fact that between 1979 and 1981, U.S. motorists cut their use of gasoline by more than 10 percent, from 80.2 billion to 71.7 billion gallons per year. Why did they do that? Economists have a theory. They relate the drop in gasoline consumption to another fact: the 50 percent rise in the retail price of gasoline, from $.86 per gallon to $1.31 per gallon, over the same period. The relationship between the price and consumption of gasoline is seen as a particular instance of a broader theory according to which an increase in the price of any good, other things being equal, tends to decrease the quantity of that good that consumers buy.

The theory as stated is a simple one. It relates quantity purchased to just one other fact, the price of the good. A more complete theory would bring in other factors that influence consumer choice, such as the prices of goods other than gasoline, consumers' incomes, changes in the average fuel economy of cars, and so on. Where does one draw the line? How much detail does it take to make a good theory?

There is no simple answer to this question, because adding detail to a theory involves a trade-off. On the one hand, if essential details are left out, the theory may fail altogether to fit the facts. On the other hand, adding too much detail defeats the purpose of understanding because key relationships may become lost in a cloud of complexity. The only real guideline is that a theory should be just detailed enough to suit the purpose for which it is intended, and no more.

By analogy, consider the models that aircraft designers use. The wind tunnel models made to test the aerodynamics of a new design need to represent the shapes of the wings, fuselage, and control surfaces accurately, but they do not need to include tiny seats with tiny tables and magazine racks. On the other hand, a full-scale model built for the purpose of training flight attendants to work on the new plane would need seats and magazine racks, but it would not need wings.

In much the same way, the theories and models presented in this book are designed to highlight a few key economic relationships. They are helpful in understanding economics in the same way that playing a flight simulation game on a computer is helpful in understanding the basics of flying. Professional economists use more detailed models, just as professional pilots train with complex flight simulators rather than with simple computer games. Nevertheless, the basic principles learned from the simple models do not contradict those that apply to the more complex ones. In the simple games, just as in the complex simulators, adjusting the rudder makes the plane turn and adjusting the elevators makes it climb or dive.

## The Use of Graphs[3]

The theories introduced so far have been stated in words. Words are a powerful tool for developing understanding, but they are even more powerful when they are supplemented by pictures. Economists support their words with pictures called graphs. An example will illustrate how economists use graphs to represent theories.

**THE PRODUCTION POSSIBILITY FRONTIER**  Recall our earlier discussion of the trade-off between education and cars. Figure 1.1 shows the trade-off in graphical form for an economy in which only those two goods are produced. The horizontal axis measures the quantity of education in terms of the number of college graduates produced per year; the vertical axis measures the production of cars. Any combination of education and cars can be shown as a point in the space between the two axes. For example, production of 10 million graduates and 5 million cars in a given year would be represented by point E.

In drawing this graph, supplies of productive resources and the state of knowledge are assumed to remain constant. Even if all available resources are devoted to education, there is a limit to the number of graduates that can be produced in a year: 20 million. The extreme possibility of producing 20 million graduates and no cars is shown by point A. Likewise, the maximum number of cars that would be produced if no resources were put into education is 18 million cars, shown by point B. Between those two extremes is a whole range of possible combinations of education and cars. Those intermediate possibilities are shown by points such as C and D, which fall along a smooth curve. The curve is known as a **production possibility frontier**.

**Production possibility frontier**

A graph that shows possible combinations of goods that can be produced by an economy, given available knowledge and factors of production.

**EFFICIENCY AND ECONOMIC GROWTH**  The production possibility frontier is a boundary between the combinations of education and cars that can be produced and those that cannot, using given knowledge and productive resources. As such, it serves nicely to illustrate the concept of efficiency in production. Points inside the frontier, such as point E, represent inefficient production. Beginning from such a point, more cars can be made without cutting the output of education (shown by a vertical move toward the frontier); more education can be produced without cutting the output of cars (a horizontal move toward the frontier); or the output of both goods can be increased (a move up and to the right toward the frontier).

Points such as A, B, C, and D that are on the frontier represent efficient production. Starting from any of those points, it is not possible to produce more of one good

FIGURE 1.1    PRODUCTION POSSIBILITY FRONTIER

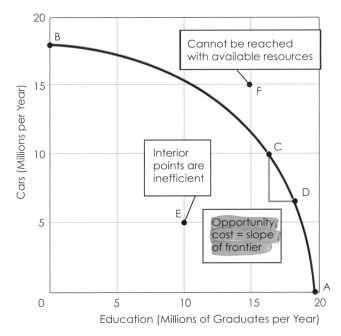

This figure shows combinations of cars and education that can be produced in a simple economy in which they are the only two products. Quantities of available factors of production and the state of existing knowledge are assumed to be fixed. If all factors are devoted to education, 20 million college graduates can be produced each year (point A). If all factors are devoted to making cars, 18 million cars can be produced each year (point B). Other combinations of the two goods that can be produced using available factors efficiently, such as those represented by points C and D, lie along a curve called a production possibility frontier. The slope of the frontier indicates the opportunity cost of education in terms of cars. Interior points, such as E, represent inefficient use of resources. Beginning from such a point, more of one good can be produced without producing less of the other. Points outside the frontier, such as F, cannot be reached using available factors of production and knowledge.

without producing less of the other. For example, in moving from C to D, output of education is increased but output of cars falls. Points such as F that lie outside the frontier cannot be reached even when the currently available knowledge and factors of production are used efficiently.

Over time, however, economic growth can stretch the production possibility frontier outward so that points such as F become possible. As mentioned earlier, the discovery of new ways of using available factors of production is one source of growth. So are additions to the total stock of factors of production—for example, through growth of the labor force. The case under discussion points to still yet another source of growth: Over time, the educational process itself improves the quality of the labor force, thus making a given number of people capable of producing more.

**OPPORTUNITY COST AND COMPARATIVE ADVANTAGE**    The production possibility frontier can also be used to represent the concept of opportunity cost. As we have seen, once the economy is producing efficiently at a point on the frontier, choosing to make more of one good means making less of the other. For example, suppose we start at point C, where 16 million students graduate each year and 10 million cars are being made. If we want to increase the output of graduates to 18 million per year, we must give up some cars and use the labor, capital, and natural resources freed in this way to build and staff classrooms. In moving from point C to point D, we trade off production of 4 million cars for the extra 2 million graduates. Over that range of the frontier, the opportunity cost of each extra graduate is about two cars. The opportunity cost of graduates, measured in terms of cars, is shown by the slope of the frontier.

As more graduates are produced, and the economy moves down and to the right along the frontier, the frontier becomes steeper and the opportunity cost of producing graduates increases. A major reason is that not all factors of production—especially not all workers—are alike. Suppose we start all the way up at point B, where no education is produced, and transfer enough resources to education to open one small college. The first people we would pull off the assembly line to staff the classrooms would be those who have a comparative advantage in teaching. By the time enough resources have been transferred to education from the auto industry to reach point D, the most suitable recruits for academic life have already been used. Increasingly, to produce still more education we have to take some of the best production workers with no assurance that they will be good teachers. The opportunity cost of increasing the output of education (shown by the slope of the frontier) is correspondingly greater.

## Theory and Evidence

Theories are of no use in explaining relationships among facts unless they fit those facts. Theory building is a matter of constantly comparing proposed explanations with evidence gleaned from observations of the actual choices people make—that is, with **empirical** evidence. When empirical evidence is consistent with the relationships proposed in a theory, confidence in the validity of the theory is increased. When evidence is not consistent with the theory, the theory needs to be reexamined. The relationships proposed in it may be invalid, or they may be valid only under circumstances different from those that prevailed when the observations were made. The theory then needs to be modified by changing the proposed relationships or adding detail.

**Empirical**

Based on experience or observation.

For example, earlier we noted that the drop in gasoline usage between 1979 and 1981 was consistent with the theory that people will buy less of something when its price goes up, other things being equal. But what about the fact that from 1976 to 1978 gasoline usage rose by 8 percent even though the price of gasoline rose by 11 percent? In seeking an explanation of this observation, an economist would first suggest that probably some of the "other things" were not equal after all. A more detailed theory that considers some of those other things is called for.

In the case of gasoline usage, such a line of inquiry proves fruitful. In the period from 1976 to 1978, two factors offset the tendency of a rising price to depress gasoline sales. First, the prices of goods and services other than gasoline rose even faster, so that gasoline actually became cheaper relative to the other things consumers bought. Second, consumer incomes rose by a strong 8 percent from 1976 to 1978, which would tend to make people buy more of many goods and services, including gasoline.

From 1979 to 1981, neither of those factors was present. During that period, gasoline prices rose twice as fast as the prices of other goods, and consumer incomes were stagnant, rising less than 1 percent. Thus, both the 1976–1978 and 1979–1981 observations are consistent with a more complete theory that takes gasoline prices, other prices, and consumer incomes into account.

Government agencies and private firms generate mountains of empirical data on economic activity. Economists constantly examine those data in an effort to confirm theories or find inconsistencies that point the way to better theories. Statistical analysis of empirical economic data is known as **econometrics**—literally, the science of economic measurement.

**Econometrics**

The statistical analysis of empirical economic data.

## Theories and Forecasts

Economic theories can help us understand things that happened in the past—trends in gasoline consumption in the 1970s, the effects of the tax reforms of the 1980s, and so on. But understanding the past is not always enough. People also want forecasts of future economic events.

Within limits, economic theory can be useful here, too. Any theory that purports to explain a relationship between past events provides a basis for predicting what will happen under similar circumstances in the future. To put it more precisely, economic theory can be used to make **conditional forecasts** of the form "If A, then B, other things being equal." Thus, an economist might say, "If gasoline prices rise, and if at the same time consumer incomes and the prices of other goods do not change, gasoline purchases will fall."

**Conditional forecast**

A prediction of future economic events in the form "If A, then B, other things being equal."

Thousands of economists make a living from forecasting. Decision-makers in business and government use economic forecasts extensively. Forecasts are not perfect, however, and forecasters sometimes make conspicuous mistakes. There are at least three reasons for the mistakes.

First, insufficient attention is sometimes paid to the conditional nature of forecasts. The news might report, for example, that "economists predict an upturn in inflation," yet inflation might not increase after all. In such a case the news report may have failed to note the forecasters' precautionary comments. The forecasters may have said that the rate of inflation would rise only if bank loans continued to expand as they had in the immediate past, but loans may not have increased after all.

Second, a forecast may be invalid because the theory on which it is based is incorrect or incomplete. Economists do not always agree on what theory best fits the facts. Some theories give more weight to one fact, others to different facts. The competing theories may imply conflicting forecasts under some conditions. At least one of the forecasts will then turn out to be wrong. Finding out which theories yield better forecasts than others is an important part of the process through which valid theories are distinguished from inadequate ones.

Third, economic forecasts can go wrong because some of the things that business managers and government officials most want to know are among the hardest to predict. For example, a competent economist could produce a fairly accurate forecast of gasoline sales, making certain assumptions about incomes and the prices of gasoline and other goods, but only a few specialists would be interested. In contrast, millions of people—including bankers, bond market traders, and families planning to buy homes—would like accurate forecasts of interest rates. Interest rates, however, happen to be among the hardest economic variables to forecast accurately.

This does not mean that economists do not try to forecast interest rates. They do try; they just do not succeed very well. Forecasts of certain other major macroeconomic variables, such as unemployment, inflation, and growth of the nation's total output, do a little better than forecasts of interest rates, but their accuracy remains low relative to the publicity they get.

Most economists take the view that well-founded conditional forecasts, for all their limitations, are a better basis for business and public policy decisions than whims and guesswork. Still, they caution against relying too heavily on forecasts. For example, in the 1970s many forecasters projected higher energy prices right through the rest of the century. When energy prices fell in the 1980s, oil companies, bankers, and even national governments that had relied on the forecasts were in trouble.

## Theory and Policy

Economists are often asked to use their theories to analyze the effects of public policies and forecast the effects of policy changes. The government may, for example, be considering new measures to aid unemployed workers, new approaches to improving air quality, or new measures to regulate international trade. How will the effects of such policies be spread through the economy? How will they affect people's lives?

Economists have their own characteristic way of thinking about public policy, just as they have their own way of thinking about other topics. In particular, economists are concerned with identifying both the direct and indirect effects of policy, as well as any indirect or unintended consequences. They are also constantly alert to both the long-run and short-term effects of policy.

- Unemployment compensation has the intended effect of aiding unemployed workers, but it also has the unintended effect of increasing the number of workers who are unemployed, because workers receiving compensation can afford to take their time finding just the right new job.
- Regulations intended to improve the fuel efficiency of automobiles encourage production of cars that weigh less, but the lighter cars are somewhat less safe.

Increased highway deaths among drivers of the lighter cars may thus be an unintended consequence of efforts to save fuel.

- Beginning in the 1930s, the federal government began to insure consumer deposits in savings and loan associations and banks. The intent was to stabilize the banking system by convincing consumers that their savings were protected. As a consequence, consumers were more willing to place funds in risky, poorly managed banks that offered high interest rates on insured deposits. This effect contributed to the massive banking crisis of the 1980s.

While policies may have unintended consequences, public policy still plays an important role in the economy. It would be wrong to conclude that the government should never act simply because its actions may do some harm as well as some good. Rather, economists simply urge that policy makers look at the whole picture, not just part of it, before they make a decision. As Henry Hazlitt once put it, the whole of economics can be reduced to a single lesson:

> *The art of economics consists in looking not merely at the immediate but at the longer effects of any act or policy; it consists in tracing the consequences of that policy not merely for one group but for all groups.*[4]

## SUMMARY

1. **What is the subject matter of economics?** *Economics* is the social science that seeks to understand the choices people make in using scarce resources to meet their wants. *Scarcity* is a situation in which there is not enough of something to meet everyone's wants. *Microeconomics* is the branch of economics that studies choices that involve individual households, firms, and markets. *Macroeconomics* is the branch of economics that deals with large-scale economic phenomena, such as inflation, unemployment, and economic growth.

2. **What considerations underlie the choice of what an economy will produce?** Producing more of one good requires producing less of something else because productive resources that are used to produce one good cannot be used to produce another at the same time. Productive resources are traditionally classified into three groups, called *factors of production*. *Labor* consists of the productive contributions made by people working with their hands and minds. *Capital* consists of all the productive inputs created by people. *Natural resources* include anything that can be used as a productive input in its natural state. The *opportunity cost* of a good or service is its cost in terms of the forgone opportunity to pursue the best possible alternative activity with the same time or resources.

3. **What considerations underlie the choice of how to produce?** Goods and services can be produced in many different ways, some of which are more efficient than others. *Economic efficiency* refers to a state of affairs in which it is impossible to make any change that satisfies one person's wants more fully without causing some other person's wants to be satisfied less fully. *Efficiency in production* refers

to a situation in which it is not possible, given the available productive resources and existing knowledge, to produce more of one good or service without forgoing the opportunity to produce some of another good or service. Once efficiency has been achieved, production potential can be expanded by increasing the availability of resources or by improving knowledge. The process of increasing the economy's stock of capital is known as *investment*. The process of looking for new possibilities—making use of new ways of doing things, being alert to new opportunities, and overcoming old limits—is known as *entrepreneurship*.

4. **What considerations underlie the choice of who will do which work?** Although a person can survive apart from all human contact, economic efficiency is greatly enhanced by cooperation with others. Three things make cooperation worthwhile: teamwork, learning by doing, and comparative advantage. Teamwork can enhance productivity even when there is no specialization. Learning by doing improves productivity even when all workers start with equal talents and abilities. Comparative advantage comes into play when people have different innate abilities or, after learning by doing, have developed specialized skills. Having a *comparative advantage* in producing a particular good or service means being able to produce it at a relatively lower opportunity cost than someone else.

5. **What considerations underlie the choice of for whom goods will be produced?** In part, deciding for whom goods will be produced revolves around issues of efficiency. *Efficiency in distribution* refers to a state of affairs in which, with a given quantity of goods and services, it is impossible to satisfy one person's wants more fully without satisfying someone else's less fully. Efficiency is part of *positive economics,* the area of economics that is concerned with facts and the

relationships among them. *Normative economics* is the area of economics that is devoted to judgments about which economic conditions and policies are good or bad.

6. **What mechanisms are used to coordinate economic choices?** The most important mechanism for achieving coordination occurs through the interaction of individuals in *markets*. Markets describe arrangements people have for trading with one another. The government plays a role in economic coordination through legislation, law enforcement, and national security. The relative importance of markets and the government in achieving coordination differs across countries.

7. **How do economists use theory, graphs, and evidence in their work?** A *theory* or *model* is a representation of the ways in which facts are related to one another. Economists use graphs to display data and make visual representations of theories and models. For example, a *production possibility frontier* is a graph that shows the boundary between combinations of goods that can be produced and those that cannot, using available factors of production and knowledge. Economists refine theories in the light of *empirical* evidence, that is, evidence gleaned from observation of actual economic decisions. The economic analysis of empirical evidence is known as *econometrics*. Economic models are often used to make *conditional forecasts* of the form "If A, then B, other things being equal."

## KEY TERMS

| | |
|---|---|
| Scarcity | Labor |
| Economics | Capital |
| Microeconomics | Natural resources |
| Macroeconomics | Opportunity cost |
| Factors of production | Economic efficiency |

Efficiency in production
Investment
Entrepreneurship
Comparative advantage
Efficiency in
    distribution
Positive economics
Normative economics

Market
Theory
Model
Production possibility
    frontier
Empirical
Econometrics
Conditional forecast

## PROBLEMS AND TOPICS FOR DISCUSSION

1. **Opportunity cost**. Gasoline, insurance, depreciation, and repairs are all costs of owning a car. Which of these can be considered opportunity costs in the context of each of the following decisions?

    a. You own a car and are deciding whether to drive 100 miles for a weekend visit to a friend at another university.

    b. You do not own a car but are considering buying one so that you can get a part-time job located 5 miles from where you live.

    In general, why does the context in which you decide to do something affect the opportunity cost of doing it?

2. **Comparative advantage in international trade**. Suppose that in the United States a car can be produced with 200 labor hours, while a ton of rice requires 20 labor hours. In Japan, it takes 150 labor hours to make a car and 50 labor hours to grow a ton of rice. What is the opportunity cost of producing rice in each country, stated in terms of cars? What is the opportunity cost of cars, stated in terms of rice? Which country has a comparative advantage in cars? Which in rice?

3. **Efficiency in distribution and the food stamp program**. The federal food stamp program could have been designed so that every low-income family would receive a book of coupons containing so many bread coupons, so many milk coupons, and so on. Instead, it gives the family a book of coupons that can be spent on any kind of food the family prefers. For a given cost to the federal government, which plan do you think would better serve the goal of efficiency in distribution? Why?

    Now consider a program that would allow families to trade their food stamps for cash (some such trading does occur, but it is restricted by law) or one in which poor families are given cash, with which they can buy whatever they want. Compare these alternatives with the existing food stamp program in terms of both positive and normative economics.

4. **Spontaneous order in the cafeteria**. Suppose that your college cafeteria does not have enough room for all the students to sit down to eat at once, so it stays open for lunch from 11:30 A.M. to 1:30 P.M. Consider the following three methods of distributing diners over the two-hour lunch period in such a way that everyone can have a seat.

    a. The administration sets a rule: Freshmen must eat between 11:30 and 12:00, sophomores between 12:00 and 12:30, and so on for juniors and seniors.

    b. The lunch period is broken up into half-hour segments, with green tickets for the first shift, blue tickets for the second, and so on. An equal number of tickets of each color is printed. At the beginning of each semester an auction is held in which students bid for the ticket color of their choice.

    c. Students can come to the cafeteria whenever they want. If there are no empty seats, they have to stand in line.

    Compare the three schemes in terms of the concepts of (i) spontaneous order and hierarchy; (ii) information and incentives; and (iii) efficiency.

5. **A production possibility frontier.** Bill Swartz has four fields spread out over a hillside. He can grow either wheat or potatoes in any of the fields, but the low fields are better for potatoes and the high ones are better for wheat. Here are some combinations of wheat and potatoes that he could produce:

| Number of Fields Used for Potatoes | Total Tons of Potatoes | Total Tons of Wheat |
| --- | --- | --- |
| All 4 | 1,000 | 0 |
| Lowest 3 | 900 | 400 |
| Lowest 2 | 600 | 700 |
| Lowest 1 | 300 | 900 |
| None | 0 | 1,000 |

Use these data to draw a production possibility frontier for wheat and potatoes. What is the opportunity cost of wheat, stated in terms of potatoes, when the farmer converts the highest field to wheat production? What happens to the opportunity cost of wheat as more and more fields are switched to wheat?

# CASE FOR DISCUSSION

## Zimbabwe's Land Questions

**HARARE, November 2003**—President Mugabe continued seizure of primarily white-owned land in urban areas. The country's white farmers own much of the country's best agricultural land; according to government figures, 4,400 whites owned 32% of Zimbabwe's agricultural land, while about one million black peasant families farmed 38%. Furthermore, whites own a disproportionate share of the country's most fertile land. The situation was created in colonial times when blacks were forced off their ancestral lands. "The land question" was the source of discontent among the majority of Zimbabweans and a major cause of the guerrilla war that led to Zimbabwe's independence in 1980. When Mugabe came to power in 1980, he promised to balance the scales for black farmers through land reform.

Land reform and redistribution is expensive. Not only does the government need to compensate farmers giving up their property, but it also needs to provide infrastructure—such as roads, schools, and hospitals—for land redistribution to be beneficial. There is also the difficulty of taking large, sophisticated farms and then subdividing them into plots to give to people without the means to farm them effectively.

President Mugabe says Britain should pay because the British government colonized the region, seizing land from African farmers in the late 19th century. While the U.K. and others have provided some aid to help the government purchase land from "willing" white farmers, donors have refused further support unless President Mugabe's land program is more clearly defined.

The white farmers themselves do not see why they should have to pay because of what happened in the past. Many say they bought their farms at market rates since Zimbabwe's independence and reject arguments rooted in colonization. While Zimbabwe's government has paid some farmers, a new law requires farmers to leave their farms before receiving compensation.

Despite promises to target the seizure of the least-productive farms, many of those on the so-called "hit-list" have been the most efficient growers of tobacco. President Mugabe's opponents accuse him of exploiting the land question to win support amid Zimbabwe's current economic crisis.

The threat of land seizures has led to a steep decline in agricultural production on white-owned farms, exacerbating food shortages and unemployment in Zimbabwe. This coupled with two years of drought threaten a famine in which up to six million of Zimbabwe's citizens could go hungry. Aid agencies estimate over one-third of the population will be unable to feed themselves by the end of the year.

Consider the following hypothetical situations involving individuals and the government in Zimbabwe:

- Shekan currently owns 100 hectares of land that he uses for tobacco farming. On this land he has hired several hands to assist in harvesting and curing the tobacco leaves. He owns capital equipment to assist in curing the tobacco leaves. Shekan pays his workers 5 Zimbabwean dollars per pound of tobacco. Shekan then sells tobacco at the market price of 7 Zimbabwean dollars per pound.
- Amadika is a middle-aged woman who works on Shekan's farm. Using Shekan's curing equipment, she gathers and cures 50 pounds of tobacco each year.
- Tatenda is a young woman who was able to gather and cure 60 pounds of tobacco on Shekan's farm. She has decided to leave the farm and attend college in the United States. Tatenda has received a full scholarship and financing from the school to cover her expenses.
- Dakarai is a young man who currently works on Shekan's farm. He is able to gather and cure 75 pounds of tobacco each year using the available capital equipment. Instead of giving all 75 pounds to Shekan, he sells 25 pounds of tobacco illegally to a cigarette manufacturer for 6 Zimbabwean dollars per pound.

## QUESTIONS

1. What might explain why Shekan pays his workers 5 Zimbabwean dollars per pound of cured tobacco while he sells it for 7 Zimbabwean dollars? What is Shekan's contribution to the tobacco production process?
2. Under President Mugabe's land management plan, Amadika is to receive 10 hectares of Shekan's property, but she receives none of the capital equipment she currently uses on Shekan's farm. When Amadika receives 10 hectares of land from Shekan's farm, will she be able to gather and cure the same amount of tobacco? Why or why not?
3. In terms of Zimbabwean dollars, what is Tatenda's opportunity cost of attending college? Why is there still a cost, even though Tatenda receives a scholarship? If she were to receive land under President Mugabe's plan, how might this affect her decision to attend school?
4. Assume that a gallon of milk costs 2 Zimbabwean dollars. What is the cost of a gallon of milk in terms of pounds of tobacco?
5. Suppose Zimbabwe's government decides that 2 dollars is too expensive for milk, and imposes a law that sets the price of milk at 1 Zimbabwean dollar per gallon. How will this affect the availability of milk in Zimbabwe?
6. Why might Dakarai sell some of his tobacco crop to Shekan at 5 Zimbabwean dollars per pound, when he can receive 6 dollars from an illegal trader?
7. President Mugabe recently denounced people, such as Dakarai, who engage in illegal trade. The government, and many Zimbabweans, see people like Dakarai as an exploiter who robs from Shekan. Discuss this issue in terms of fairness and efficiency.

## END NOTES

1. Efficiency, defined this way, is sometimes called *Pareto efficiency* after the Italian economist Vilfredo Pareto.
2. Armen A. Alchian and Harold Demsetz, "Production, Information, Cost, and Economic Organization," *American Economic Review* (December 1972): 777–795.
3. Some basic graphical concepts—axes, points and number pairs, slopes, and tangencies—are discussed in the appendix to this chapter.
4. Henry Hazlitt, *Economics in One Lesson* (New York: Arlington House, 1979), 17.

# Appendix to Chapter 1
## WORKING WITH GRAPHS

⁓

Graphs are an invaluable aid in learning economics precisely because they make use of these three special abilities of the human brain. Graphs are not used to make economics harder, but to make it easier. All it takes to use graphs effectively as a learning tool is the inborn human skill in working with pictures plus knowledge of a few simple rules for extracting the information that graphs contain. This appendix outlines those rules in brief. Additional details and exercises can be found in the *Study Guide* that accompanies this textbook.

## Pairs of Numbers and Points

The first thing to master is how to use points on a graph to represent pairs of numbers. The table in Figure lA.1 presents five pairs of numbers. The two columns are labeled "x" and "y." The first number in each pair is called the *x value* and the second the *y value*. Each pair of numbers is labeled with a capital letter. Pair A has an *x* value of 2 and a *y* value of 3; pair B has an *x* value of 4 and a *y* value of 4; and so on.

The diagram in Figure lA.1 contains two lines that meet at the lower left-hand corner; they are called *coordinate axes*. The horizontal axis is marked off into units representing the *x* value and the vertical axis into unit representing the *y* value. In the space between the axes,

**FIGURE 1A.1   NUMBER PAIRS AND POINTS**

| | x | y |
|---|---|---|
| A | 2 | 3 |
| B | 4 | 4 |
| C | 6 | 5 |
| D | 8 | 6 |
| E | 10 | 7 |

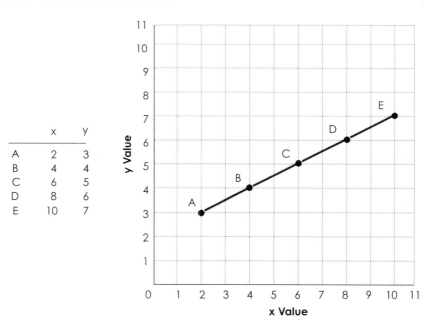

Each lettered pair of numbers in the table corresponds to a lettered point on the graph. The x value of each point corresponds to the horizontal distance of the point from the vertical axis; the y value corresponds to its vertical distance from the horizontal axis.

**FIGURE 1A.2    SLOPES OF LINES**

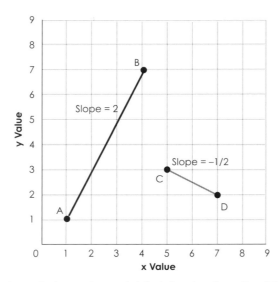

The slope of a straight line drawn between two points is defined as the ratio of the change in the y value to the change in the x value as one moves from one point to the other. For example, the line between points A and B in this Figure has a slope of +2, whereas the line between points C and D has a slope of –1/2.

each pair of numbers from the table can be shown as a point. For example, point A is found by going two units to the right along the horizontal axis and then three units straight up, parallel to the vertical axis. That point represents the *x* value of 2 and the *y* value of 3. The other points are located in the same way.

The visual effect of a graph usually can be improved by connecting the points with a line or a curve. By doing so, the relationship between *x* values and *y* values can be seen at a glance: as the *x* value increases, the *y* value also increases.

## Slopes and Tangencies

The lines or curves used in graphs are described in terms of their slopes. The **slope** of a straight line between two points is defined as the ratio of the change in the *y* value to the change in the *x* value between the two points. In Figure lA.2, for example, the slope of the line between points A and B is 2. The *y* value changes by six units between these two points, whereas the *x* value changes by only three units. The slope is the ratio 6/3 = 2.

The slope of a line between the points $(x_1, y_1)$ and $(x_2, y_2)$ can be expressed in terms of a simple formula that is derived from the definition just given:

$$\text{Slope} = (y_2 - y_1)/(x_2 - x_1)$$

Applied to the line between points A and B in Figure 1A.2, the formula gives the following result:

$$\text{Slope} = (7 - 1)/(4 - 1) = 6/3 = 2$$

A line such as that between A and B in Figure 1A.2 is said to have a **positive slope**, because the value of its slope is a positive number. A positively sloped line represents a **direct relationship** between the variable represented on the *x* axis and that represented on the

**Slope**

For a straight line, the ratio of the change in the y value to the change in the x value between any two points on the line.

**Positive slope**

A slope having a value greater than zero.

**Direct relationship**

A relationship between two variables in which an increase in the value of one variable is associated with an increase in the value of the other.

*y* axis—that is, a relationship in which an increase in one variable is associated with an increase in the other. The relationship of the age of a tree to its height is an example of a direct relationship. An example from economics is the relationship between family income and expenditures on housing.

When a line slants downward, such as the one between points C and D in Figure 1A.2, the *x* and *y* values change in opposite directions. Going from point C to point D, the *y* value changes by –1 (that is, decreases by one unit) and the *x* value changes by +2 (that is, increases by two units). The slope of this line is the ratio –1/2.

When the slope of a line is given by a negative number, the line is said to have a **negative slope**. Such a line represents an **inverse relationship** between the *x* variable and the *y* variable—that is, a relationship in which an increase in the value of one variable is associated with a decrease in the value of the other variable. The relationship between the temperature in the room and the time it takes the ice in your lemonade to melt is an example of an inverse relationship. To give an economic example, the relationship between the price of gasoline and the quantity consumers purchase, other things being equal, is an inverse relationship.

The concepts of positive and negative slopes, and of direct and inverse relationships, apply to curves as well as to straight lines. However, the slope of a curve, unlike that of a straight line, varies from one point to the next.[1] We cannot speak of the slope of a curve in general, but only of its slope at a given point. The slope of a curve at any given point is defined as the slope of a straight line drawn tangent to the curve at that point. (A **tangent** line is one that just touches the curve without crossing it.) In Figure 1A.3, the slope of the curve at point A is 1 and the slope at point B is –2.

---

[1] Economists try to be consistent, but in talking about lines and curves, they fail. They have no qualms about calling something a "curve" that is a straight line. For example, later we will encounter "demand curves" that are as straight as a stretched string. Less frequently, they may call something a line that is curved.

---

## Negative slope

A slope having a value less than zero.

## Inverse relationship

A relationship between two variables in which an increase in the value of one variable is associated with a decrease in the value of the other.

## Tangent

A straight line that touches a curve at a given point without intersecting it.

---

**FIGURE 1A.3  SLOPES OF CURVES**

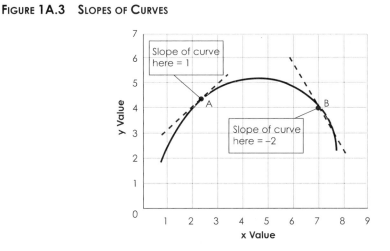

The slope of a curve at any point is defined as the slope of a straight line drawn tangent to the curve at that point. A tangent line is one that just touches the curve without crossing it. In this figure, the slope of the curve at point A is 1 and the slope at point B is –2.

## Using Graphs to Display Data

Graphs are used in economics for two primary purposes: for visual display of quantitative data and for visual representation of economic relationships. Some graphs are primarily designed to serve one purpose, some the other, and some a little of both. We begin with some common kinds of graphs whose primary purpose is to display data.

Figure 1A.4 shows three kinds of graphs often used to display data. Part (a) is *pie chart*. Pie charts are used to show the relative size of various quantities that add up to a total of 100 percent. In this case, the quantities displayed are the percentages of U.S. foreign trade accounted for by various trading partners. In the original source, the graph was drawn as part of a discussion of U.S. trade with Canada, Japan, and Western Europe. The author wanted to make the point that trade with these countries is very important. Note how the graph highlights Canadian, Japanese, and Western European trade with the U.S., and at the same time omits details not relevant to the discussion by lumping together the rest of Europe, Africa, the rest of Asia, and many other countries under the heading "rest of the world." In reading graphs, do not just look at the numbers, but ask yourself, "What point is the graph trying to make?"

Part (b) of Figure 1A.4 is a *bar chart*. Bar charts, like pie charts, are used to display numerical data (in this case, unemployment rates) in relationship to some nonnumerical classification of cases (in this case, educational attainment). Bar charts are not subject to the restriction that data displayed must total 100 percent. What point do you think the author of this graph was trying to make?

Part (c) of Figure 1A.4 is an example of a data display graph very common in economics—the *time-series graph*. A time-series graph shows the values of one or more economic quantities on the vertical axis and time (years, months, or whatever) on the horizontal axis. This graph shows the ups and downs of the U.S. unemployment rate by month over the period 1980 through 1991.

Note one feature of this time-series graph: the scale on the vertical axis begins from 3 percent rather than from 0. By spreading out the data points in the range 3 to 11 percent, one can show the trend of unemployment in greater detail. The advantage of greater detail has an offsetting danger, however. Careless reading of the graph could cause one to exaggerate the amount by which unemployment rises during a recession. For example, the unemployment line is more than three times higher above the horizontal axis in December 1991 than in March 1989. However, careful reading of the graph shows that the unemployment rate in December 1991 was actually only about 1.4 times as high as in March 1989. The moral of the story: Always examine the vertical and horizontal axes of a graph carefully.

## Using Graphs to Display Relationships

Some graphs, rather than simply recording observed facts, attempt to represent theories and models—that is, to show the relationships among facts. Figure 1A.5 shows two typical graphs whose primary purpose is to display relationships.

Part (a) of Figure 1A.5 is the production possibility frontier that we encountered in Chapter 1. The graph represents the inverse relationship between the quantity of cars that can be produced and the quantity of education that can be produced, given available knowledge and productive resources.

**FIGURE 1A.4   USING GRAPHS TO DISPLAY DATA**

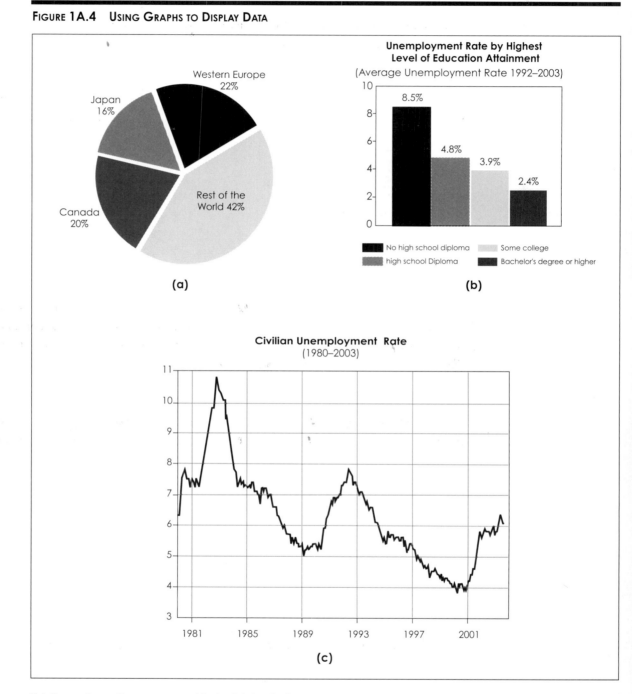

(a)

(b)

(c)

This figure shows three common kinds of data display graphs. The *pie chart* in part (a) is used when the data items sum to 100 percent. The *bar chart* in part (b), like the pie chart, is used when reporting numerical data that are associated with nonnumerical categories (in this case educational attainment). The bar chart does not require data items to sum to 100 percent. The *time-series graph* in part (c) shows the values of one or more economic quantities on the vertical axis and time on the horizontal axis.

Source: Part (a), U.S. Council of Economic Advisers, *Economic Report of the President* (Washington, D.C.: Government Printing Office, 2002), Table B-105, 397; part (b), Bureau of Labor Statistics, *Current Population Survey*; and part (c), Bureau of Labor Statistics, *The Employment Situation*.

FIGURE 1A.5  USING GRAPHS TO SHOW RELATIONSHIPS

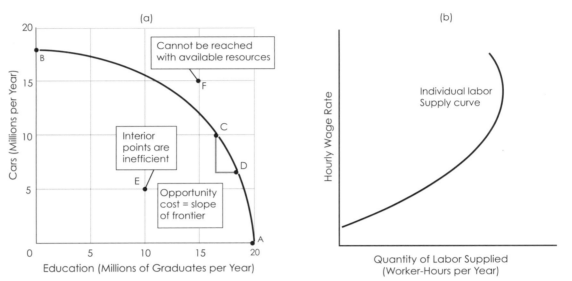

Relational graphs are visual representations of theories, that is, of relationships among facts. Two typical relational graphs are shown here. Part (a) is the production possibility frontier discussed in Chapter 1. It relates quantities of cars to quantities of education that can be produced with given factors of production and knowledge. Part (b) represents a theory of individual labor supply, according to which an increase in the hourly wage rate, after a point, will cause a person to reduce the quantity of labor supplied. Part (b) is an abstract graph in that it shows only the general nature of the relationship, with no numbers on either axis.

Part (b) of Figure 1A.5 represents a relationship between the quantity of labor that a person is willing to supply (measured in worker-hours per year) and the wage rate per hour the person is paid. According to the theory portrayed by the graph, raising the wage rate will, up to a point, induce a person to work more hours. But beyond a certain point (according to the theory), a further increase in the wage will actually cause the person to work fewer hours. Why? Because the person is so well off, he or she prefers the luxury of more leisure time to the reward of more material goods.

Note one distinctive feature of this graph: There are no numbers on the axes. It is an abstract graph that represents only the qualitative relationships between the hours of labor supplied per year and the wage rate. It makes no quantitative statements regarding how much the number of hours worked will change as a result of any given change in wage rate. Abstract graphs are often used when the point to be made is a general one that applies to many cases, regardless of quantitative differences from one case to another.

## Packing Three Variables into Two Dimensions

Anything drawn on a flat piece of paper is limited to two dimensions. The relationships discussed so far fit a two-dimensional framework easily, because they involve just two variables. In the case of the production possibility frontier, the two are the quantity of education (horizontal axis) and the quantity of cars (vertical axis). In the case of the labor supply, they are hours worked per year (horizontal axis) and wage rate per hour (vertical axis). But reality does not always cooperate with geometry. Often one must take three or more variables into account in order to understand relationships among facts.

A number of methods have been devised to represent relationships involving three or more variables. For example, a map of the United States might use coordinates of latitude and longitude to indicate position, contour lines to indicate altitude, and shadings of various colors to indicate vegetation. An architect might use a perspective drawing to give the illusion of three dimensions—height, width, and depth—on a flat piece of paper. This section deals with one simple method of packing three variables into two dimensions. Although the method is a favorite of economists—it will be used in dozens of graphs in this book—we will show its generality by beginning with a noneconomic example.

**A NONECONOMIC EXAMPLE**   The example concerns heart disease, the leading cause of death in the United States. In recent years, medical researchers have discovered that the risk of heart disease is closely linked to the quantity of cholesterol in a person's blood. Studies have indicated, for example, that a 25 percent reduction in cholesterol can cut the risk of death from heart attack by nearly 50 percent. Knowing this, millions of people have had their cholesterol levels tested, and if they were found to be high, have undertaken programs of diet, exercise, or drug therapy to reduce their risk of heart disease.

Important though cholesterol is, however, just knowing your cholesterol level is not enough to tell you your risk of dying of a heart attack in the coming year. Other variables also enter into the risk of heart disease. One of the most important of these variables is age. For example, for men aged 20 with average cholesterol levels, the mortality rate from heart disease is only about 3 per 100,000. For men aged 60, the mortality rate rises to over 500 per 100,000, still assuming average cholesterol. We thus have three variables to deal with: mortality, cholesterol, and age. How can we represent these three variables using only two-dimensional graphs?

A possible approach would be to draw two separate graphs. One would show the relationship between age and heart disease for the male population as a whole, without regard to differences in cholesterol counts. The other would show the relationship between cholesterol and heart disease for the male population as a whole, without regard to age. By looking from one diagram to the other, we could get an idea of the three-variable relationship as a whole.

However, such a side-by-side pair of graphs would be clumsy. There must be a better way to represent the three variables in two dimensions. The better way, shown in Figure lA.6, is to use cholesterol and mortality as the *x* and *y* axes, and to take age into account by plotting separate lines for men of various ages. That chart is far easier to interpret than the side-by-side pair would be. If you are a man and know your age and cholesterol count, you just pick out the appropriate line and read off your risk of mortality. If you do not like what you see, you go on a diet.[2]

The multi-curve graph is a lovely invention. One of the great things about it is that it works for more than three variables. For example, we could add a fourth variable, gender, to the graph by drawing a new set of lines in a different color to show mortality rates for women

---

[2] We could instead have started with the age-mortality chart and drawn separate lines for men with different cholesterol levels. Such a chart would show exactly the same information. We could even draw a chart with cholesterol and age on the axes, and separate contour lines to represent various levels of mortality. The choice often depends on what one wants to emphasize. Here, we emphasize the cholesterol-mortality relationship because cholesterol is something you can do something about. You cannot do anything about your age, so we give age slightly less emphasis by not placing it on one of the two axes.

FIGURE 1A.6  THREE VARIABLES IN TWO DIMENSIONS

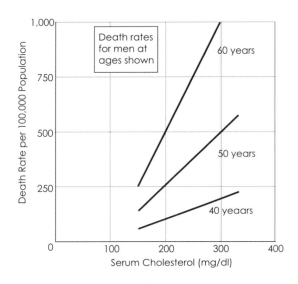

This graph shows a common way of representing a three-variable relationship on a two-dimensional graph. The three variables in this case are serum cholesterol (a measure of the amount of cholesterol in the blood), age, and death rate from heart disease for the U.S. male population. The relationship among the three variables is most easily interpreted, if all three variables are included in one graph, by drawing separate cholesterol-death rate lines for each age group. As a man ages, his cholesterol-death rate line shifts upward.

of various ages. Each line for women would have a positive slope similar to the men's lines, but would lie somewhat below the corresponding line for men of the same age, because women, other things being equal, experience lower mortality from heart disease.

**SHIFTS IN CURVES AND MOVEMENTS ALONG CURVES**   Economists use three-variable, multi-curve graphs often enough that it is worth giving some attention to the terminology used in discussing them. How can we best describe what happens to a man as he ages, given the relationship shown in Figure 1A.6?

One way to describe the effects of aging would be to say, "As a man ages, he moves from one curve to the next higher one on the chart." There is nothing at all wrong with saying that, but an economist would tend to phrase it a bit differently, saying "As a man ages, his cholesterol-mortality curve shifts upward." The two ways of expressing the effects of aging have exactly the same meaning. Preferring one or the other is just a matter of habit.

If we express the effects of aging in terms of a shift of the cholesterol-mortality curve, how should we express the effects of a reduction in cholesterol for a man of a given age? An economist would say it this way: "Cutting a man's cholesterol count through diet or exercise will move him down along his cholesterol-mortality curve."

Before you finish this book, you will see the phrases "shift in a curve" and "movement along a curve" a great many times. How can you keep them straight? Nothing could be easier.

- If you are talking about the effect of a change in a variable that is shown on one of the coordinate axes of the diagram, the effect will be shown as a movement along one of the curves.

- If you are talking about the effect of a change in a variable that is not shown on one of the coordinate axes of the diagram, the effect will be shown by a shift in one of the curves.

## Study Hints

So much for the basic rules of graphics. Once you master them, how should you study a chapter that is full of graphs?

The first—and most important—rule is to avoid trying to memorize graphs as patterns of lines. In every economics course, at least one student comes to the instructor after failing an exam and exclaims, "But I learned every one of those graphs! What happened?" The reply is that the student should have learned economics instead of memorizing graphs. Following are some hints for working with graphs.

After reading through a chapter that contains several graphs, go back through the graphs one at a time. Cover the caption accompanying each graph, and try to express the graph's "picture" in words. If you cannot say as much about the graph as the caption does, reread the text. Once you can translate the graph into words, you have won half the battle.

Next, cover each graph and use the caption as a guide. Try to sketch the graph on a piece of scratch paper. How are the graph's axes labeled? How are the curves labeled? What are the slopes of various curves? Are there important points of intersection or tangencies? If you can go back and forth between the caption and the graph, you will find that the two together are much easier to remember than either one separately.

Finally, try going beyond the graph that is shown in the book. If the graph illustrates the effect of an increase in the price of butter, try sketching a similar diagram that shows the effect of a decrease in the price of butter. If the graph shows what happens to the economy during a period of rising unemployment, try drawing a similar graph that shows what happens during a period of falling unemployment. This is a good practice that may give you an edge on your next exam.

**MAKING YOUR OWN GRAPHS**   For some students, the hardest test questions to answer are ones that require original graphs as part of an essay. Suppose the question is, "How does a change in the number of students attending a university affect the cost per student of providing an education?" Here are some hints for making your own graph.

1. Write down the answer to the question in words. If you cannot, you might as well skip to the next question. Underline the most important quantities in your answer, such as "The larger the *number of students* who attend a college, the lower the *cost per student* of providing them with an education, because fixed facilities, such as libraries, do not have to be duplicated."

2. Decide how you want to label the axes. In our example, the vertical axis could be labeled "cost per student" and the horizontal axis "number of students."

3. Do you have specific numbers to work with? If so, the next step is to construct a table showing what you know and use it to sketch your graph. If you have no numbers, you must draw an abstract graph. In this case, all you know is that the cost per student goes down when the number of students goes up. Your graph would thus be a negatively sloped line.

4. If your graph involves more than one relationship between quantities, repeat steps 1 through 3 for each relationship you wish to show. When constructing a graph with more than one curve, pay special attention to points at which you think the curves should intersect.

(Intersections occur whenever both the *x* and *y* values of the two relationships are equal.) Also note the points at which you think two curves ought to be tangent (which requires that their slopes be equal), the points of maximum or minimum value, if any, and so on.

5. When your graph is finished, try to translate it back into words. Does it really say what you want it to?

**A REMINDER**   As you read this book and encounter various kinds of graphs, turn back to this appendix now and then. Do not memorize graphs as meaningless pictures; if you do, you will get lost. If you can alternate between graphs and words, the underlying point will be clearer than if you rely on either one alone. Keep in mind that the primary focus of economics is not graphs; it is people and the ways in which they deal with the challenge of scarcity.

# Supply and Demand: The Basics

## PORSCHE FACES HARD TIMES IN THE 1990S

During the boom years of the 1980s, few status symbols could outclass a new Porsche in the driveway of a young, upwardly mobile lawyer or stockbroker. Not even German rivals Mercedes or BMW could match Porsche's flashy, sporty image, or its rocket-like performance.

But Porsche ran into trouble during the 1990s. By 1992, the German automaker's sales in the United States, its biggest single market, had fallen some 85 percent from their 1986 peak.

Chairman Arno Bohn of the Stuttgart-based company told *The Wall Street Journal* that Porsche had no intention of abandoning the U.S. market. Considering that nearly half of all Porsches in existence are on U.S. roads, to do so would be unthinkable. But even as Bohn was insisting that many people still dreamed of owning a Porsche, layoff notices were going out to Porsche employees both in Europe and North America. What caused all of Porsche's trouble? Certainly not any fault of its vaunted engineering staff. The latest Porsches are the fastest, most stylish ever. But car sales are influenced as much by economics as by engineering, and economic changes have worked against the company.

Price is a major factor. Between 1984 and 1991, the price of a Porsche in the United States doubled. In part, this reflected the fact that German industrial workers have become the world's most highly paid. And, in part, the rising value of the German mark on foreign exchange markets meant that U.S. consumers had to pay more dollars for a car, even if the cost of building it in Germany remained constant.

The competitive environment was changing, too. In the late 1980s, Japanese automakers introduced high performance sports cars of their own at prices lower than those of European models.

At the same time, the U.S. economy was hit hard by recession. And there was a new element in the recession of the early 1990s: In the past, high-paid white-collar workers—Porsche's core customer base—often rode out business downturns unscathed. This time, many of them lost their jobs. Not a good time to spend $95,000 on a new mechanical toy. Finally, tastes seemed to be changing, too. In the 1980s, the attitude among many wealthy Americans was, "If you've got it, flaunt it." By the early 1990s, even people whose incomes were untouched by recession were less eager to make a public statement of the fact by buying the most expensive car they could find.

Porsche remains a profitable, debt-free company insistent on maintaining its independence. Fortunately for Porsche, the extended economic expansion of the 1990s, coupled with its business strategies, helped Porsche turn things around, fueling a turnaround for luxury vehicles and sports cars.

Source: Based in part on Krystal Miller and Terence Roth, "Porsche, a Favorite in Times of Plenty, Struggles to Survive in a More Frugal Era," *The Wall Street Journal*, Jan. 27, 1992, B1.

⌒

L UXURY CARS ARE just one category among millions of goods and services for which prices, quantities sold, and other market conditions vary from day to day and from year to year. Whether they are goods that we ourselves buy and sell, or goods that our employers, neighbors, or family members buy and sell, the changing market conditions affect our lives in many ways. The factors determining market prices and quantities are thus a good starting point for any discussion of economics.

This chapter outlines a model of price determination in a market economy, the supply-and-demand model. Economists use the term **supply** to refer to sellers' willingness and ability to provide goods for sale in a market. **Demand** refers to buyers' willingness and ability to purchase goods.

## DEMAND

The fact that sales of Porsches fell as their price increased is an example of the law of demand in action. The **law of demand** can be stated formally as follows: In any market, other things being equal, an inverse relationship exists between the price of a good and the quantity of the good that buyers demand—that is, the amount they are willing and able to buy. Thus, the quantity demanded tends to rise as the price falls and to fall as the price rises.

We expect this to happen for two reasons. First, if the price of one good falls while the prices of other goods stay the same, people are likely to substitute the cheaper good. Second, when the price of one good falls while incomes and other prices stay the same, people feel a little richer. They use their added buying power to buy a bit more of many things, including, in most cases, a little more of the good whose price went down.

The terms *demand* and *quantity demanded,* as used in economics, are not the same as *want* or *need.* They combine the notion of willingness with that of ability to buy. I might want a Porsche, but I do not have that kind of money. Even if I did, there are other things I want more. Thus, the quantity of Porsches I demand at the going price is zero, just as it would be if I were prepared to spend $95,000 on a car but wanted a Lotus rather than a Porsche.

On the other hand, I might *need* dental surgery to avoid losing my teeth. But suppose I am poor. If I cannot pay for the surgery or find someone to pay for it on my behalf, I am out of luck. The quantity of dental surgery I demand, therefore, is zero, however, great my need for that service.

### The Demand Curve

The law of demand states a relationship between the quantity of a good that people are willing and able to buy, other things being equal, and the price of that good. Figure 2.1 represents this one-to-one relationship for a familiar consumer good, chicken.

---

**Supply**

The willingness and ability of sellers to provide goods for sale in a market.

**Demand**

The willingness and ability of buyers to purchase goods.

**Law of demand**

The principle that an inverse relationship exists between the price of a good and the quantity of that good that buyers demand, other things being equal.

The figure shows the demand relationship in two different ways. First look at part (a). The first row of the table shows that when the price of chicken is $3.00 a pound, the quantity demanded per year is 1 billion pounds. Reading down the table, we see that as the price falls, the quantity demanded rises. At $2.50 per pound, buyers are willing and able to purchase 1.5 billion pounds per year; at $1.50, 2.5 billion pounds; and so on.

**Demand curve**

A graphical representation of the relationship between the price of a good and the quantity of that good that buyers demand.

Part (b) of Figure 2.1 presents the same information in graphical form. The graph is called a **demand curve** for chicken. Suppose we want to use the demand curve to find out what quantity of chicken will be demanded at a price of $2.00 per pound. Starting at $2.00 on the vertical axis, we move across, as shown by the arrow, until we reach the demand curve at point A. Continuing to follow the arrow, we drop down to the horizontal axis. Reading from the scale on that axis, we see that the quantity demanded at a price of $2.00 per pound is 2 billion pounds per year. That is the quantity demanded in row A of the table in part (a).

The effect of a change in the price of chicken, other things being equal, can be shown as a movement from one point to another along the demand curve for chicken. Suppose that the price drops from $2.00 to $1.00 per pound. In the process, the quantity that buyers plan to buy rises. The point corresponding to the quantity demanded at the new, lower price is point B (which corresponds to row B of the table). Because of the inverse relationship between price and quantity demanded, the demand curve has a negative slope.

---

**Figure 2.1   A Demand Curve for Chicken**

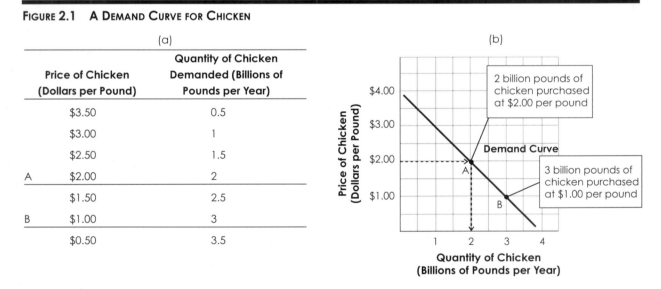

(a)

| Price of Chicken (Dollars per Pound) | Quantity of Chicken Demanded (Billions of Pounds per Year) |
|---|---|
| $3.50 | 0.5 |
| $3.00 | 1 |
| $2.50 | 1.5 |
| A   $2.00 | 2 |
| $1.50 | 2.5 |
| B   $1.00 | 3 |
| $0.50 | 3.5 |

Both the table and the chart show the quantity of chicken demanded at various prices. For example, at a price of $2.00 per pound, buyers are willing and able to purchase 2 billion pounds of chicken per year. This price-quantity combination is shown by row A in part (a) and point A in part (b).

**Change in quantity demanded**

A change in the quantity of a good that buyers are willing and able to purchase that results from a change in the good's price, other things being equal; shown by a movement from one point to another along a demand curve.

Economists speak of a movement along a demand curve as a **change in quantity demanded**. Such a movement represents buyers' reaction to a change in the price of the good in question, other things being equal.

## Shifts in the Demand Curve[1]

The demand curve in Figure 2.1 represents a relationship between two variables: the price of chicken and the quantity of chicken demanded. But changes in other variables can also affect people's purchases of chicken. In the case of chicken, the prices of beef and pork would affect demand. Consumer incomes are a second variable that can affect demand. Changes in expectations about the future are a third, and changes in consumer tastes, such as an increasing preference for foods with a low saturated-fat content, are a fourth. The list could go on and on—the demand for ice is affected by the weather; the demand for diapers is affected by the birthrate; the demand for baseball tickets is affected by the won-lost record of the home team; and so on.

How are all these other variables handled when drawing a demand curve? In brief, two rules apply:

1. When drawing a single demand curve for a good, such as the one in Figure 2.1, all other conditions that affect demand are considered to be fixed or constant under the "other things being equal" clause of the law of demand. As long as that clause is in force, the only two variables at work are quantity demanded (on the horizontal axis) and price (on the vertical axis). The effect of a change in price on quantity demanded thus is shown by a *movement along* the demand curve.

2. When we look beyond the "other things being equal" clause and find that there is a change in a variable that is not represented on one of the axes, such as the price of another good or the level of consumer income, the effect is shown as a *shift* in the demand curve. In its new position, the demand curve still represents a two-variable price-quantity relationship, but it is a slightly different relationship than before because one of the "other things" has changed.

These two rules for graphical representation of demand relationships are crucial to understanding the theory of supply and demand as a whole. It will be worthwhile to expand on them through a series of examples.

**CHANGES IN THE PRICE OF ANOTHER GOOD** We have already noted that the demand for chicken depends on what happens to the price of beef, as well as what happens to the price of chicken. Figure 2.2, which shows demand curves for both goods, provides a closer look at this relationship.

Suppose that the price of beef is initially $3.00 per pound and then increases to $4.50 per pound. The effect of this change on the quantity of beef demanded is shown in part (a) of Figure 2.2 as a movement along the beef demand curve from point A to point B. Part (b) of the figure shows the effect on the demand for chicken. With the price of beef higher than before, consumers will tend to buy more chicken *even if the price of chicken does not change.* Suppose the price of chicken is $2.00 per pound. When beef was selling at $3.00 a pound, consumers bought 2 billion pounds of chicken a year (point A′ on demand curve $D_1$). After the price of beef goes up to $4.50 a pound, they will buy 3.5 billion pounds of chicken a year, assuming that the price of chicken does not change (point B′ on demand curve $D_2$).

A rise in the price of beef would cause consumers to buy more chicken regardless of the initial price of chicken. If the price of chicken had started out at $3.00 a pound and remained there while the price of beef went up, consumers would have increased their chicken consumption from 1 billion pounds a year to 2.5 billion pounds a year. At a price of $1.00 a pound for chicken, the quantity would have risen from 3 billion pounds to 4.5 billion pounds, and so on. We see, then, that a change in the price of beef causes the entire demand curve for chicken to shift. The "other things being equal" clause of the new demand curve, $D_2$, incorporates a price of $4.50 a pound for beef, rather than the price of $3.00 a pound assumed in demand curve $D_1$.

Earlier we explained that economists refer to a movement along a demand curve as a "change in quantity demanded." The corresponding term for a shift in a demand curve is a **change in demand**. A change in quantity demanded (a movement along the curve) is caused by a change in the price of the good in question (the variable on the vertical axis). In contrast, a change in demand (a shift in the demand curve) is caused

**Change in demand**

A change in the quantity of a good that buyers are willing and able to purchase that results from a change in some condition other than the price of that good; shown by a shift in the demand curve.

**FIGURE 2.2    EFFECTS OF AN INCREASE IN THE PRICE OF BEEF ON THE DEMAND FOR CHICKEN**

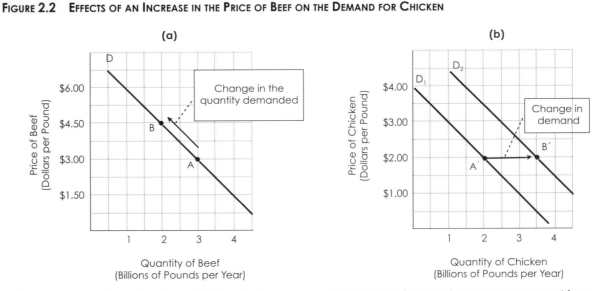

An increase in the price of beef from $3.00 to $4.50 per pound, other things being equal, causes a movement from point A to point B on the beef demand curve—a decrease in the quantity of beef demanded. With the price of chicken unchanged at $2.00 per pound, consumers will substitute chicken for beef. That will cause an increase in the demand for chicken, which is shown as a shift in the chicken demand curve from $D_1$ to $D_2$.

by a change in some variable other than the price of the good in question (one that does not appear on either axis).

In the example in Figure 2.2, people bought more chicken when the price of beef went up, replacing one meat with the other in their dinners. Economists call such pairs of goods **substitutes**, because an increase in the price of one causes an increase in the demand for the other—a rightward shift in the demand curve.

Consumers react differently to price changes when two goods tend to be used together. One example is tires and gasoline. When the price of gasoline goes up, people drive less; therefore, they buy fewer tires even if there is no change in their price. An increase in the price of gasoline thus causes a movement upward along the gasoline demand curve and a *leftward* shift in the demand curve for tires. Pairs of goods that are related in this way are known as **complements**.

Whether a given pair of goods are substitutes or complements depends on buyers' attitudes toward those goods; these terms do not refer to properties of the goods themselves. Some people might regard cheese and beef as substitute sources of protein in their diets; others, who like cheeseburgers, might regard them as complements.

One more point regarding the effects of changes in the prices of other goods is also worth noting: In stating the law of demand, it is the price of a good *relative to those of other goods* that counts. During periods of inflation, when the average level of all prices rises, distinguishing between changes in *relative prices* and changes in *nominal prices*—the number of dollars actually paid per unit of a good—is especially important. When the economy experiences inflation, a good can become relatively less expensive even though its nominal price rises, provided that the prices of other goods rise even faster.

Consider chicken, for example. Between 1950 and 2003 the average retail price of a broiler rose by almost 40 percent, from $.59 per pound to $1.05 per pound. Over the same period, however, the average price of all goods and services that consumers bought rose by 600 percent. The relative price of chicken thus fell during the period even though its nominal price rose. The drop in the relative price of chicken had a lot to do with its growing popularity on the dinner table.

**CHANGES IN CONSUMER INCOMES** The demand for a good can also be affected by changes in consumer incomes. When their incomes rise, people tend to buy larger quantities of many goods, assuming that the prices of those goods do not change.

Figure 2.3 shows the effect of an increase in consumer incomes on the demand for chicken. Demand curve $D_1$ is the same as the curve shown in Figure 2.1. Suppose now that consumer incomes rise. With higher incomes, people become choosier about what they eat. They do not just want calories, they want high-quality calories from foods that are tasty, fashionable, and healthful. These considerations have made chicken increasingly popular as consumer incomes have risen.

More specifically, suppose that after their incomes rise, consumers are willing to buy 2.5 billion pounds of chicken instead of 1 billion pounds at a price of $3.00 per

**Substitute goods**

A pair of goods for which an increase in the price of one causes an increase in demand for the other.

**Complementary goods**

A pair of goods for which an increase in the price of one results in a decrease in demand for the other.

FIGURE 2.3    EFFECTS OF AN INCREASE IN CONSUMER INCOME ON THE DEMAND FOR CHICKEN

Demand curve $D_1$ assumes a given level of consumer income. If their incomes increase, consumers will want to buy more chicken at any given price, other things being equal. That will shift the demand curve rightward to, say, $D_2$. If the prevailing market price at the time of the demand shift is $3.00 per pound, the quantity demanded increases to 2.5 billion pounds (B) from 1 billion (A); if the prevailing price is $2.00 per pound, the quantity demanded will increase to 2 billion pounds (D) from 3.5 billion (C); and so on.

pound. The change is shown as an arrow drawn from point A to point B in Figure 2.3. If the initial price of chicken had been $2.00 per pound, even more chicken would be bought at the new, higher level of income. At the original income level and a price of $2.00, the amount purchased would be 2 billion pounds, as shown by point C. After the increase in incomes, buyers would plan to purchase 3.5 billion pounds, shown by the arrow from point C to point D.

Whatever the initial price of chicken, the effect of an increase in consumer incomes is shown by a shift to a point on the new demand curve, $D_2$. The increase in demand for chicken that results from the rise in consumer incomes thus is shown as a shift in the entire demand curve. If consumer incomes remain at the new, higher level, the effects of any changes in the price of chicken will be shown as movements along the new demand curve. There is, in other words, a chicken demand curve for every possible income level. Each represents a one-to-one relationship between price and quantity demanded, given the assumed income level.

In the example just given, we assumed that an increase in income would cause an increase in the demand for chicken. Experience shows that this is what normally happens. Economists therefore call chicken a **normal good**, meaning that when consumer incomes rise, other things being equal, people will buy more of it.

**Normal good**

A good for which an increase in consumer incomes results in an increase in demand.

There are some goods, however, that people will buy less of when their incomes rise, other things being equal. For example, among your classmates, those with higher incomes are likely to go out for pizza more often than those with lower incomes. On nights when they eat pizza, they do not eat in the cafeteria, so the demand for cafeteria food falls as income rises. Similarly, when their incomes rise, people tend to buy less flour for baking at home and to buy more baked goods instead. People tend to buy fewer shoe repair services when their incomes rise; instead, they buy new shoes. Goods such as cafeteria food, flour, and shoe repair services are termed **inferior goods**. When consumer incomes rise, the demand curve for an inferior good shifts to the left instead of to the right. As in the case of substitutes and complements, the notions of inferiority and normality arise from consumer choices; they are not inherent properties of the goods themselves.

**CHANGES IN EXPECTATIONS**   Changes in buyers' expectations are a third factor that can shift demand curves. If people expect the price of a particular good to rise relative to the prices of other goods, or expect something other than a price increase to raise the opportunity cost of acquiring the good, they will step up their rate of purchase before the change takes place.

For example, suppose that in May, consumers rushed to buy airline tickets in response to a series of news reports indicating that prices would be raised for tickets ordered after June 5. The people who bought their tickets in May included many who were planning to travel late in the summer and ordinarily would have waited several more weeks before making their purchase. Thus, many more tickets were sold in May than would have been sold at the same price if consumers had not anticipated the June price rise. We can interpret the surge in ticket sales in May as a temporary rightward shift in the demand curve.

**CHANGES IN TASTES**   Changes in tastes are a fourth source of changes in demand. Sometimes these changes occur rapidly, as can be seen, for example, in such areas as popular music, clothing styles, and fast foods. The demand curves for these goods and services shift often. In other cases, changes in tastes take longer to occur but are more permanent. For example, in recent years consumers have been more health conscious than they were in the past. The result has been reduced demand for cigarettes and high-cholesterol foods, along with increased demand for fish, chicken, and exercise equipment.

# SUPPLY

## The Supply Curve

We now turn from the demand side of the market to the supply side. As in the case of demand, we begin by constructing a one-to-one relationship between the price of a

---

**Inferior good**

A good for which an increase in consumer incomes results in a decrease in demand.

good and the quantity that sellers intend to offer for sale. Figure 2.4 shows such a relationship for chicken.

**Supply curve**

*A graphical representation of the relationship between the price of a good and the quantity of that good that sellers are willing to supply.*

The positively sloped curve in Figure 2.4 is called a **supply curve** for chicken. Like demand curves, supply curves are based on an "other things being equal" condition. The supply curve for chicken shows how sellers change their plans in response to a change in the price of chicken, assuming that there are no changes in other conditions—the prices of other goods, production techniques, input prices, expectations, or any other relevant condition.

Why does the supply curve have a positive slope? Why do sellers, other things being equal, plan to supply more chicken when the prevailing market price is higher than they plan to supply when the price is lower? Without going too deeply into a discussion of microeconomic theory, we can consider some common-sense explanations here.

One explanation is that the positive slope of the supply curve represents *producers' response to market incentives.* When the price of chicken goes up, farmers have an incentive to devote more time and resources to raising chickens. Farmers who raise chickens as a sideline may decide to make chickens their main business. Some people may enter the market for the first time. The same reasoning applies in every market.

**FIGURE 2.4    A SUPPLY CURVE FOR CHICKEN**

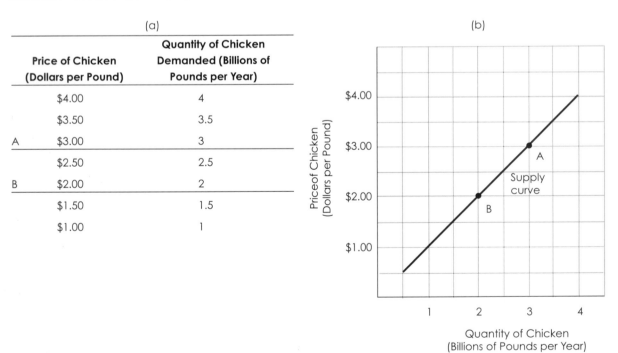

(a)

| Price of Chicken (Dollars per Pound) | Quantity of Chicken Demanded (Billions of Pounds per Year) |
|---|---|
| $4.00 | 4 |
| $3.50 | 3.5 |
| A    $3.00 | 3 |
| $2.50 | 2.5 |
| B    $2.00 | 2 |
| $1.50 | 1.5 |
| $1.00 | 1 |

Parts (a) and (b) of this figure show the quantity of chicken supplied at various prices. As the price rises, the quantity supplied increases, other things being equal. The higher price gives farmers an incentive to raise more chickens, but the rising opportunity cost of doing so limits the supply produced in response to any given price increase.

If parents are finding it hard to get babysitters, what do they do? They offer to pay more. If a sawmill cannot buy enough timber, it raises the price it offers to loggers, and so on. Exceptions to this general rule are rare.

Another explanation is that the positive slope of the supply curve reflects *the rising cost of producing additional output in facilities of a fixed size.* A furniture factory with a fixed amount of machinery might be able to produce more chairs only by paying workers at overtime rates to run the machinery for more hours. A farmer who is trying to grow more wheat on a fixed amount of land could do so by increasing the input of fertilizer and pesticides per acre, but beyond a certain point each unit of added chemicals yields less additional output.

Finally, the positive slope of the supply curve can be explained in terms of *comparative advantage and opportunity cost.* Figure 2.5a shows a production possibility frontier for an economy in which there are only two goods, tomatoes and chicken. Farmers can choose which product they will specialize in, but some farmers have a comparative advantage in growing tomatoes, others in raising chickens. Beginning

**FIGURE 2.5    THE PRODUCTION POSSIBILITY CURVE AND THE SUPPLY CURVE**

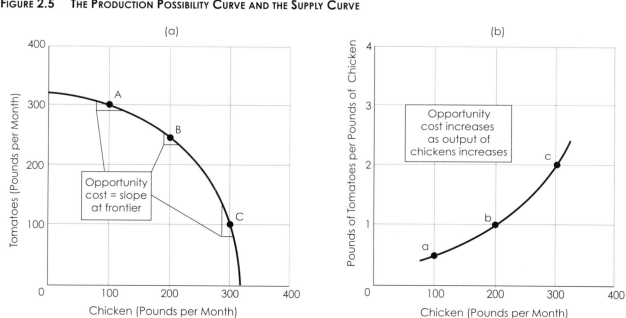

This figure offers an interpretation of the supply curve in terms of the production possibility frontier for an economy in which two goods are produced, tomatoes and chicken. Part (a) shows a production possibility frontier. The slope of the frontier at any point shows the opportunity cost of producing an additional pound of chicken measured in terms of the quantity of tomatoes that could have been produced using the same factors of production. The frontier curves because some operators have a comparative advantage in producing tomatoes and others have a comparative advantage in producing chicken. As more chicken is produced, those with the greatest comparative advantage in producing chicken are the first to stop producing tomatoes. Because the frontier gets steeper as more chicken is produced, the opportunity cost rises, as shown in part (b). The curve in part (b) can be interpreted as a supply curve, in the sense that an incentive, in the form of a higher price, will cause factors of production to be shifted from tomatoes to chicken despite the rising opportunity cost of producing chicken.

from a situation in which only tomatoes are produced, farmers with the strongest comparative advantage in raising chickens—that is, those who are able to produce chicken at relatively the lowest opportunity cost—will switch from tomatoes to chicken even if the price of chicken is low. As the point of production moves along the frontier, the price of chicken must rise to induce farmers with relatively higher opportunity costs to make the switch. The slope of the frontier at any point represents the opportunity cost of producing more chicken for a farmer who finds it worthwhile to switch from tomatoes to chicken just at that point.

In Figure 2.5 the slopes at points A, B, and C in part (a) are graphed on a new set of axes in part (b). The graph can be interpreted as a supply curve if it is noted that the price of chicken must rise relative to the price of tomatoes to induce more farmers to switch to chicken as the opportunity cost rises.

Each of these common-sense explanations fits certain circumstances. Together, they provide an intuitive basis for the positive slope of the supply curve.

## Shifts in the Supply Curve

**Change in quantity supplied**

A change in the quantity of a good that suppliers are willing and able to sell that results from a change in the good's price, other things being equal; shown by a movement along a supply curve.

**Change in supply**

A change in the quantity of a good that suppliers are willing and able to sell that results from a change in some condition other than the good's price; shown by a shift in the supply curve.

As in the case of demand, the effects of a change in the price of chicken, other things being equal, can be shown as a movement along the supply curve for chicken. Such a movement is called a **change in quantity supplied**. A change in a condition other than the price of chicken can be shown as a shift in the supply curve. Such a shift is referred to as a **change in supply**. Four sources of change in supply are worth noting. Each is related to the notion that the supply curve reflects the opportunity cost of producing the good or service in question.

**CHANGES IN TECHNOLOGY**    A supply curve is drawn on the basis of a particular production technique. When entrepreneurs reduce the opportunity costs of production by introducing more efficient techniques, it becomes worthwhile to sell more of the good than before at any given price. Figure 2.6 shows how an improvement in production technology affects the supply curve for chicken.

Supply curve $S_1$ is the same as the one shown in Figure 2.4. It indicates that farmers will plan to supply 3 billion pounds of chicken per year at a price of $3.00 per pound (point A). Now suppose that the development of a faster-growing bird reduces the amount of feed used in raising chickens. With lower costs per unit, farmers will be willing to supply more chicken than before at any given price. They may, for example, be willing to supply 4 billion pounds of chicken at $3.00 per pound (point B). The move from A to B is part of a shift in the entire supply curve from $S_1$ to $S_2$. Once the new techniques are established, an increase or decrease in the price of chicken, other things being equal, will result in a movement along the new supply curve.

**CHANGES IN INPUT PRICES**    Changes in input prices are a second item that can cause supply curves to shift. An increase in input prices, other things being equal, increases the opportunity cost of producing the good in question, and hence it tends to reduce the quantity of a good that producers plan to supply at a given price. Refer again to Figure 2.6. Suppose that starting from point A on supply curve $S_1$, the price of chicken feed increases and no offsetting changes occur. Now, instead of supplying 3 billion pounds of chicken at $3.00 per pound, farmers will supply, say, just 2 billion pounds at that price (point C). The move from A to C is part of a leftward shift in the supply curve, from $S_1$ to $S_3$.

If the price of feed remains at the new level, changes in the price of chicken will cause movements along the new supply curve. For example, farmers could be induced to supply the original quantity of chicken—3 billion pounds—if the price of chicken rose enough to cover the increased cost of feed. As you can see in Figure 2.6, that would require a price of $4.00 per pound for chicken (point D).

**CHANGES IN THE PRICES OF OTHER GOODS**   Changes in the prices of other goods that could be produced using the same factors of production can also produce

**FIGURE 2.6   SHIFTS IN THE SUPPLY CURVE FOR CHICKEN**

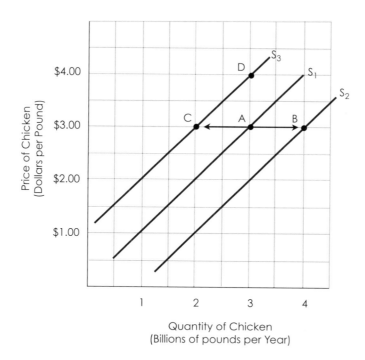

Several kinds of changes can cause the supply of chicken to increase or decrease. For example, a new production method that lowers costs will shift the curve to the *right*, from $S_1$ to $S_2$. The shift is to the right because, taking into account the new, lower cost of production per unit, producers will be willing to supply more chicken at any given price. An increase in the price of inputs, other things being equal, will shift the curve to the *left*, from $S_1$ to $S_3$. The shift is to the left because, taking into account the new, higher price of inputs, producers will be willing to supply less chicken at any given price. Changes in sellers' expectations or in the prices of competing goods can also cause the supply curve to shift.

a shift in the chicken supply curve. In our earlier example, farmers could use available resources to produce either chickens or tomatoes. Suppose that the price of tomatoes rises while the price of chicken stays at $3.00. The rise in the price of tomatoes gives some farmers who would otherwise have produced chickens an incentive to shift the use of their labor, land, and capital to the production of tomatoes. Thus, the effect of an increase in the price of tomatoes can be shown as a leftward shift in the chicken supply curve.

**CHANGES IN EXPECTATIONS**   Changes in expectations can cause supply curves to shift in much the same way that they cause demand curves to shift. Again, we can use farming as an example. At planting time, a farmer's selection of crops is influenced not so much by current prices as by the prices expected at harvest time. Expectations over a time horizon longer than one growing season also affect supply. Each crop requires special equipment and know-how. We have just seen that an increase in the price of tomatoes gives farmers an incentive to shift from chicken to tomatoes. The incentive will be stronger if the price of tomatoes is expected to remain at the higher level. If it is, farmers are more likely to buy the special equipment needed for that crop and to learn the necessary production techniques.

# THE INTERACTION OF SUPPLY AND DEMAND

Markets transmit information, in the form of prices, to people who buy and sell goods and services. Taking these prices into account, along with other knowledge they may have, buyers and sellers make their plans.[2] As shown by the demand and supply curves, buyers and sellers plan to buy or sell certain quantities of a good at any given price.

Each market has many buyers and sellers, each making plans independently. When they meet to trade, some of them may be unable to carry out their plans on the terms they expected. Perhaps the total quantity of a good that buyers plan to purchase is greater than the total quantity that suppliers are willing to sell at the given price. In that case, some of the would-be buyers must change their plans. Or, perhaps planned sales exceed planned purchases at the given price. In that case, some would-be sellers will be unable to carry out their plans.

**Equilibrium**

A condition in which buyers' and sellers' plans exactly mesh in the marketplace, so that the quantity supplied exactly equals the quantity demanded at a given price.

## Market Equilibrium

Sometimes no one is surprised: The total quantity of a good that buyers plan to purchase exactly matches the total quantity that producers plan to sell. When buyers' and sellers' plans mesh when they meet in the marketplace, no buyers or sellers need to change their plans. Under these conditions, the market is said to be in **equilibrium**.

Supply and demand curves, which reflect the plans of sellers and buyers, can be used to give a graphical demonstration of market equilibrium. Figure 2.7 uses the same supply and demand curves as before, but this time both curves are drawn on the same diagram. If the quantity of planned sales at each price is compared with the quantity of planned purchases at that price (either the table or the graph can be used to make this comparison), it can be seen that there is only one price at which the two sets of plans mesh. That price—$2.00 per pound—is the equilibrium price. If all buyers and sellers make their plans with the expectation of a price of $2.00, no one will be surprised and no plans will have to be changed.

## Shortages

**Excess quantity demanded (shortage)**

A condition in which the quantity of a good demanded at a given price exceeds the quantity supplied.

**Inventory**

A stock of a finished good awaiting sale or use.

But what will happen if for some reason people base their plans for buying or selling chicken on a price other than $2.00 a pound?[3] Suppose, for example, that they base their plans on a price of $1.00. Figure 2.7 shows that at that price buyers will plan to purchase chicken at a rate of 3 billion pounds per year, but farmers will plan to supply only 1 billion pounds. When the quantity demanded exceeds the quantity supplied, as in this example, the difference is an **excess quantity demanded** or, more simply, a **shortage**. In Figure 2.7 the shortage is 2 billion pounds of chicken per year when the price is $1.00 per pound.

In most markets the first sign of a shortage is a drop in the **inventory**, that is, in the stock of the good in question that has been produced and is waiting to be sold or used. Sellers plan to hold a certain quantity of goods in inventory to allow for minor changes in demand. When they see inventories dropping below the planned level, they change their plans. Some may try to rebuild their inventories by increasing their output, if they produce the good themselves; or, if they do not make it themselves, they may order more from the producer. Some sellers may take advantage of the strong demand for their product to raise the price, knowing that buyers will be willing to pay more. Many sellers will do a little of both. If sellers do not take the initiative, buyers will—they will offer to pay more if sellers will supply more. Whatever the details, the result will be an upward movement along the supply curve as both price and quantity increase.

As the shortage puts upward pressure on price, buyers will change their plans too. Moving up and to the left along their demand curve, they will cut back on their planned purchases. As both buyers and sellers change their plans, the market will move toward equilibrium. When the price reaches $2.00 per pound, both the shortage and the pressure to change buying and selling plans will disappear.

In the markets for most goods, sellers have inventories of goods ready to be sold. There are exceptions, however. Inventories are not possible in markets for services—haircuts, tax preparation, lawn care, and the like. Also, some goods, such as custom-built houses and machine tools that are designed for a specialized need, are not held in inventories. Sellers in these markets do not begin production until they have a contract with a buyer.

In markets in which there are no inventories, the sign of a shortage is a queue of buyers. The queue may take the form of a line of people waiting to be served or a list of names in an order book. The queue is a sign that, given the prevailing price, buyers

FIGURE 2.7    EQUILIBRIUM IN THE CHICKEN MARKET

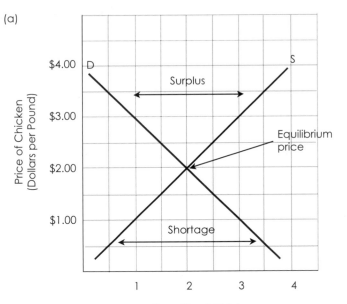

(a)

Price of Chicken (Dollars per Pound)

Quantity of Chicken
(Billions of Pounds per Year)

(b)

| Price (per Pound) | Quantity Demanded (Billions of Pounds) | Quantity Supplied (Billions of Pounds) | Shortage (Billions of Pounds) | Surplus (Billions of Pounds) | Direction of Pressure on Price |
|---|---|---|---|---|---|
| $3.50 | 0.5 | 3.5 | — | 3 | Downward |
| $3.00 | 1 | 3 | — | 2 | Downward |
| $2.50 | 1.5 | 2.5 | — | 1 | Downward |
| $2.00 | 2 | 2 | — | — | Equilibrium |
| $1.50 | 2.5 | 1.5 | 1 | — | Upward |
| $1.00 | 3 | 1 | 2 | — | Upward |
| $0.50 | 3.5 | 0.5 | 3 | — | Upward |

This figure shows the supply and demand curves for chicken presented earlier in graphical and numerical form. The demand curve shows how much buyers plan to purchase at a given price. The supply curve shows how much producers plan to sell at a given price. At only one price—$2.00 per pound—do buyers' and sellers' plans exactly match. That is the equilibrium price. A higher price causes a surplus of chicken and puts downward pressure on price. A lower price causes a shortage and puts upward pressure on price.

would like to purchase the good at a faster rate than that at which producers have planned to supply it. However, some plans cannot be carried out—at least not right away. Buyers are served on a first-come, first-served basis.

The formation of a queue of buyers has much the same effect on the market as a decrease in inventories. Sellers react by increasing their rate of output, raising their prices, or both. Buyers react by reducing the quantity they plan to purchase. The result is a movement up and to the right along the supply curve and, at the same time, up and to the left along the demand curve until equilibrium is reached.

## Surpluses

Having considered what happens when buyers and sellers initially expect a price below the equilibrium price, we now turn to the opposite case. Suppose that for some reason buyers and sellers of chicken expect a price that is higher than the equilibrium price—say, $2.50 per pound—and make their plans accordingly. Figure 2.7 shows that farmers will plan to supply 2.5 billion pounds of chicken per year at $2.50, but their customers will plan to buy only 1.5 billion pounds. When the quantity supplied exceeds the quantity demanded, there is an **excess quantity supplied**, or a **surplus**. As Figure 2.7 shows, the surplus of chicken at a price of $2.50 per pound is 1 billion pounds per year.

**Excess quantity supplied (surplus)**

A condition in which the quantity of a good supplied at a given price exceeds the quantity demanded.

When there is a surplus of a product, sellers will be unable to sell all that they had hoped to sell at the planned price. As a result, their inventories will begin to grow beyond the level they had planned to hold in preparation for normal changes in demand.

Sellers will react to the inventory buildup by changing their plans. Some will cut back their output. Others will lower their prices to induce consumers to buy more and thus reduce their extra stock. Still others will do a little of both. The result of these changes in plans will be a movement down and to the left along the supply curve.

As unplanned inventory buildup puts downward pressure on the price of chicken, buyers change their plans too. Finding that chicken costs less than they had expected, they buy more of it. In graphical terms, they move down and to the right along the demand curve. As that happens, the market is restored to equilibrium.

In markets in which there are no inventories, surpluses lead to the formation of queues of sellers looking for customers. Taxi queues at airports are a case in point. At some times of the day the fare for taxi service from the airport to downtown is more than high enough to attract a number of taxis that is equal to the demand. A queue of cabs waiting for passengers then forms. In some cities drivers who are far back in the queue try to attract riders by offering cut-rate fares. Often, though, there are rules against fare cutting. The queue then grows until the next peak period, when a surge in demand shortens it.

## Changes in Market Conditions

On a graph, finding the equilibrium point looks easy. In real life, though, it is a moving target. Market conditions—all the items that lie behind the "other things being equal" clause—change frequently. When they do, both buyers and sellers revise their plans and the point of equilibrium shifts.

**RESPONSE TO A SHIFT IN DEMAND**    We will first consider a market's response to a shift in demand. The decline in demand for beef caused by consumers' avoidance of high-cholesterol foods provides a good example. Part (a) of Figure 2.8 interprets this case in terms of the supply-and-demand model.

As the figure is drawn, the market is initially in equilibrium at $E_1$. There the price is $3.00 per pound and the quantity produced is 2 billion pounds per year. Now the changed dietary habits of U.S. consumers cause the demand curve to shift to the left, from $D_1$ to $D_2$. (There is a shift in the demand curve rather than a movement along it, because a change in tastes is not one of the items represented by the axes of the diagram.) What will happen next?

At the original price of $3.00 per pound, there will be a surplus of beef. The supply curve shows that at that price ranchers will plan to produce 2 billion pounds per year. However, according to the new demand curve, $D_2$, consumers will no longer buy that much beef at $3.00 per pound. Instead, given their new tastes, they will buy only 1billion pounds at that price.

But the price does not stay at $3.00 for long. As soon as the demand curve begins to shift and the surplus begins to develop, beef inventories rise above their planned levels, putting downward pressure on the price. As the price falls, ranchers revise their plans. They move down and to the left along their supply curve, reducing the quantity supplied as the price drops. (There is a movement along the supply curve, not a shift in the curve, because the ranchers are responding to a change in the price of beef, the variable shown on the vertical axis. Nothing has happened to change the "other things being equal" condition, such as technology, input prices, and so on, which could cause the supply curve to shift.)

As ranchers move downward along their supply curve in the direction shown by the arrow in part (a) of Figure 2.8, they eventually reach point $E_2$, where their plans again mesh with those of consumers. At that point the price has fallen to $2.25 per pound and production to 1.5 billion pounds. Although health-conscious consumers would not have bought that much beef at the old price, they will do so at the new, lower price. $E_2$ thus is the new equilibrium point.

**RESPONSE TO A SHIFT IN SUPPLY**    The original equilibrium might be disrupted by a change in supply rather than by a change in demand. For example, beginning from a condition of equilibrium, a drought in the corn belt might result in a higher price for grain for cattle feed. That would shift the supply curve to the left while the demand curve remained unchanged, as shown in part (b) of Figure 2.8.

Given the new supply curve, there will be a shortage of beef at the original price. Inventories will decline and the prices will rise in response. As the price increases, producers will move upward and to the right along their new supply curve, $S_2$, and consumers will move upward and to the left along their demand curve, $D_1$, which remains in its original position. A new equilibrium is established when the price reaches $4.50 per pound.

FIGURE 2.8  EFFECTS OF CHANGING CONDITIONS IN THE BEEF MARKET

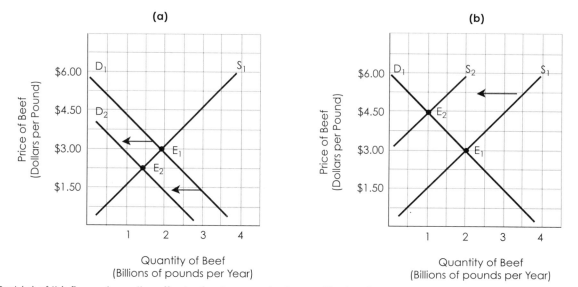

Part (a) of this figure shows the effects of a decrease in demand for beef caused by a shift in tastes away from high-cholesterol foods. Initially the market is in equilibrium at $E_1$. The change in tastes causes a shift in the demand curve. At the original equilibrium price of $3.00 per pound, there is a temporary surplus of beef. This causes inventories to start to rise and puts downward pressure on the price. As the price falls, producers move down along their supply curve to a new equilibrium at $E_2$. There both the price and quantity of beef are lower than before the shift in demand. Part (b) shows the effects of a decrease in supply caused by a drought, which raises the price of corn used to feed cattle. The shift in the supply curve causes a shortage at the initial price of $3.00 per pound. The shortage puts upward pressure on price. As the price rises, buyers move up and to the left along the demand curve until a new equilibrium is reached at $E_2$. In each case, note that only one curve needs to shift to bring about the new equilibrium.

One of the most frequent mistakes people make in learning the supply-and-demand model is to think that *both* curves must shift in order to restore equilibrium. The examples given in Figure 2.8 show clearly that this is not the case. In part (a), after the demand curve shifts, a movement along the supply curve is enough to establish the new equilibrium. No shift in the supply curve is needed. Similarly, in part (b), after the supply curve shifts, the demand curve does not need to shift to reach the new equilibrium.

In the turmoil of real-world markets, cases can be found in which both curves shift at once, but that happens only when two separate changes in conditions occur at the same time, one acting on the supply curve and the other on the demand curve. An example would be a drought that shifted the supply curve just as the market was already in the process of adjusting to a shift in the demand curve caused by changing tastes.

## Equilibrium as Spontaneous Order

The ability of markets to move toward a new equilibrium following a disturbance is an example of economic coordination through spontaneous order. In the case we have been following, the disturbance began either with a change in health consciousness among consumers or with a change in the weather. The challenge: How to coordinate the decisions of thousands of farmers, wholesalers, retailers—the whole chain of supply—to serve consumers wants under changing conditions.

No central planning agency or regulatory bureaucracy is required to accomplish the needed shift in the use of scarce resources. It is all brought about through information and incentives transmitted in the form of changing market prices. To take a real example, in 1988, as the demand for beef lagged and the drought raised the price of feed grains, ranchers culled their herds to 98 million head, down 26 percent from their peak. Meanwhile, labor, capital, natural resources, and entrepreneurial energy flowed into chicken production, where demand was booming.

The process was remarkably smooth for so vast a shift in resource use. Behind the scenes, surpluses and shortages nudged choices in the needed directions, but at no time did shortages occur in the acute form of empty meat coolers at the supermarket or lines of chicken-hungry consumers stretching down city streets. Similarly, surpluses of beef caused ranchers to cut back their herds, but they did not take the form of mountains of rotting beef that had to be dumped into landfills.

No one *intended* this process of adjustment. Equilibrium is not a compromise that must be negotiated by a committee of consumers and producers. Just as shoppers manage to equalize the length of supermarket checkout lines without the guidance of a central authority, markets move toward equilibrium spontaneously, through the small, local adjustments that people make in their efforts to serve their own interests. As Adam Smith might have put it, we have not the benevolence of Frank Perdue or the Beef Industry Council to thank for our dinner; instead it is their self-interest that puts the right food on our table.

## Market Adjustment and Entrepreneurship

The supply-and-demand model provides a clear and time-tested account of the process through which markets adjust to equilibrium in response to a change in conditions, yet in an important sense the model is incomplete. The behavior of consumers and producers as represented by demand and supply curves is overly mechanical. In the real world, people do not react so passively. As *Economics in the News 2.1* relates, they fight back when their interests are threatened. The examples cited—Rhonda Miller's better steak, Excel's vacuum-wrapped roasts, and Kroger's oven-ready meat loaves—are entrepreneurial responses to the decline in demand for beef. They show that beef producers do not just accept the shift in the demand curve and respond by sliding down the supply curve. Instead, they grab onto the demand curve and try to pull it back.

Taking entrepreneurship into account does not mean that the supply-and-demand model has to be discarded. In fact, the model provides just the framework we need to talk about what entrepreneurs are trying to do. Rhonda Miller's efforts to make a better steak have the effect of nudging the demand curve for beef to the right. Some other en-

## BEEF PRICES UP; FAST FOOD CHAINS SWITCH TO CHICKEN

Stock up the freezer if you like steak because beef prices at the supermarket are on their way up. And they're likely to stay there for a while.

U.S. cattle prices are at a record high, say economists with the U.S. Department of Agriculture . They've increased 34% since July, and this month the benchmark price of Nebraska choice steers went from $90 to $116 per 100 pounds. A year ago, the price per 100 pounds was $64.

"We've seen increases in the last 10 days," said Jim Robb, director of the Livestock Marketing Information Center in Denver. "Choice T-bone steak and New York strip steak, those prices are double what they were three weeks ago."

"Those prices will ease off a little bit but not much," said David Kay of *Cattle Buyers Weekly*. "We look as if we're going to have even tighter cattle supplies for slaughter in 2004 and even into 2005."

Prices are up because of a set of circumstances that Robb calls "completely unprecedented." First, consumer demand for beef has increased nearly 10% since 1998 after declining for 20 years.

Recent increases in consumption may be due in part because of the increasing popularity of high-protein diets, such as this summer's blockbuster South Beach diet, and the venerable Atkins diet.

Second, as Wayne Purcell of the Research Institute on Livestock Pricing at Virginia Tech points out, the U.S. banned imports of Canadian cattle and beef five months ago. The ban was imposed because of the discovery of a case of mad cow disease there last spring and reduced cattle and meat imports to the USA by 9%.

Consumers already may be feeling the impact, whether they're eating out or at home. U.S. restaurant chains such as McDonald's and Wendy's have been hyping salads and lean chicken pieces lately, and industry observers say it's no coincidence that the switch coincides with rising beef prices. Experts expect cost-cutting by other restaurant companies to offset rising food prices.

It is not clear how long it will take for the impact of the price increases to be felt at local meat counters. Retail beef prices typically trail the price paid at the stockyard anywhere from two weeks to two months. So last week's increase will not show up at supermarkets until the first weeks of November or until Christmas.

If grocers think the price hike is temporary, they may eat the difference rather than risk aggravating customers. But if grocers do raise prices, "they'll raise their everyday prices only a little, but they will keep them up for a year or so. And we just won't see beef featured in sales very much," Kay said.

Source: Elizabeth Weise, "Beef Prices On the Way Up," *USA Today*, October 24, 2003.

trepreneur might be trying to save on feed costs by developing a genetically engineered steer. If successful, the project would give the supply curve for beef a rightward shove.

# PRICE FLOORS AND CEILINGS: AN APPLICATION

Economics—both macro and micro—encompasses a great many applications of the concepts of supply and demand. Although each situation is unique, each to some extent draws on ideas developed in this chapter. This section, which uses the model to analyze the effects of government-imposed price floors and ceilings, provides some examples. Many more will be added in later chapters.

## *Price Supports: The Market for Milk*

In our earlier example of the market for beef, a decrease in demand caused a surplus, which in turn caused the price to decrease until the surplus was eliminated. Markets are not always free to respond by adjusting prices, however. The market for milk is a case in point.

Figure 2.9 shows the market for milk in terms of supply and demand curves. Suppose that initially the market is in equilibrium at point $E_1$. The wholesale price of milk is $13 per hundredweight, and 110 million hundredweight is produced per year. A trend in taste away from high-cholesterol foods—the same trend that hit the market for beef—shifts the demand curve for milk to the left. As in the case of beef, the result is a surplus, as shown by the arrow in Figure 2.9.

Here the similarity between the beef and milk markets ends. In the beef market prices are free to fall in response to a surplus, but in the milk market they are not. Instead, an elaborate set of government-imposed controls and subsidies puts a floor under the price of milk. In the figure, the government agrees to pay $13 per hundredweight for all milk that cannot be sold at that price on the open market.

With the demand curve in position $D_1$, there is no surplus; thus, the government need not buy any milk. But with the demand curve in position $D_2$, there is a surplus of 40 million hundredweight per year. Under the price support law the government

---

**FIGURE 2.9   PRICE SUPPORTS FOR MILK**

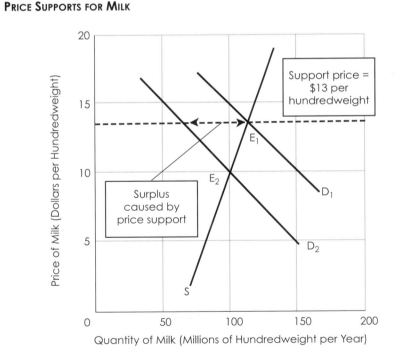

Suppose that initially the market for milk is in equilibrium at $E_1$. A shift in tastes away from high-cholesterol foods then shifts the demand curve to $D_2$. If the price were free to fall, there would be a temporary surplus that would push the price down to a new equilibrium at $10 per hundredweight. Instead, the government maintains a support price for milk at a level shown here as $13 per hundredweight. The government buys the surplus milk and stores it in the form of butter and cheese to keep the price from falling.

must buy this surplus and store it in the form of cheese, butter, and other products with long shelf lives. Since 1980, the combined costs of the support law to consumers and taxpayers has been estimated at more than $1,000 per family—enough to buy each family its own cow.

Without price supports, the shift in demand would cause the price of milk to fall to the new equilibrium price of $10 per hundredweight. When price supports are applied to a product at a level higher than the equilibrium price, however, the result is a lasting surplus condition. This happens because the support price sends misleading messages to consumers and producers. To consumers, the price of $13 says, "Milk is scarce. Its opportunity cost is high. Hold your consumption down." To producers, it says, "All is well. Incentives are unchanged. Feel free to continue using scarce resources to produce milk."

A drop in the price to $10 would send a different set of messages. Consumers would hear: "Milk is cheaper and more abundant. Although it is not cholesterol free, give in to temptation! Drink more of it!" But producers would hear: "The milk market is not what it once was. Look at your opportunity costs. Is there perhaps some better use for your labor, capital, and natural resources?"

From time to time the government has tried to eliminate the milk surplus by shifting the supply curve to the left so that it would intersect the demand curve near the support price. Under one recent program, for example, farmers were encouraged to sell their cows to be slaughtered for their meat, thereby reducing the size of dairy herds. But such programs have failed to eliminate the milk surplus. The chief reason is the dairy farmers' entrepreneurial response to the high price of milk. The government's efforts to cut the size of herds have been largely offset by increased output per cow as a result of genetic improvements and better farm management practices. For example, some dairy farms in California now have 3,000 and even 4,000 cows, compared with 50 or so on a traditional dairy farm. The cows never see a pasture—they spend their days in a pen munching high-protein alfalfa. Whereas the average Mississippi Delta cow gives 13,000 pounds of milk a year (a marvel to farmers in much of the world), its Pacific cousin yields over 21,000 pounds a year. To add insult to injury, the alfalfa they eat is grown in fields that are irrigated with government-subsidized water. Meanwhile, the government's vast inventories of butter and cheese continue to grow.

## Price Ceilings: The Case of Rent Control

In the milk market, the government maintains a support price that is above the equilibrium price. In certain other markets, a price ceiling below the equilibrium price is imposed. An example of the latter situation is rent control in housing markets.

Rent control in one form or another exists in several major U.S. cities, including New York, Washington, D.C., San Francisco, and Los Angeles. The controls vary from one city to another, but in all cases maximum rents, at least for some categories of apartments, are established by law. The purpose of rent control is to aid tenants by preventing landlords from charging "unreasonably high" rents. What is unreasonably high is determined by the relative political strength of landlords and tenants rather than by the forces of supply and demand.

**INTENDED EFFECTS**   Figure 2.10 interprets the effects of rent control in terms of supply and demand. For the sake of simplicity it is assumed that the supply of rental housing consists of units of equal size and rental value. Part (a) of the figure shows the effects of rent control in the short run. Here the short run means a period that is too short to permit significant increases or decreases in the supply of rental housing. (The short-run supply curve, which is drawn as a vertical line, indicates that a change in price will not result in any change in the quantity of apartments supplied in the short run.[4])

Under the conditions shown, the equilibrium rent per standard housing unit is $1,250 per month for each of the 200,000 units in the city. Now suppose that a rent ceiling of $500 is imposed. The result is a gain to tenants of $750 per unit per month. The total sum transferred to tenants (that is, the benefit to them from below-

**FIGURE 2.10   EFFECTS OF RENT CONTROL**

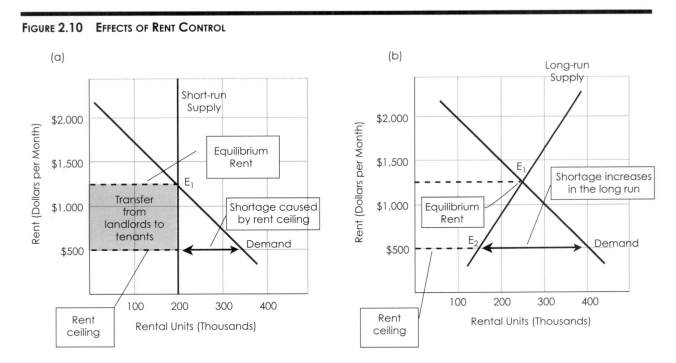

Part (a) shows the short-run effects of rent control. In the short run, the supply of rental apartments is considered to be fixed. The equilibrium rent is $1,250 per month. A rent ceiling of $500 per month is then put into effect. One possible outcome is that landlords will charge disguised rent increases, which will bring the true price back to $1,250 per month. If such disguised increases are prohibited, there will be a shortage of 350,000 units at the ceiling price. Part (b) shows the long-run effects when there is time to adjust the number of units in response to the price. If the ceiling price is enforced, landlords move down their supply curve to $E_2$. The shortage then becomes even more severe than in the short run.

market rents) is $750 per unit times 200,000 units, or $150 million, in all. In graphical terms, that sum is equal to the area of the shaded rectangle in Figure 2.10. The benefit to tenants at the expense of landlords is the principal intended effect of rent control.

**UNINTENDED EFFECTS** The policy of rent control, which does accomplish its goal of benefiting tenants at the expense of landlords, provides a classic illustration of the law of unintended consequences. In the short run, when the stock of apartments is fixed, the unintended consequences stem from the apartment shortage created by the controls. The shortage occurs because the quantity demanded is greater at the lower ceiling price than at the higher equilibrium price.

⤳ **ECONOMICS IN THE NEWS 2.2**

## RENT CONTROLS IN NEW YORK

Robert L. Bartley, "Rent Control: New York's Self-Destruction," Thinking Things Over, *The Wall Street Journal*, May 19, 2003.

Advocates of rent control view these responses as cheating and often try to outlaw them. If prohibitions are enforced, the landlord will find that there are many applicants for each vacant apartment. In that case, the landlord must decide to whom to rent the apartment. The result will often be discrimination against renters who are from minority groups, who have children, or who have unconventional lifestyles.

In the long run, rent control has other unintended effects. The long run in this case means enough time for the number of rental units to grow through construction of new units or shrink through abandonment of old ones (or their conversion to condominiums). Other things being equal, the higher the rent, the greater the rate of construction, and the lower the rent, the greater the rate of abandonment or conversion. This is reflected in the positively sloped long-run supply curve in part (b) of Figure 2.10.

If rent controls are enforced in such a way that there are no disguised charges by landlords, the number of rental units shrinks and the market moves from $E_1$ to $E_2$. At $E_2$, the unintended effects that appeared in the short run become more pronounced. The intensity of housing discrimination increases relative to the short-run case, because the difference between the number of units available and the number sought by renters increases. Graphically, that difference is shown by the horizontal gap between the supply and demand curves at the ceiling price. In the short run, there is a shortage of 50,000 units; in the long run, the shortage increases to 75,000 units.

Rent controls are often defended as being beneficial to the poor. But when all of the unintended effects of rent control are taken into account, one may question whether poor families really benefit. In cases in which disguised rent increases are possible, the true cost of rental housing is not really decreased. Further, it is hard to believe that landlords' tendency to discriminate against minority group members, single-parent families, and tenants with irregular work histories will benefit the poor. The most likely beneficiaries of rent control are stable, middle-class families who work at the same jobs and live in the same apartments for long periods.

Given the many unintended consequences of rent controls, one might legitimately wonder why the policy retains its popularity in many large cities. Why not replace rent control with some other form of housing assistance for the poor—for example, direct subsidies that would allow poor families to rent apartments at market-determined prices, as is already done in some cities? Some economists explain the popularity of rent control in terms of the political power of the middle-class tenants who are most likely to benefit from rent controls and who see helping the poor as nothing more than a convenient cover for simple self-interest. Some explain their popularity in terms of the short time horizon of government officials: The adverse effect on tenants of ending rent control would appear very quickly, whereas such benefits as increased construction of new apartments would materialize only long after the next election. And some attribute the popularity of rent control to the simple fact that many voters do not give much thought to the policy's unintended consequences.

The greater quantity demanded has several sources. First, people who would otherwise own a house or condominium may now want to rent. Second, people who would otherwise live in non–rent-controlled suburbs may now seek rent-controlled units in the city. Third, each tenant may want more space, which results in a demand for more of the standardized units shown in Figure 2.10.

The shortage creates a problem for both landlords and tenants: How will the limited supply of apartments be rationed among those who want them? Both landlords and tenants devise a number of creative responses—*entrepreneurial* responses, as an economist would say.

One response on the part of landlords is to seek disguised rent increases. These may take the form of large, nonrefundable "key deposits" or security deposits. As an alternative, they may sell old, used furniture or drapes at inflated prices as a condition for renting the apartment. Finally, the costs of certain maintenance or security services that the landlord might otherwise have paid for may be transferred to tenants.

Tenants too may get into the act. When they decide to move, they may sublet their apartments to other tenants rather than give up their leases. Now it is the tenant who collects the key money or sells the old drapes to the subtenant. The original tenant may have moved to a distant city but maintains a bank account and a post office box for use in paying the rent. The subtenant is instructed to play the role of a "guest" if the landlord telephones. This charade may become quite elaborate and can go on for decades in cities such as New York, where rent control is long established, as illustrated by *Economics in the News 2.2*.

THIS CHAPTER HAS covered the basics of the supply-and-demand model and described a few applications of that model. There are many more applications in both macro- and microeconomics. In macroeconomics, the supply-and-demand model can be applied to financial markets, labor markets, and the problem of determining the rate of inflation and real output for the economy as a whole. In microeconomics, the model can be applied to product markets, markets for productive resources, and policy issues ranging from pollution to farm policy to international trade, to name just a few. As the great economist Alfred Marshall once put it, nearly all of the major problems of economics have a "kernel" that reflects the workings of supply and demand (see *Who Said It? Who Did It? 2.1*).

When one takes a detailed look at the underpinnings of the model, it appears to fit some kinds of markets more closely than others. The fit is best for markets in which there are many producers and many customers, the goods sold by one producer are much like those sold by others, and all sellers and buyers have good information on market conditions. Markets for farm commodities, such as wheat and corn, and financial markets, such as the New York Stock Exchange, meet these standards reasonably well.

However, even in markets that do not display all of these features, the fit is often close enough so that the supply-and-demand model provides useful insights into what is going on. The rental housing market is an example: Not all rental units are, in fact, alike, even when measurement is standardized for objective characteristics such as floor space. Nevertheless, most economists would agree that valid conclusions about the effects of rent control can be arrived at by applying the supply-and-demand model to that market. Thus, the supply-and-demand model serves a precise analytical function in some cases and a broader, more metaphorical function in others. That flexibility makes the model one of the most useful items in the economist's tool kit.

# SUMMARY

1. **How does the price of a good or service affect the quantity of it that buyers demand?** Economists use the term *demand* to refer to the willingness and ability of buyers to purchase goods and services. According to the *law of demand,* there is an inverse relationship between the price of a good and the quantity of it that buyers demand. The *quantity demanded* is the quantity that buyers are willing and able to pay for. The law of demand can be represented graphically by a negatively sloped *demand curve.* A change in the quantity demanded is shown by a movement along the demand curve.

2. **How do other market conditions affect demand?** A change in any of the variables covered by the "other things being equal" clause of the law of demand causes a shift in the demand curve; this is known as a *change in demand.* Examples include changes in the prices of goods that are *substitutes* or *complements* of the good in question as well as changes in consumer incomes, expectations, and tastes.

3. **How does the price of a good affect the quantity supplied by sellers?** *Supply* refers to sellers' willingness and ability to offer products for sale in a market. In most markets an increase in the price of a good will increase the quantity of the good that sellers are willing to supply. This relationship can be shown as a positively sloped *supply curve.* The higher price gives producers an incentive to supply more, but rising opportunity costs set a limit on the amount they will supply at any given price.

4. **How do changes in other market conditions affect supply?** A change in any of the items covered by the "other things being equal" clause of the supply curve will shift the curve. Examples include changes in technology, changes in the prices of inputs, changes in the prices of other goods that could be produced with the same resources, and changes in expectations.

5. **How do supply and demand interact to determine the market price of a good or service?** In a market with a positively-sloped supply curve and a negatively-sloped demand curve, there is only one price at which the quantity of a good that sellers plan to supply will exactly match the quantity that buyers plan to purchase. That is known as the *equilibrium* price. At any higher price there will be a *surplus,* and at any lower price there will be a *shortage.*

6. **Why do market prices and quantities change in response to changes in market conditions?** A change in any market condition that shifts the supply or demand curve will change the equilibrium price and quantity in a market. For example, the demand curve may shift to the right as a result of a change in consumer incomes. This causes a shortage at the old price, and the price begins to rise. As the price rises, suppliers move up along the supply curve to a new equilibrium. No shift in the supply curve is required. On the other hand, better technology may shift the supply curve to the right. In that case, there is a surplus at the old price, and the price will fall. As the price decreases, buyers will move down along their demand curve to a new equilibrium. No shift in the demand curve is required.

7. **How do price supports and price ceilings affect the operation of markets?** A price support prevents the market price from falling when the demand curve shifts to the left or the supply curve shifts to the right. The result may be a lasting surplus. A price ceiling prevents the price from rising to its equilibrium level. The result may be a permanent shortage. The total quantity supplied may then be less than the quantity that buyers would like to purchase at the ceiling price or even at the equilibrium price.

# KEY TERMS

| | |
|---|---|
| Supply | Supply curve |
| Demand | Change in quantity |
| Law of demand | supplied |
| Demand curve | Change in supply |
| Change in quantity | Equilibrium |
| demanded | Excess quantity |
| Change in demand | demanded (shortage) |
| Substitute goods | Inventory |
| Complementary goods | Excess quantity supplied |
| Normal good | (surplus) |
| Inferior good | |

# PROBLEMS AND TOPICS FOR DISCUSSION

1. **Examining the lead-off case.** On the basis of information given in the case, analyze the decline in the quantity of Porsches sold in terms of shifts in versus movements along the demand curve for this luxury car. Specifically, how was the market for Porsches affected by the U.S. recession? By changing consumer tastes? By rising wages of German autoworkers? By the rising foreign exchange value of the German mark?

2. **A shifting demand curve.** A vending machine company has studied the demand for soft drinks sold in cans from machines. On a 70-degree day consumers in the firm's territory will buy about 2,000 cans at a price of $0.75. For each $.05 rise in price, the quantity sold falls by 200 cans per day; for each 5-degree rise in the temperature, the quantity sold rises by 150 cans per day. The same relationships hold for decreases in price or temperature. Using this information, draw a set of curves showing the demand for soft drinks on days when the temperature is 60, 70, and 85 degrees. Then draw a separate diagram with temperature on the vertical axis and quantity on the horizontal axis. Draw a line representing the relationship between temperature and quantity when the price is $0.75. Next draw additional temperature-quantity lines for prices of $0.50 and $1.00. Do the two diagrams give the same information? Discuss. (Note: If you have any trouble with this exercise, review the appendix to Chapter 1, "Working with Graphs," especially the section entitled "Packing Three Variables into Two Dimensions.")

3. **Demand and the relative price of motor fuel.** In 1979 and 1980 the nominal price of motor fuel rose much more rapidly than the general price level, pushing up the relative price of motor fuel. As we would expect, the quantity sold decreased. In 1981 and 1982 the relative price leveled off and then began to fall, but the quantity sold continued to fall. Which one or more of the following hypotheses do you think best explains the behavior of motor fuel sales in 1981 and 1982? Illustrate each hypothesis with supply and demand curves.

   a. In the 1970s the demand curve had the usual negative slope. However, in 1981 and 1982 the demand curve shifted to an unusual positively sloped position.

   b. The demand curve had a negative slope throughout the period. However, the recession of 1981 and 1982 reduced consumers' real incomes and thus shifted the demand curve.

   c. The demand curve has a negative slope at all times, but the shape depends partly on how much time consumers have to adjust to a change in prices. Over a short period, the demand curve is fairly steep because few adjustments can be made. Over the long term, it has a somewhat flatter slope because further adjustments, such as buying more fuel-efficient cars or moving closer to the job, can be made.

Thus, the decreases in fuel sales in 1981 and 1982 were delayed reactions to the price increases that occurred in 1979 and 1980.

4. **Shortages, price controls, and queues.** In 1974 and again in 1979, a decrease in worldwide oil supplies caused long lines of motorists to form at gas stations in the United States but not in European countries. Do you think the lines had anything to do with the fact that the United States had price controls that kept the price at the pump below a dollar a gallon, whereas European countries had no controls, so that prices at the pump rose the equivalent of two dollars a gallon, and even higher? Back up your reasoning with supply and demand curves.

5. **Eliminating queues through flexible pricing.** You are a member of the Metropolitan Taxi Commission, which sets taxi fares for your city. You have been told that long lines of taxis form at the airport during off-peak hours. At peak hours, on the other hand, few taxis are available and there are long lines of passengers waiting for cabs. It is proposed that taxi fares from the airport to downtown be cut by 10 percent during off-peak hours and raised by 10 percent during peak hours. How do you think these changes would affect the queueing patterns of taxis and passengers? Do you think the proposal is a good one from the passengers' point of view? From the cabbies' point of view? From the standpoint of economic efficiency? Discuss.

6. **Rent control.** Turn to part (b) of Figure 2.10, which shows the long-run effects of rent control. If the controls are enforced and there are no disguised rent charges, landlords move down the supply curve to $E_2$. Buildings are abandoned or converted because of the low rent they bring in. Now consider some alternative possibilities.

   a. Suppose that the controls are poorly enforced so that landlords, through key deposits, furni-

ture sales, or some other means, are able to charge as much as the market will bear. What will the resulting equilibrium price and quantity be, taking both open and disguised rental charges into account?

   b. Now suppose that the controls are enforced so that landlords really cannot collect more than $500 per month. However, the controls are not enforced against tenants who sublet. What will the equilibrium quantity and price be, including both the rent paid to landlords and the disguised rental payments made by subtenants to their subleasors?

# CASE FOR DISCUSSION

## *Supply and Demand for Recycled Materials*

A group of visitors to the Port of Providence, Rhode Island, were recently witnesses to one of America's export success stories: A huge freighter being loaded, not with aircraft parts, not with computers or specialty chemicals, but with tons of waste paper bound for China.

In the 1990s, the United States became for waste paper what Saudi Arabia is for oil. Much the same goes for scrap aluminum, old bottles, and other products of the rapidly spreading recycling movement. Recycling, a strictly voluntary activity until a few years ago, has now become mandatory in many cities. Already one-half of all U.S. households are served by curbside recycling programs. But recycling is not always entirely successful.

The case of aluminum cans represents recycling at its best. Mote than two-thirds of all cans are now recycled, one of the highest rates for any material. Making a new can from an old one saves up to 85 percent of the energy required to make a new can from bauxite ore. As a result, aluminum recycling has long been profitable and continues to be so.

Recycling of other materials presents greater problems. Take glass, for example. Making a new bottle from an old one, instead of from sand, saves as little as 10 percent of the energy required. The margin for profit in recycling glass therefore is very narrow. Clear glass, which is most in demand, commands a market price of $40–$45 a ton. But green, brown, and mixed glass are virtually worthless in many regions.

Even newsprint presents problems. Newsprint, like aluminum, has long been a profitable commodity for commercial recyclers. But the introduction of curbside programs can sometimes swamp local markets. Take the case of Babylon, N.Y.: Beginning in 1990, paper started coming in faster than it could be shipped to markets such as China, South Korea, and Taiwan. The town rapidly accumulated 1,200 tons of yellowing paper in an old aircraft hangar. Instead of selling the paper to dealers, the town had to pay the dealers $35 a ton to haul it away. But by 1992, market conditions had improved, and the town was again selling its newsprint for a few dollars a ton.

Critics of across-the-board recycling say that programs should be fine-tuned to market conditions. Energy and other scarce resources are wasted, they say, in costly efforts to collect and sort materials that have no economic value. Proponents of recycling, on the other hand, put their faith in the growth of demand. Several huge de-inking plants currently under construction will boost the demand for waste newsprint. And new uses for other materials, such as "glassphalt" pavement for roads, will soon absorb piles of scrap for which there have been few uses in the past.

Source: Based in part on Frank Edward Allen, "As Recycling Surges, Market for Materials Is Slow to Develop," *The Wall Street Journal,* January 17, 1992, A1.

## QUESTIONS

1. Draw supply and demand curves to illustrate the markets for clear glass and for green glass. How would these markets be affected by the growth of demand for glass to be used in "glassphalt" paving material, assuming color makes no difference for that particular use?
2. Draw supply and demand curves to illustrate the market for waste newsprint in Babylon, N.Y., (a) before 1990, showing an equilibrium price of $5 per ton; (b) in 1990–1991, when the town had to pay $35 per ton to have the paper hauled away; and (c) in 1992, when growth of demand again made it possible to sell the paper.
3. Do you think recycling should be pursued as a goal of public policy only when recycled materials can be sold profitably, or even when they cannot be sold profitably? Discuss.

## END NOTES

1. Before continuing, the reader may want to review the Chapter 1 appendix "Working with Graphs," especially the section entitled "Packing Three Variables into Two Dimensions."
2. The "plans" referred to need not be formal or thought out in detail, and are subject to change. A consumer might, for example, make out a shopping list for the supermarket based on the usual prices for various foods, but then revise it to take into account unexpected price increases or sales on certain items. On specific occasions, consumer decisions may even be completely impulsive, with little basis in rational calculation. The model of supply and demand does not require that every decision be based on precise analysis, but only that consumer intentions, on the average, are influenced by prices and other economic considerations.
3. Why might buyers and sellers enter the market expecting a price other than the one that permits equilibrium? It may be, for example, that market conditions have caused the supply or demand curve to shift unexpectedly, so that a price that formerly permitted equilibrium no longer does so. It may be that buyers or sellers expect conditions to change, but they do not change after all. Or, it may be that government policy has established a legal maximum or minimum price that differs

from the equilibrium price. Later sections of the chapter will explore some of these possibilities.

4. This is a fairly restrictive assumption. In practice, a small number of housing units can move into or out of the rental market quickly in response to changing conditions. "Mother-in-law apartments" in private homes are an example. If con-ditions in the rental market are unfavorable, the owners of such units may simply leave them vacant. Allowing for such fast-reaction units means that the short-run supply curve, while still quite steep, would not be vertical. However, a vertical short-run curve simplifies the geometry while capturing the essential features of the situation.

# Supply, Demand, and Elasticity

| | |
|---|---|
| *After reading this chapter, you will understand:* | 1. How the responsiveness of quantity demanded to a price change can be expressed in terms of elasticity<br>2. How elasticity applies to situations other than the responsiveness of the quantity of a good demanded to a change in its price<br>3. How elasticity is useful in interpreting issues of taxation and other public policies |
| *Before reading this chapter, make sure you know the meaning of:* | 1. Supply and demand<br>2. Demand, quantity demanded<br>3. Supply, quantity supplied<br>4. Substitutes and complements<br>5. Normal and inferior goods |

## A BUG IN THE SALAD BOWL

There was a time when lettuce was a seasonal food for consumers on the east coast. The transcontinental railroads and refrigerated freight cars changed all this. Produce from California and Arizona, where lettuce can be grown year round, became a standard item in supermarkets throughout the country. During the winter months, farmers in these states ship some 10,000 tons of lettuce to market every day. Densely packed and long-lasting varieties like iceberg are especially popular.

Despite the best efforts of agricultural science, however, the lettuce supply is not immune to disruption. In one recent January, an outbreak of a virus carried by the sweet potato white fly cut production by 25 percent, causing lettuce prices to rise by 300 percent. Consumers were shocked by prices of as much as $2 a head.

Paradoxically, however, the virus outbreak worked to the benefit of many farmers. Not those who lost their entire crops, of course. But many farmers who were able to ship at least some lettuce to market actually came out ahead. "Most growers have come out okay because the prices were up so much," said Wade Whitfield, president of the California Iceberg Lettuce Commission.

Although the virus outbreak caught farmers unprepared, a search for countermeasures was quickly launched. Department of Agriculture scientists searched their collections of wild lettuce strains for those that were resistant to the virus. Over time, through selective breeding and gene splicing, it should be possible to develop tasty but virus-resistant commercial varieties. Such measures take time, however, and do nothing to lessen the short-term impact on the consumer's pocketbook.

Source: Based on Ward Sinclair, "Virus Eats into Lettuce Production: Price Soars," *The Washington Post,* January 6, 1988, A7.

∽

IN THE PRECEDING chapter we saw many examples of supply and demand in action. In this chapter we will shift our focus. Instead of looking only at the direction of changes that result from changing supply and demand conditions, we will stress the size of the changes.

As the case of the lettuce virus shows, the size of the price change associated with a given change in quantity demanded is crucial. We know that a reduction in supply will cause a rise in price as consumers move up along their demand curve. But how much of a hardship will the poor crop cause for farmers? If the price rises only a little, farmers will be hit hard. But if, as in the case just described, the price rises sharply enough, the greater price per unit will more than compensate farmers as a group for the reduction in the overall size of the crop. This chapter provides a framework for approaching such questions. The methods introduced here have many applications in both macro- and microeconomics.

# ELASTICITY

The responsiveness of one economic variable to a change in another can be expressed in many ways, depending on the units of measurement that are chosen. Take the quantity of lettuce demanded by consumers. We could say that each $1 increase in the price *per carton* would reduce the quantity demanded by 100,000, 50-pound *cartons per day*. Or we could say that each $1 increase in the price *per ton* would reduce quantity demanded by 437.5 *tons per week*. Although it takes a few minutes with a calculator to verify the fact, these two statements are equivalent; only the units differ.

To avoid confusion arising from the choice of different units of measurement, it is useful to standardize. One common way of doing so is to express all changes as percentages. For example, the news item reports that a 25 percent reduction in quantity was associated with a 300 percent increase in price. These percentages would stay the same regardless of whether the original data were stated in dollars per ton, crates per week, or any other measurement.

The use of percentages to express the response of one variable to a change in another is widespread in economics. The term **elasticity** is used to refer to relationships expressed in percentages. Like equilibrium, elasticity is a metaphor borrowed from physics. Much as equilibrium calls to mind a pendulum that has come to rest hanging straight down, elasticity conjures up the image of a rubber band that stretches by a certain proportion of its length when the force applied to it is increased by a given percentage. This chapter introduces several applications of elasticity in economics.

## *Price Elasticity of Demand*

We begin with the relationship between price and quantity demanded. The **price elasticity of demand** is the ratio of the percentage change in the quantity of a good demanded to a given percentage change in its price. Figure 3.1 presents five demand curves showing different degrees of price elasticity of demand. In part (a), the quantity demanded is relatively responsive to a change in price. In this case, a decrease in price from $5 to $3 causes the quantity demanded to increase from three units to six. Because the percentage change in quantity demanded is greater than the percentage change in price, the drop in price causes total revenue from sales of the good to increase. **Revenue** is the price times the quantity sold. On a supply-and-demand diagram, revenue can be shown as the area of a rectangle drawn under the demand curve, with a height equal to price and a width equal to quantity demanded. In this case comparison of the shaded rectangles representing revenue before the price reduction ($5 per unit × 3 units = $15) and afterward ($3 per unit × 6 units = $18) shows that revenue is greater after the price has been reduced. When the quantity demanded changes by a greater percentage than price, so that a price decrease causes total revenue to increase, demand is said to be **elastic**.

**Elasticity**

A measure of the response of one variable to a change in another, stated as a ratio of the percentage change in one variable to the associated percentage change in another variable.

**Price elasticity of demand**

The ratio of the percentage change in the quantity of a good demanded to a given percentage change in its price, other things being equal.

**Revenue**

Price times quantity sold.

**Elastic demand**

A situation in which quantity demanded changes by a larger percentage than price, so that total revenue increases as price decreases.

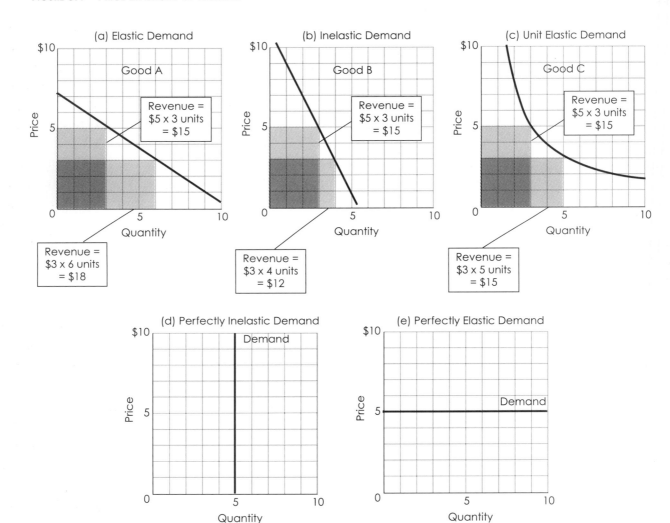

FIGURE 3.1   PRICE ELASTICITY OF DEMAND

This figure shows five examples of demand curves with various degrees of elasticity over the indicated range of variation of price and quantity. The examples illustrate elastic, inelastic, unit elastic, perfectly inelastic, and perfectly elastic demand. For the first three cases, the revenue change associated with a change in price is shown. When demand is elastic, a price decrease causes revenue to increase. When demand is inelastic, a price decrease causes revenue to decrease. When demand is unit elastic, revenue does not change when price changes.

**Inelastic demand**

A situation in which quantity demanded changes by a smaller percentage than price, so that total revenue decreases as price decreases.

Part (b) of Figure 3.1 shows a case in which the quantity demanded is relatively unresponsive to a change in price. Here, a $2 decrease in price, from $5 to $3 per unit, causes the quantity demanded to increase by just one unit—from three to four. This time the percentage change in quantity demanded is less than that in price. As a result, the decrease in price causes total revenue to fall (again note the shaded rectangles). In such a case demand is said to be **inelastic**.

Part (c) shows a case in which a change in price causes an exactly proportional change in quantity demanded, so that total revenue does not change at all. When the

**Unit elastic demand**

A situation in which price and quantity demanded change by the same percentage, so that total revenue remains unchanged as price changes.

**Perfectly inelastic demand**

A situation in which the demand curve is a vertical line.

**Perfectly elastic demand**

A situation in which the demand curve is a horizontal line.

percentage change in quantity demanded equals the percentage change in price, demand is said to be **unit elastic**.

The final two parts of Figure 3.1 show two extreme cases. Part (d) shows a vertical demand curve. Regardless of the price, the quantity demanded is five units—no more, no less. Such a demand curve is said to be **perfectly inelastic**. Part (e) shows a demand curve that is perfectly horizontal. Above a price of $5, no units of the good can be sold; but as soon as the price drops to $5, there is no limit on how much can be sold. A horizontal demand curve like this one is described as **perfectly elastic**. The law of demand, which describes an inverse relationship between price and quantity, does not encompass the cases of perfectly elastic and inelastic demand, and we do not expect market demand curves for ordinary goods and services to fit these extremes. Nevertheless, we will see that perfectly elastic and inelastic curves sometimes provide useful reference points for theory building, even though they do not resemble real-world market demand curves.

## Calculating Elasticity of Demand

In speaking of elasticity of demand, it is often enough to say that demand is elastic or inelastic, without being more precise. At other times, though, it is useful to attach numerical values to elasticity. This section introduces the most common method used to calculate a numerical value for elasticity of demand.

The first step in turning the general definition of elasticity into a numerical formula is to develop a way to measure percentage changes. The everyday method for calculating a percentage change is to use the initial value of the variable as the denominator and the change in the value as the numerator. For example, if the quantity of California lettuce demanded in the national market is initially 10,000 tons per week and then decreases by 2,500 tons per week, we say that there has been a 25 percent change (2,500/10,000 = .25). The trouble with this convention is that the same change in the opposite direction gives a different percentage. By everyday reasoning, an increase in the quantity of lettuce demanded from 7,500 tons per week to 10,000 tons per week is a 33 percent increase (2,500/7,500 = .33).

Decades ago the eminent mathematical economist R. G. D. Allen proposed an unambiguous measure of percentage changes that uses the midpoint of the range over which change takes place as the denominator. Allen's formula is not the only possible one, but it caught on and remains the most popular.

To find the midpoint of the range over which a change takes place, we take the sum of the initial value and the final value and divide by 2. In our example, the midpoint of the quantity range is (7,500 + 10,000)/2 = 8,750. When this is used as the denominator, a change of 2,500 units becomes (approximately) a 28.6 percent change (2,500/8,750 = .286). Using $Q_1$ to represent the quantity before the change and $Q_2$ to represent the quantity after the change, the midpoint formula for the percentage change in quantity is

$$\text{Percentage change in quantity} = \frac{Q_2 - Q_1}{(Q_1 + Q_2)/2}$$

The same approach can be used to define the percentage change in price. In our case, the price of lettuce increased from about $250 per ton to about $1,000 per ton. Using the midpoint of the range, or $625, as the denominator [($250 + $1,000)/2 = $625], we conclude that the $750 increase in price is a 120 percent increase ($750/$625 = 1.2). The midpoint formula for the percentage change in price is

$$\text{Percentage change in price} = \frac{P_2 - P_1}{(P_1 + P_2)/2}$$

**THE MIDPOINT FORMULA FOR ELASTICITY**   Defining percentage changes in this way allows us to write a useful formula for calculating elasticities. With $P_1$ and $Q_1$ representing price and quantity before a change, and $P_2$ and $Q_2$ representing price and quantity after the change, the midpoint formula for elasticity is

$$\text{Price elasticity of demand} = \frac{(Q_2 - Q_1)/(Q_1 + Q_2)}{(P_2 - P_1)/(P_1 + P_2)} = \frac{\text{Percentage change in quantity}}{\text{Percentage change in price}}$$

Here is the complete calculation for the elasticity of demand for lettuce when an increase in price from $250 per ton to $1,000 per ton causes the quantity demanded to fall from 10,000 tons per day to 7,500 tons per day:

$P_1$ = price before change = $250
$P_2$ = price after change = $1,000
$Q_1$ = quantity before change = 10,000
$Q_2$ = quantity after change = 7,500

$$\text{Elasticity} = \frac{(7,500 - 10,000)/(7,500 + 10,000)}{(\$1,000 - \$250)/(\$1,000 + \$250)}$$

$$= \frac{-2,500/17,500}{\$750/\$1,250}$$

$$= \frac{-.142}{.6}$$

$$= -.24$$

Because demand curves have negative slopes, this formula yields a negative value for elasticity. The reason is that the quantity demanded changes in the direction opposite to that of the price change. When the price decreases, $(P_2 - P_1)$, which appears in the denominator of the formula, is negative, whereas $(Q_2 - Q_1)$, which appears in the numerator, is positive. When the price increases, the numerator is negative and the denominator is positive. However, in this book we follow the widely used practice of dropping the minus sign when discussing price elasticity of demand. Thus, the elasticity of demand for lettuce would be stated as approximately .24 over the range studied.

A numerical elasticity value such as .24 can be related to the basic definition of elasticity in a simple way. That definition stated that price elasticity of demand is the ratio of the percentage change in quantity demanded to a given percentage change in price. Thus, an elasticity of .24 means that the quantity demanded will increase by .24 percent for each 1 percent change in price. An elasticity of 3 would mean that quantity demanded would change by 3 percent for each 1 percent change in price, and so on.[1]

**ELASTICITY VALUES AND TERMINOLOGY**   Earlier in the chapter we defined *elastic, inelastic, unit elastic, perfectly elastic,* and *perfectly inelastic* demand. Each of these terms corresponds to a numerical value or range of values of elasticity. A perfectly inelastic demand curve has a numerical value of 0, since any change in price produces no change in quantity demanded. The term *inelastic* (but not perfectly inelastic) *demand* applies to numerical values from 0 up to, but not including, 1. *Unit elasticity,* as the name implies, means a numerical value of exactly 1. *Elastic demand* means any value for elasticity that is greater than 1. *Perfectly elastic* demand, represented by a horizontal demand curve, is not defined numerically; as the demand curve becomes horizontal, the denominator of the elasticity formula approaches 0 and the numerical value of elasticity increases without limit.

## Varying- and Constant-Elasticity Demand Curves

The midpoint formula shows elasticity of demand over a certain range of prices and quantities. Measured over some other range, the elasticity of demand for the same good may be the same or different, depending on the shape of the demand curve, as shown in Figure 3.2.

Part (a) of Figure 3.2 shows a demand curve that, like most of those in this book, is a straight line. The elasticity of demand is not constant for all ranges of price and quantity along this curve. For example, when measured over the price range $8 to $9, the elasticity of demand is 5.66; when measured over the range $2 to $3, it is .33. (The calculations are shown in the figure.)

The calculations illustrate the general rule that elasticity declines as one moves downward along a straight-line demand curve. It is easy to see why. With such a demand curve, a $1 reduction in price always causes the same absolute increase in quantity demanded. At the upper end of the demand curve, a $1 change is a small percentage of the relatively high price, while the change in quantity is a large percentage of the relatively low quantity demanded at that price. At the lower end of the curve, however, the situation is reversed: A $1 change is now a large percentage of the relatively low price, while the increase in quantity is smaller in relation to the

FIGURE 3.2  ELASTICITY AT VARIOUS POINTS ALONG A DEMAND CURVE

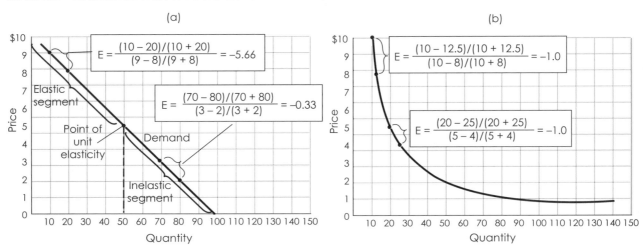

Elasticity varies along a straight-line demand curve, as part (a) of this figure illustrates. At the upper end of the curve, where the price is relatively high, a $1 change in price is a relatively small percentage change, and, because the quantity demanded is low, the corresponding change in quantity is relatively large in percentage terms. Demand is thus elastic near the top of the demand curve. At the lower end of the curve, the situation is reversed: a $1 change in price is now a relatively large change in percentage terms, whereas the corresponding change in quantity is smaller in percentage terms. Thus demand is inelastic. As part (b) shows, a curved demand curve can be drawn such that elasticity is constant for all ranges of price and quantity change.

relatively larger quantity demanded. Because it is percentages, not absolute amounts, that matter in elasticity calculations, a linear demand curve is less elastic near the bottom than near the top.

If the demand curve is not a straight line, other results are possible. There is an important special case in which the demand curve has just the curvature needed to keep elasticity constant over its entire length. Such a curve is shown in part (b) of Figure 3.2. As can be seen from the calculations in the figure, elasticity is 1.0 at every point on that curve. It is possible to construct demand curves with constant elasticities of any value. Econometric studies of demand elasticity often look for the constant-elasticity demand curve that most closely approximates buyers' average sensitivity to price changes as revealed by market data over time.

## Determinants of Elasticity of Demand

The fact that elasticity often varies along the demand curve means that care must be taken in making statements about *the* elasticity of demand for a good. In practice, what such statements usually refer to is the elasticity, measured by the midpoint formula or some alternative method, over the range of price variation that is commonly observed in the market for that good. With this understanding, we can make some generalizations about what makes the demand for some goods relatively elastic and the demand for others relatively inelastic.

**SUBSTITUTES, COMPLEMENTS, AND ELASTICITY** One important determinant of elasticity of demand is the availability of substitutes. When a good has close substitutes, the demand for that good tends to be relatively elastic, because people willingly switch to the substitutes when the price of the good goes up. Thus, for example, the demand for corn oil is relatively elastic, because other cooking oils can usually be substituted for it. On the other hand, the demand for cigarettes is relatively inelastic, because for a habitual smoker there is no good substitute.

This principle has two corollaries. One is that the demand for a good tends to be more elastic the more narrowly the good is defined. For example, the demand for lettuce in the numerical example given earlier was relatively inelastic. This could be because many people are in the habit of eating a salad with dinner and do not think of spinach or coleslaw as completely satisfactory substitutes. At the same time, however, it could be that the demand for any particular variety of lettuce is relatively elastic. If the price of Boston lettuce rises while the prices of iceberg, romaine, and red-leaf lettuce remain unchanged, many people will readily switch to one of the other varieties, which they see as close substitutes.

The other corollary is that demand for the product of a single firm tends to be more elastic than the demand for the output of all producers operating in the market. As one example, the demand for cigarettes as a whole will be less elastic than the demand for any particular brand, such as Viceroy or Winston. The reason is that one brand can be substituted for another when the price of a brand changes.

The complements of a good can also play a role in determining its elasticity. If something is a minor complement to an important good (that is, one that accounts for a large share of consumers' budgets), demand for it tends to be relatively inelastic. For example, the demand for motor oil tends to be relatively inelastic, because it is a complement to a more important good, gasoline. The price of gasoline has a greater effect on the amount of driving a person does than the price of motor oil.

**TIME HORIZON AND ELASTICITY** One of the most important considerations determining the price elasticity of demand is the time horizon within which the decision to buy is made. For several reasons, demand is often less elastic in the short run than in the long run.

One reason is that full adjustment to a change in the price of a good may require changes in the kind or quantity of many other goods that a consumer buys. Gasoline provides a classic example. When the price of gasoline jumped in the 1970s, many people's initial reaction was to cut out some nonessential driving; the quantity of gasoline demanded fell only a little. As time went by, though, consumers adjusted in many ways. One important adjustment was to buy more fuel-efficient cars. Another was to base the choice of where to live partly on the length of the drive to work or the availability of public transportation. Gradually, as such adjustments were made, the quantity of gasoline demanded fell more than it had at first.

Another reason elasticity tends to be greater in the long run than in the short run is that an increase in the price of one good encourages entrepreneurs to develop substitutes—which, as we have seen, can be an important determinant of elasticity. To take an example from history, consider the response to what has been called America's first energy crisis, a sharp increase in the price of whale oil, which was used as lamp fuel in the early nineteenth century. At first candles were the only substitute for whale-oil lamps, and not a very satisfactory one. People therefore cut their use of whale oil only a little when the price began to rise. But the high price of whale oil spurred entrepreneurs to develop a better substitute, kerosene. Once kerosene came onto the market, the quantity of whale oil demanded for use as lamp fuel dropped to zero.

A final reason for greater elasticity of demand in the long run than in the short run is the slow adjustment of consumer tastes. The case of beef and chicken, featured in the preceding chapter, provides an example. Chicken, originally the more expensive meat, achieved a price advantage over beef many years ago, but eating lots of beef was a habit. Gradually, though, chicken developed an image as a healthy, stylish, versatile food, and finally it overtook beef as the number-one meat.

## Income Elasticity of Demand

Determining the response of quantity demanded to a change in price is the most common application of the concept of elasticity, but it is by no means the only one. Elasticity can also be used to express the response of demand to any of the conditions covered by the "other things being equal" assumption on which a given demand curve is based. As we saw in the preceding chapter, one of those conditions is consumer incomes.

**Income elasticity of demand**

The ratio of the percentage change in the quantity of a good demanded to a given percentage change in consumer incomes, other things being equal.

The **income elasticity of demand** for a good is defined as the ratio of the percentage change in the quantity of that good demanded to a percentage change in income. In measuring income elasticity, it is assumed that the good's price does not change. Using $Q_1$ and $Q_2$ to represent quantities before and after the change in income, and $y_1$ and $y_2$ to represent income before and after the change, the midpoint formula for income elasticity of demand can be written as follows:

$$\text{Income elasticity of demand} = \frac{(Q_2 - Q_1)/(Q_1 + Q_2)}{(y_2 - y_1)/(y_1 + y_2)} = \frac{\text{Percentage change in quantity}}{\text{Percentage change in income}}$$

For a normal good, an increase in income causes demand to rise. Because income and demand change in the same direction, the income elasticity of demand for a normal good is positive. For an inferior good, an increase in income causes demand to decrease. Because income and demand change in opposite directions, the income elasticity of demand for an inferior good is negative.

Some of the considerations that determine price elasticity also affect income elasticity. In particular, whether a good is considered to be normal or inferior depends on how narrowly it is defined and on the availability of substitutes. For example, a study by Jonq-Ying Lee, Mark G. Brown, and Brooke Schwartz of the University of Florida looked at the demand for frozen orange juice.[2] Orange juice considered as a broad category is a normal good; people tend to consume more of it as their income rises. However, when the definition is narrowed so that house-brand and national-brand frozen orange juice are treated as separate products, the house-brand product turns out to be an inferior good. As their incomes rise, consumers substitute the higher-quality national brands, which have a positive income elasticity of demand.

## Cross-Elasticity of Demand

**Cross-elasticity of demand**

The ratio of the percentage change in the quantity of a good demanded to a given percentage change in the price of some other good, other things being equal.

Another condition that can cause a change in the demand for a good is a change in the price of some other good. The demand for chicken is affected by changes in the price of beef, the demand for motor oil by changes in the price of gasoline, and so on. Such relationships can be expressed as elasticities: The **cross-elasticity of demand** for a good is defined as the ratio of the percentage change in the quantity of that good demanded to a given percentage change in the price of another good. The midpoint formula for cross-elasticity of demand looks just like the one for price elasticity of demand, except that the numerator shows the percentage change in the quantity of one good while the denominator shows the percentage change in the price of some other good.

Cross-elasticity of demand is related to the concepts of substitutes and complements. Because lettuce and cabbage are substitutes, an increase in the price of cabbage causes an increase in the quantity of lettuce demanded; the cross-elasticity of demand is positive. Because motor oil and gasoline are complements, an increase in the price of gasoline causes a decrease in the quantity of motor oil demanded; the cross-elasticity of demand is negative. The previously mentioned study of frozen orange juice found a positive cross-elasticity of demand between house-brand and national-brand juices, indicating that the two are substitutes.

## Price Elasticity of Supply

**Price elasticity of supply**

The ratio of the percentage change in the quantity of a good supplied to a given percentage change in its price, other things being equal.

Elasticity is not confined to demand; it can also be used to indicate the response of quantity supplied to a change in price. Formally, the **price elasticity of supply** of a good is defined as the percentage change in the quantity of the good supplied divided by the percentage change in its price. The midpoint formula for calculating price elasticity of supply looks like the one for determining price elasticity of demand, but the Qs in the numerator of the formula now refer to quantity *supplied* rather than

FIGURE 3.3   CALCULATING PRICE ELASTICITY OF SUPPLY

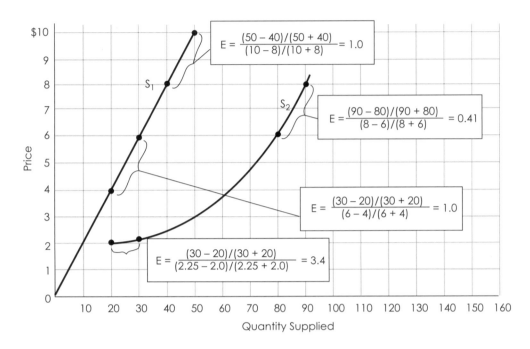

This figure gives four examples of the way price elasticity of supply is calculated. Price elasticity of supply is shown for two ranges on each of the two supply curves. Supply curve S₁ which is a straight line passing through the origin, has a constant elasticity of 1.0. Supply curve S₂, which is curved, is elastic for small quantities and inelastic for larger ones.

quantity *demanded.* Because price and quantity change in the same direction along a positively sloped supply curve, the formula gives a positive value for the elasticity of supply. Figure 3.3 applies the elasticity formula to two supply curves, one with constant elasticity and the other with variable elasticity.

In later chapters we will look in detail at the considerations that determine the elasticity of supply for various products. Two of those considered are especially important, however, and deserve some discussion here.

One determinant of the elasticity of supply of a good is the mobility of the factors of production used to produce it. As used here, *mobility* means the ease with which factors can be attracted away from some other use, as well as the ease with which they can be reconverted to their original use. The trucking industry provides a classic example of mobile resources. As a crop such as lettuce or watermelons comes to harvest in a particular region of a country, hundreds of trucks are needed to haul it to market. Shippers compete for available trucks, driving up the price paid to truckers in the local market. Independent truckers throughout the country learn—from their own experience, from trucking brokers, and from CB radios—where they can earn the best rates for hauling produce. It takes only a modest rise in the price for hauling a load of Georgia watermelons to attract enough truckers to Georgia to haul the crop to market. When the harvest is over, the truckers will move elsewhere to haul peaches, tomatoes, or whatever.

In contrast, other products are produced with much less mobile resources. Petroleum provides a good example. In the 1970s, when oil prices rose, producers had an incentive to drill more wells. However, given limited numbers of drilling rigs and other highly specialized equipment, not to mention limited numbers of sites worth exploring, the tenfold increase in oil prices during the decade caused only a slight increase in oil output. Factor mobility in this industry is limited in the other direction, too. Once a well has been drilled, the investment cannot be converted to a different use. Thus, in the 1980s, when oil prices fell again, production dropped by a much smaller percentage than price.

A second determinant of elasticity of supply is time. As in the case of demand, price elasticity of supply tends to be greater in the long run than in the short run. In part, the reason for this is connected with mobility of resources. In the short run, the output of many products can be increased by using more of the most flexible inputs—for example, by adding workers at a plant or extending the hours of work. Such short-run measures often mean higher costs per unit for the added output, however, because workers added without comparable additions in other inputs (such as equipment) tend to be less productive. If a firm expects market conditions to warrant an increase of supply in the long run, it will be worthwhile to invest in additional quantities of less mobile inputs such as specialized plants and equipment. Once those investments have been made, the firm will find it worthwhile to supply the greater quantity of output at a lower price than in the short-run case because its costs per unit supplied will be lower.

# APPLICATIONS OF ELASTICITY

Elasticity has many applications in both macro- and microeconomics. In macroeconomics, it can be applied to money markets, to the aggregate supply and demand for all goods and services, and to foreign-exchange markets, to name just a few. In microeconomics, elasticity plays a role in discussions of consumer behavior, the profit-maximizing behavior of business firms, governments' regulatory and labor policies, and many other areas. To further illustrate elasticity, we conclude this chapter with applications featuring the problems of tax incidence and drug policy.

## *Elasticity and Tax Incidence*

Who pays taxes? One way to answer this question is in terms of *assessments*—the issue of who bears the legal responsibility to make tax payments to the government. A study of assessments would show that property owners pay property taxes, gasoline companies pay gasoline taxes, and so on. However, looking at assessments does not always settle the issue of who bears the economic burden of a tax—or, to use the economist's term, the issue of **tax incidence**.

**Tax incidence**

The distribution of the economic burden of a tax.

The incidence of a tax does not always coincide with the way the tax is assessed, because the economic burden of the tax, in whole or in part, often can be passed along to someone else. The degree to which the burden of a tax may be passed along depends on the elasticities of supply and demand. Let's consider some examples.

**INCIDENCE OF A GASOLINE TAX**    First consider the familiar example of a gasoline tax. Specifically, suppose that the state of Virginia decides to impose a tax of $.50 per gallon on gasoline beginning from a situation in which there is no tax. The tax is assessed against sellers of gasoline, who add the tax into the price paid by consumers at the pump.

Figure 3.4 uses the supply-and-demand model to show the effects of the tax. Initially, the demand curve intersects supply curve $S_1$ at $E_1$, resulting in a price of $1 per gallon. The supply curve is elastic in the region of the initial equilibrium. The elasticity of supply reflects the fact that we are dealing with the gasoline market in just one state; only a slight rise in the price in Virginia is needed to divert additional quantities

**FIGURE 3.4    INCIDENCE OF A TAX ON GASOLINE**

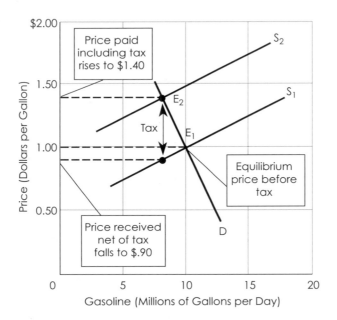

$S_1$ and D are the supply and demand curves before imposition of the tax. The initial equilibrium price is $1 per gallon. A tax of $.50 per gallon shifts the supply curve to $S_2$. To induce sellers to supply the same quantity as before, the price would have to rise to $1.50. However, as the price rises, buyers reduce the quantity demanded, moving up and to the left along the demand curve. In the new equilibrium at $E_2$, the price rises only to $1.40. After the tax is paid, sellers receive only $.90 per gallon. Thus, buyers bear $.40 of the tax on each gallon and sellers the remaining $.10. Buyers bear the larger share of the tax because demand, in this case, is less elastic than supply.

of gasoline from elsewhere in the nation. The demand for gasoline is less elastic than the supply in the region of the initial equilibrium.

The effect of the tax is to shift the supply curve to the left until each point on the new supply curve is exactly $.50 higher than the point for the corresponding quantity on the old supply curve. (We could instead say that the supply curve shifts *upward* by $.50.) Because sellers must now turn over $.50 to the state government for each gallon of gas sold, they would have to get $1.50 per gallon to be willing to sell the same quantity (10 million gallons per day) as initially. However, when sellers attempt to pass the tax on to motorists, motorists respond by reducing the amount of gas they buy. As the quantity sold falls, sellers move down and to the left along supply curve $S_2$ to a new equilibrium at $E_2$.

In the new equilibrium, the price is $1.40 per gallon—just $.40 higher than the original price. The new price includes the $.50 tax, which sellers add to their net price of $.90 per gallon—a net price that is $.10 less than before. The amount of the tax—$.50 per gallon—is shown by the vertical gap between the supply and demand curves. The economic burden of the tax is divided between buyers and sellers, but in this case it falls more heavily on the buyers.

**INCIDENCE OF A TAX ON APARTMENT RENTS**    In the preceding example, the incidence of the gasoline tax falls more heavily on buyers than on sellers because demand is less elastic than supply. If the elasticities are reversed, the results will also be reversed, as can be seen in the case of a tax on apartment rents.

In Figure 3.5, the market for rental apartments in Ogden, Utah (a small city) is initially in equilibrium at $500 per month. The supply of rental apartments is inelastic. An increase in rents will cause a few new apartments to be built, whereas a reduction will cause a few to be torn down, but in either case the response will be moderate. On the other hand, demand is fairly elastic, because potential renters consider houses or condominiums a fairly close substitute for rental apartments.

Given this situation, suppose that the local government decides to impose a tax of $250 per month on all apartments rented in Ogden, UT. This tax, like the gasoline tax, is assessed against landlords, who include the tax payment in the monthly rental they charge to tenants. As in the previous example, the tax shifts the supply curve to the left until each point on the new supply curve lies above the corresponding point on the old supply curve by the amount of the tax. (Again, we could instead say the supply curve shifts upward by the amount of the tax.) After the shift, the market reaches a new equilibrium at $E_2$. There the rental price paid by tenants rises to only $550 per month, as indicated by the intersection of the new supply and demand curves. Landlords succeed in passing only $50 of the $250 monthly tax along to tenants. Their net rental income, after turning over the tax receipts to the town government, is now just $300, down from $500 before imposition of the tax. In this case, because supply is inelastic and demand is elastic, suppliers bear most of the incidence of the tax and buyers only a little.

FIGURE 3.5   INCIDENCE OF A TAX ON APARTMENT RENTS

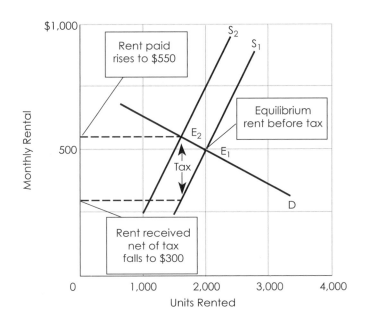

This figure shows the incidence of a tax imposed in a market in which supply is less elastic than demand. Initially, the equilibrium rent is $500 per month. A $250-per-month tax on apartment rents shifts the supply curve to $S_2$. The new equilibrium is at $E_2$. Landlords end up absorbing all but $50 of the tax. If they tried to pass more of the tax on to renters, more renters would switch to owner-occupied housing, and the vacancy rate on rental apartments would rise.

**INCIDENCE AND TAX REVENUE**   When the government considers imposing a tax on gasoline, cigarettes, apartments, or any other item, the price elasticity of demand and supply is important not only for how the burden is shared between buyers and sellers, but also for how much tax revenue the government collects. When buyers and/or sellers are more responsive to changes in price (when demand and /or supply is more elastic), a tax will generate less revenue for the government.

Figure 3.6 compares the markets for two items: milk and pork. The price elasticities of supply for these two goods are relatively similar, but the price elasticities of demand differ. Pork is a meat that has several substitutes, such as beef, chicken, and fish. Milk, however, has few substitutes, so its demand is inelastic relative to pork. The markets for milk and pork are shown in Figure 3.6. The equilibrium price of milk is $0.50 per gallon and 12 million gallons are sold each year at this price. The milk market equilibrium is point $E_1$ on the left panel of Figure 3.6. The equilibrium (shown by the point $E_1$ on the right panel of Figure 3.6) is $0.75 per pound and 12 million pounds are sold each year.

Suppose the government is considering imposing a $1.00 tax on milk or pork. The diagrams show the effects of this tax in each market. In the milk market, the $1.00 tax leads to a small decrease in the quantity from 12 to 10 million gallons

**FIGURE 3.6**

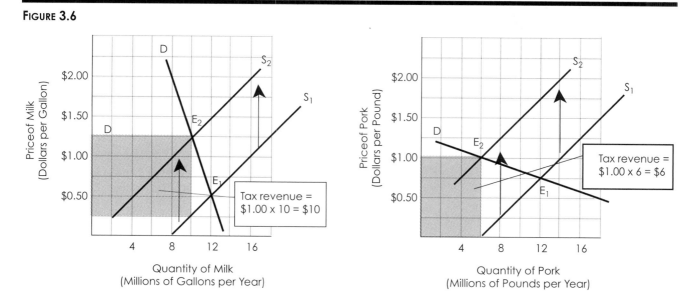

A tax imposed on a good that has an inelastic demand will generate more tax revenue. The diagrams above compare the effects of a $1.00 tax on the markets for milk (inelastic demand) and pork (elastic demand). In the market for milk, the tax reduces the equilibrium quantity by 2 million gallons, from point $E_1$ (12 million gallons) to $E_2$ (10 million gallons). Therefore, the government collects a total of $10 million from the milk tax. The same tax in pork has a very different result. In the pork market, the $1.00 tax causes a large reduction in the quantity sold, from 12 million pounds (point $E_1$) to 6 million pounds (point $E_2$). This means the government will only collect $6 million, as only 6 million pounds of pork are sold at the new equilibrium.

because demand is relatively inelastic. People buying milk are not very responsive to the change in price in terms of how much milk they buy. The government collects $1.00 on each gallon of milk sold, generating a tax revenue of $10 million from this tax because 10 million gallons are sold. In the market for pork, the tax leads to a large reduction in the quantity people buy from 12 to 6 million pounds. This reflects that the demand for pork is highly elastic. The government will collect a total of $6 million from the tax on pork, collecting $1.00 on each of the 6 million pounds sold. When comparing the two possible taxes, the government collects more revenue from the tax on milk because people don't reduce the amount of milk they buy very much.

## Elasticity and Prohibition

In the case of gasoline and apartment rents, a tax led to a reduction in the quantity consumed, which we characterized as an unintended consequence of the tax. In a few cases, the reduction in quantity consumed may be an *intended* consequence of the tax. Taxes on tobacco products are one example: because tobacco is regarded as harmful, a reduction in quantity consumed is seen as desirable. Proposals to tax environmentally harmful products, such as the chemicals thought to be responsible for ozone depletion, are another example.

## GOVERNOR SCHWARZENEGGER AND THE VEHICLE LICENSE TAX

Drivers in California must pay a Vehicle License Fee (VLF) to register and legally drive their cars once each year. In 2002, a state budget crisis left the then Governor Gray Davis in a difficult situation. Republicans in the state legislature refused to raise state income or business taxes, while Democrats refused to cut high spending in social services and education. This left the state with a projected budget shortfall of $38.2 billion. Governor Davis decided to make up for part of this shortfall by raising the VLF, doubling or tripling the fee depending the type of vehicle. Because the demand for vehicles is inelastic, people were not expected to respond to the higher registration fees by purchasing fewer cars. The result would have been an estimated $4 billion in extra state tax revenue to help fill the 38.2 billion budget shortfall. This provided the governor with a way to raise significant tax revenues without approval from the state legislature.

The VLF hikes were very unpopular for an already unpopular Governor Davis. Eventually, Governor Davis was recalled by the people of California in October 2003, and replaced with Arnold Schwarzenegger. One of Governor Schwarzenegger's first acts in office was to repeal the fee increase. How the state will address the budget crisis, and the missing $4 billion that was supposed to be generated from VLF increase, is unresolved. It is likely California will have to borrow from outside sources to make up for the shortfall and cut funding to higher education.

Prohibition is a more extreme policy aimed at reducing the quantity of a product consumed. For example, alcoholic beverages were subject to prohibition in the United States during the 1920s, and substances such a marijuana, heroin, and cocaine are subject to prohibition today. Prohibition is a common method of environmental regulation as well, with the pesticide DDT and lead additives for gasoline serving as examples.

On the surface, a policy of prohibition may seem very different from a tax, since unlike a tax, prohibition raises no tax revenue for the government. However, if we use economic analysis to look below the surface, we see some similarities as well as differences between taxation and prohibition.

First, passage of a law prohibiting production and sale of a good does not make it impossible to supply the good, but simply more expensive. After the prohibition is in effect, the supplier must consider not only the direct costs of production, but the extra costs of covert transportation and distribution systems, the risk of fines or jail terms, the costs of hiring armed gangsters to protect illegal laboratories, and so on. If the price rises by enough to cover all of these costs, the good will still be supplied. Thus, the effect of prohibition of a good is to shift its supply curve to the left until each point on the new supply curve lies above the corresponding point on the old curve by a distance equal to the extra costs associated with evading the prohibition.

Second, the effects of the prohibition, like those of a tax, depend on the elasticity of demand relative to the elasticity of supply. This is illustrated in Figure 3.7, which compares the effects of prohibition on the market for DDT and on the market for cocaine. The demand for DDT is shown as relatively elastic, because fairly effective substitutes are available at a price only a little higher than the banned pesticide. The demand for cocaine is shown as relatively inelastic, in part because once people become addicted, they will be very reluctant to curtail their use of the drug even if its price rises sharply.

In the case of elastic demand for DDT (Figure 3.7a), even a weakly enforced prohibition, represented by a shift in the supply curve from $S_1$ to $S_2$, will sharply reduce the quantity sold. A more vigorously enforced prohibition, as represented by supply curve $S_3$, may very well eliminate use of the product altogether. In either case, the amount of revenue received by suppliers is reduced. The weak prohibition cuts total revenue from $14,000 per week to $8,500 per week. The strict prohibition cuts revenue to zero.

In the case of inelastic demand for cocaine (Figure 3.7b), even a strongly enforced prohibition, represented by a shift in the supply curve to $S_2$, has relatively little effect on quantity demanded. Total revenue from the sale of cocaine rises substantially, however, from $130,000 per week at equilibrium $E_1$ to $300,000 per week at equilibrium $E_2$. As long as demand is inelastic, increasing strictness of enforcement, which drives the supply curve still higher, will also cause total revenue to increase still further.

**FIGURE 3.7   ELASTICITY AND THE EFFECTS OF PROHIBITION**

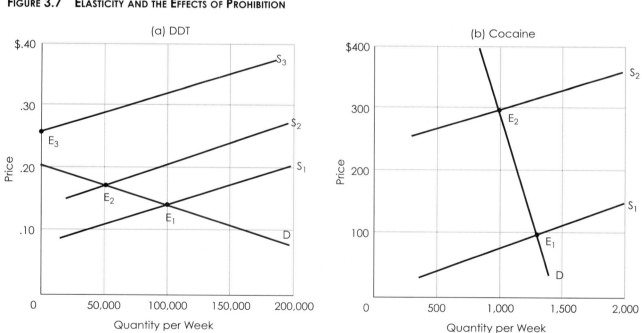

A law prohibiting production and sale of a good, like a tax on the good, shifts its supply curve to the left. The new supply curve will lie above the old supply curve at any given quantity by a distance equal to the cost of evading the prohibition. The effects on price, quantity, and revenue depend on the elasticity of demand. Part (a) uses DDT to illustrate prohibition of a good with elastic demand. A wealthy enforced prohibition ($S_2$) raises the price, reduces the quantity, and reduces total revenue. A strongly enforced prohibition reduces quantity and revenue to zero ($S_3$). Part (b) uses cocaine to illustrate prohibition of a good with inelastic demand. In this case, prohibition results in increased total revenue and expenditure on the good.

These simple conclusions based on elasticity of demand are important in understanding the intended and unintended consequences of prohibition. The intended consequence, of course, is to reduce or eliminate use of the product. As we see, the more elastic the demand for the product, the more successful is the policy of prohibition in achieving its intended effects. The unintended effects of prohibition are those associated with the change in revenue that the policy produces. These are very different in the case of elastic and inelastic demand.

Where demand is elastic, the unintended consequences are loss of profit by DDT producers, and a small rise in the cost of growing crops as farmers switch to more expensive pesticides. Neither has major social consequences. The loss of profit from producing DDT will be offset by profits from producing substitutes—very likely by the same companies. And the increased cost of growing crops is offset by the benefits of a cleaner environment.

On the other hand, where demand is inelastic, prohibition increases total expenditure on the banned product. The social consequences of this are severe. First, users of cocaine must spend more to sustain their habit. At best this means impoverishing themselves and their families; at worst it means an increase in muggings and armed robberies by users desperate for cash. Second, the impact of the prohibition on suppliers must be considered as well. For suppliers, the increase in revenue does not mean an increase in profit, but rather, an increase in expenditures to evade the prohibition. In part, the result is simply wasteful, as when drug suppliers buy an airplane to make a single one-way flight rather than using normal transportation methods. Worse, another part of suppliers' increased expenditures take the form of hiring armies of thugs to battle the police and other suppliers, further raising the level of violence on city streets.

The issue of drug prohibition, of course, involves many normative issues that reach far beyond the concept of elasticity. One such issue is people's right to harm themselves through consumption of substances such as tobacco, alcohol, or cocaine. Another concerns the relative emphasis that should be placed on prohibition versus treatment in allocating resources to reduce drug use. The analysis given here cannot answer such questions. However, it does suggest that the law of unintended consequences applies in the area of drug policy as elsewhere, and that elasticity of demand is important in determining the nature and severity of those consequences.

## SUMMARY

1. **How can the responsiveness of quantity demanded to a price change be expressed in terms of elasticity?** *Elasticity* is the responsiveness of quantity demanded or supplied to changes in the price of a good (or changes in other factors), measured as a ratio of the percentage change in quantity to the percentage change in price (or other factor causing the change in quantity). The *price elasticity of demand* between two points on a demand curve is computed as the percentage change in quantity demanded divided by the percentage change in the good's price.

2. **How is the elasticity of demand for a good related to the revenue earned by its seller?** If the demand for a good is elastic, a decrease in its price will increase total revenue. If it is inelastic, an increase in its price will increase total revenue. When the demand for a good is unit elastic, revenue will remain constant as the price varies.

3. **How can elasticity be applied to situations other than the responsiveness of the quantity of a good demanded to a change in its price?** The concept of elasticity can be applied to many situations besides movements along demand curves. The *income elasticity of demand* for a good is the ratio of the percentage change in quantity demanded to a given percentage change in income. The *cross-elasticity of demand* between goods A and B is the ratio of the percentage change in the quantity of good A demanded to a given percentage change in the price of good B. The *price elasticity of supply* is the ratio of the percentage change in the quantity of a good supplied to a given change in its price.

4. **What determines the distribution of the economic burden of a tax?** The way in which the economic burden of a tax is distributed is known as the *incidence* of the tax. The incidence depends on the relative elasticities of supply and demand. If supply is relatively more elastic than demand, buyers will bear the larger share of the tax burden. If demand is relatively more elastic than supply, the larger share of the burden will fall on sellers. If the good is subject to prohibition rather than to a tax, elasticity of demand will determine how many resources are likely to be devoted to enforcement and evasion of the prohibition.

## KEY TERMS

Elasticity
Price elasticity of demand
Revenue
Elastic demand
Inelastic demand
Unit elastic demand
Perfectly inelastic demand
Perfectly elastic demand
Income elasticity of demand
Cross-elasticity of demand
Price elasticity of supply
Tax incidence

## PROBLEMS AND TOPICS FOR DISCUSSION

1. **Examining the lead-off case.** Consider three time horizons: (a) The "very short" run means a period that is too short to allow farmers to change the amount of lettuce that has been planted. No matter what happens to the price, the quantity supplied will be the amount already planted, less the amount destroyed by the virus. (b) The "intermediate" run means a period that is long enough to allow farmers to plant more fields in lettuce, but not long enough to permit them to develop new varieties of lettuce, introduce new methods of cultivation, or acquire new specialized equipment.

(c) The "long" run means a period that is long enough to allow farmers to develop new varieties and improve cultivation techniques. Discuss these three time horizons in terms of the price elasticity of supply. Sketch a figure showing supply curves for each of the time horizons. Which time horizon or horizons are relevant to the story at the beginning of the chapter?

2. **Calculating elasticity.** Draw a set of coordinate axes on a piece of graph paper. Label the horizontal axis from 0 to 50 units and the vertical axis from $0 to $20 per unit. Draw a demand curve that intersects the vertical axis at $10 and the horizontal axis at 40 units. Draw a supply curve that intersects the vertical axis at $4 and has a slope of 1. Make the following calculations for these curves, using the midpoint formula:

   a. What is the price elasticity of demand over the price range $5 to $7?

   b. What is the price elasticity of demand over the price range $1 to $3?

   c. What is the price elasticity of supply over the price range $10 to $15?

   d. What is the price elasticity of supply over the price range $15 to $17?

3. **Elasticity and revenue.** Look at the demand curve given in Figure 2.1. Make a third column in the table that gives revenue for each price-quantity combination shown. Draw a set of axes on a piece of graph paper. Label the horizontal axis as in Figure 2.1, and label the vertical axis from 0 to $1 billion of revenue in increments of $100 million. Graph the relationship between quantity and revenue using the column you added to the table. (You may want to extend the table to show the following additional points: 1 billion units at a price of $.80; 0.5 billion units at a price of $1.00.) Discuss the relationship of your revenue graph to the demand curve, keeping in mind what you know about elasticity and revenue and about variation in elasticity along the demand curve.

4. **Elasticity of demand and revenue.** Assume that you are an officer of your campus film club. You are at a meeting at which ticket prices are being discussed. One member says, "What I hate to see most of all is empty seats in the theater. We sell out every weekend showing, but there are always empty seats on Wednesdays. If we cut our Wednesday night prices by enough to fill up the theater, we'd bring in more money." Would this tactic really bring in more revenue? What would you need to know in order to be sure? Draw diagrams to illustrate some of the possibilities.

5. **Cross-elasticity of demand.** Between 1979 and 1981 the price of heating oil rose by 104 percent. Over the same period, use of fuel oil fell slightly while use of LP gas, another heating fuel, rose. Assuming that there was no change in the price of LP gas, what does this suggest about the cross-elasticity of demand for LP gas with respect to the price of fuel oil? Draw a pair of diagrams to illustrate these events. (Suggestion: Draw upward-sloping supply curves for both fuels. Then assume that the supply curve for heating oil shifts upward while the supply curve for LP gas stays the same.)

## CASE FOR DISCUSSION

### A Novel Sales Ploy: Cut Prices

General Motors Corp. came up with a plan that might keep its 10-year-old Chevrolet Chevette alive a bit longer.

The plan was simple: cut the price.

To producers of things other than cars, that might seem a fairly obvious task. But in the auto industry, it was novel, even outlandish.

Chrysler Corporation had tried it in the spring of 1986 with its Omni/Horizon models, eight-year-old subcompacts that compete with Chevette. And it worked.

Chrysler knocked $710 off the base price of the Omni/Horizon, added some equipment and the "America" name to the car line, and offered the package for $5,499. The result was a 26.2 percent increase in sales of cars that were on Chrysler's scrap list. The company sold 165,300 Omni/Horizon models in the first nine months of 1986, compared with 130,968 during the same period in the previous year.

General Motors (GM) took the same approach with the pricing of its Chevettes for the coming year. GM trimmed nearly $800 from the price of these rear-wheel-drive, four-cylinder autos, and made standard some formerly optional equipment. The base price was $4,995.

"The car is continuing to sell fairly well, particularly in fleet sales," said Ralph Kramer, Chevrolet's director of public relations. Fleet buyers accounted for about 65 percent of the 75,761 Chevettes sold in 1985, industry analysts say.

Still, the days of the oft-maligned, oft-praised Chevette were numbered.

The level of sales was well below the minimum 100,000 per year needed to make it worthwhile to produce a line of cars. While the strategy did not, in the end, save either of these models (Chevette or Omni/Horizon), the auto industry has since made periodic use of substantial rebates to spur sales without having to cut the manufacturer's suggested retail price (MSRP).

Source: Warren Brown, "Chevette Sales Ploy: Cut Prices," *The Washington Post*, October 15, 1986, Fl. © 1986 *The Washington Post*, reprinted with permission.

## QUESTIONS

1. Using the data provided in the article, estimate the price elasticity of demand for Chrysler's Omni/Horizon. (Throughout this problem, assume that the changes in sales volume indicate movements along demand curves resulting from the change in price.)
2. If Chevette sales were to increase to 100,000 units in the year following the price cut, what would be the price elasticity of demand for the car?
3. Suppose that demand for the Chevette is elastic, so that the firm's revenues will increase if the price is cut. Does that automatically mean that the firm's profit will increase?

## END NOTES

1. As we have said, the midpoint formula (also sometimes called *arc-elasticity*) is not the only one for calculating elasticity. A drawback of this formula is that it can give misleading elasticity values if applied over too wide a variation in price or quantity. Because of this limitation, it is often suggested that the midpoint formula be used only over fairly small ranges of variation in price or quantity. Following this reasoning to its logical conclusion, there is an alternative formula for calculating elasticity for a single point on the demand curve. For a linear demand curve having the formula $q = a - bp$ (with $q$ representing quantity demanded, $p$ the price, and $a$ and $b$ being constants), the *point formula* for elasticity of demand (stated, as elsewhere, as a positive number) is

$$\text{Elasticity} = bp/(a - bp).$$

This formula allows you to compute the elasticity at a particular point. The drawback of this approach is that it will give you two different answers, depending on whether you consider an increase in price versus a decrease in price.

2. Jonq-Ying Lee, Mark G. Brown, and Brooke Schwartz, "The Demand for National Brand and Private Label Frozen Concentrated Orange Juice: A Switching Regression Analysis," *Western Journal of Agricultural Economics* (July 1986): 1–7.

# PART II

# Introduction to Macroeconomics

# In Search of Stability and Prosperity

*After reading this chapter, you will understand:*

1. The meaning of unemployment and its importance for economic policy.
2. The meaning of inflation and its impact on the economy.
3. Trends in economic growth in the United States.
4. The nature of the business cycle.

*Before reading this chapter, make sure you know the meaning of:*

1. Positive and normative economics
2. Production possibility frontier

## THE END OF THE "NEW ECONOMY"

Between 1991 and 2000, the U.S. experienced its largest post–World War II peacetime economic expansion. The growth in the technology sector and increased productivity lead many people, economists included, to claim the U.S. had entered the so-called "New Economy." In this "New Economy" people would no longer need to worry about high unemployment or economic recession. However, by 2001, this had changed. The U.S. entered a recession and lost approximately 1.9 million jobs between March and December 2001.

The health of the economy can sometimes be seen more easily on a local scale than in the flood of statistics that pour forth from government agencies. Take the case of a high school's search for a janitor. In 2000 this Colorado school placed a help-wanted ad for a janitor in the local paper. The national jobless rate was then at a record low of 3.9 percent. The ad drew 8 replies. One year later, with the national unemployment rate rising toward 5.8 percent, the school again needed a janitor. This time, its ad drew more than 350 responses. The school principal interviewed 20 of the candidates, all of whom were unemployed. The successful applicant was a 30-year-old man whose attempt to set up a landscaping business had died during the 2001 recession.

At about the same time in a different part of the country, steel workers were also feeling the pinch of the recession. The worker and his family are industrial migrants, ready to move anywhere to find good work. But in 2001, his luck hit a low point. Out of work in Pennsylvania and forced to move yet again, the former steel worker couldn't even find room in his car for the family dog. Soon he and his family were living in his father's home in Texas, collecting food stamps and waiting for better times.

☙

T HE LATEST DATA on unemployment are always headline news—and justly so. Together with the rate of inflation and the growth of real output, the level of unemployment is one of the key indicators of success in the search for economic stability and prosperity. This chapter reviews the recent performance of the U.S. economy in terms of these three key goals. The concepts introduced here will be used in subsequent chapters as the building blocks for a variety of macroeconomic theories and models.

## HIGH EMPLOYMENT

Achieving a high level of employment is a key policy goal for reasons of both positive and normative economics. In terms of positive economics, more jobs mean more output and more material satisfaction. An economy that fails to make use of labor resources that are voluntarily supplied to the market is operating inside its production possibility frontier. The lost output resulting from unemployment can at times amount to hundreds of billions of dollars.

In the minds of many people, however, billions of dollars of lost output are secondary compared with the normative costs of unemployment—the costs in terms of human lives and values. Many people's sense of self-worth is closely tied to the work they do. To find that no employer wants their contribution is psychologically damaging. The damage can be seen statistically in the tendency for rates of divorce, family violence, murder, heart disease, suicide, alcoholism, and other social and medical disorders to rise during periods of high unemployment. Many people also link the disintegration of families and neighborhood structures in poor inner-city areas to the high rates of unemployment that prevail there, especially among teenagers and members of minority groups.

All things considered, then, it is small wonder that policy makers keep a close eye on the unemployment reports. Because of their importance, it is worth seeing where those numbers come from.

## Measuring Unemployment

The Bureau of Labor Statistics, in conjunction with the Bureau of the Census, obtains the data used in calculating unemployment from a monthly sample of about 50,000 randomly selected households. Field agents go to those households and ask a series of questions about the job status of each member of the household. The questions include such things as: Did anyone work last week? Did anyone look for work? How long has the person been looking for work? How did the person go about looking?

On the basis of their answers to these questions, people are counted as employed or unemployed. A person is considered to be **employed** if he or she works at least 1 hour per week for pay or at least 15 hours per week as an unpaid worker in a family business. A person who is not currently employed but is actively looking for work is said to be **unemployed**. The employed plus the unemployed—that is, those who are either working or looking for work—constitute the **labor force**. The **unemployment rate** is simply the percentage of the labor force that is unemployed.

If people are neither employed nor actively looking for work, they are not counted as members of the labor force. This group includes many people who could work but choose not to for one reason or another. (They may be full-time students or retired, or they may work full time but without pay as homemakers.) Two groups are automatically considered to be outside the labor force: children under 16 years of age and people who are confined to prisons and certain other institutions.

Members of the armed forces are a special category. The *total labor force* includes members of the armed forces on active duty; the *civilian labor force* excludes those individuals. This distinction has an effect on the calculation of the unemployment rate. The *civilian unemployment rate* is the percentage of the *civilian* labor force that is unemployed, whereas the *total unemployment rate* is the percentage of the *total* labor force that is unemployed. Because all members of the armed forces on active duty are by definition employed, the total unemployment rate is lower than the civilian rate, usually by about a tenth of a percentage point. The civilian unemployment rate is the one that is more widely reported.

In this book, as in most other sources, the terms *unemployment rate* and *labor force* refer to the civilian labor force. However, some argue that the total unemployment rate gives a better picture of labor market conditions, considering that membership in the armed forces is, for economic purposes, much like any other job.

**Employed**

A term used to refer to a person who is working at least 1 hour a week for pay or at least 15 hours per week as an unpaid worker in a family business.

**Unemployed**

A term used to refer to a person who is not employed but is actively looking for work.

**Labor force**

The sum of all individuals who are employed and all individuals who are unemployed.

**Unemployment rate**

The percentage of the labor force that is unemployed.

Figure 4.1 presents unemployment data for the United States since 1950. The shaded band labeled "low to moderate unemployment" reflects a range of views about reasonable economic performance. During the 1950s and 1960s, the unemployment rate generally stayed within this range. Rates higher than the upper end of the range occurred in only a couple of years. In the 1970s and early 1980s, the unemployment rate took a turn for the worse. It jumped to 8.3 percent in 1975 and fell into the moderate range in only 2 of the next 12 years. Only in 1989, just before the onset of a new recession, did it again reach the levels achieved in the early 1970s. The graph shows that the falling unemployment rate during the 1990s is consistent with the job creation and economic growth experienced for much of the decade. Since the onset of the recession in March 2001, the unemployment rate has steadily risen.

**FIGURE 4.1   UNEMPLOYMENT IN THE UNITED STATES SINCE 1950**

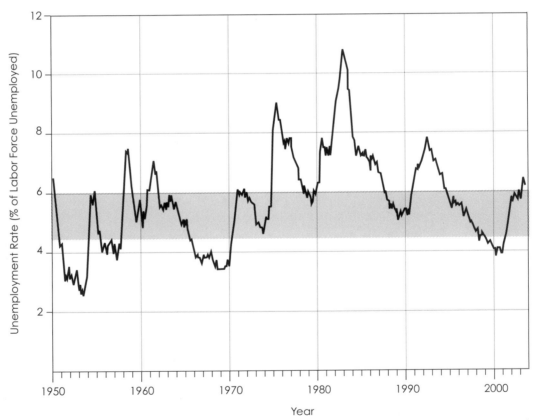

There is no one level of unemployment that is universally accepted as best for the economy. Some unemployment is always present as people change jobs and enter the labor force in a normally functioning economy. In this figure, a range of 4 to 6.5 percent unemployment is characterized as "low to moderate." Until 1975, unemployment stayed within that range, for the most part. The mid-1970s and early 1980s saw much higher rates. During the 1990s, unemployment fell steadily, only to rise sharply at the onset of the March 2001 recession.

Source: Labor Force Statistics from the Current Population Survey, Bureau of Labor Statistics, U.S. Department of Labor, 2003.

## Gray Areas in the Measurement of Unemployment

There are many gray areas in the measurement of unemployment. The official unemployment rate can be criticized for both understating and overstating the "true" number of unemployed adults. One way to understand these gray areas better is to compare the official definition of unemployment with two common-sense definitions, namely, "not working" and "can't find a job."

**"UNEMPLOYED" VERSUS "NOT WORKING"**  The official definitions of employment and unemployment differ greatly from the simple definitions of "working" and "not working." On the one hand, there are many people who work but are not officially employed. By far the largest such group consists of people who work full time at housekeeping and child care. These occupations are counted as employment if they are performed for pay, but the bulk of such work is done without pay. There are also a certain number of children under 16 who work for pay but are not counted as employed. Children under 16 working without pay for a family farm or business also are not counted as employed.

On the other hand, not everyone who does not work is counted as unemployed. There are millions of people who are not looking for work and therefore are not counted in the labor force. There are also those who are absent from their jobs because of illness, bad weather, or labor disputes. All of these are counted as employed. Finally, there are those who work part time and are counted as employed but are actively seeking full-time employment. People in this last situation are sometimes referred to as *underemployed*.

**"UNEMPLOYED" VERSUS "CAN'T FIND A JOB"**  The second common-sense definition of unemployment, "can't find a job," also only loosely fits the official definition. In some ways, the official definition overstates the number of people who cannot find jobs. Some people who are counted as unemployed are on layoffs from jobs to which they expect to be recalled, or have found jobs that they expect to start within 30 days. Other people who are counted as unemployed could easily find a job of some kind but prefer to take their time and find just the kind of job they want. (People who are not the sole income earners in their households, for example, may be in a position to look longer and be more selective than people in households with no other income.) Still other people register as unemployed to meet the requirements of income transfer programs even though they may not be qualified for any available work and only go through the motions of looking for a job. Finally, there is some doubt as to whether the description "can't find a job" fits people who could have stayed on at their last job but quit to look for a better one.

In other ways, however, the official definition of unemployment understates the number of people who cannot find jobs. For example, it does not include **discouraged workers**—people who are not looking for work because they believe no suitable jobs

**Discouraged worker**

A person who would work if a suitable job were available but has given up looking for such a job.

are available. The Bureau of Labor Statistics officially counts as a discouraged worker anyone who has looked for work within the last six months but is no longer actively looking. The description "can't find a job" could also be applied to the underemployed—those who have part-time jobs but would take full-time jobs if they could find them.

## The Employment-Population Ratio

Although the unemployment rate is the most widely publicized measure of the state of the labor market, it is not the only one. Quite aside from the problems of definition just discussed, the unemployment rate sometimes fails altogether to reflect changes in the labor market. The reason is that often the labor force grows at the same time that the number of jobs grows. For example, in December 2003, government data showed that the economy generated 57,000 new jobs, at the same time a nearly equal number of people joined the labor force. The growth of the labor force offset the increase in jobs so that the unemployment rate remained unchanged even though the percentage of the population that was employed increased. Such a pattern is frequently observed as the job market begins to improve after a period of recession, because news of possible job openings draws discouraged workers back into the labor force.

**Employment-population ratio**

The percentage of the noninstitutional adult population that is employed.

Because of this property of the unemployment rate, some economists consider another statistic, the **employment-population ratio**, to be a more revealing indicator of the health of the economy. This ratio is the percentage of the noninstitutional adult population that is employed. The denominator of the employment-population ratio, which is governed by such demographic factors as birthrates and death rates, changes slowly and predictably. Hence, this ratio is less likely than the unemployment rate to stand still while the economy moves ahead, or to give other misleading signals. In particular, during the early stages of an economic recovery when firms first start hiring new workers, the employment-population ratio will rise even though the unemployment rate may temporarily not change because of the return of discouraged workers to the labor force.

## Types of Unemployment

A change in the unemployment rate reflects a change in the flows of workers into and out of the pool of unemployed workers. Given a labor force of constant size, the unemployment rate rises when the rate of inflow into the pool of unemployed workers exceeds the rate of outflow; the unemployment rate falls when the rate of outflow from the pool exceeds the rate of inflow. The difference between the rate of inflow and the rate of outflow determines how long the average person remains unemployed. During the past 20 years, the average duration of unemployment has ranged from a low of 4.8 weeks in November 1989 to a high of 12.3 weeks in June 2003.

The duration of unemployment varies not only from year to year but also from one unemployed worker to another. As Figure 4.2 shows, depending on the state of the economy, between one-third and three-fifths of all unemployed people are out of work for less than five weeks. At the other end of the scale, 5 to 25 percent of unemployed people are out of work for six months or more. Variations in the duration of unemployment serve as a basis for distinguishing among *frictional, structural,* and *cyclical unemployment.*

**FRICTIONAL UNEMPLOYMENT** The term **frictional unemployment** refers to the short periods of unemployment that are needed to match jobs and workers. Much of this short-term unemployment is voluntary. It represents people who quit old jobs to look for new ones, people who take a week or so to move or go on vacation before starting a newly found job, and people who enter occupations, such as

**Frictional unemployment**

The portion of unemployment that is accounted for by the short periods of unemployment needed for matching jobs with job seekers.

**FIGURE 4.2  UNEMPLOYMENT BY DURATION**

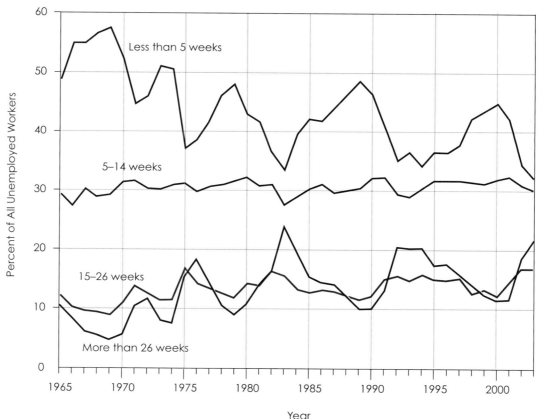

As this chart shows, there is considerable variation in the length of time people are unemployed. Depending on the state of the economy, about one-third to three-fifths of all unemployed workers spend less than five weeks out of work. On the other hand, 5 to 25 percent are out of work for six months or more.

Source: Labor Force Statistics from the Current Population Survey, Bureau of Labor Statistics, U.S. Department of Labor, 2003.

construction work, in which temporary layoffs are frequent but year-round earnings are good. Economists view a certain level of frictional unemployment as necessary in a labor market in which information is incomplete and the costs of job search are often high.

**STRUCTURAL UNEMPLOYMENT**    The term **structural unemployment** refers to a situation in which people spend long periods out of work, often with little prospect of finding adequate jobs. This prolonged joblessness occurs partly because the shifting structure of the economy has made their skills obsolete. This category of workers also includes people with few skills and little work experience. Teenagers and some minority groups are particularly affected by this type of unemployment.

For these people, structural unemployment is not merely a problem of lack of jobs. Certain types of jobs—hospital orderly jobs, fast-food work, and car washing, for example—are almost always available and require few specific skills. But structurally unemployed workers who do take such jobs often work at them only for short periods before quitting to look for something better. Working for brief periods at dead-end jobs tends to build up a pattern of poor work habits and absenteeism that makes many structurally unemployed workers unattractive to potential employers.

**THE NATURAL RATE OF UNEMPLOYMENT**    Frictional and structural unemployment are present in good years as well as bad ones. The sum of frictional and structural unemployment is often referred to as the **natural rate of unemployment**. This term can be thought of as the rate of unemployment that persists during a period of macroeconomic stability. Later in the book we will see that the natural rate can be defined more precisely as the rate that prevails when the rate of inflation is neither accelerating nor decelerating. Since the late 1980s, the natural rate of unemployment is thought to be about 5.5 to 6.0 percent.

Some economists object to using the term *natural* to refer to unemployment that is partly structural, because it seems to imply that the human suffering that accompanies structural unemployment is acceptable in some normative sense. They instead use the term *nonaccelerating-inflation rate of unemployment (NAIRU)*. The two terms are interchangeable.

**CYCLICAL UNEMPLOYMENT**    In practice, unemployment is not always at its "natural" level. As we will see later in the chapter, over time the economy undergoes cycles of expansion and contraction. As it does so, the unemployment rate changes. As a result of vigorous economic expansion, unemployment may drop below its natural rate. In such a period, the jobs are so easy to find that the duration of unemployment falls below normal, reducing the number of unemployed below the number normally unemployed for frictional and structural reasons. Even many of the hard-core structurally unemployed find jobs. On the other hand, in periods of business contraction, the unemployment rate rises above its natural rate. At such times even

---

**Structural unemployment**

The portion of unemployment that is accounted for by people who are out of work for long periods because their skills do not match those required for available jobs.

**Natural rate of unemployment**

The sum of frictional and structural unemployment; the rate of unemployment that persists when the economy is experiencing neither accelerating nor decelerating inflation.

**Cyclical unemployment**

The difference between the observed rate of unemployment at a given point in the business cycle and the natural rate of unemployment.

**Price stability**

A situation in which the rate of inflation is low enough so that it is not a significant factor in business and individual decision making.

**Inflation**

A sustained increase in the average level of prices of all goods and services.

**Consumer Price Index (CPI)**

An average of the prices of a market basket of goods and services purchased by a typical urban household.

**Real**

In economics, a term that refers to data that have been adjusted for the effects of inflation.

**Nominal**

In economics, a term that refers to data that have not been adjusted for the effects of inflation.

workers who have worked a long time for their present employer and who have excellent skills may find themselves temporarily laid off. The average duration of unemployment rises above normal frictional plus structural levels.

The difference between the actual unemployment rate at a given time and the natural rate is known as **cyclical unemployment**. When the economy slows down, cyclical unemployment is added to frictional and structural unemployment. At the peak of an expansionary period, cyclical unemployment is negative. The cyclical behavior of the unemployment rate will be examined more closely later in the chapter. First, we must explore some of the basic concepts of inflation and economic growth.

# PRICE STABILITY

**Inflation** means a sustained increase in the average level of prices of all goods and services. **Price stability**—a situation in which the rate of inflation is low enough so that it is not a significant factor in business and individual decision making—can be considered the second major goal of macroeconomic policy.

Figure 4.3 shows the trend of inflation in the U.S. economy since 1950 as measured by the annual rate of change in the **consumer price index**, a widely reported average of prices of a "market basket" of goods and services purchased by a typical urban household. As the figure shows, the inflation rate generally stayed within the low to moderate range of 0 to 3 percent throughout the 1950s and early 1960s. In fact, for the entire century from the Civil War to the mid-1960s, the peacetime inflation rate averaged only about 2 percent per year. Beginning in 1968, however, inflation rose above the 3 percent rate and became highly variable. The struggle against inflation was a dominant theme in economic policy throughout the 1980s. Considerable progress was made beginning in 1982 when the inflation rate peaked at 7 percent. By January 1992, the inflation rate had fallen to just over 2.5 percent. Since 1992, the inflation rate has consistently been in the low to moderate range.

## The Costs of Inflation

As in the case of unemployment, the costs of inflation are distributed unevenly across the population. The effects of inflation depend on one's position with regard to source of income, debtor or creditor status, and wealth, among other factors. All discussions of inflation must distinguish between effects measured in *real* terms and effects measured in *nominal* terms. Economists use the term **real** to refer to data that have been adjusted to take inflation into account; they use the term **nominal** to refer to data that are presented in the ordinary way, without adjustment for inflation.

**EFFECTS ON WAGE AND SALARY INCOME**  Most people receive the bulk of their income in the form of wages and salaries. Wage and salary earners often feel

FIGURE **4.3** INFLATION IN THE UNITED STATES SINCE **1950**

Price stability is a situation in which the rate of inflation is low enough so that it is not a significant factor in business decision making. Many economists believe that a measured inflation rate of 1 percent or less would qualify as price stability by that definition. Inflation rose sharply beginning in the late 1960s before falling again in the 1980s. The inflation rate has remained consistently low through the remainder of the 1990s and beginning of the 21st century.

Source: Consumer Price Index, Bureau of Labor Statistics, U.S. Department of Labor, 2003.

that they are badly hurt by inflation. They compare what their paychecks can buy each month at ever-higher prices with what they would be able to buy with the same paychecks if prices remained stable. However, a closer look shows that the effects of inflation on real wage and salary income are less than they are often perceived to be.

During a period of general inflation, all prices tend to rise together—including wages and salaries, which are the prices that firms pay for labor. Consider the 1970s, for example. From 1970 to 1979 the consumer price index rose by 87 percent. This means that by the end of the decade it would have taken $187 to buy the same basket of goods that could have been bought for $100 at the beginning of the decade. But wages also rose during that period. In 1970, the average hourly wage in the private nonfarm sector of the economy was $3.23; by 1979, it had risen to $6.16—that is, by

91 percent. When the 91 percent increase in the nominal wage is compared with the 87 percent increase in consumer prices, it can be seen that the real value of the average hourly wage was actually slightly greater in 1979 than it had been in 1970.

Not all workers are as well protected from inflation as others, of course. In some industries, workers are protected by "escalator clauses" that automatically raise wages when the consumer price index rises. Economists use the term **indexation** to refer to such devices. Complete indexation of wages is not widespread in the United States, however. Thus, even though wages tend to rise in step with inflation on the average, there may be individual winners and losers during any given period.

**TRANSFER PAYMENTS**   Many people receive income in the form of private pensions and government benefits. Such payments, which are not made in return for work currently performed by the person receiving them, are called **transfer payments**. At one time the recipients of transfer payments, especially retired people living on pensions that were fixed in nominal terms, were seriously hurt by inflation. Today this is less true than it once was, largely because social security, the biggest single transfer program, is fully indexed. Nominal social security benefits (that is, the number of dollars received per month) now rise automatically in step with consumer prices, thereby preserving their real value (that is, their purchasing power). Some private pensions and some forms of personal saving are not indexed, however, so inflation is still damaging to some elderly people. Transfer payments received by the nonelderly poor, such as food stamps and welfare payments, are sometimes, but not always, indexed to protect the recipients against inflation.

**INTEREST INCOME—DEBTORS VERSUS CREDITORS**   We turn next to the effects of inflation on the real income of creditors, who receive interest income from mortgage loans, corporate bonds, and the like, and on the real income of debtors, who pay that interest. The effects of inflation in this case are somewhat more complex than is true for wage income and transfer payments, but they are worth considering in some detail.

The traditional view is that inflation injures creditors and aids debtors. Suppose, for example, that I borrow $100 from you today, promising to repay the $100 of principal plus $5 interest, or $105 in all, at the end of a year. If there is no inflation during the year, I get the use of the funds for the year and you get $5 of real income in the form of the interest on the loan. But suppose that during the year the price level goes up by 10 percent. In that case I get the use of the funds for the year, and what is more, I pay you back in depreciated dollars. The $105 I give you at the end of the year will buy only about as much then as $95 will buy today. Your real income is negative, because the real value of $105 a year from now is less than the real value today of the $100 that I borrow. I, the debtor, benefit from inflation, and you, the creditor, are hurt.

However, the traditional view of the effects of inflation is incomplete in that it does not distinguish between *unexpected* and *expected* inflation. The example just

**Indexation**

A policy of automatically adjusting a value or payment in proportion to changes in the average price level.

**Transfer payments**

Payments to individuals that are not made in return for work they currently perform.

given implicitly assumes that neither I, the borrower, nor you, the lender, expected any inflation at the time the loan was made. Suppose instead that we both had expected a 10 percent increase in the price level between the time the loan was made and the time it was repaid. In that case, you would not have loaned me the $100 in return for a promise to repay just $105 at the end of the year. Instead, you would have insisted on a repayment of $115—the $100 principal, plus $10 to compensate you for the decline in purchasing power of the principal plus $5 of real interest income. I, in turn, would have agreed to those terms, knowing that the $115 payment under conditions of 10 percent inflation would be no more burdensome than the $105 payment I would have agreed to if no inflation had been expected.

This example shows that we need to distinguish between two interest concepts: the **nominal interest rate**, which is the interest rate expressed in the ordinary way, in current dollars, and the **real interest rate**, which is the nominal rate minus the rate of inflation. In the example, a 15 percent nominal interest rate, given a 10 percent rate of inflation, corresponds to a 5 percent real interest rate.

The distinction between nominal and real interest rates helps us to understand the impact of expected and unexpected inflation on debtors and creditors. *Expected* inflation, it turns out, is neutral between debtors and creditors, because the parties will adjust the nominal interest rate to take the expected inflation into account. If they would agree to a 5 percent nominal interest rate given no expected inflation, they would agree to a 15 percent nominal rate given 10 percent expected inflation, a 20 percent nominal rate given 15 percent expected inflation, and so on. All of these adjusted rates correspond to a 5 percent real rate. *Unexpected* inflation is not neutral, however. Unexpected inflation harms creditors and benefits debtors. If you lend me $100 at a 5 percent nominal rate of interest, and the price level unexpectedly rises by 10 percent over the year before I repay the loan, the real rate of interest that you realize is *minus* 5 percent.

**OTHER EFFECTS OF INFLATION**    So far our discussion of inflation has concentrated on the distributional effects of inflation. It implies that although there are losers, there are also winners; although inflation imposes costs on some people, it benefits others. The discussion would be incomplete, however, if we did not point out that inflation has some costs that are not distributional in nature, costs that place a burden on the economy as a whole without producing offsetting benefits.

One set of costs has to do with the way inflation upsets economic calculations. In an inflationary environment, households and firms have a hard time distinguishing between changes in the relative prices of goods and services and changes in the general price level. Partly for this reason, in an economy in which the rate of inflation is high and variable, as it was in the United States in the 1970s and early 1980s, business planning becomes difficult. The outcomes of investment projects that require firms to incur costs now in the hope of making profits later come to depend less on

**Nominal interest rate**

The interest rate expressed in the usual way: in terms of current dollars without adjustment for inflation.

**Real interest rate**

The nominal interest rate minus the rate of inflation.

manufacturing and marketing skills than on the ups and downs of wages, interest rates, and the prices of key raw materials. As the investment environment becomes riskier, firms may avoid projects with long-term payoffs and gamble instead on strategies that promise short-term financial gains. Similarly, households, facing more uncertainty about future price trends, may reduce their long-term saving in favor of increased current consumption. These effects are hard to measure, but many economists think that they are substantial.

Another set of costs arise from the effort to rid the economy of inflation once it has become established. The experiences of many countries in many periods suggest that bringing inflation under control often causes serious economic disruption during a transition period. The slowdown of inflation in the United States from 1980 to 1983 is a case in point. A comparison of Figure 4.3 and Figure 4.1 shows that the drop in inflation during those years coincided with a surge in the unemployment rate, which reached a peak of more than 10 percent in the summer of 1982. The increase in unemployment, in turn, represented a major loss of potential output of goods and services.

The distributional effects of inflation—its erosion of seemingly fixed paychecks, its impact on interest rates—are probably the dominant reason that inflation ranks high as an economic evil in the public mind. Most economists, however, see inflation's effects on economic calculation, business planning, and productivity as its greatest threat.

# ECONOMIC GROWTH

Economic growth is the third major goal of economic policy. Some economic growth is necessary just to provide jobs for new workers entering the labor force and thus prevent a rise in unemployment. Economic growth at a higher rate than population growth is needed to provide a rising standard of living.

## Measuring Economic Growth

Economic growth is most frequently expressed in terms of *Gross Domestic Product (GDP)*, a measure of the value of total output of goods and services produced within a nation's borders during a period of time.[1] If GDP is to provide a meaningful measure of growth over time, it, like other economic quantities, must be expressed in real terms; that is, it must be adjusted for the effects of inflation. For example, from 1997 to 2002 nominal GDP grew from $8,478.6 billion to $10,588.8 billion. However, part of the increase in nominal GDP can be attributed to the rise in the average price level during the period. Adjusted for inflation and expressed in constant 1992 dollars, the 2002, real GDP was only $9,909.4 billion. The term **real output** is frequently used as a synonym for real gross domestic product.

**Real output**

A synonym for real gross domestic product.

From 1950 through the early 1990s, the rate of growth of real GDP in the United States averaged 2-3 percent per year, a rate that most economists consider satisfactory. However, as Figure 4.4 shows, GDP did not follow a smooth upward trend. In some years, output fell below the trend; in others, it rose above the trend. The early 1980s—which, as we have already seen, was a time of high inflation and high unemployment—was characterized by a major shortfall of real GDP from its trend. Likewise, real GDP began to fall below its trend in 2000, a period of high unemployment and low inflation.

## The Benefits and Costs of Economic Growth

The benefits of economic growth are numerous. The most obvious is that growth provides consumers with a higher standard of living in the form of more goods and

**FIGURE 4.4   ECONOMIC GROWTH IN THE UNITED STATES**

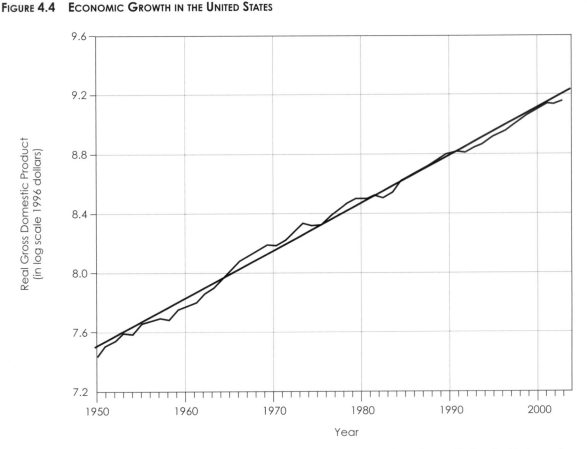

This chart shows the growth of the U.S. economy since the early 1950s. Real Gross Domestic Product is shown for each year, along with a trend line averaging 2–3 percent growth of real GDP per year over the entire period. A growth rate of 2–3 percent or more is generally considered healthy.

Source: National Economic Accounts, Bureau of Economic Analysis, U.S. Department of Commerce. The trend line is based on the average growth of real GDP between 1950 and 2002.

services. Growth also provides people with greater opportunities to choose between work and leisure. If more people choose to work, as has recently been the case in the United States, economic growth makes possible the capital investment needed to create jobs for them. Over a longer span of U.S. history, however, people have opted for more leisure. As the economy grew during the nineteenth and early twentieth centuries, it was possible to shorten the average workweek at the same time that material living standards were rising. Finally, economic growth is often credited with reducing poverty and economic injustice; a rising tide, it is said, lifts all boats.

However, economic growth has had its critics. More than a century ago the English economist John Stuart Mill worried that growth might cause the loss of "a great portion of the earth's pleasantries" (see *Who Said It? Who Did It? 4.1*). This sentiment is shared in our own time by environmentalists, who worry that economic growth is accompanied by increased pollution, destruction of wilderness areas, and the possibility of a global climatic disaster.

---

### ⌐ WHO SAID IT? WHO DID IT? 4.1
### JOHN STUART MILL ON THE STATIONARY STATE

Economic growth was a major concern of the classical economists of the nineteenth century. Then, as now, most of the leading economists were inclined to view economic growth as a good thing. However, some of them feared that the pressure of growing populations on limited natural resources would sooner or later bring economic growth to a halt. Economists portrayed the "stationary state" toward which society was moving as one of poverty and overpopulation, causing one critic to dub economics the "dismal science."

John Stuart Mill thought otherwise. Mill was one of the most remarkable figures of the nineteenth century. Eldest son of the prominent economist James Mill, John Stuart Mill began studying Greek at age 3, was tutoring the younger members of his family in Latin at age 8, and first read Smith's *Wealth of Nations* at age 13. His *Principles of Political Economy*, published in 1848, was the standard text on the subject until Alfred Marshall transformed "political economy" into "economics" at the end of the century.

Mill agreed with earlier classical economists that the economy would sooner or later reach a stationary state, but he did not view the prospect as entirely gloomy:

I cannot . . . regard the stationary state of capital and wealth with the unaffected aversion so generally manifested towards it by political economists of the old school. I am inclined to believe that it would be, on the whole, a very considerable improvement on our present condition. I confess I am not charmed with the ideal of life held out by those who think that the normal state of human beings is that of struggling to get on; that the trampling, crushing, elbowing, and treading on each other's heels, which form the existing type of social life, are the most desirable lot of human kind, or anything but the disagreeable symptoms of one of the phases of our industrial progress. . . .

If the earth must lose that great portion of its pleasantries which it owes to things that the unlimited increase of wealth and population would extricate from it, for the mere purpose of enabling it to support a larger, but not a better or happier population, I sincerely hope, for the sake of posterity, that they will be content to be stationary long before necessity compels them to.

Today Mill's sentiments have been echoed by writers who are concerned about problems of population, pollution, and resource depletion. E. F. Schumacher's *Small Is Beautiful* expressed this line of thought;[a] so did another best-selling book of the 1970s, *The Limits to Growth*, which advocated a policy of stabilizing both world population and the world capital stock by the end of the twentieth century.[b] Its proposals, set forth in the form of computer-generated charts rather than the elegant prose of a John Stuart Mill, were roundly denounced by "orthodox" economists. However, the wide audience that the book attracted indicates that growth still is not universally accepted as a good thing.

[a] E. F. Schumacher, *Small Is Beautiful* (New York: Harper & Row, 1973).
[b] Donnella H. Meadows, Dennis L. Meadows, Jorgen Randers, and William W. Behrens III, *The Limits to Growth* (New York: Signet, 1972).

Criticisms of economic growth have their merits; we have only to look around us to see that the economic growth we have experienced has brought costs as well as benefits. However, the critics can be faulted for often failing to distinguish between two issues: the *rate* of economic growth and its *direction*.

In Figure 4.5, a production possibility frontier is used to help separate the two issues. The diagram shows an economy in which two goods, clean air and cars, are produced. For an economy operating efficiently on its production possibility frontier, there is a trade-off between the two goods. More cars will make the air dirtier; fewer cars will make possible cleaner air.

As technology is improved and more resources become available, the production possibility frontier shifts outward. If the economy follows a growth path from point A to point B, people will complain that growth has led to a deterioration of environmental quality. It is not the mere fact of growth that is to blame, however. Instead, the problem lies in the *direction* of growth—that is, the combination of outputs that has been chosen. The same expansion of the production possibility frontier could have made possible a growth path from point A to point C. That growth path would be possible if more effort and expense were devoted to building cars that run more

**FIGURE 4.5   ENVIRONMENTAL QUALITY AND ECONOMIC GROWTH**

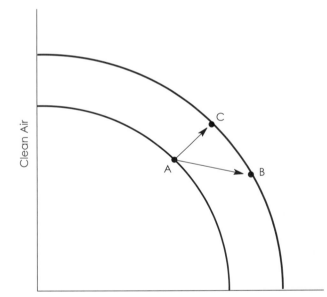

This figure shows a production possibility frontier for "cars," symbolizing material production, and "clean air," symbolizing environmental quality. In any single year, there is a trade-off between cars and clean air. More cars make the air dirtier, whereas fewer cars make possible cleaner air. Over time, improvements in technology and the availability of additional productive resources shift the production possibility frontier outward. A choice can be made between two growth paths as the frontier expands. The path from A to B shows an increase in the output of cars and a decrease in air quality. The path from A to C shows a smaller increase in the number of cars and cleaner air. The move from A to C results in more cars and cleaner air.

cleanly. Comparing point A with point C, we see that growth can bring both more cars and cleaner air (or in general, both more material output and improved environmental quality) *if people choose to go that way.* As is often the case, our problems turn out to arise not from inescapable economic laws but from the choices we make.

# THE BUSINESS CYCLE

As Figure 4.4 showed, the U.S. economy has grown substantially in recent decades, but the pace of growth has not been steady. Real GDP has moved sometimes above and sometimes below the long-term trend line. In some years real GDP has not just grown more slowly, but actually fallen. This pattern of irregular but repeated expansion and contraction of overall economic activity is known as the **business cycle**.

**Business cycle**

A pattern of irregular but repeated expansion and contraction of aggregate economic activity.

## Phases of the Business Cycle

An idealized business cycle is shown in Figure 4.6. The cycle can be divided into four phases as the economy fluctuates around the long-term growth trend. The *peak* of the cycle is the point at which real output reaches a maximum. The period during which real output falls is known as the *contraction* phase. At the end of the contraction, real output reaches a minimum known as the *trough* of the cycle. After the trough, real output begins to grow again and the economy enters an *expansion* that lasts until a new peak is reached.

According to a commonly used albeit somewhat simplified definition, a contraction lasting six months or more is a **recession**. Several recessions, of which the most recent began in March 2001 and ended in November of the same year, can be identified in Figure 4.4. As explained in *Applying Economic Ideas 4.1*, determining the beginning and ending dates of a recession is not always easy, and a recession is usually well under way before it is officially announced.

**Recession**

A cyclical economic contraction that lasts six months or more.

The nineteenth and early twentieth centuries saw a number of cyclical contractions that were much more severe than any since World War II. These were called *depressions.* The most spectacular of these was the Great Depression of the 1930s, which actually consisted of two contractionary periods separated by an incomplete recovery. During this episode, real output fell by one-third, the price level fell by one-quarter, and the unemployment rate climbed to 24 percent of the labor force. Because no succeeding contraction has come close to it in severity, the term *depression* has passed out of use in all but historical contexts.

## Unemployment, Output, and Inflation over the Business Cycle

The preceding section portrayed the business cycle in terms of real domestic product, but changes in real output are linked to changes in employment. The trend line

FIGURE 4.6 AN IDEALIZED BUSINESS CYCLE

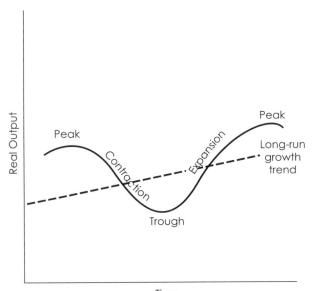

This figure shows an idealized business cycle. The cycle begins from a peak, then enters a contraction. A contraction lasting six months or more is called a recession. The low point of the cycle is known as its trough. Following the trough, the economy enters an expansion until a new peak is reached. Because real GDP varies about an upward trend, each cyclical peak tends to carry the economy to a higher level of real GDP than the previous one.

**Natural level of real output**

The level of real output that is consistent with the natural rate of unemployment.

**Okun's law**

A rule of thumb according to which each 2 percent by which real output rises above (or falls below) its natural level results in an unemployment rate one percentage point below (or above) the natural rate.

around which the idealized business cycle fluctuates represents a situation in which the economy expands at a rate that is consistent with its long-run growth potential. Under such conditions the economy is said to be at its **natural level of real output** or, alternatively, its *natural level of real domestic product.* The natural level of real output is the level that is consistent with the natural rate of unemployment.

When an expansion carries real output above its natural level, unemployment tends to fall below its natural rate. The underlying reason is simple: More workers are needed to produce the additional output. Likewise, when contraction takes real output below the natural level, unemployment rises above its natural rate because fewer workers are required.

However, the linkage between changes in real output and unemployment is not the simple one-to-one relationship implied by the assumption that "more output requires more workers." Instead, according to a widely used rule of thumb, for each 2 percent by which real output rises above its natural level, the unemployment rate tends to fall by one percentage point, and for each 2 percent by which real output falls below its natural level, the unemployment rate tends to rise by one percentage point. This rule of thumb is known as **Okun's law** after Arthur Okun, who was a member of President Kennedy's Council of Economic Advisers at the time he formulated the theory.[2]

## ⌐ APPLYING ECONOMIC IDEAS 4.1

# DATING U.S. RECESSIONS

The turning points of the business cycle are unusual among economic data in that they are determined not by a government agency, but by a private organization, the Business Cycle Dating Committee of the National Bureau of Economic Research (NBER). The NBER's prominence in the business cycle dating process dates all the way back to its founding by Wesley C. Mitchell, a pioneer in business cycle analysis. The U.S. Department of Commerce gave its stamp of approval to the NBER's work in 1961, when it began to use the organization's chronology in its publication, *Business Conditions Digest*.

Economists often use a short-hand definition of a recession as a decline in real output lasting six months or more, but the NBER's actual definition is more complex. Its notion of the cycle focuses on "expansion occurring at about the same time in many economic activities, followed by general recessions, contractions, and revivals that merge into the expansion phase of the next cycle." Clearly, this definition allows for an element of subjectivity.

The dating of the recession that began in March 2001 provides a clear illustration of the approach adopted by the NBER. The NBER Business Cycle Dating Committee announced a March 2001 business cycle peak based on real GDP, real personal disposable income, employment, and real manufacturing and trade sales figures. This information is available in the NBER's business cycle dates and press releases at http://www.nber.org/cycles/.

Based on the data reported in November 2001 release, employment peaked in March 2001, industrial production in September 2000, real sales in November 2000, and income had not yet peaked. On balance, the Business Cycle Dating Committee decided to declare March 2001 to be the cycle's peak month.

By the beginning of 2002, several key indicators reached troughs and began to turn upward. The trough for real sales in manufacturing and trade came in September 2001, and that for industrial production came in December 2001. Did that

mean that the NBER could declare an end to the recession? Not yet! For one thing, several employment indicators failed to recover by mid-2002. More importantly, it is the NBER's practice not to assign a date for the end of a recession until economic activity has recovered to its previous peak. If, as sometimes happens, there is an early, brief upturn in the economy—a false recovery from the recession—after which economic activity declines again without having reached its previous peak level, the NBER counts the new decline as a continuation of the original recession, not a new, separate recession. This is exactly what happened in the 1981–1982 recession: There was an upturn in January 1982, but then a renewed decline until November. The November 1982 trough was even lower than the January low. Economic activity did not reach its 1981 peak until mid-1983, at which point the NBER declared November to be the official end of the recession.

In the case of the 2001 recession, the recovery proceeded throughout the rest of 2002, but unusually slowly. Employment had not yet recovered, continuing to decline through July 2002. While briefly rising in the third quarter, with the exception of January 2003, employment fell through most of 2003. Despite the worsening employment situation, on November 26, 2003, the NBER Business Cycle Dating Committee met by conference call to declare November 2001 to be the official trough of the cycle. The committee's decision was somewhat controversial because of the employment figures. In the November 26, 2003 press release, the committee stated "The determination of the date of the peak in economic activity was as challenging as usual. In every episode, the major indicators peak in different months."

The table below reports how the data the Business Cycle Dating Committee looks at does not provide a clear answer. The table shows how employment, industrial production, real sales, and real income change during the business cycle. It reports the number of months the factor rose/decline during the last seven U.S. recessions.

| Recession Dates | Industrial Production | Employment | Real Sales | Real Income |
|---|---|---|---|---|
| Apr. 1960 – Feb. 1961 | –3 | 0 | –3 | +1 |
| Dec. 1969 – Nov. 1970 | –2 | +3 | –2 | +8 |
| Nov. 1973 – Mar. 1975 | 0 | +11 | 0 | 0 |
| Jan. 1980 – July 1980 | –7 | +2 | –10 | –1 |
| July 1981 – Nov. 1982 | 0 | 0 | –6 | +1 |
| July 1990 – Mar. 1991 | +2 | –1 | +1 | 0 |
| Mar. 2001 – Nov. 2001 | –6 | 0 | –7 | No peak |

Suppose, for example, that the natural level of real output is $1 trillion and the natural rate of unemployment is 6 percent. In that case, a 4 percent decrease in real output, to $960 billion, would tend to raise the unemployment rate to 8 percent. Likewise, a 2 percent increase in real output, from $1 trillion to $1.02 trillion, would push unemployment one percentage point below its natural rate, to 5 percent.[3]

Why is there a 2-to-1 ratio between changes in real output relative to its natural level and changes in the unemployment rate relative to its natural rate? Why doesn't adding 1 percent to real output cut unemployment by a full percentage point? There seem to be two basic reasons.

First, hiring and laying off workers is a costly process. Firms that hire new workers must bear the costs of advertising for applicants and screening them when they apply for employment. Also, new workers may not be fully productive until they have gone through a period of on-the-job training. Firms that lay off workers also bear costs. Some contracts call for severance payments. Some skilled workers may get other jobs after being laid off. Employers that have made many layoffs may be required by law to make higher payments to state and federal unemployment insurance funds. Because of these costs, firms tend to "hoard" labor during business downturns by cutting back their workers' hours or finding make-work projects for them instead of laying them off. Moreover, during upturns they may find it cheaper to put workers on overtime, even at time-and-a-half wages, rather than go to the trouble of finding new ones.

But labor hoarding does not fully explain the 2-to-1 ratio of Okun's law. A second explanation of the ratio lies in the way the unemployment rate itself is calculated. As we saw earlier in the chapter, the unemployment rate is the ratio of unemployed workers to the civilian labor force. During a business upturn, when firms are creating new jobs at a rapid rate, some previously unemployed workers find jobs. At the same time, however, the improved job market attracts workers who previously had not even looked for work. Not all the new entrants find work right away; some join the ranks of the unemployed instead. The upshot is that when output expands, the increase in the number of employed workers is accompanied by some growth of the labor force. As a result, a 1 percent increase in the number of jobs tends to be linked with a drop in the unemployment rate of less than one percentage point.

The rate of inflation also tends to vary over the course of the business cycle. As the economy approaches the trough of a cycle, with real output falling below its natural level, the rate of inflation tends to slow. Historically, severe business downturns such as the Great Depression produced not just a slowdown in the rate of inflation, but also an actual drop in the price level (that is, a negative rate of inflation); however there have been no such episodes since World War II. On the other side of the cycle, the rate of inflation tends to accelerate as real output moves above its natural level and the economy approaches a cyclical peak.

☜

# SUMMARY

1. **What is unemployment and why is it important for economic policy?** A person who works at least 1 hour a week for pay or 15 hours per week as an unpaid worker in a family business is considered to be *employed*. A person who is not currently employed but is actively looking for work is *unemployed*. The *unemployment rate* is the percentage of the *labor force* that is not employed. Unemployment may be classified as *frictional, structural,* or *cyclical,* depending on its cause. Structural plus frictional unemployment is known as the *natural rate of unemployment*. The *employment-population ratio* is the percentage of the adult noninstitutional population that is employed.

2. **What is inflation and what impact does it have on the economy?** *Inflation* is a sustained increase in the average level of prices of all goods and services. *Price stability* is a situation in which the rate of inflation is low enough so that it is not a significant factor in business and individual decision making. Inflation is frequently measured in terms of the rate of change in the *consumer price index*. In measuring economic quantities, a distinction must be made between *real* values, or values adjusted for inflation, and *nominal* values, or values expressed in the ordinary way, in current dollars. Applying these concepts to interest rates, we can say that the *real interest rate* is equal to the *nominal interest rate* minus the rate of inflation. Inflation disrupts the economy in two ways. First, it harms or benefits individuals according to their source of income; second, it disrupts economic calculation, thereby discouraging saving and investment. In addition, the effort to stop inflation once it has begun often entails substantial costs.

3. **What trend has economic growth followed in the United States?** Economic growth is most commonly expressed in terms of the rate of growth of *Gross Domestic Product (GDP)*, a measure of the value of the economy's total output of goods and services during a given period of time. To avoid distortions caused by inflation, gross domestic product is expressed in real terms. Real gross domestic product has grown at an average rate of about 2–3 percent since 1950, although that growth has not been steady. Economic growth is widely seen as beneficial, in that it makes possible higher living standards, jobs for those who want them, and more leisure for those who want it. Some people criticize growth as damaging to the environment. In evaluating such damage, the composition of real domestic product as it grows must be considered as well as its rate of growth.

4. **What is the nature of the business cycle?** Over time, the economy undergoes a pattern of irregular but repeated expansion and contraction of aggregate economic activity that is known as the *business cycle*. The point at which output reaches a maximum is known as the peak of the cycle. This is followed by a contraction, a trough, an expansion, and a new peak. A contraction lasting six months or more is known as a *recession*. Over the course of the business cycle, the economy sometimes rises above and sometimes falls below its *natural level of real output*. The natural level of real output is the level that is consistent with the economy's long-run growth potential and the natural rate of unemployment. According to *Okun's law*, for each 2 percent by which real output changes relative to its natural level, the unemployment rate changes by one percentage point in the opposite direction.

# KEY TERMS

| | |
|---|---|
| Employed | Employment-population |
| Unemployed |   ratio |
| Labor force | Frictional unemployment |
| Unemployment rate | Structural unemployment |

Natural rate of unem-
   ployment
Cyclical unemployment
Price stability
Inflation
Consumer Price Index
   (CPI)
Real
Nominal

Indexation
Transfer payments
Nominal interest rate
Real interest rate
Real output
Business cycle
Recession
Natural level of real
   output

## PROBLEMS AND TOPICS FOR DISCUSSION

1. **Examining the lead-off case.** Is it possible that some of the 350 people who answered the ad for the janitor's job at the Colorado high school might have been not working, but not unemployed? Under what circumstances might this be the case? If the steelworker, while living with his father in Texas, temporarily gives up looking for work until times get better, is he considered unemployed? If his wife works 5 hours a week without pay, assisting her father-in-law in a small business he runs, is she considered employed?

2. **Your personal labor force status.** What is your current labor force status? Are you a member of the labor force? Are you employed? Unemployed? Explain the basis for your answers. When was the last time your labor force status changed? Do you expect it to change soon? Give details.

3. **Employment hardship.** It has been suggested that the unemployment rate should be replaced with an "employment hardship index" that tries to measure the percentage of people who suffer hardship because of their labor force status. What kinds of people who are not now counted as unemployed might fit into this category? What kinds of people who are now counted as unemployed would not suffer hardship? Discuss.

4. **Real and nominal interest rates.** Check with your local bank to find out what interest rates currently apply to (a) one-year savings certificates and (b) three-year automobile loans. Compare these nominal interest rates with the current rate of inflation as measured by the most recently announced rate of change in the consumer price index. (That number is announced in the middle of each month for the previous month; check business periodicals for the latest data.) If the current rate of inflation were to continue unchanged, what real rate of interest would you earn on the saving certificate? What real rate of interest would you pay on the loan?

5. **Economic growth and the environment.** The pace of economic growth varies from one area of the United States to another. Some regions are growing rapidly, with people moving in, much new construction, rising incomes, and so on. Other areas are stagnant or declining, with little new construction and people moving away. Which type of area do you live in? Can you identify any environmental problems in your area that seem to be caused by economic growth? Can you identify any environmental problems that seem to be caused by economic decline? What policies could you suggest that would permit growth in your area to take place with less environmental disruption?

6. **The current state of the business cycle.** Unemployment and inflation data are announced monthly, and data on economic growth are announced on a quarterly basis. Watch your local newspaper, *The Wall Street Journal,* or business magazines such as *Business Week* for discussions of the most recent data. What changes have there been? What is happening to the employment rate? Are the employment and unemployment rates moving in the same direction or in opposite directions? What is the current rate of inflation? Is it increasing, decreasing, or staying the same?

Judging from available data, in which phase of the business cycle does the economy appear to be at the moment?

# CASE FOR DISCUSSION

## Unemployment and Politics

What did the elections of Presidents Truman, Johnson, Nixon, and Clinton have in common? Those of Presidents Kennedy and Reagan? The answer, for the first four, is that they all won as incumbent presidents in election years when the unemployment rate was falling. The other two were successful challengers in years when the unemployment rate was stagnant or rising.

Given these precedents, it is easy to imagine the dismay that ran through the first Bush administration in June 1992, when the unemployment rate hit an 8-year high, just as the election campaign was getting started in earnest. All during the spring, employers had been cautiously hiring. The National Bureau of Economic Research (NBER) had not yet officially announced the end of the recession, but almost all economists thought (correctly, it turned out) that the recovery had begun. But although the economy was growing, it was doing so at a rate of only about 2 percent per year. That was well below the average rate of growth of 4.6 percent per year for the six post–World War II elections in which the incumbent party retained power. In June, employers slashed 117,000 jobs from their payrolls. The new data made every news broadcast, and the news was bad.

Moreover, although the first President Bush could hope for good news between early summer and election time, history suggests that such news would be too little, too late. Economists like Ray Fair of Yale, who have studied the economics-politics link in detail, say that last-minute improvements are not enough. The economy's performance during the spring and summer is more important in an election year.

As it turns out, the economic numbers did improve later in the year. Unemployment fell again. An early estimate of the rate of economic growth in the third quarter, announced just before the election, turned out to be 2.7 percent, higher than forecasters had anticipated. Three weeks after the election, this was revised upward to 3.9 percent. But the third-quarter improvement was indeed too little, too late. Challenger Clinton sailed through the election by a wide margin. His job (and no easy one): Make good on campaign promises to get the economy moving well in advance of the 1996 election. This Clinton accomplished and was re-elected, despite the scandals in his personal life.

While NBER announced an official end to the November 2001 recession, the employment figures seemed to lag behind other economic indicators such as real GDP growth and real sales. This could play an important role in determining the outcome of the 2004 presidential election with the second President Bush as the incumbent.

## QUESTIONS

1. If the economy was growing at a rate of 2 percent or better in mid-1992, how is it possible that the unemployment rate was rising?
2. The unemployment rate rose by only 2.7 percentage points from its low of 5.1 percent in March 1989, to its peak in June 1992. A loss of 2.7 percent of voters would not have been nearly enough to defeat the incumbent president, however. His actual vote total fell far more than that. This implies that a rise in unemployment affects the voting behavior not just of those who are actually unemployed, but of many more people as well. Why do you think this is the case?
3. What has happened to the unemployment rate, the rate of inflation, and the rate of real economic growth since the second George Bush's inauguration? Based solely on economic criteria, do the prospects for his reelection look favorable?

# END NOTES

1. Until 1991, official economic reports emphasized a closely related measure of total production, *Gross National Product* (GNP). Later in the text we will give formal definitions of GDP and GNP, and will explain the methods by which their real and nominal values are calculated.

2. Okun's original study was based on data for the U.S. economy through the early 1960s. These data suggested a 3-to-1 ratio for his rule of thumb. Studies based on more recent data indicate that the relevant ratio is now 2-to-1.

3. We use the phrase "percentage point" because the unemployment rate itself is already expressed in percentage terms. It would be misleading to say "a 1 percent drop in the unemployment rate," which might be taken to mean a drop in the unemployment rate from 6.0 to 5.94 percent (5.94 being 99 percent of 6.0). A "one percentage point" drop in the unemployment rate clearly means a drop from 6.0 percent to 5.0 percent.

# The Circular Flow of Income and Product

## THE TWILIGHT ZONE

"For about 20 months the U.S. economy has been operating in a twilight zone: growing too fast to meet the classic definition of a recession, but too slowly to meet the usual criteria for economic recovery. There's nothing particularly mysterious about our situation. But recent news coverage and commentary—in particular, the enthusiastic headlines that followed a modest increase in growth and a modest decline in jobless claims—suggest that some people still don't get it." This was the opening of a *New York Times* column by economist Paul Krugman in August 2003.

The only way to figure out what was happening in the U.S. economy was to try to put together the pieces of the puzzle provided by the latest government statistics. An important piece of the puzzle was a newly issued report that the economy's real output had grown by an estimated 2.4 percent in the second quarter of 2003. Not a spectacular rate, but better than in the recent past. Other vital bits of information concerned what was happening in individual parts of the economy. Forecasters were especially encouraged by growth in consumer spending, the largest component of the demand for goods and services in the economy.

Would the recovery last, or was it just a spurt? Krugman noted weakness in the employment situation. Citing almost 400,000 new jobless claims filed with the government, Krugman's economic outlook was somewhat bleak.

Later, in November 2003, preliminary estimates put third-quarter real output growth at 8.2%. After these estimates were released, Krugman wrote, "I've heard it said that I should try, just once, to write something upbeat." Despite gains in the economy's total real output, the employment situation seems to be lagging behind. This has caused concern among economists like Krugman, as well as for U.S. policy makers.

I NFLATION, UNEMPLOYMENT, AND real output are three key macroeconomic indicators. But as the data just cited shows, there are many other pieces to the puzzle besides these three. Interest rates, inventories, consumer spending, exports, defense spending, even cardboard boxes—how can they all possibly fit together? How do the actions of millions of individual firms and households, each making decisions independently, interact to produce recessions, recoveries, slowdowns, and booms? This chapter identifies the major pieces of the puzzle and their relationships to one another. In so doing, it lays the foundation for all of the macroeconomic models that follow.

**Circular flow of income and product**

The flow of goods and services between households and firms, balanced by the flow of payments made in exchange for goods and services.

## THE CIRCULAR FLOW IN A SIMPLE ECONOMY

The model around which this chapter is built is the **circular flow of income and product**—that is, the flow of goods and services between households and firms, balanced by the flow of payments made in exchange for them.

To see the circular flow in its simplest form, we will begin with an economy in which there is no government, no financial markets, and no imports or exports. To make things even simpler, imagine that the households in this economy live entirely from hand to mouth, spending all their income on consumer goods as soon as they receive it, and that the firms sell all their output directly to consumers as soon as they produce it.

## The Basic Circular Flow

Figure 5.1 shows the circular flow of income and product for this ultrasimple economy. Real goods and services are shown flowing in a clockwise direction. Two sets of markets link households and firms. *Product markets,* which appear at the top of the diagram, are those in which households buy the goods and services that firms produce. *Factor markets,* which appear at the bottom, are those in which firms obtain the

**FIGURE 5.1   THE BASIC CIRCULAR FLOW**

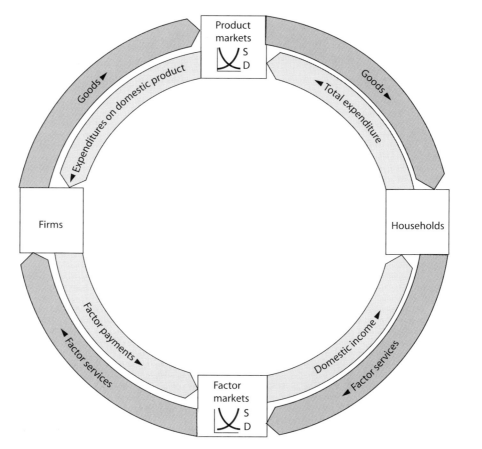

In this simple economy, households spend all their income on consumer goods as soon as they receive it and firms sell all their output to households as soon as they produce it. Goods and services flow clockwise, and the corresponding payments flow counterclockwise.

factors of production they need—labor services, capital, and natural resources—from households.

The clockwise flows of goods and services through these markets are balanced by counterclockwise flows of payments. Households make payments for the things they buy in product markets. Firms make *factor payments*—wages, interest payments, rents, royalties, and so on—in exchange for the labor services and other resources they buy.

By convention, when firms use factors of production that they themselves own, they are counted as "buying" them from the households that are the proprietors, partners, or stockholders who own the firms. All production costs therefore can be viewed as payments for factors of production purchased from households. If a firm has something left over after meeting all its costs, it earns a profit. Profits too are counted as flowing directly to the households that own the firms, even though a firm may retain some profit to increase its owners' equity rather than paying it out as dividends. For the purposes of the circular flow, then, profit is lumped together with factor payments.

## Stocks and Flows

**Flow**

A process that occurs continuously through time, measured in units per time period.

We refer to all the amounts shown as arrows in Figure 5. 1 as **flows** because they are continuously occurring processes. Flows are measured in units per time period—dollars per year, gallons per minute, or tons per month. Measurements of flows are measurements of rates at which things are happening.

**Stock**

A quantity that exists at a given point in time, measured in terms of units only.

Flows must be distinguished from stock. **Stocks** are quantities that exist at a given point in time. Stocks are measured in terms of dollars, gallons, tons, and so on at a given point in time. The amusement park ride described in *Applying Economic Ideas 5.1* provides a simple illustration of the relationship between stocks and flows.

## Money in the Circular Flow

The fluid that keeps the economy's plumbing system working is money. *Money* is what we use as a means of payment for buying goods and services. (A formal definition of money will be given in Chapter 10.) The forms of money that are most familiar to consumers are coins, paper currency, and bank account balances. Just as there is a certain stock of water in the White Water Canyon ride on any given day, there is a given stock of money in the economy at any point in time—so many dimes, so many $20 bills, and so on. For example, in January 2003, the U.S. money stock was $5.8 trillion, according to a widely used measure. Unless the government or private banks do something to change the stock of money (such as printing more $20 bills and putting them into circulation), that $5.8 trillion is what the economy has to work with, just as the stock of water in the ride is what its operators have to work with (unless they change it by opening the drain or inlet valve).

## APPLYING ECONOMIC IDEAS 5.1
### WHITE WATER CANYON

King's Dominion is a huge amusement park near Richmond, Virginia. The summer weather is hot there, which helps explain why one of the most popular rides in the park is one called White Water Canyon.

In White Water Canyon, riders are seated in a round rubber raft. After they are buckled in, the raft is swept down a twisting concrete chute through a series of wild rapids. Riders get soaked to the skin in cool water as they hit waves and shoot under waterfalls. Then they get back in line, hoping to reach the boarding point again before they dry off.

The chute down which the rafts ride looks much like a real river, but it is artificial. An electric pump circulates the water from a pond at the bottom of the chute back up to the top. The speed of the ride is controlled by the speed of the motor. When the motor runs faster, more water is pumped through the chute and the rafts are carried along at a higher speed. If the speed of the pump is reduced, the rafts slow down until they hit bottom and cease to move at all.

The system is connected to a pipeline that can be used to add water to replace water lost through splashing and evap-

oration. However, adding water does not in itself control the speed of the ride. If the pump's speed remains constant, extra water added to the system simply collects in the pond at the bottom of the chute.

This amusement park ride provides a simple illustration of the concepts of stocks and flows. The *stock* of water used in the ride is the number of gallons the system contains at any given time. When the pumps are turned off for the night, the stock of water in the system stays the same; all those gallons just trickle down into the pond at the bottom of the chute. When the pumps are turned on in the morning, the same stock of water is set in motion again.

The *flow* of water through the ride is the number of gallons per minute passing a given point in the system—say, the point at which riders board the rafts. The faster the pumps run, the faster the flow. When the pumps are turned off, the flow falls to zero even though the stock of water remains constant.

The economy's money stock, like the water in the ride, does not just lie there. To do any useful work, it must be constantly circulated through the plumbing. Economic flows, such as income and expenditures, are measures of the speed with which money is moving through the system. These economic flows are measured in dollars per year in the same way that the flow of water in the ride is measured in gallons per minute. Gross domestic product—in dollars per year—is greater than the stock of money because each unit of money can be spent more than once each year: workers spend their pay at supermarkets; supermarkets spend their revenues to meet their payrolls; checkout clerks spend their paychecks at gas stations; and so on. For example, in 2002 domestic product was flowing at just over $10 trillion per year even though the stock of money was just $5.8 trillion.

In both the White Water Canyon ride and the U.S. economy, stocks and flows are related, and changes in one are often associated with changes in the other. Yet stocks and flows can also vary independently:

- In the case of the ride, turning on the inlet valve will increase the stock of water. However, as long as the pumps continue to run at the same speed, the added water will just sit at the bottom and the rate of flow through the chute will not change. On the other hand, the flow can be increased by speeding up the pump even while the drain and inlet valves remain closed and the stock of water in the system stays fixed.

- In the case of the economy, adding more money—in the form of $20 bills, bank balances, or whatever—will not speed up the flow of income if the new money just sits in people's pockets and bank accounts. On the other hand, the flow of income can be speeded up even if the stock of money remains fixed if people increase the rate at which they pass the money from hand to hand.

The relationship between the stock of money in the economy and the flow of income is one of the crucial keys to understanding macroeconomics. We will return to this relationship repeatedly in later chapters.

## Domestic Income and Product

**Domestic product**

The total value of all goods and services produced annually in a given country.

**Domestic income**

The total income of all types, including wages, rents, interest payments, and profits, paid in return for factors of production used in producing domestic product.

Look again at Figure 5.1. Two of the flows shown there deserve special attention. The first is labeled "domestic product." **Domestic product** is the total value of all goods and services produced annually in a given country. Expenditures on domestic product constitute the dollar flow to firms that balances the flow of products from firms to product markets; an example would be the payments for clothing that manufacturers receive in return for the shirts and blouses that consumers acquire. The second important flow is labeled "domestic income." **Domestic income** is the total income of all types, including wages, rents, interest payments, and profits, received in return for supplying the factors of production used in producing domestic product. Domestic income and domestic product are, by definition, equal in this simple economy.[1] This can be verified in two ways.

First, consider household expenditures as a link between domestic income and domestic product. Households are assumed to spend all their income on consumer goods as soon as they receive it, and firms are assumed to sell all their output directly to households. The payments made by buyers must equal the payments received by sellers; thus, viewed from this side of the circular flow, domestic product must equal domestic income.

Second, consider payments for labor and other factors as a link between domestic income and domestic product. When firms receive money for the goods and services they sell, they use part of it to pay workers, owners of natural resources, and suppliers of capital. Anything left over is profit. Thus, factor payments, including profits, account for all the money earned by households, and total factor payments are equal to domestic income. From this it follows that domestic income and domestic product are equal when viewed from this side of the circular flow, too.

## Saving, Investment, and Financial Markets

The circular flow shown in Figure 5.1 is only a first step in laying out the linkages between households and firms. The next step is to add a second set of linkages that involve saving, investment, and financial markets. These linkages are shown in Figure 5.2. To simplify this and the following circular flow diagrams, the clockwise flows of goods and services are omitted.

**SAVING**   On the average, households spend less each year than they receive in income. The portion of household income that is not used to buy goods and services or to pay taxes is termed **saving**. (There are no taxes in this economy yet, but they will soon be added.)

The most familiar form of saving is the use of part of a household's income to make deposits in bank accounts or to buy stocks, bonds, or other financial instruments, rather than to buy goods and services. However, economists take a broader view of saving. They also consider households to be saving when they repay debts. Debt repayments are a form of saving because they, too, are income that is not devoted to consumption or taxes.

**Saving**

The part of household income that is not used to buy goods and services or to pay taxes.

**FIGURE 5.2   THE CIRCULAR FLOW WITH SAVING AND INVESTMENT**

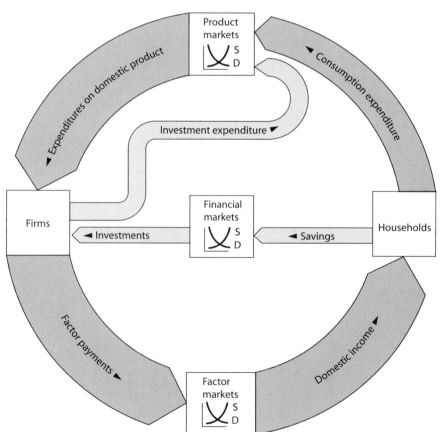

When saving and investment are added to the circular flow, there are two paths by which funds can travel on their way from households to product markets. One path is direct, via consumption expenditures. The other is indirect, via saving, financial markets, and investment. The clockwise flows of goods and services have been omitted from this diagram; only flows of funds are shown.

**INVESTMENT**   Whereas households, on the average, spend less each year than they receive in income, business firms, on the average, spend more each year than they receive from the sale of their products. They do so because, in addition to paying for the productive resources they need to carry out production at its current level, they desire to undertake *investment*. Investment includes all spending that is directed toward increasing the economy's stock of capital.

If we examine this topic more closely, we can distinguish between two categories of investment. The first, **fixed investment**, means the purchase of newly produced capital goods, such as production machinery, office equipment, and newly built structures. The second is **inventory investment**—the accumulation of stocks of raw materials prior to use or of finished products prior to sale. Inventories held by businesses are counted as part of the economy's stock of capital; they are just as necessary to the production process as capital in the form of machinery or buildings. Inventory investment can be less than zero in periods when firms are reducing their stocks of raw materials and finished products. The term *investment* used alone refers to the sum of fixed investment and inventory investment.

Investment is defined somewhat more narrowly in economics than in everyday usage. In everyday usage it means the purchase of almost any kind of asset; thus, a person or firm might be said to "invest" in corporate stocks, a previously built house, or secondhand oil tankers. However, none of these purchases is an investment in the economic sense because it adds nothing to the economy's total stock of capital goods or total inventories.

Suppose, for example, that Exxon buys a brand-new, custom-built oil tanker. That would be an investment, because the tanker is a new addition to the economy's stock of capital. A few years later Exxon decides to sell the tanker to Mobil. For carrying oil, a used tanker is just as good as a new one. Yet the purchase is not an investment in the economic sense; it is not an addition to the economy's stock of capital in the year in which it changes hands. Likewise, purchases of other used capital goods, real estate (other than new structures), mineral deposits, forests, and so on are not investments in the economic sense. They are simply transfers of assets from the balance sheet of one household or firm to that of another.

**FINANCIAL MARKETS**   As we have seen, households tend to spend less each year than they receive in income, whereas firms tend to spend more than they receive from the sale of their products. The economy contains a special set of institutions whose function is to channel the flow of funds from households, as savers, to firms, as borrowers.[2] These are known as **financial markets**. Financial markets are pictured in the center of the circular-flow diagram in Figure 5.2.

Banks are among the most familiar and important institutions found in financial markets. Banks, together with insurance companies, pension funds, mutual funds, and certain other institutions, are termed **financial intermediaries** because their role is to gather funds from savers and channel them to borrowers in the form of loans.

---

**Fixed investment**

Purchases by firms of newly produced capital goods, such as production machinery, office equipment, and newly built structures.

**Inventory investment**

Changes in the stocks of finished products and raw materials that firms keep on hand; the figure is positive if such stocks are increasing and negative if they are decreasing.

**Financial markets**

A set of market institutions whose function is to channel the flow of funds from net savers to net borrowers.

**Financial intermediaries**

A group of firms, including banks, insurance companies, pension funds, and mutual funds, that gather funds from net savers and lend them to net borrowers.

**Common stock**

A certificate of shared ownership in a corporation that gives the owner a vote in the selection of the firm's management and the right to a share in its profits.

**Bond**

A certificate that represents a promise, in return for borrowed funds, to repay the loan over a period of years, with interest, according to an agreed-upon schedule.

**Securities**

A collective term for common stocks, bonds, and other financial instruments.

**Aggregate supply**

The value of all goods and services produced in the economy; a synonym for domestic product.

**Aggregate demand**

The value of all planned expenditures.

More than half of all saving flows through financial intermediaries. The remainder is obtained directly from households through the sale of stocks, bonds, and other securities. **Common stocks** are certificates of shared ownership in a corporation that give the owner a vote in the selection of the firm's management and the right to a share in its profits. (The word *stock,* when used as shorthand for *common stock,* has nothing to do with the concept of stocks as distinguished from flows, defined earlier.) **Bonds** are certificates that represent a promise, in return for borrowed funds, to repay the loan over a period of years, with interest, according to an agreed-upon schedule. Bonds, stocks, and certain other financial instruments are collectively referred to as **securities**. A variety of markets exist in which securities are bought, sold, and resold among households, firms, and financial intermediaries. The New York Stock Exchange, located on Wall Street in New York City, is the best known of the securities markets.

# AGGREGATE SUPPLY AND DEMAND

Adding saving and investment to the circular flow raises a new issue. There are now two pathways along which funds flow from households to product markets: a direct path, through consumption expenditures, and an indirect path, through saving and financial markets to investment expenditures. Corresponding to these two paths are two separate sets of decision makers: households, which make consumption decisions, and businesses, which make investment decisions. How can we be sure that when the two types of expenditures are added together they will match the amount of available goods and services? In other words, how can we be certain that domestic income will still equal domestic product?

These questions can be answered using the familiar concepts of supply and demand in a new way. First, we define **aggregate supply** as the value of all goods and services produced in the economy. We already have another term for the same thing: *domestic product.* Next, we define **aggregate demand** as the value of all the purchases of newly produced goods and services that buyers plan to make. Thus, we can compare aggregate supply and aggregate demand to see whether, for the economy as a whole, buyers' plans mesh with sellers' plans in the same way that we compare supply and demand in the case of a single market.

## *Equilibrium in the Circular Flow*

To see how aggregate supply can be compared with aggregate demand, imagine an economy in which only three goods are produced: apples, radios, and milling machines. The firms in this economy plan to produce apples at a rate of $30,000 per year, radios at a rate of $30,000 per year, and milling machines at a rate of $40,000 per year. As they carry out their plans, output flows at a rate of $100,000 per year. This flow, which can be called either domestic product or aggregate supply, is shown in lines 1 through 4 of Figure 5.3.

FIGURE 5.3   EXAMPLES OF A SIMPLE ECONOMY IN EQUILIBRIUM

**Output Resulting from Producers' Plans**

| | | | |
|---|---|---|---|
| 1. | Total domestic product (aggregate supply) | | $100,000 |
| 2. | Apples | $30,000 | |
| 3. | Radios | 30,000 | |
| 4. | Milling machines | 40,000 | |

**Expenditures Resulting from Buyers' Plans**

| | | | |
|---|---|---|---|
| 5. | Total consumption expenditures | | $60,000 |
| 6. | Apples | $30,000 | |
| 7. | Radios | 30,000 | |
| 8. | Total planned investment | | 40,000 |
| 9. | Fixed investment (milling machines) | 40,000 | |
| 10. | Planned inventory investment | 0 | |
| 11. | Total planned expenditure (aggregate demand) | | $100,000 |

This figure shows a simple economy in which aggregate supply is exactly equal to aggregate demand. The plans of buyers and sellers match when they are carried out in the marketplace, and no unplanned changes in inventory occur. Domestic product and total planned expenditures are equal.

While producers are busy carrying out their plans, buyers are making their own plans. Consumers plan to buy apples at a rate of $30,000 per year and radios at a rate of $30,000 per year. The firms that make radios plan to buy milling machines at a rate of $40,000 per year to increase their radio-producing capacity. No one plans to increase or decrease the stocks of finished products held in inventory; therefore, planned inventory investment is zero. All of these buying plans are expressed in lines 5 through 11 of Figure 5.3. The value of all planned expenditures (consumption plus fixed investment plus planned inventory investment) is shown in line 11 as aggregate demand.

Comparing line 1 with line 11, we see that in this example buyers' and sellers' plans match perfectly. Aggregate supply and aggregate demand are equal. When the plans of buyers and sellers mesh in this way, we say that the circular flow as a whole is in *equilibrium,* just as we say that a market is in equilibrium when the plans of buyers and sellers in that market mesh.

## Disequilibrium

In practice, the plans of buyers and sellers almost never fit together as neatly as they do in Figure 5.3. In fact, it would be surprising if they did. After all, buyers and sellers do not always consult one another before production takes place. Each firm bases its production plans on the information available to it. Buyers base their plans on market prices and on their expectations about the future. Because production plans are often set before buyers' plans have been formed, there is no way to be sure the two sets of plans will mesh.

Suppose, for example, that the preceding example is changed so that consumers plan to buy only $25,000 worth of apples and firms plan to buy only $35,000 worth of investment goods (milling machines). Thus, aggregate demand is only $90,000, even though aggregate supply is still $100,000.

When these plans are tested in the marketplace, there will be some disappointment: All the radios will be sold, but $5,000 worth of apples and $5,000 worth of milling machines will be left over. What will happen to these unsold goods? Once they have been produced, they will not vanish into thin air; instead, they will pile up as inventories in the warehouses of apple farmers and machine tool companies. Those producers did not *plan* to make any inventory investments, but they nonetheless find themselves doing so. The $5,000 of unsold apples and the $5,000 of unsold milling machines are therefore classified as *unplanned* inventory investments. Because buyers' and sellers' plans do not mesh, the circular flow is said to be in *disequilibrium*.

## Reactions to Disequilibrium

In the example just given, aggregate supply exceeds aggregate demand, so there is an unplanned buildup of inventories. Because firms would not want this inventory buildup to continue, they would limit or reverse it by doing one or both of two things. First, they might cut their prices in order to stimulate sales. If they did this, the volume of the circular flow measured in nominal terms (that is, in terms of dollars' worth of goods and services at current prices) would shrink. Second, they might cut their rate of output. If they did this, the circular flow would shrink both in real terms (that is, in terms of output of goods and services adjusted for changes in prices) and in nominal terms.

At another time, aggregate demand might exceed aggregate supply. Suppose, for example, that with output the same as before, consumers plan to buy $35,000 worth of apples and firms plan to buy $45,000 worth of milling machines. When these plans are carried out in the marketplace, sales will exceed current output. The result will be unplanned depletion of inventories as stocks of apples and milling machines are used to meet the strong demand. Firms will react in a way that is opposite to their reaction to an unplanned inventory buildup. If they try to stop the inventory depletion by raising their prices, the circular flow will grow in nominal terms. If they also increase output, the circular flow will grow in both real and nominal terms.

## Equality of Domestic Income and Product

As these examples show, domestic product (aggregate supply) equals planned expenditure (aggregate demand) only when the economy is in equilibrium. However,

**Realized
expenditure**

The sum of all
planned and
unplanned
expenditures.

whether or not the economy is in equilibrium, domestic product always equals **realized expenditure**—that is, the total of planned and unplanned expenditures. This is so because unplanned inventory investment acts as a balancing item. When planned expenditure falls short of aggregate supply, inventories pile up. In that case, adding unplanned inventory investment to planned expenditure makes total realized expenditure equal to aggregate supply. On the other hand, if planned expenditure exceeds aggregate supply, inventories are run down. In that case, adding the negative unplanned inventory investment to planned consumption and investment makes total realized expenditure equal to aggregate supply. In equation form:

$$\text{Domestic product} = \text{Total planned expenditure} + \text{Unplanned inventory investment}$$
$$= \text{Total realized expenditure.}$$

Another way of writing the same thing is:

$$\text{Aggregate supply} = \text{Aggregate demand} + \text{Unplanned inventory investment.}$$

Having shown that domestic product equals total realized expenditure in this economy, we can also show that domestic product equals domestic income. As in the case of the ultrasimple economy of Figure 5.1, the equality of domestic income and product can be shown in one of two ways.

First, we can take advantage of the fact that payments for factor services and profits provide a link between domestic income and domestic product. In our examples, firms produce $100,000 worth of goods each year, all of which is either sold to investors and consumers or added to inventory. In the course of producing this quantity of goods, firms incur costs, which enter the domestic income stream as wages, interest payments, rental payments, and so on. Anything left over after all costs have been paid is profit for the firms—and this, too, is counted as going into the domestic income stream. The total of factor payments plus profits thus account for the entire $100,000 of domestic product (sales to final users plus inventory change).

Second, the equality of domestic income and product can be shown using expenditures as a link. In Figure 5.3 households plan to spend $60,000 on consumer goods (radios and apples). The other $40,000 leaves the circular flow as saving. Firms plan to invest $40,000 in milling machines, so the $40,000 is injected back into the economy as investment spending. Total expenditures (consumption plus investment) thus are equal to domestic income (saving plus consumption). Also, total expenditures, as shown earlier, are equal to domestic product.

Even if the plans of households and firms do not mesh so neatly, total realized expenditures still provide a link between domestic income and domestic product. For example, if households plan to spend just $55,000 and save $45,000, while firms plan to invest only $35,000, saving will exceed planned investment by $10,000. However, as we saw before, the $10,000 of goods that firms produce but that no one plans to buy do not vanish into thin air; instead, they pile up in inventory, where they are counted as unplanned inventory investment. When this is taken into account, total **realized investment** ($35,000 planned plus $10,000 unplanned) equals saving. Again, therefore, domestic income (saving plus consumption) equals total realized expenditure (consumption plus realized investment) and, as always, total realized expenditure equals domestic product.

**Realized investment**

The sum of planned and unplanned investment.

## ADDING GOVERNMENT TO THE CIRCULAR FLOW

The next step in our analysis of the circular flow is to add the public sector. Government is linked to the rest of the economy through taxes, expenditures, and government borrowing. These three links are added to the circular flow in Figure 5.4.

First, consider taxes. For purposes of macroeconomic theory, we need to measure the flow of funds withdrawn from the household sector by government. Clearly, taxes—including income, payroll, and property taxes—are withdrawals. However, this flow of funds from the household sector is partly offset by a flow of funds returned to households in the form of transfer payments, such as social security benefits and unemployment compensation. Therefore, to get a proper measure of the net flow of funds from households to government, we must subtract transfer payments from total taxes. The difference between taxes and transfers is called **net taxes** and is indicated in Figure 5.4 by the arrow linking households and government.

**Net taxes**

Taxes paid to government minus transfer payments made by government.

Next, consider the link between government and product markets. We have already accounted for transfers in calculating net taxes. The remainder of government spending consists of purchases of goods and services, including those bought from private firms and the wages and salaries of government employees. For purposes of the circular flow, government employees' wages and salaries are treated as if they passed through product markets on their way to households.

Finally, consider the link between government and financial markets. Governments do not always balance their budgets. The public sector as a whole, taking federal, state, and local governments together, tends to spend more than it takes in as taxes. (The federal government almost always runs a deficit. State and local governments often have surpluses, but—at least in recent decades—these have not been large enough to offset the federal deficit.)

The government deficit must be financed by borrowing in financial markets. Usually this borrowing takes the form of sales of government bonds and other securities to the public or to financial intermediaries. In Figure 5.4 the arrow from financial markets to government represents government borrowing. Over time, repeated government borrowing adds to the domestic debt. The *debt* is a stock that reflects the accumulation of annual *deficits*, which are flows.

In years when the public sector as a whole runs a budget surplus (that is, when net taxes exceed government purchases), the direction of the arrow is reversed. Governments pay off old borrowing at a faster rate than the rate at which new borrowing

**FIGURE 5.4    THE CIRCULAR FLOW WITH GOVERNMENT INCLUDED**

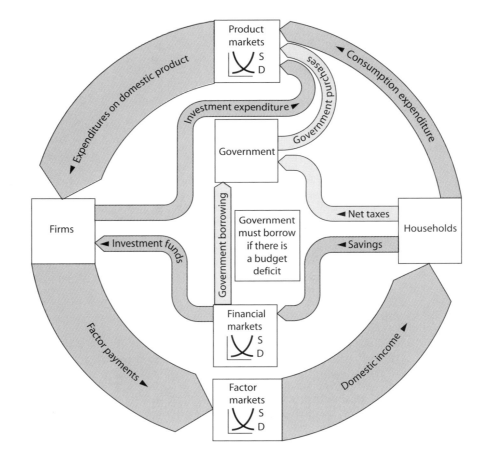

This circular-flow diagram shows three links between government and the rest of the economy. The first is net taxes (taxes minus transfer payments), which flow from households to government. The second is government pur-chases, which flow from government to product markers. If government purchases exceed net taxes (a budget deficit), the government must borrow from financial markets. The deficit case is shown here. If net taxes exceed government purchases, government repayments of past borrowing will exceed new government borrowing, resulting in a net flow of funds from government to financial markets. This case is not shown here.

occurs, thereby creating a net flow of funds into financial markets. In the United States the combined government sector last showed a budget surplus in 1979.

## Leakages and Injections

Take a moment to compare the circular flow shown in Figure 5.4 with the simpler version shown in Figure 5.1. In Figure 5.1, all of domestic income flows directly from households to product markets in the form of consumption spending. Nothing is withdrawn from the stream of income and consumption spending, and nothing is added to it. In Figure 5.4, however, additional flows have been added.

## Leakages

**The parts of domestic income—saving, net taxes, and purchases of imports— that are not used by households to buy domestic consumer goods.**

## Injections

**Those flows of funds into domestic product markets— investment, government purchases, and exports—that do not begin with the consumption expenditures of domestic households.**

First, there are two uses for income that do not result directly in purchases of goods and services. These are net taxes, which flow to government rather than to product markets, and saving, which flows to financial markets rather than to product markets. These two uses of funds are termed **leakages** from the circular flow. Because saving is defined as whatever income is left over after households buy goods and services and pay net taxes, consumption plus the two leakages always add up to domestic income.

Second, there are two kinds of expenditures, namely investment and government purchases, that do not come directly from households. These are termed **injections** into the circular flow. Because investment includes unplanned inventory investment, total realized expenditures—consumption plus injections—always equal domestic income.

## Equality of Domestic Income and Product

Adding government to the circular flow does not disturb the equality of domestic income and domestic product. Figure 5.5 shows an economy in equilibrium with the government sector added. Line 1 indicates that domestic product is $100,000. Lines 2 through 6 show the spending plans of households, firms, and government. Households

**FIGURE 5.5   EXAMPLE OF EQUILIBRIUM WITH GOVERNMENT INCLUDED**

| | | |
|---|---|---|
| 1. Domestic product | | $100,000 |
| **Expenditures** | | |
| 2. Consumption | | $70,000 |
| 3. Investment | | 15,000 |
| 4.   Planned | $15,000 | |
| 5.   Unplanned | 0 | |
| 6. Government purchases | | 15,000 |
| 7. Total expenditures | | $100,000 |
| 8. Domestic income | | $100,000 |
| **Uses of Domestic Income** | | |
| 9. Consumption | | $70,000 |
| 10. Saving | | 20,000 |
| 11. Net taxes | | 10,000 |
| 12. Total uses | | $100,000 |

This figure shows the equality of domestic income and product for an economy with government purchases and taxes included. The total of consumption plus investment plus government purchases equals the total of consumption plus saving plus net taxes. As shown here, the economy is in equilibrium and there is no unplanned inventory investment. However, the equality would hold even if total realized investment included some unplanned inventory investment.

plan to buy $70,000 worth of consumer goods and services; firms plan to buy $15,000 worth of investment goods; and the government plans to buy $15,000 worth of goods and services. Total planned expenditures come to exactly $100,000, and there are no unplanned inventory changes. When planned expenditures (aggregate demand) just equal domestic product (aggregate supply), we know that the economy is in equilibrium.

Production of $100,000 worth of goods and services generates a domestic income, consisting of wages, interest, profits, and so on, of $100,000 (line 8). Lines 9 through 11 show how this domestic income is used: $70,000 goes for consumption (as we saw before); $20,000 is saved; and $10,000 is taken in as taxes. These three uses account for the entire domestic income of $100,000.

The relationships shown in Figure 5.5 can be summarized in the following equation:

Domestic product
   = Consumption + Investment + Government purchases
   = Consumption + Saving + Net taxes
   = Domestic income.

These equations hold even if the economy is not in equilibrium. In that case, realized investment includes some unplanned inventory investment along with planned investment. But domestic product, including planned plus unplanned investment, equals domestic income whether or not the economy is in equilibrium.

## Government Influence on the Circular Flow: A Preview

A close look at Figure 5.4 suggests that the government is able to regulate the size of the overall circular flow through its control over some of the flow components. Much of the discussion in later chapters will be devoted to describing this power and how it is used. Here we will simply give a preview.

One way in which government can affect the circular flow is through its purchases of goods and services. Starting from a state of equilibrium, a reduction in government purchases would lead to unplanned inventory buildup by the firms that make the products that the government unexpectedly stopped buying. As unwanted inventories piled up, firms would react by cutting back output, reducing prices, or some of both. As they did so, the volume of the circular flow would fall in both real and nominal terms. If, on the other hand, the government increased its purchases of goods and services—again starting from equilibrium—there would be unplanned inventory depletion. Firms would react by increasing output, raising prices, or some of both. This would cause the volume of the circular flow to rise in both real and nominal terms. We see, then, that by adding to aggregate demand through increased purchases or reducing aggregate demand through lowered purchases, government can cause the level of domestic product to rise or fall.

Taxes give the government a second means of controlling the circular flow. If tax rates are increased, households will have less after-tax income to spend on consumer goods. This will reduce aggregate demand and cause an unplanned inventory buildup. In response, firms will reduce output, prices, or both, thereby reducing the volume of the circular flow. If tax rates are lowered, the process will work in reverse. With more after-tax income, consumer spending will increase. The additional aggregate demand will cause an unplanned inventory depletion, to which firms will react by increasing output, prices, or both. In this case, the volume of the circular flow and domestic product will rise. The effects of changes in taxes and government purchases, which together are known as *fiscal policy,* will be discussed later.

The government has a third, indirect means of regulating the volume of the circular flow, namely, its influence over the money stock. The Federal Reserve System, an independent unit of the federal government, can take actions that affect the stock of money in the economy. As we saw earlier in the chapter, increasing the stock of money would not necessarily cause the rate of flow of income and product to increase if the new money lay idle in people's pockets and bank accounts. However, as we will see in coming chapters, the actions through which the Federal Reserve injects new money into the economy have many indirect effects, including effects on interest rates and financial markets. If monetary policy eases the availability of loans and lowers interest rates, firms will be encouraged to step up their rate of investment spending. This, in turn, will cause the circular flow to expand. On the other hand, if monetary policy actions cause interest rates to rise, firms will be discouraged from making investments and the circular flow will tend to shrink. These matters will be discussed in detail in future chapters.

## ADDING THE FOREIGN SECTOR TO THE CIRCULAR FLOW

**Closed economy**

An economy that has no links to the rest of the world.

**Open economy**

An economy that is linked to the outside world by imports, exports, and financial transactions.

Up to this point we have developed the circular-flow model only for a **closed economy**—that is, one that has no links to the rest of the world. The U.S. economy is not closed to the rest of the world, however; it is an **open economy**—and increasingly so. Goods and services with a value equal to some 25 percent of domestic product cross the nation's borders in the form of either imports or exports, not to mention the hundreds of billions of dollars' worth of international financial transactions that take place each year. This section extends the circular-flow model to an open economy by adding a foreign sector to the household, firm, and government sectors already included.

Figure 5.6 shows that the foreign sector, like the government, is linked to the rest of the economy in three ways. Imports of goods and services provide the first link. Recall that all the components of the circular flow represents flows of money payments, not flows of goods. Payments for imports are shown by an arrow leading away from the economy to the rest of the world. Households, firms, and government all buy some imported goods and services. To keep Figure 5.6 manageable, however, only imports by consumers, which form part of total consumption expenditure, are shown.

Exports provide the second link between the domestic economy and the rest of the world. Funds received in payment for goods and services sold abroad flow into product markets, where they join funds received from sales of goods and services to

**FIGURE 5.6   THE CIRCULAR FLOW WITH THE FOREIGN SECTOR INCLUDED**

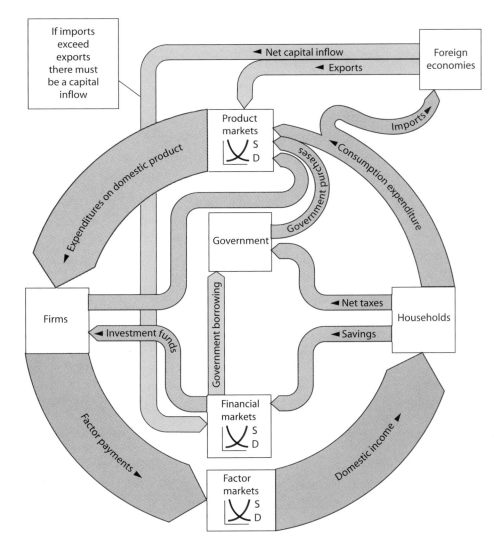

This circular-flow diagram shows three links between the domestic economy and the rest of the world. Imports are the first link. Payments for imports are shown as an arrow from households to foreign economies. Exports are the second link. Payments by foreign buyers of exports are shown as an arrow leading to domestic product markets. If too few goods and services are exported to pay for all the imports, the remaining imports must be paid for by borrowing from foreign sources or by selling real or financial assets to foreign buyers. Such transactions, known as net capital inflows, are shown as a flow into domestic financial markets. Exports might also exceed imports, in which case the arrow would be reversed to show *net capital outflows*.

domestic households, government, and firms. Receipts from the sale of exports are shown as an arrow leading into product markets. The value of exports minus the value of imports is referred to as **net exports**. If the value of imports exceeds that of exports, we can say that there are *negative net exports* or, more simply, *net imports*.

The third link between the domestic economy and the rest of the world consists of international financial transactions. These include international borrowing and lending and international purchases and sales of assets. Like imports and exports of goods and services, international financial transactions give rise to flows of dollar payments into or out of the U.S. economy. Suppose, for example, that a Japanese pension fund buys a bond issued by the U.S. government. It pays for the bond with dollars; as a result, dollars flow into the U.S. economy just as they do when a Japanese firm buys a U.S.-built computer. Much the same thing happens when a U.S. chemical company borrows $1 million from a London bank. The bank is given a promissory note and in return turns over $1 million to the U.S. firm. In both cases, there is an inflow of dollars from abroad to the U.S. economy as a result of the financial transaction.

Flows of dollars into the economy that result from net purchases of assets by foreign buyers and net borrowing from foreign financial intermediaries are known as **capital inflows**.[3] Strictly speaking, it might be better to call them *financial inflows*, because we are talking about the direction of dollar flows, not flows of capital equipment. However, the term *capital inflows* is well established.

Capital inflows have their mirror images. If a U.S. pension fund buys stock in a Swedish paper company or a U.S. bank makes a loan to a Jamaican mining concern, funds flow out of the U.S. economy. Net purchases of foreign assets and net loans to foreign borrowers by U.S. financial intermediaries are known as **capital outflows**.

There is a link between the flows of payments that arise from imports and exports of goods and services and those that arise from financial flows. The logic of this connection can be seen in a highly simplified example. Suppose you are the only person in the United States doing business with France. You want to buy French wine and, at the same time, are willing to sell U.S.-made maple syrup to the French. You place an order for $1,000 worth of wine, but you can find French buyers for only $600 worth of syrup. Does your failure to export as much as you want to import mean that you will have to cancel part of your wine order? No, because there are other ways to settle your accounts with the French: You can either borrow the $400 you need from a French bank or sell a French buyer $400 worth of common stock in your syrup company. To put it another way, you can pay for your imports via either exports or capital inflows in any combination you desire. If the tables were turned and the French wanted to buy an amount of syrup worth more than the wine you wanted to import, they would have to borrow from a U.S. financial intermediary or sell assets to a U.S. buyer. In that case there would be a capital outflow from the U.S. economy.

Later we will add details, but the principle is clear from this simple example. A country can import more than it exports if it experiences net capital inflows—that is, capital inflows that exceed capital outflows. This happens when individuals and

**Net exports**

Exports minus imports.

**Capital inflows**

Net borrowing from foreign financial intermediaries and net funds received from sales of real or financial assets to foreign buyers.

**Capital outflows**

Net lending to foreign borrowers and net funds used to purchase real or financial assets from foreign sellers.

firms in that country borrow more from abroad than foreigners borrow from them, or when they sell more assets to foreigners than foreigners buy from them. This is the case shown in Figure 5.6, and it corresponds to the experience of the United States since the early 1980s.

By the same token, a country can export more than it imports if it experiences a net capital outflow—that is, if its capital outflows are greater than its capital inflows. This happens when financial institutions in that country lend more funds to foreigners than residents of that country borrow from abroad, or when residents of the country buy more assets from foreigners than they sell to them. Thus, a country with net exports must also experience a net capital outflow. In that case, the arrow between the foreign sector and financial markets in Figure 5.6 would be reversed and labeled "net capital outflow." This would represent U.S. experience in earlier post–World War II decades.

## Equality of Domestic Income and Product in a System Including a Foreign Sector

Adding the foreign sector to the circular flow still leaves all of the basic equalities intact. As in the case of a closed economy, we can show this by means of a four-part equation, as follows:

> Domestic product
> = Consumption + Investment + Government purchases + (Exports – Imports)
> = Consumption + Saving + Net taxes
> = Domestic income.

In this four-part set of equations, consumption appears twice: First as one of the categories of expenditures on domestic product, and then as one of the uses of domestic income. If we subtract consumption from both total expenditures and total income, and then shift imports to the left-hand side, we get another useful equation:

> Investment + Government purchases + Exports = Saving + Net taxes + Imports.

This equation says that total injections equal total leakages. It is only the totals of leakages and injections that need to add up. The individual components do not have to match: saving need not equal investment, net taxes need not equal government purchases, and imports need not equal exports. For example, suppose that exports (an injection) exceed imports (a leakage) by $5,000, and at the same time, government purchases (an injection) exceed net taxes (a leakage) by $5,000. Despite these imbalances, it is possible for total leakages to equal total injections if saving (a leakage) exceeds investment (an injection) by $10,000. If *planned* investment is not at the level required to bring about this result, *unplanned inventory investment* will automatically occur at just the rate required to maintain the equality of total leakages with total (planned plus unplanned) injections.

In later chapters the relationship between total leakages and total injections will prove useful in understanding the domestic and international macroeconomic experience of the United States over the past decade.

⁀

# SUMMARY

1. **How are households and firms linked by incomes and expenditures?** The *circular flow of income and product* is the flow of goods and services between households and firms, balanced by the flow of payments made in exchange for goods and services. In the simplest case, households spend all their money on consumer goods produced by firms and firms use all the proceeds of their sales to pay wages, rent, interest, and profits to households. *Domestic product* is the value of all goods and services produced in the economy. *Domestic income* is the total income earned by households, including wages, rents, interest payments, and profits. The two are always equal, because for every dollar that firms receive from the sale of their products, they pay one dollar in factor payments and profits.

2. **How is income related to money?** In economics, the term *flow* refers to any process that occurs continuously through time, while a *stock* is the total amount of something that exists at a given point in time. The distinction between stocks and flows is useful for understanding the role of money. The *stock* of money consists of the coins, paper currency, and bank account balances used for transactions and saving. As money is spent it moves through the economy, creating various *flows*, such as income, saving, investment, and government purchases.

3. **How can the concepts of supply and demand be applied to the economy as a whole?** *Aggregate supply* is the value of all goods and services produced in the economy; it means the same thing as domestic product. *Aggregate demand* is the value of all planned expenditures in the economy. The circular flow is said to be in equilibrium when aggregate supply and aggregate demand are equal. In that case, there are no unplanned changes in inventories. If aggregate demand exceeds aggregate supply, there will be unplanned decreases in inventory (negative inventory investment). Firms will tend to react by increasing output, raising prices, or some of both. The circular flow will then expand. If aggregate supply exceeds aggregate demand, there will be unplanned increases in inventories. Firms' reactions will cause the circular flow to shrink.

4. **How do the various sectors of the economy— households, firms, government, and financial markets—fit together?** Firms are linked to households through product markets (expenditures on domestic product) and factor markets (domestic income). Both are linked to *financial markets,* through which household saving flows to firms, which use the funds to make investments. The government sector is connected to the circular flow in three ways. First, households pay *net taxes* (taxes minus transfer payments) to the government. Second, the government buys

goods and services in product markets. Third, the government borrows from financial markets to finance a deficit, or supplies funds to financial markets when it runs a surplus.

5. **How is the U.S. economy linked to the rest of the world?** The foreign sector, like the government sector, is connected to the circular flow in three ways: First, households pay foreign sellers for imported goods. Second, foreign buyers make payments to domestic firms for exported goods. Third, the foreign sector supplies funds to U.S. financial markets if the United States has negative net exports. The funds thus supplied are called *net capital inflows*. Positive net exports by the United States must be offset by *net capital outflows* to foreign financial markets.

## KEY TERMS

| | |
|---|---|
| Circular flow of income and product | Securities |
| Flow | Aggregate supply |
| Stock | Aggregate demand |
| Domestic product | Realized expenditure |
| Domestic income | Realized investment |
| Saving | Net taxes |
| Fixed investment | Leakages |
| Inventory investment | Injections |
| Financial markets | Closed economy |
| Financial intermediaries | Open economy |
| Common stock | Net exports |
| Bond | Capital inflows |
| | Capital outflows |

## PROBLEMS AND TOPICS FOR DISCUSSION

1. **Your personal money stock.** How much money do you own at this moment in the form of coins, paper currency, and the balance in your checking or savings account, if you have one? What was your flow of income in the past month? How would a change in your income affect your stock of money?

2. **Banks as financial intermediaries.** Many local banks provide leaflets advertising their services. Ask for information of this kind at a local bank. What services are provided to borrowers? To depositors? How are the two kinds of services related to the bank's activities as a financial intermediary?

3. **Planned inventory changes.** Not all changes in inventories are unplanned. Why would a firm plan to increase or decrease its inventories? How would you plan your inventories over the course of the year if you were a seller of children's toys? Of air conditioners? How would you plan your inventories of parts if you were the manager of an auto parts store in a town with a growing population? In one with a shrinking population?

4. **Disequilibrium with excess aggregate demand.** Rework the table in Figure 5.3 for the case of excess aggregate demand. (Let consumption of apples be $35,000, consumption of radios $30,000, and planned investment in milling machines $40,000.) How would producers tend to adjust to these changes? Now assume that radio dealers plan to add $5,000 to their inventories. What does this do to total aggregate demand? Will the dealers be able to carry out their plans?

5. **Reactions to disequilibrium in the circular flow.** Starting from a state of equilibrium, trace the effects of each of the following through the circular flow. What happens to inventories? How do firms tend to react? What happens to the size of the circular flow as measured in nominal terms?

   a. Business managers suddenly decide to increase investment in order to expand their firms' productive capacity.

b. The federal government reduces income tax rates.

c. Good harvests throughout the world reduce the demand for exports of U.S. farm products.

6. **Changes in real and nominal output.** In response to an increase in demand, the nation's hay farmers increase production of hay from 1 billion to 1.2 billion bales per year. At the same time, as the market moves up its supply curve, the price rises from $2 to $2.50 a bale. What happens to the output of hay measured in real terms (that is, in terms of the value of output at unchanged prices)? What happens to output measured in nominal terms (that is, in terms of the value of output with respect to the prices at which the output was sold)?

# CASE FOR DISCUSSION

## *Teetering on the Brink of Recession*

*In January 1970, the economy had just passed a business cycle peak and begun a recession. Although available data had not yet fully confirmed this fact, it was clear that the economy was weak. In these difficult circumstances, President Richard Nixon made his annual report to Congress, from which the following excerpts are taken:*

As we enter 1970, continuation of a low rate of growth of sales, production, and employment for several months seems probable. Thereafter, the performance of the economy will depend on both the continued resolve of the Government and the difficult-to-predict behavior of the private sector.

Government policy must now avoid three possible dangers. One is that after a brief lull the demand for output would begin to rise too rapidly and rekindle the inflationary process, as happened in 1967. This possibility cannot be ignored. The tax bill passed in December reduced revenues for the next

fiscal year by close to $3 billion, compared to my original proposals, requiring the Administration to reduce spending plans further. . . .

A second danger we must consider is that the moderate and necessary slowdown may become more severe. The highly restrictive stance of monetary policy is one reason for considering this possibility. Moreover, there is a question whether the rate of real output can long remain essentially flat without more adverse consequences than we have so far experienced.

A third danger is that although the economy remains on the path of slow rise, and avoids either serious recession or revived inflation, this is achieved with such tight credit conditions as to paralyze the housing industry. . . .

The goal of policy should therefore be moderately more rapid economic expansion in the latter part of 1970 than we have recently been experiencing or expect for several months ahead. Keeping the Federal budget in balance, as I have recommended, and a moderate degree of monetary restraint will help achieve this result. This combination of policies would also permit residential construction to revive and begin a rise toward the path of housebuilding required by our growing number of families.

Source: President's Council of Economic Advisers, *Economic Report of the President* (Washington, D.C.: Government Printing Office, 1970) pp. 7–8.

## QUESTIONS

1. For each of the terms used in this report, identify a corresponding flow in Figure 5.4.
2. The report notes that in late 1969 Congress cut taxes by $3 billion more than the administration requested. Explain why the president, worried about the possibility of an overly rapid expansion that might lead to inflation, responded by making further decreases in government spending.
3. Are money or interest rates directly visible in the circular flow diagram? If not, which components of the circular flow do they affect, and how?

## END NOTES

1. As we will see in the next chapter, establishing the equality of domestic income and product as measured in the official national income accounts requires a bit more detail than is shown here. Among other things, we will have to distinguish between *gross* and *net* domestic product, which are two ways of measuring this part of the circular flow, and also between *domestic* income and *national* income. However, these details of national income accounting are not critical to the discussion of macroeconomic theory in this and later chapters.

2. The version of the circular flow presented in Figure 5.2 shows households as the only source of saving and firms as the only borrowers. Reality is somewhat more complex. Later in the chapter we will see that federal, state, and local governments, as well as foreign firms and governments, participate in financial markets as savers or borrowers. In addition, it should be kept in mind that although households on the average are savers and firms on the average are borrowers, some households are borrowers and some firms are savers.

3. By *net* borrowing we mean new borrowing minus repayments of old loans. Similarly, we say *net* sales of U.S. assets to foreign buyers to allow for the possibility that foreign parties holding previously purchased U.S. assets will resell them to U.S. buyers. For example, suppose that Japanese pension fund A buys $100 million of U.S. bonds while Japanese pension fund B sells $10 million in previously purchased U.S. government bonds to a U.S. insurance company. In this case there is a *net* increase of $90 million in foreign holdings of U.S. government bonds.

# Measuring Economic Activity

## WALL STREET YAWNS AT GDP REPORT

**NEW YORK, Nov. 25**—Investors, unimpressed before Thanksgiving day, sent the Dow Jones industrial index of blue-chip stocks up only 16.15 points (17 percent increase) on the strength of a buoyant GDP report. The broader over-the-counter market, which includes stocks of many smaller companies, actually fell slightly, sending the NASDAQ index down 4.10 points (0.21 percent decrease).

The chief item of good news was a commerce department report that real gross domestic product rose at a 8.2 percent annual rate in the third quarter of 2003. It was the strongest quarterly growth in 20 years. Still, investors ran up the market in advance, buying on the rumor of economic recovery. When the good news arrived, there wasn't much to celebrate, as the party was already over.

President George W. Bush welcomed the news. Bush had promised that his economic stimulus package would get the economy moving. The third quarter report appeared to give his economic team a head start. In a radio address, Bush said, "During this season, America's families are planning for the year ahead, and they have reason to be optimistic."

Some economists doubted that the strong growth would be maintained, however. They noted that business fixed investment remained lackluster, with most new equipment purchases only replacing worn out capital. A meager $0.16 billion increase in business inventories could point either way—to optimism on the part of firms stocking up to handle further expected growth in demand in the future, or to slower than expected sales in the quarter just passed. Indeed, Wall Street's response to the GDP report indicates that investors agree.

"The number looks a little disappointing on its face, but it doesn't call the recovery into question," said Vincent Boberski, head of fixed-income research and strategy at RBC Dain Rauscher in Chicago.

Senator Darelene Hooley, a Republican senator from Oregon, was eager to give Bush credit for the recovery. "Instead of visions of sugarplums, this holiday season let's give the American people a real vision for a prosperous future," she said.

Sources: U.S. Department of Commerce, Bureau of Economic Analysis, *National Income and Product Accounts*, Table S.1, November 25, 2003; Daniel Bases, "A Day of Mixed Messages for the U.S. Economy," *Reuters*, December 3, 2003; Jennifer Loven, "Bush Touts His Role in Improving Economy," *Associated Press*, December 7, 2003.

⤳

G OVERNMENT REPORTS OF the latest data on domestic product and the price level are regularly featured in the financial press. As this report shows, the concepts of domestic product, domestic income, investment, inventories, and so on can be put to work by decision makers in business and government only if they are *measured*—that is, only if numbers are fitted to the various stocks and flows.

**National income accounts**

A set of official government statistics on aggregate economic activity.

Together, the data on aggregate economic activity published by the government are known as the **national income accounts**. The economists and statisticians whose job it is to make these measurements for the U.S. economy are widely held to be the best such team in the world. Yet, as this chapter will show, they face many problems. There are technical problems posed by sampling errors and survey methods. There are conceptual problems that arise when real-world institutions do not match the theoretical categories of economic models. Finally, there are problems of timeliness. Government decision-makers must sometimes work with preliminary data. For example, the 8.2 percent GDP growth rate reported in the news item just given was a revision of data released a month earlier that showed significantly weaker growth, just 7.2 percent. The knowledge that early data are often revised makes it necessary to balance the risks of acting on an inaccurate report against those of delaying action until more information is available.

# THE NATIONAL INCOME ACCOUNTS IN NOMINAL TERMS

We begin with an examination of the national income accounts in nominal terms—that is, in terms of the prices at which goods and services are actually sold. However, nominal measures do not tell the whole story because they are not adjusted to reflect the effects of inflation. Nevertheless, they provide a starting point. Data are collected in nominal form, and only after a set of nominal accounts have been assembled can the process of adjusting for price changes begin.

## Gross Domestic Product

**Gross domestic product (GDP)**

The value at current market prices of all final goods and services produced annually in a given country.

**Final goods and services**

Goods and services that are sold to or ready for sale to parties that will use them for consumption, investment, government purchases, or export.

The most widely publicized number in the national income accounts is gross domestic product. **Gross domestic product (GDP)** is the value at current market prices (that is, the nominal value) of all final goods and services produced annually in a given country.

The term **final goods and services** is a key part of the definition of gross domestic product. GDP attempts to measure the sum of the economic contributions of each firm and industry without missing anything or counting anything twice. To do this, care must be taken to count only goods sold to *final users*—parties that will use them for domestic consumption, government purchases, investment, or export. *Intermediate goods*—those that are purchased for use as inputs in producing other goods or services—are excluded.

Table 6.1 shows why counting both final and intermediate goods would overstate total production. The table traces the process of producing a kitchen table with a retail price of $100. The final stage of production takes place in the furniture plant, but the manufacturer does not do $100 worth of work. Instead, the manufacturer takes $40 worth of lumber, turns it into a table, and gets $60 in exchange for the labor, capital, and other factors of production used to run the furniture plant. The $40 worth of lumber is an intermediate good; the $60 contribution made by the manufacturer is the **value added** to the product at its final stage. (In practice, other intermediate goods, such as paint and fuel for heating the plant, are used in making the table. To simplify the example we assume that the table is made solely from lumber plus the manufacturer's effort.)

The second section of Table 6.1 shows the next-to-last stage of production: making the lumber. The sawmill buys $15 worth of logs, saws them into lumber that sells for $40, and gets $25 in exchange for the mill's work. The value added at the sawmill stage is $25.

Going still further back, we come to the stage at which the logs were produced. To produce $15 worth of logs, a forest products company bought $5 worth of fuel, equipment, and so on and kept $10 in exchange for the effort involved in tending the trees and harvesting the logs. That is an additional $10 of value added.

Clearly, the process of making the table could be traced back indefinitely. The last section of the exhibit sums up the value added at all stages of production prior to

**Value added**

The dollar value of an industry's sales less the value of intermediate goods purchased for use in production.

---

**TABLE 6.1   VALUE ADDED AND THE USE OF FINAL PRODUCTS IN GDP**

| | | |
|---|---:|---:|
| Final stage—manufacturing: | | |
|     Value of one table | $100 | |
|     Less value of lumber | −40 | |
|     Equals value added in manufacturing | 60 ⟶ | $60 |
| Next to final stage—sawmill: | | |
|     Value of lumber | $ 40 | |
|     Less value of logs | −15 | |
|     Equals value added at sawmill | 25 ⟶ | 25 |
| Second to final stage—timber farming: | | |
|     Value of logs | $ 15 | |
|     Less value of fuel, equipment, etc. | −5 | |
|     Equals value added in timber farming | 10 ⟶ | 10 |
| All previous stages: | | |
|     Value added in fuel, equipment, etc. | $ 5 ⟶ | 5 |
| **Total value added** | | **$100** |

This table shows why GDP must include only the value of final goods and services if it is to measure total production without double counting. The value of sales at each stage of production can be divided into the value added at that stage and the value of purchased inputs. The selling price of the final product (a $100 table, in this case) equals the sum of the values added at all stages of production.

timber farming—the fuel and equipment suppliers, their own suppliers, and so on. If production were traced back far enough, every penny could be attributed to the value added to the final product somewhere in the chain of production.

Now compare the first and last lines of the exhibit. Lo and behold, the value of the final good—the table—turns out to be a precise measure of the sum of the values added at each stage of production. This is why only final goods are counted in GDP. Adding together the $100 value of the table, the $40 value of the lumber, the $15 value of the timber, and so on would far overstate the true rate of productive activity (the true total value added) in the economy.

## The Expenditure Approach to Measuring GDP

In principle, GDP could be measured by adding together the value of each final good or service sold or by adding up the value added at each stage of production, as shown in Table 6.1. To simplify the process, however, domestic income accountants make use of the equality of domestic product and total expenditure. It is easier to gather data on the total amount spent by households, investors, governments, and buyers of exports on final goods produced in the domestic economy than it is to stand at factory gates and count goods as they roll off assembly lines. This method of measuring GDP is known as the *expenditure approach*. Table 6.2 shows how it works, using 2002 data for the U.S. economy.

**CONSUMPTION**  The first line of Table 6.2 gives total household consumption of both domestically produced and imported goods and services. The national income accounts divide consumption into three categories: durable goods, nondurable goods, and services. In principle, goods that do not wear out within a year, such as cars, furniture, and appliances, are durable, whereas goods that are used up in less than a year, such as soap, food, and gasoline, are nondurable. In practice, however, these categories are somewhat arbitrary. For example, all clothing is considered nondurable, whether the item is a pair of stockings that may last only a few weeks or a wool coat that may last ten years. The remaining category—services—includes everything that is not in the form of a physical object when sold. Examples include haircuts, legal advice, financial services, and education.

All three components of consumption contain some items that bypass the marketplace on their way to consumers. One such item is an estimate of the quantity of food produced and consumed on farms; another is an estimate of the rental value of owner-occupied homes. However, many nonmarket goods and services are not captured in the national income accounts; unpaid childcare and housework are examples.

**INVESTMENT**  The item termed *gross private domestic investment* is the sum of all purchases of newly produced capital goods (fixed investment) plus changes in business inventories (inventory investment). The fixed-investment component includes both business fixed investment—all new equipment and structures bought by firms—and the value of newly constructed residential housing. In the national income accounts, then, a homeowning household is treated like a small firm. When the house is bought, it is counted as an investment. Then, as we saw earlier, the firm's "product"—the rental value of its shelter services—is counted as part of consumption each year.

**GOVERNMENT PURCHASES**    Government's contribution to GDP at the federal, state, and local levels is treated much like consumption. The goods and factor services bought by government are considered to be "used up" as soon as they are purchased. Government purchases are valued at cost in the national income accounts. No attempt is made to measure the value added by government, because most government outputs—primary and secondary education, defense services, and police protection, to name a few—are financed by taxes and provided to the public without charge rather than sold. Transfer payments are not included in the expenditure approach to GDP, because they do not represent purchases of newly produced final goods and services.

**TABLE 6.2   NOMINAL GROSS DOMESTIC PRODUCT BY TYPE OF EXPENDITURE, 2002**
*(Dollars in Billions)*

| | | |
|---|---:|---:|
| Personal consumption expenditure | | $ 7,303.7 |
|     Durable goods | $ 871.9 | |
|     Nondurable goods | 2,115.0 | |
|     Services | 4,316.8 | |
| Plus gross private domestic investment | | 1,593.2 |
|     Fixed investment | 1,589.3 | |
|     Change in business inventories | 3.9 | |
| Plus government purchases of goods and services | | 1,972.9 |
|     Federal | 693.7 | |
|     State and local | 1,279.2 | |
| Plus net exports of goods and services | | −423.6 |
|     Exports | 1,014.9 | |
|     Less imports | 1,438.5 | |
| Equals gross domestic product (GDP) | | $10,446.2 |
| Less capital consumption allowance | | −1,393.4 |
| Equals net domestic product (NDP) | | $9,052.8 |

Gross domestic product is estimated using the expenditure approach. This involves adding together the values of expenditures on newly produced final goods and services made by all economic units to get a measure of aggregate economic activity. Net domestic product is derived from gross domestic product by excluding the value of expenditures made to replace worn-out or obsolete capital equipment.

Source: U.S. Department of Commerce, Bureau of Economic Analysis, *National Income and Product Accounts,* Table 1.1, November 2003.

**NET EXPORTS**   The last item in the GDP account is *net export*—exports minus imports. In calculating GDP, imports must be subtracted from exports to avoid double counting. Some of the goods bought by consumers, investors, and government and included in their expenditures are not produced in the domestic economy. For example, a consumer might buy a Japanese television set, an insurance company might buy Korean computers for use in its offices, and a city government might buy a Swedish-built police car. The figures for consumption, investment, and government purchases therefore overstate the final use of domestically produced goods and services to the extent that some of those goods and services were produced abroad. To correct for the overstatement in earlier lines in Table 6.2, imports are subtracted from exports at the bottom. Adding total consumption plus total investment plus total government purchases plus exports less imports yields the same sum as would be obtained by adding domestic consumption of domestically produced goods, domestic purchases of domestically produced capital goods, domestic government purchases of domestically produced goods, and total exports.

## Domestic Versus National Product

**Gross national product (GNP)**

The dollar value at current market prices of all final goods and services produced annually by factors of production owned by residents of a given country, regardless of where those factors are located.

Until 1991, a concept closely related to GDP, **gross national product (GNP)**, was featured prominently in U.S. government data. GNP differs from GDP in that it measures the total annual output of factors of production owned by residents of a given country, regardless of where those factors are located. Consider gross domestic and national product for the United States. U.S. gross *national* product includes the contribution to output of U.S. factors of production working abroad, for example, output attributable to capital invested in an English factory by the U.S. stockholders of Ford Motor Company; U.S. gross *domestic* product excludes that output. On the other hand, U.S. gross *domestic* product includes the contribution to output of foreign-owned factors located in the United States—for example, output attributable to capital invested by Honda Motor Company's Japanese stockholders in a factory in Ohio.

As a measure of the output produced by U.S. capital abroad, national income accountants use the factor income—principally in the forms of interest, dividends, and retained earnings—accruing to U.S. resident owners as a result of their firm's foreign operations. Thus, U.S. GNP includes factor income received by U.S. residents from the rest of the world, and excludes factor income paid to residents of the rest of the world.

The change in emphasis from GNP to GDP occurred for two reasons. First, GDP is more closely related to other economic statistics—for example, employment and unemployment, which focus on activity within the country's borders. Second, other leading industrial countries had featured the GDP concept for many years, and it made sense for the U.S. government to bring its national income accounts in line with those of other major countries.

In absolute magnitude, GNP and GDP differ by only a fraction of one percent. However, in periods when economic activity abroad is moving in a markedly different direction than domestic economic activity, the *rate of change* of GNP and GDP can differ significantly. For example, the U.S. Department of Commerce's first report incorporating the new approach showed a 2.0 percent growth of GNP for the third quarter of 1991, but just a 1.7 percent increase in GDP. This indicates that at the time, economic activity was growing a bit more strongly in the rest of the world than in the United States.

## Gross Versus Net Domestic Product

What makes gross domestic product "gross" is the fact that gross private domestic investment measures total additions to the nation's capital stock without adjusting for losses through wear and tear or obsolescence. For example, it includes the value of new homes and factories built each year without subtracting the value of old homes and factories that are torn down. Gross private domestic investment minus an allowance for depreciation and obsolescence yields *net private domestic investment,* a measure of the actual net addition to the nation's capital stock each year. Only net investment adds to the capital stock, thereby helping to expand the economy's production possibility frontier. The part of gross investment that covers depreciation and obsolescence is needed just to keep the frontier from shrinking inward. Although depreciation and obsolescence are hard to measure accurately, national income accountants use an approximate measure called the *capital consumption allowance.* Gross domestic product minus the capital consumption allowance yields **net domestic product (NDP)**.

**Net domestic product (NDP)**

Gross domestic product minus an allowance (called the *capital consumption allowance*) that represents the value of capital equipment used up in the production process.

The distinction between domestic and national product applies to the net, as well as the gross, product concepts. Thus, if net receipts of factor income from abroad are added to net domestic product, the result is *net national product (NNP).*

## The Income Approach to Measuring Aggregate Economic Activity

Previously, we looked at the economy in terms of a circular flow of income and product. In principle, aggregate economic activity could be measured by observing the flow at any point as it circulates. In practice, the national income accounts use two points of observation. First, as we have just seen, domestic product is measured by the expenditure approach, which is equivalent to observing the flow of aggregate economic activity at the point at which it enters product markets. Second, measurements are made of the flows of all kinds of income at the point at which they are received by households. This is known as the *income approach* to measuring aggregate economic activity. The result is shown in Table 6.3. Several items in that exhibit deserve comment.

*Compensation of employees* consists of wages and salaries plus certain *supplements.* The first supplement is employer contributions to social insurance (social

**TABLE 6.3   NOMINAL NATIONAL AND DOMESTIC INCOME, 2002**
*(Dollars in Billions)*

| | | |
|---|---:|---:|
| Compensation of employees | | $ 5969.5 |
|     Wages and salaries | $ 4996.4 | |
|     Other labor income | 973.1 | |
| Plus rental income of persons | | 142.4 |
| Plus net interest | | 684.2 |
| Plus corporate profits | | 787.4 |
|     Dividends | 434.3 | |
|     Corporate profits taxes | 213.3 | |
|     Undistributed corporate profits | 17.6 | |
|     Inventory and capital consumption adjustments | 122.2 | |
| Plus proprietors' income | | 756.5 |
| Equals national income | | 8,340.0 |
|     Less receipts of factor income from rest of world | | −287.6 |
|     Plus payments of factor income to rest of world | | 278.0 |
| Equals domestic income | | 8,330.4 |

National and domestic income is measured using the income approach. This involves adding together the values of all forms of income earned by a country's residents. U.S. national income includes some income received in return for factors of production used abroad, and excludes payments to foreign residents for the use of factors owned by them but located in the United States. Domestic income is derived from national income by subtracting receipts of factor income from the rest of the world and adding factor income paid to the rest of the world. Domestic income can thus be thought of as the total income generated as a result of producing domestic product, regardless of where the recipients reside. Note that in the case of both national and domestic income, some items, such as the portion of corporate profits that goes to pay corporate profits taxes, are counted as "earned" by households even though households never receive the income. Numbers may not be exact because of rounding.

Source: U.S. Department of Commerce, Bureau of Economic Analysis, *National Income and Product Accounts,* Tables 1.14 and 1.16, November 2003.

security). As the social security tax law is written, employees are legally required to pay only half of the tax; employers must pay the other half. Because both halves contribute to employees' retirement benefits, however, both are counted as part of employee compensation. The supplements line also includes fringe benefits other than social insurance that employers pay for, such as health insurance and private pension plans.

*Rental income of persons* consists of all income in the form of rent and royalties received by property owners. *Net interest* includes interest income received by households less interest payments made by consumers.

*Corporate profits* encompass all income earned by the stockholders of corporations, regardless of whether they actually receive that income. Dividends are the part of corporate income that stockholders actually receive. Another part of corporate profits goes to pay taxes. A third part—undistributed corporate profits—is kept by corporations for use in making investments. In measuring income, corporate profits are also adjusted for changes in inventory values and for capital consumption (depreciation). The final component of income, *proprietors' income,* lumps together all forms of income earned by self-employed professionals and owners of unincorporated business.

**National income**

The total income earned by a country's residents, including wages, rents, interest payments, and profits.

The total of these items is **national income**, the total income received by a country's residents. The term *national* is appropriate because when net interest and corporate profits are counted, the income approach includes factor income received from abroad by U.S. residents. At the same time, the income approach does not include factor income paid to foreign residents as a result of their investments in the United States. Following the procedure used in distinguishing between domestic and national product, we can calculate *domestic income,* the income concept that was featured in our discussion of the circular flow in the preceding chapter. Domestic income is equal to national income minus net receipts of factor income from the rest of the world.

## Reconciling the Income and Expenditure Approaches

In the simplified circular flows presented earlier, domestic income and domestic product are always equal. In the official national income accounts, however, the two sums fit together less neatly. Three distinctions must be kept in mind: that between national and domestic measurements, that between gross and net measurements, and that between the income and expenditure approaches. Table 6.4 shows the relationships among a number of key quantities.

The table begins with gross domestic product. Adding receipts of factor income from the rest of the world and subtracting factor income paid to the rest of the world gives gross national product. Subtracting the capital consumption allowance from gross national product gives net national product. These steps have been explained previously.

The next step is one we have not yet mentioned. It is an adjustment for the fact that part of the revenue that firms receive for their products never reaches the suppliers of factor services or the firms' owners. Instead, it is taken by government in the form of so-called *indirect business taxes,* which include sales taxes, excise taxes, and business property taxes. These taxes are treated differently than the corporate profits tax, which is viewed as being earned by owners and then taken from them by the tax collector. Indirect taxes are included in the prices at which goods and services are sold; therefore, they are part of net national product but are not counted as earned in national income.

In principle, adjusting GDP for net receipts of factor income from abroad, and then subtracting the capital consumption allowance and indirect business taxes, should yield national income. In practice, there is a further problem: GDP is measured

**TABLE 6.4   THE RELATIONSHIP BETWEEN INCOME AND PRODUCT ACCOUNTS (2002)**

| | |
|---|---:|
| Gross domestic product | 10,446.2 |
|     Plus receipts of factor income from rest of world | 278.0 |
|     Less payments of factor income to rest of world | −287.6 |
| Equals gross national product | 10,436.7 |
|     Less capital consumption allowance | −1,393.5 |
| Equals net national product | 9,043.2 |
|     Less indirect business taxes and transfers | 844.5 |
|     Less statistical discrepancy | (−108.8) |
|     Plus subsidies less current surplus of government enterprises | 32.5 |
| Equals national income | 8,340.1 |
|     Less receipts of factor income from rest of world | −278.0 |
|     Plus payments of factor income to rest of world | 287.6 |
| Equals domestic income | 8,349.7 |
|     Plus indirect business taxes[a] | 844.5 |
|     Plus statistical discrepancy | (−108.8) |
|     Less subsidies less current surplus of government enterprises | −32.5 |
| Equals net domestic product | 9,052.9 |
|     Plus capital consumption allowance | 1,393.5 |
| Equals gross domestic product | 10,446.4 |

This table shows the adjustments necessary to reconcile the income and expenditure approaches used in the national income accounts, and also shows the relationship between domestic and national income and product concepts. The table begins with gross domestic product. Adjusting for international flows of factor income gives gross national product. Subtracting the capital consumption allowance gives net national product. In theory, net national product should be equal to national income, but two adjustments must be made at this point to reconcile the income and expenditure approaches. These are an allowance for indirect business taxes and an adjustment for the statistical discrepancy. From national income, the table then returns to gross domestic product, but by a different route. Subtracting receipts of factor income from the rest of the world and adding payments to the rest of the world gives domestic income. Further adjustments then yield net and gross domestic product. Numbers may not be exact because of rounding.

SOURCE: U.S. Department of Commerce, Bureau of Economic Analysis, *National Income and Product Accounts,* Tables 1.1, 1.14 and 1.16, November 2003.

by the expenditure approach using one set of data, and national income is measured by the income approach using a different set of data. No matter how carefully the work is done, there will be some errors and omissions, and therefore the two sets of figures will not quite fit together. The difference between NNP minus indirect business taxes on the one hand, and national income, on the other, is called the *statistical discrepancy.* Most of the time this error is very small—well below 1 percent of GDP.

Having begun from GDP and arrived at national income, we now return to GDP, but by a different route. The next lines of Table 6.4 subtract factor income received from the rest of the world and add factor income paid to the rest of the world to give domestic income. Adding indirect business taxes and the statistical discrepancy to domestic income gives net domestic product. Finally, adding the capital consumption allowance gives gross domestic product, and we are back where we began.

### Personal Income

National income, as we have seen, is a measure of income earned by a country's residents, regardless of whether those households ever actually get their hands on it. For example, it includes income that is earned by capital and natural resources owned by corporations and then is retained rather than being distributed as dividends. For some purposes, it is more useful to measure what resident households actually receive than what they earn. The total income received by households is called **personal income**.

First, three items that are earned but not received by households are subtracted: contributions for social insurance (both employer and employee), taxes on corporate profits, and undistributed corporate profits. Next, transfer payments—payments received by households but not earned by them—are added. The result is personal income.

One further income measure is important: **disposable personal income**, or simply disposable income. This is the personal income that is left over after households have paid personal taxes (particularly income taxes) to federal, state, and local governments.

This completes our discussion of the national income accounts. We will now look at the linkages between the domestic economy and the economies of other nations.

**Personal income**

The total income received by households, including earned income and transfer payments.

**Disposable personal income (disposable income)**

Personal income less personal taxes (particularly income taxes).

## MEASURING INTERNATIONAL LINKAGES

The item "net exports" in the national income accounts gives a glimpse of the linkage between the domestic economy and the rest of the world. These ties have grown much stronger in recent years. In 1960, U.S. exports amounted to only 6 percent of GDP and imports less than 5 percent. By 2002, exports had grown to 9.7 percent of a much larger GDP. Imports grew even more rapidly over the same period, reaching 13.8 percent of GDP. In view of the growing importance of the foreign sector, then, it is worth taking a closer look at the international ties of the U.S. economy.

Any discussion of an economy's balance of international payments is complicated by the fact that thousands of different kinds of international payments are made every day. Payments for the goods and services that are exported and imported come to mind first, but there are many others. Equally important are the long- and short-term loans made to finance imports and exports and the payments made in international markets in connection with purchases or sales of assets, such as securities or real estate. In addition, governments and private individuals make many kinds of transfer payments to residents of other countries, including outright gifts, pension payments, and official foreign aid. Finally, the U.S. Federal Reserve System and foreign central banks engage in many kinds of official transactions. Table 6.6 shows a simplified version of the accounts used to keep track of these international transactions for the United States.

## The Current Account

The first section of the international accounts shown in Table 6.5 contains what are called **current account** transactions. These include imports and exports of goods and services, payments of factor income between countries, and international transfer payments. The main items in the current account are as follows:

**MERCHANDISE IMPORTS AND EXPORTS**  Imports and exports of merchandise (goods) are the most widely publicized items in the international accounts. During much of the nineteenth century the United States was a net importer of merchandise. From 1894 to 1970 it was a net exporter. Since 1970 it has again become largely a net importer. Table 6.5 shows a negative **merchandise balance**. The negative number indicates net merchandise imports. (News reports often refer to the merchandise balance as the *balance of trade*.)

**SERVICES**  In addition to trade in merchandise, the United States and other countries carry on a large trade in services. Travel expenditures, airline passenger fares, and other transportation services account for somewhat more than half of these services. Other services include insurance, royalties, and license fees. Certain transactions related to sales of military equipment are included under the heading of services. As the table shows, the United States was a net exporter of services in 2002.

**FACTOR INCOME**  Earlier, in drawing the distinction between domestic and national product, we noted that U.S. residents receive substantial flows of factor income from U.S. assets located abroad. These are analogous to exports, and enter the current account with a positive sign. At the same time, payments of factor income are made to residents of other countries from foreign-owned assets located in the United States. These are analogous to imports, and enter the current account with a negative sign.

**TRANSFERS**  The final item on the current account consists of net transfer receipts. This typically is a negative item in the U.S. international accounts, because transfers to other countries exceed transfers received from them. This item takes into account both government transfers, such as foreign aid and social security payments to retired workers living abroad, and private transfers, such as private famine relief and church missions.

---

**Current account**

The section of a country's international accounts that consists of imports and exports of goods and services and unilateral transfers.

**Merchandise balance**

The value of a country's merchandise exports minus the value of its merchandise imports.

## TABLE 6.5    U.S. INTERNATIONAL ACCOUNTS FOR 2002
(Dollars in Billions)

| Current Account | | |
|---|---:|---:|
| 1.  Merchandise balance | | −482.9 |
| 2.     Exports | 681.9 | |
| 3.     Imports | −1,164.8 | |
| 4.  Services, net | | 64.8 |
| 5.     Exports of services | 292.2 | |
| 6.     Imports of services | −227.4 | |
| 7.  Net receipts of factor income | | −4 |
| 8.     Income receipts from abroad | 255.5 | |
| 9.     Income payments to the United States | −259.5 | |
| 10. Transfers, net | | −58.9 |
| 11. Current account balance (lines 1 + 4 + 7 + 10) | | −481.0 |
| **Capital Account** | | |
| 12. Net change in U.S. assets abroad | | −179.0 |
|        (− indicates increase in U.S. assets abroad, | | |
|        that is, a capital outflow) | | |
| 13.     U.S. private assets | −175.3 | |
| 14.     U.S. official reserve assets | -3.7 | |
| 15.     Other U.S. government assets | −0ª | |
| 16. Net change in foreign assets in the United States | | 707.0 |
|        (+ indicates increase in foreign assets in the United | | |
|        States, that is, a capital inflow) | | |
| 17.     Foreign official assets | 94.9 | |
| 18.     Other foreign assets | 612.1 | |
| 19. Capital account balance (lines 12 + 16) | | 528.0 |
| 20. Statistical discrepancy | | −47 |
|        (sum of current and capital account balances | | |
|        with sign reversed) | | |

This table gives details of U.S. international transactions for 2002. The first section shows current account transactions, consisting of imports and exports of goods and services, together with international flows of factor income and transfer payments. The second section shows capital account transactions, consisting of international borrowing and lending, securities transactions, direct investment, and official reserve transactions. If all amounts were measured completely and accurately, the current account and capital account balances would be equal and opposite in sign. In practice, there is a statistical discrepancy indicating errors and omissions in measurement.

ªU.S. government assets other than official reserve assets (net) was equal to $32 million, the figures in the table are in billions of dollars, so this number rounds to 0.

Source: U.S. Department of Commerce, Bureau of Economic Analysis, *U.S. International Transactions Accounts Data,* Table 1 , September 2003.

**CURRENT ACCOUNT BALANCE**   When merchandise trade, services, factor income, and net transfers are combined, the result is the country's **current account balance**. (News accounts that refer to the *balance of payments* usually mean the current account balance.) Table 6.5 shows a current account deficit for the United States for 2002. The last year in which the country experienced a current account surplus was 1981.

## The Capital Account

Current account transactions are not the only ones that take place among residents of different countries. The international lending and borrowing and international sales and purchases of assets mentioned in an earlier chapter also account for an enormous volume of daily transactions. A U.S. company, for example, might obtain a short-term loan from a London bank to finance the purchase of a shipload of beer for import to the United States. The Brazilian government might get a long-term loan from Citibank of New York to help finance a hydroelectric project. A U.S. millionaire might open an account in a Swiss bank. A Japanese automaker might buy a piece of land in Tennessee on which to build a new plant. All of these transactions are recorded in the **capital account** section of Table 6.5.

Purchases of U.S. assets by foreigners and borrowing from foreign financial intermediaries by U.S. firms and individuals create flows of funds into the United States that are termed *capital inflows*. Purchases of foreign assets by U.S. residents or loans by U.S. financial intermediaries to foreigners create flows of funds out of the United States that are termed *capital outflows*.

Table 6.5 lists several types of capital account transactions. Changes in U.S. private assets include direct investments (such as construction of foreign plants by U.S. firms) and purchases of foreign securities. Changes in U.S. *official reserve assets* include foreign currency and other foreign assets acquired by the Federal Reserve System and the U.S. Treasury. Changes in other U.S. government assets relate to short- and long-term credits and other assets by government agencies other than the Federal Reserve System and U.S. Treasury. Changes in official foreign assets in the United States involve purchases of U.S. government securities by foreign central banks. Direct investment in the United States and private purchases of U.S. securities by foreign buyers are included under the heading "other foreign assets in the United States."

## Relationship of the Accounts

Capital account transactions are logically related to the current account surplus or deficit. If the United States runs a current account deficit, its earnings from the sales of exports will not be enough to pay for all of its imports. Additional funds for financing imports can be obtained through net capital inflows, that is, through U.S. borrowing

---

**Current account balance**

The value of a country's exports of goods and services minus the value of its imports of goods and services plus its net transfer receipts from foreign sources.

**Capital account**

The section of a country's international accounts that consists of purchases and sales of assets and international borrowing and lending.

from abroad that exceeds U.S. lending to foreigners or through sales of U.S. assets to foreigners that exceed purchases of assets abroad. This is the case for the U.S. international transactions shown in Table 6.5. On the other hand, a country with a current account surplus can use its extra import earnings to make net loans to foreign borrowers or net purchases of foreign assets. This would result in a negative balance on the capital account.

In principle, the balances of the current and capital accounts should be equal and opposite in sign. If there is a current account surplus of $100 billion (entered with a plus sign in the accounts), there should be a net capital outflow of $100 billion (entered with a minus sign in the accounts). The reason for this symmetry is that the two account components taken together include all the sources and uses of the funds that change hands in international transactions. Every dollar used in international transactions must have a source; thus, when the sources (+) and the uses (–) are added together, the sum should be zero.

In practice, however, government statisticians always miss some items when they tally up imports, exports, and capital flows. As a result, the numbers do not quite add up. The international accounts use the same term to refer to this quantity as is used for the similar quantity in the domestic accounts—*statistical discrepancy*. Much of the discrepancy is believed to reflect unrecorded capital flows, for example, investments made in the United States by residents of other countries, but never officially reported. Part of it also reflects a tendency for U.S. exports, especially to Canada, to be reported less fully than U.S. imports.

# MEASURING REAL INCOME AND THE PRICE LEVEL

Between 1979 and 2002, the U.S. gross domestic product, measured in nominal terms, rose from $2.6 trillion to $10.5 trillion. To anyone living through those years, however, it is clear that even though nominal GDP more than doubled, the real output of goods and services did not. Much of the increase in the dollar value of GDP reflected an increase in the prices at which goods and services were sold. To understand what really happened to output in those years, then, we must adjust the growth of nominal GDP to account for inflation.

## *Real Gross Domestic Product and the Deflator*

**GDP deflator**

A weighted average of the prices of all final goods and services produced in the economy.

To adjust nominal GDP for the effects of inflation, we need a measure of the change in the average prices of goods and services. The most broadly based measure of price changes for the U.S. economy is the GDP deflator. The appendix to this chapter explains how it is calculated. For now, we will simply define the **GDP deflator** as a weighted average of the prices of all the final goods and services that make up GDP.

**Base year**

The year that is chosen as a basis for comparison in calculating a price index or price level.

**Price level**

A weighted average of the prices of goods and services expressed in relation to a base year value of 1.0.

**Price index**

A weighted average of the prices of goods and services expressed in relation to a base year value of 100.

**BASE YEAR**   When we speak of price changes, the first question that comes to mind is: change from what? We can answer this question by choosing a convenient **base year** as a benchmark against which to measure change. The U.S. Department of Commerce currently uses 1996 as a base year for calculating the GDP deflator. The government uses two methods of calculating the GDP deflator: fixed and chained. Here, we will focus on the first method of computing GDP using fixed, or "constant," dollars.

The base year can be used in one of two ways in stating a weighted average of prices. One way is to let the base year value equal 1.0. A statement of average prices relative to a base year value of 1.0 is called a statement of the **price level**; for example, the 2002 price level, relative to the 1996 base year, was 1.106. The other way is to let the base year value equal 100. A statement of average prices relative to a base year value of 100 is known as a **price index**. Thus, using 1996 as a base year we could say that the 2002 price index was 110.6. The price level and price index are two different ways of stating the same information. In news reports the index form is used most frequently, whereas in building economic models the price level form is more convenient.

**USING THE GDP DEFLATOR**   Table 6.6 shows nominal GDP, real GDP, and the GDP deflator (stated in price level form) for the United States in each year since 1967. To convert nominal GDP for any year to real GDP stated in constant 1996 dollars, we simply divide nominal GDP by the price level for that year. For convenience, we can refer to the year for which we are making the adjustment as the *current year.* In equation form, then, the rule for adjustment can be stated as follows:

Current-year real GDP = Current-year nominal GDP/Current-year price level.

As Table 6.6 shows, applying this formula to current years after 1996 yields real GDP values measured in constant dollars of the 1996 base year that are below current-year nominal GDP. Applying the formula to current years before 1996, when the GDP deflator had values of less than 1.0, yields real-GDP values in 1996 dollars that exceed nominal GDP for those years.

For example, dividing the 1985 nominal GDP of $4,213 billion by the 1985 price level of 0.737 yields a 1985 real GDP of roughly $5,716.4 billion. (This figure does not quite agree with the one in Table 6.6 because of rounding.) Likewise, dividing the 2002 nominal GDP of $10,446.3 billion by the 1996 price level of 1.107 yields a 1996 real GDP of approximately $9,436.6 billion. Comparing the 2002 real GDP with the 1985 real GDP shows that real GDP increased about 83 percent over the period. The remainder of the increase in nominal GDP can be attributed to the 50 percent increase in the price level between 1985 and 2002. (The 2002 price level of 1.107 is approximately 50 percent higher than the 1985 price level of 0.737.)

**THE CONSUMER PRICE INDEX**   Although the GDP deflator is the most broadly based price index for the U.S. economy, it is not the best-known one. That honor

TABLE 6.6 NOMINAL GDP, REAL GDP, AND THE GDP DEFLATOR, 1967–2002

(Dollars in Billions)

| Year | Nominal GDP | Real GDP | GDP Deflator |
|------|-------------|----------|--------------|
| 1967 | 834.1 | 3,640.0 | 0.252 |
| 1968 | 911.5 | 3,795.4 | 0.263 |
| 1969 | 985.4 | 3,897.2 | 0.276 |
| 1970 | 1,039.7 | 3,911.0 | 0.291 |
| 1971 | 1,128.6 | 4,025.7 | 0.305 |
| 1972 | 1,240.4 | 4,221.6 | 0.318 |
| 1973 | 1,385.6 | 4,431.8 | 0.336 |
| 1974 | 1,501.0 | 4,415.5 | 0.366 |
| 1975 | 1,635.2 | 4,408.1 | 0.400 |
| 1976 | 1,823.9 | 4,627.8 | 0.423 |
| 1977 | 2,031.4 | 4,826.7 | 0.450 |
| 1978 | 2,295.9 | 5,066.4 | 0.482 |
| 1979 | 2,566.4 | 5,201.0 | 0.522 |
| 1980 | 2,795.6 | 5,170.1 | 0.570 |
| 1981 | 3,131.4 | 5,260.1 | 0.624 |
| 1982 | 3,259.2 | 5,163.5 | 0.663 |
| 1983 | 3,535.0 | 5,348.6 | 0.689 |
| 1984 | 3,932.8 | 5,671.8 | 0.714 |
| 1985 | 4,213.0 | 5,875.8 | 0.737 |
| 1986 | 4,452.9 | 6,056.0 | 0.753 |
| 1987 | 4,742.5 | 6,236.7 | 0.776 |
| 1988 | 5,108.3 | 6,476.0 | 0.802 |
| 1989 | 5,489.1 | 6,685.0 | 0.833 |
| 1990 | 5,803.3 | 6,799.2 | 0.865 |
| 1991 | 5,986.2 | 6,751.9 | 0.897 |
| 1992 | 6,319.0 | 6,941.4 | 0.918 |
| 1993 | 6,642.3 | 7,098.4 | 0.940 |
| 1994 | 7,054.3 | 7,369.8 | 0.960 |
| 1995 | 7,400.6 | 7,546.9 | 0.981 |
| 1996 | 7,813.2 | 7,813.2 | 1.000 |
| 1997 | 8,318.4 | 8,165.4 | 1.019 |
| 1998 | 8,781.5 | 8,550.7 | 1.032 |
| 1999 | 9,274.3 | 8,973.4 | 1.047 |
| 2000 | 9,824.7 | 9,379.3 | 1.069 |
| 2001 | 10,082.2 | 9,438.3 | 1.094 |
| 2002 | 10,446.3 | 9,779.4 | 1.107 |

This table shows nominal and real GDP and the GDP deflator for the U.S. economy for the years 1967 to 2002. The base year for the GDP deflator is 1996. To calculate real GDP in constant 1996 dollars for any current year, divide current-year nominal GDP by the GDP deflator. Your answer may differ slightly from the real GDP given in the table because of rounding.

Source: U.S. Department of Commerce, Bureau of Economic Analysis, *National Income and Product Accounts*, November 2003.

belongs to the consumer price index. Rather than taking into account the prices of all final goods and services produced in the economy, as the GDP deflator does, the **consumer price index (CPI)** considers only the goods and services that make up the "market basket" purchased by a typical urban household. For example, the CPI market basket includes cars, but not railway locomotives.

**Consumer price index (CPI)**

A price index based on the market basket of goods and services purchased by a typical urban household.

Table 6.7 presents values for the CPI (stated in index form) from 1967 to 2002. The CPI uses the period 1982–1984 rather than a single year as its base year. The appendix to this chapter explains how the CPI is calculated.

The CPI plays a key role in the economy partly because it is widely used to index wages, government transfers, and many other payments. As explained in Chapter 4, indexation of a payment means automatically adjusting it on a regular schedule for changes in the price index involved. Take, for example, the indexing of social security payments. From 2000 to 2002 the CPI rose from 177.1 to 179.9, an increase of 1.6 percent. As a result, social security payments were automatically increased by the same percentage. Millions of workers whose contracts include *cost-of-living-adjustment* (*COLA*) clauses also receive automatic raises as a result of increases in the CPI.

## Producer Price Indexes

**Producer price index (PPI)**

A price index based on a sample of goods and services bought by business firms.

Another widely publicized set of price indexes consists of **producer price indexes**. These are price averages for three classes of goods that are traded among business firms. Table 6.7 shows the producer price index for *finished goods*—investment goods sold to businesses plus other goods that are ready for final use but have not yet been sold to consumers, for example, wholesale sales of clothing to clothing stores. Other producer price indexes cover intermediate goods and crude materials ready for further processing. The producer price indexes use a base year of 1982. Because producer price indexes measure prices at early stages in the production process, they are often studied for hints of trends in consumer prices. They are also frequently used to index payments that firms agree to make to one another.

The GDP deflator, CPI, and producer price indexes by no means exhaust the possible ways of measuring changes in the price level. There are many other indexes, including regional price indexes and special-purpose indexes that give higher or lower weights to various items.

## How Good Are the National Income Accounts?

This chapter began by stressing the importance of the national income accounts to economics and warning that they are less than perfect. Now that we have surveyed the main components of the nominal and real national income accounts, it is time to try to answer the question of how good those accounts are. We will focus on four possible problem areas: the accuracy and timeliness of the data, the underground sector of the economy, bias in price indexes, and the nonmaterial aspects of the standard of living.

**TABLE 6.7    CONSUMER AND PRODUCER PRICE INDEXES, 1967–2002**

| Year | CPI | PPI (finished goods) |
|------|------|------|
| 1967 | 33.4 | 35.6 |
| 1968 | 34.8 | 36.7 |
| 1969 | 36.7 | 38.0 |
| 1970 | 38.8 | 39.3 |
| 1971 | 40.5 | 40.5 |
| 1972 | 41.8 | 41.8 |
| 1973 | 44.4 | 45.6 |
| 1974 | 49.3 | 52.6 |
| 1975 | 53.8 | 58.2 |
| 1976 | 56.9 | 60.8 |
| 1977 | 60.6 | 64.7 |
| 1978 | 65.2 | 69.8 |
| 1979 | 72.6 | 77.6 |
| 1980 | 82.4 | 88.0 |
| 1981 | 90.9 | 96.2 |
| 1982 | 96.5 | 100.0 |
| 1983 | 99.6 | 101.6 |
| 1984 | 103.9 | 103.7 |
| 1985 | 107.6 | 104.6 |
| 1986 | 109.7 | 103.3 |
| 1987 | 113.6 | 105.4 |
| 1988 | 118.3 | 108.0 |
| 1989 | 123.9 | 113.5 |
| 1990 | 130.7 | 119.1 |
| 1991 | 136.2 | 121.7 |
| 1992 | 140.3 | 123.2 |
| 1993 | 144.5 | 124.7 |
| 1994 | 148.2 | 125.5 |
| 1995 | 152.4 | 127.9 |
| 1996 | 156.9 | 131.3 |
| 1997 | 160.5 | 131.8 |
| 1998 | 163.0 | 130.7 |
| 1999 | 166.6 | 133.0 |
| 2000 | 172.2 | 138.0 |
| 2001 | 177.1 | 140.7 |
| 2002 | 179.9 | 138.9 |

This table shows two commonly used price indexes that are more narrowly based than the GDP deflator. The first is the consumer price index, which is based on a market basket of goods purchased by a typical urban household. The second is the producer price index for finished goods, which is based on a sample of finished goods traded among business firms.

**ACCURACY AND TIMELINESS** Government decision makers pay close attention to national income accounting data to get an indication of economic trends as they unfold. Unfortunately, however, there is a trade-off between the timeliness and the accuracy of data. For example, in July 2003, the U.S. Department of Commerce released an "advance" estimate of second-quarter real GDP growth equal to 2.4 percent. Later in August 2003, that estimate was revised to 3.1 percent, then again in September to 3.3 percent. Some observers think that cuts in the budgets of statistical agencies, combined with demands to speed the release of data, are making the problems of accuracy and timeliness worse. In later chapters we will see that lags in the availability of accurate data on GDP, inflation, and other economic quantities have major implications for policy makers' ability to tune economic policy to fit events as they unfold.

**THE UNDERGROUND ECONOMY** The economic activity that is measured in the national income accounts constitutes the observed sector of the economy. But a vast amount of production, consumption, and investment is never officially measured. This unobserved sector includes activities ranging from teenage baby-sitting to multimillion-dollar drug and gambling rings to the multibillion-dollar value of cooking, cleaning, and child care performed in the home. The national income accounts attempt to consider this unobserved sector when they include estimates of the rental value of owner-occupied housing and the value of food produced and consumed on farms. Those items are only the tip of the iceberg, however. The bulk of the unobserved sector is missing from the official accounts. Although no one knows exactly how big this sector is, some parts of it are known to be enormous.

Some have estimated that organized crime produces some $150 billion a year in illegal goods and services in the form of drugs, gambling, pornography, and so on. If this estimate is correct, it makes organized crime the second-largest industry in the United States after the oil industry. However, organized crime is probably not the largest sector of the so-called underground economy. The unreported income of businesses and self-employed people may add as much as $250 billion. This includes cash income that goes unreported for tax purposes (for example, a concert pianist giving occasional piano lessons) and barter transactions that involve no cash at all (for example, the pianist gets her teeth straightened in exchange for giving piano lessons to her orthodontist's child).

But even if the U.S. underground economy amounts to as much as 10 percent of officially measured GDP, that proportion is moderate by world standards. The French underground economy is thought to equal one-third of that country's GDP; in Italy, the figure may be 40 percent; and in many third world countries, the official GDP data bear only the haziest relationship to what is actually going on in the economy.

**PRICE INDEX BIASES** A third problem with the official statistics is that of price index biases. The accuracy with which changes in price levels are measured became a matter of growing concern as inflation increased in the late 1970s and indexing and automatic cost-of-living adjustments became more widespread. If the official price indexes are found to understate inflation, policy makers should perhaps make a greater effort to restore price stability. On the other hand, if price indexes overstate inflation, contracts that provide automatic adjustments for inflation may be too generous.

The problem of price index biases has been closely studied, and the results are far from reassuring. The consumer price index has been criticized for two built-in biases that have caused it to overstate inflation: substitution bias and quality bias.

*Substitution Bias.* The first reason that the consumer price index tends to overstate the true rate of increase in the cost of living is the so-called substitution bias. As the appendix to this chapter explains, the CPI is a weighted average of the prices of goods that are typically purchased by urban consumers. Because the weights used to calculate the index remain constant, they always reflect patterns of consumption at some point in the past. (They now reflect consumption patterns in the 1982 to 1984 base period.) However, because patterns change over time, the weights typically are not those of the most recent year being observed.

If changes in buying patterns were random, an obsolete set of weights would cause only random errors, not an upward bias, in the CPI. The bias results from the fact that consumer demand is influenced by changes in relative prices. As time passes, consumers tend to buy less of the goods whose prices have risen most and more of those whose prices have lagged behind the average or have actually fallen. Thus, the CPI tends to overstate the increase in the cost of living because it assigns unrealistically large weights to products whose prices have increased but that are consumed in relatively smaller amounts than formerly. For example, large increases in gasoline prices in the 1970s eventually led consumers to purchase more fuel-efficient cars, and thus to consume less gasoline. During such a period, the weight given to gasoline is too high. The market basket on which the CPI is based is periodically adjusted to reflect such changes, but the adjustments are not frequent enough to remove the bias altogether.

*Quality Bias.* A second source of bias in the consumer price index is the failure to adjust product prices for changes in quality. It would be highly misleading, for example, to say that a 2004 model car costs three times as much as a 1984 model without considering the fact that the 2004 model gets better gas mileage, can be driven longer between tune-ups, and is much safer than the 1984 model. In terms of dollars per unit of transportation service, the newer model clearly would be less than three times as expensive.

For automobiles, computers, and a few other major goods, the Bureau of Labor Statistics does try to make quality adjustments. The importance of the effort can be seen in the case of electronic equipment ranging from calculators to mainframe computers. As recently as the late 1960s, it cost over $1,000 to buy a desk-size electromechanical calculator that would add, subtract, multiply, and divide. Today half of that sum will buy a basic personal computer, and a calculator equivalent to the 1960 model can be purchased for less than $5. A study of changes in computer quality led to large adjustments in price indexes since the 1980s. However, domestic income accountants do not have the resources to make such detailed studies of all items that enter into GDP.

**NONMATERIAL SOURCES OF WELFARE**  The final problem with GDP is that it measures only material sources of welfare (which, after all, is all it tries to do). Sometimes per capita GDP is used as an indication of living standards, but when one is comparing living standards over time and across countries, nonmaterial sources of welfare are important, too.

One key nonmaterial component of the standard of living is the quality of the environment. This not only varies widely from one place to another but has changed greatly over time. Today's problems of acid rain, toxic wastes, and nuclear radiation are "bads" that, in principle, should be subtracted from GDP just as "goods" are added to it. In the same spirit, Robert Repetto of the World Resources Institute in Washington, D.C., recommends that depletion of such natural resources as oil fields and tropical forests should be subtracted along with the capital consumption allowance in calculating net domestic product. For countries such as Indonesia and Brazil, which have used huge quantities of natural resources to fuel their growth, the effect of this adjustment could cut measured rates of economic growth nearly in half.

A second nonmaterial source of welfare is the state of human health. By broad measures, especially life expectancy, standards of health in the United Stares appear to be improving. For example, since World War II the life expectancy of a typical 45-year-old American has increased from 72 years to 77, and a 65-year-old American can now expect to live to the age of 81. This increase clearly improves human welfare even for people who add nothing to measured GDP after they retire from their jobs. If the improvement in health could be measured, it would add to the growth of U.S. GDP. On the other hand, such an adjustment would make the economic picture look even bleaker in a country like Russia, where health indicators such as life expectancy and infant mortality have gotten worse in recent years.

The list of nonmaterial sources of welfare is endless. How important are satisfying work, friendship, social justice, economic equality, and freedom? Everyone knows of people who have been willing to give up income and wealth in pursuit of these things. Yet they must remain unmeasured.

For all of these reasons, then, GDP cannot be used as a measure of the true level of human welfare and can be used only with the greatest caution even for comparisons of material welfare in different times and places.

# SUMMARY

1.  **How is gross domestic product officially defined and measured?** Two domestic product concepts are featured in the official accounts of the United States. *Gross domestic product (GDP)* is defined as the value at current market prices of all *final goods and services* produced annually in a given country. *Gross national product* is the product produced by a country's factors of production, regardless of what country they are located in. *Net domestic product* is derived from GDP by subtracting a capital consumption allowance that reflects the value of capital goods worn out during the year.

2.  **How does the measurement of national income and domestic income differ from the measurement of gross domestic product?** *National income* is the sum of wages and supplements, rental income of persons, corporate profits, and proprietors' income earned by a country's residents. Domestic income equals national income minus net receipts of factor income from the rest of the world. Gross domestic product and domestic income differ by the amount of the capital consumption allowance, indirect business taxes, and the statistical discrepancy. *Personal income* is the total income that a country's resident households receive. Personal income includes transfer payments, which households receive but do not earn, and excludes contributions to social insurance, taxes on corporate profits, and undistributed corporate profits, which households earn but do not receive. Personal income less personal taxes equals *disposable personal income.*

3.  **What are the major types of international transactions?** Many types of transactions appear in the nation's international accounts. Exports less imports of goods constitute the *merchandise balance.* Adding net exports of services yields net exports of goods and services. Adding net international transfers (normally a negative number for the United States) yields the most widely publicized balance-of-payments measure, the *current account balance.* In addition, the international accounts record the capital inflows and outflows resulting from private financial transactions and official reserve transactions by the Federal Reserve and foreign central banks.

4.  **How are changes in the average level of prices measured?** The *GDP deflator* is the most broadly based measure of the *price level.* It can be viewed as a weighted average of the prices of all final goods and services that go into GDP. The *consumer price index (CPI)* includes only the market basket of goods purchased by a typical urban household. The *producer price index (PPI)* is based on goods that are typically bought and sold by business firms.

5.  **What are the limitations of official economic statistics?** The national income statistics of the United States are considered to be among the best in the world. However, they have some limitations. Potential problem areas include timeliness of data, the unobserved sector of the economy, price index biases, and nonmaterial aspects of the standard of living.

# KEY TERMS

National income accounts

Gross domestic product (GDP)

Final goods and services

Value added

Gross national product (GNP)

Net domestic product (NDP)

National income

Personal income

Disposable personal income (disposable income)

Current account

Merchandise balance
Current account balance
Capital account GDP
   deflator
Base year
Price level

Price index
Consumer price index
   (CPI)
Producer price index
   (PPI)

## PROBLEMS AND TOPICS FOR DISCUSSION

1. **Examining the lead-off case.** How are the data reported in the article measured? What do the article and subsequent revisions to data reported there suggest regarding the trade-off between the timeliness and accuracy of economic data? Why was the accumulation of inventories during the third quarter viewed as a worrisome sign by some observers?

2. **Updating the national income accounts.** Using the *Economic Report of the President* or another suitable data source, update the national income accounts in this chapter to the most recent year. Note that in some ways the official statistics are more detailed than those given in the text.

3. **Inventory in the national income accounts.** Suppose that a firm sells $10,000 worth of shoes that it has held in inventory for several years. What happens to GDP as a result? Which of its components are affected, and how?

4. **Payroll taxes in the national income accounts.** Suppose that the government raises employers' share of the social security payroll tax from 6 percent of wages to 10 percent. What happens to GDP, domestic income, national income, and personal income?

5. **International accounts.** Following the pattern of the table in Table 6.5, show how the international

accounts might look for a year in which there was a $50 billion surplus on current account, no official reserve transactions, and no statistical discrepancy. What would the capital account balance have to be?

6. **The current account deficit.** "A current account deficit is a very healthy thing. If we can get foreigners to give us real goods and services and talk them into taking pieces of paper in return, why should we want anything different?" Do you agree or disagree with this statement? Discuss.

7. **Real and nominal quantities.** In 1982 to 1984, the base period used for the consumer price index, the average earnings of construction workers were $442.74 per week. By 1989 the earnings of construction workers had reached $506.72 per week, but the consumer price index had risen to 124.0. What were construction workers' real earnings in 1989 stated in 1982–1984 dollars?

8. **Changes** in **prices and qualities.** Try to find a mail-order catalog that is at least ten years old; also find a recent catalog. Compare the ads for various items. By how much has the price of each item gone up? What changes in quality have occurred? Assuming that you could buy at list price from either the new catalog or the old one, which items would you buy from the old one and which from the new one?

## CASE FOR DISCUSSION

### *Laid-Off Steel Workers Join the Underground Economy*

**HOMESTEAD, PA.**—A half-dozen men lounge on metal folding chairs outside a storefront on Ann Street, sweating in the muggy afternoon air and talking baseball. A pay phone rings inside, and a young man runs to answer it. Moments later, he speeds off in a long, beat-up sedan.

The man is about to cheat the government. He and the other men drive people around town for a fee, but they don't pay any taxes on the fares they receive. What's more, they don't see why they should.

Most of the men used to work at the sprawling Homestead Works a half block away. Now that the steel mill has closed, their car service allows them to make a living. "It ain't bothering anyone. It ain't stealing," says Earl Jones, who was laid off last December after 36 years at the mill. How much does he make? "Ain't saying," he replies with a smile.

The men are part of a vast underground economy made up of people who work "off the books" for cash. From the tired mill towns of the Midwest to the oil patches dotting the Southwest, the underground thrives. In communities that have suddenly lost a major employer, it helps those who were laid off make ends meet, and it helps keep towns like Homestead alive.

The number of Homestead residents with off-the-books livelihoods began to increase in the early 1980s when USX Corporation's Homestead Works, which employed about 15,000 at its peak, started to lay off workers in droves. The mill's few remaining workers lost their jobs early in 1986. For most residents here, where only half the people have their high-school diplomas, the mill was all there was.

After they were laid off, many older workers retired and some of the younger ones withdrew their savings and migrated south, chasing dreams of work in more prosperous states. But many others stayed, bound by their unmarketable homes, their families,

or a strong sense of community. Unable to find legitimate jobs, they have parlayed their handyman skills underground.

One former mill worker says that half the people he knows are working off the books. For the most part, they are intensely proud people who hang the American flag from their neat front porches on holidays and respect the law, believing strongly in right and wrong. They definitely don't like the underground's seamy side—thefts and drugs. But their changed circumstances have altered the way many of them think.

"You tell me. Your kids go to bed crying at night because they're hungry. Is 'off the books' going to bother you?" asks a former steelworker.

In the fall of 2003, President Bush repealed trade legislation that would have protected steel manufacturers from international competition. While this move was very unpopular in states that still have high employment in steel manufacturing, it was lauded in states that rely on steel to produce finished goods.

Source: Clare Ansberry, "Laid-Off Steelworkers Find That Tax Evasion Helps Make Ends Meet," *The Wall Street Journal*, October 1, 1986, 1. Reprinted by permission of *The Wall Street Journal*, © Dow Jones & Company, Inc., 1986. All Rights Reserved Worldwide.

## QUESTIONS

1. What are the advantages of working "off the books" from the viewpoint of the people involved?
2. How might the failure to measure off-the-books activity affect economic policy decisions?
3. How might off-the-books work affect the statistical discrepancy in the national income accounts?

# Appendix to Chapter 6
## COMPUTATION OF PRICE INDEXES

This appendix provides further information on the GDP deflator and consumer price index. Knowing these details will make it easier to see the differences between the two indexes and to understand the source of the substitution bias, which affects each one differently.

### The GDP Deflator for a Simple Economy

A much simpler economy than that of the United States will serve to illustrate the computation of price indexes. Table 6A.1 shows price and quantity data for two years for an economy in which only three goods are produced: movies, apples, and shirts. The exhibit shows that nominal GDP grew from $1,000 in 1996 to $1,700 in 2002. But what do these figures indicate? Do they mean that people really had more of the things they wanted in 2002 than in 1996? More precisely, do they mean that people had 1.7 times as much? These questions cannot be easily answered by looking at the exhibit in its present form.

A line-by-line comparison of the two years shows that the figures on nominal product do not tell the whole story. Clearly, prices went up sharply between 1996 and 2002. Movies and apples cost more than one and a half times what they used to, and shirts nearly that much. The amounts of goods produced have also changed. Twice as many movies and shirts were produced in 2002 as in 1996, but only half as many apples.

If we wish to know how much better off people were in 2002 than in 1996, we need a way to separate the quantity changes that have taken place from the price changes. One way to do this is to ask how much the total value of output would have changed from 1996 to 2002 if prices had not changed. This approach gives the results shown in Table 6A.2. There we see

**TABLE 6A.1  NOMINAL GDP FOR A SIMPLE ECONOMY**

| 1996 | Quantity | Price | Value |
|---|---|---|---|
| Movies | 50 | $5.00 | $250 |
| Apples | 1,000 | .60 | 600 |
| Shirts | 10 | 15.00 | 150 |
| 1996 nominal GDP | | | $1,000 |
| **2002** | | | |
| Movies | 100 | $8.00 | $800 |
| Apples | 500 | .80 | 400 |
| Shirts | 20 | 25.00 | 500 |
| 2002 nominal GDP | | | $1,700 |

In this simple economy in which only three goods are produced, nominal domestic product grew from $1,000 in 1996 to $1,700 in 2002. But because prices also went up during that time, people did not really have 1.7 times as many goods in 2002 as they did in 1996.

that the 2002 output of 100 movies, 500 apples, and 20 shirts, which had a value of $1,700 in terms of the prices at which the goods were actually sold, would have had a value of only $1,100 in terms of the prices that prevailed in 1996. The $1,100 thus is a measure of real GDP for 2002. It is this measure that we should compare with the 1996 GDP of $1,000 if we want to know what really happened to output between the two years. Instead of having 170 percent as much output in 2002 as in 1996, as indicated by the change in nominal GDP from $1,000 to $1,700, the people in this simple economy really had only about 110 percent as much, as indicated by the change in real GDP from $1,000 to $1,000.

Now we know how to compute real and nominal GDP for 2002 directly from price and quantity data without using a price index to convert nominal values into real values. But although we have not explicitly used a price index, we have created one implicitly. This implicit index, or implicit GDP deflator, is the ratio of current-year nominal GDP to current-year real GDP times 100, as expressed in index form by the following formula:

$$\text{GDP delator} = \frac{\text{Current-year output valued at current-year prices}}{\text{Current-year output valued at base-year prices}} \times 100.$$

Applying the formula to the data in Tables 6A.1 and 6A.2 gives a value of 154.5 for the deflator.

### The Consumer Price Index for a Simple Economy

The consumer price index differs from the GDP deflator in two ways. First, as mentioned in Chapter 6, it takes into account only the prices of goods and services consumed by a typical urban household. Second, it is calculated according to a formula that uses base-year rather than current-year quantities. The first difference does not matter for this simple economy in which all goods are consumer goods, but the second does, as Table 6A.3 shows.

To calculate the CPI for this economy, instead of asking how much current-year output would have cost at base-year prices, we begin by asking how much base-year output would

TABLE 6A.2   NOMINAL AND REAL GDP FOR A SIMPLE ECONOMY

| Good | 2002 Quantity | 2002 Price | Value of 2000 Quantity at 1996 Price | 1996 Price | Value of 2002 Quantity at 1996 Price |
|------|------|------|------|------|------|
| Movies | 100 | $8.00 | 800 | $ 5.00 | $   500 |
| Apples | 500 | .80 | 400 | .60 | 300 |
| Shirts | 20 | 25.00 | 500 | 15.00 | 300 |
| Totals | | | $1,700 | | $1,100 |

**2002 nominal GDP = $1,700; 2002 real GDP = $1,100**

This table shows how the figures from Table 6A.1 can be adjusted to take changing prices into account. The 2002 quantities are multiplied by 1996 prices to get the value of 2002 GDP that would have existed had prices not changed. The total of 2002 quantities valued at 1996 prices is a measure of real GDP for 2002 stated in constant 1996 dollars. The implicit GDP deflator for 2002, calculated as the ratio of 2002 nominal GDP to 1996 real GDP, has a value of 154.5.

**TABLE 6A.3   A CONSUMER PRICE INDEX FOR A SIMPLE ECONOMY**

| Good | 1996 Quantity | 1996 Price | Value of 1996 Quantity at 2002 Price | 2002 Price | Value of 1996 Quantity at 2002 Price |
|------|------|------|------|------|------|
| Movies | 50 | $5.00 | 250 | $8.00 | $ 400 |
| Apples | 1,000 | .60 | 600 | .80 | 800 |
| Shirts | 10 | 15.00 | 150 | 25.00 | 250 |
| Totals | | | $1,000 | | $1,450 |

$$\text{CPI} = \frac{\$1,450}{\$1,000} \times 100 = 145.0$$

The consumer price index can be calculated as the base-year market basket of goods valued at current-year prices divided by the base-year market basket valued at base-year prices multiplied by 100. This table shows how such an index can be calculated for a simple economy. The 1996 output cost $1,000 at the prices at which it was actually sold. Had it been sold at 2002 prices, it would have cost $1,450. Thus, the CPI for 2002 is 145.0.

have cost at current-year prices. We then calculate the index as the ratio of the two different valuations of base-year quantities:

$$\text{Consumer price index} = \frac{\text{Base-year market basket valued at current-year prices}}{\text{Base-year market basket valued at base-year prices}} \times 100.$$

The CPI is calculated using base-year quantities partly because data on current prices are easier to collect than data on current output. This index, therefore, can be announced each month with little delay.

## Comparing the CPI and the GDP Deflator

As Table 6A.3 shows, the CPI for 2002 in our simple economy had a value of 145.0, whereas the GDP deflator for 2002 was 154.5. Both indexes were calculated using the same data, and both used 1996 as a base year. Which, if either, is the true measure of the change in prices between the two years?

The answer is that neither the CPI nor the GDP deflator is the only correct measure of change in the price level; instead, each answers a different question. The GDP deflator answers the question, "How much more did the 2002 output cost at the prices at which it was actually sold than it would have cost had it been sold at 1996 prices?" The CPI, in contrast, answers the question, "How much more would the 1996 output have cost had it been sold at 2002 prices instead of at 1996 prices?"

A close look at the data shows why the answers to the two questions differ. In 1996, lots of apples and few shirts were produced compared with 2002. Yet between the two years the price of apples increased 33 percent whereas the price of shirts increased 67 percent. Because the CPI uses base-year quantities, it gives a heavy weight to apples, which showed the smallest relative price increase, and a lower weight to shirts, which showed only a larger price increase. In contrast, the GDP deflator uses current-year quantities, thereby decreasing the importance of apples and increasing that of shirts.

In actuality, because people will tend to substitute purchases away from items with faster growth in prices, the CPI tends to have an upward substitution bias relative to the GDP deflator. However, that does not make the GDP deflator a true measure of change in the cost of living. It could just as easily be said that the GDP deflator has a downward substitution bias relative to the CPI or that each has an opposite bias from some "true" price index. As yet there is no foolproof way to calculate the true cost-of-living index, although some interesting attempts have been made. A discussion of these more complex types of price indexes would take us far beyond the scope of this book. However, the basic types of price indexes covered here are the ones that are most commonly used for policy-making purposes.

# PART III

# Models of Aggregate Income and Product

# The Aggregate Supply and Demand Model

1. The conditions that determine the slope of the aggregate demand curve.
2. The sources of shifts in the aggregate demand curve.
3. The conditions that determine the slopes of short- and long-run aggregate supply curves.
4. The sources of shifts in the aggregate supply curves.
5. How prices, real output, and unemployment behave as the economy responds to a change in aggregate demand.

*Before reading this chapter, make sure you know the meaning of:*

1. Supply and demand
2. Elasticity
3. Real and nominal values
4. Natural level of real output
5. Money
6. Aggregate supply and demand
7. Final goods
8. Price level

## WE WEREN'T TALKING REVOLUTION; WE WERE TALKING JOBS

Ed Paulsen's family was from South Dakota. He finished high school in 1930, as the country was sliding toward the Great Depression. He went West to pick apples in Washington state and then worked on road gangs. In 1931 he ended up in San Francisco. These are his words.

I tried to get a job on the docks. I was a big husky athlete, but there just wasn't any work. Already by that time, if you were looking for a job at a standard oil service station you had to have a college degree. It was that kind of market . . .

I'd get up at five in the morning and head for the waterfront. Outside the Spreckles Sugar Refinery, outside the gates, there would be a thousand men. You know dang well there's only three or four jobs. The guy would come out with two little Pinkerton cops: "I need two guys for the bull gang. Two guys to go into the hole." A thousand men would fight like a pack of Alaskan dogs to get through there. Only four of us would get through. I was too young a punk . . .

These were fathers, 80 percent of them. They had held jobs and didn't want to kick society to pieces. They just wanted to go to work and they just couldn't understand. There was a mysterious thing. You watched the papers, you listened to rumors, you'd get word somebody's going to build a building.

So the next morning you get up at five o'clock and you dash over there. You got a big tip. There's three thousand men there, carpenters, cement men, guys who knew machinery and everything else. These fellas always had faith that the job was going to mature somehow. More and more men were after fewer and fewer jobs. . . .

We weren't greatly agitated in terms of society. Ours was a bewilderment, not an anger. Not a sense of being particularly put upon. We weren't talking revolution; we were talking jobs.

Source: Excerpts from Studs Terkel, *Hard Times: An Oral History of the Great Depression* (New York: Pantheon Books, 1970), 29–31.

➛

THE GREAT DEPRESSION of the 1930s, when hundreds of men would fight over a day's work as a common laborer, brought many changes to law, politics, and social consciousness. It also created a revolution in economic thought. Before the Great Depression, economists had, of course, observed and analyzed the business cycles that interrupted the nation's prosperity from time to time. However, many of them saw such episodes as temporary and believed that recovery from them was automatic. Then, following the spectacular stock market crash of 1929, the economy slid into a depression from which there seemed no hope of rebounding.

Prices fell. Wages fell. Real output fell. Unemployment soared until nearly one-quarter of the labor force was out of work. These conditions lasted not months but years. Although the economy hit rock bottom in 1933, it did not return to its 1929 level of real output for a full decade. What went wrong?

The most influential attempt to answer this question proved to be that of the British economist John Maynard Keynes. Keynes brought a new perspective to the economy that emphasized the relationships among broad economic aggregates—national income and product, consumption, investment, and saving. He attempted to integrate this approach with an understanding of the role of money and interest rates in the economy, as well as with theories of employment and the labor market. He published the results in his aptly named *General Theory of Employment, Interest, and Money*, which became one of the most influential books of the century. (See *Who Said It? Who Did It? 7.1*)

By no means have all the details of Keynes's work withstood the test of time. Many of his ideas about the ability of government policy to manipulate and stabilize the economy seem overly sanguine today. Nevertheless, his general approach has left its mark. The theory presented in this and later chapters, to which many economists

---

### ☜ WHO SAID IT? WHO DID IT? 7.1
### JOHN MAYNARD KEYNES: *THE GENERAL THEORY*

John Maynard Keynes was born into economics. His father, John Neville Keynes, was a lecturer in economics and logic at Cambridge University. John Maynard Keynes began his own studies at Cambridge in mathematics and philosophy. However, his abilities so impressed Alfred Marshall that the distinguished teacher urged him to concentrate on economics. In 1908, after Keynes had finished his studies and done a brief stint in the civil service, Marshall offered him a lectureship in economics at Cambridge; Keynes accepted.

Keynes is best remembered for his 1936 work, *The General Theory of Employment, Interest, and Money*, a book that many still see as the foundation of what is today called macroeconomics. Although this was by no means Keynes's first major work, it was the basis for his reputation as the outstanding economist of his generation. Its major features are a bold theory based on broad macroeconomic aggregates and a strong argument for activist and interventionist policies.

Keynes was interested in more than economics. He was an honored member not only of Britain's academic upper class, but also of the nation's highest financial, political, diplomatic, administrative, and even artistic circles. He had close ties to the colorful "Bloomsbury set" of London's literary world. He was a friend of Virginia Woolf, E. M. Forster, and Lytton Strachey, and in 1925 he married ballerina Lydia

Lopokovia. He was a dazzling success at whatever he turned his hand to, from mountain climbing to financial speculation. As a speculator, he made a huge fortune for himself; as bursar of Kings College, he built an endowment of 30,000 pounds into one of over 380,000 pounds.

In *The General Theory*, Keynes wrote:

The idea of economists and political philosophers, both when they are right and when they are wrong, are more powerful than is commonly understood. Indeed the world is ruled by little else. Practical men, who believe themselves to be quite exempt from any intellectual influences, are usually the slaves of some defunct economist. Madmen in authority, who hear voices in the air, are distilling their frenzy from some academic scribbler of a few years back. . . . There are not many who are influenced by new theories after they are twenty-five or thirty years of age, so that the ideas which civil servants and politicians and even agitators apply to current events are not likely to be the newest.

Was Keynes issuing a warning here? Whether or not he had any such thing in mind, his words are ironic because he himself has become one of the historical economists whose ideas remain influential long after they were first articulated.

have contributed over the years, is often called new-Keynesian economics. This chapter presents some key elements of the new-Keynesian approach in a version of the familiar supply-and-demand model, adapted to the aggregate economy. Chapters that follow add progressively more detail to the model.

# THE AGGREGATE DEMAND CURVE

Aggregate demand means total planned expenditure; more precisely, aggregate demand means total planned expenditure on *final goods*. In this section, we will examine the relationship between total planned expenditure on final goods and services measured in real terms—real aggregate demand—and the average level of prices of final goods and services. When represented graphically, this relationship is known as the **aggregate demand curve**. Figure 7.1 shows a typical aggregate demand curve.

## Aggregate and Market Demand Curves

An analogy can be drawn between the aggregate demand curve for the economy as a whole and the demand curves for individual markets. Both kinds of curves represent inverse relationships between price and quantity variables. Both summarize the market choices made by many individual buyers. And, as we will show, both kinds of curves interact with other curves representing supply to determine equilibrium conditions. However, there are some important differences between the aggregate demand curve and market demand curves. Two of those differences concern the "other things being equal" conditions that lie behind the curves.

    1. The market demand curve for a good such as corn is drawn on the assumption that the prices of all other goods remain constant as the price of corn varies. No comparable assumption is made for the aggregate demand curve. As the economy moves along the aggregate demand curve, the prices of any or all goods and services produced by the economy may change as the average level of prices changes.

    2. A market demand curve is drawn on the assumption that consumers' nominal incomes remain constant at all points along the demand curve. The same is not true of nominal domestic income in relation to the aggregate demand curve. Changes in aggregate demand associated with changes in the price level cause the circular flow of income and product to expand or contract. Thus, as the economy moves along the aggregate demand curve in response to changes in the price level, nominal domestic income does not necessarily remain constant.

These points should be kept in mind as we address the question of the slope of the aggregate demand curve. It is tempting to reason that the aggregate demand curve must have a negative slope simply because the individual demand curves for all the

**Aggregate demand curve**

A graph showing the relationship between real planned expenditures on final goods and the average price level of final goods.

**FIGURE 7.1   AN AGGREGATE DEMAND CURVE**

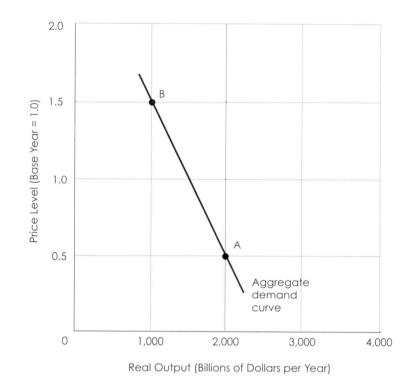

The aggregate demand curve shows the relationship between total real planned expenditure on final goods and the average price level of final goods. The curve has a negative slope because each of the major components of real aggregate demand—consumption, planned investment, government purchases, and net exports—varies inversely with the price level of final goods. Aggregate demand is relatively inelastic with respect to changes in the price level. As a result, nominal aggregate demand (real aggregate demand times the price level) increases as one moves up along the curve. For example, nominal aggregate demand is $1,000 billion at point A and $1,500 billion at point B.

goods entering into aggregate demand have negative slopes. But because the two kinds of demand curves involve different "other things being equal" assumptions, such a line of reasoning is invalid. A different approach must be taken instead.

## *The Slope of the Aggregate Demand Curve*

The best approach to understanding the slope of the aggregate demand curve is to break down aggregate demand into its principal components: consumption, investment, government purchases, and net exports. By looking at how decisions regarding the real levels of each of these components are affected by changes in the price level, we can understand why the aggregate demand curve as a whole has a negative slope.

**CONSUMPTION**   We begin by considering how the real demand for consumer goods is affected by an increase in the average level of prices. When the price level rises, firms' earnings from sales of goods and services rise by the same proportion. As those earnings are passed along to households in the form of factor payments and profits, consumers' nominal incomes also rise proportionately. This shields them, in part, from the effects of inflation.

However, even if the gain in nominal income keeps up with the increase in the price level, consumers are not fully protected from the effects of inflation. The money that they hold in currency and balances in various kinds of bank accounts has a fixed nominal value. As the price level increases, the real purchasing power of these nominal money balances falls. For example, $100 in twenty-dollar bills might initially be enough to buy a week's worth of groceries; but if a person holds onto those five twenties for a year and the average price level rises 15 percent by the end of the year, the bills will buy only enough groceries to last about six days. Because of the falling real value of nominal money balances, then, consumers become less wealthy in terms of real purchasing power and will tend to buy less real output than they would have if the price level had not risen.

Similar reasoning would apply to a period during which the price level fell. Although it has been many years since the United States has experienced a sustained drop in the price level, the effect of such a drop would be to increase the real value of consumers' nominal holdings of money. As the purchasing power of each dollar in circulation increased, real wealth would rise, real consumption would be stimulated, and real aggregate demand would increase. Taking both increases and decreases in the price level into account, then, we conclude that the real consumption component of aggregate demand varies inversely with the price level.

**INVESTMENT** Real investment will also be affected by changes in the price level, but for a different reason. As will be explained more fully in coming chapters, an increase in the price level tends to push interest rates higher. Higher interest rates raise the cost of borrowing and hence discourage firms from undertaking fixed investment. Higher interest rates also raise the costs of carrying inventories of finished products and raw materials; thus, firms may react by reducing their inventories. Therefore, an increase in the price level, via its effect on interest rates, causes the real planned investment component of aggregate demand to decrease. By similar reasoning, a decrease in the price level would cause interest rates to fall; as a result, real planned investment would tend to increase.

**GOVERNMENT PURCHASES** The effect of a change in the price level on real government purchases is not the same for all budget items or for all levels of government. Some government purchase decisions are made in real terms. For example, Congress might decide to authorize the Pentagon to buy 100 jet fighters. If the price per plane goes up, more dollars will be spent to purchase the authorized number of planes. However, other government purchase decisions are made in nominal terms. For example, the Virginia Department of Transportation may be given a budget of $50 million for road improvements. If the price of asphalt goes up, the department, constrained by its $50 million budget, will be unable to pave as many miles of roads as it had planned. Perhaps it will be able to persuade the legislature to increase it budget next year, but in the meantime the price increase results in less spending in real terms.

Generalizing from this example, we conclude that to the extent that some elements of government budgets (federal, state, and local) are set in nominal terms, the government purchases component of aggregate demand will tend to fall in real terms as the price level rises, at least in the short run.

**NET EXPORTS**   Prices can rise in one country and remain the same in others. Suppose, for example, that the United States experiences higher prices while prices in Japan stay the same. With a given exchange rate between the dollar and the Japanese yen, U.S. goods will become more expensive for Japanese buyers and Japanese goods will become relatively cheaper for U.S. buyers. As U.S. buyers switch from domestic goods to imports and U.S. exports become harder to sell abroad, the real net export component of aggregate demand falls.

A complete analysis of the effects of price-level changes on real net exports requires that one take into account changes in exchange rates and interest rates. These issues will be discussed in Chapter 18. Meanwhile, we simply note that at least under some circumstances, there will be an inverse relationship between the price level and the net export component of aggregate demand.

*Interactions among the Components*   As the price level changes, the changes in the real values of each of the components of aggregate demand interact with one another. In particular, changes in planned investment, government purchases, and net exports will affect the real incomes of households that work or supply capital to produce the goods and services that enter into those components of aggregate demand. An increase in the price level, which reduces the real demand for goods purchased for investment, use by government, and export, will cause real household income to decrease. In response to the decrease in real income, households will tend to decrease the quantities of consumer goods that they purchase. This provides an additional reason why real consumption expenditure decreases as the price level increases, beyond the impact on the real value of money balances that was mentioned earlier. These interactions among the components of aggregate demand will be explored in more detail in coming chapters.

## The Elasticity of Aggregate Demand

Our examination of real values of consumption, investment, government purchases, and net exports indicates that each component of real aggregate demand varies inversely with the price level. We conclude, then, that the aggregate demand curve as a whole must have a negative slope, as shown in Figure 7.1

It is sometimes useful to know the elasticity of a demand curve as well as whether its slope is positive or negative. For reasons that will be explained more fully in coming chapters, we will draw aggregate demand curves that are relatively inelastic with respect to changes in the average price level. This means that a given percentage change in the price level will cause a smaller percentage change in the level of real planned expenditure.

The price elasticity of demand for a single good determines what happens to revenues from sale of the good as its price changes. When the demand for a good is relatively elastic, an increase in its price will cause revenue to decrease, because a given percentage increase in the price will not increase the amount of revenue per unit enough to offset the larger percentage reduction in units sold. When demand is relatively inelastic, an increase in price will cause revenue to increase, because a given price increase will have a relatively small effect on the number of units sold.

Using similar reasoning, we can show that the elasticity of the aggregate demand curve determine how nominal aggregate demand is affected by a change in the average price level. Nominal aggregate demand means total demand for all final goods and services stated in terms of the prices at which they are actually sold. Nominal aggregate demand is equal to real aggregate demand times the price level. If aggregate demand is relatively inelastic, a given percentage increase in the price level will cause a smaller percentage decrease in real aggregate demand. As a result, nominal aggregate demand tends to increase as we move upward along a relatively inelastic aggregate demand curve.

Consider, for example, the aggregate demand curve in Figure 7.1. This curve is relatively inelastic along the segment from point A to point B.[1] At point A the price level is 0.5 and the quantity of real domestic product demanded is $2,000 billion. Nominal aggregate demand at point A thus is 0.5 × $2,000 billion, or $1,000 billion. As we move along the curve to point B, the price level rises from 0.5 to 1.5 and the quantity of real domestic product demanded falls from $2,000 billion to $1,000 billion. As a result, nominal aggregate demand at point B is $1,500 billion. Nominal aggregate demand thus is higher at point B than at point A, as would be expected for a relatively inelastic aggregate demand curve.

## Shifts in the Aggregate Demand Curve

As in the case of individual demand curves, a change in market conditions other than the price level will cause the aggregate demand curve to shift to the left or right. However, because of differences in the "other things being equal" assumptions underlying the two kinds of demand curves, the sources of the shifts are different. Among the sources of shifts in aggregate demand curves are expectations, changes in government policy, and changes in the world economy.

**EXPECTATIONS**   Expectations are one of the conditions that are held constant in drawing an aggregate demand curve. If consumers become more optimistic about the future, they may increase their real planned expenditures at any given price level.

Similarly, an increase in firms' optimism about future profit opportunities may increase real planned investment at any given price level. In either case, the aggregate demand curve shifts to the right, as illustrated by the shift from AD$_1$ to AD$_2$ in Figure 7.2. A swing toward pessimistic expectations by consumers or firms will shift the aggregate demand curve to the left.

**CHANGES IN GOVERNMENT POLICY**   Several kinds of changes in government policy can affect aggregate demand. An increase in the government purchases component of real planned expenditure, other things being equal, tends to shift the aggregate demand curve to the right. On the other hand, an increase in taxes, which cuts into consumers' disposable incomes, tends to depress the consumption component and shift the aggregate demand curve to the left. Finally, Federal Reserve policies that increase the economy's stock of money tend to shift the aggregate demand curve to the right, whereas policies that restrict the stock of money tend to shift it to the left. Policies dealing with government purchases, taxes, and the money stock are held constant in drawing a single aggregate demand curve.

**FIGURE 7.2   SHIFTS IN THE AGGREGATE DEMAND CURVE**

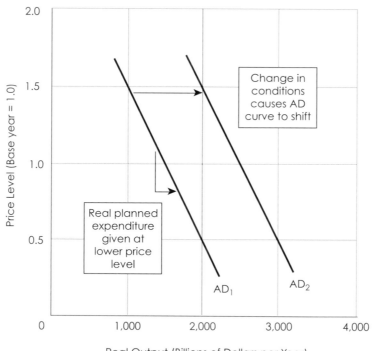

A change in economic conditions can cause the quantity of real planned expenditure associated with a given price level to change. In that case, the aggregate demand curve will shift, as shown in this diagram. Among the sources of shifts are changes in consumer or business expectations; changes in policies regarding government purchases, taxes, or money; and changes in the world economy.

**CHANGES IN THE WORLD ECONOMY** Events in foreign countries have an impact on aggregate demand in the United States via the net exports component of planned expenditure. For example, suppose that the rate of real economic growth increases in the economy of a major trading partner—say, Canada. When this happens, Canadian firms and consumers will tend to buy more imported goods, thereby boosting the real net exports component of U.S. aggregate demand. Also, changes in price levels in foreign countries will affect U.S. net exports by changing the relative prices of imported and exported goods. The effects of price-level changes may be felt, in part, through changes in the relative values of U.S. and Canadian currencies in foreign-exchange markets. The whole set of variables related to events in the world economy is held equal in drawing the aggregate demand curve.

## The Multiplier Effect

We see, then, that a shift in the aggregate demand curve can originate with a change in any of the components of demand—consumption, planned investment, government purchases, or net exports. However, the *magnitude* of the shift in the aggregate demand curve will be greater than that of the change in planned expenditure that ini-

∽ ECONOMICS IN THE NEWS 7.1
### CONSUMER CONFIDENCE SURGES

U.S. consumer confidence strengthened in November, supported by an improving job market and better returns in stocks, a survey showed on Wednesday, hinting that this holiday season may be better for retailers. The University of Michigan's final index of consumer sentiment for November rose to 93.7 from October's final reading of 89.6, market sources said. The 93.7 November reading is a high not seen in 18 months, said Steven Stanley, chief market economist at RBS Greenwich Capital Markets Inc. Eighteen months ago, he recalled, that May reading was itself a high not seen since December 2000.

The survey of consumers' mood follows a dramatic jump in confidence as gauged by the Conference Board, whose index jumped this month to highs not seen since Sept. 2002. Economists had expected the University of Michigan survey, which is released to subscribers, to rise to 94.0, given the sunnier jobs picture and a barrage of good economic news.

"It is going to be a pretty good holiday season in terms of consumer spending. We saw good consumption spending in the third quarter GDP data," said Frank Nothaft, chief economist at Freddie Mac.

But some economists warned that how consumers say they feel does not necessarily translate into actual spending.

"Your typical economic recovery is a virtuous cycle of spending, job creation, investments, and more spending. Each one fuels the other," said Chris Low, chief economist at FTN Financial, citing strong U.S. October durable goods data and a dramatic upward revision to third quarter economic growth.

Earlier Wednesday, the U.S. Commerce Department (news–web sites) said October durable goods orders jumped 3.3 percent. On Tuesday, Commerce reported that gross domestic product shot up at an 8.2 percent annual rate, the strongest advance in nearly 20 years. The University of Michigan survey's current conditions index rose to 102.5 from 99.9 and the expectations index, a gauge of perceptions about the economy over the next year, rose to 88.1 from 83.0.

The survey is based on telephone interviews with 500 U.S. households over the month on personal finances and business and buying conditions. Preliminary results, released about midway through the month, are based on the first 250 interviews.

Source: Aleksandra Rozens, "Consumer Sentiment Improves in November," *Reuters*, November 26, 2003.

tially causes the shift. The tendency for a given initial shift in any component of real aggregate demand to cause a larger shift in total real aggregate demand is known as the **multiplier effect**. The multiplier effect was first clearly explained by Keynes in *The General Theory*.

**MARGINAL PROPENSITY TO CONSUME**   The origin of the multiplier effect lies in the relationship between disposable income and consumption. Keynes argued that for each $1 change in real disposable income, households change their real consumption in the same direction by a fraction of a dollar. He called this fraction the **marginal propensity to consume**. For example, suppose that households tend to spend $.75 of every $1 of additional disposable income and save the rest. In this case, the marginal propensity to consume is .75. Given this marginal propensity to consume, a $100 million increase in disposable income for the economy as a whole will cause total consumption expenditure to rise by $75 million. Likewise, a $100 million drop in disposable income will cause consumption to fall by $75 million.

**A NUMERICAL EXAMPLE**   A numerical example can show how the multiplier effect works. Given a marginal propensity to consume of .75, let's trace the effects of a $100 million increase in planned investment arising from a shift toward greater optimism in business expectations. Specifically, we will assume that this decline takes the form of construction of new factories. The increase in planned investment initially adds $100 million to aggregate demand. It is recorded as the "first-round" effect in Table 7.1.

The $100 million increase in factory construction means $100 million of new income for construction workers, subcontractors, and materials suppliers. According to the assumed marginal propensity to consume, they will, in response, raise their consumption expenditures by $75 million. This $75 million is recorded in Table 7.1 as the "second-round" effect of the upturn in factory construction.

The repercussions of the upturn do not end here. The $75 million increase in consumption expenditures by construction workers and contractors means that their grocers, barbers, and so on will experience a $75 million increase in real income. For each dollar of added income, they too will increase their consumption expenditures by $.75. The resulting $56,250,000 increase in their real consumption is the "third-round" effect of the original upturn in factory construction.

Next, the grocers' and barbers' tailors and bartenders will feel the boost to their incomes; then the tailors' and bartenders' accountants and car dealers will be affected; and the process will continue for round after round, as shown in Table 7.1. There is, however, a limit to the *total* rise in real planned expenditures, because with each round the increase gets smaller. If the series given in the exhibit is added up over an infinite number of rounds, the total comes to $400 million, including $100 million of planned investment in the first round and a total of $300 million in consumption in all successive rounds. We can conclude that a $100 million rise in

---

**Multiplier effect**

The tendency for an initial $1 change in a component of aggregate demand to shift the aggregate demand curve in the same direction by more than $1.

**Marginal propensity to consume**

The proportion of each added dollar of real disposable income that households devote to real consumption.

**TABLE 7.1    THE MULTIPLIER EFFECT**

| Round | Increase in Real Income | Increase in Real Expenditure | |
|-------|------------------------|------------------------------|---|
| 1 | — | $100,000,000 | (investment) |
| 2 | $100,000,000 | 75,000,000 | (consumption) |
| 3 | 75,000,000 | 56,250,000 | (consumption) |
| 4 | 56,250,000 | 42,187,500 | (consumption) |
| 5 | 42,187,500 | 31,640,625 | (consumption) |
| Sum for infinite number of rounds | $400,000,000 | $400,000,000 | (Total planned expenditures) |

Households tend to devote a fraction of each dollar of added real disposable income to consumption and to reduce real consumption by the same amount when disposable income falls. The fraction, assumed to be .75 in this example, is called the *marginal propensity to consume*. This behavior tends to amplify the effects of any initial change in planned expenditure. Here planned investment in construction increases by $100 million in the first round. This causes construction workers' incomes to increase by $100 million; they then add $75 million in consumption expenditures in the second round. In turn, the people who supply the workers with consumer goods get an added $75 million of income and, as a result, increase their own consumption by $56,250,000. By the time the whole process runs an infinite number of rounds, total planned expenditure will have increased, and the aggregate demand curve will have shifted to the right by four times the initial change in planned investment.

planned expenditures will increase aggregate demand by $400 million rather than by just $100 million. In graphical terms, this means a shift of the aggregate demand curve to the right by $400.

The ratio of the total change in planned expenditure at the original level of prices to the initial change in planned expenditure is known as the **expenditure multiplier**. The size of the multiplier depends on the marginal propensity to consume. A larger marginal propensity to consume will make the change in consumption at each round larger and hence will raise the multiplier; a smaller marginal propensity to consume will make the change at each round smaller and hence will lower the multiplier. The value of the expenditure multiplier for any given marginal propensity to consume (mpc) can be calculated using the following formula:[2]

$$\text{Expenditure multiplier} = 1/(1 - \text{mpc}).$$

Thus, a marginal propensity to consume of .75 implies a multiplier of 4; an mpc of .9 implies a multiplier of 10; an mpc of .5 implies a multiplier of 2; and so on.

## THE AGGREGATE SUPPLY CURVE

We turn now to the supply side of our aggregate supply-and-demand model. *Aggregate supply* is essentially a synonym for the economy's total real output, or real

---

**Expenditure multiplier**

The ratio of the resultant shift in real aggregate demand to an initial shift in one of the components of aggregate demand.

**Aggregate supply curve**

A graph showing the relationship between real output (real domestic product) and the average price level of final goods.

domestic product. Thus, an **aggregate supply curve** shows the quantity of real domestic product supplied by the economy at various price levels. As with aggregate demand, we cannot move directly from individual market demand curves to aggregate curves. We must rethink the assumptions that lie behind the curves.

When thinking about the aggregate supply curve, one must bear in mind the distinction between the prices of final goods and those of productive inputs. The price level of final goods is stated in terms of a measure, such as the GDP deflator, that is a weighted average of the prices of the final goods that enter into GDP. An index of input prices, on the other hand, shows the average price level of the basic factors of production (labor, capital, and natural resources) and intermediate goods (energy, manufactured inputs such as steel and paper, and so on) that are used to produce GDP.

The producer price indexes are partial indexes of input prices, but the level of input prices discussed here is a broader concept because it covers labor as well as nonlabor inputs. Labor is by far the most important input, accounting for about three-quarters of all input costs for the economy as a whole. Thus, wages and salaries are particularly important elements of the average level of input prices.

## Fully Flexible Input Prices

The most important assumption underlying the aggregate supply curve concerns what firms expect to happen to the average level of input prices when a change in aggregate demand brings about a change in the average level of prices of final goods. One possibility is that when a shift in demand causes a change in the price level of final goods, input prices will change in the same proportion. There are two reasons why firms might expect this to happen.

One reason that input prices might be expected to change proportionately when a change in demand hits the market for final goods stems from the impact of such a change on wages and salaries. Suppose that the average price level of final goods rises in response to an increase in aggregate demand. If so, workers' costs of living also increase. If nominal wages and salaries were to remain the same, real wages would fall; for example, if the price level of final goods were to double, a wage of $5 per hour would buy only half the groceries or pay half the rent that it did previously. Workers would ask for raises to maintain their standard of living, and firms—which would be selling their products for twice as much per unit as before—would be able to grant the raises. If some employers tried to hold the line against wage increases, they would lose their most skilled and mobile workers to employers that were more willing to protect workers' real earnings against the effects of inflation.

The other reason is that many goods serve both as final goods and as inputs. Oil, electric power, natural gas, and other forms of energy are examples. If the forces of supply and demand raise the prices paid for these products in markets where they are sold as final goods, their prices will also rise in markets where they are sold to firms for use as productive inputs.

Suppose, then, that firms expect the prices of all inputs to rise proportionately whenever the price level for final goods rises. What will happen to total real output, that is, real domestic product, as the price level changes? The conclusion must be that the quantity of real domestic product supplied will remain constant. After all, profit-seeking firms decide how much to produce by balancing the prices they can get for their goods against the prices they must pay for the inputs they use. If both output and input prices rise by the same percentage, profit margins will be unchanged in real terms. There is therefore no reason to produce either more or less than before.

We conclude, then, that the assumption that producers expect input prices to be fully flexible implies a vertical aggregate supply curve such as the one shown in part (a) of Figure 7.3. This curve is located at the economy's natural level of real output, for reasons that will become clear as the full aggregate supply and demand model is developed. Part (a) of Figure 7.3 represents the economy's *long-run aggregate supply curve* because, in the opinion of most economists, input prices do tend to move in proportion to the prices of final goods in the long run.

**FIGURE 7.3 AGGREGATE SUPPLY CURVES**

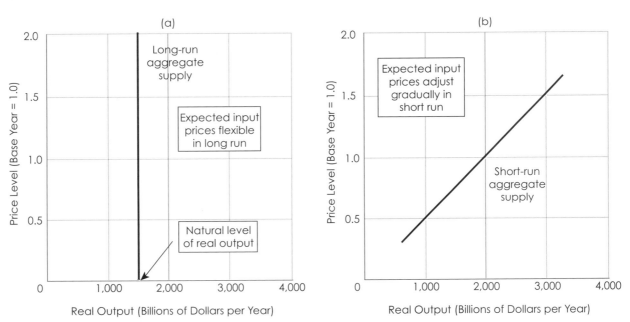

An aggregate supply curve shows the relationship between the level of final-goods prices and the level of real output (real domestic product). The slope of the aggregate supply curve depends on the way input prices are assumed to adjust to changes in the prices of final goods. In the long run, input prices are expected to adjust flexibly to changes in the prices of final goods. The long-run aggregate supply curve therefore is a vertical line drawn at the economy's natural level of real output, as shown in part (a). In the short run, input prices are assumed to adjust only gradually to changes in the prices of final goods. Thus, the short-run aggregate supply curve has a positive slope, as shown in part (b).

## Gradual Adjustment of Input Prices

There are, however, strong reasons to expect that the adjustment of input prices to changes in the prices of final goods is not instantaneous. Instead, when rising demand forces up the prices of final goods, firms may react as though they expect input prices to adjust only gradually. There are several reasons for expecting less than complete adjustment of input prices in the short run.

1. *Long-term contracts.* The prices of some inputs are fixed by long-term contracts. Union labor contracts are one example. Some firms may also rent buildings, buy fuel, or hire transportation services under long-term contracts. When the price level of final goods rises, the prices of these inputs cannot rise until it is time to renegotiate the contracts. Moreover, not all contracts have the same duration. They expire on different dates. In a system of overlapping contracts, the time required for input prices to adjust fully to a change in final-goods prices will be longer than the average length of individual contracts.

2. *Inventories.* Inventories tend to have a cushioning effect on input prices. To illustrate, suppose that a bakery experiences an increase in demand for its bread. At first it will gladly bake and sell more bread, using up its inventories of flour in the process. If prices have been rising throughout the economy, the bakery may have to pay more for the next batch of flour it orders. This change in input prices will cause it to revise its output and pricing plans, but by then a certain amount of time will have passed. Economists have sometimes argued that rational managers should adjust output prices immediately to reflect the expected replacement cost of inputs used from inventory, but in fact, many firms do not follow this practice.

3. *Incomplete knowledge.* Firms may mistake broad changes in demand for local changes affecting only their own market. For example, the bakery might think that the increased demand for bread is limited to the city it serves. Such a change would not be expected to have a perceptible effect on the price of flour, which is determined in a nationwide market. Only later will the bakery find out that the increase in demand for its bread is part of a broad increase in aggregate demand—but again, some time will have passed by then.

If firms expect input prices to adjust only partially in the short run, they will perceive improved profit opportunities when the demand for their products increases. They may take advantage of the favorable demand conditions by raising their prices, by increasing their output, or very likely by doing some of both.[3] It follows, then, that when firms expect gradual adjustment of input prices, the aggregate supply curve will, in the short run, have a positive slope, as in part (b) of Figure 7.3. The positively sloped aggregate supply curve in part (b) is termed a *short-run aggregate supply curve* because it represents the reaction of firms to a change in circumstances before input prices have had a chance to adjust fully.

Just how short is this short run, and how gradual is the gradual adjustment of prices? Although there is no simple answer, in practice, the rate at which input prices adjust will depend on a variety of circumstances and will vary from one input to another. In working with the supply-and-demand model, it is often useful to make a simplifying assumption: When prices of final goods change, firms expect that the prices of all inputs will remain unchanged for a certain period—say one year—and then move up or down all at once in accordance with the preceding change in the prices of final goods. This stepwise adjustment of input prices is, of course, only a convenient approximation to the more complex adjustment process that takes place in the real world.

## Shifts in the Short-Run Aggregate Supply Curve

The distinction between the price levels of final goods and inputs and the distinction between long-run and short-run adjustments provide a basis for understanding shifts in the aggregate supply curves. We begin with shifts in the short-run curve.

When the economy is in long-run equilibrium at its natural level of real output, markets for individual goods, services, and factors of production are also in equilibrium. In that situation the prices of final goods and services that firms sell and the prices of the inputs they use must be related in certain consistent ways:

1. In equilibrium, the prices of final goods must be at levels that will bring in sufficient revenue for firms to cover the costs of all inputs, given the prices of those inputs, and obtain a normal profit.

2. In equilibrium, the prices of labor inputs must be sufficient to balance supply and demand in labor markets. This means that, given the cost of living as determined by the prices of consumer goods, wages and salaries must be high enough to make it worthwhile for workers to acquire the skills they need for each kind of job and to show up for work each day.

Suppose that we choose as a base year one in which the economy is in long-run equilibrium. In that year the prices of inputs and final goods will be related in the ways just described. We can assign a value of 1.0 to both the average level of input prices and the average level of prices of final goods for that year. We can then measure changes relative to those base year levels.

In graphical terms, the situation in such a base year is represented by point A in Figure 7.4. Real output is equal to its natural level, which is also its long-run equilibrium level. Point A thus is on the long-run aggregate supply curve, which is a vertical line at the natural level of real output. The short-run aggregate supply curve $AS_1$ that passes through point A shows the way firms will react to changes in aggregate demand, given the prevailing level of input prices, 1.0. From point A, the economy is poised to move up or down along its short-run aggregate supply curve over a short-run time

## FIGURE 7.4  A SHIFT IN THE SHORT-RUN AGGREGATE SUPPLY CURVE

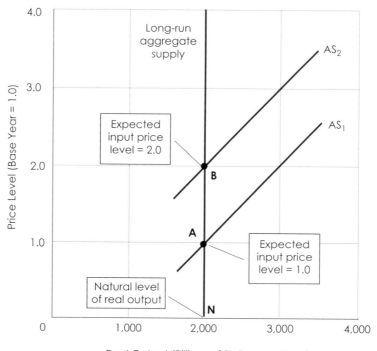

The short-run aggregate supply curve is drawn so that it intersects the long-run aggregate supply curve at the expected level of input prices. Here, the short-run aggregate supply curve $AS_1$, which intersects the long-run aggregate supply curve at point A, is based on an expected input price level of 1.0. If the expected level of input prices later increases to 2.0, the aggregate supply curve will shift upward to the position $AS_2$.

horizon for which input prices are expected to remain unchanged, and up or down along its long-run aggregate supply curve over a long-run time horizon for which input prices are expected to adjust in proportion to changes in the prices of final goods.

Over time, as economic conditions change, the economy may move to a new equilibrium. Suppose that after a number of years, the average price level of final goods has risen to 2.0 and input prices have had time to adjust fully, so that they too have risen to an average level of 2.0. Such a situation is shown as point B in Figure 7.4. In that situation, input prices and the prices of final goods will once again be in an equilibrium relationship. Firms will be selling their outputs for twice as much, enabling them to pay for their inputs, which also cost twice as much. Workers will be earning double the nominal wages and salaries they earned previously, which is just enough to allow them to maintain their original standard of living, given the doubled level of price level of consumer goods.

Given this new equilibrium situation, a new short-run aggregate supply curve, $AS_2$, can be drawn through point B. This new aggregate supply curve shows how firms will react to changes in aggregate demand if they expect input prices to remain at the new level of 2.0 for the short run. The short-run aggregate supply has shifted upward because the level of input prices that firms expect to prevail when they make short-run production plans has increased.

To summarize:

1.  The short-run aggregate supply curve intersects the long-run aggregate supply curve at a height corresponding to the level of input prices that firms expect to prevail in the short run. The expected level of input prices thus is the key "other things being equal" assumption underlying the short-run aggregate supply curve.

2.  A change in the expected level of input prices will cause the short-run aggregate supply curve to shift upward or downward to a new intersection with the long-run aggregate supply curve.

### Shifts in the Long-Run Aggregate Supply Curve

The key "other things being equal" assumption that underlies the long-run aggregate supply curve and determines its position is the economy's natural level of real output—the level of real output that can be produced with given technology and productive resources when unemployment is at its natural rate. Over time, the economy can expand its production potential through development of new technologies, growth of the labor force, investment in new capital, and development of new natural resources. Such long-run growth could be represented as an outward expansion of the economy's production possibility frontier. Using the model presented in this chapter, the same kind of expansion can be represented by an increase in the natural level of real output and a consequent rightward shift in the long-run aggregate supply curve.

In the next several chapters we will be focusing on shifts in the aggregate demand curve and the short-run aggregate supply curve. To simplify matters in discussing these shifts, we will assume that the economy's long-run aggregate supply curve will remain fixed.

## THE INTERACTION OF AGGREGATE SUPPLY AND DEMAND

Now that we have reviewed the conditions that determine the slopes of the aggregate supply and demand curves and shifts in those curves, we can put the curves together to form a complete aggregate supply and demand model. This model will be applied to many issues of theory and policy in coming chapters. In this section we illustrate its basic principles by showing how the economy responds to an increase in aggregate demand, beginning from a position of long-run equilibrium.

## Characteristics of Short- and Long-Run Equilibrium

The story begins at point $E_0$ in Figure 7.5, where the economy is in a position of both short- and long-run equilibrium. This situation is characterized by the intersection of three curves: the aggregate demand curve $AD_1$, the short-run aggregate supply curve $AS_1$, and the long-run aggregate supply curve. The significance of each of the intersections is as follows:

1. Expected input prices and prices of final goods are in their long-run equilibrium relationship at the intersection of the short-run aggregate supply curve $AS_1$ with the long-run aggregate supply curve. *The height of the intersection of the long- and short-run aggregate supply curves indicates the expected level of input prices.*

**FIGURE 7.5** **SHORT-RUN AND LONG-RUN EQUILIBRIUM**

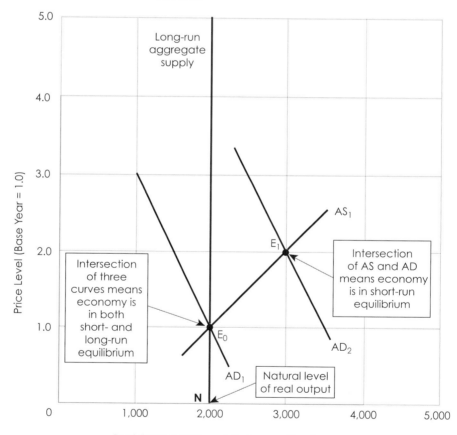

The economy is in short-run equilibrium at the point where the aggregate demand curve intersects the short-run aggregate supply curve. It can be in long-run equilibrium only at a point where the aggregate demand curve intersects the long-run aggregate supply curve. In this diagram, point $E_0$ is a point of both long- and short-run equilibrium, assuming that the aggregate demand curve is in the position $AD_1$. If the aggregate demand curve shifts to the position $AD_2$, the short-run equilibrium point moves to $E_1$. $E_1$ is not a point of long-run equilibrium because it is not on the long-run aggregate supply curve.

2.  The intersection of $AS_1$ with $AD_1$ indicates the level of final-goods prices and real domestic product for which aggregate supply equals aggregate demand, given the expected level of input prices used in drawing $AS_1$. *The intersection of the short-run aggregate supply curve with the aggregate demand curve is always the economy's point of short-run equilibrium.*

3.  The intersection of $AD_1$ with the long-run aggregate supply curve indicates the price level at which total real planned expenditures are equal to the economy's natural level of real output. *The economy can be in long-run equilibrium only at a point where the aggregate demand curve intersects the long-run aggregate supply curve.*

4.  The intersection of all three curves at $E_0$ indicates a price level and real domestic product that meet *both* the short-run and the long-run equilibrium conditions.

These four characteristics of short- and long-run equilibrium are essential to understanding the aggregate supply and demand model. Along with an understanding of the sources of shifts in each of the curves, they provide a set of basic working rules that can be applied to solve any problem that falls within the scope of the model.

## Short-Run Effects of an Increase in Aggregate Demand

Now suppose that, beginning from point $E_0$ in Figure 7.5, something causes an increase in total real planned expenditure so that the aggregate demand curve shifts to the right from $AD_1$ to $AD_2$. For the moment it does not matter just what causes the shift. It could be a change in government policy, a spontaneous increase in real consumption spending, an increase in real planned investment resulting from greater business confidence, a boom in demand for U.S. real exports, or some combination of these factors.

Whatever the cause, the immediate effect of the increase in real aggregate demand will be an unplanned decline in inventories. Seeing that their products are being bought up faster than they can be produced, firms will alter their plans accordingly. As explained earlier, their short-run reactions to the change in demand will be based on the assumption that input prices will not immediately adjust to the change in demand for final goods. Given that assumption, firms will react to the increase in demand partly by increasing output and partly by raising prices. In graphical terms, these reactions are shown by a movement up and to the right along the short-run aggregate supply curve $AS_1$, which is drawn on the assumption that input prices are expected to remain at their initial level of 1.0. As the economy moves along the aggregate supply curve, real output increases and the unemployment rate falls.

When the economy reaches point $E_1$, where $AS_1$ and $AD_2$ intersect, planned expenditure and domestic product will be back in balance and the unplanned inventory depletion will cease. This is a new position of short-run equilibrium for the economy that is applicable as long as the aggregate demand and short-run aggregate supply curves remain in the positions shown.

## Transition to a New Long-Run Equilibrium

The point at which curves $AS_1$ and $AD_2$ intersect is a point of short-run equilibrium for the economy, but it is not a point of long-run equilibrium. The reason is that the price level of final goods is not equal to the expected level of input prices at that point.

**FIGURE 7.6   SHORT-RUN AND LONG-RUN ADJUSTMENT TO AN INCREASE IN AGGREGATE DEMAND**

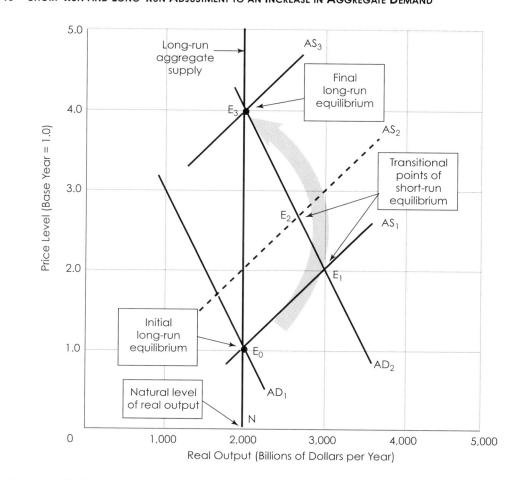

Beginning from an initial long-run equilibrium at $E_0$, a shift in the aggregate demand curve to $AD_2$ will cause the economy to move to a new short-run equilibrium at $E_1$. As it does so, real output will rise above its natural level, the price level of final goods will rise, and unemployment will fall below its natural rate. After a time, the expected level of input prices will begin to move upward in response to the increase that has taken place in the prices of final goods. As this happens, the short-run aggregate supply curve will shift upward, and the economy will move up and to the left along $AD_2$. Eventually it will reach a new equilibrium at $E_3$. As the economy moves from $E_1$ to $E_3$, the price level of final goods will continue to rise, real output will fall back to its natural level, and unemployment will rise back to its natural rate.

Expected input prices are still at level 1.0, shown by the intersection of $AS_1$ with the long-run aggregate supply curve. Prices of final goods, however, have risen to a level of 2.0 at $E_1$. This situation cannot be maintained indefinitely. Over time, input prices will gradually adjust to the change that has taken place in final-goods prices.

Figure 7.6 shows what happens as this adjustment takes place. Suppose that after a certain period (say, one year), input prices increase to a level of 2.0, catching up with the increase in prices of final goods that took place as the economy moved from $E_0$ to $E_1$. This new level of input prices will become the basis for business expectations in the subsequent year. Graphically, the increase in the expected level of input prices is shown as an upward shift in the short-run aggregate supply curve, from $AS_1$ to $AS_2$. $AS_2$ now intersects the long-run aggregate supply curve at the new expected level of input prices, 2.0.

Assuming that no further change takes place in planned expenditures, the aggregate demand curve will remain at $AD_2$. Given an unchanged level of aggregate demand, firms will react to the new, higher expected level of input prices by raising their prices and reducing their output. As they do so, the economy will move along the aggregate demand curve from $E_1$ to $E_2$, where $AS_2$ and $AD_2$ intersect. Because real output is decreasing, the unemployment rate begins to rise.

However, like $E_1$, $E_2$ is not a point of long-run equilibrium. In the process of moving to $E_2$, the prices of final goods have increased again, reaching a level of about 2.7. They are again out of balance with the expected level of input prices, which is now 2.0. Whenever the price level of final goods is above the expected level of input prices, input prices will tend to increase. Input prices thus will continue their gradual upward adjustment. As they do so, the short-run aggregate supply curve will continue to shift upward.

A succession of further intermediate positions could be shown as the aggregate supply curve shifts upward along the aggregate demand curve. To make a long story short, however, we will jump ahead to the point at which it has shifted all the way up to the position $AS_3$. When it reaches that position, its intersection with the aggregate demand curve $AD_2$ is at point $E_3$, which is also where $AD_2$ intersects the long-run aggregate supply curve. At $E_3$, then, all three curves intersect at a common point. The economy is once again in both short-run and long-run equilibrium. The gradual process through which expected input prices catch up to the prices of final goods is complete. Both input prices and output prices have reached the level of 4.0 and are in a consistent relationship to one another. Real output is back to its natural level, and unemployment is back to its natural rate. If there is no further shift in aggregate demand, the economy can remain at $E_3$ indefinitely.

## Effects of a Decrease in Aggregate Demand

Of course, events will sooner or later cause aggregate demand to change again. Beginning from the long-run equilibrium point $E_3$, let's see what will happen if the aggregate demand curve shifts all the way back to its initial position, $AD_1$. Again, it does not matter for the moment whether the decrease in demand takes the form of a decrease in consumption, planned investment, government purchases, or net exports. Nor does it matter whether the change originates with a change in government policy, or with a change in the choices made by households, firms, or buyers of exports.

Figure 7.7 shows how the firm will react to the leftward shift of the aggregate demand curve. Firms will notice the shift in aggregate demand in the form of an unplanned increase in their inventories, as demand for their own individual products decreases. At first, they may not know whether the decrease in demand is local or is

**FIGURE 7.7    SHORT-RUN AND LONG-RUN ADJUSTMENT TO A DECREASE IN AGGREGATE DEMAND**

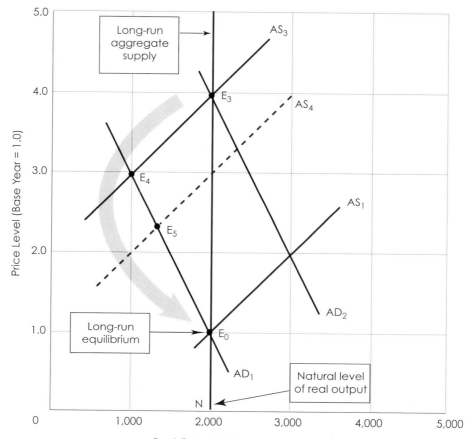

This figure begins from point $E_3$, the end point of the sequence of events described in Figure 7.6. From this point, aggregate demand is assumed to shift back to the position $AD_1$. At first, firms respond to falling demand and unexpected inventory accumulation by cutting back output and reducing prices. As the economy moves to a short-run equilibrium at $E_4$, the unemployment rate rises and final-goods prices fall. When expected input prices also begin to fall, the aggregate supply curve begins to shift downward. As it does so, the economy moves along $AD_1$, through the intermediate point $E_5$, and on down to $E_0$. If there is no further change in aggregate demand, the economy will remain in equilibrium at that point.

occurring throughout the economy. In any event, some will react by cutting output, some by reducing their prices, and many by doing some of both. The economy will move down and to the left along the aggregate supply curve $AS_3$ to a short-run equilibrium at $E_4$. There, the price level will have fallen to 3.0, and real output to $1,000 billion. Unemployment will also have increased. The economy will have experienced a serious recession.

As in the case of an increase in aggregate demand, point $E_4$ is not a possible long-run equilibrium, because final-goods prices are out of line with the expected level of input prices. This fact will soon begin to exert a downward pull on the expected and actual levels of input prices. Firms that produce intermediate goods, such as energy and semi-finished products, will find that demand for those goods is weak, and will react by cutting prices (although perhaps only when long-term contracts are up for renewal). Unemployed workers will accept lower nominal wages in order to find some work. And even workers who have kept their jobs may be willing to accept lower nominal wages when their contracts are renewed, if they realize that lower final-goods prices mean that it costs less to maintain a given standard of living.

In response to the drop in input prices, and the expectation that they will fall still more, the aggregate supply curve shifts downward. $AS_4$ is an intermediate position corresponding to an expected input price level of 3.0. However, $E_5$, at the intersection of $AD_1$ and $AS_4$, is still not a long-run equilibrium, because the level of final-goods prices there is less than 3.0. Long-run equilibrium will not be restored until the economy moves all the way back to its natural level of real output at $E_0$. During the transition from $E_4$ to $E_0$, output will be rising and unemployment falling, even though the price level of final goods continues to fall.

## Looking Ahead:
## Aggregate Supply, Demand, and the Business Cycle

If we look at the entire sequence of events shown in Figures 7.6 and 7.7, we can see that the economy has traced out something that looks very much like a business cycle:

1. Beginning from the natural level of real output, the economy expands. Domestic product rises above its natural level, unemployment falls below its natural rate, and the price level begins to rise.

2. After a time, a peak of real output is reached, after which real output, although still above its natural level, begins to fall and unemployment begins to rise.

3. If aggregate demand has shifted to the left again by the time real output returns to its natural level, the economy will continue to contract, and unemployment will rise above its natural rate. During this phase of the cycle, the price level begins to decrease.

4. Eventually real output reaches a low point, the trough of the recession. As real output moves back up toward its natural level, unemployment again falls. In principle, the economy could come to rest at the natural level of real output. If aggregate demand increases once more, however, a new cycle will begin.

⌇

## SUMMARY

1. **What are the conditions that determine the slope of the aggregate demand curve?** The *aggregate demand curve* shows the relationship between real planned expenditure on final goods and the average price level of final goods. The curve has a negative slope because each of the components of real aggregate demand—consumption, planned investment, government purchases, and net exports—varies inversely with the price level. The aggregate demand curve is relatively inelastic. As a result, the nominal value of planned expenditure (real planned expenditure times the price level) increases as one moves up and to the left along the curve.

2. **What are some sources of shifts in the aggregate demand curve?** Movements along the aggregate demand curve are associated with changes in the price level of final goods. Changes in other conditions can cause shifts in the curve. Among the sources of shifts are changes in consumer or business expectations; changes in policy regarding government purchases, taxes, and money; and changes in the world economy. Because of the *multiplier effect,* an initial $1 change in any of the components will cause the curve to shift to the right or left by more than $1.

3. **What are the conditions that determine the slopes of the short- and long-run aggregate supply curves?** An *aggregate supply curve* shows the relationship between the quantity of real output

supplied (that is, real domestic product) and the average price level of final goods. The slope of the curve depends on what assumption is made about the way firms expect input prices to be affected by changes in the prices of final goods. In the long run, actual and expected input prices tend to adjust proportionately to changes in the prices of final goods. In that case, firms have no incentive to increase or decrease output, so the long-run aggregate supply curve is a vertical line drawn at the economy's natural level of real output. In the short run, actual and expected input prices adjust only gradually to changes in the prices of final goods. Thus, in the short run, firms find it worthwhile to increase both output and prices in response to an increase in demand.

4. **What are the sources of shifts in the aggregate supply curves?** At the intersection of the long- and short-run aggregate supply curves, the price level of final goods and the expected level of input prices are equal. An increase (or decrease) in the expected level of input prices thus will cause the short-run aggregate supply curve to shift up (or down) along the long-run aggregate supply curve. The location of the long-run aggregate supply curve is determined by the natural level of real output. An increase in natural real output resulting from improved technology or greater availability of productive resources will cause a rightward shift in the long-run aggregate supply curve.

5. **How do prices, real output, and unemployment behave as the economy responds to a change in aggregate demand?** Beginning from a state of long-run equilibrium, an increase in real aggregate demand will, in the short run, cause the economy to move up and to the right along its short-run aggregate supply curve. As it does so, the prices of final goods will rise, real output will rise above its natural level, and unemployment will fall below its natural rate. After a time, the expected level of input prices will begin to rise as a result of the increases that have taken place in the prices of final goods. As that happens, the economy will move up and to the left along the aggregate demand curve, assuming no further shift in that curve. The price level of final goods will continue to rise, real output will fall back toward its natural level, and unemployment will rise back toward its natural rate. If, after the new equilibrium is reached, aggregate demand shifts to the left again, real output will drop below its natural level, and unemployment will rise above its natural rate. The level of final goods prices will fall below the expected level of input prices. Soon, the expected level of input prices, too, will begin to fall. If there is no further change in aggregate demand, the economy will return to equilibrium at the natural level of real output.

## KEY TERMS

Aggregate demand curve
Multiplier effect
Marginal propensity to
  consume
Expenditure multiplier
Aggregate supply curve

## PROBLEMS AND TOPICS FOR DISCUSSION

1. **Examining the lead-off case.** Why is a decline in real output during a recession or depression ac-companied by an increase in the unemployment rate? What must happen before unemployment can return to its natural rate? Why does this process take time, rather than being instantaneous?

2. **Elasticity of aggregate demand.** Turn to the aggregate demand curve $AD_2$ in Figure 7.1. Along that curve, as the price level rises from 0.5 to 1.5, the quantity of real output demanded declines from $3,000 billion to $2,000 billion. What happens to the aggregate quantity demanded in nominal terms over this interval? Using the formula for price elasticity of demand (the ratio of the percentage change in the quantity of a good demanded to a given percentage change in its price), what is the elasticity of aggregate demand over this interval?

3. **The multiplier effect.** Rework Table 7.1 for a $100 million reduction in real planned investment assuming a marginal propensity to consume of .9.

4. **Long- and short-run aggregate supply curves.** On a piece of graph paper draw a set of axes, such as those in Figure 7.4, but do not draw the supply curves shown there. Instead, draw a long-run aggregate supply curve based on the assumption that the natural level of real output is $3,000 billion. What is the slope of the curve? At what point does it intersect the horizontal axis? Next draw a short-run aggregate supply curve based on the assumption that the expected level of input prices is 1.5. Where does this short-run aggregate supply curve intersect the long-run aggregate supply curve that you drew?

5. **Final goods prices and expected input prices.** Given an aggregate demand curve and a short-run aggregate supply curve, how can you determine the short-run equilibrium price level of final goods? Given a long-run aggregate supply curve and a short-run aggregate supply curve,

how can you determine the expected level of input prices? Turn to Figure 7.6. Give the short-run equilibrium price level of final goods and the expected level of input prices for each of the points $E_0$, $E_1$, $E_2$, and $E_3$.

6. **Long- and short-run equilibriums.** On a piece of graph paper draw a set of axes identical to those in Figure 7.6. Draw a long-run aggregate supply curve based on the assumption that a natural level of real output is $2,500 billion. Draw a short-run aggregate supply curve that passes through the points (2,500, 1.0) and (3,500, 2.0). Label it $AS_1$. What is the expected level of input prices indicated by this supply curve? Draw an aggregate demand curve that passes through the points (2,000, 2.0) and (2,500, 1.0). Label it $AD_2$. Given these three curves, where is the economy's point of short-run equilibrium? Where is its point of long-run equilibrium? Now draw another aggregate demand curve that passes through the points (2,500, 4.0) and (4,000, 1.0). Label it $AD_2$. Given $AD_2$ and the aggregate supply curves on your diagram, where is the economy's point of short-run equilibrium? What is the relationship between the short-run equilibrium price level of final goods and the expected level of input prices? Is there a possible point of long-run equilibrium for the economy, given $AD_2$ and the long-run aggregate supply curve? If so, explain how the economy can reach that point starting from the short-run equilibrium just described.

# CASE FOR DISCUSSION

## *Setting Menu Prices at José Muldoon's*

George Hanna used to wince when his customers ordered guacamole.

"We had already introduced our menu—and then the price of avocados suddenly tripled," he recalls.

"That meant that the price we were charging for the guacamole didn't cover our cost. We'd expected the price to go up because of the season, but we didn't expect it to triple. We got burned on that one."

Hanna manages José Muldoon's, a successful Colorado restaurant featuring Southwestern and Mexican dishes. Like other restaurant managers, Hanna must set prices in his menus well in advance.

"We generally run a menu at least six to eight months," he says. "Sometimes we'll keep the same menu close to a year."

While a restaurant could change its price for a certain dish whenever its costs changed, such a tactic might irritate customers. To give customers predictable prices—and to save on printing costs—menus are not changed frequently.

That leaves Hanna with the problem of making price decisions he must stick with for a long time. If his costs of labor, food, or other inputs go up in the meantime, his profits suffer.

"I look at what costs have been over the last year, and pretty much base my cost estimates on that. My costs have been fairly stable lately, so looking at the last year works pretty well. Our restaurant also has a long track record of experience that we can draw from in estimating costs."

Source: Timothy Tregarthen, "Prices: Figuring Out What to Expect," *The Margin* (September–October 1988): 20. Reprinted with permission.

## QUESTIONS

1. Why does Hanna base his pricing decisions on the *expected* prices of his inputs rather than adjusting his prices every day in response to what actually happens to input prices?
2. Once Hanna has printed a menu that includes a fixed price for guacamole based on an expected price for avocados, what effect will an increase in demand for guacamole have on the quantity of guacamole sold?

3. At first Hanna was surprised when the price of avocados tripled. But he now expects the price of avocados to remain high. How will that expectation affect the price of guacamole on the next menu he prints? Assuming that there is no change in the demand for guacamole, what effect will an increase in the price of guacamole have on the quantity of guacamole sold?

4. Picture the following sequence of events: Beginning from a state of equilibrium, there is a nationwide increase in the demand for guacamole. The increased demand, in turn, causes an increase in demand for the avocados used in making it. As the avocado market adjusts to these increases, the price of avocados rises. Later, restaurant owners change their menu prices to reflect the change in avocado prices. What happens to the price of guacamole and the quantity sold in the short run in response to the increase in demand? What happens to the price and quantity sold in the long run?

5. In what way does the microeconomic adjustment of the guacamole market to a change in demand for guacamole resemble the macroeconomic adjustment of the economy as a whole to a change in aggregate demand? In what ways do the two processes differ?

## END NOTES

1. Elasticity varies from one point to another along a straight-line demand curve. Any straight-line demand curve becomes relatively elastic as it approaches its intersection with the vertical axis. Strictly speaking, it would be better to draw aggregate demand curves whose slope increases toward the top of the diagram. Such curves could be drawn with a constant elasticity that is less than unity throughout their length. We use straight-line aggregate demand curves in this book because they simplify the diagrams. This will cause no difficulty as long as we focus on changes occurring along the relatively inelastic part of the curve.

2. The multiplier can be derived algebraically as follows:
Let $\Delta E$ be the total impulse to planned expenditure resulting from a \$1 increase in autonomous expenditure, and let $b$ be the marginal propensity to consume. The "round by round" analysis of the multiplier shows that:

$$\Delta E = 1 + b + b^2 + b^3 + \ldots$$

Now multiply both sides of the equation by $b$ to give a new equation:

$$b\,\Delta E = b + b^2 + b^3 + \ldots$$

Subtract this new equation from the original one, giving:

$$\Delta E - b\,\Delta E = 1$$

Simplified, we get:

$$\Delta E = 1/(1 - b),$$

which is the multiplier formula given in the text.

3. Readers who have studied microeconomics can verify, using standard profit maximization models, that a rightward shift in the market demand curve for a good will, in the short run, causes an increase in both price and quantity of output under a variety of market structures.

# The Income-Expenditure Model

*After reading this chapter, you will understand:*

1. More about how consumption is related to disposable income.
2. How consumption is affected by various kinds of taxes.
3. How the equilibrium level of national income is determined in the income-expenditure model.
4. How the income-expenditure model can be used to demonstrate the multiplier effect.
5. The relationship of the income-expenditure model to the aggregate supply and demand model.

*Before reading this chapter, make sure you know the meaning of:*

1. Transfer payments
2. Government purchases
3. Net taxes
4. Planned versus unplanned investment
5. Marginal propensity to consume
6. Expenditure multiplier

## THE POWERFUL CONSUMER

Consumers have become the most important source of spending in the economy, accounting for more than two-thirds in the U.S., their greatest share in more than half a century. Not since the consumer spending boom that followed World War II have consumers spent so energetically as they have since the turn of the 21st Century. Then they were reflecting pent-up demand after years when production capacity was shifted to war.

Growth figures in 2003 provided the welcome news that other parts of the economy—notably business investment—are starting to pick up, so the consumer share may have reached a peak for now. This spending is good news for the economy. As a recovery takes hold, the biggest threat to its survival would be a downturn in consumer demand.

Sources: Floyd Norris, "Portrait of a Consumer," *The New York Times,* November 30, 2003; Louis Uchitelle, "Why Americans Must Keep Spending," *The New York Times,* December 1, 2003.

ONSUMERS HAVE ENORMOUS power over the economy. They control some two-thirds of the spending flows that pour into total domestic product. Multiplied hundreds of millions of times, their decisions can change the direction of the economy. This chapter will begin by focusing on consumers as it continues to develop the model of aggregate supply and demand. It provides a more detailed, graphical presentation of the multiplier effect, based on an analysis of income and expenditures. Finally, it shows how the graphical model of income and expenditures relates to the aggregate supply and demand graphs presented previously. As in the preceding chapter, much of what is presented here can be viewed as an outgrowth of the theory originally developed by John Maynard Keynes.

To simplify the analysis, we will make three assumptions that preserve some key features of the circular flow models at the expense of eliminating some details of the official national income accounts. First, we will eliminate the distinction between gross and net domestic product by assuming the capital consumption allowance to be zero. Second, we will eliminate the difference between net domestic income, as measured by the income approach, and domestic product, as measured by the expenditure approach, by assuming that indirect business taxes and the statistical discrepancy are zero. Finally, we will assumed undistributed corporate profits and net receipts of factor income from the rest of the world to be zero so that disposable personal income equals domestic income minus net taxes. These assumptions can be expressed in equation form as follows:

$$\text{Disposable income} + \text{Net taxes} = \text{Domestic income} = \text{Domestic product}$$

## THE CONSUMPTION SCHEDULE

The division of real disposable income between consumption and saving plays a key role in regulating the circular flow. Starting from the principle that consumers consistently spend part—but not all—of each additional dollar of income, we can show a relationship between real disposable income and real consumption expenditure like that presented in Figure 8.1. This relationship is known as the **consumption schedule** or **consumption function**.

## Autonomous Consumption

The consumption schedule shown in part (b) of Figure 8.1 does not pass through the origin; rather, it intersects the vertical axis somewhere above zero. This indicates that a certain part of real consumption expenditure is not associated with any particular level of real disposable income. The component of real consumption that is equal to the vertical intercept of the consumption schedule is called **autonomous consumption**. More generally, the term **autonomous** is applied in macroeconomics to any expenditure category that does not depend on the income level.

The $100 billion level of autonomous consumption suggests that total consumption expenditure is $100 billion even if total disposable income is zero. In practice, disposable income never falls to zero for the economy as a whole. However, individual households sometimes have zero income. When they do, they do not cut consumption to zero. Instead, they draw on past savings or borrow against future income to maintain some minimal consumption level. In this sense, the concept of autonomous consumption is rooted in actual consumer behavior.

## Marginal Propensity to Consume

Columns 1 through 4 in part (a) of Figure 8.1 show that whenever disposable income rises, some of the additional income is spent on consumption above and beyond autonomous consumption. The fraction of each added dollar of real disposable income that goes to added consumption is called the *marginal propensity to consume (mpc)*. For example, a $100 billion increase in disposable income—from $500 billion to $600 billion—raises consumption by $75 billion—from $475 billion to $550 billion. Likewise, a $100 billion decrease in disposable income—from $500 billion to $400 billion—causes consumption to fall by $75 billion—from $475 billion to $400 billion. Thus, the value of the marginal propensity to consume in this example is .75 ($75/$100).

In geometric terms, the marginal propensity to consume equals the slope of the consumption schedule. In part (b) of Figure 8.1, a horizontal movement of $100 billion in disposable income corresponds to a vertical movement of $75 billion in planned consumption. The slope of the consumption schedule, then, is $75/$100 = .75, the same as the marginal propensity to consume.

**Marginal Versus Average Propensity to Consume**   It is helpful to contrast the marginal propensity to consume with the average propensity to consume. The **average propensity to consume** for any real income level equals total real consumption divided by real disposable income. It is shown in column 6 of Figure 8.1. For income

**Consumption schedule (consumption function)**

A graph that shows how real consumption expenditure varies as real disposable income changes, other things being equal.

**Autonomous**

In the context of the income-expenditure model, refers to an expenditure that is independent of the level of real domestic income.

**Autonomous consumption**

The part of total real consumption expenditure that is independent of the level of real disposable income; for any given consumption schedule, real autonomous consumption equals the level of real consumption associated with zero real disposable income.

**Average propensity to consume**

Total consumption for any income level divided by total disposable income.

FIGURE 8.1 THE CONSUMPTION SCHEDULE

(a)

| Disposable Income (1) | Consumption Expenditure (2) | Change in Income (3) | Change in Consumption (4) | Marginal Propensity to Consume (5) | Average Propensity to Consume (6) |
|---|---|---|---|---|---|
| $ 0 | $ 100 | | | | — |
| 100 | 175 | 100 | $75 | 0.75 | 1.75 |
| 200 | 250 | 100 | 75 | 0.75 | 1.25 |
| 300 | 325 | 100 | 75 | 0.75 | 1.08 |
| 400 | 400 | 100 | 75 | 0.75 | 1.00 |
| 500 | 475 | 100 | 75 | 0.75 | 0.95 |
| 600 | 550 | 100 | 75 | 0.75 | 0.91 |
| 700 | 625 | 100 | 75 | 0.75 | 0.89 |
| 800 | 700 | 100 | 75 | 0.75 | 0.89 |
| 900 | 775 | 100 | 75 | 0.75 | 0.86 |
| 1,000 | 850 | 100 | 75 | 0.75 | 0.85 |
| 1,100 | 925 | 100 | 75 | 0.75 | 0.84 |
| 1,200 | 1,000 | 100 | 75 | 0.75 | 0.83 |

(b)

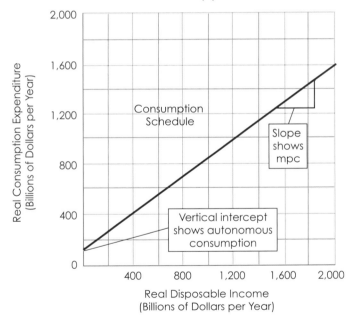

Parts (a) and (b) both present a simple example of the connection between real disposable income and real consumption. The $100 billion level of real autonomous consumption is shown in part (b) by the height of the intersection of the consumption schedule with the vertical axis. The slope of the consumption schedule equals the marginal propensity to consume.

levels below $400 billion, consumption exceeds disposable income, so the average propensity to consume is greater than 1. As disposable income increases, the average propensity to consume falls. However, because total consumption always includes a constant level of autonomous consumption—at least in the short run—the average propensity to consume is always greater than the marginal propensity to consume.[1]

**SHORT RUN VERSUS LONG RUN** In practice, the actual values of both the average and marginal propensities to consume depend on the time horizon. In the United States, consumption spending has tended to rise over long periods by about $.90 for every $1 increase in disposable income, which implies a long-run marginal propensity of about .9—or perhaps somewhat higher for the most recent past. Also, the long-run level of autonomous consumption, as implied by historical data, approaches zero. As a result, the average and marginal propensities to consume are equal in the long run.

In the short run (a year or less), however, people tend to change their consumption by less than $.90 for every $1 change in income. Also, autonomous consumption is positive in the short run; thus, the marginal propensity to consume is less than the average propensity to consume.

One reason for this is that year-to-year changes in disposable income are not always permanent. People tend to make smaller changes in their consumption in response to temporary changes in income than they do in response to permanent ones. For example, a household that is used to an annual income of $30,000 would no doubt cut back somewhat on its consumption in a year when its income temporarily dropped to $25,000. However, as long as it expected better times to return, it would probably reduce its consumption by less than it would if it expected the lower income level to be permanent. Therefore, as long as the drop in income was seen as temporary, the household would offset it to some degree by reducing its rate of saving, by dipping into past savings, or by borrowing.

Even permanent changes in income are not always perceived as permanent in the short run. Thus, a household that experiences a permanent income increase of $2,000 per year might at first treat part of the added income as temporary and consume less of it than it otherwise would. Over a longer period, as it becomes clear that the higher income level is permanent, more of the increase is likely to be consumed.

Because this book focuses mainly on short-run economic stabilization policy, the examples in this chapter use a marginal propensity to consume of .75, somewhat lower than the observed long-run mpc for the United States. However, there is nothing sacred about the value .75; under different short-run conditions, a higher or lower value might be appropriate. For a given level of autonomous consumption, a higher mpc would result in a steeper consumption schedule with the same vertical intercept; a lower mpc would result in a slope that was still positive, but less steep.

## Shifts in the Consumption Schedule

The consumption schedules that we have drawn so far show the link between real disposable income and real consumption spending. A movement along the consumption schedule shows how real consumption spending changes along with real disposable income, other things being equal. In this section, we will see what is covered by the "other things being equal" clause in this case. This will generate a list of factors that can shift the consumption schedule.

**WEALTH**    One consideration that is assumed to remain constant as we move along the consumption schedule is real wealth. A household's *wealth* is the total value of everything it owns—money, securities, real estate, consumer durables, and so on—minus the debts it owes. Wealth is a stock concept; it is measured in dollars at a point in time. Income, in contrast, is a flow; it is measured in dollars per unit of time. Of two households with equal income, we expect the one with greater wealth to spend more freely on consumer goods than the one with less wealth. Thus, anything that happens to increase the total real wealth of all households will cause an upward shift in the consumption schedule. This effect shows up as a change in autonomous consumption; the marginal propensity to consume and, hence, the slope of the consumption schedule remain unchanged.

Many people, for example, hold some of their wealth in the form of corporate stocks. A drop in the average price of all corporate stocks thus could produce a downward shift in the consumption schedule. *Applying Economic Ideas 8.1* discusses the effects on consumption of stock market crashes such as those of 1929 and 1987.

In addition, a change in the price level can affect real wealth via a change in the real purchasing power of nominal money balances. A rise in the price level means that a $20 bill or $100 in a checking account will buy less than before; a fall in the price level means that it will buy more. Thus, a rise in the price level tends to cut real autonomous consumption and shift the consumption schedule downward, whereas a fall produces an upward shift. This effect is one of the factors that give the aggregate demand curve a negative slope.

**EXPECTATIONS**    People's spending decisions depend not only on their current real income and wealth but also on their expected future real income and wealth. Any change in their expectations can cause a shift in the consumption schedule. Such changes in expectations might include higher expected earnings at a new job, an expected decrease in household expenditures due to children leaving the home after graduating, or expected prosperity for the country under a new president. When all consumers become pessimistic—as they tend to do during a recession—the consumption schedule can shift downward; when they become more optimistic, it can shift upward again.

## THE STOCK MARKET AND THE ECONOMY

The prosperity of the Roaring Twenties was marked by a soaring stock market. Then, on October 28, 1929, the market crashed. The widely watched Dow Jones average of industrial stock prices fell 38 points to close at 261, a 12.8 percent drop, and dove another 31 points the next day. Those two days of panic came to be known as the Great Crash.

Many saw the Great Crash of 1929 as the beginning of the decade-long Great Depression. But was it merely a symbol, or was it actually a factor that helped to cause the downturn?

Those who think the Great Crash simply reflected a decline that had already begun note that the peak of the 1920s expansion had been reached in August 1929. From then to October, production fell at an annual rate of 20 percent and personal income at an annual rate of 5 percent. But other arguments support the idea that the stock market crash of 1929 helped cause, or at least deepened, the Great Depression.

One argument notes that a drop in stock prices is a reduction in real personal wealth. Since wealth can affect consumption independently of changes in income, a drop in stock prices will tend to shift the consumption function downward. One rule of thumb links each $1 drop in stock market wealth to a $.05 drop in consumption. That would be enough to significantly affect the economy, especially when magnified by the multiplier effect.

A second argument emphasized the psychological impact of falling stock prices on the confidence of consumers and business managers. Because both the consumption function and the planned-investment curve are sensitive to changes in expectations, they can be shifted downward by an expectations effect as well as by a decrease in wealth. As Fred Allen, a contemporary observer, wrote: "There was hardly a man or woman in the country whose attitude toward life had not been affected by [the bull market of the 1920s] in some degree and was not now affected by the sudden and brutal shattering of hope."

Only on one other occasion has Wall Street seen a crash comparable to that of 1929. It occurred when the market fell by 508 points, or 22.6 percent, in a single day, October 19, 1987—about the same percentage decline as the two days of the Great Crash. At first, many people worried that the crash would touch off a recession. However, the effect of the 1987 crash on consumption, although measurable, was small. Other areas of spending, including investment and net exports, showed enough strength to offset the slight decline in the average propensity to consume. Although a few sectors, notably luxury cars, did suffer reduced sales, the economic expansion that had begun in 1982 continued for another two years. By the time the next recession arrived, the stock market had long since recovered from its 500-point loss of 1987.

Sources: Milton Friedman and Anna J. Schwartz, *A Monetary History of the United States* (Princeton, N.J.: Princeton University Press, 1963), Chapter 7; Peter Temin, *Did Monetary Forces Cause the Great Depression?* (New York: Norton, 1976), Chapter 3.

**NET TAXES**  Up to this point we have graphed the consumption schedule using real disposable income on the horizontal axis. For many purposes, however, it is more useful to substitute real domestic income. Recall that under the simplifying assumptions of this chapter, the level of disposable income on which consumption decisions depend will differ from the level of domestic income by the amount of net taxes. As a result, changes in net taxes become another source of shifts in the consumption schedule.[2] The type of shift produced varies, depending on how the taxes are related to income.

**Autonomous net taxes**

Taxes or transfer payments that do not vary with the level of domestic income.

**AUTONOMOUS NET TAXES**  Taxes and transfer payments that do not vary with domestic income are called **autonomous net taxes**. Personal property taxes are a major example on the revenue side of the net tax picture. On the transfer side, items ranging from interest on the national debt to government pensions are not directly linked to changes in income.

**FIGURE 8.2   DOMESTIC INCOME AND CONSUMPTION WITH AUTONOMOUS NET TAXES**

(a)

| Domestic Income (1) | Consumption with No Tax (2) | Autonomous Net Tax (3) | Disposable Income (4) | Consumption with Tax (5) |
|---|---|---|---|---|
| $ 0 | $ 100 | $100 | $–100 | $ 25 |
| 100 | 175 | 100 | 0 | 100 |
| 200 | 250 | 100 | 100 | 175 |
| 300 | 325 | 100 | 200 | 250 |
| 400 | 400 | 100 | 300 | 325 |
| 500 | 475 | 100 | 400 | 400 |
| 600 | 550 | 100 | 500 | 475 |
| 700 | 625 | 100 | 600 | 550 |
| 800 | 700 | 100 | 700 | 625 |
| 900 | 775 | 100 | 800 | 700 |
| 1,000 | 850 | 100 | 900 | 775 |
| 1,100 | 925 | 100 | 1,000 | 850 |
| 1,200 | 1,000 | 100 | 1,000 | 925 |

(b)

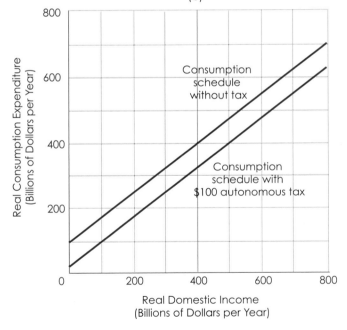

Autonomous net taxes do not change when the level of real domestic income changes. This figure shows how introducing an autonomous net tax of $100 billion shifts the consumption schedule downward when the schedule is drawn with domestic income on the horizontal axis. The amount of the shift is equal to the level of autonomous net taxes times the marginal propensity to consume.

Figure 8.2 shows how the consumption schedule is affected by introducing autonomous net taxes of $100 billion into an economy that had no taxes before. The first two columns of part (a), which are the same as those in Figure 8.1, show domestic income and the resulting level of consumption that would take place if there were no taxes. The consumption schedule assumes autonomous consumption of $100 billion and a marginal propensity to consume of .75. Columns 3 and 4 show that the $100 billion autonomous net tax reduces disposable income to a level $100 billion below that of domestic income. As column 5 shows, this $100 billion reduction cuts $75 billion from consumption at each income level in accordance with the .75 marginal propensity to consume. The remaining $25 billion of the tax is accounted for by a reduction in saving. As before, consumption is at the autonomous level of $100 billion when disposable income is zero. However, zero disposable income now corresponds to $100 billion of domestic income, as line 2 of the table shows. At a domestic income of zero, consumption is $25 billion.

Part (b) of Figure 8.2 shows the effect of the autonomous net tax in graphical terms. Introducing the tax produces a downward shift in the consumption schedule as it is drawn here, with real domestic income on the horizontal axis. The new schedule is parallel to the old one but is shifted downward by an amount equal to the marginal propensity to consume times the level of autonomous net taxes—in this case, $75 billion. The vertical intercept of the new schedule equals autonomous consumption minus the marginal propensity to consume times the level of autonomous net taxes, or $25 billion in this case.

**INCOME TAXES**    Other taxes, like the federal income tax and the social security payroll tax, are linked to income. These have a somewhat different effect on the consumption schedule, as Figure 8.3 shows.

**Marginal tax rate**

The percentage of each added dollar of real domestic income that must be paid in taxes.

Part (a) of Figure 8.3 assumes a 20 percent **marginal tax rate** on income from all sources; it also assumes autonomous net taxes of zero. As columns 3 and 4 show, this means that the tax takes $.20 of each added dollar of domestic income. Disposable income thus increases by $.80 for each added dollar of domestic income. As columns 4 and 5 show, the marginal propensity to consume of .75 applies to this $.80 of added disposable income. All told, then, for each added dollar of real domestic income $.20 goes for real taxes and $.60 of the remaining $.80 goes for real consumption.

Part (b) of Figure 8.3 shows the effect of an income tax in graphical terms. Instead of causing a downward shift that leaves the new schedule parallel to the old one, the income tax reduces the slope of the consumption schedule. With no income tax in effect, the slope of the schedule equals the marginal propensity to consume (in this case, .75). With a 20 percent marginal income tax rate, the slope is reduced to .6. The formula for the slope of the consumption schedule with an income tax in effect is:

$$\text{Slope of consumption schedule} = \text{mpc}(1 - t),$$

where t stands for the marginal tax rate

FIGURE 8.3 THE CONSUMPTION SCHEDULE WITH AN INCOME TAX ADDED

(a)

| Domestic Income (1) | Consumption with No Tax (2) | 20% Income Tax (3) | Disposable Income (4) | Consumption with Tax (5) |
|---|---|---|---|---|
| $   0 | $   100 | $   0 | $   0 | $100 |
| 100 | 175 | 20 | 80 | 160 |
| 200 | 250 | 40 | 160 | 220 |
| 300 | 325 | 60 | 240 | 280 |
| 400 | 400 | 80 | 320 | 340 |
| 500 | 475 | 100 | 400 | 400 |
| 600 | 550 | 120 | 480 | 460 |
| 700 | 625 | 140 | 560 | 520 |
| 800 | 700 | 160 | 640 | 580 |
| 900 | 775 | 180 | 720 | 640 |
| 1,000 | 850 | 200 | 800 | 700 |
| 1,100 | 925 | 220 | 880 | 760 |
| 1,200 | 1,000 | 240 | 960 | 820 |

Note: All amounts are in billions of dollars per year

(b)

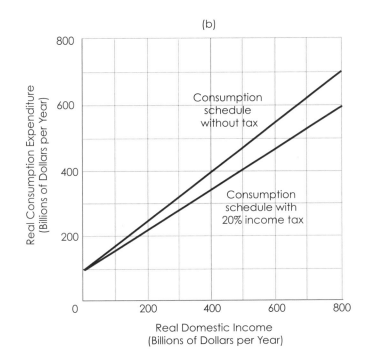

When the consumption schedule is drawn with domestic income on the horizontal axis, introducing an income tax reduces its slope. This example assumes a marginal propensity to consume of .75 and a marginal tax rate of .20. The slope of the consumption schedule with the income tax equals mpc(1 – t), where t is the marginal tax rate.

# GRAPHING THE INCOME-EXPENDITURE MODEL

Circular flow can be in equilibrium only when planned expenditure (aggregate demand) equals domestic product (aggregate supply). If planned expenditure exceeded domestic product, buyers' attempts to purchase more than was being produced would lead to unplanned decreases in business inventories. Firms would react to those decreases by increasing their output, thereby causing the level of the circular flow to rise. (They may also react by increasing prices; we will examine the effects of price changes later in the chapter.) Similarly, if planned expenditure fell short of domestic product, business inventories would build up more rapidly than planned. Firms would react by cutting their output (and/or lowering their prices).

These principles are central to Keynes' theory of equilibrium domestic income. In this section we will use them to develop a graphical model of that theory. Because Keynes saw planned expenditure primarily as a function of income rather than of prices, the model presented here is called the **income-expenditure model**.

## *The Planned-Expenditure Schedule*

First we construct a **planned-expenditure schedule** for the economy—a graph that shows the total real planned purchases of goods and services corresponding to each level of real domestic income. This curve differs from the aggregate demand curve introduced earlier in the text in that it relates the level of real planned expenditure to the level of real domestic income rather than to the price level. In constructing the planned-expenditure schedule, we will deal with each component of expenditure in turn as we did in the case of the aggregate demand curve.

**CONSUMPTION**   We have already discussed the relationship between real consumption and real domestic income. The consumption schedule serves as the foundation of the planned-expenditure schedule. The vertical intercept of the consumption schedule equals the level of autonomous consumption, adjusted, if necessary, for autonomous net taxes. Its slope equals the mpc, adjusted, if need be, for the marginal income tax rate. In this initial version of the planned-expenditure schedule, we will assume that there is no income tax and that autonomous net taxes are $100 billion, as was the case in Figure 8.2

**INVESTMENT**   The second component of planned expenditure is planned investment, including both fixed investment and planned (but not unplanned) changes in inventories. Real planned investment depends on interest rates and business expectations. In the simple model developed here, neither the interest rate nor expectations will be assumed to vary systematically with the income level. This means that planned investment is a type of autonomous expenditure along with autonomous consumption.

---

**Income-expenditure model**

A model in which the equilibrium level of real domestic income is determined by treating real planned expenditure and real domestic product as functions of the level of real domestic income.

**Planned-expenditure schedule**

A graph showing the level of total real planned expenditure associated with each level of real domestic income.

Once we know the level of planned investment for a given year, we can add it to planned consumption spending as a second component of planned expenditure, as shown in Figure 8.4. The C + I schedule in part (b) of the exhibit is the sum of the consumption and planned investment shown in columns 2 and 3 of part (a).

**GOVERNMENT PURCHASES**    The third component of planned expenditure is government purchases. In this chapter, however, we will assume that government purchases are fixed by law each year in real terms, so that they, too, are a category of autonomous expenditure.

Figure 8.4 shows how government purchases can be added to consumption and planned investment as a third component of planned expenditure. The C + I + G schedule in part (b) corresponds to the sum of columns 2 through 4 of part (a). Regardless of the domestic income level, government purchases are assumed to be limited to $150 billion.

## The Net Exports Component of Planned Expenditure

The final component of planned expenditure is real net exports, that is, real exports minus real imports. Exports can be considered autonomous from the standpoint of the domestic economy; they are determined by economic conditions in foreign countries. Imports, however, do depend on the level of domestic income. Because some of the goods that households consume are imported, imports increase when consumption expenditures rise. To calculate total planned expenditure including net exports, these imports, which are already included in the consumption component of planned expenditure, must now be subtracted.

For example, suppose that, as in Figure 8.2, the marginal propensity to consume is .75 and autonomous consumption and autonomous net taxes are each $100 billion. Suppose too that one-fifth of each added dollar of consumption expenditures is devoted to imported goods. This means that for each $1 increase in disposable income, consumption will rise by $.75 and imports will rise by one-fifth of that, or $.15. In economic terminology, there is a **marginal propensity to import** of .15. (The marginal propensity to import is expressed as a fraction of real disposable income, rather than as a fraction of consumption.)

Part (a) of Figure 8.5 shows how imports, exports, and net exports are related to domestic income. Consider imports first. As in Figure 8.2, consumption is $25 billion when domestic income is zero. One-fifth of this is spent on imported consumer goods; thus, imports are $5 billion when domestic income is zero. For each added $100 billion of domestic income, imports increase by $15 billion in accordance with the marginal propensity to import of .15. Therefore, when domestic income is $100 billion, imports are $20 billion; when domestic income is $1,000 billion, imports are $155 billion; and so on. The slope of the import schedule is .15.

Next, consider exports. These depend on the income level and the marginal propensity to import in foreign countries. In this case, we assume that foreign buyers

**Marginal propensity to import**

The percentage of each added dollar of real disposable income that is devoted to real consumption of imported goods and services.

FIGURE 8.4  THE C, I, AND G COMPONENTS OF THE PLANNED-EXPENDITURE SCHEDULE

(a)

| Domestic Income (1) | Consumption Expenditure (2) | Planned Investment (3) | Government Purchases (4) | C + I + G (5) |
|---|---|---|---|---|
| $ 0 | $ 25 | $125 | $150 | $ 300 |
| 100 | 100 | 125 | 150 | 375 |
| 200 | 175 | 125 | 150 | 450 |
| 300 | 250 | 125 | 150 | 525 |
| 400 | 325 | 125 | 150 | 600 |
| 500 | 400 | 125 | 150 | 675 |
| 600 | 475 | 125 | 150 | 750 |
| 700 | 550 | 125 | 150 | 825 |
| 800 | 625 | 125 | 150 | 900 |
| 900 | 700 | 125 | 150 | 975 |
| 1,000 | 775 | 125 | 150 | 1,050 |
| 1,100 | 850 | 125 | 150 | 1,125 |
| 1,200 | 925 | 125 | 150 | 1,200 |
| 1,300 | 1,000 | 125 | 150 | 1,275 |
| 1,400 | 1,075 | 125 | 150 | 1,350 |
| 1,500 | 1,150 | 125 | 150 | 1,425 |
| 1,600 | 1,225 | 125 | 150 | 1,500 |

Note: All amounts are in billions of dollars per year

(b)

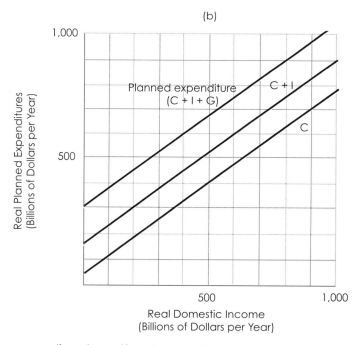

This figure shows the consumption, planned investment, and government purchases components of the planned-expenditure schedule. In the simple case represented here, consumption is the only element that varies directly with real domestic income. The slope of the C + I + G schedule thus equals the marginal propensity to consume of .75.

purchase $185 billion of exports. This quantity does not depend on the level of domestic income; hence, the export schedule in part (a) of Figure 8.5 is a horizontal line. Subtracting imports from exports yields the net export schedule. Like the import schedule, this has a slope equal (in absolute value) to the marginal propensity to import. When domestic income is zero, net exports equal $180 billion ($185 billion of exports minus $5 billion of imports). Net exports remain positive up to a domestic income of $1,200 billion; at $1,200 billion net exports are zero; and at domestic income levels above $1,200 billion they become negative.

Part (b) of Figure 8.5 adds the net export schedule to consumption, planned investment, and government purchases to yield the complete planned-expenditure schedule. The autonomous component of this schedule (shown by its vertical intercept at $480 billion) is the sum of autonomous consumption adjusted for autonomous net taxes ($25 billion), planned investment ($125 billion), government purchases ($150 billion), and net exports ($180 billion). The slope of the schedule (in this case, .6) equals the marginal propensity to consume minus the marginal propensity to import.

In this example it is assumed that there is no income tax. If there were, the calculation of the slope of the planned-expenditure schedule would have to take this into account. Using mpc for the marginal propensity to consume, mpm for the marginal propensity to import out of disposable income, and t for the marginal tax rate, the formula for the slope of the planned-expenditure schedule becomes (mpc – mpm) (1 – t).

In this example, real net exports depend only on real disposable income in the domestic economy. In practice, they also depend on real domestic income in foreign countries, which determines the level of real exports, and also on the exchange rate of the dollar relative to foreign currencies, which affects both imports and exports. We will explore these aspects of the foreign sector in more detail in later chapters.

## Determining the Equilibrium Level of Domestic Income

The planned-expenditure schedule shows how aggregate demand varies as domestic income changes, with the price level held constant. To find the equilibrium level of domestic income, all we need to do now is find the income level at which aggregate demand (that is, planned expenditure) equals aggregate supply (that is, domestic product). Figure 8.6 shows how this is done. The example is simplified by assuming a closed economy, that is, zero net exports.

**THE INCOME-PRODUCT LINE**  The first step is to add a line showing the relationship between domestic income and domestic product. Under our simplifying assumptions, domestic income and product are equal. Using the horizontal axis to represent real domestic income and the vertical axis to represent real domestic product, the relationship between the two can be shown as a straight line with a slope of 1

**FIGURE 8.5 ADDING NET EXPORTS TO THE PLANNED-EXPENDITURE SCHEDULE**

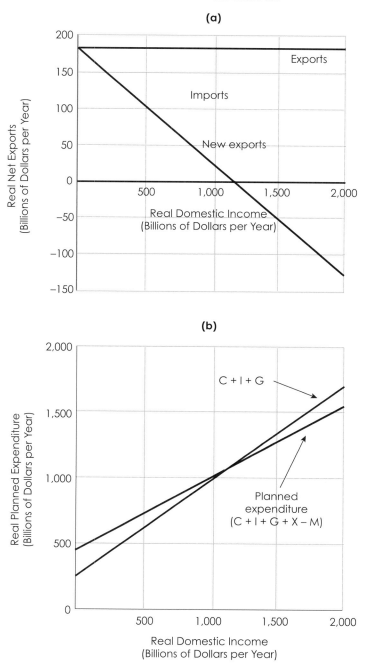

Part (a) shows how imports, exports, and net exports behave as real domestic income changes. Real domestic income in the domestic economy does not affect exports; hence, exports are represented by a horizontal line at an assumed level of $185 billion. When domestic income is zero, consumption is $25 billion; thus, imports are $5 billion. With a marginal propensity to import of .15, imports increase by $15 billion for each $100 billion increase in real domestic income. The net export line shows exports minus imports. Net exports are equal to zero at $1,200 billion. Part (b) of the exhibit shows how net exports can be added to consumption, government purchases, and planned investment to give the complete planned-expenditure schedule.

**Income-product line**

A graph showing the level of real domestic product (aggregate supply) associated with each level of real domestic income.

passing through the origin. We will refer to this line as the **income-product line**. It is simply a graphical representation of the equality of domestic income and product. (This equality is a fundamental property of the circular flow.)

**PLANNED EXPENDITURE AND DOMESTIC PRODUCT**    When the income-product and planned-expenditure lines are drawn together, as in Figure 8.6, it is a simple matter to find the income level for which real planned expenditure and real domestic product are equal. This equality occurs at the intersection of the two lines—$1,200 billion in Figure 8.6. Because *planned expenditure* is simply another term for *aggregate demand,* and *domestic product* is a synonym for *aggregate supply,* this intersection point is a point of equilibrium for the circular flow.

At no other level of domestic income can the circular flow be in equilibrium. If domestic income is lower than the equilibrium level—say, $1,000 billion—planned expenditure (aggregate demand) will exceed domestic product (aggregate supply). There will be an unplanned drop in inventories equal to the vertical distance between the planned-expenditure schedule and the income-product line. In trying to restore inventories to their planned levels, firms will increase their output, thereby causing domestic income to rise. As income rises, planned expenditure increases, but only by a fraction of the amount by which domestic product increases. The gap therefore narrows until equilibrium is restored.

If, on the other hand, domestic income is higher than the equilibrium level—say, $1,500 billion—planned expenditure will fall short of output. The unsold goods will become unplanned inventory investment equal to the gap between the planned-expenditure and income-product lines at the $1,500 billion income level. Firms will react to the unplanned inventory buildup by cutting production. Their actions will cause real domestic income and product to fall to the equilibrium level.

In Figure 8.6 the same story is told twice—graphically in part (a) and numerically in part (b). Both approaches confirm that $1,200 billion is the only possible equilibrium level for domestic income, given the underlying assumptions on which the planned-expenditure schedule is based.

## The Multiplier Effect

The level of real planned expenditure for the economy depends on many factors. First and foremost, planned spending varies as real domestic income changes. In the graphs used in this chapter, such changes are shown as movements along the planned-expenditure schedule. Other factors that affect planned expenditure—changes in expectations, consumer wealth, interest rates, taxes, government purchases, or foreign markets—cause shifts in the planned-expenditure schedule. In this section, we focus on changes in real income produced by shifts in the planned expenditure schedule under the assumption that no changes occur in the price level. This assumption will be relaxed later in the chapter.

**FIGURE 8.6   USING THE INCOME-EXPENDITURE MODEL TO FIND THE EQUILIBRIUM LEVEL OF REAL DOMESTIC INCOME**

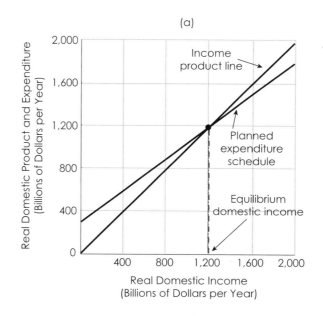

(a)

(b)

| Real Domestic Income (1) | Real Planned Expenditure (2) | Real Domestic Product (3) | Unplanned Inventory Change (4) | Tendency of Change in Domestic Income (5) |
|---|---|---|---|---|
| $ 0 | $ 300 | $ 0 | −$300 | Increase |
| 100 | 375 | 100 | −275 | Increase |
| 200 | 450 | 200 | −250 | Increase |
| 300 | 525 | 300 | −225 | Increase |
| 400 | 600 | 400 | −200 | Increase |
| 500 | 675 | 500 | −175 | Increase |
| 600 | 750 | 600 | −150 | Increase |
| 700 | 825 | 700 | −125 | Increase |
| 800 | 900 | 800 | −100 | Increase |
| 900 | 975 | 900 | −75 | Increase |
| 1,000 | 1,050 | 1,00 | −50 | Increase |
| 1,100 | 1,125 | 1,100 | −25 | Increase |
| 1,200 | 1,200 | 1,200 | 0 | No change |
| 1,300 | 1,275 | 1,300 | 25 | Decrease |
| 1,400 | 1,350 | 1,400 | 50 | Decrease |
| 1,500 | 1,450 | 1,500 | 75 | Decrease |
| 1,600 | 1,500 | 1,600 | 100 | Decrease |

Note: All amounts are in billions of dollars per year

The income-expenditure model is formed by the planned-expenditure schedule and the income-product line. This figure shows a simple way to determine the equilibrium level of real domestic income given the underlying conditions that determine the position of the planned-expenditure schedule. Any domestic income higher than the equilibrium level will cause unplanned inventory buildup and will put downward pressure on real output. Any level of domestic income below equilibrium will cause unplanned inventory depletion and put upward pressure on real output. The example is simplified by assuming a closed economy, so that net exports are zero at all levels of real domestic income.

Figure 8.7 shows the effects of a $100 billion annual increase in planned expenditure. For the moment, it does not matter whether the shift begins in the household, investment, or government sector; the effect in any case is to shift the planned-expenditure schedule upward by $100 billion, from $PE_1$ to $PE_2$.

When the planned-expenditure schedule shifts upward by $100 billion, the immediate effect is to raise planned expenditure to a level exceeding domestic product. As a result, inventories start to fall at a rate of $100 billion per year. Firms react to this unplanned inventory depletion by Increasing their output. (In a model with flexible prices, they would tend to increase both real output and prices.) As a result, the circular flow expands. Domestic income continues to rise until the gap between planned expenditure and domestic product—that is, between aggregate demand and aggregate supply—disappears. This occurs at an income level of $1,600 billion.

We see, then, that a $100 billion upward shift in the planned-expenditure schedule has caused a $400 billion increase in equilibrium real domestic income. This ability of a given vertical shift in planned expenditure to cause a greater increase in the equilibrium level of domestic income is the multiplier effect. At this point it may be

---

**FIGURE 8.7    MULTIPLIER EFFECT IN THE INCOME-EXPENDITURE MODEL**

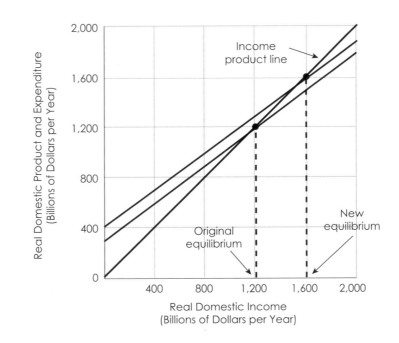

A given vertical shift in the planned-expenditure schedule produces a greater increase in the equilibrium level of real domestic income. This constitutes a graphical representation of the multiplier effect. Here a $100 billion upward shift in the planned-expenditure schedule causes a $400 billion increase in equilibrium real domestic income. The ratio of the change in equilibrium income to the initial shift in demand, which is the expenditure multiplier, has a value of 4 in this example. In this simplified example, the marginal tax rate and the marginal propensity to import are assumed to be zero.

helpful to compare the graphical demonstration of the multiplier effect in Figure 8.7 with the numerical example given in Figure 8.6.

## Modifications in the Multiplier Formula

In an earlier chapter we presented the expenditure multiplier as $1/(1 - mpc)$. The marginal propensity to consume (mpc) is the slope of the planned-expenditure schedule in a closed economy without income taxes. In this chapter we have added some details to the model that require that we modify the formula. The modifications can be derived from this general form for the multiplier:

Expenditure multiplier = 1/(1 – Slope of planned-expenditure schedule)

The formula given earlier is the simplest case. Starting from there, anything that affects the slope of the planned-expenditure schedule will affect the multiplier, as we will now show.

**THE EFFECT OF AN INCOME TAX IN A CLOSED ECONOMY**   Earlier in this chapter we saw that the addition of an income tax changes the slope of the consumption schedule from mpc to $mpc(1 - t)$, where t is the marginal tax rate. Thus the formula for the multiplier in a closed economy with a proportional income tax imposed at a marginal tax rate of t is

Expenditure multiplier = $1/[1 - mpc(1 - t)]$

This formula shows that the imposition of an income tax reduces the value of the multiplier. For example, a closed economy with a marginal propensity to consume of .8 will have an expenditure multiplier of 5 if there is no income tax. With an income tax at a 25 percent marginal rate, the denominator of the multiplier formula will be .4, and the multiplier therefore will fall to 2.5. In general, the higher the marginal tax rate, the smaller the effect of a disturbance in planned expenditure on the equilibrium level of real domestic income.

**THE EFFECT OF NET EXPORTS**   Including the foreign sector also changes the slope of the planned-expenditure schedule and, therefore, the multiplier. We represent the foreign sector with *mpm* (marginal propensity to import), which shows the share of each dollar of added disposable income that goes to imports. The slope of the planned-expenditure schedule is now $(mpc - mpm)(1 - t)$, so the formula for the expenditure multiplier becomes

Expenditure multiplier = $1/[1 - (mpc - mpm)(1 - t)1]$

For example, suppose that the marginal propensity to consume is .9, the marginal propensity to import is .15, and the marginal tax rate is .33. With no income tax or imports, the multiplier for an economy with an mpc of .9 will be 10. Adding imports will reduce the slope of the planned-expenditure schedule to .75 and, hence, reduce the multiplier to 4. Adding a marginal tax rate of .33 will further reduce the slope of the planned-expenditure schedule to .5, thereby reducing the expenditure multiplier to 2.

# THE RELATIONSHIP BETWEEN THE INCOME DETERMINATION MODELS

We now have two models for determining the equilibrium level of real domestic income and product: the aggregate supply and demand model, which treats real planned expenditure and real domestic product as functions of the price level, and the income-expenditure model, which treats them as functions of the level of real domestic income. This section briefly examines the relationship between the two models. Doing so requires that we relax the assumption that the price level does not change as planned expenditure changes.

## The Two Models in the Short Run

Figure 8.8 illustrates the relationship between the two models in the short run. Initially the economy is in equilibrium with real domestic product at its natural level and the price level at 1.0. This equilibrium is shown as $E_1$ in the aggregate supply and demand model of part (a) and as $e_1$ in the income-expenditure model of part (b). Now suppose that something happens to increase real autonomous expenditure by $500 billion; for our present purposes it does not matter whether the increase comes from autonomous consumption, planned investment, government purchases, or net exports. The increase in autonomous expenditure shifts the planned-expenditure schedule upward. This causes unplanned depletion of inventories, and the economy begins to expand.

**SHORT-RUN EQUILIBRIUM WITH FLEXIBLE PRICES**   If there were no change in the price level, a $500 billion increase in autonomous expenditure would move the planned-expenditure schedule to $PE_2$, and real output would find a new equilibrium at $3,000 billion.[3] In part (b), this equilibrium would occur at $e_2$. In part (a), a $1,000 billion increase in domestic product with no price change would put the economy at $E_2$ in accordance with the multiplier effect.

However, with flexible prices, an increase in aggregate demand causes the price level to increase as well as the level of real output. This is shown in part (a) of Figure 8.8 as a movement up and to the right along the economy's short-run aggregate supply curve, AS. As soon as the economy begins to move up along the aggregate supply curve, things start to happen in the income-expenditure model in part (b). As

## FIGURE 8.8 RECONCILING THE INCOME-EXPENDITURE AND AGGREGATE SUPPLY AND DEMAND MODELS

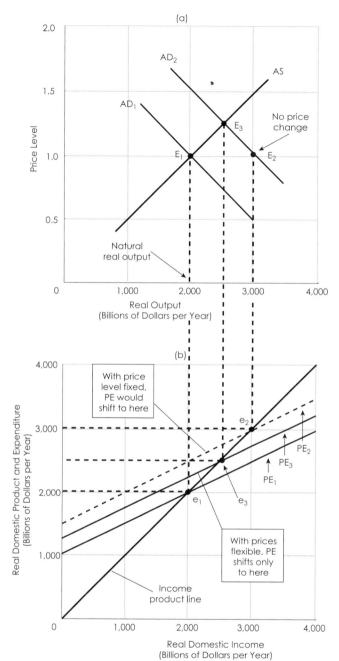

Both the income-expenditure and aggregate supply and demand models determine the equilibrium level of real domestic income and product. This exhibit shows how they can be reconciled when the effect of a change in the price level on planned expenditure is taken into account. The economy begins at $E_1$ in part (a) and as $e_1$ in part (b). Autonomous expenditure then increases by $500 billion. The aggregate demand curve shifts from $AD_1$ to $AD_2$. With no price change, the economy would end up at $E_2$ and $e_2$. However, the price level increases as the economy moves up along the aggregate supply curve to $E_3$. This causes the planned-expenditure schedule to halt its upward movement at $PE_3$. Thus, the short-run equilibrium as shown in the income-expenditure model is $e_3$, which occurs at the same level of domestic product shown by $E_3$ in part (a).

Note: All amounts are in billions of constant dollars per year.

## ⌒ ECONOMICS IN THE NEWS 8.1
### WHY AMERICANS MUST KEEP SPENDING

Nothing props up the economy more than consumers, and dips in their spending frighten forecasters. But that is all that has happened in recent years—dips, not plunges. Consumers in America spend because they feel they must spend. More than in the past, the necessities of life, real and perceived, eat up their incomes.

That treadmill spending is good news for the economy. As a recovery takes hold, the biggest threat to its survival would be a downturn in consumer spending. That is not inconceivable: The support for recent spending—the household cash generated through mortgage refinancings and tax cuts—is disappearing, and a new source of cash, from many new jobs and many new paychecks, is not yet a reality.

But do not worry, various experts say. Consumers will keep spending anyway, going deeper into debt to do so if they must. They have too many needs, some that were luxuries only yesterday. A second car and child care, for example, are now necessities for millions of households with two earners commuting to jobs. Mall-crawling, for all its popularity, is increasingly the anomaly, not the norm, in the vast realm of personal consumption.

So as the typical household keeps spending, and as other sectors of the economy revive, the country will prosper. There is considerable optimism on this point among the nation's forecasters. All but one of the 51 surveyed by Blue Chip Economic Indicators expect the economy to grow more strongly in 2004 than it has in the past 33 months—expanding at a 4 percent annual rate, up from less than 3 percent through most of the past three years.

"The economic upturn does have staying power," said Lynn Reaser, chief economist of Banc America Capital Management, the primary investment management group of the Bank of America.

Business investment, she notes, is already on the rise, profits are soaring and stock prices have gone up, reawakening the wealth effect. Above all, consumption outlays, which never flagged during the 2001 recession and the weak economic growth thereafter, surged in the third quarter, contributing significantly to economic growth. Not surprisingly, mortgage refinancing reached a peak in this quarter, as homeowners took advantage of low interest rates, and so

did the effects of the tax cuts championed by the Bush administration. Without that support, consumer spending may dip in the months ahead, but it will not plunge. Too much of a household's income goes for items now considered necessities.

This spending truly matters. Consumers are purchasing roughly $7.6 trillion a year in goods and services. Their outlays represent about two-thirds of the nation's economic activity, so when people slow their buying, the growth of the economy also slows. But that seldom happens anymore.

Look back to 1947, a total of 227 quarters. In only 20 of these three-month periods did a drop or weakness in consumer spending curb economic growth or weaken an expansion, and most of that occurred in the early decades. Only three times in the last two decades has consumer spending faltered enough to damage the economy—twice during the 1990–1991 recession and once as the slow recovery got under way. That drag disappeared in the 2001 recession, the first since the 1940s in which consumer spending rose enough to limit the contraction instead of contributing to it.

This suggests that consumers are earmarking an increasing share of their disposable income for purchases that are, or that they consider, necessary, even in recessions. "The spending you can't fool around with has gone up—for homes, health insurance, day care, car payments," said Elizabeth Warren, a Harvard Law School professor and co-author of *The Two-Income Trap* (Basic Books, 2003). She argues that the optional portion of consumer spending has become relatively small.

So even if more jobs and more paychecks fail to materialize, the typical household will keep up its spending, Ms. Warren contends. People will do so by going into debt, or deeper into debt, to acquire what they view as essentials. Such consumption will help sustain the economy in the coming presidential election year, although painfully for many households. "It is hard to construct a happy story for 2004 unless we consistently create a significant number of jobs, which we have not done yet," said Mark Zandi, chief economist at Economy.com, a research and consulting firm.

Source: (abridged, pg. 1 of 3) Louis Uchitelle, "Why Americans Must Keep Spending," *The New York Times*, December 1, 2003.

discussed previously, the rising price level reduces real autonomous consumption via its effect on the real value of nominal money balances; it reduces real planned investment via an increase in the interest rate; it may lower real government purchases if government budgets are set partly in nominal terms; and it reduces real net exports by increasing the prices of domestic goods relative to foreign goods. These effects partially offset those of the original increase in autonomous expenditure. The planned-expenditure schedule does not move all the way to $PE_2$; instead, the rise in the price level allows it to shift only as far as $PE_3$.

Because the planned-expenditure schedule shifts only to $PE_3$, equilibrium real output rises only to $2,500 billion, rather than to $3,000 billion as it would if prices remained fixed. The new short-run equilibrium in the income-expenditure model is $e_3$. This corresponds to point $E_3$ in the aggregate supply and demand model—a point on the aggregate supply curve that is above and to the right of the initial equilibrium, $E_1$.

**EFFECT ON THE AGGREGATE DEMAND CURVE**   The preceding analysis sheds light on some important features of the aggregate demand curve. The initial equilibrium, $E_1$, lies on aggregate demand curve $AD_1$ at the point at which it intersects the aggregate supply curve, AS. What about points $E_2$ and $E_3$? $E_2$ shows what would have happened to the equilibrium level of aggregate demand if the price level had remained at 1.0. $E_3$ shows what happens to it when the economy instead moves up along the aggregate supply curve. Points $E_2$ and $E_3$ both lie on a new aggregate demand curve, $AD_2$. The various points along that curve show the level of aggregate demand at different possible price levels, given the original shift in autonomous expenditure.

Our example thus confirms two points about the aggregate demand curve that were made earlier. First, we  see that the negative slope of the aggregate demand curve arises from the effects of a change in the price level on real planned expenditure. These are the same forces that limit the shift in the planned-expenditure schedule to $PE_3$. Second, we see that an initial increase in autonomous expenditure, in the form of a change in autonomous consumption, planned investment, government purchases, or net exports, causes a horizontal shift in the aggregate demand curve. This shift (the distance between $E_1$ and $E_2$ in part (a) of Figure 8.8) equals the expenditure multiplier times the initial increase in autonomous expenditure.[4] However, the actual increase in equilibrium aggregate demand is less than the horizontal shift in the aggregate demand curve, because the price level increases as the economy moves up and to the right along its short-run aggregate supply curve.

## *The Two Models in the Long Run*

So far we have looked at short-run effects. The effect of long-run adjustments is demonstrated in Figure 8.9. This exhibit begins where Figure 8.8 left off—with the economy in short-run equilibrium at $E_3$ in part (a) and at $e_3$ in part (b). The schedule $PE_2$ and the corresponding points $e_2$ and $E_2$ have been deleted to simplify the diagrams.

The economy can remain in short-run equilibrium at $E_3$ only as long as firms expect input prices to remain constant. In the long run, firms' expectations regarding input prices will adjust to the changes in prices of final goods that have already taken place, and the short-run aggregate supply curve will begin to shift upward. Expected

FIGURE 8.9   LONG-RUN EFFECTS OF EXPANSION IN THE TWO MODELS

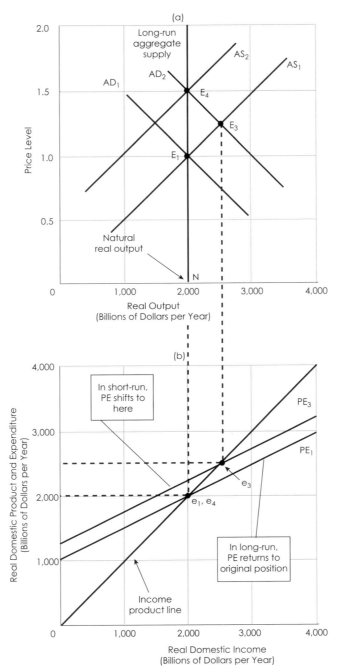

This Figure picks up where Figure 8.8 left off. The short-run equilibrium following an increase in autonomous expenditure is $E_3$ in part (a) and $e_3$ in part (b). Over time, as the input prices expected by firms adjust, the short-run aggregate supply curve shifts upward from $AS_1$ to $AS_2$, and the economy moves to a new long-run equilibrium at $E_4$. As it does, prices rise further and the planned-expenditure schedule in part (b) shifts all the way back down to its original position at $PE_1$. The final equilibrium in part (b) is $e_4$, which is identical to the initial equilibrium, $e_1$. Thus, we see that with flexible prices, a shift in the aggregate demand curve has no permanent effect on the equilibrium level of real domestic income and product.

Note: All amounts are in billions of constant dollars per year.

input prices will return to a consistent equilibrium relationship with final goods prices only when the short-run aggregate supply curve has shifted all the way from $AS_1$ to $AS_2$. The economy will then reach a new long-run equilibrium at point $E_4$ in part (a) of Figure 8.9, where aggregate demand curve $AD_2$ intersects the long-run as well as the short-run aggregate supply curve.

The move from $E_3$ to $E_4$ involves a further increase in the level of final-goods prices. As prices rise beyond the level of 1.25, real planned expenditure begins to decrease. In part (a) of Figure 8.9, this is indicated by a movement upward and to the left along the aggregate demand curve $AD_2$. The decrease in real planned expenditure reflects changes in each component of aggregate demand: a drop in consumption as real income falls and rising prices erode the real value of money, declines in real planned investment and government purchases, and falling net exports. In part (b) of the exhibit, we see that these events take the form of a downward shift of the planned-expenditure schedule; it drops below $PE_3$ and does not stop until it is all the way back to $PE_1$. At that point the depressing effects of rising prices on real planned expenditure fully offset the initial increase in autonomous expenditure. The long-run equilibrium in the income-expenditure model thus is $e_4$, which is exactly the same as the initial equilibrium, $e_1$. This result is a more elaborate restatement of a result noted in an earlier chapter: if prices for both inputs and final goods are fully flexible in the long run, a shift in aggregate demand has no lasting effect on the equilibrium level of real domestic income and product. The only lasting effect is on the levels of final goods and input prices. We will return to the implications of this proposition at several points in later chapters.

⌐)

# SUMMARY

1. **How is consumption related to disposable income?** The relationship between real consumption and real disposable income is shown by the *consumption function*. Its vertical intercept, which represents the part of real consumption expenditure that is not associated with a particular real income level, equals *autonomous consumption*. Its slope equals the marginal propensity to consume. Changes in real wealth, the average price level, or expectations can shift the consumption function.

2. **How is consumption affected by various kinds of taxes?** The basic form of the consumption function relates real consumption expenditure to real disposable income. It can be redrawn with domestic rather than disposable income on the horizontal axis by adjusting for the effect of taxes. An *autonomous net tax* shifts the consumption function downward by an amount equal to the tax times the marginal propensity to consume without changing the slope of the consumption function. An income tax reduces the slope of the consumption function to $mpc(1 - t)$, where t is the *marginal tax rate*.

3. **How is the equilibrium level of domestic income determined in the income-expenditure model?** The income-expenditure model consists of the

*planned-expenditure schedule* and the *income-product line*. Their intersection shows the equilibrium level of real domestic income, that is, the level at which planned expenditure (aggregate demand) equals domestic product (aggregate supply). At any higher level of domestic income, there will be unplanned inventory accumulation. At any lower level of domestic income, there will be unplanned inventory depletion.

4. **How can the income-expenditure model be used to demonstrate the multiplier effect?** Any shift in the planned-expenditure schedule will change its point of intersection with the income-product line. The greater the slope of the planned-expenditure schedule, the greater the change in equilibrium real domestic income that will result from a given change in autonomous expenditure. This is the multiplier effect.

5. **What is the relationship of the income-expenditure model to the aggregate supply and demand model?** The income-expenditure model relates real planned expenditure to the level of real domestic income, whereas the aggregate supply and demand model relates real planned expenditure to the price level. The key to the relationship between the two models lies in the fact that an increase in the price level causes the planned-expenditure schedule to shift downward and a decrease causes it to shift upward. An initial increase in autonomous planned expenditure shifts the aggregate demand curve to the right by an amount that depends on the size of the expenditure multiplier. In the short run, there is an increase in both real output and the price level as the economy moves up and to the right along the aggregate supply curve. In the long run, a shift in real aggregate demand has no lasting effect on the equilibrium level of real domestic income once both input and final goods prices have changed by enough to bring real domestic product back to its natural level.

## KEY TERMS

Consumption schedule (consumption function)

Autonomous consumption

Autonomous

Average propensity to consume

Autonomous net taxes

Marginal tax rate

Income-expenditure model

Planned-expenditure schedule

Marginal propensity to import

Income-product line

## PROBLEMS AND TOPICS FOR DISCUSSION

1. **Permanent and transitory changes in income.** Suppose that you won $1,000 in a lottery. How much would you spend and how much would you save? (Remember that debt repayment counts as saving.) Would you save more or less of this $1,000 windfall than of the first $1,000 of a pay increase that you expected to be permanent? Would it surprise you to learn that some surveys have found that the marginal propensity to consume from windfall income is smaller than the marginal propensity to consume from permanent income changes? Explain.

2. **Graphing the consumption schedule.** On a sheet of graph paper, draw consumption schedules for the following values of real autonomous consumption (a) and the marginal propensity to consume (mpc): a = 1,000, mpc = .5; a = 1,200, mpc = .6; a = 500, mpc = .9.

3. **Taxes and the consumption schedule.** On a sheet of graph paper, draw a consumption schedule based on the following assumptions: no taxes at all, autonomous consumption of $100 billion, and a marginal propensity to consume of .8. Label the

horizontal axis "real domestic income." Now modify this schedule for the following tax assumptions:

a. Real autonomous net taxes of $50 billion

b. An income tax with a marginal tax rate of 25 percent

c. Both (a) and (b)

*Bonus question:* Calculate the value of the expenditure multiplier for each of the preceding cases.

4. **Effects of a decrease in autonomous expenditure.** Rework Figure 8.7 for a $100 billion decrease in real autonomous planned expenditure. Explain step by step what will happen on the way to the new equilibrium.

5. **Effects of a decrease in autonomous expenditure with flexible prices.** Rework Figures 8.8 and 8.9 for a $250 billion decrease in real autonomous planned expenditure. Explain what happens at each step in the transition to a new short- and long-run equilibrium.

## CASE FOR DISCUSSION

### The Urge for New Equipment Will Keep Investment Growing

**DECEMBER, 1989**—American businesses may well fixate too shortsightedly on the quarter in front of them, but you wouldn't guess that from their views about capital spending. Investment in plant and equipment will increase next year—modestly, to be sure, with most of the strength in equipment—despite a slower-growing economy and rotten 1989 profits. What's on the minds of those executives? Brighter prospects for the next year and, yes, the next decade. The possibilities for growth around the world in the long term look better now than they did even a few months ago.

In *Fortune's* recent survey of the business mood, executives said they are more confident about the economy and more aggressive in their spending

plans than they have been in two years. That confidence surprised some analysts, partly because of the weakness in capacity use during the past few months. Putting that softness in historical context lessens the mystery. For business as a whole, utilization has barely inched down and is still near its high for the 1980s. Capital stock has been expanding better than 3 percent a year for most of this decade, but no excess capacity appears to be building up.

The real action in 1990 will be in computers. "Talk about capital spending and you are talking information processing," says Adrian Dillon, chief economist of Eaton Corp. Computers account for nearly half of equipment purchases, and after two volatile years, Dillon is expecting a substantial increase in spending.

Source: Vivian Brownstein, "The Urge for New Equipment Will Keep Business Investment Growing," *Fortune*, December 18, 1989, 33–36. © 1989 The Time Inc. Magazine Company. All rights reserved.

### QUESTIONS

1. How does an increase in capital spending by businesses affect the economy? Explain in terms of the circular flow model, the aggregate supply and demand model, and the income-expenditure model presented in this chapter. Compare and contrast the three approaches.

2. To what does *Fortune* attribute the strong prospects for business investment in 1990—to the stimulus of low interest rates, or a change in expectations, or both?

3. At the end of the second quarter of 1989, total spending on producers' durable equipment in the U.S. economy was about $400 billion. Assuming that the planned-expenditure schedule has a slope of .75, by how much will the equilibrium level of nominal domestic income increase as a result of a 5 percent increase in capital spending, assuming a constant price level? How will the effects differ if a flexible price level is assumed?

## Young, Hip, and Looking for a Bargain

The teenager: grown up enough to work part time, but not too old for birthday money or that weekly allowance. Altogether, the country's 32 million teenagers have $94.7 billion at their disposal, making them an important consumer in the U.S. economy. Factor in the jeans and video games bought by doting grandparents, or the laptops and DVD players that they recommend to aunts and uncles, and teenagers' contributions to consumer spending multiply.

Like the typical consumer who has been resilient in the face of a sluggish economy, teenagers are learning to become smart shoppers and make their dollars go further. Still, teenagers do not respond to economic factors nearly as much as older consumers do because they spend almost all of the income they earn. Teenagers with money in their pockets typically can buy whatever they want, such as clothes, consumer electronics and entertainment. Although some parents may require children to save a certain amount of their money, few teenagers have to worry about paying monthly bills.

Source: Bayot, Jennifer, "The Teenage Market: Young, Hip and Looking for a Bargain," *The New York Times*, December 1, 2003.

## END NOTES

1. The relationship between average and marginal propensity to consume can also be expressed in algebraic terms. Let $C$ represent consumption, $Y$ disposable income, $a$ autonomous consumption, and $b$ marginal propensity to consume. The consumption schedule can then be written as $C = a + bY$ and the average propensity to consume as $C/Y = (a + bY)/Y = a/Y + b$. The latter expression clearly shows that the average propensity to consume exceeds the marginal propensity to consume as long as autonomous consumption is greater than zero.

2. We continue to assume that there are no indirect business taxes. Only corporate profits taxes, payroll taxes, and personal taxes, such as personal income taxes and personal property taxes, are taken into account. Thus, it continues to be true that domestic income minus net taxes equals disposable income.

3. Later in this book will see that expansion of the economy even without a change in the price level can cause the interest rare to rise, thereby depressing planned investment. Here we assume, in effect, that the underlying change in real autonomous expenditure is strong enough to increase real autonomous expenditure by $500 billion and thus to shift the planned-expenditure curve upward by that amount— even after this interest rate effect is taken into account.

4. The qualification regarding the interest rate that was given in footnote 3 applies here as well.

# Fiscal Policy

## LOWER TAXES, GOOD, RIGHT?

One of President George W. Bush's first objectives upon taking office in 2001 was to pass broad tax cuts for consumers and businesses. Citing worsening statistics for the American economy, the Bush tax cuts, later dubbed an "economic stimulus package," gained popular and political support. Congress eventually passed the Bush tax cuts as a temporary measure to help spur a

U.S. economic recovery. With lower income taxes, consumers would spend more, and with lower corporate taxes, businesses would be encouraged to buy new capital equipment.

Following the 9/11/2001 attacks on the World Trade Center and the Pentagon, the Bush administration and Congress had another concern: funding the war on terrorism. Since the 9/11 attacks, the U.S. had engaged in wars in Afghanistan and Iraq, costing the U.S. billions of dollars in defense spending.

By the third quarter of 2003, gross domestic product was growing at a feverish pace, due to the combined effects of the temporary tax cuts and growing government spending, along with recovering consumer and business confidence. Despite improving output numbers, the U.S. job market remained sluggish. Feeling pressure from the Republican party and the administration, Congress extended the tax cuts in 2003.

These tax cuts do not come without a cost. While the Bush tax cuts may serve to stimulate spending and GDP growth in the short term, they are accompanied by huge federal budget deficits and a swelling national debt. At the end of 2003, the federal budget deficit was expected to reach $401 billion, amounting to between three and four percent of U.S. GDP.

**Fiscal policy**

Policy that is concerned with government purchases, taxes, and transfer payments.

WELCOME TO THE world of **fiscal policy**—the area of economic policy that is concerned with government purchases, taxes, and transfer payments. In this chapter, we use the models developed earlier to explore the economics of fiscal policy, including such topics as defense spending, the federal budget deficit, and the national debt. We will discuss both the short-run effects on prices and real output of changes in government purchases and net taxes and the long-run implications of fiscal policy for the way we use the $11 trillion of gross domestic product produced annually by the U.S. economy.

## THE THEORY OF FISCAL POLICY

Economists of all schools agree that fiscal policy has important effects on the economy. In the policy debates of the past half-century, however, the view of fiscal policy as a constructive tool for furthering the goals of full employment, price stability, and growth has been most closely associated with Keynes and his followers, who proposed increases in government purchases as an antidote to the Depression in the

1930s. For this reason, the theoretical case for using fiscal policy as a tool for combating economic contractions makes a suitable starting point for the chapter.

## Using Government Purchases to Combat a Contraction

In Figure 9.1, the economy has fallen into recession at point $E_1$, where the aggregate supply curve, $AS_1$, meets aggregate demand curve $AD_1$. There real domestic product is $500 billion below its natural level of $2,000 billion, and unemployment is above its natural rate. According to the aggregate supply and demand model, in the long run the expected and actual levels of input prices would gradually adjust to this level of demand. Real output would eventually return to its natural level as the aggregate supply curve shifted downward and the economy slid down and to the right along $AD_1$. But would the return to normalcy occur fast enough? Or would the reluctance of firms to lower their prices and the unwillingness of workers to accept lower nominal wages make the adjustment slow and painful?

**FIGURE 9.1   USING FISCAL POLICY TO COMBAT AN ECONOMIC CONTRACTION**

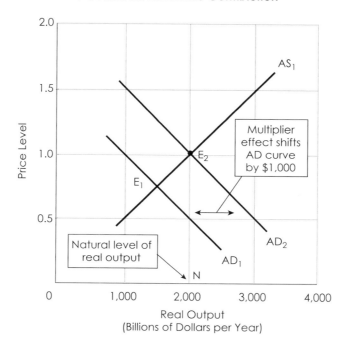

In this figure, the economy has fallen into recession at $E_1$. To reach the natural level of real output at $E_2$ without waiting for a downward shift of the aggregate supply curve, the aggregate demand curve must be shifted to the right by $1,000 billion, from $AD_1$ to $AD_2$. This can be done by increasing real government purchases and taking advantage of the multiplier effect. Given an expenditure multiplier of 4, a $250 billion increase in government purchases will bring about the required $1,000 billion shift in the aggregate demand curve. However, because the price level rises, equilibrium real domestic product does not increase by the full $1,000 billion by which the aggregate demand curve shifts. The same shift can be accomplished with a cut in net taxes, but the multiplier effect of a tax cut will be smaller than that of an increase in government purchases.

As Keynes once said, "in the long run, we are all dead." Suppose that the president and Congress, impatient with the economy's natural speed of adjustment, want to do something about the recession now. The problem is insufficient aggregate demand. Given the position of the aggregate supply curve, the aggregate demand curve needs to be shifted from $AD_1$ to $AD_2$ in order to bring real output back to its natural level at $E_2$. How can this be done?

**IDENTIFYING THE SPENDING GAP**   Although real domestic product is only $500 billion below its natural level, the horizontal gap between $AD_1$ and $AD_2$ is $1,000 billion, as shown by the arrow in Figure 9.1. This means that the equilibrium level of real planned expenditure at any given price level falls short of what is needed by $1,000 billion. If policy makers can fill that gap, they can shift the aggregate demand curve to the position $AD_2$ and bring real output to its natural level.

Of course, the gap might be filled even if policy makers did nothing. Exports might pick up; business managers might become more optimistic and increase planned investment; a rise in consumer confidence might spur consumption. But instead of waiting and hoping, policy makers could turn to the element of planned expenditure that is most directly under their control: government purchases. It is not hard to think of things that the government could spend money on—a new postal sorting station here, a stretch of interstate highway there, new vehicles for park rangers somewhere else. But just how much spending for new government purchases is needed?

**USING THE MULTIPLIER EFFECT**   To move the aggregate demand curve to the right by $1,000 billion, it is not necessary to increase government purchases by that amount. The reason is that each dollar of new government purchases is amplified by the multiplier effect. Spending $1 on a federal highway project boosts the income of construction workers, who then spend more on, say, groceries, clothing, and cats. Their spending raises the incomes of grocers, textile workers, and autoworkers, who in turn consume more. As the multiplier effect cascades through the economy, each $1 of new government purchases stimulates more than $1 of additional planned expenditure.

Let us assume that the marginal propensity to consume is .75. Using the formula for the expenditure multiplier, $1/(1 - mpc)$, we find that the value of the multiplier is 4. This means that $1 of government purchases will raise the equilibrium level of planned expenditure at a given price level by $4. (This calculation takes into account both the initial increase in government purchases and the induced increases in consumption expenditure.) Therefore, it will take $250 billion of additional government purchases to shift the aggregate demand curve to the right by $1,000 billion.[1]

**CHANGING PRICES AND AGGREGATE DEMAND**   As the aggregate demand curve shifts from $AD_1$ to $AD_2$, the economy moves up and to the right along the aggregate supply curve. In the process, the increase in prices affects real planned expenditure in ways that partially offset the multiplier effect of the original increase in government purchases. There are four reasons why a change in the price level will affect real planned expenditure:

1. Real consumption is restrained by the fact that the real value of nominal money balances falls as the price level rises.
2. Real planned investment is moderated by the higher interest rates associated with a higher price level.
3. The parts of government budgets that are set in nominal terms will command fewer real goods and services as the price level rises.
4. Real net exports will fall because domestic prices will rise relative to prices abroad.

These effects are built into the slope of the aggregate demand curve. They do not cause the aggregate demand curve to shift away from its new position at $AD_2$. Instead, they cause the economy to end up at a point on $AD_2$ at which the equilibrium level of real planned expenditure increases by less than the full $1,000 billion horizontal shift in the aggregate demand curve. In Figure 9.1 the new equilibrium is at point $E_2$. There equilibrium planned expenditure is $2,000 billion, which is only $500 billion greater than at $E_1$, despite the fact that the aggregate demand curve has shifted to the right by $1,000 billion.

In short, because a rise in the price level tends to lower every type of planned expenditure, the equilibrium level of real domestic product rises by less than the expenditure multiplier times the initial change in real government purchases.

## Using a Change in Taxes or Transfer Payments to Combat a Contraction

Government purchases are only one side of the fiscal policy equation. The other side consists of net taxes. The term *net taxes* means tax revenues collected by government minus transfer payments made by government to individuals. A tax cut or an increase in transfer payments operates in the economy via its effect on consumption.

Let us return to point $E_1$ in Figure 9.1 and see how a change in net taxes can be used to combat the contraction. As before, the problem is to shift the aggregate demand curve to the right by $1,000 billion. Suppose that in an attempt to stimulate the economy Congress votes a $100 billion increase in real social security benefits while leaving taxes unchanged. This amounts to a $100 billion cut in real net taxes. How does it affect aggregate demand?

To begin with, the action raises the real disposable incomes of social security recipients by $100 billion. In response—once again assuming an mpc of .75—they raise their consumption by $75 billion. As in the earlier case, the increase in consumer spending for groceries, cars, and the like boosts the incomes of grocers, autoworkers, and others by $75 billion; they, in turn, increase their consumption expenditures by $56,250,000,000; and so on.

We see, then, that a cut in net taxes, like an increase in government purchases, touches off an expansionary multiplier process. This is true whether the reduction in net taxes takes the form of a cut in taxes paid to government or an increase in transfer payments made by government. However, there is an important difference in the first-round impact of the two policy changes. A $100 billion increase in government purchases is itself a $100 billion *direct* addition to aggregate demand. The multiplier chain goes on from there with additional *induced* increases in consumption expenditures totaling $300 billion. Thus, the total change in planned expenditure is $400 billion. However, a $100 billion tax cut or increase in transfer payments is not in itself a direct addition to aggregate demand, because it does not represent a decision by government to buy any newly produced goods and services. Therefore, the only effect of the cut in net taxes is the induced increases in consumption expenditures. These total just $300 billion.

Generalizing from this example, we see that a cut in net taxes has a multiplier effect that is smaller than the effect of an equal increase in planned expenditure. The ratio of an induced shift in aggregate demand to a given change in real net taxes is known as the **net tax multiplier**. Mathematically, the absolute value of the net tax multiplier is given by the formula

**Net tax multiplier**

The ratio of an induced change in real aggregate demand to a given change in real net taxes.

$$\text{Net tax multiplier} = \text{Expenditure multiplier} - 1$$

Substituting $1/(1 - \text{mpc})$ for the expenditure multiplier and simplifying, we can also write this as follows:

$$\text{Net tax multiplier} = \text{mpc}/(1 - \text{mpc})$$

We can now return to Figure 9.1 and see how much of a cut in real net taxes is needed to bring the economy out of its recession. The required shift in the aggregate demand curve is $1,000 billion. Using the formula just given, an mpc of .75 yields a net tax multiplier of 3. Thus, $333 billion in tax cuts or transfer payment increases are needed to shift the aggregate demand curve to the right by $1,000 billion. In response to this shift, real output rises by $500 billion, taking into account the effects of a rising price level on the various components of real planned expenditure.

An important qualification is in order, however. The preceding analysis suggests that, on a dollar-for-dollar basis, changes in net taxes are only slightly less effective than changes in government purchases in influencing the level of aggregate demand. But in reaching this conclusion, we have assumed that households will spend the same fraction of an additional dollar received through tax cuts as they will of an additional dollar in earned income. As *Applying Economics Ideas 9.1* indicates, some economists think that this may not be the case. If they are correct, tax changes would be a much less effective fiscal policy tool than our simple model suggests.

## *Fiscal Policy and Inflation*

In previous sections we have seen how fiscal policy can be used to speed up recovery from a contraction. Now we will see that fiscal policy can also play a part in fighting inflation or, for that matter, causing inflation if used irresponsibly.

**COUNTERACTING PROJECTED INFLATION**   Consider the situation shown in Figure 9.2. The economy has been in equilibrium for some time at $E_1$, where real output is at its natural level. As the federal budget for the coming year is being prepared, forecasters warn of the possibility of inflation. The threat stems from a projected growth in the private components of aggregate demand—a surge in export demand, a boom in consumer spending, or an increase in planned investment. If something is not done, the forecasters say, the aggregate demand curve for the coming year will shift rightward to $AD_2$. That will drive the economy up and to the right along aggregate supply curve $AS_1$, to $E_2$.

**FIGURE 9.2   FISCAL POLICY AND INFLATION**

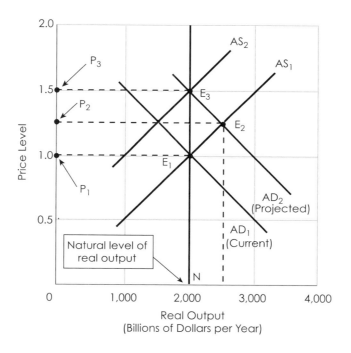

Initially the economy is at $E_1$. Forecasts show that if no policy changes are made, increases in real private planned expenditure will shift the aggregate demand curve from $AD_1$ to $AD_2$, causing the price level to rise as the economy moves to a short-run equilibrium at $E_2$. In the long run, assuming nothing is done about aggregate demand, the price level would rise still more as the aggregate supply curve shifted upward and the economy moved toward a new long-run equilibrium at $E_3$. To prevent an increase in the price level, government purchases can be cut or net taxes increased to offset the projected change in private planned expenditure, thus restoring the aggregate demand curve to position $AD_1$.

⌒ **APPLYING ECONOMIC IDEAS 9.1**

## DO TAX CHANGES REALLY AFFECT AGGREGATE DEMAND?

The net tax multiplier correctly predicts the effect of tax changes on equilibrium aggregate demand only if people treat a dollar of added disposable income received through a tax cut the same way they treat a dollar received from any other source: dividing it between saving and consumption according to the marginal propensity to consume. However, recent U.S. experience suggests that in practice saving is affected more strongly and consumption less strongly by tax changes than by other changes in disposable income.

The accompanying chart shows personal saving and total personal tax payments at all levels of government as a percentage of personal income since 1960. Tax cuts, such as the tax rebate of 1975, appear to produce an offsetting jump in saving; as a result, they add little to consumption. Likewise, tax increases, such as the tax surcharge of 1968 and the one-time increase in tax payments in April 1987, produce a jump in tax payments but an offsetting drop in saving. This implies a smaller net tax multiplier than that given by the usual formula. If a tax change were fully offset by a change in saving, it would have no multiplier effect at all. In practice, econometric studies indicate that tax changes are partly but not wholly offset by changes in saving.

Economists differ in the reasons they give for the relatively small impact of tax cuts on consumption. One far-reaching hypothesis has been put forth by Robert J. Barro of Harvard University. Barro points out that today's tax cut has implications for tomorrow's fiscal policy. If the government cuts taxes today and does not cut spending, it will have to increase its borrowing in order to cover the resulting deficit. In the future, then, taxes will have to be raised to repay this borrowing, or at least to pay interest on it. If households think ahead, Barro says, they will react to a tax cut today by increasing their saving. Income from assets that they buy with the added savings will allow them to afford the higher future taxes needed to cover today's government borrowing. To protect themselves fully against the higher future taxes, they must save 100 percent of today's tax cut. Attributing the idea to the nineteenth-century British economist David Ricardo, Barro refers to it as the "Ricardian" view of taxation.

Other economists are skeptical of the Ricardian view. They doubt that consumers are so farsighted as to adjust their saving to offset the future effects of today's tax cuts in full. They see a simpler explanation for the tendency of tax changes to be offset by changes in saving: the fact that consumers tend to save a higher percentage of temporary changes in income than of permanent changes. Some tax changes have been explicitly labeled as temporary, such as the income tax surcharge of 1968 and the tax rebate of 1975. There was also a temporary bulge in tax revenues in the second quarter of 1987. This reflected heavy realization of capital gains in late 1986 in anticipation of higher capital gains tax rates, which were scheduled to go into effect in 1987. As the chart shows, these tax changes were almost fully offset by changes in saving, at least in the short run. Even tax changes that are said to be permanent may at first be treated as if they were temporary. Only after enough time has passed for consumers to adjust to the tax changes will these changes affect consumption in proportion to the full long-run marginal propensity to consume.

A bigger puzzle is the steady decline in personal savings since 1992. Until 2001, there were only minor changes in the tax code, so the percentage of income that consumers had to pay in taxes remained steady. Exceptional U.S. growth during much of the 1990s can explain the growth in personal income taxes. When people earn more income, they may have to pay a larger percentage of their income in taxes. This leaves the trends in U.S. savings unresolved. Falling personal savings could be unrelated to fiscal policy and driven by some other factor, such as increased access to credit, permitting households to borrow more.

On the diagram, we see the plunge in personal income taxes accompanied by the Bush tax cuts mentioned at the beginning of this chapter. If consumers viewed the tax cut as temporary, they should increase their personal savings. From the graph, we see that personal savings rose slightly between 2001 and 2002, indicating that consumers may view the tax cut as temporary, or that consumers are behaving according to Ricardian equivalence.

The result will be an increase in the price level from $P_1$ to $P_2$. But inflation will not stop there. The rise in the prices of final goods will, in time, cause firms to raise their expectations regarding wages and other input prices. As a result, the short-run aggregate supply curve will shift upward to $AS_2$. As real output falls back to its natural level, the price level will continue to rise until it reaches a new long-run equilibrium at $P_3$.

＾ APPLYING ECONOMIC IDEAS 9.1

## DO TAX CHANGES REALLY AFFECT AGGREGATE DEMAND?, continued

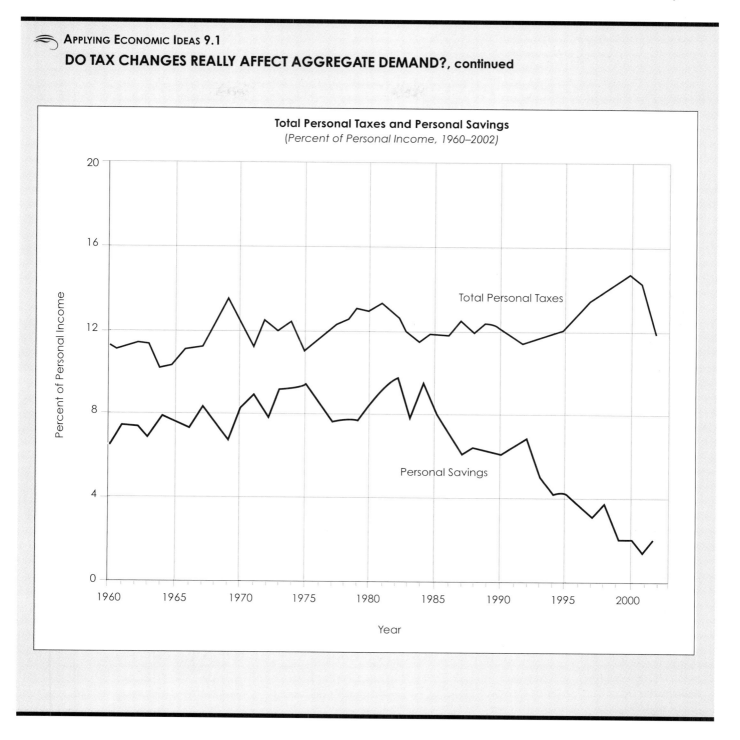

**Total Personal Taxes and Personal Savings**
*(Percent of Personal Income, 1960–2002)*

Restrictive fiscal policy is one way of warding off the inflation threat. The federal budget for the coming year can be written in such a way as to combine cuts in government purchases and increases in net taxes that will offset the projected increases in private aggregate demand. Suppose that the mpc is .75, as in our earlier examples. For each $100 by which aggregate demand is projected to shift beyond the level needed to reach the natural level of real output, government purchases can be cut by $25 or net taxes increased by $33. The right combination of cuts in government purchases, cuts in transfer payments, and increases in taxes will hold the aggregate demand curve in the desired position at $AD_1$.

**EXPANSIONARY FISCAL POLICY AS A SOURCE OF INFLATION**    In the preceding example, federal policy makers are the "good guys," crafting a sensible budget designed to restrain inflation. That is the role we would hope for them to play. However, the same diagram could be used to tell a different story.

In this scenario the economy is in equilibrium at $E_1$ and forecasters expect it to stay there. However, there is an election coming up. Members of Congress would like to please the voters by boosting federal benefits, cutting taxes, and initiating public works projects. The president, who is also up for reelection, would like to conduct the coming campaign in an atmosphere of rising real output and falling unemployment. Seeing their common interests, Congress and the president craft a strongly expansionary budget for the upcoming election year. When the expansionary budget first goes into effect, the economy moves from $E_1$ to $E_2$ in Figure 9.2. As hoped, real output expands and unemployment falls, with only a moderate increase in the price level. Voters are pleased, and everyone is reelected.

The next year, however, wages and other input prices begin to rise. As firms adjust their expectations to the new circumstances, not only does inflation of final goods prices continue but real output falls and the unemployment rate rises. The hangover from the election party sets in. This contrast between the relatively benign initial effects of expansionary policy and its less desirable long-run effects is a theme to which we will return several times in later chapters.

## *Automatic Fiscal Policy*

**Discretionary fiscal policy**

Changes in the laws regarding government purchases and net taxes.

**Automatic fiscal policy**

Changes in government purchases or net taxes that are caused by changes in economic conditions given unchanged tax and spending laws.

The type of fiscal policy discussed so far—changes in the laws regarding government purchases, taxes, and transfer payments designed to increase or decrease aggregate demand—is known as **discretionary fiscal policy**. In practice, however, the levels of government purchases and net taxes can change even if no discretionary changes are made in the laws governing them. The reason is that many tax and spending laws are written in such a way that the levels of fiscal policy variables change automatically as economic conditions vary. Such changes in government purchases or net taxes, which are known as **automatic fiscal policy**, are most closely associated with changes in real output, the price level, and interest rates.

**CHANGES IN REAL OUTPUT**    The level of real output is important because it affects both tax revenues and outlays. An increase in real output increases real revenues from all major tax sources, including income taxes, social security payroll taxes, taxes on corporate profits, and sales taxes. At the same time, an increase in real output cuts real government outlays for transfer payments. This occurs largely because increases in real output are associated with decreases in the unemployment rate. Taking both effects together, an increase in real domestic product tends to reduce the federal budget deficit in both real and nominal terms.

**CHANGES IN THE PRICE LEVEL**  An increase in the price level affects both sides of the federal budget. With real output held constant, an increase in the price level tends to increase federal tax receipts in nominal terms. At the same time, an increase in the price level tends to increase nominal expenditures. This is partly because most major transfer programs are now indexed so that they can be adjusted for changes in the cost of living and partly because inflation raises the prices of the goods and services that government buys. However, as pointed out before, some elements of government expenditures are fixed in nominal terms. This means that the increase in nominal expenditures will tend to be less than proportional to the increase in the price level.

On balance, nominal taxes rise more than nominal expenditures when the price level increases. Thus, an increase in the price level, other things being equal, reduces the deficit in both real and nominal terms.

**CHANGES IN INTEREST RATES**  An increase in nominal interest rates raises the nominal cost of financing the national debt. This is only slightly offset by increases in nominal government interest income. Therefore, on balance, an increase in nominal interest rates shifts the budget toward deficit in both nominal and real terms.

**AUTOMATIC STABILIZATION**  We have seen that when the economy expands real output rises, the price level rises, and unemployment falls. Each of these effects tends to move the government budget toward surplus in real terms, that is, to increase receipts, depress outlays, or both. Whichever side of the budget we look at, then, automatic fiscal policy operates so as to restrain aggregate demand during an expansion. By the same token, when the economy slows down, the growth rate of real output drops and unemployment rises. The inflation rate slows even if the contraction is not severe enough to cause the price level actually to fall. Thus, during a contraction the real budget swings toward deficit.

Because automatic fiscal policy operates to offset changes in other elements of planned expenditure, such budget components as income taxes and unemployment benefits are known as **automatic stabilizers**. These mechanisms serve to moderate the economy's response to changes in consumption, private planned investment, and net exports.

**Automatic stabilizers**

Those elements of automatic fiscal policy that move the federal budget toward deficit during an economic contraction and toward surplus during an expansion.

# FISCAL POLICY IN THE INCOME-EXPENDITURE MODEL

The income-expenditure model developed in the previous chapter provides an alternate way of looking at the effects of fiscal policy. This model has the advantage of focusing more directly on the multiplier effect. However, it can be misleading if it is not used cautiously, because it tends to lose sight of the effects of changes in the price level.

## Fiscal Stimulus

Part (a) of Figure 9.3 uses the fixed-price version of the income-expenditure model to show how fiscal policy can be used to avoid a recession. In drawing the figure, we assume no income or payroll taxes, no net exports, and an mpc of .75. In this case, we suppose that policy makers wish to keep the economy at its natural level of real output of $2,000 billion. However, as they prepare a budget for the coming year, their forecasters say that, given current tax and spending laws, planned expenditure will be insufficient and the planned-expenditure schedule will slip to $PE_1$, putting equilibrium domestic income at only $1,000 billion.

To keep income at the natural level, the planned-expenditure schedule must be at $PE_2$ rather than $PE_1$. If nothing is done, the shortfall of autonomous expenditure will cause a recession. The autonomous-expenditure shortfall is shown by the vertical

**FIGURE 9.3    FISCAL POLICY IN THE INCOME-EXPENDITURE MODEL**

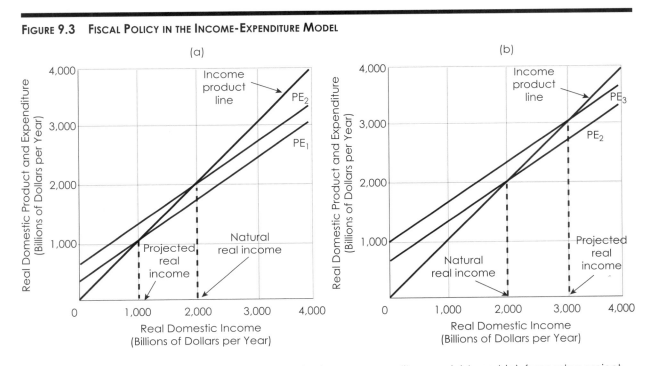

This figure illustrates fiscal policy in terms of the fixed-price income-expenditure model. In part (a), forecasters project an equilibrium real domestic income for the coming year that is $1,000 billion below the natural level. The low equilibrium value for real domestic income is caused by a $250 billion shortfall of real autonomous planned expenditure. A $250 billion increase in government purchases or a $333 billion cut in autonomous net taxes will restore autonomous expenditures to the desired level, shifting the planned-expenditure curve from $PE_1$ to $PE_2$. In part (b), the situation is reversed. A projected excess of autonomous expenditure will put the planned-expenditure curve at $PE_3$ unless something is done. The prescription for this situation is a $250 billion cut in government purchases or a $333 billion increase in autonomous net taxes.

gap between the two planned-expenditure curves. In our example the shortfall is $250 billion.

To avoid the recession, tax and spending laws must be changed so as to plug the gap. A $250 billion increase in government purchases would be one way to do this. Another would be to stimulate autonomous consumption by reducing autonomous net taxes by $333. (This figure is calculated by applying the net tax multiplier.) Either action would shift the planned-expenditure schedule from $PE_1$ to $PE_2$, as shown in the figure. Still another possibility would be to lower marginal income tax rates, thus increasing the slope of the planned-expenditure schedule without changing its vertical intercept. Such an action would also raise the equilibrium level of domestic income.

### Fiscal Restraint

Part (b) of Figure 9.3 shows how fiscal restraint can be used to stem an excess of aggregate demand that would cause real output to rise above its natural level—an occurrence that would cause inflation in a world with flexible prices. In this case we suppose that forecasts for the coming year show that under current tax and spending laws the planned-expenditure curve will be at the position $PE_3$. This will cause equilibrium domestic income to rise to $3,000 billion, which is $1,000 billion above the natural level. Unless something is done, the economy will overheat.

The excess of real domestic income is produced by a projected excess of autonomous expenditure, which is represented by the vertical gap between $PE_3$ and $PE_2$ in part (b) of Figure 9.3. Fiscal policy can be used to close this gap, as in the case of recession, but the direction of the policy change must be reversed: Government purchases must be cut or net taxes must be increased, or some of each.

Keep in mind that conclusions based on the fixed-price version of the income-expenditure model, shown in Figure 9.3, exaggerate the impact of a given change in government purchases, taxes, or transfer payments on the equilibrium level of real domestic income. In a world with flexible prices, price changes would cause additional shifts in the planned-expenditure schedule that would partially offset the impact of the fiscal policies considered here even in the short run and would fully offset them in the long run. Hence, when the price level is subject to change—as it is in the real world—the aggregate supply and demand model gives a better picture of the effects of fiscal policy than the fixed-price version of the income-expenditure model.

## THE BUDGET PROCESS

Our discussion of fiscal policy would be incomplete without at least a brief discussion of how federal officials actually go about making tax and spending decisions. In practice, the decision-making process for fiscal policy often has little to do with the theory of discretionary policy that we have just discussed. Herbert Stein, a former chairman of the Council of Economic Advisers, has gone so far as to write that "We have no long-run budget policy—no policy for the size of deficits and for the rate of growth of the public debt over a period of years." Each year, according to Stein, the president and Congress make short-term budgetary decisions that are wholly inconsistent with their declared long-run goals, hoping "that something will happen or be done before the long-run arises, but not yet."[2]

## The Federal Budgetary System

In discussing the theory of fiscal policy, it is convenient to refer to unnamed "policy makers" who manipulate taxes, transfers, and government purchases. In practice, however, no single agency is responsible for fiscal policy; budgetary authority is divided between the executive branch, headed by the president, and Congress. Also, budgetary policy must serve many goals, ranging from national security and social equity to simple political ambition, as well as price stability, full employment, and economic growth.

**Fiscal year**

The federal government's budgetary year, which starts on October 1 of the preceding calendar year.

**THE BUDGETARY PROCESS**   A brief look at the federal budgetary process will indicate where the formal authority for fiscal policy lies. The U.S. government operates on a **fiscal year** that runs from October through September; for example, fiscal 2004 runs from October 1, 2003, through September 30, 2004. About 18 months before the beginning of a fiscal year, the executive branch begins preparing the budget. The Office of Management and Budget (OMB) takes the lead in this process. It receives advice from the Council of Economic Advisers (CEA) and the Department of the Treasury. After an outline of the budget has been drawn up, it is sent to the various departments and agencies. Within the executive branch, a period of bargaining ensues in which the Pentagon argues for more defense spending, the Department of Transportation for more highway funds, and so on. During this process the OMB is supposed to act as a restraining force, keeping macroeconomic goals in mind.

By January—nine months before the fiscal year starts—the president must submit the budget to Congress. After the budget has been submitted, Congress assumes the lead in the budgetary process. Its committees and subcommittees look at the president's proposals for the programs and agencies under their jurisdiction. The Congressional Budget Office (CBO) employs a staff of professionals who advise the committees on economic matters, in somewhat the same way that the OMB and CEA advise the president. In May the House and Senate are expected to pass a first budget resolution that sets forth overall spending targets and revenue goals.

Bargaining among committees, between the House and the Senate, and between Congress and the executive branch continues throughout the summer. During this period committees prepare specific spending and tax laws; these are supposed to be guided by the May resolution. Finally, in September, Congress is supposed to pass a second budget resolution that sets binding limits on spending and taxes for the fiscal year beginning October 1. Any bills passed earlier that do not fit within these guidelines are expected to be changed accordingly.

**LIMITATIONS OF THE BUDGETARY PROCESS**   In practice, many things can—and do—go wrong with this process.

The first and most basic problem is that macroeconomic goals—full employment, price stability, and economic growth—carry little weight in the actual budgetary process. Tax and spending decisions are made in dozens of subcommittees, where they are dominated by interest group pressures, vote trading, and the desire of each member of Congress to help the folks at home.

A second problem is that Congress has not always been willing to follow its own rules. The required budget resolutions often are not passed on time; if they are passed, they are not treated as binding. Sometimes the fiscal year starts without a budget. Then agencies must operate on the basis of "continuing resolutions," meaning that they can go on doing whatever they were doing the year before. In 1995, the government shut down for six days in November when Congress failed to passed appropriations bills. According to a document released by the Clinton administration, the government shutdown cost $700–$800 million, including $400 million to furloughed federal employees who were paid, but did not report to work. The Treasury Department reported another $400 million in lost revenue over the four days that the IRS enforcement divisions were closed. More recently in 2003, lawmakers have used the threat of a government shutdown to tack provisions on to the needed appropriations bills that benefit their individual districts and states.

**Entitlements**

Transfer payments governed by long-term laws that are not subject to annual budget review.

Finally, there is the problem of so-called uncontrollable costs. These include **entitlements**, which are transfer programs governed by long-term laws that are not subject to annual budget review. Examples include social security, military retirement pay, and Medicare. Another major expense that is uncontrollable—for a different reason—is interest on the national debt. Total interest expense is determined by the size of the debt and market interest rates, which, in turn, are beyond the control of fiscal policy. Today well over half of the federal budget is in the "uncontrollable" category. Congress could control most of these costs by passing new laws to replace the current ones, but doing so is not part of the normal budgetary process.

# FISCAL POLICY AND THE FEDERAL DEFICIT

The federal budget deficit has remained a concern for federal and state lawmakers since the large U.S. deficits in the 1980s. Indeed, prior to the Great Depression (1929–1933), one of the primary goals of fiscal policy was to balance the budget. We begin this section by examining the origins of the record deficits of recent years, which lie in both discretionary and automatic elements of fiscal policy. We then turn to the controversy over the effects of the deficit on the economy as a whole.

Figure 9.4 reports the U.S. government budget over time. From the 1980s, as much was added to the cumulative deficit every two years as in the previous 30, despite the longest peacetime expansion of the post–World War II period. The recession of 1990–1991 sent the deficit higher still, but by 1997, the federal budget

**FIGURE 9.4  FEDERAL GOVERNMENT DEFICIT/SURPLUS (BILLIONS OF DOLLARS, 1962–2000)**

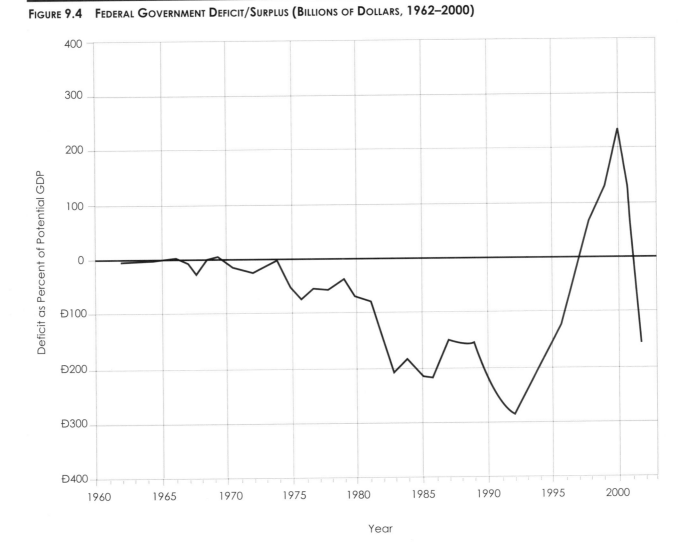

The figure plots the federal government budget (deficit or surplus), 1962–2002. From the plot, we see that budget deficits became a persistent problem in the early 1980s. A government budget deficit occurs when the federal government spends more than it collects in tax revenue. While deficits were smaller for a brief period of time, the federal government remained in the red until 1997, when the government enjoyed record surplus. These surpluses have disappeared and the government has returned to budget deficits of record levels.

Source: Congressional Budget Office, *The Economic and Budget Outlook: Fiscal Years 2004–2013*, January 2003, Appendix F, Historical Budget Data, Table 1.

achieved a budget surplus. By 2001, the recession, tax cuts, and rising defense spending brought the surpluses to an end.

## *Automatic Fiscal Policy: The Structural Versus Cyclical Deficit*

The federal budget is, however, only partly a result of discretionary policy decisions. Policy makers do not determine actual levels of government receipts and expenditures. Rather, they pass laws setting tax rates, formulas for transfer payments, and goals for purchases of goods and services. Given these laws, the actual levels of receipts and expenditures depend on the stage of the business cycle. As we have seen, the budget shifts toward deficit when the economy contracts, as tax collections fall and transfer payments rise. Similarly, during expansions the budget shifts toward surplus. As discussed at the beginning of the chapter, the federal government budget is a combination of discretionary fiscal policy decisions and economic conditions.

One way to separate the effects of discretionary policy changes from those of the business cycle is to calculate what the federal budget (surplus or deficit) would be at the natural rate of unemployment. In this section, we will use the Congressional Budget Office's estimate of the natural rate as a benchmark. The CBO's estimate of the natural rate for the United States in 2002 was 5.2 percent.

The federal budget surplus or deficit that the federal government would run, given the natural unemployment rate, is called the **structural budget**. Changes in the structural budget are interpreted as representing discretionary fiscal policy. The difference between the structural and actual budget is called the **cyclical deficit/surplus**. When unemployment rises above its natural rate, the government will run a cyclical deficit becomes positive because the structural budget exceeds the actual budget. When unemployment falls below the benchmark, the structural budget is less than the actual budget, causing a cyclical surplus. Changes in the cyclical deficit/surplus reflect changes in taxes and spending that occur automatically as real output, unemployment, and inflation change over the course of the business cycle.

Figure 9.5 shows actual and structural federal budgets for the U.S. economy in relation to nominal potential GDP in recent years. The cyclical deficit or surplus is the difference between the two. The chart highlights the dramatic decline in the structural budget (rising structural deficit) from 1981 to 1985. For a time, the increase of the structural deficit was accompanied by growth in the actual deficit (decline in the actual budget). Then, from 1983 to 1989, the actual deficit was stabilized and then began to fall, as tax revenues grew together with GDP. In 1988 and 1989, the cyclical deficit nearly disappeared, and the structural deficit declined somewhat from its peak. Predictably, the recession of 1990–1991 and the initially slow recovery raised the cyclical deficit and sent the actual deficit up once again. During the mid to late 1990s, both the actual and structural budgets rose as the U.S. economy entered a period of exceptionally high economic growth and low unemployment. The actual

**Structural budget**

The budget surplus or deficit that the federal government would incur given current tax and spending laws and unemployment at its natural rate.

**Cyclical deficit/surplus**

The difference between the structural budget and the actual federal budget. If the actual budget is above the structural budget, there is a cyclical surplus. Likewise, when the actual budget is below the structural budget, there is a cyclical deficit.

federal budget was above the structural budget, creating a cyclical surplus. With the 2001 U.S. recession, both the actual and structural budgets fell into deficits. The cyclical surplus was eliminated with the Bush tax cuts and increases in government spending.

FIGURE 9.5  ACTUAL, CYCLICAL, AND STRUCTURAL FEDERAL BUDGET (BUDGET AS A PERCENTAGE OF POTENTIAL GDP, 1960–2002)

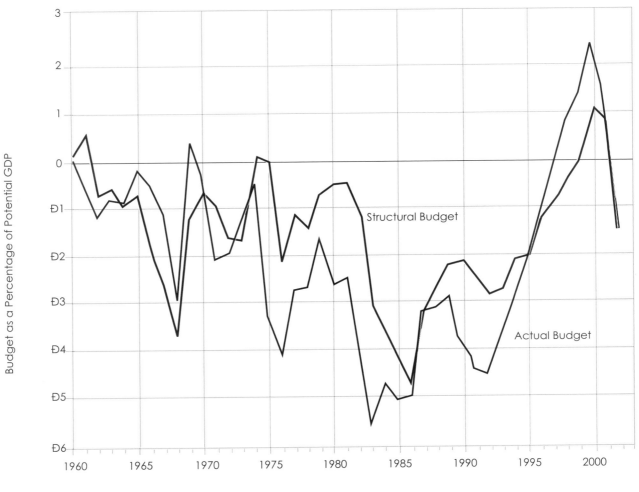

This figure breaks down the federal budget stated as a percentage of GDP into actual, cyclical, and structural components. The structural component is the estimated budget that would be produced given current tax and spending laws and a natural rate of unemployment (estimated at 5.2 percent for 2002). The cyclical component is the difference between the actual budget and the structural component. If the actual budget is less than the structural budget, this means that the government would be running a deficit, even if the economy were at the natural rate of unemployment. The structural budget decreased (so the structural budget deficit grew), on balance, after 1981. This decline is largely attributable to increased defense and entitlements spending. During the mid to late 1990s, the actual federal budget was above the structural budget, implying a cyclical surplus.

Source: Congressional Budget Office, *The Economic and Budget Outlook: Fiscal Years 2004–2013*, January 2003, Appendix F, Historical Budget Data, Table 13.

## Economic Priorities and the Deficit Since the 1980s

Earlier in the chapter we defined discretionary fiscal policy as changes in laws regarding government purchases and net taxes. The origins of the large federal deficits of the 1980s lie, to a large extent, in discretionary fiscal policies. In saying this, we are not referring to the rhetorical priorities of the Reagan and first Bush administrations, which always urged deficit reduction, but rather, we mean the actual budget priorities embodied in taxation and spending decisions jointly reached by Republican presidents and Democratic Congresses. In the 1990s, the roles were reversed: the Republican Congress had to reach compromises with a Democratic president, Bill Clinton. When the George W. Bush took office in 2000, Congress was Republican controlled, but by a narrow majority in the Senate.

**TAXES, SPENDING, AND THE DEFICIT**   Table 9.1 presents data on federal tax revenues and total federal outlays (government purchases of goods and services plus transfer payments) since the 1970s. Column 1 shows that despite a decade of rhetoric to the contrary, cutting the overall tax burden was not given high priority. True, the 1980s saw a major restructuring of tax rates, featuring reduced marginal tax rates on income, which affected primarily upper-income taxpayers, and higher social security payroll taxes, which mainly affected low- and middle-income taxpayers. Nevertheless, the share of federal taxes in GDP continued to creep upward in the 1980s, although less rapidly than in the previous decade. The popular idea that the deficit was the result of "massive Reagan tax cuts" is without foundation, except perhaps in the very restricted sense that without the tax legislation of the 1980s, federal revenues would have grown even more rapidly. The budget deficits during the early 1990s appear to the be the result of lower tax receipts resulting from the 1990–1991 recessions. By the late 1990s, higher receipt accompanying lower government expenditures led to a budget surplus.

Cutting government spending, another major rhetorical goal, was an even lower priority in reality. Column 2 shows that federal expenditures rose to an unprecedented share of GDP in the first half of the 1980s and fell back only slightly as GDP grew strongly in the later 1980s. The combined effect of trends in expenditures and revenues was a sharp increase in the budget deficit, as shown in column 7. The story told by the numbers is that the deficit increase was caused not by tax cuts but by spending increases.

The Clinton administration resisted pressure, allowing consumers and businesses to enjoy the surplus through income and corporate tax cuts. Increased receipts in the late 1990s were the result of economic growth. With higher income and profits, consumers and businesses pay more taxes to the government. At the same time, transfers to individuals declined slightly because fewer people were out of work. From columns 3 and 5, the bulk of the expenditure cuts under President Clinton are attributed to defense spending and savings from net interest.

**TABLE 9.1   FEDERAL REVENUES, OUTLAYS, AND BUDGET DEFICIT/SURPLUS AS A PERCENTAGE OF GDP**

| | (1) Receipts | (2) Total | (3) Defense Spending | (4) Transfers to Persons | (5) Net Interest | (6) Other | (7) Budget |
|---|---|---|---|---|---|---|---|
| 1971–1975 | 17.7 | 19.5 | 6.2 | 6.8 | 1.4 | 5.2 | −1.8 |
| 1976–1980 | 18.1 | 20.9 | 4.9 | 8.3 | 1.7 | 6.1 | −2.8 |
| 1981–1985 | 18.2 | 22.7 | 5.8 | 9.4 | 2.7 | 4.8 | −4.5 |
| 1986–1990 | 18.1 | 21.7 | 5.8 | 8.6 | 3.1 | 4.2 | −3.6 |
| 1991–1995 | 17.9 | 21.6 | 4.3 | 9.7 | 3.1 | 4.4 | −3.7 |
| 1996–2000 | 19.8 | 19.2 | 3.2 | 9.3 | 2.7 | 3.9 | 0.6 |

*Calendar Years*

This table shows trends in federal revenues, outlays, and budgets (deficit or surplus) as a percentage of GDP from 1971 to 2000. Column 1 shows that despite the cuts in personal income tax rates that resulted from the 1981 tax law, federal revenues rose as a share of GDP in the 1980s. Federal outlays, on the other hand, grew to record levels in the early 1980s and decreased only slightly in the later 1980s, as shown in column 2. The conclusion is that the increase in the federal deficit, shown in column 7, stems from spending increases rather than tax cuts. Turning to specific expenditure categories, we see that defense, transfer payments, and interest increased as a share of GDP during the 1980s. The big losers in the federal budget were nondefense purchases of goods and services and grants-in-aid to state and local governments. These and some smaller categories are included in column 6.

During the 1990s, falling receipts helped explain the deficits left over from tax cuts and defense spending increases under President Reagan. By the later 1990s, the federal government enjoyed a budget surplus. According to the table, this was the result of reduced expenditures and increases in receipts.

Source: President's Council of Economic Advisers, *Economic Report of the President* (Washington, D.C.: Government Printing Office, 2003), Table B-79.

**PRIORITIES AMONG PROGRAMS**   The remaining columns of Table 9.1 show what happened to the composition of federal spending by type of program. Column 3 shows that the share of GDP going to defense rose significantly in the 1980s compared with the 1970s. To put the 1980s defense buildup in perspective, however, it should be noted that the 1970s were a low point for defense expenditures in the post–World War II years. In the 1960s defense expenditures had averaged almost 9 percent of GDP. The level of Pentagon spending in the 1980s never came close to that level. When President Clinton came into office, this changed. Defense spending fell from 5.8 percent of expenditures to only 3.2 by the time he left office in 2001.

If the numbers are allowed to speak for themselves, transfer payments to persons have remained a spending priority since the 1980s, as shown in column 4 of Table 9.1. Whatever their other disagreements with Congress, the Reagan, first Bush, and Clinton administrations agreed with Congress that most transfer programs were untouchable. Two programs for the elderly, social security and Medicare, accounted for about two-thirds of total transfer payments in the 1980s and 1990s.

Column 5 of Table 9.1 shows the increasing share of GDP taken by interest on the national debt through the mid-1990s. This reflects higher interest rates as well as the growth of the debt itself relative to GDP. As the government budget went into surplus in the late 1990s, interest payments declined with the national debt.

Finally, column 6 of the table shows the big budgetary loser in the 1980s—other items, which include most discretionary nondefense spending. Within this category, nondefense purchases of goods and services—a category that includes everything from the federal judiciary to the national parks—fell from 10.8 percent of federal expenditures in 1980 to 8.8 percent in 1990. Grants-in-aid to state and local governments fell even more sharply over the same period, from 14.5 percent of expenditures to 10.4 percent. If presidential administrations' budget-cutting intentions had any impact, it was here. But these programs are such a small fraction of the total budget that cuts in them were not even enough to offset the rise in interest payments on the national debt until the late 1990s.

On balance, then, fiscal priorities of the Reagan and first Bush administrations (1981–1993) can be characterized as follows:

- A priority for slowing growth of the overall tax burden but not for actually cutting it; low priority on restricting total spending and the federal deficit.
- High priority on increasing defense spending until the very end of the decade; a slightly lower priority on increasing transfer payments, especially to the elderly; and a moderate priority on reducing discretionary nondefense spending.

The fiscal priorities of the Clinton administration (1993–2001) can be summarized as:

- A priority for slowing growth of the overall tax burden, but not for actually cutting it; high priority on restricting total spending and the federal deficit.
- High priority on reducing defense spending; a slightly lower priority on increasing transfer payments, especially to the elderly; and a moderate priority on reducing discretionary nondefense spending.

## The Deficit as a Policy Issue

In recent years, as federal red ink has reached record levels, the deficit has gained prominence as a policy issue. Ordinary people questioned in public opinion polls, joined by many professional economists, look on the deficit with foreboding. Can the government go on spending beyond its means forever? Does the deficit place a drag on economic growth? Does it represent a burden on future generations? We will see that there are sound reasons to be concerned. Before examining those reasons, however, we will look at the differing views of economists on the issue.

## *Reasons Not to Worry about the Deficit*

Economists who argue that the federal deficit is not so great a problem begin by making a series of numerical adjustments, which suggest that the federal deficit is not really as large as it seems. We will look at four of these adjustments here.

**ADJUSTING FOR THE STATE AND LOCAL SURPLUS**   The first adjustment is based on the notion that it is not the federal deficit that matters but the combined deficit or surplus of federal, state, and local governments. Although the federal government has been running record-breaking deficits, state and local governments were running substantial surpluses, at least until the 1990–1991 recession, and returned to a sizable surplus as the economy recovered. The state and local surpluses represent a flow of saving into financial markets that can be used to finance private investment and the federal deficit.

**ADJUSTING FOR THE CYCLICAL COMPONENT**   When one assesses the impact of fiscal policy on the economy, one should also adjust the federal deficit to remove its cyclical component. The reason is that the cyclical component reflects the state of the economy rather than discretionary policy decisions. For example, in 1983, when the unemployment rate averaged 9.6 percent, this adjustment would have taken some $103 billion off the deficit. By 1989, however, when the unemployment rate was near the 5.2 percent benchmark, this effect nearly disappeared. By 1992, the actual budget was once again appreciably below the structural budget. Likewise, as the economy grew through the mid- to late-1990s, the unemployment rate fell to 4.5 percent in 1998 (well below the natural rate). The actual and structural budgets went into surpluses, with the actual budget surplus rising above the structural budget surplus.

**ADJUSTING FOR INFLATION**   A final adjustment is needed to take the effects of inflation into account. Each year inflation erodes the real value of the federal debt held by the public. For example, in 1983 the nominal value of federal debt in the hands of private investors was almost $1 trillion and the inflation rate was almost 4 percent. Thus, private investors would have to buy almost $40 billion in newly issued government securities just to keep the real value of the total debt constant. This part of the deficit, it is argued, puts no real burden on the rest of the economy because, in real terms, it simply returns investors to the same position they started from. Even with recent inflation rates closer to 1.4 percent, the federal debt owned by private investors has grown to over $3 trillion, implying an inflation adjustment of $42 billion.

**THE DEFICIT AND PRIVATE SAVING**   Some economists offer another, rather different reason not to worry about the deficit. This is based on Robert Barro's argument, mentioned in *Applying Economic Ideas 9.1,* that changes in taxes tend to be fully offset by changes in private saving. If this is true, the public would respond to a tax cut by increasing saving by just the amount needed to buy the extra securities the Treasury would have to sell in order to finance the added deficit. Likewise, a tax increase made to reduce the deficit would decrease saving by the same amount, leaving no additional resources with which to finance private investment.

To be sure, most economists doubt that changes in taxes are fully offset by changes in saving. But even if there is only a partial adjustment of saving, the burden of the deficit will be eased and the case for raising taxes to cut the deficit weakened.

## Reasons to Worry about the Deficit

Despite the arguments just given, many economists—probably the majority—still worry about current and projected federal budget deficits. Let's look at some of their concerns.

**EFFECTS ON INVESTMENT**   Earlier in the chapter we saw that when the Treasury borrows to finance a deficit, it adds to total demand for the limited funds made available by private domestic saving, thereby pushing up interest rates. Private borrowers are then crowded out of financial markets. The reduction in private investment is a burden on the economy that slows economic growth and reduces the living standards of future generations. Thus, the drop in the share of net private investment in GDP from 6.9 percent in the 1970s to 4.6 percent in the 1980s is identified as one of the most harmful effects of deficits.

**BORROWING FROM ABROAD**   In defense of deficits it is sometimes said that the national debt is something "we owe to ourselves." In other words, taxes collected to repay the debt come out of the pockets of some U.S. citizens but go back into the pockets of others, leaving the country as a whole no poorer. However, it is argued, federal budget deficits push up interest rates in the United States relative to those in the rest of the world. Attracted by the high rates, foreign buyers purchase many of the securities that the Treasury sells to finance the deficit. In addition, because high interest rates on government securities push up the rates on competing private securities, many private U.S. securities also move into foreign hands.[3] In future years repaying the part of public and private debt owed to foreign investors will place a real burden on the U.S. economy. The argument that we owe it to ourselves does not apply in this case.

**THE ENLARGED STRUCTURAL DEFICIT**   It is widely acknowledged that any cyclical component of a federal deficit is less of a problem than the structural component. What worries many economists is the way the structural component grew during the 1980s even as the cyclical component fell. In 1983, just as the economy began its recovery from recession, the cyclical deficit came to $103 billion out of a total deficit of $208 billion. By 1988 and 1989, the cyclical component had all but disappeared. If the structural component had remained constant at its 1983 level, the actual deficit would have fallen to about $100 billion instead of remaining around $150 billion. Instead of shrinking, however, the structural deficit grew. By 1992, it had risen to about $200 billion, nearly double its 1983 level. The adjusted deficit rose by nearly $100 billion from 1989 to 1992.

In short, the increase in tax receipts that came from economic expansion after the recessions of the early 1980s was used not to reduce the structural deficit but to finance an increase in government expenditures. Small wonder, then, that the recession of 1990–1991 sent the actual deficit soaring to nearly $300 billion per year.

**THE CONSTRAINT PLACED ON DISCRETIONARY POLICY**   The recession of the early 1990s underlined another concern about the size of the structural deficit. According to the old Keynesian theory, government was supposed to react to a recession by raising government purchases or cutting net taxes, thereby adding to aggregate demand. The resulting deficit, and addition to the national debt, would not be worrisome if it were to be offset by budget surpluses and reduction of the debt during the subsequent business cycle peak.

However, when the country goes into a recession already running a large deficit, few policy makers are enthusiastic for large spending increases or tax cuts. Thus, it is argued, a large structural deficit handcuffs discretionary fiscal policy. Some proponents of activist fiscal policy blame the slow recovery from the 1990–1991 recession on failure of Congress to pass a fiscal stimulus package in late 1991 or early 1992. The failure can be attributed to a fear of further increasing the deficit.

**THE DANGER OF AN "EXPLODING" DEFICIT**   The growth of the structural deficit calls attention to still another worry: the increase in the part of the deficit associated with interest payments on the debt. As mentioned earlier, this part of the deficit has doubled as a percentage of the budget during the 1980s. Some economists think that under certain circumstances interest payments can experience "explosive" growth.

In the explosive-growth scenario, the amount of borrowing needed just to make interest payments on the debt is so great that the debt grows faster than domestic income even if the rest of the budget remains in balance. As the government borrows more and more each year to make interest payments, it adds to the demand for loanable funds in credit markets. This pushes interest rates higher, making it necessary to borrow even more to make the interest payments. Eventually the deficit "explodes" and threatens to swallow the entire domestic income.[4]

As the point of explosive growth approaches, the government is left with only one way out. It begins to "monetize" the deficit, which in effect means that it finances the deficit by creating new money rather than by borrowing. But financing deficits with newly created money is the classic formula for inflation. Thus, monetization of the deficit converts an explosive deficit into explosive inflation.

Is this scenario too farfetched to be a real threat? Not at all. Creating new money to cover the government deficit is the source of the runaway inflations (at annual rates of 1,000 percent per year and more) that devastated such countries as Bolivia, Argentina, Brazil, and Israel in the early 1980s. Today inflation is not running out of control in the United States; in fact, it has slowed dramatically from the double-digit rates of the late 1970s and early 1980s. Nevertheless, many economists think that continuing large federal deficits are a potential danger that cannot be ignored. In the next four chapters, we will gain a better understanding of this danger as we look at the mechanisms that are used to create and control money in the U.S. economy.

# SUMMARY

1. **How can fiscal policy be used to fight recession and inflation?** *Fiscal policy* means policy that is related to government purchases and net taxes. If a decrease in private planned expenditure threatens to send the economy into a recession, an increase in government purchases or a cut in net taxes can be used to shift the aggregate demand curve to the right, thereby restoring the economy to its natural level of real output. (In the income-expenditure model, such expansionary fiscal policy will shift the planned-expenditure schedule upward.) If an excess of private planned expenditure threatens the economy with inflation, a cut in government purchases or an increase in net taxes can shift the aggregate demand curve to the left, thereby restoring stability. (In the income-expenditure model, restrictive fiscal policy will shift the planned-expenditure schedule downward.)

2. **How are government receipts and expenditures affected by changing economic conditions?** Some changes in government receipts and expenditures reflect *discretionary* changes in the laws that govern fiscal policy. However, changes in the levels of these items can also result *automatically* from changes in economic conditions, including real output, unemployment, and the price level. In

general, economic expansion tends to raise receipts and restrain expenditures, thereby moving the budget toward surplus. Contraction tends to lower receipts and raise expenditures, thereby moving the budget toward deficit. These automatic changes in receipts and expenditures dampen the economy's response to shifts in private planned expenditure and, hence, are known as *automatic stabilizers.*

3. **How does the federal budgetary system work, and what are the limitations of that system?** In the United States authority for fiscal policy is divided between the president and Congress. Each year the president submits a budget plan, which Congress modifies and enacts into law by the beginning of the *fiscal year* on October 1. In practice, macroeconomic goals play a secondary role to political considerations in setting budget priorities.

4. **What priorities guided federal tax and spending decisions in the 1980s and 1990s?** In the 1980s, total taxes held steady as a share of GDP, despite cuts in marginal tax rates. The large deficits of the 1980s appear to have been caused not by tax cuts but by increased spending. Defense and *entitlements* accounted for the greatest spending increases. Cuts in other nondefense programs—

which now account for less than one-fifth of the budget—were not enough even to offset the growth in interest payments on the national debt. An additional implicit fiscal priority was to favor consumption over saving and investment. The Clinton administration was characterized by deep cuts to defense spending (as a share of government expenditures) and continued reduction in "other" spending. As receipts rose during the period of economic growth in the late 1990s, the federal budget went into a surplus, causing a reduction in net interest's share of government expenditure.

5. **How is the federal deficit measured, and why has it grown?** The federal deficit can be divided into a cyclical component and a structural component. The *structural deficit* is the estimated level of the deficit, given current tax and spending laws and unemployment at the natural rate. The *cyclical deficit* is the difference between the actual and structural deficits; it tends to increase during a recession and to decrease during an expansion. If unemployment drops below the natural rate at the peak of an expansion, the cyclical deficit becomes negative (that is, there is a cyclical surplus). During the expansion that followed the 1981–1982 recession, the cyclical component of the deficit declined nearly to zero while the structural component grew dramatically. The actual deficit then ballooned during the 1991–1992 recession. Both the actual and structural budgets went into a surplus during the mid- to late-1990s, only to plummet again during the 2001 recession.

6. **Are large federal deficits a threat to economic stability?** Some economists argue that if the federal deficit is adjusted for state and local government surpluses, the cyclical component of the deficit, capital expenditures, and the effects of inflation, it looks somewhat less threatening. Others claim that the deficit crowds out private invest-

ment. They are also concerned about borrowing from abroad to finance the deficit and the possibility that explosive growth of the deficit could ultimately cause severe inflation.

## KEY TERMS

Fiscal policy
Net tax multiplier
Discretional fiscal policy
Automatic fiscal policy
Automatic stabilizers
Fiscal year
Entitlements
Structural budget
Cyclical deficit/surplus

## PROBLEMS AND TOPICS FOR DISCUSSION

1. **Discretionary spending.** Suppose that the political events of 2001 had resulted in a $50 billion increase in government spending. Assuming no other changes in government policy and an expenditure multiplier of 4, how would a defense spending cut of that magnitude affect the economy? On the basis of what you have learned in this chapter, what are the drawbacks of the Bush economic stimulus package? Propose an alternative to the Bush plan and discuss its merits and weaknesses in terms of the budget.

2. **Unemployment and fiscal policy.** At point $E_1$ in Figure 9.1, real output is $1,500 billion compared with a natural level of real output of $2,000 billion. Apply Okun's law to estimate the unemployment rate at $E_1$ assuming a natural unemployment rate of 5.2 percent.

3. **Applying the multipliers.** Suppose that real output is at its natural level in the current year but forecasts show that if no action is taken, the aggregate demand curve will shift to the left by $500 billion in the coming year. Assuming an

expenditure multiplier of 2.5, what change in real government purchases will be needed to keep real output at the natural level? If a change in real net taxes is used instead, what change will be required?

4. **Impact of government purchases financed by increased taxes.** Assume that real output is currently at its natural level. For the coming year, Congress passes a budget that includes $100 million in added real government purchases to be paid for by a $100 million increase in real net taxes. What effect will this have on the aggregate demand curve? On the equilibrium level of real output? Does your answer depend on the value of the expenditure multiplier? Why or why not?

5. **A balanced budget amendment.** From time to time it has been proposed that a law or constitutional amendment be passed that will force the federal government to balance its budget every year Do you think it would be possible to keep the actual budget deficit at zero each year, or should such an amendment aim only to keep the structural deficit at zero? Discuss.

# CASE FOR DISCUSSION

## Did California Spend Its Way into a Fiscal Crisis?

At the end of 2003, California had a projected $38.2 billion state budget deficit. Unlike the federal government, California cannot simply borrow when it experiences a shortfall in receipts. State governments may borrow only if voters approve bond measures on the state ballot. With California's credit rating in jeopardy, voters may be reluctant to approve bonds to finance state deficits.

The media has been quick to blame the California's current budget crisis on excessive spending

during the 1990s. A closer examination of the data indicates that state government expenditures have grown at a slower rate since the 1989–1990 fiscal year. Much of the spending growth that occurred in the late 1990s represented the restoration of cuts made during the budget crisis of the early 1990s.

State government spending grew rapidly during 1959–1969 (8.8 percent) and 1969–1979 (6.8 percent), compared with only 1% growth between 1989 and 2002. The biggest growth in spending during the 1989–2002 period was in K–12 education, reflecting California's booming population growth.

This leaves California's governor, Arnold Schwarzenegger, in a difficult position. During his campaign, he promised that he would not raise taxes, nor would he cut funding to education. In fact, making good a campaign promise, he repealed an increase in vehicle registration fees imposed by the previous governor. The California state legislature recently passed Governor Schwarzenegger's request to put a bond measure on the ballot, but this is only a temporary solution to a growing dilemma. The problems facing California's legislature and governors are not unique. As the federal government has reduced its contributions to state and local expenditures (see Table 9.1), states are struggling to cope.

Source: David Carroll, "Did California Spend its Way into a Fiscal Crisis?" California Budget Project, May 2003.

## QUESTIONS

1. Does the reduction in vehicle license fees in California count as fiscal policy even though it takes place at the state level? Why or why not?
2. Assuming an expenditure multiplier for the economy as a whole, how would GDP be affected by $1 billion in California state budget cuts? By $650 million in California state tax increases?
3. Assume that all states cut spending and raise taxes when recession strikes. Does this make it easier or harder for the economy to recover from

recession? What would happen if the federal government followed the same policy?

4. How do recent trends in federal outlays affect state and local budgets? Suppose Congress approves a tax cut, but reduces expenditures paid to state governments by the same amount. If the state government cannot borrow, how will it respond? How will this affect state and national production?

# END NOTES

1. This is an approximation. It assumes both that there are no income taxes and that net exports and net investment are unaffected by a change in real domestic product at a given price level. In a more elaborate model that allowed for these factors, the general principles discussed in this section would still hold. However, in that model, each $1 in additional government purchases would shift the aggregate demand curve to the right by more than $1 but less than the $4 predicted by the simple expenditure multiplier calculated using a marginal propensity to consume of .75.

2. Herbert Stein, "After the Ball," *AEI Economist* (December 1984): 2.

3. These effects can also be expressed in terms of concepts that deal with international economic relations: An increase in the federal deficit, other things being equal, tends to move the capital account in the direction of a net capital inflow. This must be offset by a movement of the current account toward deficit. Thus, in an open economy, a federal deficit crowds out net exports as well as domestic investment.

4. The issue of the exploding deficit was raised in Thomas J. Sargent and Neil Wallace, "Some Unpleasant Monetarist Arithmetic," *Federal Reserve Bank of Minneapolis Quarterly Review* (Fall 1981): 1–17. Michael R. Darby refines the argument by showing that the deficit will explode if the real rate of interest (that is, the nominal market rate minus the inflation rate), adjusted for the average tax rate on federal interest payments, exceeds the long-term rate of growth of real GDP. See "Some Pleasant Monetarist Arithmetic," *Federal Reserve Bank of Minneapolis Quarterly Review* (Spring 1984).

# PART IV

# Monetary Economics

# Money
# and the
# Banking System

## WHERE LIFE IS EASY AND THE CURRENCY IS HARD

On the tiny South Pacific island of Yap, life is easy and the currency is hard.

Elsewhere, the world's troubled monetary system creaks along; floating exchange rates wreak havoc in currency markets, and devaluations are commonplace. But on Yap, the currency is a solid as a rock. In fact, it is a rock. Limestone, to be precise.

For nearly 2,000 years, the Yapese have used large stone wheels to pay for major purchases, such as land, canoes, and permission to marry. Yap is a U.S. trust territory, and the dollar is used in grocery stores and gas stations. But reliance on stone money, like the island's ancient caste system and the traditional dress of loincloths and grass skirts, continues.

Stone wheels don't make good pocket money, so for small transactions the Yapese use other forms of currency, such as beer. Beer is proffered as payment for all sorts of odd jobs, including construction. Besides stone wheels and beer, the Yapese sometimes spend "gaw," consisting of necklaces of stone beads strung together around a whale's tooth. They also can buy things with "yar," a currency made from large seashells. But these are small change.

The people of Yap have been using stone money ever since a Yapese warrior named Anagumang first brought the huge stones over from limestone caverns on neighboring Palau, some 1,500 to 2,000 years ago. Inspired by the moon, he fashioned the stones into large circles. The rest is history.

By custom, the stones are worthless when broken. Rather than risk a broken stone—or back—Yapese tend to leave the larger stones where they are and make a mental accounting that the ownership has been transferred— much as gold bars used in international transactions change hands without leaving the vault of the New York Federal Reserve Bank.

Just three decades ago, Yap was little changed from the way it had been for centuries. But now things are changing. To help preserve the tradition of stone money, Andrew Ken, a Yapese monetary thinker, is trying to persuade the Yap government to start a stone money exchange. This would allow the Yapese to trade their boulders for dollars, or buy them back, whenever they wish. "We're losing because we can't liquidate," Ken complains. Currently, the U.S. dollar is the official currency of the Yap Islands, but the stone money is still used for traditional exchanges such as the purchase of land or in village ceremonies.

Source: Art Pine, "Fixed Assets, or: Why a Loan in Yap Is Hard to Roll Over," *The Wall Street Journal,* March 29, 1984, 1. Reprinted by permission of *The Wall Street Journal,* © 1984 Dow Jones & Company, Inc. All Rights Reserved Worldwide.

〜

MONEY IS THE fluid that moves in the circular flow of income and product. Money can take many forms: giant stones on the Pacific island of Yap; gold coins throughout much of the world in earlier centuries; electronic entries in banks' computers in the United States today; and even in computer simulation games such as Sims and EverQuest.

Although we have mentioned money often, in this and the following chapters we give it center stage. We will begin by defining money and explaining how it is measured. Next we will explore the banking system. Later in this text we will see how the Federal Reserve, a government agency, controls the stock of money. We will also turn to a discussion of the demand for money and how that demand interacts with supply. Finally, we will see that changes in the money stock can have a strong impact on the decisions of households, firms, and government units. By the end of these discussions, it will be clear why a stable monetary system is a crucial part of national economic policy.

# MONEY: WHAT IT IS AND WHAT IT DOES

**Money**

An asset that serves as a means of payment, a store of purchasing power, and a unit of account.

**Money** is best defined in terms of what it does: It serves as a means of payment, a store of purchasing power, and a unit of account. Money serves these functions regardless of its name or form—U.S. dollars, Japanese yen, or Yapese stone wheels can all function in all three ways.

## The Functions of Money

As a means of payment, money reduces the costs of carrying out transactions. Using money avoids the complexities of barter. Imagine a market in which farmers meet to trade produce of various kinds. Apples will get you peppers, cauliflower will get you beets, and turnips will get you garlic. But what if you want garlic and have only potatoes? What you need is a universal means of exchange—one that all sellers will accept because they know that others will also accept it; one that is in limited supply so that you know its exchange value will remain constant; and one that is easily recognized and hard to counterfeit. The Yapese find that stone wheels work well for large transactions, and they use "yar" or "gaw" for small ones. In the United States, coins and paper currency serve as pocket money while bank deposits, which can be transferred by check or computer networks, are used for bigger business deals.

As a store of purchasing power, money makes it possible to arrange economic activities in a convenient manner over time. Income-producing activities and spending decisions need not occur simultaneously. Instead, we can accept money as payment for our work and keep the money handy until we want to spend it. The U.S. dollar is a fairly good store of purchasing power, although in some periods its purchasing power has been undermined by inflation. Yapese stone wheels evidently work even better—they have held their value for centuries.

Finally, as a unit of account money makes it possible to measure and record economic stocks and flows. A household's needs for food, shelter, and clothing can be expressed in dollar terms. The nation's output of movies, apples, and airplanes can be added together in dollar terms. Without money as a unit of account, private and public economic planning would be virtually impossible.

## Money as a Liquid Asset

Anything of value can serve as a store of purchasing power if it can be sold and the proceeds can be used to buy something else. Money, however, has two important traits that no other asset has, at least not to the same extent. One is that money itself can be used as a means of payment without first having to be exchanged for something else. A house, a corporate bond, or a blast furnace may have great value, but they can rarely be traded without first being exchanged for an equivalent amount of money. The other trait is that money can neither gain nor lose in nominal value; this is necessarily so, because money is the unit of account in which nominal values are stated. Thus, a house, a bond, or a blast furnace may be worth more or fewer dollars next year than this year, but the nominal value of a dollar is always a dollar—no more and no less.

**Liquidity**

An asset's ability to be used directly as a means of payment, or to be readily converted into one, while retaining a fixed nominal value.

An asset that can be used as or readily converted into a means of payment and is protected against gain or loss in nominal value is said to have **liquidity**. No other asset is as liquid as money. In fact, a comparison of the definitions of money and liquidity suggests that any perfectly liquid asset is, by definition, a form of money.

## Measuring the Stock of Money

For purposes of economic theory and policy, we need to know not only what money is but also how it can be measured. In all modern economies the stock of money is controlled by government. As we will see, if government fails to supply enough money, real output and employment will decrease, at least temporarily. On the other hand, flooding the economy with too much money causes inflation. Because the money stock cannot be controlled if it cannot be measured, the problem of measurement is an important one.

**Currency**

Coins and paper money.

**Transaction deposit**

A deposit from which funds can be freely withdrawn by check or electronic transfer to make payments to third parties.

**CURRENCY AND TRANSACTION DEPOSITS** We begin with a rather restrictive definition that views money as consisting of just two highly liquid types of assets: currency and transaction deposits. **Currency** includes coins and paper money. **Transaction deposits**—popularly known as *checking accounts*—are deposits from which money can be withdrawn by check or electronic transfer without advance notice and used to make payments.

In the United States, currency consists of the familiar Federal Reserve notes, which are issued in denominations of $1, $2, $5, $10, $20, $50, and $100, and of coins minted by the Treasury. Coins and paper money were formerly backed by precious metals. Until 1934, the U.S. government issued both gold coins and paper currency that could be exchanged for gold on demand; silver coins and silver-backed paper money survived until the mid-1960s. Today, coins and paper money are simply tokens whose value is based on the public's faith in their usefulness as means of paying for goods and services. In this regard, the use of dollars in the United States is no different from the use of stone wheels on the island of Yap.

**Commercial banks**

Financial intermediaries that provide a broad range of banking services, including accepting demand deposits and making commercial loans.

**Thrift institutions (thrifts)**

A group of financial intermediaries that operate much like commercial banks; they include savings and loan associations, savings banks, and credit unions.

**Depository institutions**

Financial intermediaries, including commercial banks and thrift institutions, that accept deposits from the public.

**M1**

A measure of the money supply that includes currency and transaction deposits.

Transaction deposits are available in a number of forms. One major type of transaction deposit is the *demand deposit*. By law, demand deposits cannot pay interest, but banks compensate demand-deposit customers with various services. Until the mid-1970s, demand deposits were the only kind of transaction deposit available in the United States and were offered only by **commercial banks**. They have since been joined by a variety of interest-bearing checkable deposits, notably negotiable order of withdrawal or NOW accounts. These are available to consumers through commercial banks and **thrift institutions (thrifts)**—savings and loan associations, savings banks, and credit unions. Banks and thrifts are referred to collectively as **depository institutions**. (We will look at these institutions in more detail later in the chapter.)

As Table 10.1 shows, in the fall of 2002 demand deposits made up roughly half of the total transaction deposits, with all other checkable deposits accounting for the other half. Currency plus all forms of transaction deposits totaled $1,202.2 billion as of November 2002. The sum of currency and transaction deposits is known as **M1**.

Some readers may find it odd that credit cards are not included in the monetary aggregates. After all, from the consumer's point of view, paying for a purchase with a credit card is a close substitute for paying by cash or check. *Applying Economic Ideas 10.1* discusses the nature of credit cards and explains why they do not figure in the measurement of the nation's money stock.

**THE BROADLY DEFINED MONEY STOCK**   The rationale behind the narrow definition of the money stock, M1, is that almost all transactions are made with either

**TABLE 10.1   COMPONENTS OF THE U.S. MONEY STOCK, NOVEMBER 2002 (BILLIONS OF DOLLARS, SEASONALLY ADJUSTED)**

| | | |
|---|---|---|
| Currency | | $623.6 |
| + Travelers checks | | $7.5 |
| + Transactions deposits | | $571.1 |
| Demand deposits | $294.5 | |
| Other checkable deposits | $276.6 | |
| **= M1** | | **$1,202.2** |
| + Savings deposits (including MMDAs) | | $2,743.6 |
| + Small-denomination time deposits | | $898.1 |
| + Retail money market fund shares | | $933.4 |
| **= M2** | | **$5,777.3** |

This table breaks down the U.S. money supply into its components as of November 2002. It gives two of the most commonly used money supply measures. M1 is the total of currency and transaction deposits; M2 includes M1 plus other highly liquid assets.

Source: Board of Governors of the Federal Reserve System, *H.6 Statistical Release*, December 18, 2003.

## ～ APPLYING ECONOMIC IDEAS 10.1

### "PLASTIC MONEY"

Recent innovations in banking have streamlined how people make payments and have reduced their reliance on using paper currency. For instance, instead of writing a check as a means of payment, individuals can use a debit card or a credit card.  Many people wonder how this "plastic money"—the MasterCards, VISA cards, and other bank cards that so many people carry these days—fits into M1 and M2. Just what role do these cards play in the payments system?

*Credit cards*, the most common type of plastic money, are not really a form of money at all. What sets credit cards apart from currency, bank deposits, and other forms of money is the fact that they are not a store of value. Instead, they are documents that make it easy for their holders to obtain a loan.

When you go into a store, present your credit card, and walk out with a can of tennis balls, you have not yet paid for your purchase. What you have done is borrow from the bank that issued the card. At the same time, you have instructed the bank to turn over the proceeds of the loan to the store. Later the bank will send money to the store (either in the form of a check or by crediting the amount to the store's account). This will pay for the tennis balls. Still later you will send money to the bank to pay off the balance on your credit card account.

Another common form of plastic money is a *debit card*. A debit card directly withdraws money from the payer's bank account and deposits these funds into the receiver's account. The funds are verified electronically, which substantially reduces the time and cost needed to clear a check. Similarly, many students in colleges today can use their student identification card as a stored-value card, or "smart card." Stored-value cards are much like debit cards except that they generally draw on funds stored with the card's administrator (such as the college/university issuing student I.D. cards) rather than in a bank account. Because stored-value and debit cards draw on funds the cardholder has deposited (in a checking or school account), they are considered money.

Many businesses operating on the internet accept electronic cash and electronic checks. These are much like their paper counterparts, cash and checks, except the transactions take place electronically over the internet.  For example, rather than writing a paper check to pay for something in a store, you can order the same good over the internet and provide your check number to paybank account information to pay.

The obvious drawback to electronic money is that it increases the likelihood of fraud. It is more difficult to verify the person's identity without photo identification or other personal information. Also, businesses using electronic money gain access to additional personal information not usually provided when using paper cash or checks.

---

currency or transaction deposits. However, if one chooses to focus on the function of money as a store of value rather than as a means of payment, there are a number of other assets that are almost as liquid as the components of M1 and serve as close substitutes for them.

Shares in money market mutual funds are one example. A *money market mutual fund* is a financial intermediary that sells shares to the public. The proceeds of these sales are used to buy short-term, fixed-interest securities such as Treasury bills. Almost all the interest earned on securities bought by the fund is passed along to shareholders. (The fund charges a small fee for its services.) Shareholders can redeem their shares in a number of ways—by writing checks on the fund (usually in amounts above a minimum of $500), by telephone transfer, or by transfer to another fund.[1] Because the proceeds from sales of shares are invested in very safe short-term assets, a money market mutual fund is able to promise its shareholders a fixed nominal value of $1 per share, although the interest paid on the shares varies with market rates. Except for the minimum-amount requirement on checks, then, money market mutual

**Savings deposit**

A deposit at a bank that can be fully redeemed at any time, but from which checks cannot be written.

**Time deposit**

A deposit at a bank or thrift institution from which funds can be withdrawn without payment of a penalty only at the end of an agreed-upon period.

**M2**

A measure of the money supply that includes M1 plus retail money market mutual fund shares, money market deposit accounts, and saving deposits.

**Equation of exchange**

An equation that shows the relationship among the money stock (M), the income velocity of money (V), the price level (P), and real domestic product (y); written as MV = Py.

**Velocity (income velocity of money)**

The ratio of nominal domestic income to the money stock; a measure of the average number of times each dollar of the money stock is used each year for income-producing purposes.

fund balances are almost as liquid as those of ordinary transaction accounts. Money market funds grew rapidly in the late 1970s and early 1980s, when market interest rates rose while rates paid by banks and thrifts were limited by federal regulations.

Banks and thrifts also offer a number of other accounts that serve as reasonably liquid stores of purchasing power. **Savings deposits** are a familiar example. Although checks cannot be written on these deposits, they are fully protected against loss in nominal value and can be redeemed at any time. In addition to conventional savings deposits, since late 1982 banks and thrifts have been allowed to compete with money market mutual funds by offering so-called *money market deposit accounts (MMDAs)*. These accounts have limited checking privileges and offer higher interest rates than the transaction accounts included in M1. Their volume grew very rapidly after their introduction. As Table 10.1 shows, savings deposits and MMDAs together totaled $2,743.6 billion in November 2002.

Banks and thrifts also offer **time deposits.** In the case of small-denomination time deposits (up to $100,000), funds typically must be left on deposit for a fixed period, ranging from less than a month to many years, in order to earn the full interest rate, and they normally cannot be transferred to another person before maturity. This feature makes them less liquid than savings deposits or MMDAs, but in return they usually pay a higher interest rate. They, too, are protected against loss of nominal value.

Retail money market mutual fund shares, MMDAs, savings deposits, and small-denomination time deposits are added to M1 to create a measure of the money supply known as **M2.** As Table 10.1 shows, M2 amounted to $5,777.3 billion in November 2002.

Besides M1 and M2, there are other, still broader measures. M3 includes such items as large-denomination time deposits ($100,000 and up) and other liquid assets.

## Why Money Matters

In presenting alternative measures of the money stock, we might seem to have wandered rather far afield from our main macroeconomic themes of price stability, real output, and employment. In fact, however, these key variables are closely related to money. Much of the next three chapters will be devoted to showing why this is so, but a preliminary overview can be given here.

**THE EQUATION OF EXCHANGE**　The relationship between money and other key variables can be stated in the form of the following equation, which is termed the **equation of exchange**:

$$MV = Py$$

where M stands for a measure of the money stock, P for the price level, and y for real domestic product. The remaining variable, V, stands for **velocity** or, more fully, the **income velocity of money.** Velocity can be thought of as the average number of times each dollar of the money stock is spent each year for income-producing transactions. It can also be thought of as the ratio of nominal domestic product to the money stock.[2] For example, if a country had a money stock of $200 billion and a real domestic product of $1,000 billion, velocity would be 5, indicating that each dollar of the money stock changed hands about 5 times a year for purchases of final goods and services.

The equation of exchange shows that any change in the money stock must affect the price level, real output, velocity, or some combination of these variables. Thus, control over the money stock gives the government another policy instrument with which to influence key macroeconomic variables. Later chapters will show in detail the means by which policy makers can influence the money stock. They will also discuss the effects of changes in the money stock on other variables.

**WHICH "M" IS BEST?**    As we have seen, there are various measures of the money stock. All of these measures are determined by establishing a cutoff point along a range of financial assets with varying degrees of liquidity, from currency at one end to long-term securities at the other. No hard-and-fast answer can be given to the question of which M is "best" without also asking, "Best for what?"

As mentioned earlier, the basic idea of M1 is to measure the money stock available for use as a means of payment. However, it does not do this perfectly. On the one hand, some consumers use interest-bearing transaction accounts, such as NOW accounts, primarily as a store of purchasing power. This savings motive is reflected in the fact that some of these accounts have a low *turnover rate*—that is, the ratio of the volume of transactions per year to the average balance is low. On the other hand, as we have seen, money market mutual funds and MMDAs have limited checking features that allow them to serve as means of payment. These assets are not included in M1 partly because they have even lower turnover rates, but they are still used for some transactions. Thus, M1 is far from perfect as a measure of means-of-payment money.

Similar problems plague M2, which is intended to measure the stock of money as a short-term, highly liquid store of purchasing power. M2 includes items such as savings and small-denomination time deposits, which have fixed nominal values despite their low turnover rates. But the cutoff line between M2 and M3—for example, the $100,000 cutoff for time deposits—is arbitrary.

For purposes of macroeconomic modeling and policy, the best money stock measure would be the one with the most predictable velocity and, hence, the most predictable relationship to the variables lying on the right-hand side of the equation of exchange—that is, real output and the price level. For many years economists were confident that M1, whatever its imperfections, was the best available measure in this regard. In the 1980s, as banking institutions and ways of doing business changed, M1 began to lose its close relationship to other economic variables, and M2 became a better measure. In this book, unless we specify otherwise, the term *money* can be understood to refer to M2.

# THE BANKING SYSTEM

As Table 10.1 shows, less than 30 percent of M2 consists of currency issued by the federal government and money market mutual funds. Most of the other components of M2—transaction deposits, savings deposits and MMDAs, and small-denomination time deposits—are issued by commercial banks and thrifts. For this reason, an understanding of monetary theory and policy requires a knowledge of the structure and operations of depository institutions.

## Types of Depository Institutions

There are four principal types of depository institutions in the United States. They differ in the types of loans and deposits in which they specialize, although their operations increasingly overlap.

The largest group of depository institutions is *commercial banks*. These usually include the word *bank* in their names. One of their specialties is making commercial loans—that is, loans to businesses, frequently short term. They also make consumer loans and home mortgage loans. Until the 1970s, commercial banks were the only institutions that could offer checking accounts, and they still hold the bulk of transaction deposits. They also raise funds by offering savings and time deposits and other financial instruments. Large commercial banks provide many services, such as wire transfers and international banking facilities, to business customers.

*Savings and loan associations* (also known as *savings and loans* or *S&Ls*) specialize in home mortgage lending, although they also make other real estate loans, consumer loans, and a limited number of commercial loans. Household savings and time deposits have traditionally been their main source of funds, but today they also offer fully checkable deposits as well as MMDAs with limited checking privileges. Although they may not use the word *bank* in their names, some savings and loan associations shape their operations to resemble those of commercial banks as closely as regulations permit.

*Mutual savings banks* are a type of depository institution that emerged in the nineteenth century to serve the needs of working-class households needing a depository for their small amounts of savings. Some still have names that reflect these origins, such as "Dime Savings Bank." Mutual savings banks offer the same range of deposits as savings and loan associations, but they tend to offer more diversified types of loans.

*Credit unions* are small financial intermediaries organized as cooperative enterprises by employee groups, union members, or certain other groups with shared work or community ties. They specialize in small consumer loans, although a few also make mortgage loans. They offer both transaction and savings deposits.

Since the mid-1970s, the traditional distinctions among these four types of institutions have eroded. Today, both from the viewpoint of the consumer and in macroeconomic terms, there is no real difference between a transaction deposit in a commercial bank and one in a thrift institution. Therefore, we will use the terms *bank* and *banking system* to refer to all depository institutions except when there is a particular reason to single out one type of institution.

## The Banking Balance Sheet

The operations of a commercial bank can best be understood by reference to its balance sheet. A firm's or household's **balance sheet** is a financial statement showing what it owns and what it owes, or, to use more technical language, its *assets, liabilities,* and *net worth.* **Assets,** which are listed on the left-hand side of the balance sheet, are all the things that the firm or household owns or to which it holds a legal claim. **Liabilities,** which are listed on the right-hand side of the balance sheet, are all the legal claims against a firm by non-owners or against a household by nonmembers. **Net worth,** also listed on the right-hand side of the balance sheet, is equal to the firm's or household's assets minus its liabilities. In a business firm, net worth represents the owners' claims against the business. *Equity* is another term that is often used to refer to net worth. In banking circles net worth is often referred to as *capital.*

The balance sheet gets its name from the fact that the totals of the two sides always balance. This follows from the definition of net worth. Because net worth is defined as assets minus liabilities, liabilities plus net worth must equal assets. In equation form, this basic rule of accounting reads as follows:

$$\text{Assets} = \text{Liabilities} + \text{Net worth}$$

Table 10.2 shows a total balance sheet for U.S. commercial banks. Balance sheet items for thrift institutions would differ in amount, but the concepts involved would be the same.

**ASSETS**  On the assets side of the balance sheet, the first line lists the non-interest-bearing deposits that banks maintain with the Federal Reserve System (which we will look at in more detail shortly), as well as vault cash, which is currency that banks keep in their own vaults. Deposits at the Federal Reserve plus vault cash constitute a bank's **reserves.** Historically, banks held reserves of cash or deposits that could be quickly converted into cash because at any moment some depositors might want to withdraw their funds. Today the minimum level of reserves is not left to the judgment of banks; rather, federal regulations require banks to hold reserves equal to a certain percentage of transaction deposits. The Federal Reserve's power to regulate the level of reserves in the banking system is a major tool of monetary policy. Other *cash assets, also included in line one of the balance sheet and sometimes known as secondary reserves,* give banks the liquidity to meet unexpected needs.

The next two items on the assets side of the balance sheet show the banks' main income-earning assets. The largest item is loans made to firms and households. In addition, commercial banks hold a substantial quantity of securities, including secu-

---

**Balance sheet**

A financial statement showing what a firm or household owns and what it owes.

**Assets**

All the things that the firm or household owns or to which it holds a legal claim.

**Liabilities**

All the legal claims against a firm by nonowners or against a household by nonmembers.

**Net worth**

The firm's or household's assets minus its liabilities.

**Reserves**

Cash in bank vaults and banks' non-interest-bearing deposits with the Federal Reserve System.

**TABLE 10.2 TOTAL BALANCE SHEET FOR U.S. COMMERCIAL BANKS, DECEMBER 10, 2003 (BILLIONS OF DOLLARS)**

| Assets | | Liabilities | |
|---|---|---|---|
| Reserves and cash items | $322.2 | Transaction deposits | $624.2 |
| Securities | $1,841.2 | Nontransaction deposits | $4,122.2 |
| Loansᵃ | $4,373.3 | Bank borrowing | $1,426.9 |
| Other assets | $792.0 | Other liabilities | $574.4 |
| | | | |
| Total assets | $7,328.7 | Total liabilities | $6,747.7 |
| | | Net worth | $581.0 |
| | | Total liabilities plus net worth | $7,328.7 |

This table shows the total balance sheet for all U.S. commercial banks as of December 10, 2003. Assets of banks include non-interest-bearing reserves and interest-bearing loansᵃ and securities. Liabilities include deposits of all kinds and other borrowings. Net worth equals assets minus liabilities. The balance sheets of thrift institutions would show the same basic categories but would differ in details.

ᵃLosses from loans are included in "Other assets"; loans are reported gross of these losses.

Source: Board of Governors of the Federal Reserve System, *H.8 Statistical Release*, December 19, 2003.

rities issued by federal, state, and local governments. The final item on this side includes some smaller income-earning items plus the value of the banks' buildings and equipment.

**LIABILITIES**  The first two items on the liabilities side of the banks' balance sheet are various kinds of deposits. They are liabilities because they represent funds to which depositors hold a legal claim. Funds that banks have borrowed are also liabilities. A small portion of these are borrowed from the Federal Reserve and the rest from private sources. Because the banks' total liabilities are less than their assets, they have a positive net worth. This sum represents the claim of the banks' owners against the banks' assets.

## The Federal Reserve System

We have already mentioned the Federal Reserve System, or the *Fed*, as it is known in financial circles. The Fed is the central banking system of the United States. It provides banking services to private banks and to the federal government. It is one of the chief regulators and supervisors of the banking system. Its responsibility for monetary policy makes it a major partner with Congress and the executive branch in macroeconomic policy making.

The Fed was established in 1913 as an independent agency of the federal government and therefore is not under the direction of the executive branch. It is subordinate to Congress, but Congress does not intervene in its day-to-day decision making.

The reason for making the Fed independent was to prevent the U.S. Treasury Department from using monetary policy for political purposes. In practice, however, the Fed's monetary actions are coordinated with the Treasury's fiscal actions. The chair of the Fed's Board of Governors is in frequent contact with the secretary of the Treasury, the chair of the President's Council of Economic Advisers, and the director of the Office of Management and Budget. By law, the Fed also presents a formal report on monetary policy to Congress twice a year. It also explains how its monetary policy objectives are related to economic conditions and to the economic goals set by the administration and Congress.

**FEDERAL RESERVE BANKS**   The Federal Reserve System is composed of 12 Federal Reserve district banks. Each serves a particular district of the country. The cities in which Federal Reserve Banks are located are Boston, New York, Philadelphia, Cleveland, Richmond, Atlanta, Chicago, St. Louis, Minneapolis, Kansas City, Dallas, and San Francisco. An additional 25 cities, including Seattle, Denver, Cincinnati, Miami, and others, have branches of the Federal Reserve Bank in their district.

Each Federal Reserve bank is a separate unit chartered by the federal government. Its stockholders are commercial banks that are members of the Federal Reserve System. Although Federal Reserve banks issue stock to their members, they are not typical private firms in that they are neither operated for profit nor ultimately controlled by their stockholders. The Federal Reserve banks earn income from their holdings of federal securities and, since 1981, from charges for services provided to banks and thrift institutions. Each year the Fed district banks return all their income, minus operating costs, to the Treasury.

Each bank is managed by a nine-member board. Six of those members are selected by the member banks; the other three are appointed by the Fed's Board of Governors. Each board sets the policies of its own bank under the supervision of the Board of Governors. The Board of Governors also approves the appointments of each Reserve bank's top officers.

The Federal Reserve banks perform a number of important functions in the banking system. These include operating a wire system for electronic funds transfers, clearing checks, handling reserve deposits, and making loans to depository institutions. They also issue paper currency in the form of Federal Reserve notes and supply Treasury coins. Finally, they provide banking services to the Treasury.

**THE BOARD OF GOVERNORS**   The head of the Federal Reserve System is its Board of Governors. The Board, which supervises the 12 Federal Reserve banks, is comprised of seven members who are appointed by the president and confirmed by the Senate. Each governor serves a single 14-year term, with one term expiring every other year. The president appoints one of the board members to serve as chair for a four-year term.

The Board of Governors has the power to approve changes in the interest rate on loans made to banks and thrifts by the Fed district banks. It also sets, within limits determined by law, the minimum level of reserves that banks and thrifts are required to hold relative to certain deposits. The Board supervises and regulates many types of banking institutions, including state-chartered member banks, bank holding companies, and U.S. offices of foreign banks. It also approves bank mergers and implements consumer credit regulations.

**THE FEDERAL OPEN MARKET COMMITTEE**   Authority over purchases and sales of government securities held by the Fed—its most important monetary policy tool—rests with the Federal Open Market Committee (FOMC). The FOMC is made up of the seven members of the Board of Governors plus five district bank presidents. The president of the Federal Reserve Bank of New York is a permanent member; the remaining four seats rotate among the other 11 district banks. The committee meets eight times a year (and also confers by telephone) to set a general strategy for monetary policy. Committee decisions regarding changes in the Fed's holdings of securities are carried out through the open market trading desk at the Federal Reserve Bank of New York.

**MEMBER AND NONMEMBER BANKS**   Approximately two-fifths of the 8,621 commercial banks in the United States belong to the Federal Reserve System. National banks must be members; state-chartered banks may join if they meet certain requirements. The member banks serve as stockholders of their district Federal Reserve Bank. Until 1980, member banks enjoyed certain privileges and received free services from the Fed, but in return they were subject to generally stricter regulation than nonmember banks.

In 1980 Congress passed the Depository Institutions Deregulation and Monetary Control Act, which did away with many of the distinctions between member and nonmember banks and between commercial banks and thrift institutions. As a result, since 1980 member banks, nonmember commercial banks, savings and loans, savings banks, and credit unions have all been subject to more uniform reserve requirements. In return for tighter regulation of reserves, thrift institutions won the right to compete more directly with commercial banks in making certain types of loans and offering transaction accounts. Nonmember depository institutions achieved access to Fed services such as check clearing, wire transfers, and loans on the same terms as member banks. In 1982 small depository institutions were exempted from reserve requirements. Thus, as a result of the Monetary Control Act, the distinction between banks and thrift institutions became less important.

**THE FED'S BALANCE SHEET**   Table 10.3 shows a balance sheet for the Federal Reserve System. Government securities are by far the Fed's largest asset. These security

**TABLE 10.3  CONSOLIDATED BALANCE SHEET OF THE FEDERAL RESERVE BANKS, DECEMBER 17, 2003 (BILLIONS OF DOLLARS)**

| Assets | | Liabilities | |
|---|---|---|---|
| Securities | $690.95 | Fed notes in circulation | $681.65 |
| Loans to banks | $0.05 | Bank deposits (reserves) | $26.51 |
| Other assets | $63.81 | Other liabilities plus net worth | $46.65 |
| Total assets | $754.81 | Total liabilities plus net worth | $754.81 |

The Federal Reserve banks have liabilities to the general public in the form of Federal Reserve notes and to banks and thrifts in the form of reserve deposits. The Fed's main assets are government securities. Loans to banks with which to meet reserve requirements are small, but they are a key aspect of banking and monetary policy.

Source: Board of Governors of the Federal Reserve System, *H.41 Statistical Release*, December 18, 2003.

holdings play a key role in the Fed's control of the money stock. Loans to banks and thrifts are small compared with other assets, but they are listed separately because they are important for policy purposes. Normally these loans are made to depository institutions on a short-term basis to enable them to meet their reserve requirements. However, in special circumstances longer-term loans are made to banks and thrifts that are experiencing a seasonal need for funds or are having financial difficulties. Other assets include some denominated in foreign currencies; these are important in carrying out the Fed's functions in the international monetary system.

Federal Reserve notes, which account for almost all of the nation's stock of currency, are the Fed's largest liability. These are followed by the reserves deposited with the Fed by banks and thrifts. Other liabilities include deposits of the Treasury and of foreign central banks. Because the Fed's assets exceed its liabilities, it has a positive net worth.

# ENSURING THE SAFETY AND STABILITY OF THE BANKING SYSTEM

Banks play a vital role in our economy, yet we often take them for granted until they experience problems. Unfortunately, parts of the banking system have experienced serious problems in recent years. Headlines about bank and thrift failures and financial wrongdoing have become all too common. This section looks at the sources of these failures and also at the policies used by government to ensure that the problems of individual institutions do not threaten the safety and stability of the banking system as a whole.

## Risks of Banking

Banks earn a profit by lending the proceeds from the deposits they receive or by using the proceeds to buy securities at interest rates higher than those they pay to depositors. Banks have been earning profits in this way for hundreds of years, but there are some well-known risks involved.

One is the risk of loan losses. What happens if a bank makes a loan to a customer who is unable to repay it? When a loan goes bad, the bank's net worth is reduced by an equal amount. (In balance-sheet terms, writing off the bad loan is a reduction in assets. Liabilities—that is, deposits and borrowing—do not change. Therefore, net worth, which equals assets minus liabilities, must fall.) If loan losses are too great, the bank's net worth may fall below zero. At that point the bank will no longer have enough assets to pay off all of its depositors and other creditors. A bank whose liabilities exceed its assets is said to be *insolvent* and usually must cease doing business.

A second risk that banks face is *insufficient liquidity,* that is, having insufficient liquid assets to cover withdrawals. When a depositor withdraws funds from a bank, the bank pays partly by drawing on the reserves it holds on deposit with the Fed or as vault cash and partly by drawing on other liquid assets that it holds for this purpose. Under normal conditions, new deposits approximately offset withdrawals, and the bank does not need to draw on its less liquid assets, such as loans and long-term securities, to cover withdrawals. If an unexpected wave of withdrawals occurs, however, the bank may use up all of its liquid assets. It will then have to convert some of its less liquid assets into cash. This may not be easy, especially if the wave of withdrawals takes place when business conditions are unfavorable, requiring the bank to sell the assets at less than the value at which they are entered on the bank's books. For example, a bank might have paid $1,000,000 for bonds issued by a state government agency. Later, because of unfavorable market conditions, it might have to sell them for just $800,000. Sales of assets at less than book value have an effect on the balance sheet similar to that of loan losses: In accordance with the basic equation of accounting, the reduction in the value of assets causes an equal reduction of the bank's net worth. If net worth falls below zero, the bank becomes insolvent.

Whether the bank's troubles begin with loan losses or with insufficient liquidity, there is a danger that they may trigger a run on the bank. A *run* is a situation in which depositors begin to withdraw their funds because they fear that the bank may become insolvent. Because large withdrawals force the bank to sell assets at less than their book values, depositors' fears become self-fulfilling and the bank fails.

In the worst possible case, the whole banking system, not just one bank, could get into trouble. If many banks faced loan losses or runs at the same time, they could not help one another with temporary loans of reserves. If large banks failed, smaller banks, which keep deposits in the large ones or make other loans to them, might be brought down, too. If many banks simultaneously tried to meet deposit outflows by selling their holdings of securities, the market price of the securities might fall, adding to their losses. A general bank *panic,* in which the stability of the whole system would be threatened, could ensue.

## Policies to Ensure Safety and Soundness

During the nineteenth century, a number of bank panics were touched off by recessions. As a result, both state and federal governments experimented with policies designed to ensure the safety and soundness of the banking system. Out of these efforts has evolved a system that is based on three basic tools: bank supervision and regulation, loans to troubled banks, and deposit insurance.

## The U.S. Banking System

**SUPERVISION AND REGULATION**   Bank examinations are the oldest tool for ensuring the safety and soundness of the banking system. These examinations, conducted by state or federal officials, are intended to ensure that banks do not make unduly risky loans, that they value their assets honestly, and that they maintain an adequate level of net worth. Honest bookkeeping, prudent lending, and adequate net worth help banks to survive business downturns without becoming insolvent. A variety of federal and state agencies—including the Federal Reserve, the Federal Deposit Insurance Corporation (FDIC), and the Office of the Comptroller of the Currency (part of the Treasury) or OCC for short—share responsibility for supervision and regulation.

Supervision and regulation do not always ensure sound banking practices. Examinations do not always spot bad loans. Sometimes examiners are deceived by fraudulent operators of banks and thrifts; in other cases they do no better than bank managers in spotting weak loans. In the case of thrifts, capital requirements were watered down by Congress and not enforced by regulators; many institutions were allowed to operate without an adequate cushion of net worth.

At the end of 1990, all banking regulatory agencies began phasing in so-called risk-based capital standards. Under these regulations, relatively risky assets require proportionately more capital as backing. This regulation has been introduced in compliance with an international agreement known as the Basel Accord, which is discussed further later in this chapter. More recent legislation at both the domestic and international level has tightened capital requirements still further.

**LENDER OF LAST RESORT**   Bank inspections, introduced more than a century ago, were not by themselves enough to prevent banking panics. In 1907 an especially severe panic took place, eventually leading to the establishment of the Federal Reserve System in 1913. Among other duties, the Fed has the power to aid the banking system in times of trouble by acting as a lender of last resort. For example, when the stock market experienced a record 22.6 percent loss on October 19, 1987, the Fed quickly announced that it stood ready to lend extra funds to any banks that needed additional cash because of customers' stock market losses. As discussed in *Economics* *in the News 10.1*, the Fed played an essential role in maintaining the soundness of the U.S. banking system following the 9/11 terrorist attacks in 2001.

Loans by the Fed to troubled institutions are useful primarily as a device to help fundamentally sound and solvent banks during temporary periods of insufficient liquidity. They cannot solve the problems of banks and thrifts that have fallen into insolvency because of imprudent management practices leading to massive loan losses.

**DEPOSIT INSURANCE**  Even with its power as a lender of last resort, the Fed failed to prevent a major bank panic in 1933, during the Great Depression. In 1934, in response to that crisis, Congress established the Federal Deposit Insurance Corporation (FDIC). Since the Monetary Control Act of 1980, all deposits are insured up to $100,000 per account (and even more in special cases.)

The idea of deposit insurance is to short-circuit runs on banks. If deposits are insured, depositors need not run to the bank to withdraw their funds; even if the bank fails, the government will pay them their money or arrange for the transfer of their deposits to a solvent bank. Also, if runs can be avoided, the problems of one or a few banks will not touch off a panic that threatens the whole system. Depository institutions are supposed to bear the cost of deposit insurance through premiums charged by the insurance funds. However, in recent years, premiums have fallen short of costs and taxpayers have had to cover the insurance funds' losses.

⌐ **ECONOMICS IN THE NEWS 10.1**
### 9/11: THE FED AS A LENDER OF LAST RESORT

The September 11, 2001 attacks on the World Trade Center in New York and the Pentagon in Washington, D.C. caused severe disruptions in the financial system that left banks short on funds. The Fed's actions during the crisis highlight its importance not only as a lender of last resort, but as a central authority in the payments system.

At 11:45 A.M., just three hours after the attacks, the Federal Reserve issued the following press statement: "The Federal Reserve System is open and operating. The discount window is available to meet liquidity needs." The discount window refers to a "window" where banks may go to take out loans from the Fed. Today, loan disbursements are made electronically through this "discount window." In addition, the Federal Reserve's staff contacted banks in the days surrounding the attacks to promote borrowing from the Fed as banks faced difficulty in honoring payments and extending lines of credit to their customers.

A series of events prevented timely payments both in the business and banking sectors. The physical damage to communications, computers, and general operations in New York slowed payments dramatically. The Federal Aviation Administration (FAA) halted air traffic, preventing the delivery of checks to banks by air. As a result, the volume of interbank transfers, essential in the bank payments system, fell 43% between September 10 and 11, 2001.

The Federal Reserve System responded by acting in its original role as a lender of last resort, providing large sums in the form of loans to the banking system. Between September 5 and September 12, Fed loans to banks increased from $195 million to $45.6 billion. As the president of the Federal Reserve Bank of St. Louis, William Poole, stated: "In the absence of Fed intervention, we would have seen a cascade of defaults as firms due funds that were not arriving would be unable to meet their obligations."

Sources: Kristin Van Gaasbeck, "Circling the Wagons: The Fed's Response to 9/11," presented at the *Western Economics Association International 78th Annual Meeting*, Denver, CO, July 12, 2003; William Poole, "The Role of Government in U.S. Capital Markets," lecture presented at the Institute of Governmental Affairs, University of California, Davis, October 18, 2001.

## ECONOMICS IN THE NEWS 10.2
### GLOBAL BANKING CRISES

The international banking system's stability has become increasingly important and increasingly difficult to maintain. Because each country has its own banking regulations, it is difficult to maintain international banking standards. The "International Banking" section below discusses a few examples of past international banking crises and of attempts to regulate the international banking system. The table below highlights recent international banking crises and reports the estimated losses attributed to bank failures. For each country, the cost as a share of the economy's Gross Domestic Product (GDP) is reported.

From the table, we see that the 1980s U.S. S&L crisis cost relatively little as a percentage of the economy's resources (GDP). Also, the table shows how devastating banking crises can be, illustrating the importance of adequate bank regulation.

### COST OF INTERNATIONAL BANKING CRISES (1980–PRESENT)

| Country | Dates | Estimated Cost as a % of GDP |
|---|---|---|
| Argentina | 1980–82 | 55% |
| Indonesia | 1997–present | 50–55% |
| Thailand | 1997–present | 42% |
| Cote d'Ivoire | 1988–1991 | 25% |
| Mexico | 1995–present | 15% |
| Japan | 1990s | 12% |
| Hungary | 1991–1995 | 10% |
| Russia | 1998–1999 | 5–7% |
| United States | 1984–1991 | 3% |
| Turkey | 1982–1985 | 2.5% |
| New Zealand | 1987–1990 | 1% |

Source: Daniela Klingebiel and Luc Laewan, eds., "Managing the Real and Fiscal Effects of Banking Crises," World Bank Discussion Paper No. 428 (Washington: World Bank, 2002).

One problem with deposit insurance is that it could encourage banks to take on excessive risk, since they know their depositors are insured by the government. The savings and loans (S&L) crisis of the 1980s offers a perfect example of this problem. Deposit insurance encouraged some banks and thrifts to take undue risks with their depositors' money; the depositors did not object, knowing that the federal government would bail them out if the institution failed. Losses at savings and loans associations were so large that the Federal Savings and Loan Insurance Corporation (FSLIC), the deposit insurance fund for S&L and mutual savings banks at the time, itself was forced into insolvency. Since 1989, the FDIC currently provides deposit insurance for S&Ls and mutual savings banks.

## International Banking

Bank failures in one country have severe consequences for that country's trading partners. For this reason, in 1987 several countries attempted to establish a set of standard requirements for the international banking system. The resulting Basel Accord imposed regulations to help prevent banks from declaring bankruptcy. The Basel Accord guidelines also make recommendations regarding bank balance sheet management. In practice, the accord has been difficult to enforce because of varying accounting definitions and loopholes in the agreement.

As we saw for the U.S. banking system, safeguards are needed to prevent widespread bank failures. In the United States, this responsibility rests with the Fed, FDIC, and other regulators. Unfortunately, many countries do not have adequate resources to provide credible deposit insurance. While the FDIC regulates and examines the banks it insures, few insurance funds abroad have this power. Also, few central banks have enough funds to act as a lender of last resort in the case of a bank panic. For this reason, the International Monetary Fund (IMF) has assumed the role of a lender of last resort. Much like the Federal Reserve may approve loans to failing banks, the IMF provides loans to countries that do not have the necessary resources to finance bailouts, or even those unable to honor government debt obligations. However, it has been criticized for imposing requirements that are not in the best interest of countries relying on the IMF to borrow. For instance, the IMF was criticized for its handling of the East Asian financial crisis that involved Indonesia, Korea, Malaysia, Philippines, Taiwan, and Thailand. As shown in *Economics in the News 10.2*, while Malaysia did not receive direct aid from the IMF, it fared better than other countries such as Korea and Indonesia that did receive IMF loans.

⌐

# SUMMARY

1. **What is money, and what does it do?** *Money* is an asset that serves as a means of payment, a store of purchasing power, and a unit of account. Because money can be used as a means of payment and has a fixed nominal value, it is said to be *liquid*.

2. **How is the stock of money in the economy measured?** A narrow measure of the money stock, *M1*, includes *currency* (coins and paper money) plus *transaction deposits* (deposits on which checks can be freely written). A broader and more widely used measure, *M2*, includes the components of M1 plus money market mutual fund shares, money market deposit accounts, *savings*

*deposits*, small-denomination *time deposits*, and certain other liquid assets. The relationship between money and other economic variables can be stated as the *equation of exchange*: $MV = Py$, in which M stands for the money stock, V for *velocity*, P for the price level, and y for real domestic product.

3. **What is the structure of the U.S. banking system?** The U.S. banking system consists of four types of *depository institutions*. The most important are *commercial banks*, which specialize in commercial loans and transaction deposits. In addition, there are three types of *thrift institutions*: savings and loan associations, savings banks, and credit unions. The Federal Reserve System is the

nation's central bank. It provides services to depository institutions, holds much of their required *reserves,* and, together with other federal agencies, regulates the banking system.

4. **How are the safety and stability of the banking system maintained?** Banks fail if they become insolvent—that is, if their assets fall below the level of their liabilities. This may happen because of loan losses or because deposit withdrawals have exhausted liquid assets. The government has three principal tools for ensuring the safety and soundness of the banking system: supervision and regulation; loans to banks and thrifts experiencing liquidity problems; and deposit insurance.

## KEY TERMS

| | |
|---|---|
| Money | Time deposit |
| Liquidity | M2 |
| Currency | Equation of exchange |
| Transaction deposit | Velocity (income |
| Commercial banks | velocity of money) |
| Thrift institutions (thrifts) | Balance sheet |
| Depository institutions | Assets |
| M1 | Liabilities |
| Savings deposit | Net worth |

## PROBLEMS AND TOPICS FOR DISCUSSION

1. **Examining the lead-off case.** What characteristics of stone wheels make it possible for them to serve as money in the Yap economy? Why are other forms of money used for some transactions? Discuss.

2. **The functions of money.** Money serves three functions: as a means of payment, a store of purchasing power, and a unit of account. How does inflation undermine each of these functions?

3. **Barter in the modern economy.** For most purposes, money lowers the cost of making transactions relative to barter—the direct exchange of one good or service for another. However, barter has not disappeared, even in an advanced economy such as that of the United States. Can you give an example of the use of barter in the U.S. economy today? Why is barter used instead of money in this case?

4. **Plastic money.** Do you use any credit cards? Does their use reduce the amount of money you need? Which forms of money do you need less of because you have a credit card? How do credit cards differ from debit cards?

5. **The banking balance sheet.** The National Information Center is a database with banking information maintained by the Federal Reserve System. You can download balance sheet information at http://www.ffiec.gov/nic/. Do an institution search for your bank or thrift and download the balance sheet information for this institution. How does this balance sheet compare with that of all commercial banks as given in Table 10.2? *Bonus question:* Obtain the balance sheets of a bank and a thrift and compare them.

6. **Current monetary data.** Every Thursday the Federal Reserve reports certain key data on money and the banking system. These reports are available from the Board of Governors of the Federal Reserve System *H.6 Statistical Release.* Obtain the most recent H.6 release online at http://www.federalreserve.gov/releases/ and answer the following questions:

   a. What items are included in M2 that are not included in M1? What was the total of such items in the most recent month for which data are reported? Which of these money measures grew most quickly in the most recent month for which data are reported?

b. Demand and other transaction deposits at these banks account for about what percentage of M1? What percentage of M1 is held in the form of currency and travelers checks?

7. **Recent bank failures.** The FDIC maintains a list of recently failed banks online at http://www.fdic.gov/bank/. Go to this list and download the information for a recently failed bank. Why did the institution fail? How did federal authorities respond to the failure?

# CASE FOR DISCUSSION

## *Makeshift Money in the French Colonial Period*

*The following letter was written by de Meulle, governor of the French province of Quebec in September 1685:*

My Lord—

I have found myself this year in great straits with regard to the subsistence of the soldiers. You did not provide for funds, My Lord, until January last. I have, notwithstanding, kept them in provisions until September, which makes eight full months. I have drawn from my own funds and from those of my friends, all I have been able to get, but at last finding them without means to render me further assistance, and not knowing to what saint to pay my vows, money being extremely scarce, having distributed considerable sums on every side for the pay of the soldiers, it occurred to me to issue, instead of money, notes on [playing] cards, which I have had cut in quarters. I send you My Lord, the three kinds, one is for four francs, another for forty sols, and the third for fifteen sols, because with these three kinds, I was able to make their exact pay for one month. I have issued an ordinance by which I have obliged all the inhabitants to receive this money in payments, and to give it circulation, at the same time pledging

myself, in my own name, to redeem the said notes. No person has refused them, and so good has been the effect that by this means the troops have lived as usual. There were some merchants who, privately, had offered me money at the local rate on condition that I would repay them in money at the local rate in France, to which I could not consent as the King would have lost a third; that is, for 10,000 he would have paid 40,000 livres; thus personally, by my credit and by my management, I have saved His Majesty 13,000 livres.

[Signed] de Meulle
Quebec, 24th September, 1685

Source: From *Canadian Currency, Exchange and Finance During the French Period*, vol. 1, ed. Adam Shortt (New York: Burt Franklin, Research Source Works Series no. 235, 1968).

## QUESTIONS

1. What indication do you find that the playing-card notes issued by the governor served as a means of payment? Why were they accepted as such?
2. What indicates that the notes served as a store of value? What made them acceptable as such?
3. Did the invention of playing-card money change the unit of account in the local economy?

# END NOTES

1. Money market mutual funds, which compete with banks and thrifts for household savings, make every effort to make their services as convenient as those of their competitors. They provide statements, checkbooks, deposit slips, and so on that closely resemble those used by banks and thrifts. Technically, however, their liabilities are shares in the fund's portfolio of assets, not deposits. Therefore, money market mutual funds are not considered to be depository institutions. Only retail, or consumer, money market mutual funds are included in M2—those owned by corporations are not.
2. This can be demonstrated as follows: First, the right-hand side of the equation, the price level times real domestic product, can be replaced by y, standing for nominal domestic product. Next, both sides of the equation can be divided by M to give V – y/M.

# Central Banking and Money Creation

1. How banks create money.
2. Why the size of the money stock is limited by the quantity of bank reserves.
3. The instruments available to the Fed for controlling the money stock.
4. How closely the money stock can be controlled.
5. The activities that the Fed undertakes in the international sphere.

1. M1, M2
2. Balance sheets
3. Federal Reserve System
4. Federal Open Market Committee
5. Bank reserves

## INSIDE THE FED

As powerfully as the moon affects the tides, the Federal Reserve System influences American finance and business. Like the moon, the Fed is mysterious, unseen most of the time, and only partly illuminated the rest of the time. Here H. Robert Heller, who served on the Fed's board of governors under chairmen Paul Volcker and Alan Greenspan, tells what it was like to be a member of this august group.

One of the most breathtaking moments of my life was the first time I walked into a meeting of the Federal Open Market Committee. Volcker had administered the oath of office to me at 8:55 A.M. on August 19, 1986. Then the door to the boardroom, which adjoins his office, opened, and we walked into an FOMC meeting, which began at nine o'clock. Everybody was already seated at the table, and they all rose. It was sort of like being inducted into the College of Cardinals.

Then the discussion started. I was trying to keep track of the various positions. There was a broad range of views, with some advocating a little easier monetary policy, and some a little tighter. And I thought, "My God, what if I'm the swing vote?" Cold sweat started running down my back. Finally, when it came to the roll call, to my enormous surprise almost everybody agreed to ease monetary policy slightly.

I began to realize that the FOMC is an enormous consensus builder. That makes it very different from the Supreme Court. Five-to-four decisions are the rule there. What we tend to see here is either 12-0 or 11-1 decisions. Though people walk into the meeting with somewhat divergent views, the sharp edges are worn off in discussion. Eventually a consensus emerges and is formulated by the chairman. Following further discussion and possible modification of the chairman's proposal, it is put to a vote. You think: Can I associate myself sufficiently with the consensus to vote yes, or am I so opposed that I must say, "This policy would be unacceptable." I never dissented, and I'm proud of that, because I believe I helped to build that consensus.

Source: Robert F. Norton, "A Rare Glimpse Inside the Fed," *Fortune*, September 11, 1989, 155–156. 1989 The Time Inc. Magazine Company. All rights reserved.

⁐

ONLY A VERY few people ever sit on the Federal Open Market Committee. Most people's interactions with the banking system are limited to writing checks, getting an auto loan, or getting cash from an automatic teller machine. Yet, as this chapter will show, each depositor's and each borrower's actions ultimately influence and are influenced by decision makers throughout the financial system, including those who sit at the very top.

This chapter draws on the workings of the banking system. We begin by examining how banks create money in a simplified system. Then we discuss the tools that the Federal Reserve uses to control the money stock within the country. Finally we look briefly at the Fed's role in international financial markets.

# THE CREATION OF MONEY

The bulk of the U.S. money supply consists of the liabilities of banks and thrift institutions. In this section we will see how these institutions create money on the basis of reserves supplied by the Federal Reserve System.

## A Simplified Banking System

As we have done in building models of other parts of the economy, we will begin with a simplified situation and add details later. Our simplified banking system is as follows:

1. The system consists of ten identical banks.
2. The banks' only assets are loans and reserve deposits at the Fed; there is no vault cash.
3. The banks' only liabilities are demand deposits; their net worth is zero.
4. Demand deposits are the only form of money in the banking system.
5. The system is regulated by a simplified Federal Reserve System that has the power to set uniform reserve requirements on all deposits.
6. The Fed's only assets are government securities, and its only liabilities are the reserve deposits of member banks. Banks do not borrow reserves from the Fed.

Simplified as it is, this 10-bank system can show us a great deal about the mechanics of money creation in the U.S. banking system.

**Required reserves**

The minimum amount of reserves that the Fed requires depository institutions to hold.

**RESERVES: REQUIRED AND EXCESS**    The Federal Reserve System sets a minimum percentage of certain categories of deposits that each bank or thrift must hold as reserve deposits with the Fed or as vault cash. These are called **required reserves**. The ratio of required reserves to total deposits is the **required-reserve ratio**. If the bank holds more than the minimum amount of required reserves, the balance is known as **excess reserves**. In equation form, the relationships among required reserves, excess reserves, deposits, and the required-reserve ratio can be stated as follows:

**Required-reserve ratio**

Required reserves stated as a percentage of the deposits to which reserve requirements apply.

$$\text{Required reserves} = \text{Deposits} \times \text{Required-reserve ratio}$$

and

$$\text{Excess reserves} = \text{Total reserves} - \text{Required reserves}$$

For our simplified banking system, we will assume a required-reserve ratio of 10 percent on all deposits.

**Excess reserves**

Total reserves minus required reserves.

**BALANCE SHEET EQUILIBRIUM**    As profit-seeking firms, banks want to earn all the interest they can; thus, they normally keep excess reserves to a minimum in order to make as many loans or buy as many securities as possible. The situation in which required reserves equal total reserves represents a state of equilibrium.

Although in practice, banks do not maintain reserves exactly at their equilibrium level at all times, in our simplified banking system we will assume that they quickly bring their excess reserves back to zero following any disturbance.

## Mechanics of Money Creation

Now we are ready to examine the mechanics of money creation in our simplified banking system. As the following example will show, money creation is governed by the required-reserve ratio, the amount of reserves supplied, and banks' efforts to maximize their profits.

**INITIAL BALANCE SHEETS**  Assume that each bank in the system starts out with a balance sheet that looks like this:

### Initial Balance Sheet of a Representative Bank

| Assets | | | Liabilities | |
|---|---|---|---|---|
| Reserves | | $ 10,000 | Demand deposits | $100,000 |
| Required | $10,000 | | | |
| Excess | 0 | | | |
| Loans | | 90,000 | | |
| Total assets | | $100,000 | Total liabilities | $100,000 |

Also assume that the Fed's initial balance sheet looks like this:

### The Fed

| Assets | | Liabilities | |
|---|---|---|---|
| U.S. government securities | $100,000 | Reserve deposits | $100,000 |

Starting from this point, we will look at the effects of an injection of reserves into the banking system. Each bank receives new reserves every time a customer deposits funds that were withdrawn from another bank. However, this does not increase the reserves in the banking system as a whole. For total reserves to be increased, new reserves must come from outside the system. The chief source of new reserves is the Fed.

Suppose that the Fed decides to increase the amount of reserves available to the banking system by $10,000. It usually does this by adding to its holdings of government securities, buying such securities from a securities dealer. Such an action is called an **open market operation** (in this case, an open market purchase) because the Fed, acting through the Federal Reserve Bank of New York, goes to the securities market and bids against other buyers to purchase the securities. Suppose the Fed buys $10,000 in securities from a dealer and pays for them through a wire transfer to

**Open market operation**

A purchase (sale) by the Fed of government securities from (to) the public.

the dealer's bank, which we will call Albany National Bank.[1] The *wire transfer* is an electronic instruction made through the Fed's computer network that credits Albany National Bank's reserve account at the Fed with $10,000 and simultaneously directs the bank to credit the same amount to the dealer's demand-deposit account.

At this point the Fed's initial goal of injecting $10,000 of new reserves into the system has been achieved. The balance sheets of the Fed and Albany National Bank now look like this (changes from the previous balance sheet are shown in parentheses):

### The Fed

| Assets | | Liabilities | |
|---|---|---|---|
| U.S. government securities | $110,000 (+10,000) | Reserve deposits | $100,000 (+10,000) |

### Albany National Bank

| Assets | | | Liabilities | |
|---|---|---|---|---|
| Reserves | | $ 20,000 (+10,000) | Demand deposits | $110,000 (+10,000) |
|     Required | $11,000 (+1,000) | | | |
|     Excess | 9,000 (+9,000) | | | |
| Loans | | 90,000 | | |
| Total assets | | $110,000 (+10,000) | Total liabilities | $110,000 (+10,000) |

**LENDING OUT THE EXCESS RESERVES** Note how the $10,000 in new reserves at Albany National Bank is divided between required and excess reserves. Deposits have gone up by $10,000, meaning that the bank must hold $1,000 more in required reserves. The other $9,000 in new reserves need not be held against deposits and hence is listed as excess reserves. Albany National Bank is no longer in equilibrium; it can increase its profits by lending out the excess reserves.

Of course, in order to make a loan the bank must find a borrower. Suppose that on the morning on which Albany gets its new reserves James Anderson walks in and applies for a $9,000 auto loan. The loan is granted and the $9,000 is credited to Anderson's checking account balance. (If Anderson had no checking account at Albany, he could ask the bank to pay him the proceeds of the loan in the form of a check or even currency. In that case, some of the intermediate steps in the following process would differ, but the end result would be the same.) At the moment at which the loan is completed—but before Anderson pays for the car—Albany National Bank's balance sheet looks like this:

**Albany National Bank**

| Assets | | | Liabilities | |
|---|---|---|---|---|
| Reserves | | $ 20,000 | Demand deposits | $119,000 |
| Required | $11,900 | | | |
| | (+900) | | | |
| Excess | 8,100 | | | |
| | (−9000) | | | |
| Loans | | 99,000 | | |
| | | (+9,000) | | |
| Total assets | | $119,000 | Total liabilities | $119,000 |
| | | (+9,000) | | (+9,000) |

**CHECKING AWAY THE LOAN PROCEEDS**   In crediting Anderson's account with $9,000, Albany National Bank has created a new $9,000 asset (the loan) matched by a new $9,000 liability (the deposit). Because of the new deposit, its required reserves have risen by $900. At this point Albany still has $8,100 in excess reserves. Why, then, does it not use those reserves to make yet another loan?

The reason the bank cannot safely make new loans greater than the original amount added to its excess reserves is that it knows Anderson will not leave the $9,000 sitting in his account; instead, he will write a check to pay for his new car. Let's see what happens when he does so.

We will call the dealer who sells the car Joyce Barnard and assume that she keeps her checking account at Bethel National Bank. When Barnard deposits Anderson's Albany National Bank check in her Bethel account, Bethel sends it to the Fed for clearance. *Clearing the check* simply means that the Fed credits $9,000 to Bethel's reserve account and subtracts $9,000 from Albany's reserve account. The Fed then puts the check in the mail so that Albany can forward it to Anderson for his records. When all these transactions have taken place, the two banks' balance sheets look like this:

**Albany National Bank**

| Assets | | | Liabilities | |
|---|---|---|---|---|
| Reserves | | $ 11,000 | Demand deposits | $110,000 |
| | | (−9,000) | | (−9,000) |
| Required | $11,000 | | | |
| | (−900) | | | |
| Excess | 0 | | | |
| | (−8,100) | | | |
| Loans | | 99,000 | | |
| Total assets | | $110,000 | Total liabilities | $110,000 |
| | | (−9,000) | | (−9,000) |

**Bethel National Bank**

| Assets | | | Liabilities | | |
|---|---|---|---|---|---|
| Reserves | | $ 19,000 | Demand deposits | | $109,000 |
| | | (+9,000) | | | (+9,000) |
| Required | $10,900 | | | | |
| | (+900) | | | | |
| Excess | 8,100 | | | | |
| | (+8,100) | | | | |
| Loans | | 99,000 | | | |
| Total assets | | $109,000 | Total liabilities | | $109,000 |
| | | (+9,000) | | | (+9,000) |

A careful look at these balance sheets reveals two important things. First, we clearly see why Albany National Bank could not safely lend out more than its initial $9,000 of excess reserves. It knew that the $9,000 deposit it created by writing the loan to Anderson would not stay on its books for long. As soon as the check cleared, $9,000 of deposits and reserves would be lost (unless the car dealer also kept an account at Albany). Only $900 loss in deposits (10 percent of the total change in deposits) could be taken from required reserves; it needed the $8,100 of excess reserves to make up the difference.

Second, we see that Albany's loss is Bethel's gain. Albany lost $9,000 in reserves ($900 required and $8,100 excess) when the check was written and cleared, and Bethel gained exactly the same amounts. The check-clearing process thus has left the banking system's total reserves unchanged.

**KEEPING THE EXPANSION GOING WITH ANOTHER LOAN**   The clearing of Anderson's check put Albany National Bank back in equilibrium, with $10,000 more in total assets and $10,000 more in liabilities than it started with. But now Bethel is out of equilibrium, with $8,100 in excess reserves. The logical thing for Bethel to do is to make a loan of its own using its excess reserves. (We now know that the proceeds of this loan will be checked away quickly, so we will skip the intermediate balance sheet.) After Bethel's borrower has written a check for $8,100, which is deposited in, say, Cooperstown National Bank, Bethel's and Cooperstown's balance sheets looks like the balance sheets at the top of the next page.

**FURTHER ROUNDS IN THE EXPANSION OF DEPOSITS**   We need not go through all the rounds of the expansion process in detail, because a clear pattern has emerged. The initial open market purchase of securities by the Fed injected $10,000 of new reserves into the system. The first bank to receive the funds kept $1,000 (10 percent) as required reserves and lent out the remaining $9,000. When the loan proceeds were checked away, they became $9,000 in new deposits and reserves for a second

### Bethel National Bank

| Assets | | | Liabilities | |
|---|---|---|---|---|
| Reserves | | $ 10,900 | Demand deposits | $109,000 |
| | | (−8,100) | | |
| Required | $10,900 | | | |
| | (unchanged) | | | |
| Excess | 0 | | | |
| | (−8,100) | | | |
| Loans | | 98,100 | | |
| | | (+8,100) | | |
| Total assets | | $109,000 | Total liabilities | $109,000 |

### Cooperstown National Bank

| Assets | | | Liabilities | |
|---|---|---|---|---|
| Reserves | | $ 18,100 | Demand deposits | $108,100 |
| | | (+8,100) | | (+8,100) |
| Required | $10,810 | | | |
| | (+810) | | | |
| Excess | 7,290 | | | |
| | (+7,290) | | | |
| Loans | | 90,000 | | |
| Total assets | | $108,100 | Total liabilities | $108,100 |
| | | (+8,100) | | (+8,100) |

bank, which kept $900 (10 percent) and lent out the remaining $8,100. The next bank, in turn, would be able to lend out $7,290, the next one $6,561, and so on round after round. The loans create new deposits at each round; therefore, the money supply, made up entirely of deposits, expands by $10,000 + $9,000 + $8,100 + $7,290 + $6,561, and so on. In the end, the whole process creates $100,000 in new deposits.

To summarize the process of deposit expansion, let's compare the beginning and final balance sheets for the ten-bank system as a whole. Initially the balance sheet looked like this:

### Initial Balance Sheet of a Representative Bank

| Assets | | | Liabilities | |
|---|---|---|---|---|
| Reserves | | $ 100,000 | Demand deposits | $1,000,000 |
| Required | $100,000 | | | |
| Excess | 0 | | | |
| Loans | | 900,000 | | |
| Total assets | | $1,000,000 | Total liabilities | $1,000,000 |

After the injection of $10,000 in new reserves, the combined balance sheet for the ten banks looks like this:

**Final Balance Sheet for the 10-Bank System**

| Assets | | | Liabilities | |
| --- | --- | --- | --- | --- |
| Reserves | | $ 110,000 | Demand deposits | $1,100,000 |
| | | (+10,000) | | (+100,000) |
| Required | $110,000 | | | |
| | (+10,000) | | | |
| Excess | 0 | | | |
| Loans | | 990,000 | | |
| | | (+90,000) | | |
| Total assets | | $1,100,000 | Total liabilities | $1,100,000 |
| | | (+100,000) | | (+100,000) |

We see, then, that the expansion of deposits continues until excess reserves have disappeared. By the time the new reserves have become fully absorbed, total demand deposits will have expanded by $100,000. On the assets side of the balance sheet, this $100,000 of new liabilities will be offset by $10,000 in new required reserves and $90,000 in new loans.

## Contraction of Money Supply

When the Fed withdraws reserves from the banking system, the whole process works in reverse. For example, assume that all the banks are back in the initial position in the last example and that the Fed decides to withdraw, say, $1,000 in reserves. It can do this by making an open market sale of $1,000 of securities from its portfolio. Now suppose that the securities are bought by a dealer who pays for them with a wire transfer from an account at Denver National Bank. To complete the transfer, the Fed deducts $1,000 from Denver's reserve account. At that point Denver's balance sheet looks like this:

**Denver National Bank**

| Assets | | | Liabilities | |
| --- | --- | --- | --- | --- |
| Reserves | | $ 9,000 | Demand deposits | $99,000 |
| | | (−9,000) | | (−1,000) |
| Required | $9,900 | | | |
| | (−100) | | | |
| Excess | −900 | | | |
| | (−900) | | | |
| | | 90,000 | | |
| Total assets | | $99,000 | Total liabilities | $99,000 |
| | | (−1,000) | | (−1,000) |

The loss of $1,000 in deposits when the dealer bought the security reduced required reserves by only $100, whereas Denver's total reserves fell by $1,000 when the Fed completed the transaction. This leaves the bank with negative excess reserves—that is, a $900 reserve deficiency—that it must attempt to correct. In our simplified banking system, Denver must make up the deficiency by reducing its loans. It therefore leaves the next $900 it receives in loan payments in its reserve account. (We assume that if the bank did not have the reserve deficiency, it would make new loans as old ones were paid off, keeping its total loan holdings steady.) In the real world, a bank with a reserve deficiency has a number of other options. One is to sell other assets, such as government securities. Another is to borrow reserves from a bank that has excess reserves. Still another is to borrow from the Fed itself. We will return to these options later.

When Denver National Bank reduces its loan holdings to make up its reserve deficiency, it drains reserves from some other bank in the system. For example, suppose that Maria Espinosa writes a check on Englewood National Bank to pay off $900 that she borrowed from Denver. At the moment when the wire transfer is complete, the balance sheets of the Denver and Englewood banks will look like this:

**Denver National Bank**

| Assets | | | Liabilities | |
|---|---|---|---|---|
| Reserves | | $ 9,900 | Demand deposits | $99,000 |
| | | (+900) | | |
| Required | $9,900 | | | |
| | (unchanged) | | | |
| Excess | 0 | | | |
| | (+900) | | | |
| Loans | | 89,100 | | |
| | | (−900) | | |
| Total assets | | $99,000 | Total liabilities | $99,000 |

**Englewood National Bank**

| Assets | | | Liabilities | |
|---|---|---|---|---|
| Reserves | | $ 9,100 | Demand deposits | $99,100 |
| | | (−900) | | (−900) |
| Required | $9,910 | | | |
| | (−90) | | | |
| Excess | −810 | | | |
| | (−810) | | | |
| Loans | | 90,000 | | |
| Total assets | | $99,100 | Total liabilities | $99,100 |
| | | (−900) | | (−900) |

At this point, then, Denver has made up its reserve deficiency, but $810 of it has been passed along to Englewood. Now it is Englewood's turn to reduce its loan holdings. Using an $810 loan repayment that it has received from some other bank, Englewood will build up its reserves by the required amount, but a $729 deficiency will appear somewhere else. The contraction process will continue until deposits in the banking system as a whole have been reduced by $10,000—10 times the original loss of reserves that resulted from the Fed's open market security sale.

### The Money Multiplier for the Simplified Banking System

As these examples have shown, the total amount of demand deposits that the banking system can hold depends on the total amount of reserves supplied by the Fed and on the required-reserve ratio. In equation form, with rr standing for the required-reserve ratio, the relationship is as follows:

$$\text{Total demand deposits} = (1/rr) \times \text{Total reserves}$$

Thus, when total reserves were $100,000, the total money stock (consisting entirely of demand deposits in our example) was $1 million. When the Fed injected $10,000 of new reserves into the system, bringing total reserves to $110,000, the money stock rose by $100,000, to $1.1 million. When the Fed withdrew $1,000 of reserves through an open market sale, reducing total reserves to $99,000, the money stock fell by $10,000, to $990,000.

The term 1/rr in the equation just given is called the **money multiplier** and is the ratio of the equilibrium money stock to total reserves. In our simplified banking system, in which the required-reserve ratio was 10 percent, the value of the money multiplier was 10. Each injection or withdrawal of reserves by the Fed thus increases or decreases the money stock by ten times the change in reserves.

**Money multiplier**

The ratio of the equilibrium money stock to the banking system's total reserves.

# THE INSTRUMENTS OF MONETARY POLICY

The Fed has a major role in providing services to the banking system and in ensuring the system's safety and stability. Our discussion of money creation here shows that the Fed has another power, namely, the power to control the money stock. Now that we know how money is created, we can examine the policy instruments that give the Fed this power.

### Open Market Operations

The preceding section illustrated the most important of the policy instruments that the Fed uses to control the money stock: open market operations. If the Fed wants to expand the money stock, it instructs the Open Market Trading Desk at the Federal

Reserve Bank of New York to buy government securities. This is known as an *open market purchase. Economics in the News 11.1* presents an eyewitness account of an open market purchase of securities by the Fed.

Sometimes, as in the news item, the Fed makes an outright purchase of securities, but more frequently it buys the securities subject to a repurchase agreement. In such an arrangement the dealer selling the securities to the Fed agrees to buy them back at a later date. Open market operations involving repurchase agreements have only a temporary effect on bank reserves; reserves return to their initial level as soon as the "repurchase" part of the agreement is carried out. Such actions are used to make relatively small day-to-day adjustments in bank reserves.

Whichever form the purchase takes, the Fed pays for the securities by means of a wire transfer that adds funds to the reserves of the seller's bank. Because these are newly created reserves and not just a transfer of reserves from one bank to another, they add to the banking system's total reserves. Further, each dollar of reserves added to the banking system permits the volume of deposits subject to reserves to expand by several dollars. The amount of the expansion—the number of dollars added to the money stock per dollar of added reserves—is determined by the money multiplier. In the real world, however, the factors determining the value of the money multiplier are more complex than in the simplified system discussed in the preceding section.

If the Fed wants to decrease the money stock, it reverses this process: It instructs the Trading Desk to carry out an open market sale of securities, either outright or subject to a repurchase agreement. When a dealer buys securities from the Fed and pays for them with a wire transfer of funds from its deposit at a commercial bank, reserves will be drained from the banking system. The money supply will contract by an amount equal to the money multiplier times the size of the open market sale.

Although open market operations are the most frequently used tool for controlling the money stock, they are not the only one. If we remove some of the simplifying assumptions used so far in this chapter, we can see how these other tools work.

## The Discount Rate

In our simplified banking system, banks can acquire new reserves only by attracting additional deposits. In practice, however, banks and thrifts that want additional reserves either to meet the Fed's requirements or to expand their loans have another option: borrowing reserves.

One possibility is to borrow reserves from another bank. The market in which banks make short-term loans of reserves to other banks is known as the **federal funds market**. The interest rate charged on such loans is called the **federal funds rate**. Transactions in this market, in which the usual loan term is 24 hours, total billions of dollars per day. As described in *Economics in the News 1.1*, the federal funds rate is very important. The Fed indicates its policy stance through setting a target for the federal funds rate, the **federal funds rate target**. The Fed's policy-making body,

**Federal funds market**

A market in which banks lend reserves to one another for periods as short as 24 hours.

**Federal funds rate**

The interest rate on overnight loans of reserves from one bank to another.

**Federal funds rate target**

The Fed's target for the federal funds rate, announced by the Federal Open Market Committee (FOMC).

## ⌐ ECONOMICS IN THE NEWS 11.1

### "THE FED'S IN!"

Scene: Morning. The trading desk at Aubrey Lanston & Co., a major New York bond dealer. There is the usual pandemonium associated with financial trading. Dealers are on the phone, sometimes on many phones at once. They are all shouting.

Suddenly, the Fed light flashes on. The room goes quiet. Bond dealer Richard Kelly grabs the direct line to the Fed. The message is quick, guarded.

"We're taking offerings of bills. Regular delivery."

Click.

"The Fed's in!" Kelly shouts. The pandemonium resumes. On a scale of one to deafening, it's gone from a 6.0 to 9.8.

Lanston is one of 44 primary bond dealers in New York that got the same call. Traders working the eighth-floor Open Market Desk at the New York Federal Reserve Bank would have reached all of them with the same message in the space of a minute.

The message means that the Fed is buying short-term securities—Treasury bills—in the open market. "Regular delivery" means the Fed will take them the next day. Traders from the Fed will call the firms back in a few minutes to let the dealers know how much time they have to get their offers together. It won't be much; the Fed will have finished its dealing, buying more than a billion dollars worth of bills, by that afternoon.

"As soon as we hear from the Fed, we'll call our customers who might have bills they want to sell, and we'll also evaluate our own holdings to see whether we want to make an offer. Then, at the appointed time, we'll call back and make our offers to sell."

When Kelly calls back with an offer of securities already held by Lanston or from Lanston's customers, he'll list specific amounts of bills and the "discounts"—percentage reductions from the face values of the bills—at which Lanston or its customers are willing to offer them. The discount determines the price at which the bill is offered—the higher the discount, the lower the price of the bill.

Once the Fed has received offers from Lanston and the other primary dealers, staffers at the stately old New York Federal Reserve Bank will compare offers. They'll take the best—those that offer the highest discounts—for the total quantity the Fed is buying that day.

If the Fed chooses to take any of the bills offered by Lanston, it will place funds directly in Lanston's account. Those funds will constitute new reserves of the banking system. Because some of the purchases will be from Lanston's customers, Lanston will transfer those funds to its customers' banks all over the country.

Open market operations—purchases and sales of U.S. Treasury and federal agency securities—are the Federal Reserve's principal tool for implementing monetary policy. The short-term objective for open market operations is specified by the Federal Open Market Committee (FOMC). Changes in the FOMC's guidelines for open market operations affect both the quantity of bank reserves and the federal funds rate, which is the interest rate at which depository institutions lend balances at the Federal Reserve to other depository institutions overnight. Before 1994, the FOMC was highly secretive about its directives regarding open market operations. Beginning in 1994, the FOMC began announcing changes in its policy stance, and in 1995 it began to explicitly state its target level for the federal funds rate. Since February 2000, the statement issued by the FOMC shortly after each of its meetings usually has included the Committee's assessment of the risks to the attainment of its long-run goals of price stability and sustainable economic growth as well as a target for the federal funds rate.

Sources: Timothy Tregarthen, "Making Money at the Fed," *The Margin* (November–December 1988): 6; Federal Reserve Board, "Policy Tools: Open Market Operations," (December 2003) available at http://www.federalreserve.gov/policy.htm.

---

**Discount window**

The department through which the Federal Reserve lends reserves to banks.

the Federal Open Market Committee (FOMC), is responsible for making decisions regarding this target. In the next chapter, we will return to the role of the federal funds rate as a part of the Fed's policy strategy.

Funds that banks borrow from one another through the federal funds market have no effect on total bank reserves; this type of borrowing just moves reserves around from one bank to another. Funds that commercial banks borrow directly from the Fed through the so-called **discount window** are another story, however.

Banks borrow from the Fed in two kinds of situations. Most often they borrow for short periods to adjust their reserves when unexpected withdrawals have left them with less than the required amount of reserves. These banks are not in danger of insolvency, but are temporarily short on reserves. Banks with healthy balance sheets qualify for primary credit, and are charged the **discount rate**. Since January 2003, to discourage banks from borrowing too often or too much through the discount window, the Fed sets the discount rate above the federal funds rate target. Typically, the discount rate is one percentage point above the federal funds rate.

In addition to primary credit, the Fed sometimes makes loans to troubled banks to give them time to get their affairs in order. Since these banks are less likely to be able to repay the Fed, they must pay a higher interest rate, above the discount rate. Typically, the interest rate is one-half of a percentage point above the discount rate charged on primary credit loans.

The discount rate is a second policy instrument for controlling the money supply, although a less powerful one than open market operations. If the Fed wants to encourage more discount borrowing, it lowers the discount rate. As the discount rate falls relative to the federal funds rate, the cost of discount borrowing falls relative to the cost of borrowing from other banks and the volume of discount borrowing expands. However, because of the administrative pressures that the Fed uses to discourage excessive discount borrowing, there is a limit to how much discount borrowing banks will want to undertake. If the Fed wants to reduce borrowing from the discount window, it raises the discount rate.

## Changes in Required-Reserve Ratios

Changes in required-reserve ratios are a third potential policy instrument that the Fed can use to control the money supply. Earlier in the chapter we showed that the total volume of demand deposits in a simplified banking system is determined by the formula

$$\text{Total demand deposits} = (1\,/rr) \times \text{Total reserves}$$

where *rr* stands for the required-reserve ratio. Similar but somewhat more complex formulas apply to the relationship between required-reserve ratios and all of the elements of M1 and M2 in the actual U.S. banking system. Thus, a reduction in required-reserve ratios will increase the money stock that can be created on the basis of a given quantity of reserves, and an increase in the ratios will decrease the money stock for a given quantity of reserves.

Although changes in required-reserve ratios have never been used for day-to-day control over the money supply, there have been times in the past when the Fed changed the ratios when it wanted to make a strong move toward expansion or contraction of the money supply. For example, in late 1990, the Fed eliminated a 3 percent reserve requirement on non-personal saving and time deposits. In April 1992, it reduced the

---

**Discount rate**

The interest rate charged by the Fed on loans of reserves to banks.

required reserve ratio on transaction deposits from 12 percent to 10 percent. These changes were made, in part, to speed recovery from the 1990–1991 recession, although they also reflected a belief that lower reserve requirements would reduce bank's cost, encourage bank lending, and strengthen the role of banks in the financial system. More recently, the Fed has not used the reserve requirement as an instrument to control the money supply, because it poses difficulties in bank balance sheet management.

## Other Factors Affecting the Money Multiplier and Reserves

In our simplified banking system, the money multiplier is a constant and the Fed has full control over bank reserves. In practice, however, the situation is more complex; both the money multiplier and reserves can vary for reasons beyond the Fed's control.

Consider, for example, the multiplier for the most important monetary aggregate, M2. M2 includes both transaction deposits, on which reserves are required, and saving and time deposits, on which no reserves are required. The total amount of M2 that banks can create per dollar of reserves (that is, the M2 multiplier) thus depends, among other things, on the relative amounts of reservable and nonreservable deposits that banks' customers decide to hold. If people decide to move their funds from transactions deposits to savings or time deposits, the M2 multiplier rises. If they move them from savings and time deposits to transactions deposits, the M2 multiplier falls.

Total reserves in the banking system can also be affected by choices made by bank customers. In our simplified banking system, reserve deposits at the Fed were the only form of reserves. In the real world, however, part of reserves are held in the form of vault cash. If bank customers decide to withdraw larger than normal amounts of currency from their accounts, as they typically do at Christmas time and during summer vacations, total bank reserves fall. If bank customers reduce their holdings of currency, reserves rise.

Such changes in reserves and the money multiplier make the Fed's job more difficult. When reserves or the money multiplier unexpectedly increase, the Fed must offset the increase with open market sales of securities or a rise in the discount rate. When reserves or the money multiplier fall, the Fed must buy securities on the open market or lower the discount rate. Such offsetting actions allow the Fed to maintain fairly close control over the money stock, but the control is not as direct or precise as in our simplified banking system.

# CENTRAL BANKING IN THE INTERNATIONAL ECONOMY

The preceding section of this chapter looked at three instruments of monetary policy—open market operations, changes in the discount rate, and changes in reserve ratios—all of which operate entirely within the domestic economy. In this section we turn to a fourth instrument of monetary policy—operations in the foreign-exchange

**Foreign-
exchange
market**

A market in which
the currency of one
country is traded
for that of another.

market, in which U.S. dollars, Japanese yen, European euros, British pounds, and the currencies of other countries are exchanged for one another. In this section, we take a preliminary look at the mechanics of the central bank activities in the **foreign-exchange market** and the relationship between those activities and domestic monetary policy. Succeeding chapters add details relating exchange rates to the balance of payments, interest rates, inflation, and economic growth.

Like its fellow central banks in other countries, the Fed has the right to use foreign-exchange market transactions as an instrument of monetary policy. However, for a variety of reasons, the Fed has not used this instrument as actively in recent years as have central banks abroad. Keep in mind as you read this section that although foreign-exchange market operations are a minor instrument of monetary policy for the Fed, they are a very important instrument, often the most important, for many other central banks.

## The Structure of the Foreign-Exchange Market

As a traveler you may have had occasion to exchange U.S. dollars for Canadian dollars, Mexican pesos, or the currency of some other country. This trading in paper currencies is a small corner of the largest set of markets in the world—the foreign-exchange market, in which hundreds of billions of dollars are traded each day. Such trading reflects the fact that virtually every international transaction in goods, services, or financial assets is preceded by the exchange of one currency for another.

Large transactions in the foreign-exchange market, like large domestic transactions, are conducted with transaction deposits in commercial banks. A key role is played by large banks in the world's money centers—London, Zurich, Tokyo, and other cities—which are known as *trading banks*. These banks have branches all over the world and accept deposits denominated in many different currencies.

Suppose that Bloomingdale's department store in New York needs to buy euros to purchase Italian goods. Italy is part of the European Monetary Union (EMU), a group of countries that uses a single currency known as the euro. Bloomingdale's can ask Chase Manhattan Bank to debit its dollar-denominated account and credit a deposit of equal value to an account in Rome, Italy, denominated in euros that it can use to pay an Italian supplier. Similarly, if a German pension fund wants to buy U.S. Treasury bills, it can exchange a deposit denominated in euros at a German or U.S. trading bank for a deposit denominated in dollars and use those dollars to buy the Treasury bills. The trading banks make a profit on these transactions by charging an *asked* price for the currency they sell that is slightly higher than the *bid* price they pay for the currency they buy.

## Supply and Demand in the Foreign-Exchange Market

What determines the number of euros that a customer gets in exchange for its dollars? Why, on a given day, is the exchange rate 0.85 euros per dollar rather than 0.75

or 1? The answer is that the rate depends on supply and demand. Here, we will consider a simplified illustration of the foreign-exchange market in which dollars are exchanged for euros.

*Current account transactions* include imports and exports of goods and services and international transfer payments, and *capital account transactions (or financial account transactions, as they can also be called)* involve international purchases and sales of assets and international borrowing and lending. Both play a role in determining the supply and demand for dollars in the foreign-exchange market.

In the example given earlier, a U.S. department store wanted to buy Italian leather shoes. To buy the leather shoes, it must first buy euros. An importer of goods or services to the United States enters the foreign-exchange market as a *supplier* of dollars. The supply curve for dollars shown in Figure 11.1 combines the transactions of all importers. In this diagram the supply curve has a positive slope, indicating that

**FIGURE 11.1  THE FOREIGN-EXCHANGE MARKET FOR DOLLARS AND EURO**

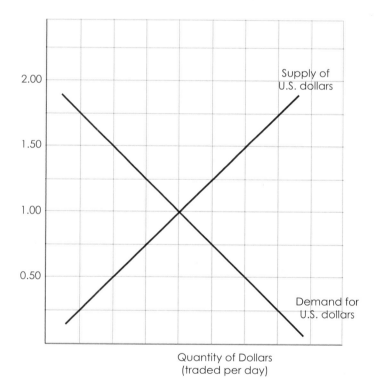

This diagram represents the foreign-exchange market in which U.S. dollars are exchanged for European euros and euros are exchanged for dollars. The exchange rate is expressed as the number of euros required to purchase one U.S. dollar. The supply curve of dollars reflects the activities of U.S. importers of European goods and services. They sell dollars to obtain the euros they need in order to buy Italian leather shoes, German automobiles, and so on. The demand curve for dollars reflects the activities of European buyers of exports from the United States. They use euros to buy the dollars they need to buy Boeing aircraft, American wheat, and so on. The demand curve also includes the effects of net capital inflows to the United States. For example, a German pension fund that wants to buy U.S. government bonds first needs to exchange euros for dollars to use in purchasing the bonds.

an increase in the exchange rate of the dollar relative to the euro (meaning that more euro can be bought per dollar) will increase the number of dollars supplied.[2]

On the other side of the market, a Spanish grocery chain that wishes to buy wheat exported from the United States must buy U.S. dollars to carry out the transaction. A buyer of U.S. exports enters the foreign-exchange market as a *demander* of dollars. The demand curve shown in Figure 11.1 includes the demand for dollars of all European buyers of U.S. exports.

In addition to current account transactions, U.S. and European firms and individuals carry out numerous capital account transactions. For example, a German pension fund that wishes to buy U.S. Treasury bills must first buy dollars to use in paying for those securities. A *capital inflow* (or *financial inflow*) to the United States thus is associated with a demand for dollars above and beyond the demand arising from current account transactions. What about a *capital outflow*, such as a purchase of foreign securities by a U.S. buyer? Such a transaction could be counted as a source of dollars supplied to the foreign-exchange market, but to simplify the diagram, a different approach is taken in Figure 11.1. There, capital outflows are first subtracted from capital inflows to arrive at a figure for *net capital inflows*. Only these net capital inflows (the excess of inflows over outflows) are added to the current account demand for dollars in drawing the dollar demand curve. As discussed in earlier chapters, the United States has experienced a net capital inflow each year for more than a decade. Still another source of demand for dollars, net purchases by central banks on the official reserve account, will be discussed in a future chapter.

**PRICES IN THE FOREIGN-EXCHANGE MARKET**  Foreign-exchange rates—the prices of currencies in terms of other currencies, as determined by supply and demand—are published daily in financial newspapers. Figure 11.2 shows the foreign-exchange rate quotations for a typical day. A few currencies are commonly quoted in U.S. dollars per unit of foreign currency (Australian, EMU members, New Zealand, and the United Kingdom), while most are quoted in units of foreign currency per U.S. dollar. For example, the exchange rate between the euro and the dollar can be quoted in terms of euro per dollar, as was done in labeling the vertical axis in Figure 11.1. On the other hand, the price can be quoted in terms of dollars per euro, as is commonplace in foreign exchange rate quotes. Most currencies are quoted on a *spot* basis, that is, for immediate delivery. Some of the major currencies are also traded on a *forward* basis, meaning that the currencies will be exchanged at an agreed-upon future date at a price that is set today.

As supply and demand conditions change from day to day, exchange rates also change, as shown by the difference between the rates for successive days in Figure 11.2. A number of factors can contribute to such changes. For example, expansion of the U.S. economy would increase the demand for all sorts of goods, including goods imported from Mexico. Sales of dollars by U.S. importers to acquire the pesos needed to purchase those goods would cause the supply curve for dollars to shift to the right. Part (a) in Fig-

**FIGURE 11.2   FOREIGN-EXCHANGE RATES (DAILY RATES FOR WEEK ENDING NOVEMBER 21, 2003)**

| Country | Monetary Unit | Nov. 17 | Nov. 18 | Nov. 19 | Nov. 20 | Nov. 21 |
|---|---|---|---|---|---|---|
| *Australia | dollar | 0.7105 | 0.7212 | 0.7229 | 0.7238 | 0.7227 |
| Brazil | real | 2.9485 | 2.948 | 2.945 | 2.9465 | 2.924 |
| Canada | dollar | 1.3143 | 1.3025 | 1.304 | 1.3031 | 1.3042 |
| China, P.R. | yuan | 8.2769 | 8.2767 | 8.2767 | 8.2769 | 8.277 |
| Denmark | krone | 6.3341 | 6.253 | 6.244 | 6.246 | 6.2435 |
| *EMU members | euro | 1.1744 | 1.1893 | 1.1909 | 1.1895 | 1.1913 |
| Hong Kong | dollar | 7.764 | 7.758 | 7.76 | 7.7615 | 7.764 |
| India | rupee | 45.55 | 45.62 | 45.63 | 45.78 | 45.75 |
| Japan | yen | 108.98 | 108.11 | 109.06 | 108.99 | 108.87 |
| Malaysia | ringitt | 3.8 | 3.8 | 3.8 | 3.8 | 3.8 |
| Mexico | peso | 11.18 | 11.168 | 11.198 | 11.188 | 11.204 |
| *New Zealand | dollar | 0.6257 | 0.6339 | 0.6385 | 0.6425 | 0.6406 |
| Norway | krone | 6.9874 | 6.893 | 6.8565 | 6.867 | 6.851 |
| Singapore | dollar | 1.727 | 1.719 | 1.7132 | 1.7183 | 1.72 |
| South Africa | rand | 6.7346 | 6.6275 | 6.615 | 6.57 | 6.525 |
| South Korea | won | 1183 | 1181 | 1178 | 1191.9 | 1195.7 |
| Sri Lanka | rupee | 96.8 | 97.25 | 95.85 | 95.7 | 96 |
| Sweden | krona | 7.6407 | 7.54 | 7.5385 | 7.549 | 7.52 |
| Switzerland | franc | 1.3245 | 1.3055 | 1.3032 | 1.302 | 1.2985 |
| Taiwan | dollar | 34.01 | 34 | 34 | 34.03 | 34.05 |
| Thailand | baht | 39.95 | 39.96 | 39.93 | 39.91 | 39.95 |
| *United Kingdom | pound | 1.6885 | 1.6998 | 1.6982 | 1.7024 | 1.7025 |
| Venezuela | bolivar | 1600 | 1600 | 1600 | 1600 | 1600 |

In the foreign-exchange market, the dollar is traded for the currencies of other countries. The monetary unit (name of the currency) is also shown. Exchange rates vary from day to day according to supply and demand conditions. This figure shows the daily foreign-exchange quotations for the week ending on November 21, 2003. Exchange rates may be quoted in U.S. dollars per unit of the foreign currency (such as $1.6885 per British pound) or units of the foreign currency per dollar (6.3341 Danish krone per U.S. dollar).

* U.S. dollars per unit of foreign currency

Source: Board of Governors of the Federal Reserve System, *H.10 Statistical Release*, November 21, 2003.

ure 11.3 shows how a U.S. recession would decrease the demand for goods imported from Mexico and, hence, cause the supply curve for U.S. dollars to shift to the left.

Expansion of Mexico's economy would increase the demand for goods exported from the United States. Mexican importers' purchases of the dollars needed to buy those goods would cause the demand curve for dollars to shift to the right. A recession in Mexico would cause the demand curve for dollars to shift to the left.

An increase in any condition making U.S. assets more attractive to Mexico's buyers would increase net capital inflows to the United States and produce a rightward shift in the demand curve for dollars. Examples might include an increase in the profit potential of U.S. corporations, which would make their stocks more attractive, or an increase

FIGURE 11.3 THE FOREIGN-EXCHANGE MARKET FOR DOLLARS AND MEXICAN PESOS

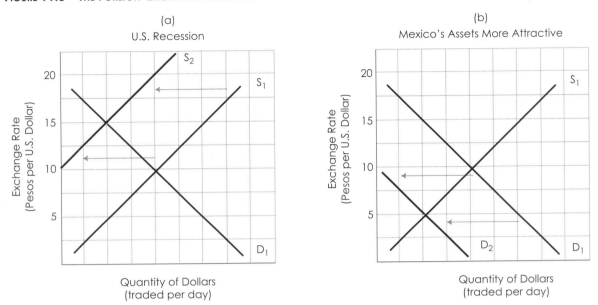

This diagram represents the foreign-exchange market in which U.S. dollars are exchanged for Mexican pesos and pesos are exchanged for U.S. dollars. The exchange rate is expressed as the number of pesos required to purchase one U.S. dollar. The supply curve of dollars reflects the activities of U.S. importers of Mexican goods and services. Therefore, as shown in part (a), when the U.S. economy goes into a recession, U.S. importers will buy fewer goods and services from Mexican businesses. This leads to a decrease in supply of U.S. dollars because American importers do not need to exchange as many U.S. dollars for pesos. The result is an increase in the exchange rate from 10 pesos to 15 pesos per U.S. dollar.

Part (b) illustrates how the foreign exchange market is affected when Mexico's assets become more attractive for foreign investors, including U.S. investors. This results in a decrease of net capital inflow into the U.S. and a leftward shift in the demand for U.S. dollars. In this case, the exchange rate will decrease from 10 pesos to 5 pesos per U.S. dollar.

in interest rates on U.S. government securities. Similarly, any condition making Mexico's assets more attractive to U.S. buyers, such as an increase in Mexico's interest rates relative to U.S. interest rates, would reduce net capital inflows and, hence, would shift the dollar demand curve to the left. This case is shown in part (b) of Figure 11.3.

These are only a few of the factors that can affect supply and demand in the foreign-exchange market. Changes in exchange rates have an important effect on the prices of goods and services in international trade. *Economics in the News 11.2* discusses what happened when the U.S. dollar lost value relative to the euro and how this affects Europeans' travel to the U.S.

## Central Bank Intervention in the Foreign-Exchange Market

Exchange rates are not mere numbers; they have major impacts on the economy. For example, if the value of the dollar rises relative to that of the yen, as it did during the first half of the 1980s, more yen can be bought for a dollar. Japanese goods thus

## Economics in the News 11.2
## WHERE TO SPEND VACATION?

**DECEMBER 22, 2003**—For 21-year-old Yannick Stolk, a trip to the United States from her hometown near Antwerp, Belgium, was too big an expense.

Until now.

The euro has risen nearly 19 percent against the U.S. dollar this year, and European tourists like Yannick are cashing in on the dream trip that has suddenly become, well, 19 percent cheaper.

At American cruise operator Royal Caribbean Cruise Ltd., European bookings for 2004 are up 120 percent from last year, and 40 percent of those bookings are for U.S. destinations such as Miami and the U.S. Virgin Islands. "The price sensitivity is definitely working to our advantage," said Gary Burton, senior vice president of marketing at Royal Caribbean.

International visitors' contribution to the U.S. economy this year is estimated at $65.8 billion, with the projection for next year at $69.4 billion, according to the Travel Industry Association of America. "Forty-five percent of that money comes from European travelers," Cathy Keefe, TIA spokeswoman, told Reuters.

The British pound also reached a five-year high against the U.S. dollar last Thursday, prompting Britons to hop on planes to New York in order to pick up the designer items on their Christmas lists. "All the designer products are so much cheaper in the U.S. now. New York is an absolute hotspot for Christmas shopping, so they get an international holiday, plus they save money on their shopping at the same time," said Jessica Potter, spokeswoman at ebooker.com, a British online travel agency that handles reservations for flights, hotels, and car rentals. "Bookings are significantly up this year, and flight availability has become difficult for us to find," said Potter, who visited the U.S. for a shopping spree herself. "Levis and Reebok—they are so much cheaper there now!" she said.

The euro has risen 50 percent from its lowest point three years ago, making the United States and all its tourist attractions a better value for Europeans. "The only reason I'm here is that it's cheaper," said Marc Stolk, Yannick's father, after a day of hiking and biking around the Everglades in Florida. "I've been wanting to come for a while, but when it was one euro to one dollar, it was too expensive."

But with one euro now translating to $1.24, the number of Europeans visiting the United States is on a climb from the 9.4 million European visitors last year, according to the Orlando/Orange County Visitors Bureau. Of the top 25 tourism generating countries, Sweden and the United Kingdom are expected to gain the biggest market share in the United States in 2003, according to the Travel Industry Association. The Stolks stayed at the Everglades Youth Hostel in Florida City, where 90 percent of the guests are European, and holiday bookings are up 30 percent from last year, the owner of the hostel told Reuters.

"Historically, the strength of foreign currency has always favored travel to the U.S.," said Jose Estorino, senior vice president of marketing at the Orlando/Orange County Convention and Visitor's Bureau, which is investing $1.7 million in an upcoming marketing campaign in the United Kingdom. The campaign, which is scheduled to launch just after Christmas, will include direct mail at targeted households, advertisements on television, in newspapers, in the tunnels of the underground transportation system, and on buses. "We expect the economic impact of the campaign to be $225 million in the next year," Estorino said.

In the meantime, Marc Stolk said he is enjoying his affordable holiday. "And if the euro keeps going up, I'll come back to see California."

Source: Jui Chakravorty, "Euro Vacationers Find America Affordable," *Reuters*, December 22, 2003.

become relatively inexpensive for U.S. consumers. Imports from Japan increase, and U.S. firms competing with those imports face possibly devastating competition. At the same time, U.S. goods and services become relatively more expensive to Japanese buyers, not because the price in dollars has gone up, but because it now takes more yen to buy those dollars. U.S. exporters thus experience a decline in demand for their products when the value of the dollar rises relative to that of the yen.

When the dollar falls in value relative to the yen, as it did after February 1985, these effects are reversed. More dollars must be spent to import a given quantity of Japanese goods. The price that U.S. consumers pay for imports rises, and U.S. firms face less competition than before. U.S. exporters benefit from a fall in the value of the dollar, because Japanese buyers now find it easier to buy their products.

Because exchange rates affect the welfare of consumers and firms, their level is a matter of concern for policy makers. Consequently, from time to time central banks in the United States and other countries intervene in the foreign-exchange market in an attempt to stabilize exchange rates by offsetting market pressures that tend to raise or lower the exchange values of their currencies. The relatively infrequent foreign-currency operations of the U.S. government are directed by the Treasury, which has overall responsibility for the management of international financial policy, in close cooperation with the Federal Open Market Committee. They are carried out by the Fed through its foreign trading desk in New York.

Suppose, for example, that equilibrium has been established at an exchange rate of 125 yen to the dollar, as shown by point $E_1$ in Figure 11.4. Firms and consumers have adjusted to this exchange rate, and the Treasury would like to avoid a sudden change. However, the U.S. economy now begins to expand strongly, shifting the dollar supply curve to the right, from $S_1$ to $S_2$. If no action were taken, a new equilibrium

**FIGURE 11.5   EFFECTS OF INTERVENTION IN THE FOREIGN-EXCHANGE MARKET**

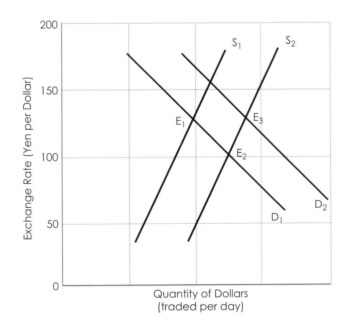

The Federal Reserve can intervene in the foreign-exchange market to resist changes in currency values. In this case, the exchange rate is initially in equilibrium at a rate of 125 yen per dollar. Expansion of the U.S. economy increases U.S. demand for imports from Japan, thus increasing the supply of dollars and shifting the supply curve to the right, from $S_1$ to $S_2$. By itself, this shift would lower the equilibrium exchange rate to 100 yen per dollar. However, the Fed intervenes by purchasing dollars with yen. This has the effect of shifting the demand curve for dollars to the right, thereby preventing a decrease in the exchange rate.

would be established at an exchange rate of 100 yen to the dollar—point $E_2$ in the exhibit. What could the Fed do to stabilize the exchange rate at 125 yen?

**MECHANICS OF INTERVENTION**   If it wanted to support the price of the dollar relative to the yen, the Treasury would instruct the Fed to intervene in a way that would increase the quantity of dollars demanded. The mechanics of such an action would be similar to those of an open market operation. What makes intervention possible is the fact that on the assets side of its balance sheet the Fed holds foreign securities along with its holdings of U.S. government securities; these include yen-denominated securities issued by the Japanese government.

To resist downward pressure on the exchange rate, the Fed first would sell some yen-denominated securities to a securities dealer in Tokyo. It would receive payment in the form of a yen-denominated transaction deposit at the Bank of Japan, that country's central bank. The Bank of Japan acts as the Fed's agent in this transaction. To acquire dollars the Fed sells the yen-denominated deposit to a Tokyo branch of one of the New York trading banks. The bank would pay for the yen deposit by drawing on the reserves of dollars it had on deposit with the Fed in the United States. The end result of this series of transactions would be a purchase of dollars by the Fed whose effect is to increase the demand for dollars. It would shift the demand curve to the right, from $D_1$ to $D_2$. A new equilibrium would be established at $E_3$, where the exchange rate is unchanged because supply and demand have increased equally.

If at another time the Fed wanted to counter upward pressure on the value of the dollar, it would have to reverse these transactions. In that case it would buy a yen-denominated deposit from the New York trading bank and pay for it with a wire transfer crediting the appropriate number of dollars to the bank's reserve account at the Fed. The Fed would then use the yen deposit to buy Japanese government securities for its portfolio. This set of trades would tend to nudge down the value of the dollar in the foreign-exchange market.

**EFFECTS ON THE DOMESTIC MONEY STOCK**   Foreign-exchange market intervention as described in the preceding section would affect the U.S. banking system's reserves at the same time that they influenced the dollar's exchange value. If the Fed were to buy foreign currencies in order to push down the value of the dollar and invest the funds in foreign government securities, it would increase the U.S. banking system's reserves in exactly the same way that it does when it buys U.S. government securities on the open market. If it were to sell foreign currencies obtained by reducing holdings of foreign government securities in order to support the value of the dollar, bank reserves would be depleted just as they are when the Fed conducts an open market sale of U.S. government securities. Thus, the Fed's actions in the exchange market potentially affect bank reserves and domestic monetary policy.

On the relatively rare occasions when the Fed does act in the foreign-exchange markets, it routinely acts to offset the effects of its foreign-exchange activities on domestic bank reserves by engaging in a special type of open market operation known as *sterilization*. To sterilize a sale of foreign currencies, which tends to decrease U.S. bank reserves, the Fed simultaneously makes an equal open market purchase of U.S. government securities. The open market purchase restores total reserves to their previous value. To sterilize a purchase of foreign currencies, which tends to increase bank reserves, the Fed carries out an offsetting domestic open market sale. The central banks of many other countries also use sterilization to limit the impact of foreign-exchange market operations on the domestic money supply. However, not all do so. In Chapter 14, we will examine what is called *exchange-rate based stabilization policy,* an approach used by the central banks of many emerging market countries. Central banks that take this approach want to strengthen, not weaken, the impact of foreign exchange rates on the domestic economy. For that reason, they do not use sterilization.

In concluding this section, it is worth emphasizing that foreign-exchange markets and exchange rates are very important to the Fed's decision making even though it does not often intervene to affect them and even though it uses sterilization when it does. The reason is that any decisions the Fed makes about domestic monetary policy that affect domestic interest rates, real output, and the price level also influence the value of the dollar via their effects on supply and demand in the foreign-exchange market. At the same time, movements in exchange rates that have their origin elsewhere in the world have far-reaching effects on the U.S. domestic economy. For these reasons, the Fed must take developments in the foreign-exchange market into account in determining domestic monetary policy. One rarely reads a newspaper article related to domestic monetary policy that does not also discuss effects on the international value of the dollar or a story on the value of the dollar that does not end by discussing U.S. monetary policy and interest rates.

## SUMMARY

1. **How do banks create money?** Banks can make loans whenever their *reserves* exceed the minimum amount of *required reserves* set by the Fed. When a bank makes a loan, it credits the proceeds to the borrower's transaction account. When the borrower spends this newly created money, the recipient deposits it in another bank, which in turn can use its excess reserves to make another loan. In this way, each dollar of new reserves that the banking system receives becomes the basis for a multiple expansion of deposits.

2. **Why is the size of the money stock limited by the quantity of bank reserves?** Banks can create money only to the extent that they have *excess reserves*. The total quantity of deposits that the banking system can create is thus limited by the total quantity of reserves available and the *required-reserve ratio*. In a simplified banking system, the number of dollars of deposits that can be

created for each dollar of reserves equals 1/rr, where rr is the required-reserve ratio. The ratio 1/rr is the *money multiplier* for the simplified banking system.

3. **What instruments are available to the Fed for controlling the money stock?** *Open market operations,* in which the Fed affects the banking system's reserves through purchases or sales of government securities, are the Fed's principal instrument of monetary control. An open market purchase injects reserves into the banking system and allows the money stock to expand; an open market sale drains reserves and causes the money stock to contract. Changes in the discount rate charged by the Fed on loans of reserves to banks are a second instrument of monetary control. An increase in the *discount rate* reduces the quantity of reserves borrowed. This absorbs excess reserves and thus tends to cause the money stock to contract. Lowering the discount rate encourages borrowing of reserves and thus tends to allow the money stock to expand. Changes in required-reserve ratios are a third means of controlling the money stock. A decrease in the required-reserve ratio creates excess reserves and allows the money stock to expand; an increase in the ratio causes the money stock to contract.

4. **How well can the money stock be controlled?** The Fed is able to control the money stock reasonably closely through the use of open market operations and changes in the discount rate. However, its control is not perfect; unpredicted variations in the money multiplier or in total reserves can cause unexpected changes in the money stock.

5. **What activities does the Fed undertake in the international sphere?** From time to time, the Fed intervenes in the *foreign-exchange market* to counteract upward or downward pressure on the

dollar's value relative to other currencies. It can lower the exchange value of the dollar by selling dollars and buying foreign currencies; and it can raise the value of the dollar by buying dollars and selling foreign currencies. Intervention in the foreign-exchange market can potentially affect the U.S. banking system's reserves and, hence, the domestic money stock. These effects on the domestic money stock are routinely avoided because the Fed offsets the reserve impact of its interventions through domestic open market operations, a practice known as *sterilization*. However, sterilization does not completely break the linkage between domestic and international monetary and financial developments. The Fed intervenes in foreign exchange markets relatively infrequently, but this instrument of monetary policy is much more important for the central banks of some other countries.

## KEY TERMS

Required reserves
Required-reserve ratio
Excess reserves
Open market operation
Money multiplier
Federal funds market

Federal funds rate
Federal funds rate target
Discount window
Discount rate
Foreign-exchange
  market

## PROBLEMS AND TOPICS FOR DISCUSSION

1. **Examining the lead-off case.** What are the duties of the Federal Open Market Committee? Who are the committee's voting members? Why is it considered such a powerful body? A vote to ease monetary policy means a vote to increase the growth of the money stock compared with the growth that would otherwise occur. What

methods for implementing such a decision are available to the Fed?

2. **Multiple expansion of deposits.** Rework the deposit expansion examples in this chapter on the basis of the following assumptions:

   a. An injection of $5,000 in reserves via an open market purchase

   b. An injection of $20,000 in reserves with a 20 percent rather than 10 percent required-reserve ratio

   c. Withdrawal of $500 in reserves via an open market sale

3. **Currency and the money stock.** Use a balance sheet approach to trace the effects of a withdrawal of $1,000 in currency from a bank. Assume that reserves are initially held half in the form of vault cash and half in the form of reserves on deposit with the Fed. Also assume that after the initial currency withdrawal there are no further changes in currency holdings by the public.

4. **The federal funds rate and the discount rate.** The *Federal Reserve Bulletin,* published monthly by the Fed, gives the values of the discount and federal funds rates and data for total and borrowed reserves. What has happened to the difference between these rates recently? Has the discount rate been changed? What has happened to the volume of borrowed reserves? Have they moved in the direction you would expect given the behavior of interest rates?

5. **The foreign-exchange market.** Find the most recent foreign-exchange quotations from the Board of Governors, *H.10 Statistical Release,* available at http://www.federalreserve.gov/releases/. How has the value of the dollar changed relative to other major currencies compared with the data given in Figure 11.2?

# CASE FOR DISCUSSION

## *Dollar Finds Little Joy*

**LONDON (DECEMBER 23, 2003)**—The dollar steadied against the euro and dipped versus the yen on Tuesday ahead of Christmas holidays in many markets, as investors juggled a heightened U.S. security alert, economic expectations, and intervention worries. Tokyo markets were shut for a holiday on Tuesday and several countries begin Christmas holidays on Wednesday. But the recent downtrend for the dollar continued, following a heightened U.S. security alert at the weekend and persistent worries about the U.S. ability to attract investment flows to cover its current account deficit.

"Security is an ongoing theme, and we have seen some rise in risk aversion on the back of the security alert," said Mitul Kotecha, head of global foreign exchange research at Credit Agricole Indosuez. "Data today will confirm robust U.S. growth, but underlying negative factors for the dollar remain in place." The dollar steadied at $1.24 per euro early in the day on Friday, compared with record lows of $1.2447 set on Monday, the U.S. currency's 14th record low in 17 trading sessions.

The dollar eased 0.10 percent against the yen to 107.40, just over half a yen above three-year lows set earlier this month. Traders remain wary of yen-weakening intervention by the Japanese authorities during the thin holiday period, after Japan spent record amounts this year in order to curb the strength of the yen and protect the country's export-led recovery.

Sterling was steady against the dollar and the euro after data showing UK growth of an upwardly revised 0.8 percent in the third quarter but a widening in the current account deficit during the same quarter, to 8.1 billion pounds.

### Markets Alert

The U.S. government raised its security alert on Sunday to orange, the second-highest level, saying there was a high risk of an attack in the holiday period. Geopolitical tensions have weighed on the dollar for much of 2003—before, during and after the Iraq (news–web sites) war. The dollar is nearing the end of the year down more than 15 percent against the euro and nearly 10 percent against the yen.

European trade chief Pascal Lamy said on Tuesday the euro's current value was "not yet worrying," but it was essential that currency movements did not happen too fast. Euro zone data showed investment capital poured into the euro zone in October, with combined portfolio and investment inflows rising to 18.2 billion euros in October from 1.0 billion inflow in September.

U.S. final third quarter GDP (news–web sites), due at 8:30 A.M. EST, is expected to be unrevised at a healthy 8.2 percent annual growth. The final University of Michigan consumer sentiment survey for December, due at 9:45 A.M. EST, is forecast to be revised up to 91.0 from the preliminary 89.6, though still below November's reading of 93.7.

"Economic data has not been having an impact on the dollar since early November," said Jane Foley, currency strategist at Barclays Capital. "Sentiment is still clearly dollar-negative."

## QUESTIONS

1. Explain why a slowdown in the U.S. would tend to make the dollar fall relative to the yen and euro. How would the drop in U.S. interest rates, affect this outcome?
2. What actions could the Fed take to intervene in an attempt to prop up the dollar relative to the yen and euro?
3. What actions could the Bank of Japan (Japan's central bank) take to intervene in an attempt to prop up the dollar relative to the yen and euro? Why might it be interested in doing so?
4. What effects would a lower value for the dollar, relative to the yen and euro, have on the U.S. economy? Who would benefit from the low value of the dollar? Who would be hurt?

## END NOTES

1. Only one of the nearly 40 primary security dealers is a bank; the remainder are nonbank institutions. For clarity, we assume in this discussion that the Fed does business only with nonbank dealers. Open market operations carried out through a bank dealer have exactly the same final effects, but some of the intermediate steps are different.
2. The slope of the current account supply curve for dollars depends on the price elasticity of demand for European goods imported into the United States. The preliminary conclusions drawn in this section will be restated to apply to a broader variety of circumstances in that chapter.

# The Supply and Demand for Money

## "MR. CHAIRMAN . . ."

The Chairman of the Federal Reserve Board is required by law to report to Congress twice each year on issues of monetary policy. The following are excerpts from the testimony of Fed Chairman Alan Greenspan before the Senate Committee on Banking, Housing, and Urban Affairs.

*July 16, 2003*

Mr. Chairman and members of the Committee, I am pleased to present the Federal Reserve's semiannual Monetary Policy Report to the Congress. When in late April I last reviewed the economic outlook before this Committee, full-scale military operations in Iraq had concluded, and there were signs that some of the impediments to brisker growth in economic activity in the months leading up to the conflict were beginning to lift. Many, though by no means all, of the economic uncertainties stemming from the situation in Iraq had been resolved, and that reduction in uncertainty had left an imprint on a broad range of indicators.

Stock prices had risen, risk spreads on corporate bonds had narrowed, oil prices had dropped sharply, and measures of consumer sentiment appeared to be on the mend. But, as I noted in April, hard data indicating that these favorable developments were quickening the pace of spending and production were not yet in evidence, and it was likely that the extent of the underlying vigor of the economy would become apparent only gradually.

In the months since, some of the residual war-related uncertainties have abated further and financial conditions have turned decidedly more accommodative, supported, in part, by the Federal Reserve's commitment to foster sustainable growth and to guard against a substantial further disinflation. If the past is any guide, domestic financial developments, apart from the heavy dose of fiscal stimulus now in train, should bolster economic activity over coming quarters.

To be sure, industrial production does appear to have stabilized in recent weeks after months of declines. Consumer spending has held up reasonably well, and activity in housing markets continues strong. But incoming data on employment and aggregate output remain mixed. A pervasive sense of caution reflecting, in part, the aftermath of corporate governance scandals appears to have left businesses focused on strengthening their balance sheets and, to date, reluctant to ramp up significantly their hiring and spending. Continued global uncertainties and economic weakness abroad, particularly among some of our major trading partners, also have extended the ongoing softness in the demand for U.S. goods and services.

When the Federal Open Market Committee (FOMC) met last month, with the economy not yet showing convincing signs of a sustained pickup in growth, and against the backdrop of our concerns about the implications of a possible substantial decline in inflation, we elected to ease policy another quarter-point. The FOMC stands prepared to maintain a highly accommodative stance of policy for as long as needed to promote satisfactory economic performance. In the judgment of the Committee, policy accommodation aimed at raising the growth of output, boosting the utilization of resources, and warding off unwelcome disinflation can be maintained for a considerable period without ultimately stoking inflationary pressures.

Source: Testimony by Alan Greenspan, Chairman, Board of Governors of the Federal Reserve System, before the Committee on Financial Services of the United States House of Representatives, July 15, 2003.

⌐

W E NOW KNOW what money is, how it is measured, and how it is related to reserves, but this testimony of Federal Reserve Chairman Greenspan underscores an important relationship to which we have so far paid little attention: that between monetary policy and interest rates. In this chapter we will use the tools of supply and demand to analyze this relationship.

## THE DEMAND FOR MONEY

### The Demand for Money as Demand for a Stock

By now the concept of demand is a familiar tool of analysis, but there are some key differences between the demand for money and previous applications of the concept. One difference lies in the fact that money is a *stock*, not a *flow*. When we discuss the demand for chicken, we do so in terms of pounds of chicken demanded *per year*. When we discuss aggregate demand, we speak in terms of constant dollars of total planned expenditure *per year*. But when we speak of the demand for money, we are talking about the quantity of money that people want to hold *at a particular point in time*, or, more precisely, the quantity they want to hold of the assets that enter into *M2:* currency, transaction deposits, savings deposits, MMDAs, savings and small-denomination time deposits, money market mutual funds, repurchase agreements, and certain other items.

Another difference between the demand for money and the demand for other goods lies in the fact that people do not "buy" money in the same sense that they buy other goods—at least not if we use the term "buy" to mean paying a certain price stated in money. However, people can obtain money by exchanging other assets for a form of money, for example, by selling bonds in exchange for bank deposits or selling a painting in exchange for currency. When we speak of the factors determining the demand for money, then, we mean the factors that determine why people choose to hold money rather than nonmonetary assets. The most important of these are nominal income and opportunity cost.

## Money Demand and Nominal Income

Other things being equal, people want to hold a stock of money that varies in proportion to their income. In a feudal society, the peasant living on a subsistence income had a few copper coins in a jar in the cupboard, whereas the lord of the manor, with a princely income, kept bags of gold coins in his strong room. In modern times, the average college student's stock of money may consist of a few Federal Reserve notes in her purse, whereas her parents, who earn higher income from full-time jobs, hold substantial balances in their checking accounts. Looking at matters from the viewpoint of the economy as a whole, the total stock of money held by all households and firms tends to vary in proportion to the level of nominal domestic income, other things being equal.

The desire to hold a stock of money related to income arises in part from the use of money as a means of payment for transactions ranging from the purchase of a candy bar to the purchase of a house. Because the nominal volume of transactions made in the economy varies in proportion to nominal domestic income, other things being equal, so does the quantity of money used by households and firms to carry out those transactions. The demand for money also reflects its nature as a readily accessible liquid store of value. As the incomes of households and firms rise, so does their wealth, and they will want to hold part of that wealth in liquid nontransaction balances, such as savings deposits, that are also included in M2.

The proportionality of demand for money to income can be expressed as the desired ratio of money to nominal domestic income, or, equivalently, as the desired ratio of nominal domestic income to money. The ratio of nominal domestic income to money is termed the *income velocity of money*. Thus, to say that people want to hold a stock of liquid assets that varies in proportion to nominal domestic income, other things being equal, is equivalent to saying that they desire to maintain a certain constant income velocity of money as nominal domestic income varies. For example, suppose a person with an income of $20,000 per year keeps an average balance of $2,000 in currency and bank account balances. We would say that such a person's "personal income velocity" was 10. If her income increased to $40,000 per year, and at the same time she increased her average holdings of currency and bank balances to $4,000, her personal income velocity would stay constant at 10.

## Opportunity Cost and the Demand for Money

Let us turn now to the "other things being equal" clause in our assertion that the quantity of money demanded varies in proportion to nominal domestic income. The key item covered by the "other things being equal" clause in this statement is the *opportunity cost* of holding money. The opportunity cost arises from the fact that wealth held in the form of money could be held in some other form instead—some form that would earn a higher rate of interest.

Consider money in the sense of M2. Some of the components of M2—currency and demand deposits—pay no interest at all. Others, like NOW accounts and MMDAs, do pay interest. However, even these typically pay less interest than less liquid assets, such as government or corporate securities. In part, then, the opportunity cost of holding money consists in the difference between the interest rate that could be earned on nonmonetary assets and the interest rate earned on monetary assets.

In addition, it should be kept in mind that purchase of interest-bearing assets is not the only alternative use of funds held in the form of M2. The funds a person holds as currency or savings deposits could also be used to purchase corporate stock, from which income is received in the form of dividends and capital gains rather than interest. The funds could be used to buy real assets, such as a car or a house, from which implicit income is received from the useful services they give. Or the funds could be used to repay debt, say an auto loan or a home mortgage, thereby avoiding payment of interest. Avoiding a dollar of interest payments is just as worthwhile as earning a dollar of interest income.

Despite the opportunity cost of holding assets in the form of money, however, people still hold some money. They do so because the alternative assets that earn higher interest have the disadvantage of lower liquidity. They cannot be used directly as a means of payment, and their nominal value is subject to change.

Clearly, the trade-off between the advantages of holding money (its liquidity) and the disadvantages of doing so (the opportunity cost) is a matter of degree. The higher the opportunity cost, the less money people will want to hold for a given level of nominal income. The same principle can also be expressed in terms of velocity: The higher the opportunity cost of money, the higher its velocity.

## Measuring the Opportunity Cost of Money

The principle that velocity varies directly with the opportunity cost of money is simple enough to state. However, in order to observe the principle in action, we must have some way of measuring the opportunity cost of holding money. That turns out to be not quite so simple.

The approach to measuring the opportunity cost of money is to use a particular nonmonetary asset as a benchmark for comparison of the interest rate on money and alternative assets. Treasury bills with a maturity of three months are a frequently chosen benchmark. The logic of using three-month T-bills as a benchmark stems from the fact that, in terms of their degree of liquidity, they lie just outside the spectrum of assets included in M2. T-Bills are, in that sense, a close substitute for money. The T-bill rate can then be compared with the M2 interest rate, or, more exactly, with a weighted average of the interest rates on the various components of M2.[1]

Note that if all components of M2 paid interest, and if their interest rates always varied point-by-point with changes in the T-bill rate, the measured opportunity cost of money would never change. (To illustrate, suppose the rate on interest savings accounts rose from 2 to 6 percent while the T-bill rate rose from 4 to 8 percent.) In practice, however, this is not the case, partly because some M2 components pay no interest, and partly because banks do not adjust deposit rates fully to reflect changes in market rates. Thus, a 1 point rise in the T-bill rate tends to be associated with less than a 1 point rise in the weighted average M2 rate.

## The Money Demand Curve

The general ideas expressed in our discussion of portfolio balance can be used to construct a money demand curve for the economy as a whole, as in Figure 12.1. Such a curve shows the total quantity of money that all firms and households want to hold under given conditions.

In drawing a money demand curve, we place the quantity of money (M2) on the horizontal axis. On the vertical axis, we place an appropriate nominal market interest rate, such as the three-month Treasury bill rate.

Part (a) of Figure 12.1 shows two money demand curves. Each curve has a negative slope. The negative slope reflects the fact that, other things being equal, people want to hold less money and more nonmonetary assets as market interest rates rise. As market interest rates fall, people tend to reduce their holdings of nonmonetary assets in order to gain the liquidity benefits of holding more money.

**SHIFTS IN THE MONEY DEMAND CURVE**   Money demand curves, like other demand curves, are drawn on the basis of "other things being equal." The most important condition that is held equal for a given money demand curve is the level of nominal domestic income. As we have explained, the quantity of money people desire to hold at any given interest rate tends to vary in proportion to nominal domestic income. Thus, if there is a change in nominal domestic income, the money demand curve will shift.

**FIGURE 12.1 A MONEY DEMAND SCHEDULE FOR A SIMPLE ECONOMY**

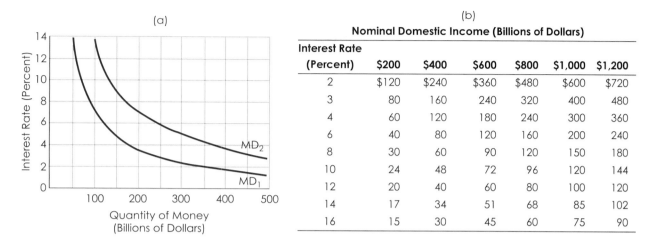

| Interest Rate (Percent) | Nominal Domestic Income (Billions of Dollars) | | | | | |
|---|---|---|---|---|---|---|
| | $200 | $400 | $600 | $800 | $1,000 | $1,200 |
| 2 | $120 | $240 | $360 | $480 | $600 | $720 |
| 3 | 80 | 160 | 240 | 320 | 400 | 480 |
| 4 | 60 | 120 | 180 | 240 | 300 | 360 |
| 6 | 40 | 80 | 120 | 160 | 200 | 240 |
| 8 | 30 | 60 | 90 | 120 | 150 | 180 |
| 10 | 24 | 48 | 72 | 96 | 120 | 144 |
| 12 | 20 | 40 | 60 | 80 | 100 | 120 |
| 14 | 17 | 34 | 51 | 68 | 85 | 102 |
| 16 | 15 | 30 | 45 | 60 | 75 | 90 |

This figure shows how the amount of money demanded varies in a simple economy as the level of nominal domestic income and the interest rate on a representative nonmonetary asset (or weighted rate on a collection of such assets) vary. The entries in part (b) show the amount of money demanded at the interest rate corresponding to each row and the nominal domestic income corresponding to each column. Each column can be graphed to get a money demand curve for a given level of nominal domestic income. $MD_1$ corresponds to the fourth column ($600 billion) and $MD_2$ to the last column ($1,200 billion).

Suppose, for example, that nominal domestic income doubles because real incomes double while the price level is unchanged, because prices double while real income is unchanged, or as a result of a combination of both kinds of change. Whatever the cause of the doubling of nominal domestic income, every household and firm will, on the average, undertake twice the nominal volume of transactions as before. Other things being equal (that is, at any given level of the interest rate), they would want to hold twice as much money to facilitate these transactions. They would also tend to double the nontransactions balances they hold as a liquid store of purchasing power. Therefore, as shown in part (a) of Figure 12.1, a doubling of nominal domestic income will cause the money demand curve to shift to the right, from $MD_1$ to $MD_2$.

Part (b) of Figure 12.1 presents the same relationships in numerical form. Each column of the table represents a single money demand curve. The columns show what happens to the quantity of money demanded as the interest rate changes while nominal domestic income remains the same. Each row of the table, on the other hand, shows how the demand for money responds to a change in nominal domestic income at a given interest rate. The general principle is that when the interest rate is held constant, the quantity of money demanded is proportional to nominal domestic income.

**MONEY DEMAND AND VELOCITY** The data in part (b) of Figure 12.1 imply that at any given nominal interest rate there will be a certain ratio of nominal domestic income to the quantity of money demanded. For example, consider the row of the table corresponding to an interest rate of 12 percent. Reading along that row, we see that when nominal domestic income is $200 billion, the quantity of money demanded is $20 billion; when nominal domestic income is $400 billion, the quantity of money demanded is $40 billion; and so on. For an interest rate of 12 percent, then, the ratio of nominal domestic income to the quantity of money demanded—that is, the income velocity of money—is 10 to 1 for all levels of nominal domestic income. Looking at other rows in the table, we see that velocity is 5 to 1 when the interest rate is 6 percent, 2.5 to 1 when the interest rate is 3 percent, and so on.

## SUPPLY AND DEMAND IN THE MONETARY SECTOR

Having looked in some detail at the demand for money, we are ready to put demand together with supply. The result is a graph such as that shown in Figure 12.2. The horizontal axis shows the money stock, measured in dollars; the vertical axis shows the market interest rate as a percentage per year. The money demand curve in Figure 12.2 shows the amount of money that people want to hold at each given interest rate

**FIGURE 12.2   EQUILIBRIUM IN THE MONETARY SECTOR**

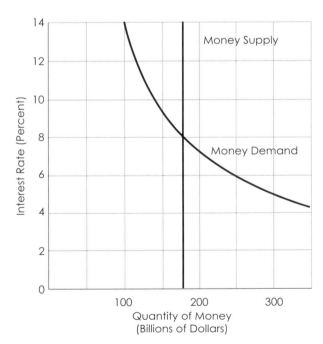

The money demand curve shown here is based on the data given in part (b) of Figure 12.1, assuming a nominal domestic income of $1,200 billion. The money supply curve assumes that the Fed sets a money supply target of $180 billion and adjusts total reserves to maintain this quantity of money regardless of what happens to interest rates. Under these conditions, the equilibrium interest rate is 8 percent.

assuming nominal domestic income of $1,200 billion. An increase in nominal domestic income will shift the money demand curve to the right, and a decrease will shift it to the left.

The money supply is under the control of the Federal Reserve. The exact shape of the money supply curve depends on how the Fed chooses to use its tools of monetary control. The supply curve in Figure 12.2 assumes that the Fed sets a target for the money stock ($180 billion in this case) and uses open market operations to stabilize reserves so as to keep the money stock on target regardless of what happens to the interest rate. This assumption results in a vertical money supply curve. A more advanced discussion of the monetary sector could incorporate other possible shapes for money supply curves, but it will not be necessary to do so for present purposes.

The supply and demand curves in Figure 12.2, which look like many other market supply and demand curves we have drawn, are, in a sense, a "market for money." Using that term might be confusing, however, since the term "money market" is widely used in the financial press to refer to the market for short-term fixed-interest securities—which, as we have seen, are not included in "money" (M2) as defined by economists. To avoid confusion, we will refer to the supply-and-demand situation shown in Figure 12.2 as the "monetary sector."

## Equilibrium in the Monetary Sector

The supply and demand curves in Figure 12.2 intersect at an interest rate of 8 percent. At that rate, the amount of money supplied by the banking system (which is determined, in turn, by the amount of reserves the Fed supplies to the banking system) just equals the amount people want to hold. There is neither upward nor downward pressure on interest rates.

No other interest rate would permit such an equilibrium. Suppose, for example, that the interest rate were just 4 percent. With such a low implied opportunity cost of money, people would want to hold more of it. They would try to obtain more money by borrowing from banks, but as long as the total quantity of bank reserves is constant, the banking system as a whole cannot increase the total quantity of deposits.[2] However, any one bank can acquire the added reserves it would need to expand loans and deposits by borrowing those reserves from other banks in the federal funds market. Competition among banks would drive up the federal funds rate. Other short- and long-term market interest rates tend to adjust quickly to changes in the federal funds rate, so that the whole family of interest rates would rise to the level corresponding to 8 percent on the vertical axis of Figure 12.2. The monetary sector would then be back in equilibrium.

In Figure 12.2, a rising interest rate brings the monetary sector back into equilibrium by reducing the amount of money demanded rather than by increasing the amount of money supplied. As long as the Fed provides no more reserves to the banking system, banks cannot supply any more money. Even though any one person can add money to his or her portfolio by borrowing or by selling some other asset, this will not affect the amount of money in the banking system as a whole.

The same story can be told in reverse for the case in which the interest rate is higher than its equilibrium value. In that event, people would not be willing to hold all the money that banks want to supply. Banks cannot force people to hold deposits. They can, however, attempt to put excess reserves to work by lending them in the federal funds market. Under such circumstances, competition among banks will drive the federal funds rate down, and other interest rates will fall as a consequence. As the interest rate falls, the public becomes willing to hold the quantity of money that banks would like to supply, given the amount of reserves available to the system.

## Effects of a Change in the Money Supply

Our description of the monetary sector is useful for a number of purposes. Let us begin by using it to analyze the effects of shifts in the money supply curve.

Figure 12.3 shows the monetary sector in equilibrium at $E_1$ with a money supply of $180 billion and an interest rate of 8 percent. Starting from this point, the Fed decides to increase the money supply to $360 billion. Assuming a money multiplier of 10, it can do this by injecting 518 billion of new reserves into the banking system by means of open market purchases.

**FIGURE 12.3   EFFECTS OF AN INCREASE IN THE MONEY SUPPLY**

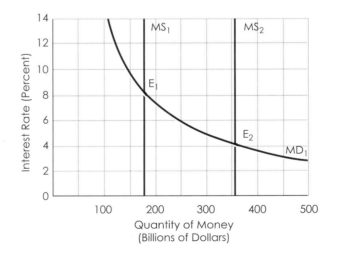

The money stock starts out at $180 billion, putting the money supply curve in the position $MS_1$. An open market purchase by the Fed injects new reserves into the banking system. Banks' competitive efforts to put the new reserves to work drive rates down, first in the federal funds market and then in other markets. As the money supply expands, the economy moves toward a new equilibrium, $E_2$, where the interest rate has fallen by enough to make people willing to hold the larger quantity of money.

The immediate impact of the open market operation is to boost banks' excess reserves. To restore their balance sheets to equilibrium, banks set out to convert the excess reserves into earning assets. The quickest way to do so is to lend the excess reserves in the federal funds market. Their attempts to do so will drive down the federal funds rate. Soon the decline in interest rates will spread to other markets, including the markets for consumer and business loans.

As the volume of borrowing expands, the quantity of deposits supplied to the public increases. In Figure 12.3 this is shown as a shift in the money supply curve from $MS_1$ to $MS_2$. At point $E_1$ people were content to hold the old quantity of money, $180 billion, in their portfolios. Now falling interest rates reduce the opportunity cost of holding money and make people willing to absorb the increased quantity supplied by banks. Thus, as the injection of reserves shifts the money supply curve to the right, falling interest rates cause people to move downward and to the right along their money demand curve. In time a new equilibrium is reached at point $E_2$, where the money stock is greater and the interest rate lower than before.

If the Fed withdraws reserves from the banking system through an open market sale, the same process operates in reverse. Banks find themselves with less than the required quantity of reserves. At first, they will try to obtain the reserves they need in the federal funds market. However, with total reserves fixed, their attempts to do so will only drive up the federal funds rate. As that happens, banks may decide to restore their balance sheets to equilibrium by reducing their holdings of securities or loans. To do so, they sell securities or raise interest rates on loans by enough to reduce the rate of new lending below that at which old loans are paid off. As interest rates rise through the economy, people become willing to hold a smaller quantity of money in their portfolios. A new equilibrium is reached in which the money supply is smaller and the interest rate higher than before.

## Effects of an Increase in Income

In discussing the effects of a change in the money supply, we have assumed that the level of nominal domestic income remained constant. Let us reverse that assumption and see what happens to the monetary sector when nominal domestic income changes while the money supply curve stays put.

Figure 12.4 sets the stage. It shows the market in equilibrium at $E_1$ with an interest rate of 4 percent and a money supply of $180 billion. Nominal domestic income is assumed to be $600 billion, which puts the money demand curve in the position $MD_2$.

Now assume that nominal domestic income rises to a level of $1,200 billion. As we saw earlier in the chapter, an increase in nominal domestic income, other things being equal, shifts the money demand curve to the right. The new position of the money demand curve is $MD_2$.

At the new, higher income level, people will want more money with which to carry out transactions and to hold as a liquid store of value. They will attempt to

**FIGURE 12.4   EFFECTS OF AN INCREASE IN NOMINAL DOMESTIC INCOME**

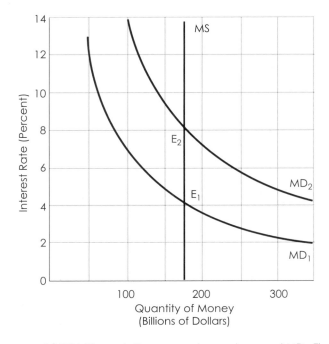

A nominal domestic income of $600 billion puts the money demand curve at MD₂. The equilibrium interest rate is 4 percent given this income and the money supply of $180 billion. If an increase in nominal income to $1,200 billion shifts the money demand curve to MD₂, there will be an excess demand for money at the initial interest rate. People will try to increase the quantity of money they hold, in part by borrowing from banks. As a result of competition among banks for reserves to meet the increased loan demand, interest rates will rise, first in the federal funds market, and then in the loan market and other markets.

obtain the additional money partly by borrowing from banks. Banks, in turn, will try to get the reserves they need to support the added loans and deposits by borrowing in the federal funds market. But the federal funds market only moves reserves around from one bank to another. The banking system as a whole cannot increase its total deposits given the total reserves supplied by the Fed. Competition among borrowers thus will not increase the money stock as a whole, but will instead drive up interest rates. The higher interest rates will make people willing to get along with the limited money stock available despite their higher incomes. Thus, the economy will move to a new equilibrium at E₂. There nominal domestic income and the interest rate are higher than before and the money stock has not changed.

If nominal domestic income falls, the same process will occur in reverse. With lower incomes, people will require less money. If the interest rate does not change, they will reduce their demand for deposits, in the process tending to pay off old loans without taking out an equal volume of new ones. Banks will attempt to lend the resulting excess reserves in the federal funds market, but because many banks are doing so at once, their efforts will cause the federal funds rate to fall. Other rates, including, eventually, loan rates, will be pushed down as well. When interest rates fall enough to make people content to hold the existing money stock even at a lower level of nominal domestic income, the monetary sector will be back in equilibrium. The interest rate will be lower than before; nominal domestic income will be lower; and the money stock will not have changed.

## The Monetary Sector, Interest Rates, and the Aggregate Demand Curve

In the preceding section we saw that an increase in nominal domestic income tends to raise the equilibrium interest rate, because it shifts the money demand curve to the right. This is true regardless of the form of the increase in nominal domestic income.

One possibility is an increase in real income with no change in the price level. In this case people will want to hold a greater quantity of money in part to make the transactions connected with the production and sale of a larger volume of real output, and in part to add to real savings-type balances. The money demand curve will shift to the right, as shown in Figure 12.4, and the interest rate will rise.

On the other hand, the increase in nominal income may take the form of a higher price level with no change in the real income level. In that case the physical volume of transactions will not change, but more money will be needed to carry out the transactions because goods and services will have higher prices. Also, with a higher price level, more nominal savings balances will be needed to maintain the real value of those balances. Thus, an increase in the price level is also capable of shifting the money demand curve to the right and driving up the equilibrium interest rate.

In practice, changes in nominal domestic income usually reflect some combination of changes in the price level and changes in real income. However, separating the two effects helps us understand the nature of the economy's aggregate demand curve. One of the reasons for the negative slope of the aggregate demand curve is that, other things being equal, a rise in the price level tends to increase the interest rate, thereby depressing the level of planned investment expenditure. We now see why this is so. A higher price level pushes up the interest rate because it shifts the money demand curve. A given money stock can be considered one of the "other things being equal" conditions that lies behind the economy's aggregate demand curve.

We can also see why the aggregate demand curve is relatively inelastic with respect to the price level. As the price level increases, the interest rate rises. As we saw earlier in the chapter, an increase in the interest rate causes velocity to rise. According to the equation of exchange, if velocity rises while the quantity of money remains constant (as it does at all points on a given aggregate demand curve), nominal domestic product (that is, real domestic product multiplied by the price level, the right-hand side of the equation of exchange) must rise. In graphical terms, this means that nominal output must be rising as an increase in the price level carries the economy upward along a given aggregate demand curve. This can occur only if the percentage decrease in real output as the economy moves along the curve is less than the percentage increase in price. And a percentage change in quantity demanded that is smaller than the associated percentage change in price is the definition of relatively inelastic demand.

## Monetary Policy Instruments and Targets

Because monetary policy has such an important effect on inflation, output, unemployment, exchange rates, and other variables, it is prominently featured in financial news. *Economics in the News 12.1* is typical in its emphasis on the power of monetary policy. However, in light of what we have learned about monetary policy so far, there is something in this news story that does not seem quite right. The story focuses on the ability of the Fed to control *interest rates,* whereas, up to this point, we have emphasized the Fed's control of the money stock. In doing so, we have shown changes in interest rates only as an indirect effect of shifts in the money supply curve. So which interpretation is right—do central banks control the quantity of money, or do they control interest rates?

In fact, there is no contradiction between the analysis we read in the newspapers and the theory presented in this chapter. They are simply different ways of looking at central bank actions. The economic viewpoint focuses on *policy instruments,* whereas reports in the financial press focus on *policy targets.* The next section will explain the importance of this distinction.

**TARGETS AND INSTRUMENTS**   A *policy instrument* is any variable over which the central bank has direct administrative control. In Chapter 11, we looked at two major policy instruments and two minor ones:

*Major monetary policy instruments*
- Open market purchases and sales of domestic securities
- Purchases and sales of foreign currency

*Minor policy instruments*
- Changes in the required reserve ratio
- Changes in the discount rate

A *policy target,* on the other hand, is a variable that the central bank aims to affect by making change in policy instruments. Interest rates are an important example of a policy target. For example, as was shown in Figure 12.3, the Fed can use an open market purchase to increase the monetary base and shift the MS curve to the right. As banks and the nonbank public adjust their behavior to the change in money supply, market interest rates will fall.

The Fed, like the central banks of many other countries, guides day-to-day operations by setting an **operating target** in the form of a market interest rate—the federal funds rate at which banks make short-term loans of reserves among one another. The

**Operating target**

A financial variable for which the Fed sets a short-term target, which it then uses as a guide in the day-to-day conduct of open market operations.

**FIGURE 12.5**

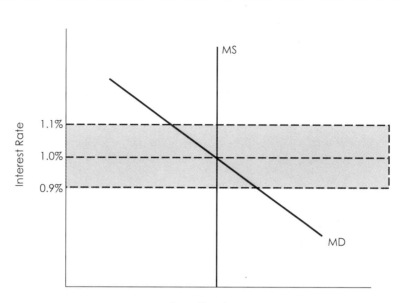

Quantity of Money

This figure shows how the Fed could set an operating target of 1 percent, plus or minus 1/10 percent, for the federal funds rate. If market forces tended to push the rate above the operating target, the Fed would use an open market purchase of securities (a policy instrument) to increase the money supply, thereby bringing the interest rate back within its target range. Similarly, an open market sale of securities would be used if the interest rate fell too low.

federal funds rate is extremely sensitive to open market operations and changes in other policy instruments. It reacts to the Fed's actions within moments of when they are taken.

Figure 12.5 shows how the Fed can control and use open market operations, its most important policy instrument, to achieve its operating target for the federal funds rate. Suppose, for example, that operating target for the federal funds rate is 1 percent, plus or minus 1/10 percent. In Figure 12.5, the target range is shown as a band around a horizontal line that is the announced target. In order to keep the interest rate within the target range, the central bank needs to use its policy instruments to move the MS curve to a position such that it intersects the MD curve no lower than .9% and no higher than 1.1%.

Holding the interest rate within its target range is not just a matter of "set it and forget it." Market conditions are constantly changing in ways that push the money supply and demand curves around. For example, the level of domestic income changes from day to day depending on the weather, the calendar, and more basic economic trends, thereby shifting the demand curve. Also, the money multiplier can change from day to day or week to week, for example, when people withdraw additional currency from ATM machines on holidays. Each day the Fed reviews market conditions and determines what open market purchases or sales are needed when market conditions threaten to push the interest rate above or below the target range.

## ☜ ECONOMICS IN THE NEWS 12.1

### THE ALL-POWERFUL FED CHAIRMAN?

JANUARY 17, 2001—What do you get when you cross a god-father with a Federal Reserve chairman? Someone who makes you an offer you can't understand.

Sorry; an old joke, and one that's somewhat unfair to Alan Greenspan. Still, the Fed chairman does talk in a code that, while usually easy to decipher, bears only a distant resemblance to English. Moreover, he has a weakness for Delphic statements, seeming to imply that he knows more than he chooses to say clearly.

So Mr. Greenspan may bear some of the blame for the current rash of conspiracy theories surrounding the Fed's recent decision to cut interest rates. There isn't any real mystery about why the Fed acted; but those who insist that there must be more there than meets the eye have gained some undeserved credibility from the Fed's tradition of inscrutability.

When the Fed cut interest rates by half a percentage point on Jan. 3, jumping the gun on its scheduled meeting later this month, it surprised everyone. But we shouldn't have been that surprised; indeed, I was kicking myself for not having guessed that such a move was about to happen. All the ingredients were there: new signs of weakness in the economy, and evidence of an incipient panic in the financial markets. The Fed has always believed in the occasional usefulness of "slap in the face" interventions, dramatic moves that pull investors up short. So there was nothing particularly strange about that sudden rate cut.

But there are many people who won't accept the obvious explanation, who insist that the Fed acted on secret information about a looming recession or financial crisis—so many that last week Roger Ferguson, the Fed's vice chairman, went out of his way to deny those rumors.

Why would commentators want to invent elaborate and unnecessary stories about hidden Fed knowledge? One reason is political: ardent tax-cutters, who hope to use recession fears to stampede Congress into giving them what they want, are eager to put as much negative spin on the economy as possible.

Another reason is personal: those who were skeptical about the glories of the "new economy" have spent the last few years in the doghouse. Now that some economic clouds have finally appeared, they don't want the sun to shine on their parade.

Finally, there's the CNBC effect. Providing business news has itself become a big business. But all-news channels, which struggle to stay interesting while covering the same material hour after hour, often find themselves emphasizing entertainment values over the usually prosaic truth. Even the Weather Channel has fallen into the habit of hyping each storm as if it were soon to be a major motion picture. And now that CNBC can no longer run breathless tales about the economic boom, it has started to feature equally breathless (and potentially self-fulfilling) speculations about economic crisis.

The result has been to put Mr. Greenspan himself in a no-win situation. If he doesn't cut rates as fast as Wall Street wants, analysts fret that he has gotten behind the curve. But if he does cut rates aggressively, rumors fly about the dark secrets that prompted his action.

So it was certainly a good idea for someone from the Fed to ask, as Mr. Ferguson did, the rhetorical question "What does the Fed know that we don't know?" and answer, truthfully, "Very little, if anything."

The real "secret of the temple" is that the Fed, Mr. Greenspan included, basically has no more knowledge about what is going on than any economic analyst equipped with a telephone and a modem. What the Fed has that the rest of us don't is not knowledge but power.

Ironically, the belief that the Fed has special knowledge actually reduces the institution's power: rumors that Mr. Greenspan cut rates because he knows something we don't diminished what would otherwise have been a salutary effect on market psychology. Still, despite all that, the Fed's move has already made a noticeable difference, stemming the rout in the Nasdaq and producing a striking recovery in the corporate bond market. Another few shots in the arm like that and talk of recession might well evaporate.

The key thing to realize is that Alan Greenspan is just a man, no wiser or better informed than many others. But he controls the money supply—and that's enough.

Source: Paul Krugman, "Secrets and Truth," *The New York Times,* January 17, 2001.

---

Understanding how central banks use interest rates as an operating target explains the headlines. When the headline says "Fed Increases Interest Rates," it should be interpreted as journalistic shorthand for something like this: "The Fed has decided to increase its operating target for the federal funds rate. To move the rate up to its new target range, the Fed will carry out open market sales of securities or other actions designed to reduce reserves of the banking system and bring about the changes in the behavior of commercial banks and the public that will result in changes in the money stock."

Interest rates are the key operating target of the Fed and the central banks of many countries, but they are not the only possible one. Some central banks focus their day-to-day operations not on an interest rate target, but rather, on a target value for the exchange rate of their currency relative to some other currency. We looked briefly at exchange rate targeting in Chapter 11 and we will return to this topic in Chapter 14.

It is also important to emphasize that the concerns of central bankers extend beyond short-term operating targets like interest rates or exchange rates. Over a somewhat longer time horizon than day-to-day operations, they set *intermediate targets* for key economic variables like inflation, unemployment, or economic growth. Even the central bank's intermediate targets are not the whole story of monetary policy. In a broader context, the central bank is only one of a number of policy-making units within a country's government. Its real job is to work together with the country's ministry of finance, its parliament, its president, and other leaders to pursue the ultimate policy goal of economic stability and prosperity for all citizens. The complex relationships among monetary policy instruments, targets, and ultimate goals will be explored further in Chapter 14.

## SUMMARY

1. **How do nominal income and interest rates affect the demand for money?** Other things being equal, the quantity of money people desire to hold varies in proportion to nominal domestic income. Because the components of M2 pay a lower interest rate on average than nonmonetary assets, there is an opportunity cost associated with holding money, which varies directly with market interest rates. Therefore, for a given nominal domestic income, the quantity of money demanded varies inversely with market interest rates.

2. **What are the characteristics of the money demand curve?** The demand for money can be represented by a downward-sloping curve on a graph in which the horizontal axis measures the quantity of money and the vertical axis measures

the interest rate. An increase in nominal domestic income shifts the money demand curve to the right, and a decrease shifts it to the left.

3. **How is the equilibrium interest rate affected by a change in the money stock?** An expansion of bank reserves shifts the money supply curve to the right. As banks seek to convert their excess reserves into income-earning assets, competition drives interest rates down. This in turn increases the quantity of money that the public is willing to hold. The economy thus moves down along the money demand curve to a new equilibrium in which the interest rate is lower. A decrease in bank reserves causes a reversal of this sequence of events.

4. **How is the equilibrium interest rate affected by a change in nominal domestic income?** An increase in nominal domestic income increases the

quantity of money that people would like to hold at any given interest rate, thereby shifting the money demand curve to the right. People attempt to obtain more money by borrowing more from banks, causing banks to compete for the limited available supply of reserves. This competition drives interest rates up until a new equilibrium is reached at which people are satisfied to hold the existing quantity of money at the new level of nominal domestic Income.

5. **What targets has the Fed used as guides for its open market operations?** The Fed implements monetary policy by use of *policy instruments,* of which open market operations are the most important. As a guide to the conduct of open market operations, it sets an *operating target* for the federal funds rate—an important interest rate that influences the level of all other market interest rates. If market forces tend to push the interest rate above its target level, the Fed makes open market purchases of securities to boost the money stock, and if market forces tend to push interest rates below the target, the Fed makes open market sales. The operating target for interest rates is adjusted from time to time in light of intermediate policy targets and ultimate policy goals, such as price stability, full employment, and economic growth.

## KEY TERM

Operating target

## PROBLEMS AND TOPICS FOR DISCUSSION

1. **Examining the lead-off case.** In the excerpt at the beginning of the chapter, Fed Chairman Green-

span notes that in mid-2003 the economy was expanding in real terms and the price level was slowly rising. He assured us that the stance of monetary policy was to remain highly accommodative. Would the Fed need to reduce bank reserves to "tighten" monetary policy, that is, to cause interest rates to increase to accommodate the 2003 economy? Or would it be enough just to slow or stop the growth of reserves? Explain in terms of money supply and demand curves. Later in the year the growth of nominal GDP rose substantially. Under those circumstances, what would the Fed have to do to cause interest rates to fall?

2. **Velocity.** Using the Federal Reserve Economics Database (FRED) available on the St. Louis Fed Web site http://research.stlouisfed.org, find the values of M2, nominal GDP, and the three-month Treasury bill rate for the two most recent years reported. Calculate velocity for the two years. If the T-bill rate changed from one year to the next, did velocity change in the same direction? If the Treasury bill rate was unchanged, did velocity also remain unchanged?

3. **Money demand and the price level.** Some economists draw a different type of money demand curve from the one used in this book. They begin with a diagram that shows the quantity of money demanded on the horizontal axis and the price level on the vertical axis. Sketch these axes on a sheet of graph paper. Number the vertical axis from 0 to 10 and the horizontal axis from 0 to $500 billion. Assume a constant real domestic income of $200 billion and a constant nominal interest rate of 4 percent. Using part (b) of Figure 12.2 as a guide, draw a curve showing how the quantity of money demanded varies as the price level changes. (Remember that nominal domestic income equals real domestic income times the price level.) How does this version of the money demand curve shift if the interest rate rises from 4 to 6 percent?

4. **Effects of a decrease in the money supply.** Rework the example given in Figure 12.3 for the case of a decrease in the money supply from $180 billion to $120 billion.

5. **Effects of a decrease in nominal domestic income.** Rework the example given in Figure 12.4 for the case of a decrease in nominal domestic income from $600 billion to $400 billion. (Use part (b) of Figure 12.2 to draw the demand curve for a nominal domestic income of $400 billion.)

6. **Recent monetary policy.** View the statements issued from the FOMC's meetings at http://www .federalreserve.gov/fomc/. Go to the statement for the most recent meeting. Did the FOMC choose to change the federal funds rate target? What reasons did it cite for its decision?

# CASE FOR DISCUSSION

## *Deciphering Bond Prices and Interest Rates*

One of the jobs of a journalist specializing in reporting on financial markets is to interpret each day's movements in security prices and interest rates. In this job, the reporter is aided by a few fixed principles but must nevertheless rely on some creative guesswork.

One of the fixed principles is that the prices of fixed-income securities such as long-term bonds will move in the opposite direction to market interest rates. The reason for the inverse relationship between interest rates and bond prices can be made clear by an example. Suppose ABC Corporation sells a 30-year bond with $1,000 face value at a time when the market interest rates on loans and securities of such a maturity is 10 percent. The bond will consist of a promise to make a fixed payment of $100 per year to the holder of the bond for 30 years, plus a final payment of $1,000 at the end of that period. The fixed annual payment, expressed as a percentage of the bond's face value, is called the bond's coupon rate. Suppose that a year later, market conditions change. Interest rates on securities and loans of all kinds are lower. Under the new conditions ABC Corporation sells additional 30-year bonds with a coupon rate equal to the new market interest rate of 8 percent (that is, the new bonds promise the holder just $80 per year per $1,000 of face value).

Once the new bonds are issued, how much will investors be willing to pay for the old bonds? Obviously, more than for the new ones, because the old bonds pay $100 per year, whereas the new ones pay just $80 per year. Specifically, an investor who would be willing to pay $1,000 for one of the new bonds would be willing to pay about $1,250 for an old bond with the same face value—a difference in price that reflects the difference in the coupon rate of the two bonds.

But the fact that bond prices are inversely related to market interest rates is only the starting point for the journalist's daily analysis of bond prices. The hard part of the job is to explain why interest rates change.

To give a specific example, on December 11, 2003, bond prices rose and interest rates fell. What new developments in world financial markets might have caused this to happen? Reporters considered the following possibilities:

- Retail sales rose 0.9 percent in November 2003 when analysts had looked for a gain of 0.7 percent, while sales excluding autos climbed 0.4 percent, as expected. October's 2003 sales were revised up, making the whole report reasonably upbeat.
- A rise in jobless claims to 378,000 last week from 365,000 the week before. Analysts had looked for a dip to 360,000 and were worried the figures pointed to another month of subdued payroll gains.

- The FOMC's eye-catching statements from December 11, 2003 indicated the Fed expects inflation to stay low.

Reporters characterized the first of these developments as "bullish"—that is, as tending to push bond prices higher. On the other hand, the second development, possibly poor labor market conditions that may threaten consumer spending, was characterized as "bearish"—that is, as tending to push bond prices lower. The final statement indicates that the FOMC would be unlikely to raise its federal funds rate target in 2004 because it expects that inflation will remain low. The fact that bond prices actually rose was interpreted to mean that the bullish news had more impact than the bearish news. The market was said to have "shrugged off" the poor labor market numbers, perhaps because such a development had already long been considered possible, and therefore was already fully reflected in bond prices and interest rates.

Because each day brings some bullish and some bearish news, bond-marker journalists can almost always find some explanation of why prices and interest rates moved as they did.

## QUESTIONS

1. Suppose, as in the example given, that ABC Corporation issues a 30-year bond with a 10 percent coupon rate. A year later, market interest rates have risen sharply, and ABC sells new 30-year bonds with a coupon rate of 12.5 percent. Assuming the new bonds have a market price equal to their face value of $1,000, approximately what will be the market price of the old bonds under these conditions?

2. Taking into account the factors that affect the demand for money, and assuming a fixed supply of money, explain how each of the following would affect interest rates and bond prices: (a) a decrease in exports; (b) an increase in inflation, assuming no change in real domestic income; and (c) an increase in government purchases.

3. Look for articles related to bond prices and interest rates in recent issues of *The Wall Street Journal* or in the financial pages of another national newspaper. What is the current direction of change of bond prices? Of interest rates? What "bullish" or bearish news is cited to explain these movements?

## END NOTES

1. Suppose, for example, that total M2 is $1,000 billion, consisting of $800 billion of savings deposits paying 5 percent interest and $200 billion of currency paying zero interest. The weighted average interest rate on M2 as a whole, in this simplified example, would be 4 percent.

2. To be precise, we should say that banks cannot increase the total quantity of deposits subject to reserves. To simplify matters, we will assume that all deposits are subject to a uniform required-reserve ratio.

# An Integrated View of Monetary and Fiscal Policy

| *After reading this chapter, you will understand:* | |
|---|---|
| | 1. How changes in the money stock affect real output, the price level, and unemployment. |
| | 2. What is meant by the *neutrality* of money. |
| | 3. How fiscal policy affects interest rates and planned investment. |
| | 4. The international implications of fiscal policy. |
| | 5. *Keynesian* and *monetarist* views of the Great Depression. |

| *Before reading this chapter, make sure you know the meaning of:* | |
|---|---|
| | 1. Elasticity |
| | 2. Real and nominal interest rates |
| | 3. Leakages and injections |
| | 4. Natural level of real output |
| | 5. Multiplier effect |
| | 6. Monetary sector |

## BALANCING FISCAL AND MONETARY POLICY

The following passages are excerpted from the 2003 *Economic Report of the President*, transmitted by President George W. Bush to Congress in February 2003.

The U.S. economy grew at an annual rate of 3.4 percent through the first three quarters of 2002. (The advance release for GDP in the last quarter of 2002 became available only after this Report went to press.) Although output rebounded after the terrorist attacks of September 2001, job growth during the recovery has remained unsatisfactory. However, the continued recovery in output over the past year, and especially the robust improvements in productivity, foreshadow a return to more vibrant job creation in the future.

The contraction of 2001, although one of the mildest on record, turned out to have started earlier and to have been more severe than data available before July 2002 had indicated. The revised data that became available at that time revealed that output had dropped moderately in each of the first three quarters of 2001 before the rebound began in late 2001 and early 2002. Output fell by a cumulative total of 0.6 percent from the peak at the end of 2000 to the trough in the third quarter of 2001, much less than in most previous recessions. The mildness of the recession—in spite of the effects of terrorist attacks, continued declines in the stock market, and concerns over corporate governance—reflects in large part the benefits derived from the flexibility of the market-driven U.S. economy.

Monetary and fiscal policy also provided support for demand in the face of these adverse developments. In 2001, faced with signs of a slowing of economic activity, the Federal Reserve reduced the target Federal funds rate 11 times during the year, for a total reduction of 4.75 percentage points, to 1.75 percent. The Federal Reserve then held the Federal funds rate steady through most of 2002, until a half-percentage-point cut on November 6 brought it down to 1.25 percent.

Recent U.S. fiscal policy has pursued the goal of promoting economic growth. Among the central components of a pro-growth fiscal policy are measures to limit the share of output commanded by the government, and measures to reduce disincentives to work, save, and invest. The Economic Growth and Tax Relief Reconciliation Act (EGTRRA), enacted in June 2001, lowered marginal tax rates for all taxpayers. This tax cut will have important incentive effects that will lead to higher incomes and improved long-term living standards. EGTRRA also provided important support for economic activity in the short term, because of the way in which the tax rate reductions were set in place and the timing of the act's passage.

⌐

IN PRECEDING CHAPTERS, we looked at the monetary sector of the economy in isolation. In this chapter we return to the broader themes of inflation, real output, and employment and see how these are shaped by developments in the monetary sector. The passages just quoted from the 2003 *Economic Report of the President* emphasize the interaction between monetary and fiscal policy. The long-term goals of high employment, price stability, and economic growth require the president, Congress, and the Federal Reserve to work together. By combining a monetary sector model with the aggregate supply and demand model and the analysis of fiscal policy developed earlier, we will gain a better understanding of why both monetary and fiscal policy play important roles in economic policy, and why the two branches of policy need to be carefully coordinated.

# THE TRANSMISSION MECHANISM

**Transmission mechanism**

The set of channels through which monetary policy affects real output and the price level.

The set of channels through which monetary policy affects the economy is known as the **transmission mechanism**. We will begin with the most important aspect of the transmission mechanism, which is the effect of monetary policy on the planned-investment component of aggregate demand acting by way of changes in interest rates.

## *Planned Investment and the Interest Rate*

Business firms constantly plan to make investments both in fixed capital and in inventories. To do so, they must somehow acquire the funds needed to finance the investments. Many firms are fortunate enough to have steady flows of profits, some of which can be used for investment before the rest is paid out to owners. Others obtain funds by borrowing—either directly from the public or through financial intermediaries.

Whatever the source of a firm's investment funds, acquiring new fixed capital or inventory always involves an opportunity cost. The opportunity cost of investment is the real interest rate that must be paid for funds that are obtained from outside the firm or that could be earned by investing the firm's own funds elsewhere. There is no free source of funds. A firm that spends its own profits on new office equipment could have earned interest on those funds by depositing them in a bank, buying government securities, or lending them to another firm. A firm that borrows in order to buy capital goods must pay the real interest rate charged by lenders.

At any given time, there may be dozens or hundreds of investment opportunities available to a firm. A regional sales office could be built in a distant city. Production equipment could be modernized. Larger inventories of raw materials could be kept on hand to guard against supply disruptions. Somehow the firm's managers must decide which projects to undertake and how far to carry each one. In doing so, they must balance the potential benefits, in terms of increased profits, against the opportunity cost of obtaining the investment funds.

Suppose, for example, that a firm decides to improve the insulation in the roof of its warehouse. A consultant estimates that 6 inches of insulation will reduce the firm's fuel costs by $2,000 per year. Doubling the added insulation to 12 inches will save another $1,000 per year, bringing the total yearly savings to $3,000. Each six inches of insulation costs $10,000. How much insulation should be used—12 inches, 6 inches, or none?

The correct choice can be made by comparing the return on investment, stated as a percentage of the cost of the investment, to the opportunity cost of capital—that is, the real rate of interest. In this case the return on investment takes the form of a reduction in fuel costs. The first 6 inches of insulation brings a reduction of $2,000 per year, or 20 percent of its cost. Installing it, therefore, will be worthwhile as long as the interest rate is less than 20 percent. The second 6 inches will reduce fuel costs by another $1,000 per year, or 10 percent of its cost. Adding it will be worthwhile only if the interest rate is less than 10 percent. Thus, we see that the firm will install 12 inches of insulation if the interest rate is below 10 percent, 6 inches if it is 10 percent or more but less than 20 percent, and none if it is 20 percent or more.

As simple as it is, this example illustrates a basic principle: Other things being equal, the lower the opportunity cost of investment, the higher a firm's rate of planned investment. Generalizing from this principle, we can draw a **planned-investment schedule** for a firm and, by extension, for the economy as a whole. Such a schedule shows the amount of planned investment associated with each real interest rate.

Part (a) of Figure 13.1 shows the planned-investment schedule for our hypothetical firm based on the example just given. At real interest rates of 20 percent or more, it will not be worthwhile to do any insulating. As soon as the real interest rate drops below 20 percent, the first $10,000 of insulation becomes worthwhile. The second 6 inches of insulation begins to pay for itself when the interest rate falls below 10 percent. Given the 15 percent rate shown in the diagram, investment is cut off at $10,000.

Part (b) of Figure 13.1 shows an investment schedule for the economy as a whole. With tens of thousands of firms and millions of potential investment projects, the stairsteps of the single-firm, single-project investment schedule are smoothed out. In this schedule, a 15 percent real interest rate is associated with $225 billion of real planned-investment spending per year for the economy as a whole.

Any change in the real interest rate, other things being equal, will produce a movement along the planned-investment schedule. In part (b) of Figure 13.1, for example, a decrease in the interest rate to 10 percent will increase real planned investment to $250 billion. Likewise, an increase in the interest rate to 20 percent will reduce real planned investment to $200 billion.

Of course, the real interest rate is not the only factor that affects investment decisions. Anything else that affects the expected profitability of an investment—forecasts of product demand, expected changes in technology, trends in labor supply—will also cause the amount of investment to change. Increased optimism about profit opportunities thus will cause the planned-investment schedule to shift to the right, while increased pessimism will cause it to shift to the left.

**Planned investment schedule**
───────────

A graph showing the relationship between the total quantity of real planned investment expenditure and the real interest rate.

**FIGURE 13.1  PLANNED-INVESTMENT SCHEDULES FOR A HYPOTHETICAL FIRM AND FOR THE ECONOMY AS A WHOLE**

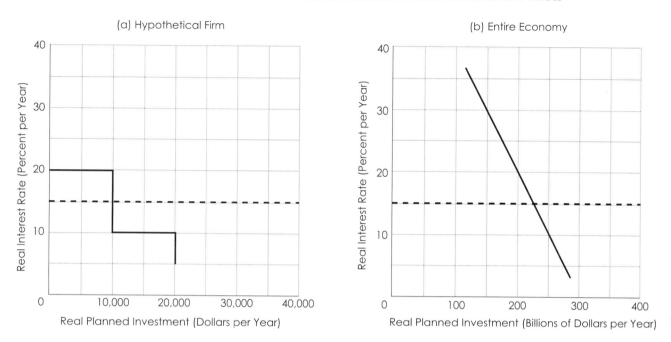

Part (a) shows planned investment for a hypothetical firm; part (b) shows a planned-investment schedule for the economy as a whole. At a 15 percent real interest rate, the hypothetical firm will invest at a real rate of $10,000 per year, and real planned investment for the economy as a whole will be $225 billion per year. Both for the firm and for the economy, the amount of real planned investment rises as the real interest rate falls, other things being equal.

## Other Aspects of the Transmission Mechanism

When expansionary monetary policy causes nominal market interest rates to fall, the associated decline in real interest rates will induce a movement of the economy downward along the planned investment schedule. This stimulates the planned investment component of aggregate demand. The planned investment schedule thus is central to the transmission mechanism of monetary policy. However, a change in monetary policy also causes other reactions in the economy that boost aggregate demand, thus contributing additional force to the transmission mechanism.

Consider the effects of monetary policy on net exports via the exchange rate. A decrease in U.S. interest rates, other things being equal, will decrease the demand for dollars in the foreign exchange market. This happens because lower interest rates make U.S. assets less attractive to foreign investors. A decrease in demand for the dollar causes the exchange rate of the dollar to fall relative to foreign currencies. With the exchange rate lower, U.S. exports become relatively cheaper for foreign buyers, while imports become relatively more expensive for U.S. buyers. Increased exports and lower imports both add to the net exports component of aggregate demand. A second aspect of the transmission mechanism, therefore, runs from expansionary monetary policy, to lower interest rates, to a lower exchange rate for the dollar, to increased net exports.

Consumption, too, can be stimulated by a decrease in interest rates, especially consumption of items like automobiles and other consumer durables that tend to be bought on credit. This third aspect of the transmission mechanism, then, runs from expansionary monetary policy, to lower interest rates generally (including interest rates on consumer loans), and thus to increased consumption.

Finally, some economists think expansionary monetary policy is transmitted to a significant degree through channels that do not involve interest rates at all, or do so only indirectly. In this view, an expansion of the highly liquid assets that make up the money stock causes people to reevaluate their strategies for investments in all kinds of assets. Some of this impact of monetary policy may spill over into the stock market. As increased demand pushes up stock prices, firms find it easier to sell new stock to finance investment. Also, rising stock prices increase people's wealth, in turn further stimulating consumption.

In sum, the transmission mechanism for monetary policy operates through many channels, some of central importance, and some minor. In the remainder of this section, we will simplify by focusing on the planned investment schedule as the key element of the transmission mechanism. A more complete analysis would show other elements at work as well.

## SHORT-RUN EFFECTS OF MONETARY POLICY

Figure 13.2 shows the interest-investment transmission mechanism at work in response to a one-time expansion in the money stock.

Initially the monetary sector is in equilibrium at point $E_1$ in part (a) of the figure. The money supply curve is in the position $MS_1$, and the money demand curve is at $MD_1$; thus, the equilibrium nominal interest rate is $R_1$. According to the planned-investment schedule in part (b), interest rate $R_1$ will result in a level of real planned investment indicated by $I_1$. This level of planned investment is built into aggregate demand curve $AD_1$ in part (c) along with given conditions regarding consumption, government purchases, and net exports. The initial equilibrium point in part (c) is thus $e_1$, at the intersection of $AD_1$ and the aggregate supply curve, AS. Equilibrium real output is $y_1$, and the price level is $P_1$.

Now assume that the Fed raises its target value for the money stock. This is shown in part (a) of Figure 13.2 as a rightward shift of the money supply curve to the position $MS_2$. The shift is accomplished by means of an injection of new reserves into the banking system via open market purchases.

## FIGURE 13.2   SHORT-RUN EFFECTS OF EXPANSIONARY MONETARY POLICY

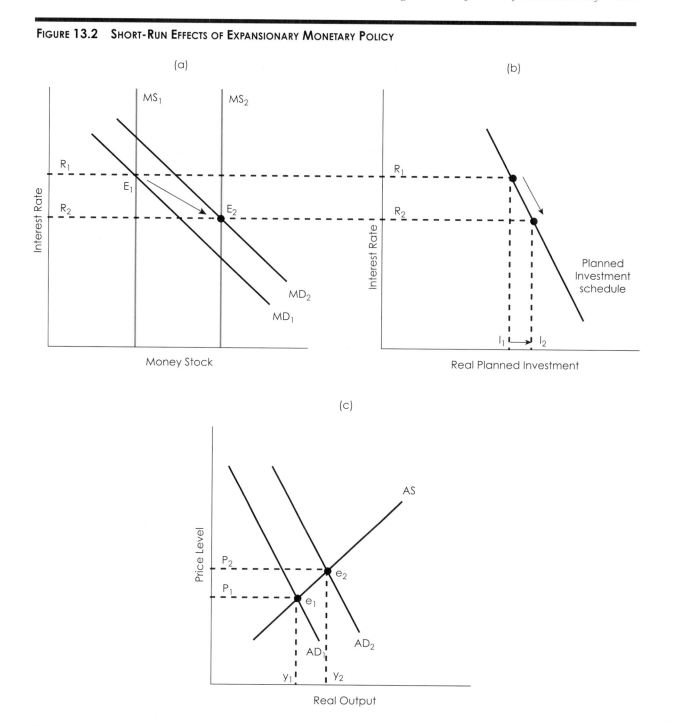

A one-time increase in the money stock shifts the money supply curve from MS$_1$ to MS$_2$. The interest rate begins to fall. Real planned investment begins to increase as the economy moves down and to the right along the planned-investment schedule. The increase in planned investment shifts the aggregate demand curve from AD$_1$ to AD$_2$, raising real output and the price level. The resulting rise in nominal domestic income shifts the money demand curve to the right from MD$_1$ to MD$_2$. This shift is enough to limit the drop in the interest rate but not sufficient to prevent it altogether. In the new short-run equilibrium, the interest rate is lower and real investment, real output, and the price level are all higher than they were initially.

As banks compete to put their new reserves to work, the interest rate falls. The falling interest rate lowers the opportunity cost of investment; thus, firms move downward and to the right along the planned-investment schedule shown in part (b). The increase in real planned investment, in turn, causes the aggregate demand curve to shift to the right, as shown in part (c). In response to the boost in demand, real output and the price level both increase and the economy moves upward and to the right along its short-run aggregate supply curve.

As the economy expands, the increase in prices and real output causes nominal domestic income to rise. Bringing the story full circle, the rise in nominal domestic income causes the money demand curve to shift to the right, from $MD_1$ to $MD_2$. This limits the fall in the interest rate, but the curve does not shift enough to prevent the interest rate from falling somewhat. The monetary sector comes into equilibrium at point $E_2$, where the new money supply and demand curves intersect. At the new equilibrium interest rate, $R_2$, real planned investment is $I_2$. This level of planned investment, together with the same underlying conditions as before regarding real consumption, government purchases, and net exports, puts the aggregate demand curve in the position $AD_2$. The new short-run equilibrium for the economy thus is $e_2$ in part (c), where real domestic product is $y_2$ and the price level is $P_2$.

To summarize, expansionary monetary policy has the following effects in the short run:

1.  A reduction in the interest rate
2.  An increase in the level of real output
3.  An increase in the price level

Contractionary policy produces an opposite set of short-run effects, as can also be shown using Figure 13.2. Starting at $E_2$ in the monetary sector, the Fed lowers its money stock target, shifting the money supply curve to the left. All the arrows are now reversed. A rising interest rate causes a reduction in planned investment. Falling planned investment shifts the aggregate demand curve to the left, causing prices and real output to fall. This, in turn, means that nominal income declines, causing the money demand curve to shift to the left as well, but not enough to prevent some increase in the interest rate. In the new short-run equilibrium, the monetary sector returns to $E_1$ and the economy as a whole returns to $e_1$.

## LONG-RUN EFFECTS AND THE NEUTRALITY OF MONEY

Previously we explained the distinction between the positively sloped short-run aggregate supply curve and the vertical long-run aggregate supply curve. Movements along the short-run curve are based on firms' expectation that input prices will not change immediately in response to a change in aggregate demand. However, a change in the prices of final goods will eventually affect the level of input prices. As the actual and expected values of input prices adjust to changes in the prices of final goods, the short-run aggregate supply curve shifts upward until the economy returns to equilibrium at the natural level of real output.

The economy will undergo such a process of long-run adjustment when the money stock changes and then remains at its new level. This process is shown in Figure 13.3.

As Figure 13.3 shows, expansionary monetary policy lowers interest rates and stimulates aggregate demand. As the aggregate demand curve shifts rightward, from $AD_1$ to $AD_2$, the economy moves to a new short-run equilibrium at $e_2$. Now let us see what happens next.

As the economy moves from $e_1$ to $e_2$, the average level of final-goods prices increases. After a time, this causes input prices to increase as well. This happens partly because some goods serve as both inputs and final goods and partly because the rise in the price level raises the cost of living, putting upward pressure on wage rates. Once this process begins to affect firms' expectations regarding input prices, the assumption

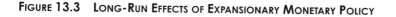

**FIGURE 13.3    LONG-RUN EFFECTS OF EXPANSIONARY MONETARY POLICY**

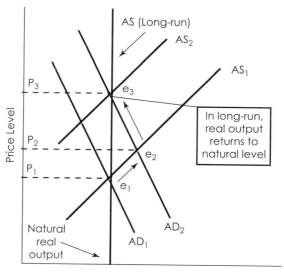

A one-time increase in the money stock causes real output to rise temporarily above its natural level, reaching point $e_2$. The economy cannot remain at this point indefinitely, however. As expected input prices begin to adjust upward, the aggregate supply curve will shift from $AS_1$ to $AS_2$. The economy will move along aggregate demand curve $AD_2$ until it reaches a new long-run equilibrium at $e_3$. As it does so, nominal domestic income will continue to rise, pushing interest rates up until they return to their initial level. Thus, in the long run, a one-time increase in the money stock will only induce a proportional increase in the price level and leave real output and the interest rate unchanged. This result is known as the *neutrality of money.*

underlying the initial short-run aggregate supply curve, $AS_1$, no longer holds. The price level rises above the level that it reached at $e_2$. The short-run aggregate supply curve shifts upward to $AS_2$. As it does so, the economy moves up and to the left along aggregate demand curve $AD_2$ until it returns to the natural level of real output at $e_3$. At that point both final-goods prices and input prices have adjusted upward in proportion to the initial increase in the money stock. For example, if the money stock increases by 10 percent, both final-goods prices and input prices will also increase by 10 percent.

For reasons discussed in the preceding chapter, the aggregate demand curve is relatively inelastic. Therefore, as the economy moves up and to the left along the curve, the percentage increase in price is greater than the percentage decrease in real output, which means that nominal domestic income and product will increase. In the monetary sector, the increase in nominal domestic income will put upward pressure on real interest rates, eventually pushing them all the way back up to the level they were at before expansionary monetary policy was undertaken. Real planned investment, which had increased while interest rates were lower, decreases again as interest rates rise until investment, too, is back where it started.

The preceding analysis shows that a one-time increase in the money stock has the following long-run effects:

1. An increase in the equilibrium levels of both final-goods and input prices in proportion to the change in the money stock
2. No change in the equilibrium level of real output
3. No change in the equilibrium interest rate

**Neutrality of Money**

The proposition that in the long run a one-time change in the money stock affects only the price level and not real output, employment, interest rates, or real planned investment.

This set of conclusions is often referred to as the principle of the **neutrality of money**. Money is neutral in the sense that one-time changes in its level do not affect the long-run equilibrium values of real variables such as real output, real planned investment, employment, or real interest rates. In the long run, a one-time change in the money stock affects only price levels.

The principle of the neutrality of money has a long history in economics. It was stated clearly by Adam Smith's friend David Hume (see *Who Said It? Who Did It? 13.1*). It can also be stated in terms of the equation of exchange. If the terms are rearranged, the equation of exchange can be written in the form $P = MV/y$. As we know, the value of velocity depends on the interest rate. Because the long-run equilibrium value of the interest rate is not affected by a one-time change in the money stock, velocity, too, will be unaffected by such a change. Thus, the equation just given tells us that if $y$ is held constant at its natural level and $V$ is unchanged, a one-time change in the money stock will produce a proportional change in the price level. For example, a doubling of the money stock has the long-run effect of doubling the price level from $P_1$ to $P_3$.

# MONEY AND FISCAL POLICY

In Chapter 9, we examined the effects of fiscal policy on planned expenditure and the equilibrium level of real output. We saw that an increase in government purchases or a decrease in net taxes causes an increase in aggregate demand. Since that time, we have introduced the monetary sector, which links changes in money, real output, and the price level to interest rates, and from there to planned investment. Now, in this section, we will put all of this together to show how changes in fiscal policy interact with developments in the monetary sector.

## The Crowding-Out Effect

Figure 13.4 presents the expanded analysis of the effects of fiscal policy, taking the monetary sector into account. Initially the economy is in equilibrium at point $e_1$ in part (c). Real output is at its natural level, $y_1$; the price level is at $P_1$ and stable. The monetary sector, shown in part (a), is in equilibrium at $E_1$ with an interest rate of $R_1$. This interest rate results in real planned investment at the level $I_1$, as shown in part (b). This level of planned investment, together with consumption, government purchases, and net exports, determines the level of total planned expenditure.

## FIGURE 13.4 THE CROWDING-OUT EFFECT

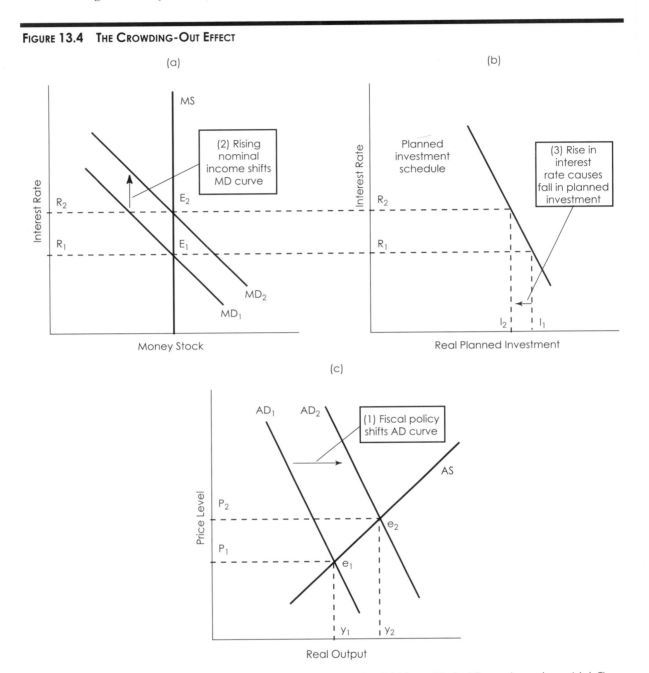

Expansionary fiscal policy shifts the aggregate demand curve to the right from $AD_1$ to $AD_2$, as shown in part (c). The resulting increase in nominal domestic income shifts the money demand curve to the right from $MD_1$ to $MD_2$, as shown in part (a). As interest rates rise, real planned investment will decrease and the economy will move to the left along the planned-investment schedule shown in part (b). The tendency of expansionary fiscal policy to reduce private planned investment is known as the *crowding-out effect*.

Now the government undertakes expansionary fiscal policy in the form of, say, an increase in real government purchases. (A cut in taxes or an increase in transfer payments would have essentially the same effects.) The result is a rightward shift of the aggregate demand curve. The economy begins to expand. The price level and real output both increase as the economy moves up and to the right along the short-run aggregate supply curve.

Next consider the effects on the monetary sector, shown in part (a) of Figure 13.4. Because both prices and real output are increasing, nominal domestic income must also be rising. The money demand curve therefore shifts to the right. With the money supply curve unchanged, interest rates rise. As they do so, firms move up and to the left along the planned-investment schedule shown in part (b). The level of real planned investment begins to fall, partly offsetting the initial expansionary effect of the decrease in government purchases.

**Crowding-out effect**

The tendency of expansionary fiscal policy to raise the interest rate and thereby cause a decrease in real planned investment.

This tendency for an increase in government purchases to cause a decrease in real private planned investment is known as the **crowding-out effect**. The crowding out of real investment spending limits the expansion of real output. In Figure 13.4 the economy reaches a new short-run equilibrium at point $e_2$ in part (c), where real output is at $y_2$ and the price level at $P_2$. This point corresponds to point $E_2$ in part (a) of the figure. In the new short-run equilibrium, both the price level and real output are lower than they would be if the indirect effect of government purchases on interest rates and investment had not been taken into account.

In an earlier chapter we discussed the effects of fiscal policy in terms of the multiplier effect. Now we see that because of crowding out, a given increase in government purchases shifts the aggregate demand curve by less than the expenditure multiplier would imply. Suppose, for example, that the expenditure multiplier is 4 and the change in government purchases is $100 billion. Multiplying these two numbers would lead one to expect a $400 billion shift. But in practice the shift is less because the expansionary effect of the increase in government purchases is partially offset by a decrease in private planned investment.[1] What is more, the price increases caused by the shift in aggregate demand push interest rates up still higher and further reduce planned investment.

## Fiscal Policy in the Long Run

Fiscal policy is no more able than monetary policy to permanently raise real domestic product above its natural level. Figure 13.5 picks up where Figure 13.4 left off; it shows the long-run effects of expansionary fiscal policy.

Expansionary policy has shifted the aggregate demand curve in part (c) from $AD_1$ to $AD_2$, moving the economy to a short-run equilibrium at $e_2$. Compared with the situation in the initial equilibrium, $e_1$, real output is above the natural level and the level of final-goods prices has increased. Over time, as the rise in the prices of final goods begins to affect the expected level of input prices, the short-run aggregate supply curve shifts upward. As the economy moves up and to the left along the aggregate demand curve $AD_2$, prices continue to rise, but real output falls back toward the natural level. A new long-run equilibrium is reached at $e_3$.

Because the aggregate demand curve is relatively inelastic, nominal domestic income increases in the course of the move from $e_2$ to $e_3$. As nominal domestic income rises, the money demand curve must shift farther to the right, from $MD_2$ to $MD_3$ in part (a) of Figure 13.5. This causes further crowding out of private planned investment. A continued increase in the interest rate pushes firms farther up and to the left along the planned-investment schedule, as shown in part (b). A new long-run equi-

**FIGURE 13.5  CROWDING OUT IN THE LONG RUN**

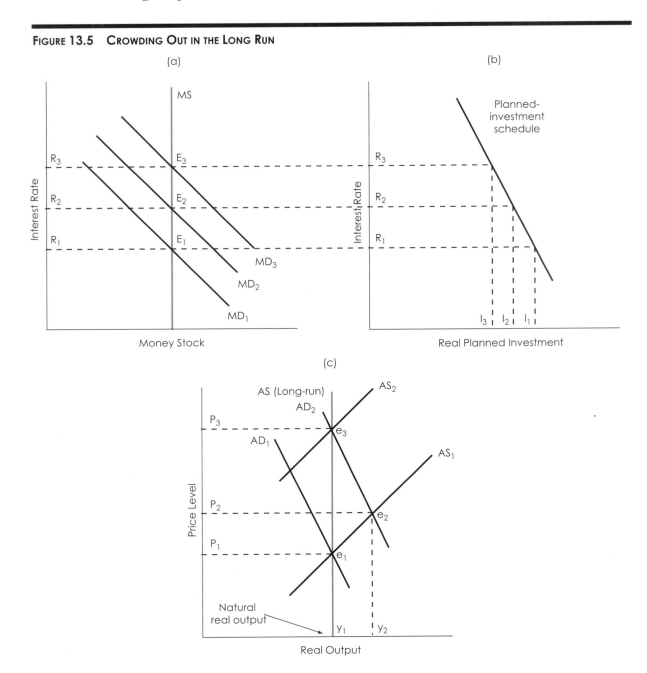

Point $e_2$ in part (c) of this figure is only a short-run equilibrium. As the aggregate supply curve shifts upward and the economy moves to a new long-run equilibrium at $e_3$, nominal domestic income continues to rise. The money demand curve shifts farther to the right from $MD_2$ to $MD_3$, as shown in part (a). As it does, the economy moves farther to the left along the planned-investment schedule, as shown in part (b). Thus, the crowding-out effect intensifies in the long run as real output returns to its natural level.

librium is not reached until the expansionary effects of the original fiscal policy action are completely crowded out. The aggregate demand curve remains in its new position, $AD_2$, but the economy's movement upward and to the left along this curve brings real domestic product all the way back to its natural level.

In one respect, the long-run effects of fiscal policy are similar to those of monetary policy: In both cases there is a higher price level in the new long-run equilibrium but no permanent change in real output. However, there is one important difference. Monetary policy is said to be "neutral" because a one-time increase in the money stock (and perhaps even a lasting change in the rate of money growth) has no long-run effects on any real variables—real output, planned investment, or real interest rates. But fiscal policy is not "neutral" in this sense. Even though expansionary fiscal policy does not change the long-run equilibrium level of real output, it does change the long-run equilibrium values of the real and nominal interest rates and real planned investment.

## The Importance of the Fiscal-Monetary Policy Mix

We have now seen that both fiscal and monetary policy can be used to stimulate aggregate demand and encourage economic expansion, but with opposite effects on interest rates and investment. Other things being equal, expansionary monetary policy tends to lower interest rates and encourage planned investment. On the other hand, tax cuts or increases in government purchases, while also stimulating aggregate demand, do so in a way that raises interest rates and reduces private planned investment—the crowding-out effect. All this suggests that in order to maintain the private investment in machinery, technology, and human resources needed for healthy economic growth in the long run, policy makers must carefully balance the mix of fiscal and monetary policy.

Unfortunately, the natural dynamics of democratic politics make it difficult to maintain the needed monetary-fiscal balance. When economic stimulus is needed, both the president and Congress are quick to suggest a fiscal remedy. After all, lower taxes and higher spending on schools, roads, or social benefits are a form of medicine that is always easy to swallow. The difficulty comes when the fiscal remedy has done its work and the economy is growing again. At that point, unless some fiscal restraint is exercised, monetary policy may be called upon to do too much of the work of slowing the growth of aggregate demand to avoid unwanted inflation. If a clash between excessively expansive fiscal policy and severe tightening of monetary policy does develop, interest rates will be forced up, investment will be discouraged, and the nation's long-term economic health will be threatened.

The issue of fiscal-monetary balance assumed particular importance in 2003–2004. Although strong economic growth usually causes the budget deficit to decrease, it failed to do so during the recovery from the 2001 recession—a recovery that was stimulated, in part, by aggressive tax cuts early in the administration of President

George W. Bush. *Economics in the News 13.1* summarizes some of the issues facing policy makers at that time.

## Monetarism vs. Keynesianism: A Historical Note

One of the key events in the formation of modern macroeconomics was the Great Depression, which affected the United States from 1929 to 1939. In the first four years of the Depression, real output and prices fell by more than a third and the unemployment rate rose to over a quarter of the labor force. Although there had been

---

⁕ ECONOMICS IN THE NEWS **13.1**
### DEALING WITH THE DEFICIT

Testifying before Congress in February 2004, Federal Reserve Chairman Alan Greenspan began by noting that "the most recent indicators suggest that the economy is off to a strong start in 2004, and prospects for sustaining the expansion in the period ahead are good." The economy was growing, inflation was low, and the financial health of businesses had improved. However, he went on to warn, "This favorable short-term outlook for the U.S. economy . . . is playing out against a backdrop of growing concern about the prospects for the federal budget." More specifically, the federal deficit, which had risen to $375 billion in fiscal year 2003 was projected to rise to a record level of over half a trillion dollars in fiscal year 2004.

Where did this enormous deficit come from? Greenspan noted three sources. First, the Iraq war added tens of billions of dollars to military spending. Second, there were increased expenditures on domestic programs, ranging from agricultural subsidies to education. Greenspan attributed these increases in discretionary spending partly to a weakening of fiscal discipline in Congress as a result of the budget surplus years of the 1990s.

Spending was not the whole story, however. The Bush Administration's tax cuts, which for a time had been helpful in stimulating the recovery from the 2001 recession, were now contributing to the growing budget deficit. Greenspan noted that the ratio of federal debt to GDP—a key indicator of long-term fiscal health—had already begun to edge up after falling during the 1990s. This meant a weakening of the starting point from which lawmakers would have to address future fiscal challenges.

The greatest of these challenges, in Greenspan's view, will be the growth in Social Security and Medicare costs as the country prepares for the retirement of the baby-boom generation. He warned "under a range of reasonably plausible assumptions about spending and taxes, we could be in a sit-uation in the decades ahead in which rapid increases in the unified budget deficit set in motion a dynamic in which large deficits result in ever-growing interest payments that augment deficits in future years. The resulting rise in the federal debt could drain funds away from private capital formation and thus over time slow the growth of living standards." In short, he warned of a looming crowding-out effect on an unprecedented scale.

What could be done? As Greenspan pointed out, the alternatives are not terribly attractive. Social Security and Medicare spending, under current law, are expected to rise from 7 percent of GDP in 2004 to 12 percent in 2030. Covering these outlays with increased taxes would not simply mean reversing the Bush tax cuts, but going beyond this to raise the tax burden to a historic high. Greenspan proposed instead slowing the growth of benefits by a combination of increased retirement age and revision of the formula under which retirees are protected against the effects of inflation. That suggestion, however, set off a storm of protest from all corners of the Washington political establishment, where Social Security cuts are regarded as the "third rail" of politics. But doing nothing and letting the deficit grow would force such a severe tightening of monetary policy that interest rates would rise sharply, threatening investment.

"The dimension of the challenge is enormous," Greenspan said in conclusion. "The one certainty is that the resolution of this situation will require difficult choices and that the future performance of the economy will depend on those choices."

Source: Testimony of Chairman Alan Greenspan, Economic outlook and current fiscal issues, before the Committee on the Budget, U.S. House of Representatives, February 25, 2004. Downloaded from www.federalreserve.gov.

serious economic contractions many times during the nineteenth century, there had never been a depression of this magnitude and duration. It forced economists to re-examine their theories from the ground up.

John Maynard Keynes (*Who Said It? Who Did It? 7.1*) was the most influential theorist of the Depression era. Among other things, he had clear views on the relationship between monetary and fiscal policy. Certainly Keynes recognized that monetary policy could affect interest rates, interest rates planned investment, and planned investment GDP. But he thought these effects would be weak. "There are not many people," he wrote, "who will alter their way of living because the rate of interest has fallen from 5 to 4 percent."[2]

If interest rates had little effect on investment, Keynes thought, investment might remain inadequate to bring the economy to full employment even if nominal interest rates fell near zero, as they can during a severe contraction. Even if the central bank greatly increased bank reserves and the money supply, people would simply accumulate liquid assets rather than using them to finance investment in plants and equipment. Keynes called this situation a **liquidity trap**. (The *Case for Discussion* at the end of this chapter explores the possible relevance of the liquidity trap to low-inflation economies like Japan and the United States today.)

If a liquidity trap made monetary policy powerless during a severe contraction, what could policy makers do to return the economy to full employment? For Keynes and his followers, the answer was clear: An increase in government purchases should be used to fill the gap between the actual and full-employment aggregate demand. Keynes did not think that monetary policy would always be ineffective. After the economy returned to full employment and interest rates rose back to normal levels, and even higher, in times when an overheated economy brought on inflation, monetary policy would play its traditional role. But because of the depression context in which Keynes wrote, the special case of "impotent monetary policy—potent fiscal policy" became the best remembered of his ideas.

After World War II many Keynesian economists forecast a new depression and economic stagnation. They thought that private investment would dry up with the end of wartime government spending. They were wrong: The postwar recovery of the United States and Western Europe was rapid. Central banks in most of the major economies pursued easy monetary policies during those years, and inflation was more widespread than depression. The countries that were able to control inflation did so only by using standard policies of monetary restraint. Economists began to take renewed interest in the role of money in the economy.

The new emphasis on money was strongest among a group of economists led by Milton Friedman (*Who Said It? Who Did It? 13.2*). Friedman's research led him to think that movements in the money supply had a much greater effect on economic events, even under depression conditions, than the early Keynesians had been willing to admit. Because of the emphasis Friedman and his followers placed on monetary policy, their school of thought came to be known as **monetarism**.

**Liquidity trap**

A situation in which interest rates near zero lead to accumulation of liquid assets instead of stimulating planned investment.

**Monetarism**

A school of economics that emphasizes the importance of changes in the money stock as determinants of changes in real output and the price level.

~ WHO SAID IT? WHO DID IT? 13.2

## MILTON FRIEDMAN AND MONETARISM

In October 1976, Milton Friedman received the Nobel Memorial Prize in economics, becoming the sixth American to win or share that honor. Few people were surprised. Most people wondered why he had had to wait so long. Perhaps it was because Friedman has built his career outside the economics establishment, challenging almost every major doctrine of that profession.

Friedman was born in New York in 1912, the son of immigrant garment workers. He attended Rutgers University, where he came under the influence of Arthur Burns, then a young assistant professor and later chairman of the Federal Reserve Board. From Burns, Friedman learned the importance of empirical work in economics. Statistical testing of all theory and policy prescriptions became a key feature of Friedman's later work. From Rutgers, Friedman went to the University of Chicago for an M.A. and then east again to Columbia University, where he received his Ph.D. in 1946. He returned to Chicago to teach. There he and his colleagues of the "Chicago school" of economics posed a major challenge to the economists of the "eastern establishment."

If one could single out a recurrent theme in Friedman's work it would be his belief that the market economy works—and that it works best when left alone. This can be seen in his best-known work, *A Monetary History of the United States*. Written with Anna Schwartz, this book attacks two major tenets of Keynesian economics: (1) that the market economy is unstable without the guiding hand of government, and (2) that monetary policy was tried and found useless as a cure for the Great Depression. Friedman and Schwartz found both beliefs to be far from the truth. "The Great Depression," Friedman later wrote, "far from being a sign of the inherent instability of the private enterprise system, is a testament to how much harm can be done by mistakes on the part of a few men when they wield vast power over the monetary system of the country."

Friedman strongly favors a hands-off policy by government in almost every area. In his view, the problem is not that government is evil by nature, but that so many policies end up having the opposite of their intended effects: "The social reformers who seek through politics to do nothing but serve the public interest invariably end up serving some private interest that was not part of their intention to serve. They are led by an invisible hand to serve a private interest." Transport regulation, public education, agricultural subsidies, and housing programs are among the many policy areas in which Friedman believes that the government has done more harm than good and for which a free competitive market would do better.

Friedman's research led to a reinterpretation of the Great Depression. In *A Monetary History of the United States*, Friedman and Anna J. Schwartz explained why what began as a fairly ordinary business contraction in the summer of 1929 turned into a four-year downward spiral from which complete recovery took an entire decade.[3] Their analysis focused on the collapse of the banking system and a precipitous decline in the money stock early in the Depression. In the monetarist view, it was not the inherent impotence of monetary policy that caused the Great Depression, but rather the terrible impact on the economy of serious monetary policy errors. If the Fed had used its policy instruments—especially open market purchases of securities—more aggressively, the downturn that began in 1929 might never have been more than a brief cyclical contraction.

The debate between monetarists and Keynesians over monetary vs. fiscal policy raged throughout the 1960s and 1970s. Some monetarists went so far as to stand Keynes on his head, insisting that the crowding-out effect would be so strong and complete that fiscal policy would be impotent to affect the economy, so that "only money matters." On the other side, some Keynesians advocated using fiscal policy to fine-tune the economy with a degree of short-term precision that now seems implausible. In recent years, the debate has died out or taken other directions than the oversimplified "monetary vs. fiscal policy" issue. Mainstream economic policy makers in all countries today acknowledge the importance of prudent management of both monetary and fiscal policy if the goals of long-term economic growth and stability are to be achieved.

# FISCAL POLICY IN AN OPEN ECONOMY

In earlier discussions, we have seen that monetary policy affects imports, exports, capital flows, and the foreign-exchange value of the dollar. It does so partly via effects on domestic income, which in turn affect the level of imports, and partly via effects on interest rates, which in turn affect capital flows. In this chapter we have shown that fiscal policy also affects both domestic income and interest rates. This being the case, we would expect fiscal policy also to have international implications—and so it does.

## Leakages and Injections

The international implications of fiscal policy can be understood in terms of the concepts of leakages and injections from the circular flow. The basic relationship between leakages and injections in equation form is as follows:

$$S + T + M = I + G + X$$

where S stands for saving, T for net taxes, M for imports, I for investment, G for government purchases, and X for exports. For our present purposes, it is useful to rearrange the terms of the equation in the following form:

$$(X - M) = (T - G) + (S - I)$$

The terms of this equation can be interpreted as follows: I and S, as before, stand for investment and saving. The term $(T - G)$ represents the government budget. If the government spends (G) more than it collects in tax revenue (T), then there is a *government budget deficit* and $(T - G)$ will be a negative number. The term $(X - M)$ can be interpreted in two ways. First, it represents the economy's *current account*—the amount by which exports of goods and services exceeds imports. If the U.S. imports more than it exports, then $(X - M)$ will be a negative number and there is a *current account deficit*. Second, it represents net capital flows. An excess of imports over exports must be financed by a *net capital inflow* into the U.S.—that is, by net borrowing from abroad plus net sales of assets to foreign buyers—so that the value of the current account deficit and the value of capital inflows are equal.[4]

The modified leakages-injections equation also has a simple interpretation in terms of the circular flow of income and product (see Figure 5.6). The terms S, domestic saving, and X – M, net capital inflows, represent *sources* of funds to financial markets; they appear in the circular flow diagram as the two arrows pointing into financial markets. The terms I, investment, and G – T, the government budget deficit, represent *uses* of funds drawn from financial markets; they are shown in the circular flow diagram by the two arrows pointing outward from financial markets.

## Sources of a Current Account Deficit

The leakages-injections equation shows that the economy will experience a current account deficit under either of the following two circumstances:

1. If domestic investment is high relative to domestic savings.
2. If the government runs a budget deficit.

The current account deficit is not necessarily a bad thing. If the U.S. has investment opportunities that attract foreign capital inflow, this will correspond to a current account deficit. On the other hand, a current account deficit could reflect poor fiscal management of the federal budget. The following discussion considers the U.S.

current account deficit and its sources since the early 1980s. Figure 13.6 shows the path of the federal budget and the current account since 1960.

## The Twin Deficits of the 1980s

In which of these ways did the U.S. economy respond to the increase in the government budget deficit during the 1980s? An examination of the evidence suggests that much of the adjustment was borne by the current account deficit. This gave rise to the phenomenon of the "twin deficits"—the record deficits in the federal budget *and* the balance of payments on current account that were both recorded in the mid-1980s.

Figure 13.6 shows the path of the two deficits over time. Until the 1970s, the federal budget and the current account were both close to balance. In the early 1970s, and then more decisively in the early 1980s, the federal budget moved sharply into deficit, followed shortly by a move toward deficit in the current account. The mecha-

**FIGURE 13.6   THE U.S. CURRENT ACCOUNT AND FEDERAL BUDGET (1960–2003)**

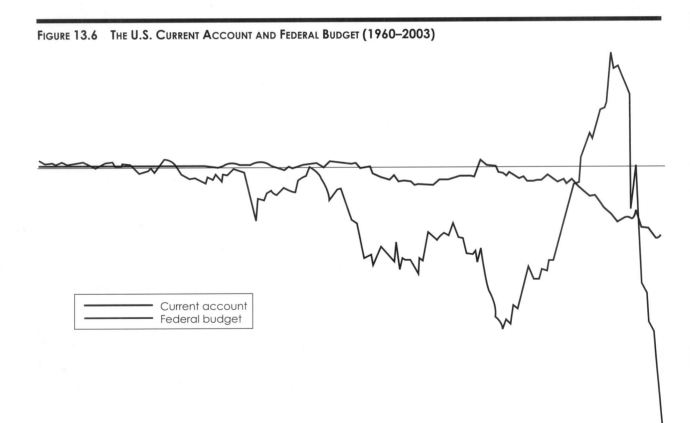

As this chart shows, until the 1970s the U.S. government budget and current account were close to balance on average. Beginning in the 1970s and then more strongly in the 1980s, the government budget swung toward deficit. The current account balance, although lagging somewhat behind, moved in the same direction, giving rise to the twin deficits. In 1997, as the federal budget moved into surplus, the current account deficit still grew. When the government experienced budget deficits again beginning in 2002, the current account continued to move further into deficit.

Source: Bureau of Economic Analysis, U.S. Department of Commerce, 2003.

nisms giving rise to the lagged association between the federal budget deficit and the current account deficit can be summarized as follows:

1. The move toward fiscal stimulus raised U.S. interest rates.
2. Higher U.S. interest rates encouraged a net capital inflow, which, in turn, increased the demand for dollars in the foreign-exchange market and raised the foreign-exchange value of the dollar.
3. The higher value of the dollar encouraged imports and discouraged exports, thereby (with a lag) widening the U.S. current account deficit.

There were other changes in leakages and injections as well during this period. Saving and investment both declined in the 1980s, although not at the same rates; if saving and investment had changed exactly in step with each other, the current account deficit would have tracked the budget deficit more closely. By the late 1980s, the increase in net capital inflow and decline in the federal budget deficit allowed investment to recover somewhat despite a further decline in domestic saving.

The twin deficits have provided additional ammunition for critics of the budget priorities of the 1980s and early 1990s. Those priorities—increased outlays for entitlements and defense with no increase in the share of GDP going to taxes—were described in an earlier chapter. Critics charge that the resulting fiscal policy has left the nation burdened with debts owed to foreign lenders, has caused export industries to lose market share in an increasingly competitive world economy, and has starved domestic firms of investment capital via the crowding-out effect.

## The U.S. Current Account in the 1990s and Beyond

In 1991 and 1992, the current account and federal budget deficits broke with the earlier pattern and moved in opposite directions. One cause was the U.S. government's receipt in 1991 of huge payments from foreign governments that had agreed to share the burden of the 1990–1991 Gulf War. In addition, the 1990–1991 recession was characterized by high interest rates, driving up the cost of borrowing. Consequently, private investment fell to a new low during this period.

Beginning in 1992, the federal budget deficit began to shrink, corresponding to the longest peacetime expansion experienced in the U.S. Expansions help reduce the need for government expenditure and increase the government's tax revenue because people are earning more income. As a consequence, the federal budget experienced surpluses by 1997.

However, these federal budget surpluses did not correspond to a recovery in the current account. Indeed, the current account deficit grew larger during this period, with a sharp decline just as the federal budget was balanced in 1997. From the injections-leakages equation above, we see that this is the result of high investment combined with a continued decline in domestic saving. (As shown in Figure 13.7, the U.S. personal savings rate declined steadily during the late 1980s, but fell sharply through

FIGURE 13.7   U.S. PERSONAL SAVINGS RATE (1960–2003) (SHADED AREAS INDICATE TWIN DEFICITS)

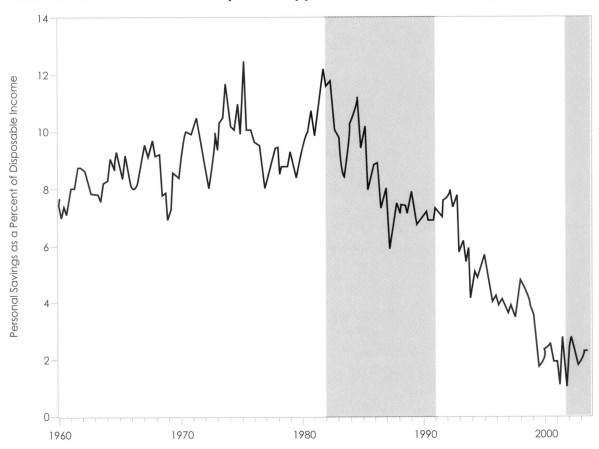

As this chart shows, until the 1970s, the U.S. government budget and current account were close to balance on average. Beginning in the 1970s and then more strongly in the 1980s, the government budget swung toward deficit. The current account balance, although lagging somewhat behind, moved in the same direction, giving rise to the twin deficits. In 1997, as the federal budget moved into surplus, the current account deficit still grew. When the government experienced budget deficits again beginning in 2002, the current account continued to decrease.

Source: Bureau of Economic Analysis, U.S. Department of Commerce, 2003.

the 1990s.) As the U.S. economy expanded, so did investment opportunities that attracted a net capital inflow into the U.S., reflected in a further decline in the U.S. current account.

Following the September 2001 terrorist attacks, wars in Afghanistan and Iraq, tax cuts passed by President Bush and Congress, and the 2001 recession, the government experienced budget deficits again beginning in 2002. As the "twin deficit" concept would lead us to expect, the increased budget deficit has been accompanied by a further move toward deficit on the current account. The current account deficit would have had to increase even more if not partially offset by a small increase in saving and a decrease in investment relative to the high rates of the 1990s.

We can summarize the changes over the decade up to 2004 as follows: In the earlier part of this period, the large financial inflows associated with the current account deficit represented the response of foreign investors to exceptional U.S. private investment opportunities during the technology boom of the 1990s. Later, during the administration of George W. Bush, the current account deficits and associated net financial inflows grew further, but their composition changed. Instead of private inflows to finance growth and capital formation, by 2003 and 2004 much of the inflow took the form of purchases of U.S. government securities by foreign central banks—especially those of China and Japan. How long the United States can continue to count on such financing for its budget deficits remains unclear at the time this is written. Basing their reasoning on the leakages and injections equation, some economists warn that if Asian central banks were to stop financing U.S. budget deficits, interest rates in the United States would rise sharply.

# SUMMARY

1. **How do changes in the money stock affect real output, the price level, and unemployment?** An increase in the money stock initially lowers interest rates. The resulting increase in real planned investment shifts the aggregate demand curve to the right. As the economy moves up and to the right along the aggregate supply curve, in the short run real output increases, the price level increases, and the unemployment rate falls. A decrease in the money stock has the opposite effects.

2. **What is meant by the neutrality of money?** An increase in the money stock can cause real output to rise above its natural level only in the short run. As input prices rise, the economy returns to the natural level of real output at a higher price level than initially. In the new equilibrium the prices of both final goods and inputs will have changed in proportion to the increase in the money stock, but the values of all real variables—interest rates, planned investment, real output, and employment—will be unaffected. This proposition is known as the *neutrality of money*.

3. **How does fiscal policy affect interest rates and planned investment?** Expansionary fiscal policy shifts the aggregate demand curve to the right. Real output and the price level rise in the short run, as does nominal domestic income. The increase in nominal domestic income shifts the money demand curve to the right, causing both real and nominal interest rates to increase. This rise in interest rates *crowds out* some real planned investment. As the economy returns to a long-run equilibrium at the natural level of real output, a further rise in the price level causes nominal domestic income to rise still higher, putting additional upward pressure on interest rates. Thus, there is a further depressing effect on real investment, and the crowding-out effect intensifies in the long run.

4. **How did Keynesian and monetarist economists view the relationship of monetary to fiscal policy?** Keynes and his early followers thought that the transmission mechanism from money to GDP via interest rates and investment was weak, especially under depression conditions. They thought that the economy would be unable to recover from a depression on its own and that only expansionary fiscal policy could do the job. After World War II,

*monetarists,* led by Milton Friedman, argued that monetary policy is important even under depression conditions. They saw the Fed's policy mistakes following the 1929 crash as a major factor in the length and severity of the Depression. The debate over the relative importance of monetary and fiscal policy continued throughout the 1960s and 1970s. Today most economists see proper management of both monetary and fiscal policy as essential to economic stability and prosperity.

5. **What are the effects of fiscal policy in an open economy?** In a closed economy, assuming no change in the saving rate, an increase in the government budget deficit will lead to a change in investment—the crowding-out effect. In an open economy, the economy may compensate for an increase in the budget deficit through an increase in the current account deficit and a corresponding rise in net capital inflows. This appears to have happened in the United States in the 1980s, when the economy experienced "twin deficits"— a federal budget deficit and a current account deficit. When the federal budget balance moved into surplus in the late 1990s, current account deficits continued because of high investment relative to saving in the United States. In the early 2000s, the twin deficits returned.

## KEY TERMS

Transmission mechanism

Planned-investment schedule

Neutrality of money

Crowding-out effect

Liquidity trap

Monetarism

## PROBLEMS AND TOPICS FOR DISCUSSION

1. **Examining the lead-off case.** Using government data sources such as the *Economic Report of the President* or current news sources, determine what has happened to inflation, the unemployment rate, the rate of growth of real GDP, and the federal budget deficit since 2000.

2. **Long-run effects of contractionary monetary policy.** Use a set of diagrams similar to Figures 13.2 and 13.3 to trace the long-run effects of a one-time contraction of the money stock beginning from equilibrium at the natural level of real output.

3. **Effects of a tax increase.** Use a set of diagrams similar to Figure 13.5 to trace the effects of a contractionary fiscal policy such as a tax increase. What happens to real output, unemployment, the price level, interest rates, and real planned investment in the short run and in the long run?

4. **Crowding out and the money supply curve.** Use a set of diagrams similar to Figure 13.4 to investigate how the crowding-out effect is influenced by the shape of the money supply curve. First use a positively sloped curve and then a horizontal curve. Discuss the policy implications of your results.

5. **The twin deficits.** Using data sources such as the *Economic Report of the President* or the *Survey of Current Business,* determine what has happened to the current account deficit and the federal budget deficit, both expressed as a percentage of GDP. Have the two deficits moved in the same direction or in opposite directions? Discuss in terms of the theory presented in this chapter.

## CASE FOR DISCUSSION

### Germany's Budget Woes

For decades following World War II, the Germany economy was the engine that pulled the train of European economic growth. But today, the engine is on a sidetrack. The German economy is in its worst slump in half a century, and politicians face a dilemma in deciding how to get things moving again.

The issue of fiscal-monetary policy mix lies at the heart of the German dilemma. As the chart below shows, since the growth slowdown started, the German government has let its budget deficit increase, from a small surplus in 2000 to a level near 4 percent of GDP today. To some extent, the growth of the deficit reflects cyclical factors—a decline in tax revenues and an increase in jobless benefits as the economy has slumped. But it also reflects a conscious policy decision in Berlin to use tax relief and increased spending to stimulate aggregate demand in order to get growth going again.

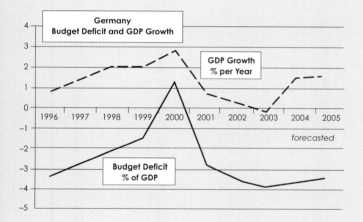

Unfortunately, Germany's fiscal policy has run head first into budget rules set by the EU for the 12 member economies of the euro zone. Those rules state that a country must not run a budget deficit of more than 3 percent of GDP, subject to potentially large fines. Ironically, Germany itself insisted on such strong rules when the euro zone was formed, fearing irresponsible fiscal policy on the part of some of its European neighbors.

Setting a limit for budget deficits would make sense if a country that had hit the limit, but still needed to stimulate aggregate demand, could simply switch its mix away from fiscal policy toward an easing of monetary conditions. But doing so lies beyond the power of the German central bank. Since Ger-

many gave up its beloved mark in favor of the euro, there is no way to ease German monetary conditions without also easing them for the eleven other countries of the euro zone. And the European central bank, so far, has refused to do so.

The reason is inflation. Germany's own inflation is low, expected barely to exceed 1 percent in 2004. As recently as the end of 2003, there were fears of actual deflation. But elsewhere in the euro zone things are different. Several other EU countries, including Greece, Spain, Portugal, and Italy, have inflation rates that are above the 2 percent target set by the European Central Bank. Any shift toward more expansionary monetary policy for the benefit of Germany would quickly spill over into those countries and push them even higher above the inflation ceiling.

Is there a way out? Not an easy one. Late in 2003, Germany, together with France, another high-deficit euro-zone member, reached an uneasy compromise with EU policy makers that will let them continue to violate the deficit ceiling without invoking the feared penalties. But there will be no monetary bale-out, and prospects for German growth in 2004 and 2005 look only marginally brighter than in the preceding three years. In the long run, structural reforms of labor markets and tax law may make the German economy flexible enough to start growing again while meeting EU macroeconomic targets. But don't expect that to happen any time soon. For the foreseeable future, the tension between fiscal policy, set at the level of country governments, and monetary policy, set for the euro zone as a whole, will surely continue.

## QUESTIONS

1. In the days when Germany had its own currency, the mark, how would a switch toward smaller deficits and faster growth of the money stock have affected interest rates? Investment? Aggregate demand? GDP?

2. Some economists think a uniform deficit limit of 3 percent of GDP for all euro zone countries is

unrealistic. They say the limit should be higher for countries that are in recession. Explain how an alternative "full employment deficit limit" might be defined and implemented.

3. In the United States, the Fed sets monetary policy for the whole country, but each state has a substantial role in determining taxes and government spending. In what ways do you think the situation of an individual state that grows slower than the U.S. national average is similar to that of Germany within the EU? In what ways does it differ? Discuss.

## END NOTES

1. In an earlier chapter we assumed, as a working approximation, that the change in government purchases times the expenditure multiplier would equal the horizontal shift in the aggregate demand curve. Now we can see why this was only an approximation: There would be some crowding out even if the economy moved horizontally to the right on the aggregate supply and demand diagram with the price level unchanged. Even with no change in the price level, there would be some increase in nominal domestic income as a result of the increase in real domestic product. That alone would be enough to shift the money demand curve to the right, although not as far as the shift to MD2 shown in Figure 13.4. Thus, the interest rate would rise somewhat, and there would be some crowding out of private investment. This fixed-price portion of the crowding-out effect keeps the aggregate demand curve from shifting to the right by the full amount of the change in government purchases times the multiplier. However, the amount of the shift can still be thought of as equal to the change in autonomous expenditure times the expenditure multiplier, provided that the change in autonomous expenditure is interpreted as the increase in government purchases minus the change in planned investment resulting from the fixed-price component of crowding out.

2. John Maynard Keynes, *The General Theory of Employment, Interest, and Money* (New York: Harcourt, Brace, and World, 1936), 94.

3. Milton Friedman and Anna Jacobson Schwartz, *A Monetary History of the United States, 1867–1960* (Princeton, NJ: Princeton University Press, 1963).

4. The concepts of current and capital account balances were introduced in an earlier chapter. This discussion simplifies matters somewhat by assuming that international transfer payments and the statistical discrepancy are both zero. It also ignores some technical differences in accounting conventions between the domestic income and product accounts and the balance of payments statistics.

# PART V

Price Stability,
Employment, and
Economic Growth

# Policies
# for Price
# Stability

*After reading this
chapter, you will
understand:*

1. How inflation or deflation can arise from changes in aggregate demand.
2. How inflation or deflation can arise from shifts in the short-run aggregate supply curve.
3. What types of policy can be used to achieve price stability.

*Before reading this
chapter, make sure you
know the meaning of:*

1. Indexation
2. Price level
3. Base year
4. Phillips curve
5. Okun's law
6. Liquidity trap

## THE GREAT INFLATION OF THE 1970S

If the 1930s were the decade of the Great Depression, the 1970s perhaps should be called the "Great Inflation." Like the Great Depression, the Great Inflation brought lasting changes to economic thought and policy. What went on in this turbulent decade?

The seeds of the Great Inflation were sown in the 1960s. Under President Lyndon Johnson, federal outlays for the Vietnam War rose steadily, but because the war was unpopular at home, Johnson was reluctant to raise taxes. Many economists see the resulting fiscal stimulus as a key factor in the inflation that followed in 1968. The inflation rate rose to 4.2 percent per year; in 1969, it reached 5.4 percent.[1] In comparison with what was to come, 5.4 percent inflation was moderate—but it was more than three times the 1.7 percent average rate for the decade from 1958 to 1967.

In 1970 and early 1971, the inflation rate continued to creep upward. Then, in August 1971, President Richard Nixon announced a dramatic new economic program. The centerpiece was a 90-day freeze on all prices and wages, followed by further wage and price restraints. This attempt to control prices worked for a time. The inflation rate fell in late 1971 and during 1972. Prices and wages were subject to some degree of control under three presidents for the rest of the decade.

However, in 1973, when the power of wage and price controls to restrain inflation was already waning, the world received a major inflationary shock. In the aftermath of a war with Israel, the Arab members of the Organization of Petroleum Exporting Countries (OPEC) doubled the price of oil—a major U.S. import and a key component of the consumer price index. Inflation accelerated again, with the added complication of retail price controls on gasoline, which led to long waiting lines at gas stations.

In 1974, the inflation rate reached 11 percent and the United States discovered an unpleasant new fact. In the past, inflation had been thought to have a silver lining in the form of low unemployment. But the nation then learned that it could suffer from both high unemployment and high inflation at the same time. In the 1974 to 1975 recession, the unemployment rate rose to nearly 9 percent while the inflation rate fell only slightly. A new concept was born: the "misery index," the sum of the rates of inflation and unemployment. The misery index hit a value of 18 during the 1974 to 1975 recession, and throughout the subsequent recovery it never fell below 13. This was miserable indeed compared with the indexes of 6 or lower to which people had grown accustomed in the 1960s.

Despite the fiscal stimulus of the Vietnam War and the inflationary shock of the oil crisis, the Fed could have curbed inflation by restraining the growth of the money stock. However, just as it had failed to prevent a drop in the money stock from 1929 to 1933, thereby worsening the Great Depression, during the 1970s the Fed failed to prevent rapid growth of the money stock, thus adding fuel to the Great Inflation.

Finally, in October 1979, the Fed put on the brakes and the economy subsequently went through the windshield. In 1980, as the economy entered a brief recession, both inflation and unemployment rose. The misery index soared to an all-time high of 20. On top of this, OPEC chose 1979 to 1980 to more than double the world oil price for the second time. After a temporary recovery from the 1980 recession, in 1981 the economy entered its most severe downturn since the Great Depression of the 1930s.

Inflation receded during the 1980s, and the misery index returned to single digits. More recently, inflation has been brought under control, remaining around 2 percent since the mid-1990s. Americans now read about inflation abroad and think complacently that "it can never happen here." In fact, the possibility of a deflation became a growing concern during the early twenty-first century.

⁓

THE UNITED STATES was not the only country affected by the Great Inflation of the 1970s. As Figure 14.1 shows, the median rate of inflation for all advanced economies rose into double digits for much of that decade before beginning to recede in the 1980s. In the developing world, inflation did not begin to come under control until the middle of the 1990s. In the previous chapter, we saw how Keynesian and monetarist interpretations of the Great Depression had a profound impact on the development of macroeconomic theory. In a similar way, the Great Inflation of the 1970s refocused macroeconomic theory on the problem of inflation. This chapter will look at key elements of macroeconomic theory and policy related to problems of price stability, including not only the problem of inflation but more recent concerns about deflation as well.

## INFLATION AND DEFLATION IN THE AGGREGATE SUPPLY AND DEMAND MODEL

Throughout this text we have refined our understanding of sources of shifts in the aggregate demand and supply curves. The sources of such shifts can be summarized as follows:

1. Shifts in the aggregate demand curve may originate in its real consumption, planned investment, government purchases, or net export components. Expansionary monetary or fiscal policy shifts the aggregate demand curve to the right; contractionary monetary or fiscal policy shifts it to the left.

FIGURE 14.1  CONSUMER PRICE INFLATION

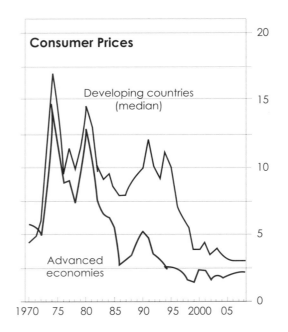

In the 1970s, inflation rates rose into double digits in both advanced and developing economies. In the former, inflation was brought under control by the end of the 1980s. In many developing countries serious inflation continued into the 1990s.

Source: IMF, *World Economic Outlook*, April 2003, Figure 1.1, p. 1.

2. The long-run aggregate supply curve is a vertical line drawn at the level of natural real output. A change in the level of natural real output shifts the curve.

3. The positively sloped short-run aggregate supply curve is drawn on the assumption that the expected level of input prices adjusts only gradually to changes in aggregate demand and in final goods prices. The height of the intersection of a short-run aggregate supply curve with the long-run aggregate supply curve indicates the expected level of input prices on which that short-run curve is based. An increase in the expected level of input prices shifts the short-run aggregate supply curve upward; a decrease in the expected level of input prices shifts it downward.

We now turn to some of the relationships among inflation, real output, and unemployment that can be derived by applying these principles to specified changes in economic conditions.

## Demand-Pull Inflation

We begin with the case of **demand-pull inflation**, by which we mean inflation caused by an upward shift in the aggregate demand curve while the short-run aggregate supply curve remains fixed or shifts upward at no more than an equal rate. We have

**Demand-pull inflation**

Inflation caused by an upward shift of the aggregate demand curve while the aggregate supply curve remains fixed or shifts upward at no more than an equal rate.

already encountered the simplest form of demand-pull inflation, which occurs when there is a one-time rightward shift in the aggregate demand curve beginning from an initial state of equilibrium. The response is a movement up and to the right along the short-run aggregate supply curve to a new short-run equilibrium. In the process, real output and the price level of final goods increase while the unemployment rate decreases. After a lag, expectations regarding input prices will adjust and the short-run aggregate supply curve will begin to shift upward. If the aggregate demand curve remains in its new position, the economy will move up and to the left along it to a new long-run equilibrium in which real output returns to its natural level.

However, a one-time expansionary policy action is not the only possibility. Instead, continuing expansionary fiscal or monetary policy may allow aggregate demand to keep growing. In this case, as the short-run aggregate supply curve is driven upward by firms' expectations of ever-higher input prices, the aggregate demand curve keeps pace with it. Real output does not fall back toward its natural level; rather, it is kept above that level by ongoing demand-pull inflation. This possibility is illustrated in Figure 14.2, where the economy follows a path from $E_1$ to $E_2$ to $E_3$ and beyond.

The scenario shown in Figure 14.2 has major implications for economic policy. In the short run, starting from a state of long-run equilibrium, an expansionary fiscal or monetary policy is effective in stimulating real economic growth and lower unemployment. The initial cost of such a policy is a small amount of inflation. However, the initial gains in real output can be sustained only at the cost of ongoing demand-pull inflation.

Once the initial benefits of the expansion have been realized, policy makers will face a dilemma. One choice is to stop the stimulus. If they do this, inflation will cease but output will fall back to its natural level, and unemployment will rise to its natural rate. The other alternative is to continue the expansionary fiscal or monetary policy. In that case, real output can be held above its natural level for some time and unemployment kept below its natural rate. Choosing this path, however, will mean year after year of inflation. Although it is not directly apparent from Figure 14.2, a rate of inflation that is steady in percentage terms from year to year may not be enough to hold unemployment below its natural rate. Later in the text we will show that under certain plausible assumptions regarding the way expectations of inflation are formed, inflation must accelerate to a higher percentage rate year after year to keep unemployment below its natural rate for an extended period.

**Cost-push inflation**

Inflation that is caused by an upward shift in the aggregate supply curve while the aggregate demand curve remains fixed or shifts upward more slowly.

## Cost-Push Inflation and Supply Shocks

Demand-pull inflation occurs when the aggregate demand curve shifts upward while the aggregate supply curve remains fixed or shifts upward at no more than an equal rate. However, inflation can also occur as a result of an upward shift in the aggregate supply curve while the aggregate demand curve stays in place or shifts upward more slowly. This type of inflation is known as **cost-push inflation**, because upward shifts

**FIGURE 14.2   DEMAND-PULL INFLATION**

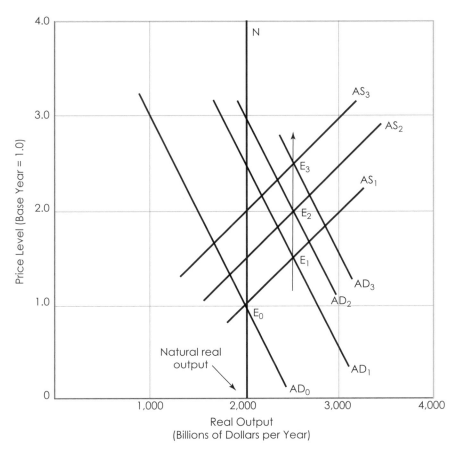

Demand-pull inflation begins when a rightward shift in the aggregate demand curve pulls the economy up and to the right along the short-run aggregate supply curve, from $E_0$ to $E_1$ in this figure. Subsequently, the short-run aggregate supply curve will begin to shift upward as increases in final-goods prices filter through to cause expected increases in wages and other input prices. If expansionary policy continues to shift the aggregate demand curve upward, as shown here, real output can be kept above its natural level, which corresponds to the long-run aggregate supply curve N, for a sustained period. However, the cost of maintaining this high level of real output is inflation.

**Supply shock**

An event, such as an increase in the price of imported oil, a crop failure, or a natural disaster, that raises input prices for all or most firms and pushes up workers' costs of living.

in the aggregate supply curve are linked with increases in firms' expected costs of production, which in turn, depend strongly on input prices.

**Supply shocks** are one source of cost-push inflation. A supply shock is an event independent of changes in aggregate demand that raises the average level of input prices that firms expect. The sudden increases in the cost of imported oil that hit the U.S. economy in 1974 and from 1979 to 1980 are examples of such events. A rise in the price of oil increases expected input prices through several channels. First, petroleum products themselves are inputs to many production processes in such forms as heating fuel, motor fuel for transportation, and chemical feedstocks. Second, firms anticipate that prices of substitute energy sources, such as natural gas and electric power, will rise when oil prices rise. Finally, firms anticipate that increased prices for oil and other energy sources will affect the cost of living and that nominal wages will sooner or later have to be adjusted to reflect those changes.

The oil price increases of the 1970s were particularly dramatic examples of supply shocks, but lesser supply shocks occur frequently. The effects of the weather on farming, construction, and transportation may increase firms' anticipated costs of doing business. Natural disasters, such as earthquakes or hurricanes, raise costs of doing business in the affected areas and may affect input prices in wider areas via changes in demand for such key inputs as construction materials. Finally, changes in the foreign-exchange value of the dollar can affect the prices of inputs that are traded on world markets. A fall in the value of the dollar relative to foreign currencies makes imported inputs (say, imported cotton used by a U.S. textile mill) more expensive; it may also increase demand for U.S. exports of intermediate goods such as chemicals that are traded on the world market, thereby driving up their prices.

Supply shocks can work both ways, however. The increases in world oil prices in the 1970s raised input prices expected by U.S. firms, but the subsequent decreases in oil prices during the early 1980s reduced expected input prices. Similarly, unusually good weather leading to bumper crops or an increase in the foreign-exchange value of the dollar would tend to cause a decrease in expected input prices. During the mid- to late-1990s, the U.S. experienced high economic growth accompanied by low inflation rates. Many economists have explained the decline of inflation in the 1990s in terms of beneficial supply shocks. Americans enjoyed historically low oil prices and technological progress that substantially reduced production costs.

Figure 14.3 illustrates the effects of a supply shock. In the figure the economy begins in long-run equilibrium at $E_0$. The price level for final goods and the expected level of input prices are equal at 1.0, and real output is at its natural level of $2,000 billion. At this point, something—say an increase in world oil prices—causes an increase in the average expected level of input prices. As firms adjust their expectations, the short-run aggregate supply curve shifts upward from $AS_0$ to $AS_1$, as shown in Figure 14.3. With the higher expected level of input prices but no matching increase in aggregate demand, firms must revise their plans. They find that it is no longer profitable to produce as much as before. As they cut back their output, each industry moves up and to the left along its industry demand curve. As this happens, the economy as a whole moves upward and to the left along aggregate demand curve $AD_0$ to a new short-run equilibrium at $E_1$. $E_1$ cannot, however, be a position of long-run equilibrium because real output is below its natural level and unemployment is above its natural rate.

**RECOVERY VIA DOWNWARD PRICE ADJUSTMENT** What happens next depends on what happens to the aggregate demand curve. If there are no policy changes, the aggregate demand curve will stay at $AD_0$. In this case, unplanned inventory

**Figure 14.3   Effects of a Supply Shock**

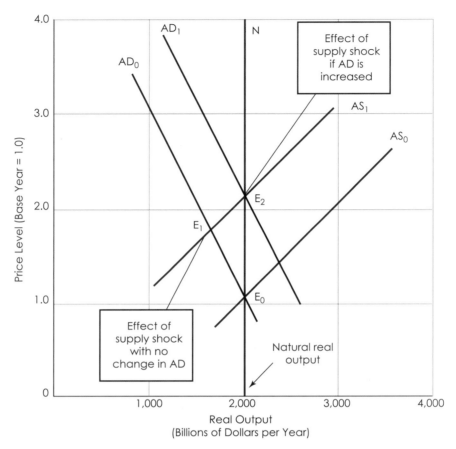

A supply shock is said to occur when an event external to the workings of the domestic economy—say, bad weather or an increase in the price of imports—raises the expected level of input prices. In this figure, a supply shock shifts the short-run aggregate supply curve upward from $AS_0$ to $AS_1$ while the aggregate demand curve initially stays at $AD_0$. The result is a cost-push inflation. The price level rises, real output falls, and the unemployment rate rises. If aggregate demand remains unchanged, the economy will eventually return to $E_0$. Alternatively, expansionary policy can be used to shift the aggregate demand curve to $AD_1$. This will move the economy to $E_2$ and hasten the recovery of real output, but it will worsen the inflationary consequences of the supply shock.

accumulation, excess capacity of firms, and excess unemployment will tend to put downward pressure on wages and prices. Some unemployed workers will accept jobs at lower wages than they had hoped for. Firms will find that although energy prices remain high, the average level of prices for final goods has not risen by as much as they initially expected input prices to increase. (In graphical terms, this is shown by the fact that the intersection of $AS_1$ and $AD_0$, which marks the short-run equilibrium level of final goods prices, is lower than the intersection of $AS_1$ with the long-run aggregate supply curve, N.) Because firms will expect the level of input prices to adjust downward, with a lag, toward the prevailing price level of final goods, the short-run aggregate supply curve will begin to shift downward from $AS_1$. In time, as it does so, the economy will move back down along $AD_0$ from $E_1$ to $E_0$. The price level will fall back to where it was before oil prices rose, and output will return to its natural level.

This path to recovery from a supply shock is likely to be slow, however. To follow it, the average price level of both inputs and final goods must fall while energy prices, the assumed source of the supply shock, remain high. For this to happen, there must be a major adjustment in relative prices. Real wages and the prices of goods and services other than energy must fall more than the average in order to bring the average down. This is likely to be a painful process for everyone—and until it is completed, unemployment will remain above its natural rate and output below its natural level.

**RECOVERY VIA A SHIFT IN AGGREGATE DEMAND**    There is another way to recover from a supply shock. If expansionary monetary or fiscal policy is used to shift the aggregate demand curve from $AD_0$ to $AD_1$, the economy can move to a new long-run equilibrium at $E_2$. In fact, if the expansion of aggregate demand follows the supply shock quickly enough, the economy may be able to avoid any major loss in real output. Instead of moving first to $E_1$, it will move straight up along the long-run aggregate supply curve, N, from $E_0$ to $E_2$. Monetary or fiscal stimulus used to moderate the impact of a supply shock on real output is known as **accommodating policy**.

Recovery from a supply shock through accommodating policy is likely to be faster than recovery through adjustment of relative prices. Also, the cost of recovery in terms of lost real output will probably be lower. But the cost in terms of increases in the price level will be greater. If policy makers accommodate a supply shock with a boost to aggregate demand, the price level will end up permanently higher, whereas if they keep the lid on aggregate demand, the impact of the supply shock on the average price level will be temporary. Moreover, there is a danger that aggregate demand may continue to expand, leading to an overshoot of the long-run equilibrium and a bout of demand-pull inflation.

There is no consensus on the best way to react to supply shocks. The response depends partly on the extent of one's dislike for inflation on the one hand and for unemployment on the other. Some economists have suggested that temporary supply shocks, such as crop failures or natural disasters, should not be accommodated by raising aggregate demand. They reason that the aggregate supply curve will soon shift back down as the damage is repaired. However, they suggest, a long-lasting supply shock, such as the oil price increases of the 1970s, might best be accommodated at least partially by raising aggregate demand. It may be worth suffering the resulting permanent increase in the price level to avoid a prolonged transition period of low real output and high unemployment.

## Inflationary Expectations as a Source of Cost-Push Inflations

Supply shocks are not the only source of cost-push inflation. Cost-push inflation can also be caused by past experiences of demand-pull inflation. To get this result, we

**Accommodating policy**

Expansionary monetary or fiscal policy used to increase aggregate demand in order to moderate the effects of a supply shock on real output.

must modify our assumptions regarding how firms form their expectations about the level of input prices. Up to this point, we have supposed that firms expect input prices in the current year to be at a level consistent with that of final goods prices in the previous year. However, in an economy that has experienced inflation for several years in a row, firms are more likely to expect the level of input prices to increase this year by a percentage equal to last year's inflation rate. Put another way, when firms have seen inflation in the past, they will expect more inflation in the future and will make their plans accordingly.

Figure 14.4 shows what happens when inflationary expectations become established in the economy. We begin from a situation of ongoing demand-pull inflation similar to that shown in Figure 14.2. An expansionary fiscal or monetary policy has held output above its natural level for some time. The economy is moving upward along the arrow through $E_1$ and $E_2$. After several years of inflation, firms and workers expect more inflation in the future and have adjusted their plans to cope with it as best they can. Their plans are reflected in a series of upward-shifting short-run aggregate supply curves that keep pace with the upward-shifting aggregate demand curve.

What happens now if the government decides to stop inflation by halting the growth of aggregate demand? (We are talking not about reducing the level of aggregate

**FIGURE 14.4 INFLATIONARY RECESSION**

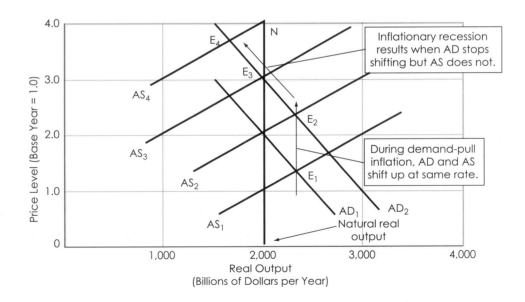

An inflationary recession occurs when aggregate demand slows or stops growing following a period of sustained inflation. In this figure, the aggregate demand curve stops shifting after the economy reaches $E_2$. Firms expect the level of input prices to continue to rise; thus, the short-run aggregate supply curve moves on up to $AS_3$ in the next year and to $AS_4$ in the year after that. As it does, the economy enters a recession during which the price level continues to rise. For a time the inflation rate may actually increase as real output falls.

demand but only about stopping its growth.) In terms of Figure 14.4, the effect will be to stop the upward shift of the aggregate demand curve, leaving it in the position $AD_2$.

Halting the growth of aggregate demand, however, will not stop inflation in its tracks. Firms and workers have grown used to inflation and expect it to continue. Workers expect their costs of living to rise further and will have made contracts with their employers giving them offsetting wage increases each year. Firms expect their input prices to rise further and will have become used to passing the increases along to their customers. As long as firms expect their input prices to continue rising and set their prices and output plans on that basis, the short-run aggregate supply curve will continue to shift upward.

## Inflationary Recession

**Inflationary recession**

An episode in which real output falls toward or below its natural level and unemployment rises toward or above its natural rate while rapid inflation continues.

With the aggregate supply curve moving upward while the aggregate demand curve stays put, real output starts to fall and unemployment begins to rise. Meanwhile, the price level keeps going up. The economy will soon reach $E_3$ in Figure 14.4. There real output and unemployment have returned to their natural levels. This is not the end of the story, however. Because firms experienced continued inflation as the economy moved from $E_2$ to $E_3$, they are not likely to expect inflation to stop now. As long as they anticipate that prices of final goods will keep on rising, firms will continue to form their expectations regarding input prices on that basis. As a result, the aggregate supply curve will keep drifting upward, as shown by $AS_4$ in Figure 14.4. As the economy moves along the aggregate demand curve toward $E_4$, the economy experiences an **inflationary recession**, an episode in which inflation, rising unemployment, and falling real output all occur at the same time.[2]

What can be done to bring the economy out of an inflationary recession? A "cold turkey" approach would be to sit tight and keep the lid on aggregate demand. Rising unemployment, declining sales, and an unplanned inventory buildup would, in time, cause firms and workers to revise their expectations about the rate of inflation for both inputs and final goods. Prices of raw materials would begin to fall. Workers, seeing first a slowing of the rise in the cost of living, and then an actual decline, would accept lower nominal wages. Lower levels of expected input prices would cause the aggregate supply curve to begin shifting downward. Slowly the economy would slip back down along the aggregate demand curve toward an equilibrium at $E_3$. But the experience would be a painful one.

A more moderate approach would be to slow the growth of aggregate demand gradually rather than stopping it cold. With luck, this could bring the economy to a "soft landing" at the natural level of real output. It might take longer to slow inflation this way, but a severe recession might be avoided.

In practice, there is a danger that policy makers will overreact to an inflationary recession. Instead of easing the economy to a soft landing, they may first react to pressures to "do something" about inflation (by stopping the growth of aggregate demand altogether) and then react to pressures to "do something" about unemployment by renewing the rapid growth of aggregate demand before inflationary expectations have been broken. Such a "stop-go" policy will result in a highly unstable path for the economy over time.

The truth is that no one knows a quick, painless way to stop inflation once it has become part of public expectations. As we will see, many economists think the best preventative is to keep inflation from getting started in the first place. This is a theme to which we will return in the last section of this chapter.

## Deflation and Recession

**Deflation**

A situation in which the average price level falls for a sustained period of a year or more.

In recent years, as inflation has receded throughout the world, economists have become concerned with the possibility of **deflation**—a situation in which the average price level falls for a sustained period. Deflation has not occurred in the United States since the early years of the Great Depression, when the price level fell by a third from 1929 to 1933. However, other countries, most notably Japan, have experienced deflation in the early twenty-first century. At first it might seem that if inflation is bad, deflation must be good, but that turns out not to be the case. As discussed in *Economics in the News 14.1,* Japan's recent deflation, like the U.S. deflation of the 1930s, has been accompanied by high unemployment and stagnant real GDP. As a result of this experience, deflation is considered a risk that all low-inflation countries need to think about.

Deflation is most likely to occur during a recession caused by a decrease in aggregate demand, as illustrated in Figure 14.5. Unlike the situation shown in the preceding figure, where the recession began on a basis of prior inflationary expectations, the situation illustrated in Figure 14.5 begins from a condition in which there is no prior inflation, either actual or expected.

The deflationary episode begins when a decrease in aggregate demand causes a decrease in real output. The aggregate demand curve falls from $AD_1$ to $AD_2$ and the economy's level of output moves to point $E_2$. Eventually, the economy's rising unemployment and falling real output will put downward pressure on input prices. To see why, consider how high unemployment affects the wages workers receive. If factory owners see lines of able-bodied workers outside of their factories, they will be able to pay lower wages to their current workers. Workers who are already employed will accept these wage cuts for fear of losing their jobs. In a climate of high unemployment, it would be difficult to find another job. As the decline in wage rates begins to affect all producers' expected input prices, the AS curve will shift downward (from $AS_1$ to $AS_2$), until the economy returns to the natural level of output at $E_3$.

If this adjustment process works, then why did the Great Depression last for a full decade and why has Japan's recent stagnation lasted despite several years of falling prices? A number of factors tend to make deflation persist once it gets started. First, there are several barriers that prevent input prices from falling. In the

### ➜ ECONOMICS IN THE NEWS 14.1

## DEFLATION IN JAPAN

From the 1960s through the 1980s, the Japanese economy was the envy of the world. As Japanese cars, consumer electronics, and industrial goods flooded the world and set new standards of quality, its economy boomed. Japan became the world's second-largest economy, and it became the first Asian country whose living standards were on a par with those of North America and Western Europe. Books with titles like *The Japanese Century* became best sellers.

Then, in the 1990s, all this began to fall apart. As the accompanying figures how, growth of real GDP and industrial production slowed to a crawl, and in several years actually declined. Unemployment, which had been very low, began to rise and the famous Japanese system of guaranteed lifetime jobs came under severe strain. The slowdown in real economic activity was accompanied by a dramatic change in the behavior of prices. Japan had never been a high-inflation economy, but now prices began actually to decline. Japan became the first major economy since the 1930s to experience sustained deflation.

The damage done by deflation in Japan extended beyond the usual macroeconomic indicators of real output, prices, and employment. The financial sector, and in particular, Japan's once mighty banks, suffered severely. During the boom years, banks had made huge loans secured by mortgages on commercial real estate. As deflation began to undermine both the prices of that real estate and the profits of the companies that owned it, the banks suffered massive losses. Only a permissive and supportive policy by the Bank of Japan (the country's central bank) staved off a financial panic.

To be sure, the Japanese government did not stand idly by. It applied all of the conventional tools of expansionary policy. Beginning in 1993, the government budget, which had been in balance or surplus on average during the 1990s, swung sharply into deficit. Deficits were so large and persistent that net government debt soared from less than 15 percent of GDP in 1991 to over 70 percent of GDP in 2002, but GDP growth did not budge.

On the monetary front, policy was also highly expansionary. The central bank lowered short-term interest rates all the way to zero—as low as they could go. However, although expansionary monetary policy led to steady growth of bank reserves, the growing reserves were not translated into new loans. With money so cheap, financial and nonfinancial companies simply accumulated huge quantities of liquid assets—a classic liquidity trap.

In early 2004, as this is written, the Japanese economy is finally showing signs of life, helped in part by even more aggressive expansionary policy that includes strong measures to keep the exchange rate low and stimulate exports. But even if this turns out to be the beginning of a lasting recovery, Japan's deflationary decade at the turn of the twenty-first century stands as a warning to policy makers throughout the world: Deflation is dangerous. Better to prevent it before it starts, because deflation, once entrenched, is hard to fight.

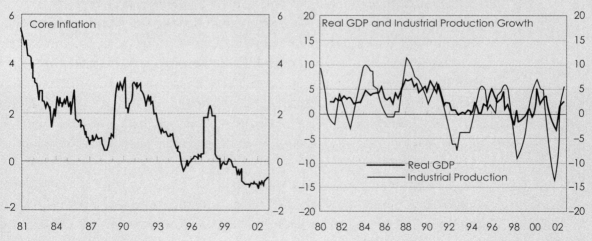

*Twelve-Month Percent Change* — Core Inflation

*Four-Quarter Percent Change* — Real GDP and Industrial Production Growth (Real GDP, Industrial Production)

Source: International Monetary Fund, *Deflation: Determinants, Risks and Policy Options*, April 2003, Box 4.3, p. 43.

**FIGURE 14.5**    **DEFLATION AND RECESSION**

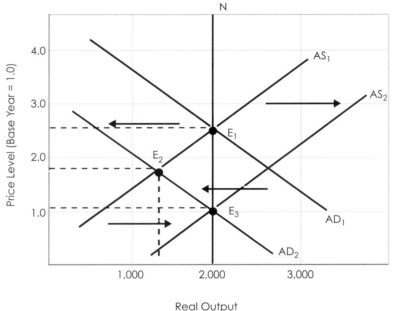

This figure shows how a decrease in aggregate demand causes a recession, accompanied by a deflation (falling prices). In this figure, the aggregate demand curve shifts to the left and the economy reaches $E_2$. High unemployment and low real output put downward pressure on input prices, and the short-run aggregate supply curve falls to $AS_2$. The increase in aggregate supply spurs economic recovery, as the economy returns to the natural rate of output at $E_3$.

case of an inflationary recession, we saw how prices can grow rapidly when producers anticipate higher inflation rates. While it is easy for input prices to rise, it is relatively difficult for them to fall. Producers face barriers to imposing wage cuts, such as minimum wage laws and union contracts. A union certainly would not argue with higher wages, but it will probably dispute wage cuts. Even without these institutional barriers, producers may worry that lower wages discourage workers from working hard. Consider two fast food restaurants. One pays its workers $8.00 per hour, and another pays $6.00 per hour. Which restaurant provides better service? Probably the one paying its workers more, because its employees have more to lose if they are fired.

A second set of factors that makes deflation hard to reverse centers on monetary policy. As discussed in the previous chapter, interest rates play a key role in transmitting the effects of monetary policy to the real economy via their effects on investment. Unfortunately, there is a natural lower bound to nominal interest rates: They can go no lower than zero. For a bank to loan money at a negative interest rate—to pay borrowers to take money off its hands—would be an absurdity. Loan demand would be infinite, because borrowers could profit simply by borrowing money and storing it in a safe. Once a central bank lowers interest rates to zero, the economy risks becoming stuck in a classic liquidity trap. Something like this seems actually to have happened in Japan. How to conduct economic policy under conditions of deflation is an issue explored further in the *Case for Discussion* at the end of the chapter.

Finally, there is a danger that deflation can lead to a financial panic. The problem is that banks and other institutions use real estate, business equipment, and even financial assets as collateral for loans. If deflation undermines the value of collateral, borrowers may default on loans, thereby threatening the solvency of financial institutions.

# THE PHILLIPS CURVE

**Phillips curve**

A graph showing the relationship between the inflation rate and the unemployment rate, other things being equal.

Up to this point, our analysis has suggested a negative relationship between inflation and real output and, in turn, employment. The expansion of aggregate demand can be used to hold real output above its natural level and unemployment below its natural rate, but at the cost of sustained inflation. Deflation, on the other hand, tends to be accompanied by falling real output and high unemployment. This association between low unemployment and demand-pull inflation can be represented in the form of a graph called a **Phillips curve**, named for the British economist A. W. H. Phillips, who first described it in a 1958 paper[3] (see *Who Said It? Who Did It? 14.1*).

---

**⤳ WHO SAID IT? WHO DID IT? 14.1**

**A. W. H. PHILLIPS AND THE PHILLIPS CURVE**

A. W. H. Phillips was an economist whose reputation was based largely on a single paper on the right topic published at the right time. In the late 1950s, the connection between inflation and unemployment was a major unsolved problem of macroeconomic theory. The curves that Phillips drew in his famous article in *Economica* suggested a simple, stable relationship between inflation and unemployment. Phillips's paper did not present a theory for explaining the relationship, but his curves became the peg on which all future discussions of the problem would be hung. Every subsequent article on inflation and unemployment discussed the shape of the Phillips curve, the point on the Phillips curve that best served as a policy target, how the Phillips curve could be shifted, and so on. Today the term is so familiar that Phillips's name enjoys a sort of immortality, even though his own interpretation of the curve has fallen into disfavor.

Phillips was born in New England, but most of his academic career was spent in London. He taught at the London School of Economics during the 1950s and 1960s, moving to Australian National University in 1967: Phillips's training in electrical engineering seems to have influenced his approach to economic problems. In the mid-1950s, he was suggesting the use of an "electric analog machine or simulator" as an aid to the study of economic dynamics. This idea seems to have foreshadowed the widespread use of electronic computers in modern economic research.

FIGURE 14.6    THE PHILLIPS CURVE AS A POLICY MENU

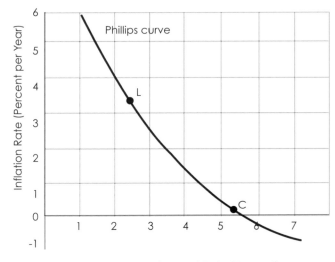

When A. W. H. Phillips first drew attention to the inverse relationship between inflation and unemployment, his "Phillips curve" was treated as a policy menu. Liberals argued that a point such as L should be chosen; this would "buy" a permanent reduction in unemployment at the cost of a little inflation. Conservatives seemed to favor a point such as C, which would offer stable prices at the cost of more joblessness.

## The Phillips Curve as a Policy Menu

A sample Phillips curve is drawn in Figure 14.6. During the 1960s, when the Phillips curve first attracted economists' attention, it was viewed as a menu of policy choices. Political liberals sometimes argued that policy makers should choose a point such as L on the Phillips curve; this point would "buy" full employment and prosperity at the price of a modest inflation rate. Conservatives expressed horror at the thought of any degree of inflation and argued for a point such as C, which would achieve price stability at the expense of some jobs.

However, the problem with viewing the Phillips curve as a policy menu was that the choices it offered kept changing while the meal was in progress. As the 1960s unfolded, economists began to notice that inflation-unemployment points for recent years did not fit the curves they had plotted using data from the 1950s. It became common to speak of an upward drift of the Phillips curve: a given level of inflation would "buy" increasingly smaller reductions in unemployment.

Still, had the upward drift of the Phillips curve been caused by factors outside their control, policy makers could have chosen their preferred point from a new, higher Phillips curve. With the advent of the 1970s, however, economists' perception of the Phillips curve started to change. It began to appear that shifts in the Phillips curve were caused by the very policies that had sought to move the economy along the curve.

## *The Phillips Curve and the Natural Rate of Unemployment*

The distinction between the long-run and short-run effects of changes in aggregate demand on prices, output, and unemployment provides the key to this new view of the Phillips curve. A once-and-for-all rise in the level of aggregate demand leads to only a temporary reduction in unemployment. The reason is that the expected levels of wages and other input prices adjust to changes in the level of final-goods prices, thereby pushing up the aggregate supply curve. Thus, real output can rise above its natural level only as long as the short-run aggregate supply curve does not completely catch up with the shifting aggregate demand curve.

Earlier we defined the natural rate of unemployment as the rate that prevails when the economy is experiencing neither accelerating nor decelerating inflation. We can also say that the natural rate of unemployment is the rate that prevails when the expected inflation rate equals the actual inflation rate. This can happen with real output at its natural level and the expected and actual inflation rates both zero. However, unemployment can also be at its natural rate when the economy is in a moving equilibrium with a constant inflation rate to which everyone has become accustomed.

This modern view of the Phillips curve is illustrated in Figure 14.7. Two short-run Phillips curves are shown, each corresponding to a different expected inflation rate. If no inflation is expected, the Phillips curve takes the position $Ph_1$. The intersection of this Phillips curve with the horizontal axis indicates the natural rate of unemployment, here taken to be 6 percent. If the actual inflation rate unexpectedly

**FIGURE 14.7   SHORT-RUN AND LONG-RUN PHILLIPS CURVES**

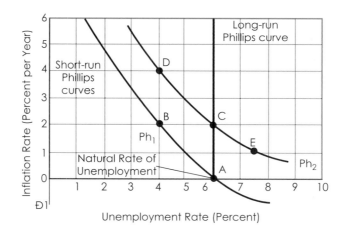

In the modern view of the Phillips curve, there is an inverse relationship between unemployment and inflation only in the short run. Unexpected inflation lowers the unemployment rate, but only until people's expectations adjust to the new inflation rate. Any change in the expected inflation rate shifts the short-run Phillips curve. The long-run Phillips curve is a vertical line drawn at the natural rate of unemployment, here assumed to be 6 percent. The long- and short-run curves intersect at the expected inflation rate for which the short-run curve is drawn.

goes up to 2 percent per year, the economy will initially move upward and to the left along this Phillips curve from point A to point B. This will correspond to a movement upward and to the right along the economy's short-run aggregate supply curve; real output and the price level will rise as inflation gets under way and the unemployment rate falls.

If the inflation rate remains at 2 percent per year, people will sooner or later adjust their expectations accordingly. In terms of the diagrams in the chapter on inflation, the rising short-run aggregate supply curve will catch up with the aggregate demand curve. As this happens, real output will return to its natural level and unemployment to its natural rate. From that point, the aggregate demand and short-run aggregate supply curves and their intersection point move upward along the vertical long-run aggregate supply curve at a constant 2 percent rate. In Figure 14.7, this causes an upward shift of the short-run Phillips curve to $Ph_2$. As a result, the economy moves to point C.

From point C, the economy can move upward or downward along the new short-run Phillips curve, depending on what happens to the actual inflation rate. If inflation increases to 4 percent while people expect it to remain at 2 percent, the economy initially will move to point D. If inflation slows to 1 percent while people expect it to remain at 2 percent, the economy at first will move from point C to point E. However, these movements along the short-run Phillips curve will not represent new long-run equilibrium points. As soon as people get used to the new inflation rate, the short-run Phillips curve will shift again.

### The Long-Run Phillips Curve

A further implication of the newer view of the Phillips curve is that it must be vertical in the long run. This follows from the notions that unemployment attains its natural rate whenever the actual and expected inflation rates are equal, and that any given steady rate of inflation will be expected to continue. Such a long-run Phillips curve is shown in Figure 14.7 as a vertical line drawn at the natural rate of unemployment. Each short-run Phillips curve intersects the long-run Phillips curve at the expected inflation rate for which the short-run curve is drawn. Thus, unemployment will be at its natural rate only when the actual and expected inflation rates are equal.

The concepts of a vertical long-run Phillips curve and a short-run Phillips curve that shifts upward as inflation accelerates have now become the established view of the relationship between inflation and unemployment. The old view that the Phillips curve could be treated as a policy menu, along which low unemployment could be "purchased" at the expense of a moderate but steady rate of inflation, is no longer accepted. In retrospect, past attempts of policy makers to keep unemployment low by persistently using expansionary monetary and fiscal policy are seen as one of the causes leading to the Great Inflation of the 1970s. *Applying Economic Ideas 14.1* illustrates the consequences of such overly expansionary policy in the United States in the 1960s. In the low-inflation environment of the early twenty-first century, such a strategy seems distinctly unattractive.

# STRATEGIES FOR LASTING PRICE STABILITY

In the first section of this chapter, we looked at the mechanisms that get inflation started or cause the economy to slip into deflation. These included both demand-pull and cost-push elements. Now we turn to strategies that aim to cure inflation or deflation once they have become established, and once they have been brought under control, to maintain lasting price stability.

## *What Policy Instruments Are Available?*

In the aggregate supply and demand model, changes in the price level can be brought about either by shifts in the AD curve (demand-pull inflation) or the AS

---

⌢ **APPLYING ECONOMIC IDEAS 14.1**
**INFLATION IN THE KENNEDY–JOHNSON ERA**

John Kennedy came to the presidency in 1960 with the stated intent of getting the country moving again after two recessions in the later years of the Eisenhower administration. Lyndon Johnson, his successor, was equally determined to pursue an expansionary policy. Economists are still debating the relative impact of the tax reductions, heavy defense spending, and accelerating monetary growth that characterized the Kennedy–Johnson years. But there is no doubt that this combination of policies was as expansionary as anyone could have wished. The result was a sustained period of growth and low unemployment.

The accompanying diagram shows the unemployment inflation record for the economy during the Kennedy–Johnson era. The pattern is just what the accelerationist theory would lead us to expect. At first, the expansionary policy produced major gains in employment with little additional inflation. But starting in 1964, the year of the tax cut, each successive drop in unemployment was accompanied by a bigger jump in prices. By the end of Johnson's term in office, inflation was rising higher and higher each year just to keep unemployment from growing. Although it may have seemed in the first years of this expansionary cycle that the economy was moving upward along a fixed Phillips curve "menu," by the end of the 1960s policy makers were playing catch-up as the Phillips curve shifted steadily upward.

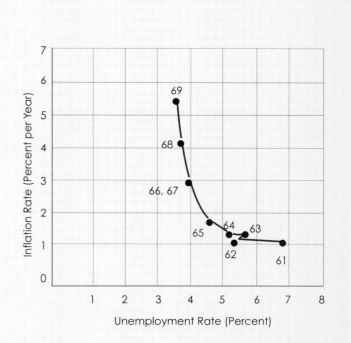

Source: President's Council of Economic Advisers, *Economic Report of the President* (Washington, D.C.: Government Printing Office, 1987), Tables B-35 and B-58. Annual average civilian unemployment rate and percentage change in annual average CPI.

curve (cost-push inflation). It stands to reason, then, that a complete strategy for price stabilization should make use of policy instruments that act both on the demand and the supply side of the economy.

We have looked in considerable detail at demand-side policy instruments in earlier chapters. The principal fiscal policy instruments of demand management are changes in government purchases and changes in net taxes. We recall that changes in net taxes can mean either changes in tax rates governing payments to the government, or changes in transfer payments, such as unemployment benefits or Social Security benefits. For monetary policy, we have seen that open market purchases of government securities are the principal policy instrument used by the Federal Reserve to control aggregate demand via changes in the money supply. Supplementary instruments occasionally used by the Fed include changes in the discount rate and, at least in the past, changes in required reserve ratios. Finally, we have noted that intervention in foreign exchange markets via purchases or sales of foreign currencies is a powerful instrument of monetary policy used by central banks in many other countries, although it has not been much used by the Fed in recent years.

Up to this point, we have given less attention to policy instruments that might be used to control shifts in the aggregate supply curve. Our earlier discussion of shifts in the AS curve emphasized supply shocks like natural disasters or shifts in world commodity prices that lie outside the control of national governments. But policy makers do have some instruments available through which they can control aggregate supply.

**WAGE AND PRICE CONTROLS**    Direct administrative controls over wages and prices are one instrument that can be used to control movements in the aggregate supply curve. The case for wage and price controls is strongest when they are used in conjunction with restrictive demand management as a temporary measure to fight an inflationary recession. When policy makers apply the brakes to aggregate demand after a period of rapid inflation, firms and workers do not expect inflation to stop right away. When the government imposes price and wage controls, it is hoped that workers and firms will believe that the controls are really going to stop inflation, for in that case they will lower their inflationary expectations much sooner than they would if they had to learn from experience.

This reduction in expected inflation—if it happens—will remove the cost-push element from the inflationary recession. Knowing that they need not push for higher wages to beat inflation, workers will find their current wages acceptable. Knowing that their input prices will not be rising, firms will be less inclined to reduce output and raise prices. A larger part of the reduction in the growth of nominal GDP will take the form of a slowdown in price increases than would otherwise be the case. The drop in real output and the rise in unemployment will be smaller than they would otherwise be. As a result, the transition to price stability will be quicker and less painful than it would be without controls.

Wage and price controls do not always have the desired effects, however. The problem is that they are often used as a substitute for demand management policy rather than as a supplement to it. The government either tries to use wage and price controls to fight inflation without simultaneously slowing the growth of aggregate demand, or leaves controls in force after the transition is over and a new boom is under way. Therefore, wage and price controls either will be ineffective or will lead to shortages, rationing, and black markets.

There have been several experiments with wage and price controls in the United States. One took place during World War II. The high level of wartime government spending made it hard to control aggregate demand. Strict price controls were used to suppress inflation. The results were predictable: Rationing was introduced for gasoline, tires, sugar, and many other goods, and widespread black markets emerged.

Another experiment with wage and price controls took place from 1971 to 1974 during the Nixon administration. The Nixon controls were a mixed success at best. They were first introduced when inflation already was falling and may have helped to speed the decline somewhat. But they were left in place after prices began to rise again in mid-1972. At that point, they proved useless or worse.

Although wage and price controls can theoretically play a constructive role in managing inflation, they have been used inappropriately so often that they have gone out of fashion among policy makers. The number of countries that applies such controls today is much smaller than was the case a generation ago.

**CONTROL OF EXCHANGE RATES**   A second instrument that can be used to control the aggregate supply curve is the exchange rate of the domestic currency relative to foreign currencies. This instrument is especially powerful in small, relatively open economies. In such economies, the prices of imported goods are an important component of input prices and the prices of imported consumer goods are a key determinant of the cost of living, which in turn affects the level of nominal wages in domestic labor markets. If central bank intervention in foreign exchange markets causes the domestic currency to appreciate, the prices of imported goods decrease when stated in domestic currency. Accordingly, downward pressure is placed on the aggregate supply curve. When the currency depreciates, the aggregate supply curve tends to shift upward. In contrast to wage and price controls, which have fallen out of fashion, the use of exchange rates as an instrument of supply-side macroeconomic policy has increased in recent decades. We will return to this topic later in the chapter.

**MINOR SUPPLY-SIDE INSTRUMENTS**   Other minor instruments are sometimes used to affect conditions of aggregate supply. For example, changes in tax rates may have such an effect, to the extent that businesses perceive taxes as an element of cost, or to the extent that tax rates affect workers' wage demands when bargaining with employers. Policies that affect commodity prices can also be used for macroeconomic purposes. An example would be the U.S. strategic petroleum reserve. Releasing supplies of crude oil from the reserve can, in principle, offset the inflationary impact of an increase in world oil prices. These instruments are not likely to have strong, lasting effects on the aggregate price level, however.

## The Importance of Credibility

Regardless of the specific instrument used, it is important to remember that all efforts to affect the position of the aggregate supply curve act through *expectations*. To the extent that businesses expect wages and other input prices to rise in the future, the AS curve will shift upward, thwarting efforts to control inflation. To the extent that announced policies to stabilize prices are seen as *credible,* the position of the AS curve will stabilize and the work of policy makers in slowing inflation or resisting deflation will be easier.

For this reason, policy makers often accompany efforts at price stabilization with aggressive public relations efforts to persuade the public that they are serious in pursuing their announced policy goals. Changing the faces of policy makers sometimes helps. For example, the appointment of Paul Volcker, known to be influenced by monetarist ideas, as Chairman of the Federal Reserve in 1979 sent a signal to financial markets that tolerance for inflation was at an end. Countries that have used exchange rates to control inflation have often accompanied a stabilization campaign with issuing a new currency with a new name. In other cases, policy makers have signaled the seriousness of their attention by making changes in basic laws. For example, a country whose past inflation had been fueled by excessive money growth by a weak, politically subservient central bank might announce a new law that makes the central bank independent of political control.

As we turn from a listing of individual instruments to a discussion of the way instruments can be combined into a coherent price stabilization strategy, we will see that the issue of credibility is always of key importance.

## Inflation Targeting

**Inflation targeting**

A strategy for price stability in which policy makers adopt an explicit target range for the rate of inflation over an intermediate time horizon.

One of the most widely used strategies for achieving price stability is known as **inflation targeting**. As the name implies, adopting this strategy means that the central bank, and policy makers in other branches of government as well, adopt an explicit target range for the rate of inflation as the principal aim of macroeconomic policy over an intermediate time horizon.

**RELATIONSHIP TO OTHER TARGETS AND GOALS** Under an inflation-targeting regime, the target for the rate of inflation occupies an intermediate position between short-term operating targets and long-term policy goals. The price level cannot serve as a short-term operating target for monetary policy because the government's policy instruments affect the price level only indirectly and with a lag. For monetary policy, the transmission mechanism runs from policy instruments that affect the size of the money stock through interest rates and investment to aggregate demand. For fiscal policy, the transmission mechanism runs either through changes in government purchases, which are themselves a component of aggregate demand, or through changes in consumer expenditures caused by changes in tax rates. In either case, shifts in aggregate demand affect the price level, but not immediately. As we have seen, an increase in aggregate demand at first causes real output to increase while causing a moderate rise in prices, and later causes a further increase in prices as the aggregate supply curve shifts upward and real output returns to its natural level. Because the transmission mechanism from monetary and fiscal policy to prices is long and indirect, inflation-targeting countries cannot expect to keep the rate of inflation exactly on target on a month-to-month basis. Instead, the usual approach is to set a target range for inflation of, say, between 2 and 4 percent, averaged over a one- or two-year time horizon.

The rate of inflation is an intermediate policy target in another sense, as well. Most policy makers view price stability not so much as something that is desirable for its own sake, but as a condition that should be established to facilitate the more fundamental goals of growth in real income and full employment. Figure 14.8, based on a sample of 103 countries over a 30-year period, shows that low-inflation countries perform consistently better in terms of economic growth. Inflation rates well under 10 percent per year appear optimal, although there are a few cases of countries that have done well with inflation in the low single digits. Countries with inflation rates over 100 percent have, on the average, experienced decreasing real GDP.

**FIGURE 14.8  INFLATION-GDP GROWTH: 103-COUNTRY AVERAGE**

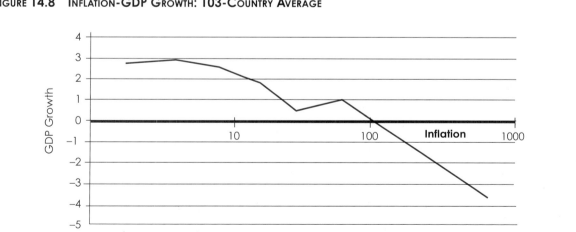

Source: Atish Gosh and Steven Phillips, *Inflation, Disinflation, and Growth,* IMF Working Paper 98/68, May 1998.

A too-low a rate of inflation can also be harmful to economic growth, although the sample on which Figure 14.8 is based does not show this clearly. Other data indicate that countries that experience deflation usually have stagnant or falling GDP, as in Japan during the past decade. Germany's recent experience provides another example. German inflation has been the lowest in the European Union, less than 1 percent per year. At the same time, Germany has experienced higher unemployment than its neighbors and virtually no growth of real GDP. To provide a cushion against the danger of falling into deflation, inflation-targeting countries usually aim for a rate of price increase in the low single digits rather than setting a target of zero inflation, which would be needed for complete price stability.

**INFLATION TARGETING, EXPECTATIONS, AND CREDIBILITY**   Earlier we emphasized the importance of credibility to all price stabilization policies. If consumers and businesses expect the government to set reasonable inflation goals and stick to them, the inflationary expectations that shift the aggregate supply curve and destabilize the economy can be kept under control.

No country can avoid some variations in the rate of inflation caused by unpredictable supply shocks or demand disturbances linked to sudden swings in consumer or business confidence. Inflation targeting aims to maximize the stabilizing effects of expectations when such disturbances occur. Suppose, for example, a country whose inflation has averaged 3 percent per year is hit by a sudden rise in the quarterly inflation rate to 5 percent. In a country where consumers and businesses had low confidence in government policy, they might take actions to protect themselves from more inflation to come. These efforts at self-defense by consumers and businesses would push the aggregate supply curve upward and make the fears of future inflation self-fulfilling. On the other hand, if the country had a well-established inflation target of 2 to 4 percent averaged over a one- or two-year period, private decision makers could be confident that the temporary surge of inflation would be offset by monetary or fiscal policy as needed. Expecting inflation to fall back within the target range, they would not panic. The resulting stability of the aggregate supply curve would make the job of demand management easier, and in that case, predictions of price stability would be self-fulfilling.

**INFLATION TARGETING AND THE FED**   Inflation targeting is the official policy of the European euro zone, the United Kingdom, Canada, Australia, and many emerging market countries. In the United States, however, the Fed has not fully embraced inflation targeting. True, the Fed attaches great importance to keeping inflation low while at the same time avoiding the risk of deflation. It has been highly successful in doing so. Since 1992, the annual inflation rate as measured by the GDP deflator, considered the broadest price-level indicator, has held steady between 1 and 3 percent. Looking at the data alone, an observer might well conclude that the Fed had an inflation target of 2 percent plus or minus 1 percent. Yet the Fed has announced no such target. Instead, it has insisted that an explicit inflation target might limit its flexibility in reacting to unforeseen circumstances.

Some Fed watchers expect this to change. They expect the Fed to announce openly the policy it seems to have been following implicitly. They think doing so will provide an even more stable framework for forward-looking expectations in financial markets than is provided by the excellent record of the Fed's discretionary policy over the past decade.

## Exchange-Rate Based Stabilization Policy

**Exchange-rate based stabilization policy (ERB)**

A policy that uses the exchange rate as the principle operating target for macroeconomic policy

Another widely used price stabilization strategy uses the exchange rate of the country's currency as its principal target. This approach is usually called **exchange-rate based stabilization policy (ERB)**. ERB policy has been used by many emerging market economies, for example by Argentina and Brazil in the 1990s and Ecuador more recently. Several countries undergoing the process of transition from socialist planned economies to a market system have also used ERB policy, including Estonia, Latvia, Lithuania, Hungary, and Bulgaria. Some developed countries, for example Denmark and, before the introduction of the euro, the Netherlands, have also used ERB policy.

**OPERATING AND INTERMEDIATE TARGETS UNDER ERB POLICY** The first thing to note about ERB policy is that the exchange rate, unlike the rate of inflation, can be used as an operating target on a day-to-day basis. As we have seen, a country's central bank can influence the exchange rate directly through the instrument of buying and selling foreign currency in exchange for its own domestic currency. Sales of foreign currency tend to strengthen the exchange rate of the domestic currency or slow an undesired tendency toward depreciation caused by market forces. Purchases of foreign currency have the opposite effect. In addition, the central bank's use of domestic open market operations to influence interest rates has a strong effect on the exchange rate via their effects on financial inflows or outflows. In fact, interest rates and exchange rates are so closely linked that it is a maxim of central banking that monetary policy can be used either to achieve an operating target for the exchange rate or an operating target for the interest rate, but not for both at once.

Countries that use ERB policy define the operating target for the exchange rate in different ways. Some declare an exactly fixed value of the exchange rate as their target. Others use a target zone, say 10 pesos per dollar plus or minus 2 percent. Still others use an adjustable target, for example, one that includes a steady, planned rate of depreciation of the exchange rate at 5 percent per year. Because the principles involved in meeting any of these targets are similar, we will not take the time to discuss the relative merits of these policy variants.

In using the exchange rate as an operating target, central banks that use ERB policy also have their eyes on intermediate targets and long-term policy goals. A stable exchange rate makes a very strong contribution to the intermediate target of price stability. This is especially true in relatively small countries that are open to international trade and financial flows. In such countries, a depreciation of the currency is quickly passed through into domestic price inflation because it causes increases in the prices of imported industrial inputs and in the cost of imported consumer goods that influence workers' wage demands. Stabilizing the value of the currency provides an "anchor" for price expectations. If the central bank's commitment to the exchange rate target is credible, the stable expectations will provide a good basis for achieving the long-term goals of economic growth and full employment. If the central bank's credibility is weak because of political instability or unfavorable factors in the external economic environment, attempted ERB stabilization may fail.

ERB policy can have an especially powerful effect in a country that suffers from the extremely rapid inflation known as **hyperinflation**. When inflation reaches rates of thousands of percent per year, as it did in the 1980s and 1990s in countries like Argentina, Brazil, Bolivia, and others, people lose faith almost completely in the value of the local currency. They continue to use it for making day-to-day purchases, but they keep their savings in a safe currency like the dollar or the euro. Contracts for major purchases and often for wages are also made in the foreign rather than the domestic currency. Under these conditions, a credible program to fix the exchange rate of the local currency at a specific value against the dollar or the euro has a powerful effect on expectations. Inflation may end almost overnight as people once again find they can safely use the domestic currency for all their needs. *Applying Economic Ideas 14.2* provides an example of successful use of ERB policy to end the 1996–1997 hyperinflation in Bulgaria.

**Hyperinflation**

Very rapid inflation.

## Problems with ERB Stabilization

Despite the successful use of ERB stabilization policy by many countries, the policy is not without dangers. Some attempts to apply ERB policy without taking potential problems into account have ended in failure.

Conflicts between fiscal and monetary policy are one problem area. Under ERB stabilization, monetary policy must be focused exclusively on maintaining the target exchange rate. The central bank cannot do that and, at the same time, make easy credit available to the government to finance its budget deficit. In fact, excessive growth of the money supply because of central bank lending to finance budget deficits is often the cause of the very hyperinflation that ERB stabilization aims to end. Conflicts arise when a country's central bank tries to implement ERB stabilization while its government does not have the political discipline to control spending and enforce tax collection in order to keep the budget deficit under control. Sooner or later a crisis breaks out in which the government must default on its debt, or the

⬆ **APPLYING ECONOMIC IDEAS 14.2**

## BULGARIA'S SUCCESSFUL EXCHANGE-RATE BASED STABILIZATION

In the early 1990s, during the first years of its transition from Communism to a market system, Bulgaria's economy performed better than the average for countries in Eastern Europe and the former Soviet Union. There was some inflation, but not as severe is in Russia or neighboring Romania. There was an initial drop in real output, but not as deep a decline as in nearby Ukraine or Georgia.

However, Bulgaria's good start was followed by delays in introducing key economic reforms, especially in the financial sector. In 1996, the economy slowed down and the banking system came close to collapse. In a desperate attempt to save commercial banks, the Bulgarian central bank pumped money into the economy in a way that brought on rapidly

escalating inflation. By the end of 1996, a full-scale inflationary crisis was underway. Protesters took to the streets, the government fell, and a caretaker government took over pending new elections. By early 1997, when the new government set to work, there was a full-fledged inflationary crisis. As the figure shows, prices were rising at a rate of more than 100 percent per month. Clearly, strong medicine was called for.

The new Bulgarian government chose to apply one of the most stringent of all forms of exchange-rate based stabilization policy. In March 1997, it announced that it would introduce a *currency board*—a form of monetary policy that would obligate the central bank to maintain an absolutely fixed exchange rate. Because the European Union was the country's largest trading partner, the Bulgarian lev was pegged to the German mark. Later, when the euro replaced the mark, the peg was transferred to the euro.

As soon as the currency board was announced, an interesting thing happened. As the figure shows, the new policy stopped inflation dead in its tracks—not in July, when it was implemented, but right away in March, as soon as it was announced! Since that time, Bulgaria has enjoyed low inflation and one of the best rates of real economic growth in the region.

The successful Bulgarian experience with ERB stabilization illustrates a point about the importance of credibility to price stabilization policy: If people *believe* that their government is politically committed to stability and has a technically valid plan for implementing its commitment, then the promise of stabilization becomes self-fulfilling. That, at least, is what seems to have happened in Bulgaria.

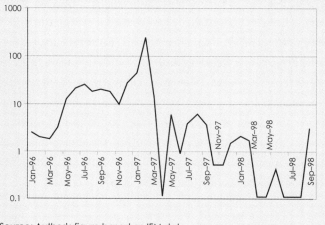

Source: Author's figure based on IFM data.

central bank must abandon its exchange rate target, or both. The painful crisis of the Argentine economy at the end of 2001, which included both a default and a devaluation, provides a case in point.

Countries that link their currencies to that of a strong partner like the dollar or the euro must consider another potential problem as well. Once a small country links its currency to that of a larger neighbor, the smaller country's economy becomes exposed to all the economic shocks that affect the larger partner. For example, consider the case of Ecuador, which has adopted the U.S. dollar as its currency in a bid to end hyperinflation. If the dollar depreciates relative to the euro or the Japanese yen, Ecuador experiences an increase in the cost of imports, even though it did nothing to cause the depreciation. Similarly, if the U.S. Fed were to find it necessary to raise interest rates to resist inflation sometime in the future, Ecuador's interest rates would rise as well, harming investment and slowing its growth.

For these reasons, economists advise that ERB stabilization policy is most likely to work if the small country's economy has strong ties to its larger currency partner in other ways besides the exchange rate. It is helpful if a large share of its imports and exports take place with the currency partner. It is helpful if labor and capital markets allow relatively free flow of resources between the two countries. It is helpful if their business cycles are synchronized. And it is helpful if the two countries are similarly affected by shocks like changes in international commodity prices. In all of these respects, conditions were favorable for the successful policy linking the Bulgarian currency to the euro. The same conditions were much less favorable for the linkage of Argentina's peso to the U.S. dollar, helping to explain its ultimate failure.

The preceding cautionary words do not mean that ERB policy can never be used unless initial conditions are ideal. Rather, it means that exchange rate policy should not be applied rigidly without consideration of the context. There are compromises in ERB policy that can help to cushion a country against some of the dangers. For example, in the 1990s Latvia chose to link its currency not to that of a single partner, but to a weighted average of other currencies. In the same period, Hungary chose to use a pre-announced, gradually slowing rate of depreciation of its currency, rather than an immediate fixed exchange rate, to slow its excessive inflation to the desired level. And in the 1980s, Israel temporarily fixed its exchange rate in order to end an inflationary crisis, but phased out the fixed exchange rate in favor of inflation targeting before a crisis of the Argentine type had a chance to develop. In short, despite some spectacular failures, ERB stabilization policy, applied intelligently and flexibly, remains a valuable option in the policy maker's toolkit.

## SUMMARY

1. **What are the characteristics of inflation or deflation that arise from shifts in aggregate demand?** Inflation caused by an increase in aggregate demand is known as *demand-pull inflation*. In the short run, an increase in aggregate demand will move the economy up and to the right along its short-run aggregate supply curve. As increases in final goods prices come to be reflected in expected input prices, the aggregate supply curve shifts upward. If continued expansionary policy shifts the aggregate demand curve upward at the same rate, the economy can be held above its natural level of real output for an extended period, but at a substantial cost in terms of inflation. During times of economic contraction, a decrease in aggregate demand can move the economy down and to the left along its aggregate supply curve. Prices fall as output contracts, and the economy enters a period of *deflation*.

2. **How can inflation arise from shifts in the short-run aggregate supply curve?** If the short-run

aggregate supply curve shifts upward while the aggregate demand curve stays in place or shifts upward more slowly, the economy will experience *cost-push inflation*. Real output will fall, and the economy will enter an *inflationary recession*. One source of cost-push inflation is a *supply shock*, such as an increase in the price of a key input such as petroleum. Another is the momentum of inflationary expectations generated by previous demand-pull inflation.

3. **How are inflation and unemployment related?** The short-run relationship between inflation and unemployment is shown by the *Phillips curve*, which shows that for a given expected inflation rate, lower actual inflation rates tend to be linked with higher unemployment rates. The intersection of the short- and long-run Phillips curves corresponds to the expected rate of inflation: an increase in the expected inflation rate tends to shift the short-run Phillips curve upward. The long-run Phillips curve is a vertical line at the natural rate of unemployment. Unemployment will be at its natural rate only when the actual inflation rate equals the expected inflation rate.

4. **What types of policies can be used to achieve lasting price stability?** Lasting price stability requires using the instruments of monetary and fiscal policy to avoid undue swings in aggregate demand. The government's control over aggregate supply is less direct. Instruments like wage and price controls and exchange rate policy can sometimes help, but the most important task is to achieve a degree of credibility that stabilizes expectations. Credibility is enhanced if price stabilization policy conforms to an over all strategy. Two proven stabilization strategies are *inflation targeting* and *exchange-rate based stabilization policy*.

## KEY TERMS

Demand-pull inflation
Cost-push inflation
Supply shock
Accommodating policy
Inflationary recession
Deflation
Phillips curve
Exchange-rate based
 stabilization policy
Inflation targeting
Hyperinflation

## PROBLEMS AND TOPICS FOR DISCUSSION

1. **Examining the lead-off case.** Given the information provided about the "Great Inflation" in the case at the beginning of this chapter, would you describe the nature of that inflation as demand-pull, cost-push, or a mixture of the two? Discuss.

2. **Expected input prices.** Three aggregate supply curves are shown in Figure 14.2. What is the expected level of input prices associated with each?

3. **Favorable supply shocks.** Supply shocks are not always bad. Use aggregate supply and demand curves to explain the short-run and long-run effects of a favorable supply shock, such as a decline in world oil prices. Could a supply shock ever cause deflation?

4. **Price expectations and real output.** Use the aggregate supply and demand model to show that real output can be above its natural level only when the current level of final-goods prices is above the level of expected input prices. Show too that real output can be below its natural level only when the current level of final-goods prices is below the level of expected input prices.

5. **Publicity and policy changes.** Assume that the economy has been going through a long period of demand-pull inflation. The government decides to try to stop the inflation by means of restrictive

monetary and fiscal policies. Should it make the required policy changes with as little fanfare as possible, or should it publicize them widely? Will it make any difference? Why or why not?

6. **Forecasting inflation.** What do you expect the inflation rate to be next year? Do you know what it was last year? Last month? On what sources do you rely for information about past and present inflation and for forming your expectations about the future? Do you think this course will affect your ability to forecast inflation in the future? Discuss.

7. **The current rate of inflation.** Inflation data given in this chapter refer to year-to-year percentage changes in the consumer price index. Use the most recent *Economic Report of the President* (available online at www.gpoaccess.gov/eop/) to determine the rate of inflation for 2004 (and later years, if applicable). Has inflation remained relatively steady—in the 1 to 3 percent range experienced throughout the later 1990s and early 2000s? If not, can you suggest any reason for the change based on the theories presented in this chapter?

# CASE FOR DISCUSSION

## *How Much Should We Worry About Inflation?*

In early May of 2003 the Federal Reserve signaled its concern about what it called the "minor risk" that today's 1 percent inflation could turn into a deflationary period of falling prices. Testifying before Congress later in the month, Fed Chairman Alan Greenspan reiterated that concern. And in late 2003, he told a group of world bankers that while the development of deflationary forces was a low probability event, the Fed would lean over backward to make certain they are contained.

### Why the Concern About Inflation?

The combination of weak demand for goods and services and competitive pressures from an overhang of excess capacity can squeeze profit margins and force price discounts. The accompanying slack demand for labor will tend to slow the pace of money wage increases and lead to further price weakness. This is how recessions and sluggish recoveries painfully bring down the rate of inflation. And when inflation is already low, prices can actually begin falling.

Falling prices and the expectation of further declines can, in turn, exacerbate the weakness of demand. Consumers may delay some purchases in hopes of getting better prices. Potential home buyers and business investors are discouraged from borrowing for fear they will have to repay their debts out of earnings and revenues diminished by the decline in prices. A reduction in interest rates could overcome this barrier to investment. But, since interest rates can't fall below zero, many of those who worry about deflation fear that the Federal Reserve will have little power left to support demand and fight deflation if interest rates are already low when deflation begins.

### What Can We Do About It?

The breathless tone of some of the media discussion about deflation reflects exaggerated fears. There are a number of monetary and fiscal tools available to stimulate demand and fight deflation, even after the short-term interest rate targeted by the Fed has been pushed down to zero (it is now 1¼ percent). Fed governor Ben Bernanke discussed some of these tools in a November speech. For example, the Fed could act to push down the interest rates on longer-term government securities, thereby promoting lower rates on private loans and bonds, which are still significantly above zero. One powerful way to do this, he suggests, would be for the Fed to announce that it stands ready to make unlimited purchases of medium or even long-term Treasury securities at a price that would achieve some targeted low interest yield. Bernanke also suggested that, among other measures, the Fed could make interest-free loans to banks, accepting as collateral private debt obligations and, if it became necessary, could ask the Congress for authority to purchase such obligations itself. (This latter approach, however, would have to be very carefully crafted because the Fed would then be allocating capital among individual private firms.)

If such monetary policy measures were not enough, the Federal government could generate additional demand with a large, temporary stimulus of tax relief and spending measures. Since households are likely to spend a smaller fraction of a temporary than a permanent tax cut, the size of the reduction should be calibrated accordingly. As Bernanke suggests, the addition to the deficit created by the stimulus could be financed by direct Fed purchases of Treasury securities, so as to prevent the added deficit from raising interest rates and to avoid a large increase in the publicly held federal debt.

While likely harmful in a prosperous or rapidly recovering economy, these measures could be safe and highly useful in an economy with low inflation or deflation and plagued with chronically weak demand.

### Is Japan a Model of What Inflation Can Do?

Japan's decade-long stagnation has, in the last four or five years, been accompanied by falling prices. But Japan should not be taken as an example of what inevitably follows from a modest deflation. In the first place, as economist Adam Posen has pointed out, Japan has used only some of the range of monetary tools available to fight deflation, and those belatedly. And with respect to fiscal policy, the Japanese have for some time been reluctant to undertake aggressive stimulus, on grounds that their debt has already grown sharply relative to GDP. But this objection could be overcome by having the Bank of Japan buy the government securities needed to finance the stimulus—as suggested above for the U.S.

Japan also has some deep structural problems that are inhibiting the growth of investment that is desperately needed to help end stagnation. While Japan has developed a number of world-class export industries, a recent study (2000) by the McKinsey Global Institute showed that a substantial fraction of domestic output is produced by firms with productivity far below those in corresponding U.S. industries. The study documented the regulations, restrictions, land policies, subsidies, and tax incentives that have provided an anti-competitive shelter for inefficient business practices and firms. The potential for modernizing "catch-up" investment in a wide range of domestically oriented industries has been inhibited by this web of protective devices, and political opposition has kept the pace of liberalization slow.

Since the bubble burst more than ten years ago, the Japanese banking system has become saddled with a massive volume of bad loans. Successive efforts to get the bad loans off the books and recapitalize the banks have been frustrated or watered down by entrenched interests within the Japanese Diet, because such a process might force many protected "zombie" firms into bankruptcy. It is difficult to determine the extent to which productive new investments have been deterred by an inability to get bank financing, rather than by the combined effects of stagnant aggregate demand and the protections afforded to existing business establishments. But it's probably much more the latter than the former.

### Conclusion

Deflation, while not a likely forecast for the U.S., needs to be recognized as a downside risk, and the Fed is right to do so. But let's keep it in perspective. In particular, what has happened to Japan is not a model. The U.S. financial system is not hamstrung with a debilitating burden of bad loans. Compared to Japan, it shelters many fewer sectors from competition and imposes smaller barriers to investments that challenge existing industry structures. From a macroeconomic standpoint, the Federal Reserve has made explicit its intent to move promptly to counteract faltering demand, and its willingness to adopt innovative monetary tools should short-term interest rates fall to zero. Most important, it seems quite likely that the appearance of deflationary forces would lead to a substantial further economic stimulus. Indeed, in the current political climate, the main concern is not that the response would be insufficient, but that it would go beyond the needed temporary stimulus, providing yet another permanent tax cut and loading more debt burdens on future generations.

Source: Charles L. Schultz, "How Much Should We Worry about a U.S. Deflation?" Brookings Institution, June 4, 2003.

## QUESTIONS

1. Why is it important for U.S. policy makers to avoid a deflation? Is deflation a problem the Federal Reserve seems concerned about?
2. If an economy were suffering from a fall in aggregate demand that caused deflation, and if the central bank refused to provide the stimulus needed to raise aggregate demand, what other actions could the government take to bring the economy out of its slump? Does this support the Keynes' view? Does it support the monetarist view?
3. Suppose that an economy is suffering from a deflation. By cutting interest rates, the central bank can only reduce the real interest rate so much, with the real interest rate potentially remaining at a very high level. Thinking like a monetarist, can you think of some extreme action that the central bank could undertake that would drastically increase the purchases that consumers want to make and would therefore start to make prices increase? Would Keynes believe this approach would work?

## END NOTES

1. All figures for inflation given here are year-to-year percentage changes in the consumer price index.
2. This situation is sometimes called *stagflation*, but the term is not apt. The term *stagflation*—a combination of "stagnation" and "inflation"—was coined in the 1970s to describe a situation of slow or zero growth in real output, high inflation, and unemployment in excess of its natural rate. The term *inflationary recession* is more suitable for periods that combine high inflation rates with actual drops in real output. The 1974 to 1975 and 1980 recessions were inflationary recessions in this sense.
3. A. W. H. Phillips, "The Relationship between Unemployment and the Rate of Change of Money Wage Rages in the United Kingdom, 1861–1957," *Economica*, new series, 25 (November 1958): 283–299.

# Economic Growth, Productivity, and Saving

*After reading this chapter, you will understand:*

1. How the economy can grow while maintaining price stability.
2. How insufficient growth of aggregate demand can cause a *growth* with deflation.
3. How expansion of aggregate demand at a faster rate than natural real output can cause inflation.
4. Trends in U.S. productivity growth.
5. What policies are available to promote economic growth.

*Before reading this chapter, make sure you know the meaning of:*

1. Leakages and injections
2. Cyclical and structural deficits
3. Crowding-out effect
4. Demand-pull and cost-push inflation
5. Inflation targeting

## MECHANIZATION REDRAWS PROFILE OF AMERICAN AGRICULTURE

IMMOKALEE, FLA.—Chugging down a row of trees, the pair of canopy shakers in Paul Meador's orange grove here seem like a cross between a bulldozer and a hairbrush, their hungry steel bristles working through the tree crowns as if untangling colossal heads of hair. In under 15 minutes, the machines shake loose 36,000 pounds of oranges from 100 trees, catch the fruit, and drop it into a large storage car. "This would have taken four pickers all day long," Mr. Meador said.

Canopy shakers are still an unusual sight in Florida's orange groves. Most of the crop is harvested by hand, mainly by illegal Mexican immigrants. Nylon sacks slung across their backs, perched atop 16-foot ladders, they pluck oranges at a rate of 70 to 90 cents per 90-pound box, or less than $75 a day.

But as globalization creeps into the groves, it is threatening to displace the workers. Facing increased competition from Brazil and a glut of oranges on world markets, alarmed growers here have been turning to labor-saving technology as their best hope for survival.

"The Florida industry has to reduce costs to stay in business," said Everett Loukonen, agribusiness manager for the Barron Collier Company, which uses shakers to harvest about half of the 40.5 million pounds of oranges reaped annually from its 10,000 acres in southwestern Florida.

The spread of mechanization could redraw the profile of Immokalee, which today is a rather typical American farming town. Seventy-one percent of the population of 20,000 is Latino—with much of the balance coming from Haiti—and 46 percent of the residents are foreign born, according to the 2000 census. About 40 percent of the residents live under the poverty line, and the median family income is below $23,000—less than half that of the United States as a whole. Philip Martin, an economist at U.C. Davis, points to the poverty as an argument in favor of labor-saving technology. He estimates that about 10 percent of immigrant farm workers leave the fields every year to seek better jobs. Rather than push more farmhands out of work, he contends, introducing machines will simply reduce the demand for new workers to replenish the labor pool.

And there are some beneficiaries among workers: those lucky enough to operate the new gear. Perched in the air-conditioned booth of Mr. Meador's canopy shaker, a jumpy ranchera tune crackling from the radio, Felix Real, a former picker, said he can make up to $120 a day driving the contraption down the rows, about twice as much as he used to make.

Yet many Immokalee workers are nervous. "They are using the machines on the good groves and leaving us with the scraggly ones," said Venancio Torres, an immigrant from Mexico's coastal state of Veracruz, who has been picking oranges in Florida for three years.

Source: Eduardo Porter, "In Florida Groves, Cheap Labor Means Machines," *The New York Times,* March 22, 2004.

⟨⟩

A N INCREASINGLY COMPETITIVE world economy is putting pressure on industry, agriculture, and service providers throughout the American economy. The response varies. Some firms disappear as jobs are moved abroad. Some survive by turning to low-cost sources of labor, including both legal and illegal immigrants. But if the U.S. economy is to maintain and improve its high living standards over the long run, it must do what the orange growers of Immokalee, Florida have done: increase productivity both by investment in new equipment and by training workers to perform higher paying, high-skill jobs.

In this chapter, we will look at the issue of productivity using the same aggregate supply and demand tools that we applied in the chapter on inflation. We will begin by discussing the policies required for long-run economic growth without excessive inflation. Next we will look at the record of productivity growth in the U.S. economy and likely future trends. Finally, we will discuss policies for promoting economic growth.

# ECONOMIC GROWTH WITH PRICE STABILITY

As we saw in earlier chapters, real output can rise above its natural level in the short run in response to an increase in aggregate demand. It can also fall below its natural level during a recession. Long-run growth, on the other hand, deals not with these short-run ups and downs relative to the natural level of real output but with growth in natural real output itself as a result of increased hours worked and increased productivity—that is, more output per worker-hour.

## *Effects of the Growth of Natural Real Output*

Figure 15.1 shows the effects of the growth of natural real output in terms of aggregate supply and demand. The economy starts out in equilibrium at $E_0$ with a natural real output of $1,500 billion per year, represented by the long-run aggregate supply curve $N_0$. Over time the labor force grows and productivity increases. The result is a rightward shift in the long-run aggregate supply curve to $N_1$.

As natural real output grows, the economy does not move up along its short-run aggregate supply curve as it does when aggregate demand shifts while natural output remains constant. Instead, the short-run aggregate supply curve shifts to the right along with the long-run curve. As long as there is no change in the expected level of productivity-adjusted input prices, the intersection of the long-run and short-run curves will remain at the same price level, 1.0 in this case.[1] This happens because the conditions causing the growth of real output—more workers, more capital, better technology, improved management, and so on—make it possible for output to grow with no increase in input costs per unit of output.

In Figure 15.1, the economy at first is able to produce $1,500 billion of goods and services at a price level of 1.0. The shift in natural real output means that the economy can now potentially produce $2,500 billion of goods and services at the same price level. In order to actually achieve this, however, there must be appropriate growth of aggregate demand. If, as shown in the figure, the aggregate demand curve shifts to the right by the same amount as natural real output, firms will be able to sell all the output produced at the new natural level without cutting their prices. Under these conditions the economy will move smoothly from $E_0$ to $E_1$. At these points, as well as all points in between, the economy will remain in long-run equilibrium. Prices will be stable; productivity-adjusted input prices will remain at the level expected by business managers; real output will keep up with its rising natural level; and unemployment will be steady at its natural rate.

## Managing the Growth of Demand

Figure 15.1 shows the ideal condition of steady economic growth with no inflation or excessive unemployment. However, the economy does not always run smoothly; a number of things can go wrong. One possibility is that steady economic expansion may be thrown off course by shocks to aggregate demand originating in consump-

**FIGURE 15.1   GROWTH WITH STABLE PRICES**

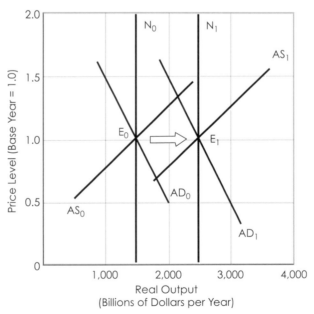

Over time, growth of the labor force and of output per worker-hour causes natural real output to rise. As an increase in natural real output shifts the long-run aggregate supply curve from $N_0$ to $N_1$, the short-run aggregate supply curve also shifts to the right. If aggregate demand is allowed to grow at the same rate, the economy will move smoothly from its initial equilibrium at $E_0$ to a new equilibrium at $E_1$. Prices will be stable, and unemployment will remain at its natural rate.

tion, investment, or net exports. Alternatively, fiscal and monetary policy may be mismanaged in a way that disturbs the smooth growth of the economy. In this section, we will look at what happens when demand grows too rapidly or too slowly.

**GROWTH WITH DEFLATION** Figure 15.2 shows what happens when aggregate demand fails to keep up with natural real output. As before, the economy starts from an equilibrium at $E_0$. Natural real output then rises from $1,500 billion to $2,500 billion, as shown by the shift of the long-run aggregate supply curve from $N_0$ to $N_1$. The short-run aggregate supply curve also shifts rightward, to $AS_1$. This time, however, tight monetary and fiscal policy keep the lid on aggregate demand. With the aggregate demand curve stuck at $AD_0$, the economy cannot reach the intersection of $AS_1$ with $N_1$.

What will happen? If real output initially increases in line with the increases in hours worked plus the growth of productivity while aggregate demand remains unchanged, unplanned inventory buildup will take place. Firms' managers are disappointed; they are producing more than before, but they cannot sell all their output at the prices that prevailed previously. To keep stocks of unsold goods from building up, firms cut their prices, hoping to boost sales. At the same time, they cut back their production plans. They increase output somewhat, but not by as much as the growth

**FIGURE 15.2 GROWTH WITH DEFLATION**

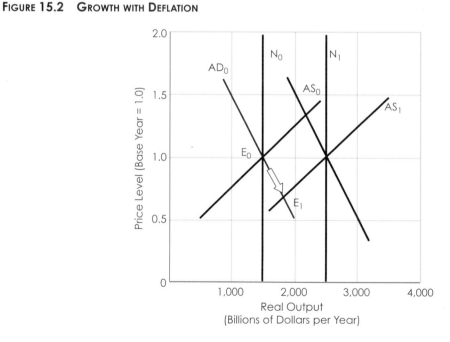

In the case shown here, natural real output grows while aggregate demand remains fixed. Thus, as the long- and short-run aggregate supply curves shift to the right, the aggregate demand curve remains unchanged. The economy moves down and to the right along the aggregate demand curve and at the same time moves down and to the left along the new short-run aggregate supply curve, $AS_1$, as it shifts to the right. The economy experiences falling prices and ends up at $E_1$, where unemployment is higher than its natural rate even though real output has grown. This is sometimes called a *growth recession*.

of natural real output. Thus, as the long-run aggregate supply curve shifts from $N_0$ to $N_1$ and the short-run aggregate supply curve shifts with it, firms' price and output cuts are moving them downward and to the left along the new aggregate supply curve, $AS_1$. The economy thus moves to $E_1$, where the aggregate demand curve $AD_0$, which has not moved from its original position, intersects $AS_1$.

What happens to employment as the economy moves from $E_0$ to $E_1$? Firms have increased their output, but not by as much as natural real output has grown. Given the new investment that has been made and other productivity gains, the economy could produce $2,500 billion in real output; but at $E_1$, output is only about $1,800 billion. The feeble growth in real output means that not enough jobs will be created to absorb all the new workers entering the labor force. Thus, the unemployment rate will rise. If workers resist cuts in nominal wages even though the prices of goods they buy are falling, adjustment will be even slower.

A situation in which real output grows, but not by enough to keep the price level from falling or unemployment from rising above its natural rate, is a form of deflation. Unlike the Japanese deflation examined in the preceding chapter, real output does not actually fall, but it does not grow enough to keep up with potential real output. Because this situation combines rising output with rising unemployment, it is sometimes called a **growth recession**.

**Growth recession**

A situation in which real output grows, but not quickly enough to keep unemployment from rising.

**GROWTH WITH INFLATION** Growth with deflation results from overly cautious economic policy. The economy has the capacity to grow, but policy makers do not give it the room it needs. In the United States, however, policy makers have more often made the opposite mistake: They have pushed the economy beyond the ability of natural real output to grow. The result has been growth with inflation.

The situation of growth with inflation is another form of the demand-pull inflation discussed in an earlier chapter. The difference, as Figure 15.3 shows, is that growth of natural real output is now shifting the long-run aggregate supply curve to the right. As it does so, the short-run aggregate supply curve shifts with it. But while natural real output grows from $1,000 billion to $2,000 billion, an expansionary policy boosts the level of aggregate demand even more forcefully. The new aggregate demand curve, $AD_1$, intersects the new short-run aggregate supply curve, $AS_1$, at $E_1$. The actual level of real output rises above its natural level and unemployment falls below its natural rate.

In moving from $E_0$ to $E_1$, the economy experiences demand-pull inflation, which will affect expectations in the following period. When the expected level of productivity-adjusted input prices rise, the short-run aggregate supply curve will be pushed upward at the same time that growth in natural real output carries both the short- and long-run aggregate supply curves farther to the right. On balance, the short-run curve will end up in the position $AS_2$. To keep real output above its natural level by the same amount, the aggregate demand curve would have to shift to a position such as $AD_2$. In moving from $E_1$ to $E_2$, output would stay exactly the same dis-

## FIGURE 15.3 GROWTH WITH INFLATION

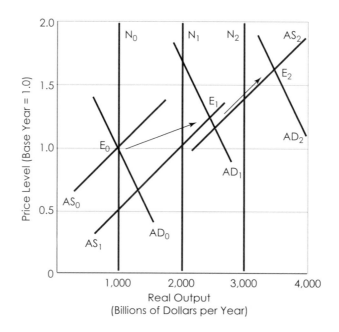

In this example, aggregate demand is allowed to grow more rapidly than natural real output. As the economy grows, it also experiences demand-pull inflation. As the economy moves from $E_0$ to $E_1$, the unemployment rate falls and there is only mild inflation. If aggregate demand is expanded aggressively to try to keep unemployment below its natural rate, inflation will accelerate. On the other hand, a prudent inflation-targeting policy could maneuver the economy to a steady, moderate rate of inflation with continued economic growth and unemployment at the natural rate.

tance above its natural level, keeping unemployment steady at a value somewhat below the natural rate. However, prices will rise by more than they did during the move from $E_0$ to $E_1$. Over time, inflation could get out of control, accelerating to a point at which it could not easily be stopped without a painful inflationary recession.

There is an alternative to this scenario of accelerating inflation, however. Starting from point E1 in Figure 15.3, policy makers could moderate the growth of aggregate demand so that in each coming period the new AD curve intersected the aggregate supply curve AS exactly at the natural level of real output. The result would be similar to the scenario of growth with price stability shown in Figure 15.1, except that the short-run aggregate supply curve would shift upward a little in each period, and there would be a steady, moderate rate of inflation.

Many economists believe that a little bit of inflation as an accompaniment to economic growth is not a bad thing. As we saw in the preceding chapter, countries that use inflation targeting usually aim not for zero inflation, but for an inflation rate around 2 or 3 percent per year. Such moderate inflation has its advantages. One is that moderate inflation provides a cushion against the danger of deflation in case the economy encounters a contractionary shock. Another advantage of moderate inflation is that it can ease the adjustment of relative wages. At any time, some industries are growing while others experience relative decline. If wages and prices in declining industry do not actually have to fall, but can instead stay steady or grow more slowly than those in expanding sectors, adjustment of relative prices will go more smoothly.

# RECENT TRENDS IN ECONOMIC GROWTH AND PRODUCTIVITY

**Labor productivity**

A measure of how much workers produce in a given period of time, usually measured as output per hour of work.

Up to this point, we have treated the rate of growth of natural real output as a given. Now we will give it a closer look. We can begin by breaking the sources of growth of natural real output into two components: the growth of total labor inputs, on the one hand, and the growth of output per unit of labor, or **labor productivity**, on the other.

The growth of total labor inputs tends to be determined by social and demographic factors that differ from one country to another, but that do not change rapidly within any one country. One source of growth of labor inputs is, of course, population growth. Population in the United States is now growing at about 1 percent per year or less, largely thanks to immigration. Population in most other advanced countries is stable or slowly declining. Another possible source of increased labor input is increased labor force participation. In the United States, for example, from 1960 to 1989, labor force participation by women increased from 37 percent to 57 percent, more than offsetting a smaller decline in labor force participation among men. Since 1990, labor force participation trends of various groups have roughly balanced out, so that the total rate has not changed much. Over the same period, both population growth and increased labor force participation have been offset, in part, by a decrease in average weekly hours worked from about 39 in 1960 to about 34 today. Taking all these trends together, total hours worked in the U.S. economy have grown moderately.

As Figure 15.4 shows, growth of labor productivity has shown substantial variability over the past half century, in contrast to the relatively steady trend of total hours worked. Setting aside substantial short-term cyclical variations, productivity trends can be broken into three longer periods. From 1948 to 1973, productivity grew at an average rate of about 2.8 percent. Then, from 1974 to 1991, productivity growth fell by more than half, to an average annual rate of just 1.3 percent. Since 1992, the productivity slowdown has been reversed. During the later 1990s, productivity growth recovered to a rate of more than 2 percent per year, and from 2000 through early 2004, it grew at the unusually strong rate of more than 4 percent per year.

## Explaining the Productivity Slowdown and Its Reversals

The productivity slowdown of the 1970s and 1980s and the more recent productivity boom have been the subject of extensive study. The following factors are among those most often cited as contributing to varying productivity trends:

**FIGURE 15.4   U.S. PRODUCTIVITY GROWTH PERCENT PER YEAR: THREE-YEAR MOVING AVERAGE**

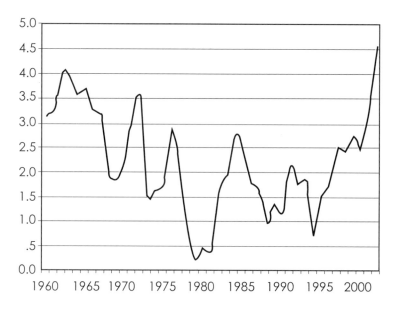

From 1948 through 1973, productivity grew at an average annual rate of 2.8 percent. From 1974 to 1991, productivity growth slowed substantially, to an average of just 1.3 percent per year. Since 1992, productivity growth has recovered, reaching its highest rates in half a century during the early 2000s.

Source: *Economic Report of the President,* 2004, table B-50.

- **Changes in the labor force.** Many analyses of the productivity slowdown point to the entry of millions of women and young people into the labor force during the 1970s. These new workers were, on the whole, skilled and motivated, but they tended to have less experience than those who already held jobs. At the same time, by their sheer number they pulled down the ratio of capital to labor. By the 1990s, these demographic changes had worked their way through, allowing historic productivity trends to resume.

- **Supply shocks.** Some economists believe that the oil price shocks of the 1970s contributed to the productivity slowdown by rendering much of the economy's capital stock obsolete. Many inefficient older trucks, planes, furnaces, generators, and so on had to be retired or placed on standby because high oil prices made them too costly to operate. The effect was almost the same as if the equipment had been destroyed by fire or flood. Moreover, it is argued, the oil price shocks made it necessary to rechannel much investment into finding ways to get by with less oil—either through the design of more energy-efficient equipment or through the production of substitute energy sources—rather than into other productivity-enhancing areas of research. By the end of the 1980s, the effects of these supply shocks had run their course, leaving a leaner, more efficient capital stock as a basis for further growth.

- **Research and technology.** During the 1970s, research and development spending fell from a high of 3 percent of GDP to a low of 2.2 percent in 1977. Some economists have seen the R&D slowdown as a major culprit in the stagnation of productivity. In the 1980s and even more in the 1990s, these trends were reversed and replaced by a technology boom, as businesses made huge investments in computers and communications technology. At first the impact of these on economy-wide productivity was disappointing, but after a period of learning and organizational change the new technologies began to pay off in a big way. Some economists see the spurt of productivity in the early 2000s as a delayed result of technology investments of the preceding decade.

- **Inflation.** As we saw in the preceding chapter, inflation is an enemy of economic growth. The productivity slowdown of the 1970s occurred at the same time as the speedup of inflation. Inflation disrupted business planning and labor-management relations, and distorted the impact of taxes on business and investment income. This not only reduced total investment but also tended to channel investment toward uses that did little to enhance productivity, such as housing and tax shelters, and away from more productive projects. Since 1992, inflation has returned to the moderate range of 1 to 3 percent. Many economists think it is not coincidental that the slowdown in inflation coincided with the revival of productivity growth.

## International Productivity Trends

The United States was not the only country to experience a productivity slowdown in the 1970s. Rather, the slowdown affected most of the major industrialized countries simultaneously. For example, the rate of increase in output per worker-hour in manufacturing, one frequently cited measure of productivity, fell from 3.2 percent per year in the period from 1960 to 1973 and to 1.4 percent per year in the period from 1973 to 1979 in the United States. However, over the same period the annual rate of growth of manufacturing output per worker-hour fell from 10.3 percent to 5.5 percent in Japan; from 6.4 to 4.6 percent in France; from 6.4 to 2.6 percent in Sweden; and from 4.2 to 1.2 percent in the United Kingdom.[2]

On the other hand, the revival of productivity growth in the United States has not been duplicated in many other advanced countries. Productivity growth has continued to lag in the European Union, a development that some observers blame on overly rigid central regulation and insufficiently flexible labor markets. And, as discussed in *Economics in the News 15.1,* Japan, which used to be seen as a world productivity leader, has fallen behind.

## Measurement Problems

A major reason that productivity is so hard to understand is that the whole field is plagued by extraordinary measurement problems. Productivity numbers attempt to

## ⬛ ECONOMICS IN THE NEWS 15.1

### TALE OF TWO ECONOMIES

One of the most remarkable developments of the last 10 years was the dual reversal of fortune by the world's two largest economies—the simultaneous economic ascendance of the United States and decline of Japan. Fiscal and monetary policies certainly contributed in both instances. However, new research shows that microeconomic factors, especially the different organization and strategies of the two countries' information technology sectors, may have been more important.

Information technology may matter less than "New Economy" promoters once claimed, but the strength and length of the 1990s U.S. boom clearly owed much to IT. According to first-rate analysis by the Commerce Department, IT companies, while constituting less than 8 percent of the GDP, accounted for nearly 30 percent of U.S. economic growth from 1995 to 2000. Harvard's Dale Jorgenson and the Fed's Kevin Stiroh trace more than three-fourths of increased U.S. productivity growth to IT advances and strong business investment to deploy those advances.

Throughout the '80s, many Americans envied Japan its technological prowess, but there is a strong case that Japan's IT weakness magnified its slow growth and weak productivity gains in the '90s. One of Japan's top economists, Rizaburo Nezu of the Fujitsu Research Institute, has recently documented the various and complex ways in which, less than a generation after Japanese firms pioneered the miniaturization and marketing of electronics, Japan has "disappeared from world IT competition."

Today, the world's 10 largest IT companies include six American firms but only one Japanese company, the mobile phone and ISP giant NTT DoCoMo. Japan's domestic macroeconomic troubles cannot explain this. IT companies draw on global markets and technologies. For the last decade, companies could borrow money in Tokyo to develop or buy IT technologies more cheaply than in New York. And since 1990, Japanese firms have invested in R & D and in IT hardware at higher rates than their U.S. counterparts.

Yet the '90s saw Japanese IT fail spectacularly, market segment by market segment. The main culprits were the flawed strategies and organization of Japanese IT companies. The semiconductor industry is, in many ways, the very heart of IT development. Twelve years ago, U.S. and Japanese firms each controlled more than 40 percent of the world market. Over the next decade, their corporate strategies diverged; by 2000, American chip makers accounted for 55 percent of global semiconductor sales, and Japanese companies were left with just 25 percent. Leading chip makers in Japan (and Europe) tried to produce all kinds of chips. This strategy required them to diffuse their R & D resources. As they fell behind technologically, their market share eroded. Their counterparts in America (and Korea) concentrated on a few, select classes of chips and vastly expanded their market share.

American firms today control two-thirds of the world PC market and 80 percent of global server sales. In each case, Japanese producers account for less than 5 percent. Again, contrasting production strategies may explain the Japanese's also-ran status. The American companies that have come to dominate PC and server sales—Dell, IBM, Sun Microsystems, Compaq, and HP—concentrate on procurement, logistics, and after-sales service and leave most of the computer design and production to firms like Taiwan's Quanta and Acer. Japan's once-great computer makers—Fujitsu, Toshiba, and Sony—have persisted in doing almost everything at home and for themselves, an increasingly improvident strategy in an era of globalization.

Source: Robert Shapiro, "The IT Split," *Slate*, August 21, 2002 (abbreviated from original article).

measure output per unit of input. That is simple enough when the output is a tangible good for which quality does not change over time, such as coal or lumber. But much of the economy does not fit this pattern.

For one thing, an increasing portion of the economy is devoted to producing goods for which quality changes are more important than quantity changes. Computers are the classic example, but quality changes in such areas as pharmaceuticals, aircraft, and even automobiles are hardly less striking. National income statisticians try to capture some of these quality changes in their measures of output, but their efforts are not fully successful. Economist John Kendrick of Georgetown University, a leading expert on productivity, thinks that failure to adjust fully for quality changes leads to a 0.36 percentage point understatement in the annual rate of growth of real GDP.[3] This, in turn, reduces estimates of productivity growth.

Moreover, the measurement problems get worse when we turn from goods-producing industries to services, which now account for some two-thirds of GDP. After 1973, official measures of productivity in the service sector fell to nearly zero, and according to some data, even became negative. But what do the numbers pertaining to service-industry productivity actually mean?

In the opinion of a growing number of economists, they mean very little. The basic problem is the impossibility of measuring the output of services in quantity terms. Suppose, for example, that an insurance company raises its premiums without changing the numbers of people it employs or types of policies that it offers. Perhaps the increase reflects the need to cover increases in the risks to which policyholders are exposed, say, a rising crime rate. In that case, it could be argued that the increased revenue reflects greater service to customers, and hence, an increase in productivity. But perhaps the premium increase simply reflects higher costs. In that case, output per worker is unchanged. Not knowing how to measure output, the government reports no productivity figures for the insurance industry at all.

No productivity figures are reported for health care, real estate, or stock brokerage services, either. In all, figures are reported for industries employing only 30 percent of all service workers. In other industries, the reported figures are tainted by questionable measures. For example, in banking, output is counted in terms of the number of trust accounts maintained and number of checks cleared, with no adjustment for the dollar volume of each transaction. Nor is there any attempt to measure the improvement in quality resulting from the many new services banks have added in recent years.

Small wonder that a productivity expert like Michael Darby, formerly chief economist at the Commerce Department, says frankly, "At our current state of knowledge, we don't really know what's happening to service-sector productivity. It could well be growing faster than manufacturing productivity, instead of much slower."[4]

## POLICIES FOR PROMOTING ECONOMIC GROWTH AND SAVING

Throughout this book, we have listed growth of real output as one of the fundamental goals of macroeconomic policy. All economists, regardless of which school of thought they belong to, see growth as important both to improvement in material welfare and to maintenance of national security. Accordingly, a variety of policies designed to promote growth have been advanced.

One element of growth policy commands widespread agreement: As we saw in the first section of this chapter, policy makers must allow a rate of growth of aggregate demand that will at least roughly match that of natural real output. If demand is permitted to grow too rapidly, higher inflation rates will return, and rapid inflation, as we have seen, may have been one of the villains of the productivity slowdown of the 1970s. On the other hand, if demand grows too slowly, the economy may slip into deflation.

In addition to policies designed to match the growth of actual and natural real output, policies have been proposed that are intended to promote the growth of natural real output itself. First we will consider the use of conventional monetary and fiscal policy tools to promote such growth. We then consider policies that aim to increase the economy's growth potential by encouraging saving and investment.

## Economic Growth and the Fiscal-Monetary Policy Mix

There is more than one way to achieve a given level or rate of growth of aggregate demand. But although a mix of expansionary fiscal policy and tight monetary policy might produce the same growth rate of aggregate demand as a mix of tight fiscal policy and expansionary monetary policy, the two policy mixes have different effects on interest rates. Our basic macroeconomic model suggests that an easy monetary/tight fiscal policy mix leads to lower real and nominal interest rates than a tight monetary/easy fiscal policy mix. Because the easy monetary/tight fiscal policy mix yields lower real interest rates, it also results in more real investment.

The economists President Kennedy brought to Washington in the early 1960s relied in part on this principle to help fulfill Kennedy's campaign pledge to "get the country moving again." They saw no problem with federal budget deficits as a means of pulling the economy out of a recession, but they firmly believed that the deficit should disappear as the economy approached its natural level of real output. If it did not, the deficit would crowd out private investment and slow economic growth.

In the 1990s, the idea of shifting the policy mix toward tighter fiscal and easier monetary policies to promote growth has again become popular. In one form or another, the concept was endorsed by all three major candidates in the 1992 presidential elections. For example, the first President Bush declared that "the primary economic goal of my Administration is to achieve the highest possible rate of economic growth." He announced a plan to promote growth through a combination of spending cuts to eliminate the federal budget deficit, combined with tax incentives to further stimulate investment. Victorious candidate Bill Clinton also pledged deficit reduction as a key to faster growth, taking the political risk of stating that cutting the deficit would require tax increases. This strategy paid off. As we saw in earlier chapters, the U.S. federal budget returned to surplus in the 1990s for the first time in a generation. The surpluses reversed the crowding-out effect of deficits and helped finance the technology investments that have since boosted productivity growth.

The budget surpluses of the 1990s disappeared in the first decade of the twenty-first century, however. President George W. Bush used expansionary fiscal policy, in the form of broad tax cuts, to speed recovery from the 2001 recession. Later, a sharp rise in federal spending, including both the enormous cost of financing the Iraq war and growth in domestic spending, pushed deficits to record levels. By 2004, the federal budget deficit had reached an all-time record. Federal Reserve chairman Alan Greenspan was once again warning that the fiscal-monetary policy mix was seriously out of balance.

## Growth and Saving

As noted in earlier chapters, investment must be financed either by saving that takes place within the country, or by inflows of capital from abroad. Accordingly, economists concerned with growth have noted with alarm a sharp decline in net national saving in the United States. One measure of net national saving is net private saving less the government budget deficit. By this measure, net national saving fell from nearly 8 percent of net domestic product (NDP) in the 1971 to 1980 period to less than 5 percent in the 1981 to 1985 period and just 3 percent in the 1986 to 1990 period. New saving revived somewhat in the later 1990s, reaching a peak of 5.5 percent of GDP in 2000. From that point, it quickly declined again to a new low of just 0.7 percent in the first quarter of 2003.

As we already know, the swing from deficits to surplus and back to deficits in the federal budget are one contributing factor to the saving shortfall of recent years. That is not the whole story, however. Personal saving has also decreased substantially in recent years, as shown in Figure 15.5. As the figure shows, U.S. personal saving averaged around 7.25 percent of disposable income for the period 1960 to 1980. In the early 1980s, it edged up to 7.75 percent, but since 1986 it has decreased. The personal savings rate fell dramatically in the late 1990s, falling below 2 percent of disposable income before edging up just slightly in the early 2000s.

Private and government savings are also important in terms of trade and borrowing from abroad. Recall the relationship between private savings (S), investment (I), the government budget (T – G), and the current account (X – IM):

$$(X - IM) = (T - G) + (S - I)$$

Budget deficits have a negative effect on the current account, causing it to fall further into deficit. If the U.S. runs a federal budget deficit, then (T – G) is negative, causing a decrease in the current account (X – IM). The current account also represents net capital flows. An excess of imports over exports must be financed by a net capital inflow into the U.S.—that is, by net borrowing from abroad plus net sales of assets to foreign buyers—so that the value of the current account deficit and the

**FIGURE 15.5    PERSONAL SAVINGS RATE**

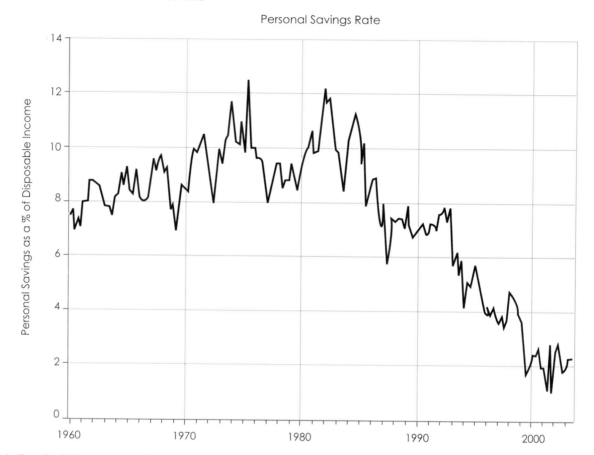

Personal Savings Rate

As the chart shows, personal saving averaged around 7.25 percent of disposable income for the period 1960 to 1980. In the early 1980s, it edged up to 7.75 percent, but since 1986, it has decreased. The decline in personal savings continued through the periods of federal budget surpluses in the late 1990s, falling dramatically below 2 percent of disposable income in the late 1990s. The downward trend in personal savings since the mid-1980s seems to reflect a longer-term trend.

Source: Bureau of Economic Analysis, U.S. Department of Commerce, 2003.

value of capital inflows are equal. As we saw in earlier chapters, the record federal budget deficits of 2003 and 2004 have been financed largely by financial inflows in the form of purchases of U.S. government securities by Asian central banks.

Government policy makers and independent economists have recommended a variety of policies to promote saving. Some emphasize increasing the rate of return on saving, for example, by making income from savings wholly or partially tax exempt. Tax-deferred Individual Retirement Accounts are an example of such a policy. Other economists suggest that saving can be promoted by raising taxes on consumption goods, either through a broad value-added tax of the kind used in Europe, or through increased taxes on tobacco, alcohol, and gasoline.

## How Much Saving Is Enough?

In the debate over the saving shortfall and policies to deal with it, one question is almost never asked: How much saving is enough? Participants in the debate almost universally agree that more saving is better. What is more, they do not always limit themselves to positive economic arguments regarding the effects of saving on capital accumulation and growth. Many commentators are given to sweeping normative declarations to the effect that low savings "cheat the future" and to condemnations of a culture that allegedly "bombards us with messages to buy things—not save." In short, a low saving rate is perceived as a sign of moral weakness.

But there are some counterarguments to these claims. First, the primary reason saving is valued is that it promotes more rapid economic growth. Yet there is a long tradition in economics that questions the unlimited desirability of economic growth itself. This antigrowth tradition is manifested today in certain parts of the environmental movement, which identify excessive growth of material output, combined with inadequate attention to nonmaterial sources of human welfare, as the root of many current problems.

Second, the welfare of future generations is constantly evoked in the debate over saving. But as long as growth of per capita real income does not come to a stop altogether (and it has not done so), future generations will be richer than our own. Saving thus is a transfer from the relatively poor present to the relatively rich future. Why is such a transfer desirable, considering that most people favor transfers from the rich to the poor rather than from the poor to the rich within any given generation? This question is never asked or answered by proponents of a higher saving rate.

Finally, why should the private component of national saving be a matter of public policy in the first place? After all, personal and business saving are not the result of decisions reached in some big town meeting—they are the outcome of millions of individual decisions by households and business managers. In the case of households, we are willing to leave people free to choose whether to eat better (consumption) or live in a better house (saving), and free to choose how much of their lifetime income to enjoy themselves and how much to leave to their children. In the case of firms, we are content to leave stockholders, acting through their agents in corporate management, free to choose between reinvestment of earnings and distribution of dividends. If we are content to leave all these microlevel choices up to individuals, why should we not be content with whatever national saving rate results from adding together their outcomes?

The debate over the saving shortfall would be more enlightening if the question of how much saving is enough were at least considered.

# SUMMARY

1. **How can the economy grow while maintaining price stability?** As growth of natural real output shifts the long-run aggregate supply curve to the right, the short-run aggregate supply curve will shift with it, provided there is no change in the expected level of productivity-adjusted input prices. If aggregate demand is allowed to grow at the same rate as natural real output, the aggregate demand curve will shift along with the others. Under these conditions output will grow smoothly, final-goods prices will be stable, and unemployment will remain at its natural rate.

2. **How can insufficient growth of aggregate demand lead to growth combined with deflation?** If aggregate demand does not keep up with the growth of natural real output, firms will be unable to sell all the output they are able to produce. Unplanned inventory buildup will put downward pressure on prices and cause the actual level of real output to grow more slowly than the natural level. The result is growth with deflation, or a *growth recession*, during which real output grows but the unemployment rate rises.

3. **How can expansion of aggregate demand at a faster rate than natural real output cause inflation?** If aggregate demand grows faster than natural real output, demand-pull inflation will result. If inflation targeting is used to hold price increases to a moderate rate, lasting prosperity is possible. However, if growth of aggregate demand is excessive, inflation will accelerate. This condition may be difficult to reverse without triggering an inflationary recession.

4. **What factors explain substantial swings in the rate of U.S. productivity growth over the past half century?** From the end of World War II until the early 1970s, productivity growth averaged 2.8 percent per year. From 1973 to 1991, it fell to less than half of that, before recovering during the later 1990s. Explanations for these fluctuations include changes in the age and gender composition of the labor force, supply shocks caused by oil price increases, inflation, changes in spending on research and development, and trends in technology. No one of these factors seems to fully explain the swings in productivity. Problems in measuring productivity, especially in the service sector, add to the difficulties of fully understanding productivity trends.

5. **What policies are available to promote economic growth?** According to our basic macroeconomic model, growth will be promoted by a policy mix that includes a structurally balanced budget and a monetary policy leading to relatively low interest rates. Economic growth can be promoted by other policies encouraging saving and investment, as well. In addition, growth could potentially be stimulated by tax policies designed to encourage saving and investment.

# KEY TERMS

Growth recession
Labor productivity

# PROBLEMS AND TOPICS FOR DISCUSSION

1. **Examining the lead-off case.** How do improvements in technology increase the rate of economic growth? What adjustment of monetary and fiscal policy is needed when technology investments cause the growth of natural real output to accelerate? What are the possible sources of saving needed to finance investments in technology? Who gains, and who loses when technological change occurs?

2. **Stagflation.** Endnote 1 describes an episode of what could be called "stagflation." Draw a set of aggregate supply and demand curves to illustrate this situation.

3. **Growth with inflation.** Figure 15.3 illustrates growth with inflation. What would happen to the economy if, starting from the situation represented by point $E_2$, policy makers were to stop the growth of aggregate demand while natural real output continued to grow? Use aggregate supply and demand curves to illustrate your answer.

4. **Personal saving.** Most people have negative saving when they are young (that is, they consume more than their income), have positive saving during their prime working years, and then have negative saving again in retirement. Do you expect your own saving to follow this pattern? Why or why not?

# CASE FOR DISCUSSION

## The Great American Savings Shortfall

At the turn of the twenty-first century, American consumers helped to keep the economy afloat through a relatively short recession in 2001. Fiscal tax cuts and the Fed's lowering interest rates encouraged people to borrow and spend. While this helped spur economic recovery in 2001, it leaves us in a quandary: Don't we need to save now to afford the coming surge in retirements from the baby boom generation? The personal savings rate in the U.S. hovers around 2%. How do policy makers boost saving without threatening economic recovery?

There is little agreement regarding what to do about the saving rate. Some advocate traditional economic incentives, including a cut in capital gains taxes (such as those implemented by President George W. Bush), tax-favored family savings plans,

and reforms to Social Security. Others recommend alternatives such as investment tax credits to encourage business saving. Frank Levy of the University of Maryland and Richard C. Michel of the Urban Institute maintain that the problem is less about tax incentives than about culture—a culture, they say, that "bombards us with messages to buy things—not save—every day." In this context, they see the key to increased saving as "a change in national outlook."*

Levy and Michel suggest that we think of saving as cholesterol. "Both are the byproduct of immediate gratification, neither involves short-run cost, both accrue slowly with real dangers for the future." If the president is serious about the saving shortfall, they say, he should talk as plainly about it as doctors talk about cholesterol. Why not publish national guidelines on what people ought to save—a simple schedule that relates annual savings to family income and age? "In a word, with guidelines on everything from salt intake to safe sex, a problem without guidelines is not seen as a problem," Levy and Michel conclude.

*Frank Levy and Richard C. Michel, "Why America Won't Save," *The Washington Post*, February 4, 1990, p. C1.

## QUESTIONS

1. How would you define "undersaving"? Are you yourself undersaving? Is the country as a whole? How would you go about determining the ideal rate of national saving? Or is more saving always better, without limit?

2. The article suggests that saving, like eating a healthy diet, involves a trade-off between present and future gratification. Use a production possibility frontier to illustrate this trade-off. Label the horizontal axis "saving" and the vertical axis "consumption." First draw a frontier that is based on a fixed current income. Mark a point A on the frontier that represents a relatively low saving rate and a point B that represents a relatively high rate. Next draw two frontiers that represent

future income levels—one based on saving rate A and the other on saving rate B. Why will the two future frontiers not be the same? Is it possible to draw the frontiers in such a way that the higher current saving rate will permit both higher saving and higher consumption in the future?

3. Do you think Levy's and Michel's proposal for national saving guidelines would have a significant impact on the national saving rate? How would you go about determining the proper guidelines? Would you favor voluntary guidelines, compulsory guidelines, or none at all? Discuss.

# END NOTES

1. To understand why input prices must be adjusted for changes in productivity, imagine that nominal wages and other nominal input prices remained constant, but output per worker-hour doubled throughout the economy. In that case, a typical firm's cost of producing any given level of output would fall by half, thereby shifting the firm's individual supply curve downward and increasing the quantity of output the firm would be willing to produce under any given conditions of market demand. For the economy as a whole, this would produce a downward shift of the short-run aggregate supply curve relative to the long-run aggregate supply curve. However, if nominal wages doubled at the same time output per worker-hour doubled, unit costs of production at the new natural level of output would remain the same as they were to begin with, and there would be no such shift. In that case, we would say that productivity-adjusted wages were constant. The same kind of adjustment can be made for any input.

2. U.S. Department of Labor, Bureau of Labor Statistics, "International Comparisons of Manufacturing Productivity and Labor Cost Trends," USDL 89–322, June 30, 1989, Table 1.

3. "Are GNP Estimates Understated?" *The Margin* (January–February 1990): 13.

4. As quoted in Alfred L. Malabre, Jr., and Linkley H. Clark, Jr., "Productivity Statistics for the Service Sector May Understate Gains," *The Wall Street Journal*, August 12, 1992.

# GLOSSARY

**Accommodating policy**   Expansionary monetary or fiscal policy used to increase aggregate demand in order to moderate the effects of a supply shock on real output.

**Aggregate demand**   The value of all planned expenditures.

**Aggregate demand curve**   A graph showing the relationship between real planned expenditures on final goods and the average price level of final goods.

**Aggregate supply**   The value of all goods and services produced in the economy; a synonym for domestic product.

**Aggregate supply curve**   A graph showing the relationship between real output (real domestic product) and the average price level of final goods.

**Appreciation (of a currency)**   An increase in the value of a country's currency relative to another's.

**Assets**   All the things that the firm or household owns or to which it holds a legal claim.

**Automatic fiscal policy**   Changes in government purchases or net taxes that are caused by changes in economic conditions given unchanged tax and spending laws.

**Automatic stabilizers**   Those elements of automatic fiscal policy that move the federal budget toward deficit during an economic contraction and toward surplus during an expansion.

**Autonomous**   In the context of the income-expenditure model, refers to an expenditure that is independent of the level of real domestic income.

**Autonomous consumption**   The part of total real consumption expenditure that is independent of the level of real disposable income; for any given consumption schedule, real autonomous consumption equals the level of real consumption associated with zero real disposable income.

**Autonomous net taxes**   Taxes or transfer payments that do not vary with the level of domestic income.

**Average propensity to consume**    Total consumption for any income level divided by total disposable income.

**Balance sheet**    A financial statement showing what a firm or household owns and what it owes.

**Base year**    The year that is chosen as a basis for comparison in calculating a price index or price level.

**Bond**    A certificate that represents a promise, in return for borrowed funds, to repay the loan over a period of years, with interest, according to an agreed-upon schedule.

**Business cycle**    A pattern of irregular but repeated expansion and contraction of aggregate economic activity.

**Capital**    All means of production that are created by people, including tools, industrial equipment, and structures.

**Capital account**    The section of a country's international accounts that consists of purchases and sales of assets and international borrowing and lending.

**Capital account net demand curve**    A graph that shows the net demand for a country's currency that results at various exchange rates from capital account transactions.

**Capital inflows**    Net borrowing from foreign financial intermediaries and net funds received from sales of real or financial assets to foreign buyers.

**Capital outflows**    Net lending to foreign borrowers and net funds used to purchase real or financial assets from foreign sellers.

**Change in demand**    A change in the quantity of a good that buyers are willing and able to purchase that results from a change in some condition other than the price of that good; shown by a shift in the demand curve.

**Change in quantity demanded**    A change in the quantity of a good that buyers are willing and able to purchase that results from a change in the good's price, other things being equal; shown by a movement from one point to another along a demand curve.

**Change in quantity supplied**    A change in the quantity of a good that suppliers are willing and able to sell that results from a change in the good's price, other things being equal; shown by a movement along a supply curve.

**Change in supply**    A change in the quantity of a good that suppliers are willing and able to sell that results from a change in some condition other than the good's price; shown by a shift in the supply curve.

**Circular flow of income and product**    The flow of goods and services between households and firms, balanced by the flow of payments made in exchange for goods and services.

**Closed economy**    An economy that has no links to the rest of the world.

**Commercial banks**    Financial intermediaries that provide a broad range of banking services, including accepting demand deposits and making commercial loans.

**Common stock**  A certificate of shared ownership in a corporation that gives the owner a vote in the selection of the firm's management and the right to a share in its profits.

**Comparative advantage**  The ability to produce a good or service at a relatively lower opportunity cost than someone else.

**Complementary goods**  A pair of goods for which an increase in the price of one results in a decrease in demand for the other.

**Conditional forecast**  A prediction of future economic events in the form "If A, then B, other things being equal."

**Consumer Price Index (CPI)**  An average of the prices of a market basket of goods and services purchased by a typical urban household.

**Consumption schedule (consumption function)**  A graph that shows how real consumption expenditure varies as real disposable income changes, other things being equal.

**Cost-push inflation**  Inflation that is caused by an upward shift in the aggregate supply curve while the aggregate demand curve remains fixed or shifts upward more slowly.

**Cross-elasticity of demand**  The ratio of the percentage change in the quantity of a good demanded to a given percentage change in the price of some other good, other things being equal.

**Crowding-out effect**  The tendency of expansionary fiscal policy to raise the interest rate and thereby cause a decrease in real planned investment.

**Currency**  Coins and paper money.

**Current account**  The section of a country's international accounts that consists of imports and exports of goods and services and unilateral transfers.

**Current account balance**  The value of a country's exports of goods and services minus the value of its imports of goods and services plus its net transfer receipts from foreign sources.

**Cyclical deficit/surplus**  The difference between the structural budget and the actual federal budget. If the actual budget is above the structural budget, there is a cyclical surplus. Likewise, when the actual budget is below the structural budget, there is a cyclical deficit.

**Cyclical unemployment**  The difference between the observed rate of unemployment at a given point in the business cycle and the natural rate of unemployment.

**Demand**  The willingness and ability of buyers to purchase goods.

**Demand curve**  A graphical representation of the relationship between the price of a good and the quantity of that good that buyers demand.

**Demand-pull inflation**  Inflation caused by an upward shift of the aggregate demand curve while the aggregate supply curve remains fixed or shifts upward at no more than an equal rate.

**Depository institutions**    Financial intermediaries, including commercial banks and thrift institutions, that accept deposits from the public.

**Depreciation (of a currency)**    A decline in the value of a country's currency relative to another's.

**Direct relationship**    A relationship between two variables in which an increase in the value of one variable is associated with an increase in the value of the other.

**Discount rate**    The interest rate charged by the Fed on loans of reserves to banks.

**Discount window**    The department through which the Federal Reserve lends reserves to banks.

**Discouraged worker**    A person who would work if a suitable job were available but has given up looking for such a job.

**Discretionary fiscal policy**    Changes in the laws regarding government purchases and net taxes.

**Disposable personal income (disposable income)**    Personal income less personal taxes (particularly income taxes).

**Domestic income**    The total income of all types, including wages, rents, interest payments, and profits, paid in return for factors of production used in producing domestic product.

**Domestic product**    The total value of all goods and services produced annually in a given country.

**Econometrics**    The statistical analysis of empirical economic data.

**Economic efficiency**    A state of affairs in which it is impossible to make any change that satisfies one person's wants more fully without causing some other person's wants to be satisfied less fully.

**Economics**    The social science that seeks to understand the choices people make in using scarce resources to meet their wants.

**Efficiency in distribution**    A situation in which it is not possible, by redistributing existing supplies of goods, to satisfy one person's wants more fully without causing some other person's wants to be satisfied less fully.

**Efficiency in production**    A situation in which it is not possible, given available knowledge and productive resources, to produce more of one good without forgoing the opportunity to produce some of another good.

**Elastic demand**    A situation in which quantity demanded changes by a larger percentage than price, so that total revenue increases as price decreases.

**Elasticity**    A measure of the response of one variable to a change in another, stated as a ratio of the percentage change in one variable to the associated percentage change in another variable.

**Empirical**   Based on experience or observation.

**Employed**   A term used to refer to a person who is working at least 1 hour a week for pay or at least 15 hours per week as an unpaid worker in a family business.

**Employment-population ratio**   The percentage of the noninstitutional adult population that is employed.

**Entitlements**   Transfer payments governed by long-term laws that are not subject to annual budget review.

**Entrepreneurship**   The process of looking for new possibilities—making use of new ways of doing things, being alert to new opportunities, and overcoming old limits.

**Equation of exchange**   An equation that shows the relationship among the money stock (M), the income velocity of money (V), the price level (P), and real domestic product (y); written as MV = Py.

**Equilibrium**   A condition in which buyers' and sellers' plans exactly mesh in the marketplace, so that the quantity supplied exactly equals the quantity demanded at a given price.

**Excess quantity demanded (shortage)**   A condition in which the quantity of a good demanded at a given price exceeds the quantity supplied.

**Excess quantity supplied (surplus)**   A condition in which the quantity of a good supplied at a given price exceeds the quantity demanded.

**Excess reserves**   Total reserves minus required reserves.

**Exchange controls**   Restrictions on the freedom of firms and individuals to exchange the domestic currency for foreign currencies at market rates.

**Exchange-rate based stabilization policy**   A policy that uses the exchange rate as the principle operating target for macroeconomic policy.

**Expenditure multiplier**   The ratio of the resultant shift in real aggregate demand to an initial shift in one of the components of aggregate demand.

**Factors of production**   The basic inputs of labor, capital, and natural resources used in producing all goods and services.

**Federal funds market**   A market in which banks lend reserves to one another for periods as short as 24 hours.

**Federal funds rate**   The interest rate on overnight loans of reserves from one bank to another.

**Federal funds target**   The Fed's target for the federal funds rate, announced by the Federal Open Market Committee (FOMC).

**Final goods and services**   Goods and services that are sold to or ready for sale to parties that will use them for consumption, investment, government purchases, or export.

**Financial intermediaries**  A group of firms, including banks, insurance companies, pension funds, and mutual funds, that gather funds from net savers and lend them to net borrowers.

**Financial markets**  A set of market institutions whose function is to channel the flow of funds from net savers to net borrowers.

**Fiscal policy**  Policy that is concerned with government purchases, taxes, and transfer payments.

**Fiscal year**  The federal government's budgetary year, which starts on October 1 of the preceding calendar year.

**Fixed investment**  Purchases by firms of newly produced capital goods, such as production machinery, office equipment, and newly built structures.

**Flow**  A process that occurs continuously through time, measured in units per time period.

**Foreign-exchange market**  A market in which the currency of one country is traded for that of another.

**Frictional unemployment**  The portion of unemployment that is accounted for by the short periods of unemployment needed for matching jobs with job seekers.

**GDP deflator**  A weighted average of the prices of all final goods and services produced in the economy.

**Gross domestic product (GDP)**  The value at current market prices of all final goods and services produced annually in a given country.

**Gross national product (GNP)**  The dollar value at current market prices of all final goods and services produced annually by factors of production owned by residents of a given country, regardless of where those factors are located.

**Growth recession**  A situation in which real output grows, but not quickly enough to keep unemployment from rising.

**Hyperinflation**  Very rapid inflation.

**Income elasticity of demand**  The ratio of the percentage change in the quantity of a good demanded to a given percentage change in consumer incomes, other things being equal.

**Income-expenditure model**  A model in which the equilibrium level of real domestic income is determined by treating real planned expenditure and real domestic product as functions of the level of real domestic income.

**Income-product line**  A graph showing the level of real domestic product (aggregate supply) associated with each level of real domestic income.

**Inconvertibility (of a currency)**  A situation in which a country's currency can be exchanged for foreign currency only through a government agency or with a government permit.

**Indexation**   A policy of automatically adjusting a value or payment in proportion to changes in the average price level.

**Inelastic demand**   A situation in which quantity demanded changes by a smaller percentage than price, so that total revenue decreases as price decreases.

**Inferior good**   A good for which an increase in consumer incomes results in a decrease in demand.

**Inflation**   A sustained increase in the average level of prices of all goods and services.

**Inflationary recession**   An episode in which real output falls toward or below its natural level and unemployment rises toward or above its natural rate while rapid inflation continues.

**Inflation targeting**   A strategy for price stability in which policy makers adopt an explicit target range for the rate of inflation over an intermediate time horizon.

**Injections**   Those flows of funds into domestic product markets—investment, government purchases, and exports—that do not begin with the consumption expenditures of domestic households.

**Inside lag**   The delay between the time a policy change is needed and the time a decision is made.

**Inventory**   A stock of a finished good awaiting sale or use.

**Inventory investment**   Changes in the stocks of finished products and raw materials that firms keep on hand; the figure is positive if such stocks are increasing and negative if they are decreasing.

**Inverse relationship**   A relationship between two variables in which an increase in the value of one variable is associated with a decrease in the value of the other.

**Investment**   The act of increasing the economy's stock of capital—that is, its supply of means of production made by people.

**Labor**   The contributions to production made by people working with their minds and muscles.

**Labor force**   The sum of all individuals who are employed and all individuals who are unemployed.

**Labor productivity**   A measure of how much workers produce in a given period of time, usually measured as output per hour of work.

**Law of demand**   The principle that an inverse relationship exists between the price of a good and the quantity of that good that buyers demand, other things being equal.

**Leakages**   The parts of domestic income—saving, net taxes, and purchases of imports—that are not used by households to buy domestic consumer goods.

**Liabilities**   All the legal claims against a firm by nonowners or against a household by nonmembers.

**Liquidity**   An asset's ability to be used directly as a means of payment, or to be readily converted into one, while retaining a fixed nominal value.

**Liquidity trap**   A situation in which interest rates near zero lead to accumulation of liquid assets instead of stimulating planned investment.

**M1**   A measure of the money supply that includes currency and transaction deposits.

**M2**   A measure of the money supply that include M1 plus retail money market mutual fund shares, money market deposit accounts, and saving deposits.

**Macroeconomics**   The branch of economics that studies large-scale economic phenomena, particularly inflation, unemployment, and economic growth.

**Marginal propensity to consume**   The proportion of each added dollar of real disposable income that households devote to real consumption.

**Marginal propensity to import**   The percentage of each added dollar of real disposable income that is devoted to real consumption of imported goods and services.

**Marginal tax rate**   The percentage of each added dollar of real domestic income that must be paid in taxes.

**Market**   Any arrangement people have for trading with one another.

**Merchandise balance**   The value of a country's merchandise exports minus the value of its merchandise imports.

**Microeconomics**   The branch of economics that studies the choices of individuals, including households, business firms, and government agencies.

**Model**   A synonym for theory; in economics, often applied to theories that are stated in graphical or mathematical form.

**Monetarism**   A school of economics that emphasizes the importance of changes in the money stock as determinants of changes in real output and the price level.

**Money**   An asset that serves as a means of payment, a store of purchasing power, and a unit of account.

**Money multiplier**   The ratio of the equilibrium money stock to the banking system's total reserves.

**Multiplier effect**   The tendency for an initial $1 change in a component of aggregate demand to shift the aggregate demand curve in the same direction by more than $1.

**National income**   The total income earned by a country's residents, including wages, rents, interest payments, and profits.

**National income accounts**   A set of official government statistics on aggregate economic activity.

**Natural level of real output**   The level of real output that is consistent with the natural rate of unemployment.

**Natural rate of unemployment**   The sum of frictional and structural unemployment; the rate of unemployment that persists when the economy is experiencing neither accelerating nor decelerating inflation.

**Natural resources**   Anything that can be used as a productive input in its natural state, such as farmland, building sites, forests, and mineral deposits.

**Negative slope**   A slope having a value less than zero.

**Net domestic product (NDP)**   Gross domestic product minus an allowance (called the *capital consumption allowance*) that represents the value of capital equipment used up in the production process.

**Net exports**   Exports minus imports.

**Net taxes**   Taxes paid to government minus transfer payments made by government.

**Net tax multiplier**   The ratio of an induced change in real aggregate demand to a given change in real net taxes.

**Net worth**   The firm's or household's assets minus its liabilities.

**Neutrality of Money**   The proposition that in the long run a one-time change in the money stock affects only the price level and not real output, employment, interest rates, or real planned investment.

**Nominal**   In economics, a term that refers to data that have not been adjusted for the effects of inflation.

**Nominal exchange rate**   The exchange rate expressed in the usual way: in terms of current units of foreign currency per current dollar.

**Nominal interest rate**   The interest rate expressed in the usual way: in terms of current dollars without adjustment for inflation.

**Normal good**   A good for which an increase in consumer incomes results in an increase in demand.

**Normative economics**   The area of economics that is devoted to judgments about whether economic policies or conditions are good or bad.

**Okun's law**   A rule of thumb according to which each 2 percent by which real output rises above (or falls below) its natural level results in an unemployment rate one percentage point below (or above) the natural rate.

**Open economy**   An economy that is linked to the outside world by imports, exports, and financial transactions.

**Open market operation**   A purchase (sale) by the Fed of government securities from (to) the public.

**Operating target**   A financial variable for which the Fed sets a short-term target, which it then uses as a guide in the day-to-day conduct of open market operations.

**Opportunity cost**   The cost of a good or service measured in terms of the forgone opportunity to pursue the best possible alternative activity with the same time or resources.

**Outside lag**   The delay between the time a policy decision is made and the time the policy change has its main effect on the economy.

**Perfectly elastic demand**   A situation in which the demand curve is a horizontal line.

**Perfectly inelastic demand**   A situation in which the demand curve is a vertical line.

**Personal income**   The total income received by households, including earned income and transfer payments.

**Phillips curve**   A graph showing the relationship between the inflation rate and the unemployment rate, other things being equal.

**Planned-expenditure schedule**   A graph showing the level of total real planned expenditure associated with each level of real domestic income.

**Planned investment schedule**   A graph showing the relationship between the total quantity of real planned investment expenditure and the real interest rate.

**Positive economics**   The area of economics that is concerned with facts and the relationships among them.

**Positive slope**   A slope having a value greater than zero.

**Price elasticity of demand**   The ratio of the percentage change in the quantity of a good demanded to a given percentage change in its price, other things being equal.

**Price elasticity of supply**   The ratio of the percentage change in the quantity of a good supplied to a given percentage change in its price, other things being equal.

**Price index**   A weighted average of the prices of goods and services expressed in relation to a base year value of 100.

**Price level**   A weighted average of the prices of goods and services expressed in relation to a base year value of 1.0.

**Price stability**   A situation in which the rate of inflation is low enough so that it is not a significant factor in business and individual decision making.

**Producer price index (PPI)**   A price index based on a sample of goods and services bought by business firms.

**Production possibility frontier**   A graph that shows possible combinations of goods that can be produced by an economy given available knowledge and factors of production.

**Purchasing power parity**   A situation in which a given sum of money will buy the same market basket of goods and services when converted from one currency to another at prevailing exchange rates.

**Real**   In economics, a term that refers to data that have been adjusted for the effects of inflation.

**Real exchange rate**   The nominal exchange rate adjusted for changes in the price levels of both countries relative to a chosen base year.

**Real interest rate**   The nominal interest rate minus the rate of inflation.

**Realized expenditure**   The sum of all planned and unplanned expenditures.

**Realized investment**   The sum of planned and unplanned investment.

**Real output**   A synonym for real gross domestic product.

**Recession**   A cyclical economic contraction that lasts six months or more.

**Required-reserve ratio**   Required reserves stated as a percentage of the deposits to which reserve requirements apply.

**Required reserves**   The minimum amount of reserves that the Fed requires depository institutions to hold.

**Reserves**   Cash in bank vaults and banks' non-interest-bearing deposits with the Federal Reserve System.

**Revenue**   Price times quantity sold.

**Saving**   The part of household income that is not used to buy goods and services or to pay taxes.

**Savings deposit**   A deposit at a bank that can be fully redeemed at any time, but from which checks cannot be written.

**Scarcity**   A situation in which there is not enough of a resource to meet all of everyone's wants.

**Securities**   A collective term for common stocks, bonds, and other financial instruments.

**Slope**   For a straight line, the ratio of the change in the $y$ value to the change in the $x$ value between any two points on the line.

**Sterilization**   The Fed's use of open market operations to offset the effects of exchange market intervention on domestic reserves and on the money stock.

**Stock**   A quantity that exists at a given point in time, measured in terms of units only.

**Structural budget**   The budget surplus or deficit that the federal government would incur given current tax and spending laws and unemployment at its natural rate.

**Structural unemployment**   The portion of unemployment that is accounted for by people who are out of work for long periods because their skills do not match those required for available jobs.

**Substitute goods**   A pair of goods for which an increase in the price of one causes an increase in demand for the other.

**Supply**   The willingness and ability of sellers to provide goods for sale in a market.

**Supply curve**   A graphical representation of the relationship between the price of a good and the quantity of that good that sellers are willing to supply.

**Supply shock**   An event, such as an increase in the price of imported oil, a crop failure, or a natural disaster, that raises input prices for all or most firms and pushes up workers' costs of living.

**Tangent**   A straight line that touches a curve at a given point without intersecting it.

**Tax incidence**   The distribution of the economic burden of a tax.

**Theory**   A representation of the way in which facts are related to one another.

**Thrift institutions (thrifts)**   A group of financial intermediaries that operate much like commercial banks; they include savings and loan associations, savings banks, and credit unions.

**Time deposit**   A deposit at a bank or thrift institution from which funds can be withdrawn without payment of a penalty only at the end of an agreed-upon period.

**Transaction deposit**   A deposit from which funds can be freely withdrawn by check or electronic transfer to make payments to third parties.

**Transfer payments**   Payments to individuals that are not made in return for work they currently perform.

**Transmission mechanism**   The set of channels through which monetary policy affects real output and the price level.

**Unemployed**   A term used to refer to a person who is not employed but is actively looking for work.

**Unemployment rate**   The percentage of the labor force that is unemployed.

**Unit elastic demand**   A situation in which price and quantity demanded change by the same percentage, so that total revenue remains unchanged as price changes.

**Value added**   The dollar value of an industry's sales less the value of intermediate goods purchased for use in production.

**Velocity (income velocity of money)**   The ratio of nominal domestic income to the money stock; a measure of the average number of times each dollar of the money stock is used each year for income-producing purposes.

# INDEX